IV

MEMOIR OF SAMUEL SLATER

LIBRARY OF
EARLY AMERICAN BUSINESS AND INDUSTRY

MEMOIR

OF

SAMUEL SLATER

THE FATHER OF AMERICAN MANUFACTURES

CONNECTED WITH A

HISTORY OF THE RISE AND PROGRESS

OF THE

COTTON MANUFACTURE

IN ENGLAND AND AMERICA

BY

GEORGE S. WHITE

[1836]

REPRINTS OF ECONOMIC CLASSICS

AUGUSTUS M. KELLEY · PUBLISHERS
NEW YORK · 1967

FIRST EDITION 1836

(Philadelphia: *At No. 46 Carpenter Street*, 1836)

Reprinted 1967 by

Augustus M. Kelley · Publishers

Library of Congress Catalogue Card Number

66-18322

PRINTED IN THE UNITED STATES OF AMERICA

by SENTRY PRESS, NEW YORK, N. Y. 10019

Drawn by Mr Lincoln.   Engraved by J.B. Neagle.

CRESCIT SUB PONDERE VIRTUS

Samuel Slater

Printed by E.W Rogers

MEMOIR OF SAMUEL SLATER,

The Father of American Manufactures.

CONNECTED WITH A

HISTORY OF THE RISE AND PROGRESS

OF THE

COTTON MANUFACTURE

IN

ENGLAND AND AMERICA.

WITH REMARKS ON THE

MORAL INFLUENCE OF MANUFACTORIES IN THE UNITED STATES.

BY GEORGE S. WHITE.

"Facts truly stated are the best applauses or most lasting reproaches."
"The history of the origin and development or progress of every subject is of great importance, because every thing relating to it can then be shown concentrated, as it were in a mirror, be clearly seen, and correctly judged of."

ILLUSTRATED BY THIRTY ENGRAVINGS.

PHILADELPHIA:
PRINTED AT NO. 46, CARPENTER STREET.
1836.

ADVERTISEMENT.

Being always convinced that without an investigation of the early state and progress of manufactures in Philadelphia, my work would be very imperfect, I resolved on publishing the volume in this city, expecting that, during my residence for the necessary attention to the printing, I should be able to examine the evidences of its early attention to manufactures. But I was not aware of the amount of interest on this subject, which had been manifested in Pennsylvania, from its early settlement. As an entire stranger in the city, I should have been much cramped in my investigations, had it not been for the liberal assistance afforded me by Dr. Mease, who entered into my design with ardour, and with enthusiastic patriotism. I am especially indebted to that gentleman, for opening to me avenues of information, which have enabled me to obtain as much useful matter as would of itself fill a volume :— my limits oblige me to make a selection. But I thus publicly express my obligations to Dr. Mease for the constant and unwearied pains he took to afford me every facility for the attainment of my object, which, as I had no personal claims on his attention, must have arisen from the deep interest he took in the subject. I fear that I have presumed on his goodness, and intruded on time which would otherwise have been devoted to a valuable work that he is preparing for the press, and thereby retard a publication anxiously expected by the citizens of Pennsylvania : in so doing I ought not only to apologise to him, but to ask pardon of the public, considering that he is himself engaged in preparing for the press a work on the Geography and Statistics of Pennsylvania.

To other gentlemen of this favoured city, I return thanks, without taking the liberty of designating them; which, however, if I felt authorised to do, their names would add greatly to the respectability of my work.

Philadelphia, April 18*th*, 1836.

CONTENTS.

LIST OF ENGRAVINGS.

DEDICATION.

REVEREND SIR,

This memoir of a distinguished layman of the church, in your diocess, who has achieved an important enterprise for our country, is dedicated to you, as his father in God. From his personal acquaintance, and from the knowledge he had, of your useful and abundant services, in the cause of religion, he frequently expressed to me and others a high and permanent regard for you.

If he could now express a wish on the subject, he would approve of my design, at least so far as my presenting this volume to your notice, if he believed it to be in any way worthy of your patronage. I have been anxious for an opportunity respectfully to express my reverence and high estimation, for a character so long beloved, and viewed as a model of what a bishop ought to be. You have emphatically taught us how to live, how to labour, how to suffer, as well as how to pray. You have demonstrated to New England, that prelacy may exist without arrogance or ostentation, and that ecclesiastical authority can be exercised without spiritual tyranny or oppression. No one can be better situated to judge of the moral condition of manufacturing establishments ; for your ministerial labours have been extended to nearly every village and hamlet in your diocess. To you, therefore, I can appeal for the correctness of the article on that subject.

It has been my humble supplication, that you may live long to preside in the councils of the church, and teach those in authority how to rule in the fear of God.

Whenever, in obedience to the inspired penman, my mind is led to the contemplation :—" Of whatsoever things are true ; whatsoever things are just ; whatsoever things are honest ; whatsoever things are pure ; whatsoever things are lovely ; whatsoever things are of good report : whatever is virtuous and praiseworthy :"— your example, (which I have observed the last twenty-five years) appears before me, as a practical demonstration of these heavenly principles.

It is only the fear that my work will be very imperfect and unworthy of your notice, which prevents my enjoying the highest pleasure and gratitude in thus publicly assuring you with how much veneration and devotion,

I am, Rt. Rev. Sir, your friend and servant,

GEORGE S. WHITE.

To the Subscribers of " The Memoir of Slater," in New England.

When I first made the proposals of this work, I only promised rising of 300 pages without engravings, at $2 00, and when encouraged by your patronage to proceed in the undertaking, I ventured only two or three engravings, not even hoping that I should be able to obtain a steel engraving of the portrait of Mr. Slater.

Your favourable encouragement emboldened me both to proceed in the work, and enlarge my design, till I have produced a volume which is sold at $3; and after paying 75 cents a copy to the agent, the remaining is only sufficient to pay all actual expenses attending the work. An inferior edition can, if desired, be printed to be afforded at $2; but several gentlemen advised me not to do it till I had offered my first subscribers and patrons, the " History of Manufactures" in its best form. In obedience with that advice, and with this explanation, Mr. Kennie offers the volume ; but for the responsibility of the change in the price, I only am responsible.

GEORGE S. WHITE,
Canterbury, Conn.

PREFACE.

In want of facts, it appears to have been a common propensity of our race to resort to fiction. The ancients, thus influenced, were prone to recur to fabulous ancestry, and to attribute all their *improvements* and *inventions* to deified powers. So, instead of awarding to merit its due, and creating a spirit of enquiry and emulation, all their arts were gratuitously attributed to their fabled Apollo. At this distant period of the world we can perceive at once, that this was done by a prevailing ignorance and through a defect of a suitable means for conveying useful and permanent information.

We know enough of human nature to conclude that it will be nearly the same under similar circumstances, and that so far as it is acted upon by them, similar results may be expected from similar causes.*

* "The Rhode Island papers announce the death, on Monday last, of *Samuel Slater, Esq.*—long known as one of the most enterprising and respected citizens of that state, and as the father of the cotton manufacturing business in this country. The first cotton-mill built in the United States was erected by him, in Pawtucket, and was yet in operation at the time of our last visit. There is a curious anecdote, connected with the original machinery of this factory, which, as it is strictly true, we will relate for the edification of Doctors Abercrombie and Macnish, and other enquirers into the philosophy of dreams. Mr. Slater was an ingenious mechanist, and all the machinery was constructed under his immediate direction. Of course, in the earliest infancy of the business, and before the machinery to be constructed was itself thoroughly understood, or the means for making it as ample as could have been desired, imperfections to a greater or less extent were to be anticipated. At length, however, the work was complete, and high were the hopes of the artist and his employers. All was ready, but the machinery would not move, or at least it would not move as intended, or to any purpose.

Ignorance and superstition produce precisely the same dark and dangerous disguises and consequences, in our day, as they did anciently.

With the aid of letters, and every facility for printing, as yet not a single publication has been presented to the American public to give an account, and perpetuate the rise and progress, of the cotton and other manufactures in this country.

To such an extent have they advanced and probably will advance, without correct information the liability is, for the whole account of their rise and progress at some future period to run into fiction and fable; and the man who was most instrumental in introducing them, instead of being viewed as a plain practical mechanic, using honest means for his own benefit, and at the same time promoting the best interests of this country, to be ranked among fictitious characters, and to have his name and fame some way mysteriously associated with the business which he has permanently established.

Information is surely needed on these points, and this is the author's apology for collecting, compiling, and presenting to the public, a work, including the *Memoir* of *Samuel Slater*, and giving a general account of the rise and progress of manufactures in this country. In going into this unoccupied field much labour was requisite to collect materials. They have been obtained from a variety of sources, all of which the author wishes to acknowledge with due deference.

General credit is due to the following writers:—Hamilton's Report to Congress, 1790; Niles's Register; Edinburgh Encyclopedia;

The disappointment was great, and the now deceased mechanist was in great perplexity. Day after day did he labour to discover, that he might remedy the defect—but in vain. But what he could not discover waking was revealed to him in his sleep.

" It was perfectly natural that the subject which engrossed all his thoughts by day, should be dancing through his uncurbed imagination by night, and it so happened that on one occasion, having fallen into slumber with all the shafts and wheels of his mill whirling in his mind with the complexity of Ezekiel's vision, he dreamed of the absence of an essential band upon one of the wheels. The dream was fresh in his mind on the following morning, and repairing bright and early to his works, he in an instant detected the deficiency !

" The revelation was true, and in a few hours afterwards, the machinery was in full and successful operation. Such is one feature in the history of American manufactures. The machinist has since led an active and useful life—sustaining in all the relations of society an unblemished reputation."— *Com. Advertiser.*

Baines's History of the Cotton Manufactures; " Spinning Master's Assistant ;" Results of Machinery ; Babbage's Economy of Manufactures ; History of Derbyshire ; Zec. Allen on Mechanics, and his Practical Tourist: and Ure's Philosophy of Manufactures. To others I am indebted for very important assistance and encouragement, whose names I do not feel at liberty to publish ; but the impression of their kindness is recorded on a tablet that but one event can erase.

With all the help afforded me, I have considered it little short of presumption, for one, whose studies have been so devoted to another department, to attempt mechanics. I have been led into the subject gradually and accidentally ; at first I only intended a memoir of my friend ; but finding his whole life so connected with manufactures, it became necessary that I should have a general knowledge of the subject. Those whose opinions had weight with me, said, the public needed an historical essay on the rise and progress of manufactures ; at last a volume is produced. Whether the public will receive my labours in good part, remains to be proved.

The difficulty of understanding the processes of manufactures, has unfortunately been greatly overrated. To examine them with the eye of a manufacturer, so as to be able to direct others to repeat them, does undoubtedly require much skill and previous acquaintance with the subject; but merely to apprehend their general principles and mutual relations, is within the power of almost every person possessing a tolerable education. Those who possess rank in a manufacturing country can scarcely be excused if they are entirely ignorant of principles whose developement has produced its greatness. The possessors of wealth can scarcely be indifferent to processes which nearly or remotely have been the fertile source of their possessions. Those who enjoy leisure can scarcely find a more interesting and instructive pursuit than the examination of the workshops of their own country, which contain within them a rich mine of knowledge, too generally neglected by the wealthier classes.

The more knowledge is accumulated and perfected, the more easily it is acquired and recollected. I find this to be the case in the study of mechanics; what appeared complex and obscure to me at first, now appears pleasing and easy to be understood. The subject is not so inexplicable as many imagine.

Arnott says : "The laws of physics have an influence so extensive, that it need not excite surprise that all classes of society are at last discovering the deep interest they have to

understand them.   The *lawyer* finds that in many of the causes
tried in his courts, an appeal must be made to physics,—as in the
cases of disputed inventions : accidents in navigation, or among
carriages, steam engines, and machines generally : questions
arising out of the agency of winds, rains, water currents, &c.
The *statesman* is constantly listening to discussions respecting
bridges, roads, canals, docks, and mechanical industry of the
nation.   The *clergyman* finds ranged among the beauties of nature, the most intelligible and striking proofs of God's wisdom and
goodness :—the *sailor* in his ship has to deal with one of the most
admirable machines in existence : *soldiers*, in using their projec-
tiles, in marching where rivers have to be crossed, woods to be
cut down, roads to be made, towns to be besieged, &c., are trusting chiefly to their knowledge of physics : the *land-owner*, in
making improvements on his estates, building, draining, irrigating,
road making, &c.   The *farmer* equally in these particulars, and
in all the machinery of agriculture : the *manufacturer* of course ;
the *merchant* who selects and distributes over the world the products of manufacturing industry—all are interested in physics ;
then also the *man of letters*, that he may not, in drawing illustrations from the material world, repeat the scientific heresies and
absurdities, which have heretofore prevailed. It is for such reasons,
that natural philosophy is becoming daily more and more a part
of common education.   In our cities now, and even in an ordinary
dwelling house, men are surrounded by prodigies of mechanic art,
and cannot submit to use these, as regardless of how they are produced, as a horse is regardless of how the corn falls into his manger.
A general diffusion of knowledge, owing greatly to the increased
commercial intercourse of nations, and therefore to the improvements in the physical departments of astronomy, navigation, &c.,
is changing every where the condition of man, and elevating the
human character in all ranks of society."

It is my design to make this work permanently interesting and
valuable, and render it subservient to the cause of domestic
industry.   I have raised an argument in favour of the immense
importance of manufacturing establishments of every description ;
and I think the work is calculated to promote a patriotic attention
to the general enterprise and prosperity of the country.

The following remarks, first made in reference to Edmund Burke,
are not inapplicable to one who was his great admirer :—

" Few things interest the curiosity of mankind more, or prove
so instructive in themselves, as to trace the progress of a powerful
mind, by the honourable exertion of its native energies, rising, in

the teeth of difficulties, from a very private condition to important standing in society, with power to influence the destiny of nations. Such a person, as sprung not from the privileged few, but from among the mass of the people, we feel to be one of ourselves. Our sympathies go along with him in his career. The young imagine that it may possibly be their own case ; the old, that with a little more of the favour of fortune it might have been theirs ; and, at any rate, we are anxious to ascertain the causes of his superiority, to treasure up his experience, to profit by what he experienced to be useful, to avoid what he found to be disadvantageous. And the lesson becomes doubly instructive to that large class of society who are born to be the architects of their own fortune ; when it impresses the great moral truth, that natural endowments, however great, receive their highest polish and power, their only secure reward, from diligent study—from continued, unwearied application : a plain, homely faculty, within the reach of all men, one which is certain to wear well, and whose fruits bear testimony to the industry of the possessor, and to the intrinsic value of the possession."

Should the present attempt enable the citizens of the United States to appreciate more justly the powers of one to whom this country is under very important obligations, the writer will not deem his labour misapplied. His testimony at least is impartial. He has no party purpose to answer, no influence to court, no interest to push ; except it be the common interest felt by every generous mind, of rendering to a distinguished and deserving character those honours which are its due.*

The great importance of manufactures, is exciting a vast interest in England, and on the continent of Europe ; this year has produced valuable publications in this new department of literature, and a series of volumes are promised by Dr. Ure, the author of the Philosophy of Manufactures. France is alive to the all absorbing subject, which they perceive has given England a preeminence among the nations of the earth; the comparative advantages between the two nations are nicely drawn, but in view of these, England boasts that she shall be able to maintain her superiority, against France and the world.

* At Grand Cairo in Egypt, they have such a profound respect to new inventions, that whoever is the discoverer of any new art or invention is immediately clad in cloth of gold, and carried in triumph throughout the whole city, with trumpets and other musical instruments playing before him, and presented to every shop to receive the joyful acclamations and generous presents of his fellow citizens.

Will any one, with the whole of this absorbing topic before him, doubt, whether England could have advanced, and gained ground against the nations on the continent which had long been superior to her, without the cherishing protection and patronage which has been carefully granted to every branch of her trade and commerce? Those who are well informed on this subject, can have no remaining doubts. Home manufactures, in order to their existence and perfection, must be protected—either by prohibitory duties, or by a preference and patronage of the people; the latter mode is the most effectual and the most advisable, in the present state of American finances. And what American, who feels the importance attached to the growing interest of the United States, who will not exercise patriotism enough, so far to prefer our own manufactures as to render us entirely independent of Europe in any emergency? Are we for ever to be the dupes of European influence, and the fantastic vagaries of their customs and fashions, ever varying, for the express purpose of making merchandise of our weakness and vanity, and the faculty of imitation? Let us rather assume a national character, a national costume. If we are to be guided by fashion, let that fashion be American; the produce of American soil, of American invention and skill, and of American industry and enterprise. The day is past and gone, when any of our citizens will think it best to have our *work-shops* in Europe; indeed America will soon learn the extent of her resources to be such, as to render her independent of the old world, and thus establish our independence on a basis that can neither be shaken by the implements of war, nor by the stratagems of peace. For it is now avowed that those strifes are in full operation, aiming at universal conquest. A conquest made of our resources, rendering our labour and skill and raw materials ineffective, would effectually impoverish and ruin us as a people, making us the dupes of superior energy and capital. America is already alive to those circumstances, but she must never be off her watch-tower—for the enemy is ever on the alert, making a breach at every weak point, and taking advantage of our inadvertence and inactivity.

But if Americans make good use of their natural capabilities, and take advantage of their free institutions, they may cope with the whole world, in deriving the benefits of skill and enterprise; and thus establish on a permanent basis, such establishments of industry and wealth as shall render America independent of the world.

" A machine, receiving at different times and from many hands, new combinations and improvements, and becoming at last of signal benefit to mankind, may be compared to a rivulet swelled in its course by tributary streams, until it rolls along, a majestic river, enriching in its progress provinces and kingdoms. In retracing the current, too, from where it mingles with the ocean, the pretensions of even ample subsidiary streams are merged in our admiration of the master flood, glorying, as it were, in its expansion. But as we continue to ascend, those waters which, nearer the sea, would have been disregarded as unimportant, begin to rival in magnitude, and divide our attention with, the parent stream ; until at length, on our approaching the fountains of the river, it appears trickling from the rock, or oozing from among the flowers of the valley. So also, in developing the rise of a machine, a coarse instrument, or a toy, may be recognised as the germ of that production of mechanical genius, whose power and usefulness have stimulated our curiosity to mark its changes, and to trace its origin. And the same feeling of reverential gratitude, which attached holiness to the spots whence mighty rivers sprung, also clothed with divinity, and raised altars in honour of, the inventors of the saw, the plough, the potter's wheel, and the loom. To those who are familiar with modern machinery, the construction of these implements may appear to have conferred but slight claim to the reverence in which their authors were held in ancient times, yet, artless as they seem, their use first raised man above the beasts of the field; and, by incalculably diminishing the sum of human labour, added equally to the power and enjoyment of the barbarous tribes of those ages to which their discovery is referred. In their rudest form, they are nearly all the mechanical aids that were necessary for the wants of nations, of shepherds and of husbandmen. For refinement, in the formation of even these simple contrivances, or for the invention and use of more complex mechanism, we must look to communities that have made considerable advances in the career of civilisation ; to those regions where men, congregating in large masses, create numerous artificial wants, and, by this peculiarity in their social position, excite the natural rivalry of individuals to devise expedients to remove them. Accordingly it is found, that the dense population of some eastern countries, had there produced a state of society eminently calculated to call forth the resources of inventive power. From a remote period, the great wealth of the Egyptians, particularly, had generated a taste for luxurious magnificence, which that people early displayed in the erection of colossal and sumptuous buildings. The remains of their vast pyramids, temples, and palaces, evince a skilful practice of numerous devices to abridge and facilitate labour, and to give a permanence, almost eternal, to their gorgeous structures."—*Stuart's Anecdotes.*

" The introduction of new inventions seemeth to be the very chief of all human actions. The benefits of new inventions may extend to all mankind universally, but the good of political achievements can respect but some particular cantons of men; these latter do not endure above a few ages, the former for ever. Inventions make all men happy without either injury or damage to any one single person. Furthermore, new inventions are, as it were, new erections and imitations of God's own works."—*Bacon.*

March 1, 1836.

INTRODUCTION.

A retrospective view of the colonial policy of Great Britain may not be inapplicable to some introductory remarks to this work.

It has always been the well known policy of that powerful nation, to supply her colonies with the home manufactures. They have of course, as a part of this plan, prevented the introduction of machinery and of all mechanical operations and improvements. Through the influence of fashion, as well as by other means, they have rendered their various dependencies entirely subservient to the mother country; affording them a constant supply, not only of articles of necessity, but those of ornament and fashion. This was the avowed condition of the North American colonies, previous to the war of the revolution.* Chatham said, he "would

---

* The state of the country, the state of the government, and the state of manufactures at this period, may be learned from the following letter written by John Adams, Dec. 19, 1816.

Extract of a letter from President Adams to Wm. E. Richmond, Esq. Providence. Dec. 14th, 1819.

Sir,—I have received your polite favour of the 10th, the subject of which is of great importance. I am old enough to remember the war of 1745, and its end. The war of 1755, and its close. The war of 1775, and its termination. The war of 1812, and its pacification. Every one of these wars has been followed by a general distress, embarrassments on commerce, destruction of manufactures ; fall of the price of produce and of lands, similar to those we feel at the present day—and all produced by the same causes:—I have wondered that so much experience has not taught us more caution. The British merchants and manufacturers, immediately after the peace, disgorged upon us all their stores of merchandise and manufactures—not only without profit, but at a certain loss for a time—with the express purpose of annihilating all our manufactories and ruining all our manufacturers. The cheapness of the articles allures us into extravagances, and at length produces universal complaint. What would be the consequences of the abolition of all restrictive, exclusive, and monopolising laws, if adopted by

not have the Americans make a " *hobnail*;" and they will not have " a razor to shave their beards," was an expression in debate, by a member of the English parliament. Such was the condition of these colonies, previous to their declaration of independence ; hence, the inhabitants found themselves bare even of necessary clothing, and of common utensils for the use of their domestic economy. This rendered the war more oppressive, and increased the privations of the Provincials, altogether beyond the sufferings of a state of warfare in modern times. The citizens had, from their first settlement, looked to the other side of the Atlantic for their clothing, their luxuries, &c. ; in fact, for every thing, except their fire wood, meats, and bread stuffs. So that at the commencement of their resistance, they were nearly left without a tool to work with ; the women were driven to the use of thorns, when their supply of pins failed them. All kinds of hardware and crockery were generally unattainable. Even the article of leather, was very imperfectly prepared. So that not only the army were badly shod, but many of the citizens were *bare-footed*, and *bare-headed*. The following remarks will show, that these restrictions on trade constituted a part of the complaints and grievances of the colonies. It was not easy for them to see by what principle their removal to America should deprive them of such rights and privileges. They could not comprehend the justice of restrictions so materially different from those at " home ;" or why they might not, equally with their elder brethren in England, seek the best markets for their products, and like them manufacture such articles as were within their power, and essential to their comfort. But the selfish politicians of Britain, and her still more selfish merchants and manufacturers, thought otherwise. A different doctrine was accordingly advanced, and a different policy pursued. Acts were therefore early passed, restricting the trade with the

all the nations of the earth, I pretend not to say : but while all the nations with whom we have intercourse, persevere in cherishing such laws, I know not how we can do ourselves justice without introducing, with great prudence and discretion however, some portions of the same system. The gentlemen of Philadelphia have published a very important volume upon the subject, which I recommend to your careful perusal. Other cities are co-operating in the same plan. I heartily wish them all success, so far as this, at least— that congress may take the great subject into their most serious deliberation, and decide upon it according to their most mature wisdom.

JOHN ADAMS.

Note—A meeting was held in London, to assist cotton manufacture, headed by Earl Grosvenor, Lord Folkstone, H. Brougham, Sir Robert Peel, &c., and liberal subscriptions collected.

plantations, ⌐as well as with other parts of the world, to British built ships belonging to the subjects of England, or to her plantations. Not contented with thus confining the colonial export trade to the parent country, parliament in 1663 limited the import trade in the same manner. These acts, indeed, left free the trade and intercourse between the colonies. But even this privilege remained only a short period. In 1672 certain colonial products, transported from one colony to another, were subjected to duties. White sugars were to pay five shillings, and brown sugars one shilling and sixpence, per hundred ;—tobacco and indigo one penny, and cotton wool a half-penny, per pound. The colonists deemed these acts highly injurious to their interests. They were deprived of the privilege of seeking the best market for their products, and of receiving in exchange the articles they wanted, without being charged the additional expense of a circuitous route through England. The acts themselves were considered by some as a violation of their charter rights; in Massachusetts they were, for a long time, totally disregarded. The other colonies viewed them in the same light. Virginia presented a petition for their repeal; and Rhode Island declared them unconstitutional, and contrary to their charter. The Carolinas, also, declared them not less grievous and illegal. The disregard of these enactments on the part of the colonies—a disregard which sprung from a firm conviction of their illegal and oppressive character—occasioned loud and clamorous complaints in England. The revenue it was urged would be injured; and the dependence of the colonies on the parent country would, in time, be totally destroyed. Here much interesting matter might be introduced, but nothing more than a general sketch is intended.

A similar sensibility prevailed on the subject of *manufactures*. For many years after their settlement, the colonies were too much occupied in subduing their lands, to engage in other business. When, at length, they turned their attention to them, the varieties were few, and of coarse and imperfect texture. But even these were viewed with a jealous eye. In 1699, commenced a systematic course of restrictions on colonial manufactures, by an enactment of parliament, " That no wool, yarn, or woollen manufactures of their American plantations, should be shipped there, or even laden, in order to be transported thence, to any place whatever." Other acts followed, in subsequent years, having for their object the suppression of manufactures in America, and the continued *dependence* of the colonies on the parent country. In 1719, the house of commons declared, " That the erecting of manufactories in the colonies, tended to lessen their dependence on Great Britain." In 1731, the board of trade reported to the house of commons, "That there were more trades carried on, and manufactures set up, in the provinces on the continent of America, to the northward of Virginia, prejudicial to the trade and manufactures of Great Britain, particularly in New England;" they suggested "whether it might not be expedient, in order to keep the colonies properly *dependent* upon the parent country, and to render her manufactures of service to the government, "to give those colonies some encouragement." From the London company of hatters, loud complaints were made to parliament, and suitable restrictions demanded upon the exportation of hats, which were manufactured in New England, and exported to various places, to the serious injury of their trade. In consequence of these representations, the exportations of hats from the colonies to foreign countries, and from one plantation to another, were prohibited ; and even restraints, to a certain extent, were imposed on their manufacture. In 1731, it was enacted, that hats should neither be shipped, nor even laden upon a horse-cart or other carriage, with a view to transportation to any other colony, or to any place whatever ; no hatter should employ more than two apprentices at once, nor make hats, unless he had served as an apprentice to the trade seven years ; and, that no negro should be allowed to work at the business at all. The complaints and the claims of the manufacturers of iron were of an equally selfish character. The colonists might reduce the iron ore into pigs—they might convert it into bars—it might be furnished them duty free ; but the English must have the profit of manufacturing it, beyond this incipient stage. Similar success awaited the representations and petitions of this trade. In this year, 1750, parliament allowed the importation of pig and bar iron from the colonies, into London, duty free ; but prohibited the erection or continuance of any *mill* or other *engine*, for slitting or rolling iron, or any *plating* forge, to work with a tilt-hammer, or any furnace for making steel, in the colonies, under the penalty of two hundred pounds. Every such mill, engine, or plating forge, was declared a *common nuisance* ; and the governors of the colonies, on the information of two witnesses, on oath, were directed to cause the same to be removed within thirty days, or to forfeit the sum of £500. It appears that no sooner did the colonies, emerging from the feebleness and poverty of their early settlements, begin to direct their attention to commerce and manufactures, than they were subjected by the parent country to many vexatious regulations, which seemed to indicate, that with regard to those subjects, the colonies were expected to follow that line of policy, which she in her wisdom should mark out for them. At every indication of colonial prosperity, the complaints of the commercial and manufacturing interests of Great Britain; were loud and clamorous. Repeated demands were made upon the government, to correct the growing evil, and to keep the colonies in due subjection. "The colonies," said the complainants, "are beginning to carry on trade; they will soon be our formidable rivals; they are already setting up manufactures; they will soon set up for independence." To the increase of this feverish excitement in the parent country, the English writers of those days contributed not a little. As early as 1670, in a work entitled, "Discourse on Trade," published by Sir Joshua Child, is the following language, which expresses the prevailing opinion of the day:—"New England is the most prejudicial plantation to this kingdom; of all the American plantations, his majesty has none so apt for the building of shipping, as New England; nor any comparably so qualified for the breeding of seamen, not only by reason of the natural industry of that people, but principally by reason of their fisheries; and in my poor opinion, there is nothing more prejudicial, and in prospect more dangerous to any mother kingdom, than the increase of shipping in her colonies." Such was their condition, that if they made a hat, or a piece of steel, an act of parliament calls it a nuisance; a tilting hammer, a steel furnace, must be removed as a nuisance. Cutting off our trade with all parts of the world, was a principal reason that originated the declaration of independence. All Europe, who dreaded America, were urging England forward in her restrictive policy with the colonies.

These restrictions led to grievances, and complaints from the colonies, which finally ended in their independence.

As soon as the United States were recognised and acknowledged in her national compact, other nations as well as England crowded their manufactures into the new and hungry market. The country was then bare of European commodities. The flooding of the country with foreign articles rendered it unnecessary and impracticable to establish manufactures in any part of the Union. The condition of Europe soon called for the products of the soil, and the activity of commerce caused the merchants to flourish, and these, by furnishing a market, enriched the farmers and other inhabitants. This enabled them to give enormous prices for European and India goods: so nothing was done of importance, even to lay a foundation for future supplies of American domestic goods.

French and English fabrics were introduced, by all the interest
of commercial men, and they were encouraged by all the rage of
fashion. With such seeming kindness, the power of the states
were rendered inoperative, and their resources expended. Their
condition was similar to that of the Corsicans, who after they had
gained and substantiated their independence under the patriotic
and heroic Paoli, were swindled out of their liberty and reduced
to servitude by an influx of Italian silks and trinkets from Naples.
(*See Boswell's History of Corsica.*)

Nothing but a particular exigence, and the state of European
affairs, during the reign of Napoleon, prevented the ruin of this
republic, by the astonishing importation of foreign productions.
The non-intercourse and non-importation laws raised the prices
of all articles, before any energetic means were used to manufacture for ourselves. The rage for English goods, and for the
luxuries of the East, had become so general, that no cost could
prevent their use, and not merely a common use, but even an
extravagant expenditure.

The daughters of the self-denying matrons, known to fame, in
the stories of the first resistance to Great-Britain, in renouncing
the use of *tea*—used profusely the best hyson and gunpowder
imperial ; so that these expensive kinds were more generally used,
in the States, than in any other country in the world. Instead of
the homespun coats and gowns formerly prided in, British broad
cloths and French silks, were in common use, and the thirst and
demands of fashion were insatiable. The people had passed from
one extreme to another. No laws, either of non-importation or
non-intercourse, could prevent such articles finding a way into
our principal cities, and from thence into our country villages,
where they brought an exorbitant price. So that millions of
dollars were taken from us annually, to supply our wives and
daughters with chips from Italy, and bonnets from Leghorn.

Even the war of 1812 with Great Britain, did not stop the use,
but rather increased the desire for every thing foreign.

The restrictive policy failing, the state of the treasury urged
to the expedient of an equalised tariff, upon the goods of all foreign
nations at peace with the United States. This policy soon restored
the exhausted revenue, and enabled the government to sustain the
war, till a peace could be had on honourable terms.

The suddenness of the peace, unexpected and unforeseen,
caused a flood of every description of articles, so that the markets
were completely glutted. Many goods on hand, fell to one third
of their previous prices on the merchant's hands. This dis-

couraged the infant establishments, which had been called into existence, by the emergency of war, to supply our necessities; they were not only disheartened but ruined, and many companies failed and lost their all. This state of affairs even threatened their total dissolution; a few only weathered the storm, and maintained a firm standing. To the undaunted perseverance of those few establishments, we owe the present progress and triumph of our improved manufactures.

By the introduction of the best and latest machinery, and with the advantages of New England water-power, they have survived every attack, surmounted every obstacle, and overcome every difficulty. Irish linens and India cottons, which once supplied our markets, are now but little known. An immense quantity of our cotton cloths are sold at a very low price, and are consumed in all parts of the Union, both plain and printed; as well as large exportations to South America, where they are in high repute, and have driven the British and India goods out of those markets.

Samuel Slater, the father of our manufacture of cotton, lived to see this astonishing change, and the successful operation of what he had first introduced, by unwavering firmness, under various and now unknown discouragements; which may teach us " Not to despise the day of small things." Slater commenced with seventy-two spindles, in a clothier's shop at Pawtucket, and did not find ready sale for his yarn after he had spun it. The first students of the university of Oxford in England first recited in a barn, in the time of Alfred; and the most splendid establishments, as well as the greatest of empires, commenced from small beginnings. We cannot, at present, foresee the wonderful extension of our manufactures; they are destined to supersede all that have ever existed before them in any part of the world.

A cold indifference on this subject exists, even in the manufacturing districts. There is not that decided preference, and patriotic attachment, to our own productions, as there undoubtedly ought to be, but a deplorable infatuation, after every thing foreign and *far fetched.*

" Are you sure that it is *not* American?" is the question often put, when articles are offered for sale. Domestic goods have been treated with too much contempt, even by those who earn their bread by their production. This apathy, this monstrous destitution of patriotism, must be removed, and the predilection for the fabrics of Europe and India goods, must be frowned down, before our manufactures of fine goods and silks can be established on a permanent basis. If they ever arrive at greater perfection; if they are to be enabled to vie with the old world, with their accumulated capitals and cheapness of labour, they must be nurtured and cherished at home. This would be the most "judicious" course. Let us all unite, as the heart of one man, in the resolution, to prefer, and use nothing but the work of our own hands, and the business will be completed : we have the power to say it shall be done. This will be the final and effectual "tariff," that shall settle this subject of long and loud debate. This course must follow the "compromise or pacification," and all will be well. Employment will be necessary for our immense increase of population, and the influx of strangers, from every part of the world, invited to our shores, by the promise of liberty and plenty, must find work to exercise their various abilities and habits of industry. Many of them are valuable mechanics and artisans, of infinite variety of skill, well adapted to assist in the rapid improvements now commencing, unexampled in ancient or modern history. Who knows but other Slaters may come over to us, and assist in feeding and clothing the population that is forming new states in the vast wilderness, destined to be great empires, to exist for many generations—when Rome, and Paris, and Berlin, shall be no more. The prospect of national greatness is as sure as that of national existence. We are too contracted in our conceptions, when we talk of the southern and eastern interests. The rise and progress of empires and nations yet unborn, are connected with our prosperity.

Columbus first led the way, and opened a path for the oppressed to find freedom and peace. The old world had become tyrannical and despotic, and the groans of the children of men had come up into the ears of the Lord God of the universe. He inspired his servant with wisdom and courage, and afforded him all necessary means to open a new world to the eyes of astonished millions, to whom it was marvelous and almost miraculous. The wisdom of the wise men was turned backward, their knowledge turned to foolishness. All the maxims of political and spiritual tyranny were turned upside down ; and Luther and others, exhibiting a mighty spirit of reformation, believed there would be deliverance, though they saw not the way. Their faith saved them, and it has happened according to their word. The iron arm has been broken ; and the weak and despised have fled for refuge, and have found a quiet habitation.

May Americans remember their mercies and deep responsibilities! Let us lay aside every weight, and the sin that doth so easily beset us ; and let us run with patient perseverance in every good work, and we shall become the praise of the whole earth.

Had Columbus been discouraged, and turned back, at the mutiny of his crew, or had he then hearkened to the timid caution of his friends, we never should have reaped the wonderful harvest of benefits, from their disinterested labours, that we now enjoy. It is by constant self-denial and unconquered perseverance, that we can obtain any great object : we shall reap if we faint not, but if we are not faithful to the end, we cannot obtain the reward.

The strong and prominent trait of character in Slater, was his unwavering and steadfast perseverance, and his constant application to the fulfilment of his object. Had he failed in constructing the Arkwright machinery, or had he finally failed in his extensive business, the cause of manufactures would have been retarded ; indeed, no one can calculate the evil consequences of such an event ; but he held on his way ; he fainted, but yet pursued. And he has left us an example, to those engaged in the same cause, or in a similar enterprise, to be stedfast, unmoveable, and faithful ; till America shall rival, in the perfection of her manufactures, as she does now in the freedom of her institutions, the nations of the earth! We are richly supplied, and we possess, in a high and superabundant degree, all the natural capabilities for the purpose ; all that is necessary, is the application of them to the proper object. Those philosophers who deny the bounties of Providence, in their rich and exhaustless abundance, by teaching that this globe is unable to support and sustain the natural increase of its inhabitants, have the most contracted and degraded view of the resources of nature, and the arrangement of her laws, not to insist upon the inspiration. They contradict the realities of all ages, by an unbelieving scepticism, fostered by a selfish policy, and a misrepresentation of matters of fact. We have resources for hundreds of millions. He is the true patriot who developes those mines and riches, and who gives employment to the species, to dignify society and ornament the country. We envy not those self styled patriots, whose thirst for office and distinction allows them to deceive and cajole their fellow citizens, by prejudicing them against the talented and enterprising part of society. Thus teaching them discontent, and prejudicing them against the necessary arrangements to promote the general welfare, making them the tools of their sordid and selfish policy ; and yet these *patriots* imagine that their exaltation is essential to the honour and safety of their country. The path-way of virtue and truth, which only leads to honour and immortality, is too hard for their tender feet. They are astonished that any person should go the round about way of self-denial, and they declare that none do, *with which a conscientious regard to actions and motives is always connected.* A state of society, not founded on the principles of honest industry, must be degraded and low ; and, like the inhabitants of South America, must be wretched and miserable. Mankind must be usefully and honourably employed, in order to be virtuous and happy. In proof of this position, compare the condition of South America with the United States, and more especially with that part of the United States, where manufacturing establishments have come into being and risen to eminence. The mighty contrast in the condition and character of the people, is altogether greater than that formed by the hand of nature in the two countries themselves. South America, particularly that part in the neighbourhood of the La Plata, in the hands of New Englanders, would at once become the paradise of the world, did they retain their moral and intellectual habits. Without these habits, we can pronounce what they would be, from what a resident well acquainted with the country affirms the South Americans are. With governments in distraction, and so enfeebled as to exert no force except by the sword and bayonet, vice, disorder, and confusion, every where prevail. The finest fields in the world for agriculture are suffered to remain barren and desolate, or to be traveled by wandering herds. Indolence and ignorance enfeeble the hands and put out the eyes of the inhabitants. Roaming in poverty, filth, and pollution, they are totally blind to their advantages and privileges : they are tossed about by every wind of prejudice and passion. Trained to view labour as a degradation, while trampling the most prolific fields and possessing every thing requisite, and of the first qualities, for food and clothing, they would be obliged to go naked and starve, were it not for the industry of other nations. As it now is, robbers and assassins fill their streets, and thousands are disappearing by the only species of industry for which they have an adaptation, that of destroying each other. The inhabitants of New England, barren and rugged as she is, comparing her with this picture, and contrasting it with their own condition, will bless that Providence which has placed them as they are, and see at once that an introduction of the manufacturing interest has added in no small degree to their dignity and happiness.

Slater, by the introduction of machinery, and by his arrangements in the various deparments of the manufacturing establishments, opened the means of employment, and excavated a mine more valuable than those of Peru, or than all the precious metals of the earth; because the human capabilities are brought into exercise. This gives to man his full enjoyment, in the pursuit of happiness. In contrast with South America, it is pleasing to see the spirit of enterprise and improvement rising in every part of our country. This spirit, if not now universal, is rapidly becoming so. We see it breaking out every where, in the middle states, in the northern, in the southern, in the western; and like the kindling of fire, we see it gathering strength, as it rises and spreads. Who does not see in this rising spirit, a subject of national felicitation? Perhaps the greatest this country ever had before ; certainly greater than any other country ever possessed. Was even the spirit of liberty itself, which produced the revolution, and gave us our independence, more a subject of national congratulation? Who can estimate the value of this new born spirit which now animates our country, when we consider our great and rapidly increasing population, their characteristic ardour in every lucrative pursuit, and the boundless scope which our country affords for the range of this spirit? Here we have every thing to invite to enterprise and encourage hope; the great and growing market afforded by our commerce and our manufactures is rendering every article of produce valuable and productive. Thus every department of wealth aids and unites in replenishing the boundless resources of our happy country.

" An object is not insignificant, because the operation by which it is effected is minute: the first want of men in this life, after food, is clothing, and as this machinery enables them to supply it far more easily and cheaply than the old methods of manufacturing, and to bring cloths of great elegance and durability within the use of the humble classes, it is an art whose utility is inferior only to that of agriculture. It contributes directly and most materially to the comforts of life, among all nations where manufactures exist, or to which the products of manufacturing industry are conveyed ; it ministers to the comfort and decency of the poor, as well as to the taste and luxury of the rich. By supplying one of the great wants of life with a much less expenditure of labour than was formerly needed, it sets at liberty a larger proportion of the population, to cultivate literature, science, and the fine arts. To England, these inventions have brought a material accession of wealth and power. They are not confined in their application to one manufacture, however extensive, but that they have given nearly the same facilities to the woollen, the worsted, the linen, the stocking, and the lace manufactures, as well as to silk and cotton ; and that they have spread from England to the whole of Europe, to America, and to parts of Africa and Asia : it must be admitted that the mechanical improvements in the art of spinning have an importance which it is difficult to over-estimate.   By the Greeks, their authors would have been thought worthy of deification ; nor will the enlightened judgment of moderns deny that the men to whom we owe such inventions deserve to rank among the chief benefactors of mankind."—*Baines.*

  " Cotton spinning, the history of which is almost romantic, has been made poetical by Dr. Darwin's powers of description and embellishment.   In his ' Botanic Garden' he thus sings the wonders of Arkwright's establishment on the Derwent, at Cromford."

> ——" Where Derwent guides his dusky floods
> Through vaulted mountains, and a night of woods,
> The nymph Gossypia treads the velvet sod,
> And warms with rosy smiles the wat'ry god,
> His pond'rous oars to slender spindles turns,
> And pours o'er massy wheels his foaming urns,
> With playful charms her hoary lover wins,
> And wields his trident while the monarch spins.
> First, with nice eye, emerging Naiads cull
> From leathery pods the vegetable wool :
> With wiry teeth *revolving cards* release
> The tangled knots, and smooth the ravel'd fleece :
> Next moves the *iron hand* with fingers fine,
> Combs the wide card, and forms the eternal line ;
> Slow, with soft lips, the *whirling can* acquires
> The tender skeins, and wraps in rising spires ;
> With quickened pace *successive rollers* move,
> And these retain, and those extend the *rove ;*
> Then fly the spokes, the rapid axles glow,
> While slowly circumvolves the labouring wheel below."

BELPER.

MEMOIR OF SAMUEL SLATER.

CHAPTER I.

"Nothing is here for tears, nothing to wail,
    Or knock the breast; no weakness, no contempt,
    Dispraise or blame; nothing but well and fair,
    And what may quiet us, in death so noble."
                                          MILTON.

In writing the volumes of biography so frequently presented to
the world, the motives of their authors have been various, and the
subjects diversified. Mankind take an interest in the history of
those, who, like themselves, have encountered the trials, and discharged the duties of life. Too often, however, publicity is given
to the lives of men, splendid in acts of mighty mischief, in whom
the secret exercises of the heart would not bear a scrutiny. The
memoirs are comparatively few of those engaged in the business
and useful walks of life.

Biography, of late years, has been rendered interesting, chiefly,
by an extensive and learned correspondence ; so that the compilers
have scarcely room for narrative or reflection. These collections
of letters from eminent persons are read with avidity, as a matter
of curiosity, and as an indulgence to the inquisitive desire to
enter into the private moments and opinions of individuals extensively known to fame. It is of a man well known in the
business transactions of this country that we write. Notwithstanding his business and acquaintance were so extensive, and his
success so complete, the materials for writing his memoir are scanty

and few. This is a complaint with all writers of biography who write the lives of persons that have passed through life in a uniform course, being little subjected to serious and important changes. To make it up from letters is out of the question, as there are only a few in existence, excepting those on business ; so that this volume will be a counterpart to the publications above referred to.* So that if I had not been favoured, in a personal acquaintance with my deceased friend, I could not, in any satisfactory manner, have accomplished my purpose, in wishing to give the public an account of a man whom they have long heard of, as the father of our manufactures ; and as one who had been successful in establishing the cotton business, on an improved and permanent basis.

I am writing of a man of business; not of a man devoted to literature, or what has been called the liberal arts ; whose fame has been spread by means of publications, or who had in any way sought publicity, or made claim to any pretensions, *but of one who all his lifetime avoided it.* It is well known, that the late Samuel Slater, Esq. of Webster, Massachusetts, and for many years a resident citizen in the village of Pawtucket, Rhode Island, was a native of England. I have the most direct information of the place of his birth, and of his parentage. His father, William Slater, inherited the paternal estate, called " Holly House," near

---

* " The life of this gentleman presents nothing of that eclat and splendour by which mankind are most commonly attracted and fascinated ; nothing of the 'pomp and circumstance,' or stirring incidents of war; of murder and pillage, burning and havoc, which, pursued on the large scale, makes the man a hero ; but, followed on a less extensive plan, would brand him as a felon. His glory is not the flitting ignis fatuus that rises from the charnel house, to dazzle and mislead ; but the bright, cheering, and durable halo of a well spent life ; passed in successful efforts to better the condition of our race ; in the cultivation and extension of those useful arts, which, by multiplying our comforts and conveniences, advance the empire of civilisation, and add to the sum of human enjoyment. If the mass of mankind were wise ; if the chosen few, who sit in moral judgment on the actions of the great, and record their sentence on the page of history, were just—then would the false tinsel of military glory fade before the touchstone of truth, and that 'shadow of renown,' which has followed the destroyers of our race, 'from Macedonia's madman to the Swede,' be no longer regarded. The true interests of humanity, and the dictates of political justice and wisdom, require, alikè, that this should be the case ; and that none but the real benefactors of mankind should be held up as objects of our gratitude, or examples for our imitation."—*Short sketch of the life of Samuel Slater.*

Belper, in the county of Derbyshire, England. This estate is now owned and occupied by his son, William Slater.

The father of Samuel Slater was one of those independent yeomanry, who farm their own lands, now almost peculiar to that part of the country, as a distinct class from the tenantry of England. He did not, however, confine himself altogether to the business of agriculture, but added to his estate by the purchase of lands. He did so for the sale of timber, and was in fact a timber merchant.

Being a neighbour of Jedediah Strutt, of whom we shall have occasion to speak, he once made a considerable purchase for him containing a water-privilege, on which there is now a very extensive establishment. He was otherwise engaged with Mr. Strutt in making purchases of consequence, who had a high opinion of his abilities and integrity as a man of business. This acquaintance, and these transactions, led to the connection of Mr. Strutt with Samuel, who was the fifth son, and is said to have resembled his father in his person, and to have inherited his talents. This enterprising son transplanted a branch of the Slater family into the new world, where we trust they will grow and prosper for many generations. The mother of Mr. Slater was a fine looking woman, and lived a short time since with her third husband, whom she survived, and often observed, she had been favoured with " three good husbands." She had by her first husband, William Slater, a large family; William, who now lives on the paternal estate with many children, bids fair to keep up the family name on the other side of the Atlantic. John Slater, son of the subject of this memoir, visited him a few years since, at the Holly House farm, the place of his father's nativity, and viewed the establishment where his honoured parent served his long and important apprenticeship, as he did also the other mills owned by Messrs. Arkwright and Strutt, at Crumford, six miles from Belper. When on my last visit to Mr. Slater at Pawtucket, in 1833, he showed me the prints of Arkwright and Strutt, and pointing to that of Strutt, said, "Here is my old master," and pronounced it a good likeness.

Perhaps nothing could have had more influence on the subject of this memoir, to induce him to leave his business, than the desire to visit his aged mother, of whom he spoke always most affectionately, and corresponded with her.* And to have viewed

* The following letter is just such an one as we should expect an affectionate son would write to his mother, on the loss of a beloved and interesting

the place and scenes of his early days ; his brothers and sisters, and their little ones, to the third generation; his school-fellows,

child. And it is expressive of that strong parental affection, which was peculiarly striking in Mr. Slater toward all his offspring. Towards his mother, Mr. Slater retained the fondest affection.

Extract of a letter sent by S. Slater to his mother at Belper, England, March 28th, 1801.

Providence, R. I.

Dearly Beloved Parent,—In December last, I answered yours of June, 1800, in which I wrote you, that my little family enjoyed a good state of health. But now, under the most weighty load of sorrow and affliction, I have to inform you that my first born and only son, William, was numbered among the dead, January 31st, aged four years and five months. He was taken sick with a severe cold, on Jan. 23d ; the next day he had a bad cough, but was playful, and anxious to ride about four miles, to see one of my particular acquaintances. Therefore, to gratify him, I told him to go and tell the boy to put the horse in the chaise, and we would ride ; accordingly he readily went to give his orders ; but finally, we did not go to ride, and he never went out of the house afterwards. In the evening he was very much troubled with a shrill cough, and rested but little during the night. On the 25th he still grew worse, and on the 26th, in the afternoon, we called for a physician; he gave him some powerful medicine, but the operation of it was trifling, and his cough and hoarseness kept increasing during the day and night following. On the 27th, he was more troubled with hard breathing ; and of course a more particular attention was paid by the physician, and medicine increased, but, alas ! to no purpose. During this day and night, and on the 28th also, all our efforts and hopes were baffled. On the morning of the 29th, the physician judged him very dangerous, and from his knowledge of my great love and affection for my delightful child, he informed me that his case was very precarious, and said he knew I should take every method to have him restored. He said if I wished for further medical aid to assist and advise with him, he was entirely willing. Therefore I sent immediately for the most eminent physician, and on his arrival, they conversed, and pronounced his disorder the quinsey. They proceeded to give large and strong doses of medicine, which put him in the most deplorable misery ; together with his most excruciating disorder. By this time his breath was so far stopped that he could not remain more than two or three minutes in one place, and remained so that day and all night following. On the morning of the 30th, his load of affliction was increased, but he bore all with calmness, and appeared lovely. Towards noon death had approached very near unto him, and about one o'clock his eyes were nearly closed, his little fingers stiff and almost cold, and his breath seemingly gone. He remained in that state till nearly three o'clock, then he appeared to revive for a little while, and sat up in the bed, and called for things to eat, and did eat freely ; which gave us some flattering hopes of his recovery. But, behold, he was again seized as violently as ever, and remained so until the morning of the 31st, when, about three o'clock, he was summoned to quit this habitation of sorrow and trouble, for that of joy

This Indenture Witnesseth. That Samuel Slater of Belper in the County of Derby,

doth put himself Apprentice to Jedediah Strutt of New Mills in the Parish of Duffield in the said County of Derby Cotton Spinner,

to learn his Art and with him (after the Manner of an Apprentice) to serve from the day of the date of these presents unto the full End and

During which Term the said Apprentice his Master faithfully shall serve his Secrets keep his lawful commands every where gladly do he shall do no Damage to his said Master nor see to be done of others; but to his Power shall let or forthwith give Warning to his said Master of the same he shall not waste the Goods of his said Master nor lend them unlawfully to any. he shall not commit fornication nor contract Matrimony within the said Term he shall not play at Cards Dice Tables or any other unlawfull Games whereby his said Master may have any loss With his own Goods or others during the said Term without Licence of his said Master he shall neither buy nor sell he shall not haunt Taverns or Play Houses nor absent himself from his said Master's Service day or Night unlawfully. But in all things as a faithfull Apprentice shall behave himself towards his said Master and all his during the said Term.

And the said Jedediah Strutt in consideration of the true and faithful Service of the said Samuel Slater

his said Apprentice in the Art of Cotton Spinning which he useth, by the best Means that he can, shall teach and instruct or cause to be taught and instructed, Finding unto the said Apprentice Sufficient Meat Drink Washing and Lodging during the said Term And for the true Performance of all and every the said Covenants and Agreements either of the said Parties bindeth himself unto the other by these Presents In Witness whereof the Parties above named to these Indentures interchangeably have put their Hands and Seals the Eighth Day of January and in the Twenty Third Year of the Reign of our Sovereign Lord GEORGE THE THIRD by the Grace of God of Great Britain France and Ireland KING Defender of the Faith &c and in the Year of our Lord One Thousand Seven Hundred and Eighty Three

Samuel Slater

Jed Strutt

J. Lockur
Geo. Williams

B

Five Pence
Pr. Pair

Stamp

Seal

Seal

his playmates, his schoolmaster, Jackson, who was then living; the sons and grandsons of his old master, Strutt; the old mill; the meadows and orchards, &c. that surrounded Holly house. He left them all, in the bloom of youth, and retained a vivid recollection of every particular. These early remembrances would cause the tear to escape, even in his old age. But the state of his health, the multiplicity of his concerns, and his *concentrativeness*, bound him to Webster, and forbade the thought of a voyage across the Atlantic. He refrained, denied himself, sent his love by his son, and never returned to his father's land. But he ever retained a strong affection and lively concern in the welfare of his native country.

As is usual, Samuel went on trial to Mr. Strutt, previous to his indenture of apprenticeship, and during this probation his father fell from a load of hay. This fall was the occasion of his death. During his father's sickness, and perceiving that he was dangerously ill, he wished his father to article him to Mr. Strutt, as both parties were satisfied. As a proof that his father had confidence in him, and that there was stability in the boy, he said to him, "You must do that business yourself, Samuel, *I have so much to do, and so little time to do it.*" It is believed that this was his last interview with his beloved parent.

He lost his father in 1782, when he was fourteen years of age, at a time when a father's care and advice are much needed. A boy left without guardianship, or watchful eye to restrain him, is frequently exposed and led into temptation and ruin. Young Slater, however, had an indulgent and faithful mother, and elder brothers, so that he was not left entirely to his own resources. The plate opposite is an engraved copy from the original indenture, which is preserved in the family, as a relic of their father's early fidelity, and as a proof of his favoured means of knowledge..

Mr. Strutt was then building a large cotton factory at Milford, and was a partner with Sir Richard Arkwright, in the cotton spinning business; the latter having been induced to this connection by the prospect which Strutt's machines afforded, of an increased consumption of yarn. Samuel Slater asked Mr. Strutt, before he went into the business, whether he considered it a *permanent* business. Mr. Strutt replied, " It is not probable, Samuel,

and perfect peace for ever. And we thereby are deprived of one of our brightest earthly gems, the glittering of which, time will never efface. But the Lord gave him, and he hath taken him away; and from henceforth and for ever, blessed be his name."

that it will always be as good as it is now, but I have no doubt it
will always be a *fair* business, if it be well managed." It will be
recollected, that this was before Mr. Peel invented the printing
cylinder. Indeed the whole cotton business of England was, at
that time, confined to a small district in Derbyshire, and its whole
amount not greater than that which is done at the present day in
a single village in New England.

In the early part of our young apprentice's time, he manifested
the bent of his mind, for he frequently spent his Sundays alone,
making experiments in machinery. He was six months without
seeing his mother, or brothers and sisters, though he was short of
a mile from home. Not that he lacked in filial or fraternal affections ; but he was so intent, and so devoted to the attainment of
his business. To show the expertness and the propensity of his
mind, the following circumstance is related. Mr. Strutt endeavoured to improve the *heart-motion*, that would enlarge or raise the
yarn in the middle, so as to contain more on the bobbin. Jedediah Strutt was unsuccessful in his experiments, and Samuel saw
what was wanting, and went to work the next Sunday, (the only
time he had to himself,) and formed such a motion, (a diagram
of which is given below) to the satisfaction of his master, who
presented him with a guinea.

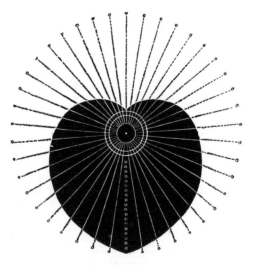

Mr. Strutt was an economist, and enforced his maxims on
Samuel, cautioning him against waste, and assuring him that it was

by savings that a fortune in business was to be made.* During this time, Samuel became an excellent machinist, as he had an opportunity of seeing the latest improvements. Arkwright and Strutt were in company, and it was at a time when there was much excitement and lawsuits on the patent rights; so that he was initiated into all the crooks and turns of such controversies. This may have prevented him applying for a privilege as the introducer of Arkwright's patents into the United States.

Slater served his indenture with Mr. Strutt, and faithfully performed his part of the contract to the last day of the term, and there was a good understanding between the parties to the last. This accomplishment of his *full time* was characteristic of him, and was praiseworthy and beneficial, as it laid the foundation of his adaptation to business, and finally to his perfect knowledge of it. He was different from those restless youths, who think they know every thing before they have cut their eye teeth, and who set up for themselves before their beards are grown, without either knowledge or capital, and who fail and defraud their creditors, during the time they ought to have been serving an apprenticeship. Such boys break their engagements, forfeit all confidence, and follow the example of Franklin, in that particular, though they cannot be compared to him in any thing else. And in this, Franklin was to be blamed; I praise him not. He himself acknowledges it to have been a great error in his life. A conscientious regard to contracts is a principle by which every person ought to be influenced, and without which, there is no hope of their arriving at eminence in their profession. Mr. Slater told me a short time before his death, that after his time was out, he engaged with Mr. Strutt to have the oversight of the erection of some new works, in addition to the mill, and this general employment, with his close observation (for he always saw and heard every thing, nothing could escape his notice,) and retentive memory, was of great service to him in afterwards assisting him to erect his first mill in Pawtucket. If he had been confined to one branch of business, as is usual with an apprentice in England, his knowledge would have been inadequate to perform what he

* The following anecdote is told:—"When Mr. Slater was yet a boy, with Mr. Strutt, he passed by some loose cotton on the floor without picking it up; Mr. Strutt called him back and told him to take up the cotton, for it was by attending to such small things that great fortunes were accumulated; and Mr. Strutt observed to his wife, by way of still impressing the subject on the mind of his favourite apprentice, 'that he was afraid that Samuel would never be rich.'"

did on his first coming to America. But his residing in Strutt's family, his being the son of his deceased friend and neighbour, as well as his close application to business, his ingenious experiments, and his steady habits, gave him the character of the "industrious apprentice."

He had the confidence of his master, and became his *right-hand man*, and he might have attained the highest eminence by a continuance in England. Mr. Strutt afterwards declared that had he known his intentions, nothing should have induced him to part with him. But Mr. Slater told me that he contemplated trying America for some time; and that his object was, to get a general knowledge of the business, in order to come to this country and introduce the manufacture of cotton, on the Arkwright improvement, and that he remained after the time of his indenture with that special object in view.

There were early indications that he designed embarking in business for himself, and it is said, that he used to enquire of Arkwright and others, if they thought the business would be overdone in England. Yet it does not appear that he ever made known to any person his intention of leaving England. The father of Samuel Slater must have been a man of considerable property and business for those times, from the fact of his supporting so large a family respectably, and giving them such an education as was equal to any children who were calculated for business, sixty years ago. After making provision for his widow, he left to each of his children what was then a considerable sum for persons in business. There was included, in Samuel's portion, two houses in Belper, a nail store, and another building; all of which sold as they were, under many disadvantages, for nearly two thousand dollars. He did not touch this property when he left home, but probably reserved it for a retreat in case of failure of his object in coming to the United States. He had always that kind of generalship which provides for a retreat in case of accident, or as he would say, " to lay up for a rainy day."

Few persons who are extravagant when apprentices, ever gain in business; and it has been said, that few who saved money then but what succeeded in after life. The following copy of a note*

* " *Four-pence Stamp.*

£2 2s.—I promise to pay to Samuel Slater, or order, upon demand, the sum of two pounds two shillings, for value received, with lawful interest for the same, as witness my hand this tenth day of January, 1768.

Signed in the presence of us,   WILLIAM ASHMOLE.
Wm. More, J. Pratt."

which I have in my possession, shows the early savings of Slater : economy and indefatigable industry were the foundation principle of his fortune. Not by speculation, or by any circumstances peculiarly favourable to the accumulation of wealth, but by the dint of persevering attention to business for half a century.

The motive, or inducement, and first occasion of his thinking of leaving Mr. Strutt, and what finally determined him, was his observing* in a Philadelphia paper, a reward offered by a society for a machine to make cotton rollers, &c. This convinced him that America must be very bare of every thing of the kind, and he prepared himself accordingly. He probably knew the risk he should run in attempting to leave England as a *machinist,* and it was characteristic of him, never to talk of his business—where he was going, or when he intended to return. John Slater, a surviving brother, says he remembers his coming home, and telling his mother that he wished his clothes, as he was going by the stage to London ; this was the last time his mother, or any of the family, saw him, till his brother John joined him in Pawtucket. He was aware, that there was danger of his being stopped, as the government restrictions were very severe, and very unjust ; the officers were very scrupulous in searching every passenger to America. He therefore resolved not to take any pattern, nor have any writing or memorandum about him, but trusted wholly to his acquirements in the business and to his excellent memory. His appearance was also in his favour, it being that of an English farmer's son, rather than that of a mechanic. He told me himself he had nothing about him but his indenture, which he kept concealed, and this was his only introduction and recommendation in the new world.

Though he left home for London, without making known his intentions, he did not design leaving his friends in suspense ; he therefore prepared a letter for his mother informing her of his destination ; which, however, he did not venture to put in the

---

* During the last year or two of his apprenticeship, his thoughts as to his future course, and the establishment of the business on his own account, were turned towards this country, by various rumours and reports which reached Derbyshire, of the anxiety of the different state governments, here, to encourage manufactures. The newspaper account of a liberal bounty (£100) granted by the legislature of Pennsylvania, to a person, who had imperfectly succeeded in constructing a carding machine, to make rolls for jennies, and the knowledge that a society had been authorised by the same legislature for the promotion of manufactures, induced him finally to push his fortune in the western hemisphere.

post-office, till just before he went on board the ship bound to New York.

While waiting in London till the captain was ready to embark, which appears to have been a week or ten days, he spent his time in seeing the curiosities; the Cathedrals, the Tower, and other London shows. Of these he often spoke, in familiar conversation, with a great deal of interest. He told of a circumstance that happened to him in London :—a Jew accosted him, perceiving him to be from the country, and told him, in a private manner, that he had some silk stockings, that he would sell remarkably low, but he wished the bargain to be *between themselves;* which overture our young adventurer listened to rather incautiously; and found, on examination, after he went to his tavern, that he had bought *stockings without feet.* When he told this anecdote, he said, it served to "sharpen his eye teeth." Few countrymen, strangers in London, spend even a short time there, without experiencing some similar adventure ; the above, however, was not of serious importance, and served only to laugh at, as a proof of his credulity.

Young people should be cautious how they spend their time in great cities, without the acquaintance of some of the resident inhabitants. The best way for strangers who only remain a short time in a city, is to put up at one of the most respectable hotels.

We cannot help reflecting on the unforeseen changes which take place in human life. When we are boys, we know not where our lot will be cast, nor what will be our destiny in this changing world. Nor is it proper we should—it is wisely ordered that it should be otherwise ; " sufficient for the day is the evil thereof." It is for us to do our every day's duty, and leave the event ; "what a man soweth, that shall he also reap." If we do well, we shall receive the reward of our labours, even in the pleasure of well doing. If young Slater had foreseen the difficulties he had to encounter, before he spun the first cotton yarn in America, he never would have undertaken it; but it is well that we have no such foresight, and that our strength is according to our day. Those who have left their native country, know something of the trials of parting. Young Slater's heart was full, when he looked the last time on Holly House, and all that was within; but a youthful ambition fired his soul, and enabled him to overcome his feelings. He took a last look of his mother, he tore himself away from his brothers and sisters, with whom he had taken sweet counsel, and with whom he was closely united in fraternal affection. The emigrant can understand all this, and feel it most intensely, and it is better felt than expressed ; words are cold and imperfect to delineate such beatings of the heart, or the natural attachment we feel to our nation, " for with all its faults, we love it still;" it is our country, and no trifling consideration should cause a person to leave his native land for another.   But emigration is the fashion of the day, for the traveling organ was never more active, not even in Arabia.

The cotton business was then in its infancy ; if Mr. Slater had continued in England, and used the same exertions, and the same economy as he has done here, he would have realised a fortune there, equal to what Arkwright did himself; as the father of Sir Robert Peel did, and several others far inferior to Samuel Slater— in business talents, and mechanical genius.   He himself entertained this opinion ; but he was afraid the cotton spinning would be overdone in England, and listened to the overtures held out from the United States; we shall see how far his footsteps were prospered, and how far the country has been benefited by his labours. He brought with him all Arkwright's improvements in use at that time, and made articles equal to those made in England.   He was not ashamed to send his first yarn home to Mr. Strutt, as it would bear a comparison with his, and with any made elsewhere.*

Mrs. Mary Wilkinson, of Providence, R. I., has a pattern of cotton check cloth, and presented me with a part of an apron, of the first check made by Mr. Slater, which she says she paid for in covering his rollers with leather ; a specimen of which is in the Philadelphia Museum.   I keep it by me as a curiosity, and it is quite equal to the same article made in England.   Genius usually receives its early bias from some circumstances, in the general character of the age, and some in the particular condition of the person to whom it belongs : this observation is exemplified in the genius of Slater.

There were early indications of the genius of Samuel : when a child he gave a patient attention to whatever he attempted.   The "boy is the father of the man ;" he was his mother's best boy to wind worsted, for which purpose he made himself a polished steel spindle ; his inclination led him to the machine shop.   His schoolmaster admired him as a good writer, and as good at arithmetic ; observing that scholars well versed in duodecimals and vulgar fractions, made more business men, than attention to the other rules.   Such early acquisitions gave indications of his great cal-

* A specimen of the first yarn, stocking and twist, is deposited in the Philadelphia Museum.

culation, and his talents as an accountant, in which he afterwards so much excelled.

When Jedediah Strutt, the partner of Arkwright, applied to his neighbour Slater for one of his sons, expressing a wish to have the eldest, which after some consultation was refused, Mr. Slater, who had perceived his son Samuel's inclination, told his friend he had better take Samuel on trial, then not fourteen years of age, observing that he "wrote well, and was good at figures." This proved a judicious selection, which is a matter of great importance in a parent apportioning his sons to proper employments. None could have been more appropriate nor more successful, than the choice which was made in this instance. It appears there were strong and early developments of the bent of his mind. He became extraordinary for comprehensive calculations, and never forgot his good, plain, old-fashioned hand-writing.

Samuel was put to school to a Mr. Jackson, a very approved teacher in Belper, of whom he acquired the rudiments of a common business education, and like most of Mr. Jackson's scholars, learned to write a good hand, and a free and easy style. He always in after life spoke of this worthy gentleman with gratitude and affection, and maintained a correspondence with him after he came to America. This old schoolmaster, who was proud of his scholar, never forgot him ; and the following letters were preserved by Mr. Slater.

BELPER, 21st Feby. 1790.

Dear Sir,—I am glad to have so favourable an account of your health when your letters left the western world, the seat of patriotism and independence; your long and dangerous voyage I shall pass over in silence, as I suppose the reflection will now afford you pleasure. There is something truly pleasing in thinking upon calamities which we have surmounted and are passed away. You are in a sphere of action now where you are likely to see a considerable portion of this dirty globe: let me enjoin you to keep an exact and regular journal of every day's transactions and observations. It will be an amusement for you at the time you do it. The other advantages of it I need not point out, your own good sense will soon point them out: I know from your particular turn, that you are well fitted for it. A number of observations will often occur to you which would not be noticed by most other people—make private remarks upon the leading features in the characters of all you have to deal with. I hope to live to see you in Britain once again. Be particularly careful of your health ; the countries you are likely to visit, demand some adherence to regularity and care. I shall at all times be happy to hear of your welfare. I have no local news to send you ; I think Derbyshire wears much the same aspect (the difference of seasons allowed for) as when you turned your back upon it. At all events I can assure you, that the morals of a particular set are not at all improved since you left them. I am far from being well ; I have the scurvy very ill, and am at this time troubled with a cold; however, I intend this night drinking your health in a bumper. Let us hear from you as often as convenient; your opportunities will be frequent, perhaps as in your nautical travels you will frequently meet with ships bound to England.

I am, dear sir, with every sincere wish for your welfare,

Yours, &c. THOMAS JACKSON.

The Historical Society of Rhode Island voted, to request Mr. Slater to give them such particulars as he should think proper, in relation to his coming to this country;* and the following was found among his papers; which shows, that had he lived, he intended to have granted their petition. " Samuel Slater was born in the town of Belper, in the county of Derby, June 9th, 1768. In June 28th, 1782, being about fourteen years of age, he went to live with Jedediah Strutt, Esq., in Milford, near Belper, (the inventor of the Derby ribbed stocking machine, and several years a partner of Sir Richard Arkwright in the cotton spinning business,) as a clerk; who was then building a large factory at Milford, where said Slater continued until August 1789. During four or five of the late years, his time was solely devoted to the factory as general overseer, both as respected making machinery and the manufacturing department. On the 1st day of September 1789, he took his departure from Derbyshire for London, and on the 13th he sailed for New York, where he arrived in November, after a passage of sixty-six days. He left New York in January 1790, for Providence, and there made an arrangement with Messrs. Almy and Brown, to commence preparation for spinning cotton at Pawtucket.

* PROVIDENCE, R. I. Dec. 13th, 1834.

Sir—At a late meeting of the board of trustees of the Rhode Island Historical Society, a resolution was passed of which the subjoined is a copy. Any communication that you may feel inclined to make in consonance with the request, will, if addressed to me, be promptly laid before the board.

I am, sir, respectfully yours,

THOMAS H. WEBB.

In board meeting—At the instance of the secretary, it was resolved, that Mr. Samuel Slater be requested to draw up and present to this society, a history of the first introduction of cotton spinning into this country, together with an account of the difficulties attendant thereupon, and of such other incidents in respect thereunto, as he may deem important or interesting to have preserved for the information of posterity.

A true copy from the records.   Attest,

THOMAS H. Webb,

Mr. Samuel Slater.   Secretary R. I. Hist. Soc.

"On the 18th day of the same month, the venerable Moses Brown took him out to Pawtucket, where he commenced making the machinery principally with his own hands, and on the 20th of December following, he started three cards; drawing and roving, and seventy-two spindles, which were worked by an old fulling mill water wheel in a clothier's building, in which they continued spinning about twenty months; at the expiration of which time they had several thousand pounds of yarn on hand, notwithstanding every exertion was used to weave it up and sell it.

" Early in the year 1793, Almy, Brown and Slater built a small factory in that village, (known and called to this day the old factory,) in which they set in motion, July 12, the *preparation* and seventy-two spindles, and slowly added to that number as the sales of the yarn appeared more promising, which induced the said Slater to be concerned in erecting a new mill, and to increase the machinery in the old mill." The above was written by Mr. Slater a short time before his death, and it is to be regretted that he did not live to give a full account of the progress of his business.

From the preceding account of Samuel Slater's early history, connections, and his enterprise and perseverance in laudable pursuits, it appears that he came to this country in honour and respectability. From his connections, advantages, and business turn, it is obvious that he might and in all probability would have reached a fortune in his own country. In leaving his own country with such promising appearances, and making America the theatre of his operations, he manifests in his early life a spirit of enterprise which all admire. With a keen discernment, he undoubtedly had premonitions of future prosperity, and ultimately of planting himself permanently in America.

———

The invention ascribed to Arkwright, and on which his renown for mechanical genius mainly rests, is said, by Mr. Baines, " To have been previously described, with the utmost distinctness, in the specification of the machine invented by John Wyatt, and that cotton had for some years been spun by those machines. The patent for the invention was taken out, in the year 1738, in the name of Lewis Paul, with whom Mr. Wyatt had connected himself in partnership, but there is evidence to show that the latter was the inventor."

The following accounts of Messrs. Arkwright and Strutt will be read with much interest, and this place appears to be appropriate for their insertion.

RICHARD ARKWRIGHT, was one of those great characters, whom nature seems to have destined, by the endowment of superior powers, to be the benefactor of their fellow-creatures. Born of parents who were classed among the inferior rank of society, and brought up to one of the most humble occupations in life, he yet, by the aid of genius and perseverance, rose to affluence and honour. Richard Arkwright, who was the youngest of thirteen children, was born in Preston, in Lancashire, some time in the year 1732. In that neighbourhood there was a considerable manufactory of linen goods, and of linen and cotton mixed, carried on; and his acquaintance with the operations he witnessed there, seems in early life to have directed his thoughts to the improvement of the mode of spinning. This, however, he did not accomplish, till many years had elapsed, for prior to the year 1767, he followed his trade, which was that of a barber; but at that period he quitted his original business and situation at Wirksworth, and went about the country buying hair. Coming to Warrington, he projected a mechanical contrivance for a kind of perpetual motion. A clock-maker of that town, of the name of John Kay, dissuaded him from it, and suggested that much money might be gained by an engine for spinning cotton, which Kay promised to describe. Kay and Arkwright then applied to Peter Atherton, Esq. of Liverpool, for assistance in the construction of such an engine, who, discouraged by the mean appearance of the latter, declined, though he soon afterwards agreed to lend Kay a smith and watch-tool maker to prepare the heavier part of the engine, whilst Kay himself undertook to make the clock-maker's part of it, and to instruct the workmen. In this way Arkwright's first engine, for which he afterwards took a patent, was made. Mr. Arkwright experienced many difficulties before he could bring his machine into use; and even after its completion had sufficiently demonstrated its value, its success would have been for ever retarded if his genius and application had been less ardent. His circumstances were far too unfavourable to enable him to commence business on his own account, and few were willing to risk the loss of capital on a new establishment. Having at length, however, the good fortune to secure the co-operation of Mr. Smalley, of Preston, he obtained his first patent for spinning cotton by means of rollers; but their property failing, they went to Nottingham, and there, by the assistance of wealthy individuals, erected a considerable cotton-mill turned by horses; but this mode of procedure being found too expensive, another mill, on a larger scale, was erected at Cromford, the machinery of which was put in motion by water. This patent right was contested about the year 1772, on the ground that he was not the original inventor. He obtained a verdict, however, and enjoyed the patent without further interruption, to the end of the term for which it was granted. Soon after the erection of the mill at Cromford, Mr. Arkwright made many improvements in the mode of preparing the cotton for spinning, and invented a variety of ingenious machines for effecting this purpose in the most correct and expeditious manner; for all which he obtained a patent in the year 1775. The validity of this second patent was tried in the court of king's bench, 1781, and a verdict was given against him on the ground of the insufficiency of the specification; but in 1785 the question was again tried in the court of common pleas, when he obtained a verdict. This verdict, however, raised up an association of the principal manufacturers, who instituted another cause, by writ of *scire facias*, in the court of king's bench, when Mr. Arkwright was cast, on the ground of his not being the original inventor. Conscious that this was not the case, he moved for a new trial; the rule, however, was refused, and on the 14th of November, 1785, the court of king's bench gave judgment to cancel the letters patent. The improvements and inventions in cotton spinning, for which we are indebted to the genius of Sir Richard Arkwright, and which complete a series of machinery so various and complicated, are so admirably combined and so well adapted to produce the intended effect in its most perfect form, as to excite the admiration of every person capable of appreciating the difficulty of the undertaking. And that all this should have been accomplished by the single efforts of a man without education, or even mechanical experience, is most extraordinary, and affords a striking instance of the wonderful powers displayed by the human mind when its powers are steadily directed to one object. Yet this was not the only employment of this eminent man; for at the same time that he was inventing and improving machinery, he was also engaged in other undertakings, which any person, judging from general experience, must have pronounced incompatible with such pursuits. He was taking measures to secure to himself a fair proportion of the fruits of his industry and ingenuity; he was extending the business on a larger scale; he was introducing into every department of manufacture, a system of industry, order, and cleanliness, till then unknown in any manufactory where great numbers were employed together. These advantages he so effectually accomplished, that his example may be regarded as the origin of almost all similar improvements. When it is considered that during this entire period he was afflicted with a violent asthma, which was always extremely oppressive, and threatened sometimes to put an immediate termination to his existence, his great exertions must excite astonishment. For some time previous to his death, he was rendered incapable of continuing his usual pursuits, by a complication of diseases, which at length deprived him of life, at Cromford, on the 3d of August, 1792, in the sixtieth year of his age. In the infancy of the invention, Sir Richard Arkwright expressed ideas of its importance, which to persons less acquainted with its merits appeared ridiculous; but he lived long enough to see all his conceptions more than realised in the advantages derived from it, both to himself and to his country; and the state to which those manufactures dependent on it have been advanced since his death, makes all that had been previously effected appear comparatively trifling. The merits of Sir Richard Arkwright may be summed up by observing, "that the object in which he was engaged, is of the highest public value; that though his family were enriched, the benefits which have accrued to the nation have been incalculably greater; and that upon the whole he is entitled to the respect and admiration of the world."—*Rees's Cyclopedia. Arkwright and Cotton.*

JEDEDIAH STRUTT, the ingenious inventor of the machine for making ribbed stockings, was a native of Normanton, where he was born in the year 1726. His father, who was a farmer and maltster, is represented as a severe man, who paid but little attention to the welfare of his offspring, whose education

JEDEDIAH STRUTT.

he neglected during their early years, and in whose establishment in the world when arrived at the years of maturity, he took no interest. Nature, however, had invested them with understandings superior to those of the class of society in which they ranked, and notwithstanding the many disadvantages under which they laboured, their abilities became conspicuous in their ultimate success and prosperity. This remark is more strictly applicable to his son Jedediah. Early in life he discovered an ardent desire for his own improvement, which at last grew into an habitual and strong passion for knowledge; and unassisted by the usual aids for the acquisition of learning, he, by the powers of his own genius alone, acquired a considerable acquaintance with literature and science. In the year 1754, Mr. Strutt took a farm at Blackwell, in the neighbourhood of Normanton, and married. Soon after this, about the year 1755, an event occurred which may be considered as the foundation of his future prosperity—it was to him that moment which the poet describes as the

" ———— tide in the affairs of men,
Which taken at the flood leads on to fortune."

Wm. Woolat, his wife's brother, who was a hosier, informed him of some unsuccessful attempts that had been made to manufacture ribbed stockings on the stocking-frame, which excited his curiosity, and induced him to investigate that curious and complicated machine, with a view to effect what others had attempted in vain. After much attention, labour, and expense, he succeeded in bringing the machine to perfection, and in the year 1756, in conjunction with his brother-in-law, obtained a patent for the invention, and removed to Derby, where he established an extensive manufacture for ribbed stockings. The advantages resulting from this invention were not confined to the patentees, for a very short time after the patent was obtained, another was granted to the Messrs. Morris of Nottingham, for a machine on a similar principle, but applied to the making of silk lace, a business which since has been carried on to a very great extent. Subsequently, the principle of the invention has been applied to a considerable variety of other work. About the year 1771, Mr. Strutt entered into partnership with the celebrated Sir Richard Arkwright, who was then engaged in the improvement of his improved machinery for cotton spinning. But though the most excellent yarn, or twist, was produced by this ingenious machinery, the prejudice which often opposes new inventions was so strong against it, that the manufacturers could not be prevailed upon to weave it into calicoes. Mr. Strutt, therefore, in conjunction with Mr. S. Need, another partner, attempted the manufacture of this article in the year 1773, and proved successful; but after a large quantity of calicoes had been made, it was discovered that they were subject to double the duty (six-pence per yd.) on cottons with linen warp, and when printed, were prohibited. They had, therefore, no other resource than to ask relief of the legislature, which after great expense, and a strong opposition from the Lancashire manufacturers, they at length obtained. In the year 1775, Mr. Strutt began to erect the cotton works at Belper, and afterwards at Milford, at each of which places he resided many years. These manufactures were carried on for a number of years by Mr. Strutt himself, and since by his sons and grandsons.

Mr. Need was partner of Mr. Strutt of Derby, and Mr. Strutt having seen Arkwright's machine, and declared it to be an admirable invention, only wanting an adaptation of some of the wheels to each other, both Mr. Need and Mr. Strutt entered into partnership with Arkwright. Mr. Strutt was brought up a farmer, but having a passion for improvement, and a mechanical genius, he succeeded in adapting the stocking-frame to the manufacture of ribbed stockings. He established an extensive manufacture of ribbed stockings at Derby, and after his connection with Mr. Arkwright he erected cotton works at Milford, near Belper; he raised his family to great wealth. Some of the circumstances connected with Arkwright's settling at Nottingham, were communicated by the late Mr. Wm. Strutt, the highly gifted and ingenious son of Jedediah Strutt, to the editor of the "Beauties of England and Wales."

Even to the present time, the course of improvement has not stopped. Mules have been constructed, which do not require the manual aid of a spinner, the mechanism being so contrived as to roll the spindle-carriage out and in at the proper speed, without a hand touching it; and the only manual labour employed in these machines, which are called "self-acting mules," is that of the children who join the broken threads. The first machine of this nature was invented by the ingenious Mr. William Strutt, F. R. S., of Derby, son of Jedediah Strutt, the partner of Arkwright; and the following mention is made of it in a memoir of that gentleman, written by his son, Mr. Edward Strutt, at present member for Derby. William Strutt died on the 29th of December, 1830, and the memoir appeared shortly after in a periodical journal :—" Among his other inventions and improvements, we may mention a self-acting mule for the spinning of cotton, invented more than forty years ago, but we believe the inferior workmanship of that day prevented the success of an invention, which all the skill and improvement in the construction of machinery in the present day has barely accomplished." This William Strutt was the early companion of Slater, they were boys in the mill together.

CHAPTER II.

THE STATE OF MANUFACTURES PREVIOUS TO 1790.

" Neither affecting to conceal the smaller rills by which the stream was fed, nor to bring them so much into view as to deprive the principal object of its consequence."

In collecting the facts relative to the early attempts at manufacture of cloths of various descriptions, I was much impressed with the struggles which were to be made against obstacles nearly of an insurmountable nature. The commencement was with imperfect machinery, obtained at great expense; ignorance of their operations; difficulties of constructing even from patterns and models, by such persons, who had no practical knowledge, and no means of knowing the theory or philosophy of the machinery. In addition to these perplexities, they had to encounter the free importations of articles from Europe, at a much lower rate than the home manufacturers could afford them. No wonder that they did not succeed, but we may be astonished that they persevered in their attempt. And we can now perceive, that from those small beginnings the present brightened prospects received their foundation. From the best information that I can gather, the jenny spinning, (with cards for rolls, and roving by hand), was first commenced in Beverly or Bridgewater, Mass.; and to the honour of that state it must be recorded, that the proprietors received assistance from the legislature. But even legislative protection could not support those small establishments against the superior machinery of England. Much individual sacrifice was endured, but these losses and vexatious experiments eventuated in the public good. We can now only record, to the praise of those brave spirits of untiring enterprise who laid the foundation of our present prosperity, such facts which must be their lasting praises. Few can now imagine the privations and disappointments, that attended these incipient measures; but immense establishments have grown out of them, matured and perfected by all the improvements of the age.*

* The manufacturing business in this country, small as it began, is now the first business of the age. It has already whitened the fields at the south with the growing of cotton; and covered the hills of the north with flourishing flocks; while the north is made alive with the busy hum of industry, and

Previous to the war of the revolution, notwithstanding the restrictions which the colonies laboured under, manufactures kept gaining ground; but the war greatly retarded and embarrassed many branches. Silk had made a good beginning at the south, as well as at the north; and was receiving encouragement from the mother country, in order to rival the French, in that important national resource. Other manufactures in their incipient state, were discouraged, and entirely failed. There was a great want of mechanics, and but few emigrations from Europe. Even tools and implements of husbandry were exceedingly scarce, and sold at enormous prices.

Every attempt therefore to recommence, or begin anew any domestic manufacture, had not only to contend with importations from the East Indies, and from Europe ; but the want of machinery, and the lack of artisans skilled in the various branches. This is evident in the first attempts of the jenny spinning, and the carding of rolls for woollen cloths. The evidence that will be

a great proportion of its population provided with an honest and lucrative employment; and with suitable economy, made contented and happy with the luxury of abundance. It was the being a witness of such mighty and benevolent changes in the condition of our country, and in the character and appearance of its inhabitants, that operated, not as a moderate impulse with the writer to present to the public the biography of the man who, amid disasters and difficulties, first put their springs in motion; and to present before the public some of the surprising results.

The following document is the earliest of any direct proof of an association to aid domestic industry, and as such it is worthy of preservation : " A number of inhabitants of the city and liberties of Philadelphia, having entered into an agreement of co-partnership, under the name of the United Company of Philadelphia, for promoting American manufactures, this is to certify, that Tench Coxe hath paid his full subscription of ten pounds towards the joint stock of the said company, whereby he is entitled to a vote in the business of the company ; of all the profits arising from the said manufactures, agreeable to the articles :—As witness my hand this eighth day of November 1775.   JOSEPH STILES, Treasurer."

The above Mr. Coxe was appointed to congress, as R. Peters's letter from the house of assembly, Philadelphia, shows :

Honourable Tench Coxe, Esq.

Sir,—I have the honour to enclose a copy of the minute of the general assembly, by which it will appear that you are appointed a delegate to represent this state in congress, until the constitution for the government of the United States shall be in operation.   I am, sir,

Your very obedient serv't,

RICHARD PETERS, Speaker.

incidentally produced in this volume, will show the weak and deficient state of all kinds of manufactures, previous to 1790. This period will be considered the era of their national commencement. It was in this year that the legislature of Massachusetts resolved more effectually to aid the Beverly company.* About the same time, Jan. 15th, 1790, the house of representatives in congress called on the secretary of the treasury to collect information on the subject, which led to a full and extensive enquiry, and resulted in the report of Alexander Hamilton, Dec. 5, 1791.

In examining American writers on this subject, I find no individual who commenced so early, and who continued with such unwavering perseverance, in the patriotic promotion of the growth of cotton, as the only redundant staple which this country could produce; and in the commencement and forwarding the cotton manufacture, under every disadvantage and embarrassment—I find no one appearing at the head and front of these measures equal to Tench Coxe. From his refutation of Lord Sheffield,† to his last draft of petition to congress on behalf of the tariff he continued the same undeviating champion, through an active and useful life, of domestic industry and economy ; and not even Hamilton himself deserves greater praise, in laying the foundation and in raising the superstructure of the American system, than that enlightened and energetic statesman. Incessantly engaged as he was, in those departments of government which demanded the exertion of all his energies, we find him always with the labouring oar ; and there can be no doubt that Washington's first secretary of the treasury is indebted for those valuable statistics, which enabled

---

* The following advertisement, April 3d, 1782, is from the Pennsylvania Gazette. A brief notice of the patriotic individual, who undoubtedly made the first " Jeans, fustians," &c. in America, will be inserted in the Appendix :—

" PHILADELPHIA MANUFACTURES—suitable for every season of the year, viz: Jeans, Fustians, Everlastings, Coatings, &c., to be sold by the subscriber at his dwelling house and manufactory, (which is now standing), in South Alley, between Market street and Arch street, and between Fifth and Sixth streets, on Hudson's square.   SAMUEL WETHERILL."

† The misconceptions in regard to American affairs, which prevailed in many parts of Europe in the year 1791, and particularly in the British dominions, were deemed to be very great: they appeared to be founded, in no small degree, on the disquisitions of Lord Sheffield. Tench Coxe demonstrated the errors of this writer, (whose observations had gone through six editions, from 1783 to 1791), first in the " Museum," and then in his " View of the United States."

him to draw up his report on manufactures, to the important assistance of Tench Coxe. If my limits would allow me to insert his correspondence with every department of government, the above remarks would be clearly demonstrated; but I must confine myself to a few.

The various disorders of 1787, and the want of a national system, affected very severely a number of persons in the large towns who were engaged in the different branches of manufactures. These were more numerous and much more important than was at that time perceived by persons of the closest observation. The laws of some of the states imposed considerable duties upon the fabrics of all the rest, in some instances as high as the impost on similar articles manufactured in foreign countries. The remains of the excessive importations of the four preceding years were constantly offered for sale at prices lower than their cost in Europe, and less than they could be made for in America. From a deep sense of these inconveniences, exertions were commenced in various parts of the United States, by persons of all descriptions, to relieve the manufacturing citizens; which appeared the more desirable to many, because the necessary measures tended at the same time to promote the great cause of union among the states, and to repress habits of expense which the war, and the peace likewise, though from very different causes, had introduced into most of the towns, and too many parts of the country. The citizens of Philadelphia took a very active part in these salutary measures, and instituted a society, which afterwards proved of considerable utility, to carry their views into execution. An address was delivered by Tench Coxe to an assembly of the friends of American manufactures, convened for the purpose of establishing a society* for the encouragement of manufactures and

---

* *The Plan of the "Pennsylvania Society for the Encouragement of Manufactures and the Useful Arts," founded in* 1787.

The wealth and prosperity of nations principally depend on a due attention to agriculture, manufactures and commerce. In the various stages of her political existence, America has derived great advantages from the establishment of manufactures and the useful arts. Her present situation in the world calls her, by new and weighty considerations, to promote and extend them. The United States, having assumed the station of an independent government, require new resources to support their rank and influence, both abroad and at home. Our distance from the nations of Europe,—our possessing within ourselves the materials of the useful arts, and articles of consumption and commerce,—the profusion of wood and water, (those powerful and necessary agents in all arts and manufactures,) the variety of natural productions with which this extensive country abounds, and the number of people

the useful arts, in the University of Pennsylvania, on Thursday, the 9th of August, 1787, and published at their request.

in our towns, and most ancient settlements, whose education has qualified them for employments of this nature,—all concur to point out the necessity of our promoting and establishing manufactures among ourselves. From a conviction of the truth and importance of these facts, a number of persons have agreed to associate themselves. Every member, on his admission, shall pay to the treasurer the sum of ten shillings, and the same sum annually, which shall go into the general fund, to defray the necessary expenses of the society, to confer premiums, and to accomplish every other salutary measure consistent with the design of the institution. For the better employment of the industrious poor, and in order to render the society as useful as possible, a subscription, for sums of not less than ten pounds, from any one person or company, shall be immediately opened to all persons whatever, for the purposes of establishing factories in such places as shall be thought most suitable; to be called, " The Manufacturing Fund."

The Hon. Tench Coxe, Esq., Philadelphia.

Boston, June 14, 1792.

My dear sir,—I have perused with renewed pleasure your remarks on the state of the Union, which you have obligingly inclosed to me. I shall think it useful on every account to cause them to be republished in our gazettes. The principles and facts are valuable as an acquisition to our political literature. But their tendency to foster an affection for the Union, in which self-love so plainly co-operates with patriotism, and their efficacy against the silly charges of our own malcontents, render them peculiarly useful and seasonable. A Briton, too, is ready enough to believe that the civilised world reaches no further than the Land's-End. You have furnished good physic to cure him of his prejudices. It has been too long the fashion to listen to the rant of eloquent ignorance. Our newspapers were formerly stuffed with declamation, almost without a single fact. Your publication not only furnishes knowledge to the public mind, but it establishes principles of discipline, which will assist in producing more for itself. Accordingly I beg you to accept my thanks for your work.

The bank mania, though checked, is not cured. This state has rejected a proposal for a state bank. But the defeated still hope success in some other form. Happily, our interests as a state are better founded than our opinions. Trade prospers, ships are in demand; the rate at which they are chartered is said to be high beyond what has been known in common times.

Produce sells readily, and at a good price; yet the merchants complain that trade is overburdened. In short, there is scarcely any thing that seems to languish.

I am, with sentiments of esteem and regard, your obliged and obedient humble servant, FISHER AMES.

The Hon. Tench Coxe, Esq., Philadelphia.

Boston, July 11th, 1793.

My dear sir,—You will please, with my thanks for the inclosure of the ingenious remarks on the scheme of a manufacturing town, to accept an

From the petition to the legislature of Massachusetts, and other collateral facts, the evidence is conclusive that cotton spinning in this country, further than the hand-card and one thread wheel, was carried through its first struggles by the Beverly company in Massachusetts.   What was done in Bridgewater, must have been a small concern.   In accordance with the general spirit of enterprise and indefatigable exertions among the citizens of Massachusetts, in all local and national concerns, the Beverly company, with tremendous obstacles in view and at the risk of their fortunes, made an attempt to accomplish an object which they knew would ultimately promote and extend the wealth and establish the independence of the united colonies—who had just emerged from European oppression, and declared to the world that they were, of right, free and independent ; the monarchs of the world having acknowledged their national existence.   The eagle-eyed legislature of the old Plymouth colony foresaw, that, without protection of their national industry, their independence was but a name, and that they had

apology for the delay of an answer.   Knowing that printers are more fond of publishing amusing than instructive tracts, I had doubts of the punctual insertion of the piece, and I chose to delay my answer till it had been done. The Centinel has at length given it to the public.   While the discussion of the subject affords pleasure and instruction to the political economists, it coincides perfectly well with the prevailing temper and views of the eastern states.   Even if it should be doubted whether manufacturing companies will prove profitable to the adventurers, yet as a very efficient means of introducing and perfecting the arts among us, there can be no question of their ultimate usefulness.   The spirit of enterprise has of late been uncommonly ardent.   Your observations are well adapted to the making it both inquisitive and cautious.   I cannot forbear noticing, also, the great propriety and advantages of interesting the hopes of our citizens in the operations of a government of sufficient energy to protect and reward their industry and enterprise.   So much is done by incendiaries to make the people hate and fear it, I think it a task worthy of a patriot and philosopher, to hold up the bright side of the case.   You have done so well heretofore, especially in the refutation of Lord Sheffield, that the federal men have placed a reliance on your continued attention to the same subjects, as time and circumstances may render their further elucidation necessary.   It is not many years since the encouragement of the arts was deemed an Utopian scheme in our country. One would think experience had fully proved the solidity of the principles of the advocates for manufactures.   But even yet the southern gentlemen hold it up as a bugbear of usurpation of power, and dissipation of public money.   You have stated facts which ought to have the effect of undeceiving them ; and if the spirit of party could be reasoned down, I should suppose you had done it.   I am, dear sir, with sentiments of esteem, &c. &c.

FISHER AMES.

lost the bravest of their sons, had fought and conquered, and still remained subservient to the aggrandisement of their enemies.

Rhode Island caught her spirit of manufacturing from the Beverly company, which had been formed in Massachusetts, and from this company she received her patterns of machinery and the mode of operating the machinery; though it must be acknowledged, that both states were indebted to foreign emigrants for instruction and assistance in spinning and weaving, and also in preparing the cotton.

At the recent great meeting in Boston, on the subject of opening a rail road to Albany, the infant difficulties of domestic manufactures were thus adverted to by Mr. Hallet:—

" We talk now of the future, in regard to railways, with doubt, as of an experiment yet to be tested, and many look upon the calculations of the sanguine as mere speculating dreams. Here is a new avenue about to be opened to the development of resources, and yet men hesitate to go forward. Let us test what we can reasonably anticipate in this, by what we know has happened, in the development of resources once deemed quite as visionary, through another medium of industry and enterprise—domestic manufactures. There is not an adult among us who cannot remember the time when it was a source of mortification to be dressed in homespun. Now, our own fabrics are among the best and richest stuffs of every day consumption, and the products of our looms are preferred even in foreign countries. Forty years ago, who would have dared to conjure up the visions of such manufacturing cities as Lowell, and Fall River, your Ware, Waltham, and the hundreds of flourishing villages which now constitute the most prosperous communities in this commonwealth? How small and feeble was the beginning of all this! In 1787, the first cotton mill in this state was got up in Beverly, by John Cabot and others, and in three years it was nearly given up, in consequence of the difficulties which the first beginning of the development of the vast resources of domestic industry, in our state, had to encounter. I hold in my hand," said Mr. Hallet, "a document of uncommon interest, on this subject, found in the files of the Massachusetts senate; which will show the early struggles of domestic manufactures, and the doubts entertained of their success, more forcibly than any fact that can be stated. It is the petition of the proprietors of the little Beverly cotton mill, in 1790, for aid from the legislature to save them from being compelled to abandon the enterprise altogether.

Petition of the Proprietors of the Beverly Cotton Manufacture.

" To the senate and house of representatives of the commonwealth of Massachusetts, in general court assembled, June 2, 1790—The proprietors of the Beverly Cotton Manufactory beg leave to represent, that the establishment of a manufacture of cotton, in imitation of the most useful and approved stuffs which are formed of that material in Europe, and thence continually imported into this country at a very great expense, has been attempted by the said proprietors. This attempt commenced in the year 1787, from a consideration of the extensive public advantages to be obtained by it; and on this occasion your petitioners may be permitted to declare that in that view of the subject, the hazard of their private property, and the many obstacles which have since deprived them of every hope of present emolument to themselves, were overlooked. The design has been prosecuted, although it has proved much more arduous and expensive than was at first conceived, and under very discouraging circumstances, so far as to demonstrate that it is practicable ; and that the manufacture, being once established, will be sufficiently lucrative to support and extend itself, and will afford not only a supply for domestic consumption, but a staple for exportation. The general use within the United States of imported cotton goods is well known to this court. It may be necessary to suggest for their reflection, that articles of this extensive consumption among us have been provided by foreigners, whose commerce we have thus encouraged, and that in this, as in other instances, we have been draining our country of a circulating medium to contribute to the wealth and populousness of Great Britain. Removing the occasion of this destructive traffic is not the only public advantage to be derived from the manufacture of cotton, as undertaken by the said proprietors. The raw material is procured in exchange for fish, the most valuable export in the possession of this state, and, at this time, in great need of encouragement. It must be evident that the cod fishery will be essentially encouraged by extending the demand for the imports to be obtained by it. This manufacture finds employment and support for a great number of persons, and among others for infirm women and children. In its immediate operation, and in the commerce and navigation connected with it, this honourable court will not fail to discover the beneficial influence of this manufacture, and especially upon the landed interest, by the increase of people and national wealth, which may be expected from it. The said proprietors, in the prosecution of their design, have necessarily incurred a variety of expenses and losses, which succeeding adventurers cannot be liable to. Among those experienced by us, are the following, viz:—The extraordinary price of machines unknown to our mechanics, intricate and difficult in their construction, without any model in the country, and only to be effected by repeated trials, and long attention ; one instance among many of the kind is a carding machine, which cost the proprietors eleven hundred dollars, and which can now be purchased for two hundred dollars. The extraordinary loss of materials in the instruction of their servants and workmen, while so many are new, and the additional losses sustained by the desertion of these, when partly informed, and by the increase of wages to prevent it, in consequence of the competition of rival manufactories. The present want of that perfection and beauty in their goods, which long established manufactories can exhibit, from the skill of their workmen, but principally from the use of machines which your petitioners have as yet found too expensive for them to procure ; (meaning the Arkwright patents). But not to trouble your honours with details which would encroach too much on the time of this court, your petitioners have ever conceived that the government of this commonwealth would at least indemnify them for these extraordinary expenses and losses ; which cannot be reimbursed by any future success of their design, since the models of machines, and the essential information obtained at their expense, is open to every succeeding adventurer. The expenditure of the said proprietors has already amounted to nearly the sum of £4,000, the value of their remaining stock is not equal to £2000, and a further very considerable advancement is absolutely necessary to obtain that degree of perfection in this manufacture, which alone can ensure its success. This necessary addition to their stock will enable the proprietors to rival in beauty, perfection, and cheapness, the European manufactures ; and in that case, they shall willingly trust in the prudence and patriotism of their countrymen for a preference. But the proprietors having already hazarded, some their whole fortunes, and others very large sums, are obliged to declare, that, without aid from this honourable court, no further advancement can be made. And, mortifying as it is, they feel themselves in the necessity of relinquishing a design highly beneficial to the public, and undertaken by them from the purest motives. The intended aid by a grant of land, made by a former legislature to the said petitioners, has not in any degree answered the purpose of it. Your proprietors now pray, that, in lieu of that grant, some more real and ready assistance may be afforded them ; submitting to the wisdom of the honourable court the particular mode of effecting it. Your petitioners conceive that the establishment of a manufacture, which gives encouragement to the most valuable branch of commerce possessed by this state, which must in its operation increase the number of people, and prevent those emigrations which have become so frequent, and are so dangerous to the landed interest ; a manufacture which, once established, will retain amongst us large sums of our circulating medium, and greatly increase the wealth of our country, cannot fail of the attention and protecting influence of this honourable court, and in this confidence they still anticipate the success of their design ; and as in duty bound will ever pray, &c.

JOHN CABOT, } Managers.
JOSHUA FISHER, }

" This petition," said Mr. Hallet, in a discussion of a proposed rail road, in Faneuil Hall, Boston, " was referred to the committee of both houses for the encouragement of arts, agriculture, and manufactures, (of which Nathaniel Gorham was chairman,) and with all the lights which that intelligent committee then had on this subject, destined to become one of the greatest means of developing resources ever opened to national prosperity, they cautiously reported that ' from the best information we can obtain, we are of opinion that the said manufactory is of great public utility. But owing to the great expenses incurred in providing machines, and other incidents usually attending a new business, the said manufactory is upon the decline, and unless some public

assistance can be afforded, is in danger of failing. Your committee therefore report, as their opinion, that the petitioners have
a grant of one thousand pounds, to be raised in a lottery :' on
condition that they give bonds that the money be actually appropriated in such a way as will most effectually promote the
' manufacturing' of cotton piece goods, in this commonwealth.
. . . . Where now is the little Beverly cotton
mill? And what has been the mighty development of resources
in domestic industry in forty-five years, since the date of that
petition, when the wisest men among us had got no farther than
to a belief that the said manufactory was of great public utility !
Is there any vision of the great public utility of railways," said
Mr. Hallet, "which can go beyond what now is, and what will be
in forty years, that can exceed in contrast what we know once
was and now is, in the development of resources by the investment of capital and industry in domestic manufactures? The
petitioners for the little Beverly cotton mill were doubtless deemed
to be absurdly extravagant, when they hinted that the manufacture of cottons would one day, not only afford a supply for
domestic consumption, but a staple for exportation. But what do
we now see ? Our domestic fabrics find a market in every clime,
and vessels, lying at your wharves, are receiving these goods to
export to Calcutta.

" The world is beginning to understand the true uses of wealth,
to develope the resources of the country ; and it is in great enterprises, which benefit the public more than those immediately concerned in them, that we have a practical demonstration of the
doctrine of the greatest good of the greatest number. Much is
said, and more feared, about the divisions of the rich and the poor.
But in truth, in our happy institutions, we need have no poor,
forming a distinct class among the citizens. Where is your populace, your rabble ? is an enquiry which has often puzzled the
foreigner who has passed through our streets when thronged by a
multitude. We have no populace—no rabble, but free and independent citizens. What has made them so ? The development of our resources. What has stopped the tide of emigration
that once threatened to depopulate New England? The development of our resources. Go on developing these resources, and
there need be no fear of setting the poor against the rich, for there
will be no poor to set against them. All will be rich, for they
will have enough ; and no man is in reality any richer for possessing what he cannot use. When men of capital are found hoard-
ing it, holding it back from enterprises, and cautious of doing any

thing to develope the resources of a community, there is then just cause to fear the operation of unequal and injurious distinctions. Take from industry and enterprise the means of acquiring wealth, cut off commerce, manufactures, canals, and railways, and you will lay the surest foundation possible for the despotism of one class over another. But open all these great resources to all—extend your facilities of intercourse throughout the country, and you cannot repress the energies of men ; you cannot keep them poor long enough to mark them as a class. Your gradations in society will be stepped over, forward and backward, so often, that no distinct line can be kept up. This is the vast moral power, which is exerted on society by the investment of capital for public benefit, without unjust privileges ; in great projects. Here are the true uses of wealth, in a government like ours, and this great specific lies at the bottom of the philosophy of our political economy. Develope the resources of the country—place the means of wealth within the reach of industry, and you produce the happy medium in society. All will then move forward evenly, as on the level of a rail road, with occasional inclined planes and elevations, but none that can stop the powerful locomotives which impel forward every New Englander—enterprise and moral energy."

The action on this petition, and the previous grant of land, are the first acts on record of direct legislative encouragement to domestic manufactures in the state of Massachusetts ; and therefore it is a document of great interest highly honourable to the enterprise of the citizens of Massachusetts, and to the sagacity of her legislature. Some assistance appears to have been granted to Mr. Orr* of Massachusetts, and it is thought to have been done previous to the grant to Beverly.

---

* In 1786, Robert and Alexander Barr, brothers, from Scotland, were employed by Mr. Orr, to erect carding, spinning, and roping machines in his works at East Bridgewater, where they were made. On the 16th Nov. 1786, the general court of Massachusetts, to encourage the machinists, made them a grant of 200*l.*, lawful money, for their ingenuity, and afterwards added to the bounty by giving them six tickets in the state land lottery in which there were no blanks.

In March 1787, Thomas Somers, (an English midshipman,) under the direction of Mr. Orr, also constructed a machine, or model, and by a resolve of the general court of the same date 20*l.* lawful money, was placed in the hands of Mr. Orr to encourage him in the enterprise.

The above machines and model remained in Mr. Orr's possession, for the inspection of all disposed to see them ; and he was requested by the

As there are several claimants from states and individuals, for the honour of having commenced the first carding and spinning of cotton, it will probably be more satisfactory to the parties concerned, and to the public, to insert their own accounts of their first operations, from which a judgment can be formed of the merits of the case.

" *To the Board of Managers of the Pennsylvania Society for promoting Manufactures and Useful Arts.*

"The report of the committee for manufactures :—This committee, considering that the business in which they are engaged had attracted the public notice, and that it would be expected some account should be given of the progress and present state of the institution, in August began an enquiry into the state of their funds, their stock of goods, machines, and utensils, by which they are enabled to lay before you the following statement, and they flatter themselves it affords a pleasing prospect of future success. It is now about twelve months since this society was formed, and subscriptions were entered into, some of which, for various causes, have not yet been paid. They therefore state the amount of the subscriptions received to the 23d August, and show the manner in which the money hath been applied.

" Amount of cash received of contributors, when
exchanged for specie. £1327 10s. 6d.
From this, deduct for machines, utensils and
fitting up the house for the manufactory, £453 10s. 2d.
_____
Which leaves a circulating capital of £874 0s. 4d.
_____

" With a view to meet one idea of the subscribers, the employment of the poor, and to promote the other objects of the institution, the committee purchased a quantity of flax, and employed between two and three hundred women in spinning linen yarn during the winter and spring, and also engaged workmen to make

general court to exhibit them, and to give all information and explanation in his power respecting them.

It is believed that the above, in 1786, was the first jenny and stock card made in the United States.

It is said that the first muskets ever made in America were made by Mr. Orr. Also the first nails made by machinery were manufactured at Bridgewater, Massachusetts.

a carding engine, and four jennies, of forty, forty-four, sixty, and eighty spindles, for spinning of cotton ; and, as soon as the season would permit the house to be fitted up, they were set to work. It is unnecessary to observe on the difficulties which occur in so arduous an undertaking as attempting to establish manufactures in a country not much acquainted with them—such as finding artists, and making machines without models, or but imperfect ones. The committee have further had various obstructions thrown in their way by foreign agents, of which you have already been informed. From these causes, it happened, that it was the 12th of April, 1788, before the first loom was set to work ; the number has been since increased to twenty-six, and in them have been wrought the following goods, to August 23d :—

"Of jeans, 2959½ yards, corduroys, 197½, federal rib, 67, beaver fustian, 57, plain cottons, 1567½, linen, 725, tow linen, 1337½— total 7111 yards. Besides in the looms two hundred yards of jeans, corduroys, cottons, and linen ; out of which manufactured goods they had sold, at this time, of jean, dyed cotton and linen yarn, fine and tow linen, &c. to the amount of four hundred and forty-eight pounds, five shillings, and eleven pence half-penny, besides which, in order to show the state of the factory to the 23d of August, 1788, in a clearer light, they subjoin the following statement of the stock account :—

STOCK, DR.

To cash,	£1327 10 6½
To debts due sundry persons,	375 9 0
To profit,	72 4 9½
	£1775 4 4

CR.

By utensils, &c.	£453 2 6
Goods on hand at the bleachers and printers,	732 14 11
Materials and linen yarn on hand,	550 2 6
Outstanding debts,	38 16 9
	£1775 4 4

"In addition to the enumerated articles manufactured to the 23d of August, we annex the following to Nov. 1 :—Jeans, 759½ yards, corduroys, 383½, flowered cotton, 39, cottons, 2095, flax linens, 123, tow linens, 494, bird eye, 123—total, 4016 yards. And about two hundred and forty yards of different kinds of goods now in the looms, the whole amounting to eleven thousand three hundred and sixty seven yards; and there has also been manufactured by the twisting mill, about one hundred and eighty five pounds of plain, coloured, and knitting thread; since the first of August, also, a hundred and ninety yards of cottons have been printed; and it may be observed, that the want of proper bleach-yards, and the difficulty of procuring persons well skilled in bleaching, contributed to prevent the quantity being printed which was intended.

"The committee have now laid before you a statement of their proceedings, and might adduce many arguments to prove the propriety, and indeed the necessity, of giving every encouragement to establish this valuable branch of internal trade; but they apprehend that the motives which gave birth to the association have not lost their energy, either from the result of these experiments, or the prospect of future success, and they do not hesitate to add, that every view of the subject fully proves the peculiar importance of the cotton manufacture to this country, and the possibility (with proper exertions) of giving it a permanency, which, they doubt not, will prove a source both of private and public wealth. Impressed with these sentiments, and feeling sensibly our late dependence on foreign nations for many of the most useful articles of life, it is certain that, unless there are great exertions of virtue and industry, we must still remain in the same disadvantageous situation; whilst on the other hand, if we pursue the plan of establishing manufactures amongst ourselves, we thereby open an extensive field of employment for persons of almost every description.*

Samuel Wetherill, Jr.

Chairman pro tem."

---

* The views which led to the early encouragement of manufactures, are in part expressed in the following extract from Hamilton's Report.

"The expediency of encouraging manufactures in the United States, which was not long since deemed very questionable, appears at this time to be pretty generally admitted. The embarrassments about the period of 1791, are very generally acknowledged. The obstructions of our external trade have led to serious reflections on the necessity of enlarging the sphere of our domestic commerce; the restrictive regulations, which in foreign markets abridge the vent of the increasing surplus of our agricultural produce, serve to beget an earnest desire that a more extensive demand for that surplus may be created at home; and the complete success which has rewarded manufacturing enterprise in some valuable branches, conspiring with the promising symptoms which attend some less mature essays in others, justify

Notwithstanding the laudable and persevering efforts made by the people of Massachusetts and Rhode Island, and soon after, of Pennsylvania, New York, and Connecticut, they entirely failed, and saw their hopes and prospects prostrate. In looking for the causes of such disasters, we find no deficiency of enterprise or exertion, none of funds, and none of men who were ready and willing to engage in the business, and no lack of patronage from the governments, they having learned from experience the privations during

a hope, that the obstacles to the growth of this species of industry, are less formidable than they were apprehended to be; and that it is not difficult to find, in its further extension, a full indemnification for any external disadvantages which are or may be experienced, as well as an accession of resources, favourable to national independence and safety.

" It ought readily to be conceded, that the cultivation of the earth—as the primary and most certain source of national supply; as the immediate and chief source of subsistence to man; as the principal source of those materials which constitute the nutriment of other kinds of labour; as including a state most favourable to the freedom and independence of the human mind; one, perhaps, most conducive to the multiplication of the human species—has intrinsically a strong claim to pre-eminence over every other kind of industry. But that it has a title to any thing like an exclusive predilection, in any country, ought to be admitted with great caution. That it is even more productive than every other branch of industry, requires more evidence than has yet been given in support of the position. That its real interests, precious and important as without the help of exaggeration they truly are, will be advanced rather than injured by the due encouragement of manufactures, may, it is believed, be satisfactorily demonstrated. And it is also believed, that the expediency of such encouragement, in a general view, may be shown to be recommended by the most cogent and persuasive motives of national policy."

" The only thing that reconciled the British ministry to the peace of independence was the prospect of our becoming one of their best customers. The prejudices of Americans, who thought the country too young for manufacturing, and that the arts, by introducing luxury, would also introduce vice, and wean them from that simplicity of manners which was believed exclusively to belong to the agricultural life ; the predilection which nearly half the community, especially the rich, had for the fabrics of the mother country, and the influence which the merchants have had in our councils, all continued to prevent the introduction of clothing manufactories into these states. Time, however, and experience, have demonstrated, that luxury and vice may find their way into a country where manufacturing is discouraged; that, by a spirit of traffic, foreign luxuries are introduced, and a restless migratory life robs a nation of its innocence and simplicity. Years have weaned many from European attachments, and the intelligent part of the merchants perceive that commerce would increase by multiplying and diversifying the objects of our industry."—*Mease.*

revolutionary war. All must be attributed to the fact, that, during all the incipient struggles, Great Britain had in operation a series of superior machinery, which Massachusetts and Rhode Island had endeavoured to obtain in vain. The present state of the American manufactures shows what has grown out of such disastrous beginnings, and furnishes one among the many evidences which may be found, not to despair in the day of adversity.

The following is the account, furnished by Wm. Anthony, of the commencement of Cotton Spinning in Rhode Island :—

" About the year 1788, Daniel Anthony, Andrew Dexter, and Lewis Peck, all of Providence, entered into an agreement to make what was then called "home-spun cloth." The idea at first was to spin by hand, and make jeans with linen warp and cotton filling, but hearing that Mr. Orr, of Bridgewater, Massachusetts, had imported some model of machinery from England, for the purpose of spinning cotton, it was agreed that Daniel Anthony should go to Bridgewater and get a draught of the model of said machine ; he, in company with John Reynolds, of East Greenwich, who had been doing something in the manufacturing of wool, went to Bridgewater, and found the model of the machine spoken of, in possession of Mr. Orr, but not in operation. It was not the intention of Mr. Orr* to operate it, but he only kept it for the inspection of those who might have an inclination to take draughts. The model of the machine was very imperfect, and was said to be taken from one of the first built in England. A draught of this machine was accordingly taken, and laid aside for a while. They then proceeded to build a machine of a different construction called a jenny ; I understood that a model of this machine was brought from England, into Beverly, Massachusetts, by a man of the name of Summers. This jenny had twenty-eight spindles ; the wood work was built by Richard Anthony, the spindles and brass were made by Daniel Jackson, an ingenious coppersmith of Providence. This jenny was finished in 1787. It was first set up in a private house and afterwards removed to the market house chamber in Providence, and operated there.

"Joshua Lindly of Providence was then engaged to build a carding machine, for carding the cotton agreeably to the draught presented, also obtained from Beverly. This machine was something similar to the one now used for carding wool, the cotton being taken off the machine in rolls, and roped by hand ; after some

* Mr. Orr received a compensation from government for presenting it for inspection. It was therefore called the State's Model.

delay this machine was finished. They then proceeded to build a spinning frame after the draught obtained at Bridgewater. This machine was something similar to the water-frame now in use, but very imperfect; it consisted of eight heads of four spindles each, being thirty-two spindles in all, and was operated by a crank turned by hand. The first head was made by John Baily, an ingenious clock-maker of Pembroke, Massachusetts, the other seven heads, together with the brass work and spindles, were made by Daniel Jackson of Providence, the wood work was made by Joshua Lindly of said Providence. In 1788, Joseph Alexander and James M'Kerris, natives of Scotland, arrived in Providence, both being weavers, and understanding the use of the fly-shuttle; they were engaged to weave corduroy. Mr. Alexander to weave a piece in Providence, and Mr. M'Kerris went to East Greenwich to work there. A loom was accordingly built after the directions of Mr. Alexander, and put in operation in the market house chamber; this was the first fly-shuttle ever used in Rhode Island. A piece of corduroy was there woven, the warp being linen and the filling cotton, but as there was no person to be found who could cut the corduroy, and raise the pile which makes the ribs on the face of the cloth, and give it the finish, it was thought best to abandon that kind of cloth. Mr. Alexander left Providence, and went to Philadelphia; Mr. M'Kerris continued to work in Greenwich for some years. This appears to be the beginning of the jenny spinning in Rhode Island, and undoubtedly originated with the above company.

" The spinning frame (the one attempted from the state's model), after being tried for some time in Providence, was carried to Pawtucket and attached to a wheel propelled by water—the work of turning the machine was too laborious to be done by hand, and the machine was too imperfect to be turned by water. Soon after this, the machine was sold to Mr. Moses Brown of Providence, but as all the carding and roping was done by hand it was very imperfect, and but little could be done. This was the situation of cotton manufacturing in Rhode Island, when Mr. Samuel Slater arrived in this country; then all this imperfect machinery was thrown aside, and machinery more perfect built under his direction. About the time the above machinery was being made, John Fullem, a native of Ireland, a stocking weaver by trade, settled in East Greenwich. He had a stocking loom, and his object was to weave stockings for the inhabitants generally; but not succeeding there to his wishes, he went to Providence, and sold his loom to Moses and Smith Brown, and still continued to operate it under the superintendence of Smith Brown ; but the business was found unprofitable, and was abandoned.

"About the time the above machinery was put into operation, Herman Vandausen, a native of Germany, came to East Greenwich, and undertook the business of calico printing, being a calico printer by trade ; he went to work, cut his types on wood, and began to print ; his object was to print for the people generally, and many people wove coarse cotton cloth in their families, and had it printed. The calico looked much like that imported from India in that day, and was not much, if any, inferior to that cloth. Some samples of the cloth printed by Mr. Vandausen was shown (by a gentleman that now lives in Providence) to Mr. John Brown, who was then about trading to India. Mr. Brown gave some encouragement of assistance, but as it was found cheaper to import than to make them here, the business was given up."

In addition to the communication of Wm. Anthony, in conversation with Joseph Anthony, of Providence, R. I., the oldest son of Daniel Anthony, he fully concurred in the above statement. He stated that his brother Richard Anthony made the first jenny in Rhode Island, probably under the direction of his father, who it is thought spun the first yarn from jennies, by the assistance of his sons. There were thirty spindles on the jenny. The carding machine produced a roll eighteen inches long. It was then taken by a woman, and roped on a hand wheel. The same Daniel Anthony made hand-cards during the revolutionary war ; but no machinery was obtained till after the independence of the states. David Buffum bought a jenny, and Joseph Anthony spun on it at Newport two years, and obtained warp at Slater's mill, but they failed in their attempt. These were the machines purchased by Moses Brown, and referred to in the following letter to Mr. Slater.

Extract of a letter to Samuel Slater from Moses Brown.

PROVIDENCE, 10th of 12th month, 1789.

We have two machines of this kind, one of thirty-two spindles, the other of twenty-four. They have been worked, and spun about one hundred and fifty skeins of cotton yarn, from five to eight skeins of fifteen lays round a reel of two yards to the pound; but the person whom we let the mill to, being unacquainted with the business, and the mills probably not perfected, he could not make wages in attending them, and therefore they are at present still. We then wrought hand roping and the carding machine was not in order. We have since got a jenny, and are putting on fine cards to the machine : these with an eighty-four and a sixty spinning jenny, and a doubling and twisting jenny, compose the principal machinery about our manufactory. We have from Ireland a man and his wife, who are spinners on the jennies, but we are destitute of a person acquainted with the frames. We shall be glad to be informed what quantity of yarn your mills spin in a day on one spindle. What number of spindles a lad can, or does attend, and at what age? How your roping is made, what fineness, whether twisted harder or softer than for jennies? Whether the cotton is soaped before carding, as that for the jenny, or not at all? What the wooden rollers in the mills are covered with? Ours have been done with calf-skin. How the taking up is regulated. Ours is by leather strings? On what the spools play and run, on irons?

The following document will show the extent to which the firm of Almy & Brown had carried their operations about this period :

An Account of the Cotton Goods manufactured by Almy & Brown, of Providence, state of Rhode Island, since the commencement of the business, say about the 11th of 6th month, 1789, to the 1st of 1st month, 1791.

Corduroy,	45 pieces,	1090	yds. sold from 3s. 6d. to 4s. per yd.		
Royal Ribs, Denims, &c.	25 "	558	"	3s.	4s.
Cottonets,	13 "	324	"	2s. 6d.	3s.
Jeans,	79 "	1897	"	2s.	2s. 6d.
Fustians,	26 "	687	"	1s. 8d.	2s.

Total 189 pieces. 4556 yds.

From the 1st day of the 1st month, 1791, to the present date.

Velverets,	30 pieces,	669	yds. sold from 4s. to 4s. 4d.		
Thicksets,	30 "	745	"	3s. 6d.	4s.
Corduroy,	45 "	1001	"	3s. 6d.	4s.
Fancy Cords,	26 "	664	"	3s. 6d.	4s.
Royal Ribs, Denims, &c.	55 "	1284	"	3s.	4s.
Jeans,	74 "	1769	"	2s.	2s. 6d.
Fustians,	66 "	1691	"	1s. 8d.	2s.

Total 326 pieces. 7823 yds.

ALMY & BROWN.

Providence, 10th month, 15th, 1791.

Andrew Dexter was an English goods merchant in Boston, and removed to Providence in 1785. His store was near where the Arcade now stands. He was the brother of Samuel Dexter, of Boston, who was secretary of the treasury and of the war department, and a senator of the United States. This gentleman assisted in the commencement of making machines for manufacturing cotton. His debtor account with the business commenced Sept. 8th, 1788, in which I find a machine for calendering cotton goods ; the first charge is dated March 8th, 1790 ; this calender was put up in Moses Brown's barn, and worked by a horse. The extracts here furnished from his leger show the connection existing between Dexter, and Almy and Brown, and the operatives employed by them; and very fairly elucidate the very limited nature of the manufacturing business in general. The extracts are all certified as true copies, by George H. Peck.

Moses Brown to Andrew Dexter, Dr.

	£.	s.	d.
1789.			
May 18. To my obligation of this day, ...	45	00	00

To spinning jenny complete, sold him per agreement
at the bills, viz:

	£	s	d
To Nathaniel Gilmer's bill, forging 60 spindles, and other iron work	3	1	9
8lb. 7oz. steel for spindles, at 10d.		7	
	3	8	9
To Elijah Bacon's bill for stuff, . . .		18	9
To Oliver Carpenter's bill for 60 whirls,		10	
To Daniel Jackson's bill, ...	4	13	9
To Joshua Lindley's bill, ...	11	8	3
To cash paid for wire at several times,		3	9
To James Burrell's bill for cylinder,	2	8	
To Job Danforth's bill for stuff, . . .		8	6
To cash paid for pulleys 1s. 4d., do. for wire and line, 6d.	1	10	
To do. do. for screws 11d., do. for wire, 2s. 4d.	3	3	

————24 4 10

£69 4 10

1789.   *Cr.*

June 27. By one and half chest tea, received of Brown and
Benson on his acct. nt. wt. as per bill,

383
188
————571lb. at 1s. 8d.   47 11 8

Nov. 5. By 1329lb. beef received of Judge Aldridge,   16s. 8d.   11 1 6
By one calf-skin.   12

Jan. 25. By 128¾lb. sole leather at 14d. 7 9 7½
1790.

By half the hide and tallow, 300½lb.; the whole being
601lb. 2 10 1

£69 4 10

1790.   —

Dr. Jenny, Carding and Spinning Frame, completed at the joint and
equal expense of Lewis Peck and Andrew Dexter.

To Lewis Peck's bill,   61 11 5
To Andrew Dexter, do.   78 3 7
————   £139 15

Extract of Almy & Brown's account in Andrew Dexter's Leger.

1791. April 16,   1 piece of Jean 20¼ yards
                4   do.   do. 100¼ do.
                1   do.   do. 26½ do.
1792. July 12,   114¾ cotton, at 2s. 7½d.   ——£15 2s.

The above is a true copy from the late Andrew Dexter Esqr's. Leger.
      Providence, Nov. 24th, 1835.
                           GEORGE H. PECK.

From the above documents, there is undeniable proof that Hargreaves' jennies were in use, in various places in the United States, previous to 1790, and that mixed goods of linen and cotton were wove principally by Scotish and Irish weavers. But I have not been able to ascertain, beyond a doubt, who first introduced the jenny, or by whom they were first used for spinning in America.

Moses Brown says—" We had, in 1789, got several jennies and some weavers at work on linen warps, and found the undertaking much more arduous than I expected, both as to the attention necessary and the expense, being necessitated to employ workmen of the most transient kind, and on whom little dependence could be placed."*

" During this time, 1790, linen warps were wove, and the jenny spinning was performed in different cellars of dwelling houses." There have been made by Almy & Brown, (Moses Brown found money, they being poor) since the 1st of January, 1790, to November following, velverets, velverteens, corduroys, thicksets, a variety of fancy cut goods, jeans, denims, velures, stockinets, pillows of fustian, &c., 326 pieces, containing 7823 yards, there

* The difficulties under which these incipient measures towards the establishment of the business were pursued, can hardly be conceived at the present day, even by a practical and experienced machinist or manufacturer. The basin of the Narragansett Bay, and the small but invaluable streams that fall into it on every side, did not form then, as they now form, a continuous hive of mechanical industry, enterprise, and skill, where every sort of material, and every, even the most minute, subdivision of handicraft ingenuity, could be procured at will. There were no magazines or workmen. With the exception of scythes, anchors, horse shoes, ploughs, nails, cannon shot, and a few other articles of iron, there was no staple manufacture for exportation from Rhode Island. The mechanism then applied in these manufactures was almost as simple as the first impulse of water or steam. The compounds of gyration now obtained, in almost endless variety, by the application of the ellipsis, was then almost or wholly unknown in this country. No sheetings, shirtings, checks, or ginghams, were made previous to 1790.

are also several other persons who manufactured cotton and linen by the carding machines and jennies." We hear nothing of the use of jennies after this period, and they produced but little advantage to the community; as Moses Brown observes :—" Our commencing the business at a period, when from the great extent of it in England and Ireland, and other causes, many became bankrupts, their goods were sold at auction, and shipped to America in large quantities, the two or three last years, lower than ever before. Add to this, which is much the greatest difficulty, British agents have been out in Providence, and, I presume, some other manufacturing towns, with large quantities of cotton goods for sale, and strongly soliciting correspondence of people in the mercantile line to receive their goods at a very long credit, say eighteen months, which is six or nine more than has been usual heretofore ; for the discouragement of their manufactory here. This bait has been too eagerly taken by our merchants, who, from their activity in business, mostly trade equal to or beyond their capital, and so are induced by the long credit to receive the goods, in expectation of turning them to advantage before the time of payment. But the great quantities some have on hand, we have reason to expect, will disappoint them; but others, being induced by the same motive, are supplied, and thus the quantities of British goods of these kinds on hand, exceeding the market, obstruct the sale of our own manufactures, without the merchant trading in them getting his usual profits by them. This English trade, therefore, in time, would be reduced for want of profits ; but when the actual sales of British goods fail, of the cotton manufacture, they are sent and left here on commission. This, I am informed, by good authority, was the policy of the English manufacturers, formed into societies for that purpose."

The abilities of the manufacturing interest of Great Britain to intercept the sale of our own goods, at a price as low as theirs has been heretofore sold by our importing merchants, the actual combination of them to discourage other countries, forms a very great discouragement to men of abilities to lay out their property in extending manufactories ; the preparation for which, even before they can be perfected, must be left, if they cannot be continued. Such was the incipient state of the attempt at jenny spinning, in 1790 ; and nothing but the introduction of the " water-frame spinning," which had superseded the jennies in England, could have laid a foundation for the cotton manufacture in the United States. But that had happily commenced, by an individual who was personally and practically acquainted with all its branches, and who had uncommon determination and perseverance to accomplish his purpose. The following description of *jenny spinning*, is from the Edinburgh Encyclopedia, under the article "Cotton Spinning."

" The jenny, in its manner of action, resembles the ancient spinning with the distaff and spindle, but is so contrived, that one person works a number of spindles at once. It was the earliest improvement on spinning, after the *one-thread wheel*, and was the invention of Richard Hargreaves, weaver in Lancashire, in the year 1767. The jenny is now entirely superseded by the mule. For jenny spinning, the elementary process was called *batting* ; it was next soaped, in order to make it more easily stretched in the roving and spinning; the soaping was performed by immersing the cotton in a solution of soap in water; it was next put into a screw press, and afterwards dried in a stove.

"Hand cards first, and stock cards afterwards, were employed before the invention of the cylinder cards.

" The roving was performed, on similar principles to the spinning jenny, on a machine called a *billy*, which was driven by means of bands from a cylinder, which receives its motion from a vertical fly-wheel, driven by hand at one end of the machine.

" The *jenny* is a machine, similar in its operation to the *roving billy*, but differs from it in construction in this respect, that the *clasp* is attached to the carriage, while the spindles are disposed in the rails of the frame which remain at rest. The drawing out of the clasp stretches the roves so as to reduce them into the size proper for the yarn, at the same time the spindles twine it. During the return of the carriage, the yarn is built on the spindles by levers and wires, and formed like the rovings into cops. It is wrought with the hand by one grown-up person, assisted by a boy or girl, called a *piecer*, in order to mend such threads as break. The yarn, when taken off the spindles, is sometimes reeled, but more frequently given to the weaver in cops, who has it wound on the bobbins preparatory to being placed in the shuttle."

James Hargreaves, a weaver of Stand Hill, near Blackburn, was the inventor of the jenny. Such a machine, it is probable, would not be at once perfected; its construction would probably occupy the author, who was a poor man, and had to work for his daily bread, some years ; and as Hargreaves went to Nottingham in 1790, before which time his machine had not only been perfected, but its extraordinary powers so clearly proved, notwithstanding his efforts to keep it secret, as to expose him to persecution and the attacks of a mob, it is reasonable to think that the invention was conceived, and that the author began to embody it, as early as 1764. Hargreaves, though illiterate and humble, must be regarded as one of the greatest inventors and improvers in the cotton manufacture. His principal invention, and one which showed high mechanical genius, was the jenny.

Hargreaves is said to have received the original idea of this machine, from seeing a one-thread wheel overturned upon the floor, when both the wheel and the spindle continued to revolve. The spindle was thus thrown from a horizontal into an upright position ; and the thought seems to have struck him, that if a number of spindles were placed upright, and side by side, several threads might be spun at once.

He contrived a frame, in one part of which he placed eight rovings in a row, and in another part a row of eight spindles. With this admirable machine, though at first rudely constructed, Hargreaves and his family spun weft for his own weaving. Aware of the value of the invention, but not extending his ambition to a patent, he kept it as secret as possible for a time, and used it merely in his own business.   A machine of such powers could not however, be long concealed ; but when it became the subject of rumour, instead of gaining for its author admiration and gratitude, the spinners raised an outcry that it would throw multitudes out of employment, and a mob broke into Hargreaves' house, and destroyed his jenny.   So great was the persecution he suffered, and the danger in which he was placed, that this victim of popular ignorance was compelled to flee his native county, as the inventor of the fly-shuttle had been before him.   Thus, the neighbourhood where the machine was invented, lost the benefit of it ; yet without preventing its general adoption—the common and appropriate punishment of the ignorance and selfishness which oppose mechanical improvements.   The number of spindles in the jenny was at first eight, when the patent was obtained it was sixteen ; it soon came to be twenty or thirty, and no less than one hundred and twenty have since been used.   Before quitting Lancashire for Nottingham, Hargreaves had made a few jennies for sale, and the importance of the invention being universally appreciated, the interests of the manufacturers and weavers brought it into general use, in spite of all opposition.

It is mentioned, that Crompton, the inventor of the mule, learned to spin upon a jenny of Hargreaves' make, in 1769.

Notwithstanding the outrage and violence against him, Hargreaves was enabled to live in comfort though not in affluence, on the fruits of his invention.

CHAPTER III.

FROM SAMUEL SLATER'S LEAVING ENGLAND TO HIS MARRIAGE
WITH HANNAH WILKINSON, OF NORTH PROVIDENCE, R. I.

" He that wishes to be counted among the benefactors of posterity, must add, by his
own toil, to the acquisition of his ancestors."

The preceding chapter is designed to show, that every attempt
to spin cotton warp or twist, or any other yarn, by water power,
till 1790, had totally failed, and every effort to import the patent
machinery of England had proved abortive.* Much interest had
been excited in Philadelphia, New York, Beverly, Massachusetts,
and in Providence, Rhode Island ; but they found it impossible to
compete with the superior machinery of Derbyshire. Distrust
and despondency had affected the strongest minds ; disappointment and repeated losses of property, had entirely disheartened
those brave pioneers in the production of homespun cloth. At
this moment, Mr. Slater had left Belper, and was on his passage
to America, with a full and decided plan to construct and erect
the Arkwright machinery in the United States. The evidence
adduced in this chapter, is designed to show, that previous to 1790,
no such machinery existed in this country; and that Samuel
Slater, without the aid of any one who had ever seen such
machinery, did actually, from his personal knowledge and skill,
put in motion the whole series of Arkwright's patents ; and that
he put them in such perfect operation, as to produce as good yarn,
and cotton cloth of various descriptions, equal to any article of the
kind produced in England at that time. This is the claim that
we make for the subject of this memoir, and if we are successful
in proving this point, we lay a foundation for sufficient praise for
any one individual.

Mr. Slater's passage from London to New York extended to
sixty-six days. This was a considerable imprisonment to a lands-
man who had never seen a ship before.

---

* Tench Coxe entered into a bond with a person who engaged to send him,
from London, complete brass models of Arkwright's patents; the machinery
was completed and packed, but was detected by the examining officer, and
forfeited, according to the existing laws of Great Britain, to prevent the
exportation of machinery.

Immediately on his arrival, he was introduced to the New York Manufacturing Company, and engaged in their employment. But the state of their business was low and inferior, compared with what he had been accustomed to in his own country; so that he was dissatisfied with his prospects, and he did not like the water privileges which were shown him in this section of the country, to commence any new works.

A captain of one of the Providence packets informed him of Moses Brown, who was endeavouring to do something in the cotton business, and advised Mr. Slater to write by him and offer his services; which advice he followed, and turned his attention from Philadelphia, to which he had been first directed, as appears by the following letter, dated—

NEW YORK, December 2d, 1789.

Sir,—A few days ago I was informed that you wanted a manager of *cotton spinning*, &c. in which business I flatter myself that I can give the greatest satisfaction, in making machinery, making good yarn, either for *stockings* or *twist*, as any that is made in England; as I have had opportunity, and an oversight, of Sir Richard Arkwright's works, and in Mr. Strutt's mill upwards of eight years. If you are not provided for, should be glad to serve you; though I am in the New York manufactory, and have been for three weeks since I arrived from England. But we have but *one card, two machines*, two spinning jennies, which I think are not worth using. My encouragement is pretty good, but should much rather have the care of the perpetual carding and spinning. *My intention* is to erect a *perpetual card and spinning*. (Meaning the Arkwright patents.) If you please to drop a line respecting the amount of encouragement you wish to give, by favour of Captain Brown, you will much oblige, sir, your most obedient humble servant,   SAMUEL SLATER.

N. B.—Please to direct to me at No. 37, Golden Hill, New York.

Mr. Brown, Providence.

It appears from the above letter, that Mr. Slater claimed to have a full knowledge of the business of Messrs. Arkwright and Strutt; that he could make the machinery, and superintend the works when erected; and that such were the works he wished to be engaged in; that he could make as good yarn either for *stocking* or *twist*, as any that was made in England at that time. The machinery in New York was very inferior, jennies on the Hargreave's plan; but the Arkwright patent was not in existence, and every attempt to establish it had been unsuccessful, as appears by the following letter:—

PROVIDENCE, 10th 12th month, 1789.

Friend,—I received thine of 2d inst. and observe its contents. I, or rather Almy & Brown, who has the business in the cotton line, which I began, one being my son-in-law, and the other a kinsman, want the assistance of a person skilled in the frame or water spinning. An experiment has been made, which has failed, no person being acquainted with the business, and the frames imperfect.

We are destitute of a person acquainted with water-frame spinning; thy being already engaged in a factory with many able proprietors, we can hardly suppose we can give the encouragement adequate to leaving thy present employ. As the frame we have is the first attempt of the kind that has been made in America, it is too imperfect to afford much encouragement; we hardly know what to say to thee, but if thou thought thou couldst perfect and conduct them to profit, if thou wilt come and do it, thou shalt have all the profits made of them over and above the interest of the money they cost, and the wear and tear of them. We will find stock and be repaid in yarn as we may agree, for six months. And this we do for the information thou can give, if fully acquainted with the business. After this, if we find the business profitable, we can enlarge it, or before, if sufficient proof of it be had on trial, and can make any further agreement that may appear best or agreeable on all sides. We have secured only a temporary water convenience, but if we find the business profitable, can perpetuate one that is convenient. If thy prospects should be better, and thou should know of any other person unengaged, should be obliged to thee to mention us to him. In the mean time, shall be glad to be informed whether thou come or not. If thy present situation does not come up to what thou wishest, and, from thy knowledge of the business, can be ascertained of the advantages of the mills, so as to induce thee to come and work ours, and have the *credit* as well as advantage of perfecting the first water-mill in America, we should be glad to engage thy care so long as they can be made profitable to both, and we can agree. I am, for myself and Almy & Brown, thy friend,

MOSES BROWN.

Samuel Slater, at 37, Golden Hill, New York.

In the above letter, Moses Brown offers Samuel Slater, if he could work the machinery they had on hand, *all the profits of the business.* On the proviso, that he was what he professed, and would erect machinery such as he described, he should become concerned with him as they might agree.

He holds out to him the promise of the *credit,* as well as the *advantages* of perfecting the first *water-mill* in America. Under these inducements and assurances, Mr. Slater left New York, expecting to find the water-frame ready for operation. When he came to Providence, he assured Mr. Brown that he could do all that he had promised in his letter; for proof of which he showed him "his indenture" with Mr. Strutt, who had been a partner with Arkwright, and who spun the best yarn, both for stockings and twist, that was at that time spun in England. Moses Brown took Mr. Slater to Pawtucket, and showed him the machinery that he had described in his letter, which they had failed to operate, not finding any person who had wrought on the Arkwright patent, or had seen any one that had wrought on it.

Moses Brown told me, that, " when Samuel saw the old machines, he felt down-hearted, with disappointment—and shook his head, and said ' these will not do ; they are good for nothing in their present condition, nor can they be made to answer.' It appears that Mr. Anthony had tried them, and was unsuccessful ; and different persons, who had seen these works, have informed me that they were worth nothing more, than so much old iron ;" these were the words of Wm. Almy, when speaking to me on the subject.   Such particulars may to some appear frivolous ; but such transactions as tend to illustrate the progress of the wealth or manners of our country, merit the utmost attention.   Even minute events are objects of consequence when they tend to establish important points in national history, and national aggrandisement.   After various disapointments, it was proposed that Mr. Slater should erect the series of machines, called the Arkwright patents, which he would not listen to, till he was pro- mised a man to work on wood, who should be put under bonds not to steal the patterns, or disclose the nature of the works.   " Under my proposals," says he, " if I do not make as good yarn, as they do in England, I will have nothing for my services, but will throw the whole of what I have attempted over the bridge."

The following document will show what was finally determined on between the parties:—

" The following agreement, made between William Almy and Smith Brown of the one part, and Samuel Slater of the other part,—Witnesseth that the said parties have mutually agreed to be concerned together in, and carry on, the spinning of cotton by water, (of which the said Samuel pro- fesses himself a workman, well skilled in all its branches ;) upon the follow- ing terms, viz :—that the said Almy and Brown, on their part, are to turn in the machinery, which they have already purchased, at the price they cost them, and to furnish materials for the building of two carding machines, viz :—a breaker and a finisher ; a drawing and roving frame ; and to extend the spinning mills, or frames, to one hundred spindles.   And the said Samuel, on his part, covenants and engages, to devote his whole time and service, and to exert his skill according to the best of his abilities, and have the same effected in a workmanlike manner, similar to those used in England, for the like purposes.   And it is mutually agreed between the said parties, that the said Samuel shall be considered an owner and proprietor in one half of the machinery aforesaid, and accountable for one half of the expense that hath arisen, or shall arise, from the building, purchasing, or repairing, of the same, but not to sell, or in any manner dispose of any part, or parcel thereof, to any other person or persons, excepting the said Almy and Brown;

neither shall any others be entitled to hold any right, interest, or claim, in any part of the said machinery, by virtue of any right which the said Slater shall or may derive from these presents, unless by an agreement, expressed in writing from the said Almy and Brown, first had and obtained—unless the said Slater has punctually paid one half of the cost of the said machinery with interest thereon ; nor then, until he has offered the same to the said Almy and Brown in writing upon the lowest terms; that he will sell or dispose of his part of the said machinery to any other person, and instructed the said Almy and Brown, or some others by them appointed, in the full and perfect knowledge of the use of the machinery, and the art of water spinning. And it is further agreed, that the said Samuel, as a full and adequate compensation for his whole time and services, both whilst in constructing and making the machinery, and in conducting and executing the spinning, and preparing to spin upon the same, after every expense arising from the business is defrayed, including the usual commissions of two and a half per cent. for purchasing of the stock, and four per cent. for disposing of the yarn, shall receive one half of the profits, which shall be ascertained by settlement from time to time, as occasion may require; and the said Almy and Brown the other half—the said Almy and Brown to be employed in the purchasing of stock, and disposing of the yarn. And it is further covenanted, that this indenture shall make void and supersede the former articles of agreement, made between the said Almy and Brown and the said Slater, and that it shall be considered to commence, and the conditions mentioned in it be binding upon the parties, from the beginning of the business ; the said Samuel to be at the expense of his own time and board from thenceforward. And it is also agreed that if the said Almy and Brown choose to put in apprentices to the business, that they have liberty so to do. The expense arising from the maintenance of whom, and the advantages derived from their services during the time the said Almy and Brown may think proper to continue them in the business, shall be equally borne and received as is above provided for in the expenses and profits of the business. It is also to be understood, that, whatever is advanced by the said Almy and Brown, either for the said Slater, or to carry on his part of the business, is to be repaid them with interest thereon, for which purpose they are to receive all the yarn that may be made, the one half of which on their own account, and the other half they are to receive and dispose of, on account of the said Slater, the net proceeds of which they are to credit him, towards their advance, and stocking his part of the works, so that the business may go forward.

"In witness whereof the parties to these presents have interchangeably set their hands, this fifth day of the fourth month, seventeen hundred and ninety.

WM. ALMY.
SMITH BROWN.
SAMUEL SLATER.

Witnesses—
Oziel Wilkinson, Abraham Wilkinson."

In accordance with this agreement of copartnership, I find a bill of account, settled Dec. 3d, 1792, signed Almy & Brown, in account with Samuel Slater ; which contains the following item of credit to Samuel Slater :—" Nov. 25th, 1792. By the one half of the proceeds from the sales of yarn spun at the mills, and of credit taken to our account, and accounted for by us as sold— £882 4s. 11½d. Providence Dec. 3d, 1792. ALMY & BROWN."

I find also these charges on the same settlement :—

1792, Feb. 17.
   To the one half of our account against spinning mills
      for machinery, &c. up to Feb. 11th, 1792,   £252 1 6
   To one half of do. for stock up to same date,   210 19 1¾

The above documents show what was finally determined on between the parties in the business.

The following letter from Mr. Smith Wilkinson, written at my request, corroborates the above :—

POMFRET, May 30th, 1835.

Mr. Samuel Slater came to Pawtucket early in January 1790, in company with Moses Brown, Wm. Almy, Obadiah Brown, and Smith Brown, who did a small business in Providence, at manufacturing on billies and jennies, driven by men, as also were the carding machines. They wove and finished jeans, fustians, thicksetts, velverets, &c. ; the work being mostly performed by Irish emigrants. There was a spinning frame in the building, which used to stand on the south-west abutment of Pawtucket bridge, owned by Ezekiel Carpenter, which was started for trial (after it was built for Andrew Dexter and Lewis Peck) by Joseph and Richard Anthony, who are now living at or near Providence. But the machine was very imperfect, and made very uneven yarn. The cotton for this experiment was carded by hand, and roped on a woollen wheel, by a female.

Mr. Slater entered into contract with Wm. Almy and Smith Brown, and commenced building a water frame of 24 spindles, two carding machines, and the drawing and roping frames necessary to prepare for the spinning, and soon after added a frame of 48 spindles. He commenced some time in the fall of 1790, or in the winter of 1791. I was then in my tenth year, and went to work for him, and began at tending the breaker. The mode of laying the cotton was by hand, taking up a handful, and pulling it apart with both hands, and shifting it all into the right hand, to get the staple of the cotton straight, and fix the handful, so as to hold it firm, and then applying it to the surface of the breaker, moving the hand horizontally across the card to and fro, until the cotton was fully prepared.

The first frame of 24 spindles, was much longer erecting than anticipated, because cards and other things, even tools to work with, could not be obtained; all these were made by Mr. Slater's own hands, or by his directions. He laboured night and day under every disadvantage, to accomplish his purpose, but the hope of future reward sweetened his labour.*

Mr. Slater once said to me, when speaking of labour, that he had laboured sixteen hours a day, for twenty years successively, and he might have added, in the most laborious occupations.

The assertions which have been made in public, representing that Mr. Slater brought with him from England, models and patterns, drawings of machinery, &c., we know, from the best possible

---

* In the fourth of July oration of Edward Everett, is the following valuable letter, and its accompanying remarks:—"I quote a sentence from it, in spite of the homeliness of the details, for which I like it the better, and because I wish to set before you, not an ideal hero wrapped in cloudy generalities, and a mist of vague panegyric, but the real, identical man, with all the peculiarities of his life and occupation. 'Your letter,' says he, 'gave me the more pleasure, as I received it among barbarians and an uncouth set of people. Since you received my letter of October last, I have not slept above three or four nights in a bed; but after walking a good deal all day, I have lain down before the fire, upon a little hay, straw, fodder, or a bearskin, whichever was to be had—with man, wife, and children, like dogs and cats; and happy is he who gets the berth nearest the fire. Nothing would make it pass off tolerably, but a good reward. A doubloon is my constant gain every day, that the weather will permit my going out, and sometimes six pistoles. The coldness of the weather will not allow of my making a long stay, as the lodging is rather too cold for the time of year. I have never had my clothes off, but have lain and slept in them, except the few nights I have been in Fredericksburg.' If there is an individual, in the morning of life, in this assembly who has not yet made his choice, between the flowery path of indulgence, and the rough ascent of honest industry—if there is one who is ashamed to get his living by any branch of honest labour, let him reflect, that the youth who was carrying the theodolite and surveyor's chain, through the mountain passes of the Alleganies, in the month of March—sleeping on a bundle of hay before the fire, in a settler's log cabin, and not ashamed to boast that he did it for his doubloon a day, is George Washington; that the life he led trained him up to command the armies of United America; that the money he earned was the basis of that fortune which enabled him afterwards to bestow his services, without reward, on a bleeding and impoverished country. For three years, was the young Washington employed, the greater part of the time, and whenever the season would permit, in this laborious and healthful occupation; and I know not if it would be deemed unbecoming, were a thoughtful student of our history to say, that he could almost hear the voice of Providence, in the language of Milton, announce its high purpose—

   ' To exercise him in the wilderness :—
   There he shall first lay down the rudiments
   Of his great warfare, ere I send him forth
   To conquer.' "

authority, to be incorrect; he told me that he had not a single pattern or memorandum to assist him in his calculations in constructing his first machinery; but he was favoured with an excellent memory, which never failed him in a single particular, until he accomplished his purpose. This was corroborated by the testimony of Moses Brown and William Almy.

It was then that his mathematical talents were put to the test. Whoever is acquainted with " The Carding or Spinning Master's Assistant, or the theory and practice of cotton spinning, showing the use of each machine employed in the whole process,—how to adjust and adapt them to suit the various kinds of cotton, and the different qualities of yarn; and how to perform the various calculations connected with the different departments of cotton spinning," will be satisfied that Mr. Slater's first work, in Pawtucket, was a proof of his knowledge and experience, as well as of his mathematical and mechanical genius. At the same time, it will be evident how much assistance he might have derived from such a publication; but nothing of the kind was then in existence. It is only within a few years that such helps have been prepared. Mr. Slater had seen the spinning frames that were constructed under the auspices of Arkwright himself, and had been brought to a very high state of improvement. The machines which have been generally used, since his time, are constructed upon the *very same principle;* any alterations that have been made, are chiefly upon the form or framing of the machine: as that which was formerly made of wood, is now made of cast iron, which gives it a more neat and handsome appearance, and also renders it more durable. In reference to the introduction of this machinery, Mr. Burgess observed, in a speech in congress, in 1825, and also at a public dinner in Pawtucket, R. I., June 16, 1828—" At the commencement of our present national government, a man arrived in this very place (I do not call his name, because it belongs to history, and must be known to all); and he brought with him that art, in those manufactures, which enables England, in the progress of its improvements, so to multiply labour, and accumulate wealth, that she did, by the aid of her machinery, in the close of the last, and the beginning of the present century, stand between the military despotism of one part of Europe, and the entire liberties of the world."

The annexed plate represents the machinery which Mr. Slater erected, and operated in the old fulling mill at Pawtucket. The clothier's shop alluded to by Mr. Wilkinson, was washed away Feb. 15, 1807; but the two frames which Mr. Slater first made and

CARDING, DRAWING, ROVING and SPINNING.

operated, are now in the *old mill* in Pawtucket, and are frequently shown to visiters as choice curiosities. I conversed with the son of E. Carpenter, in whose shop S. Slater built his machinery, who was the clothier, and then a boy; he was permitted to see the first yarn spun, about which he told me, and observed that listing was used for belts. The following description will aid in understanding the engraving.

Water-spinning. It received this name, from being the first done by a water-wheel, and was patented by R. Arkwright.

Carding. After the cotton is picked, the usual process is to card it; first, by a carding machine, called a *breaker ;* and a second time on another, called a *finisher.* The breaker consists of a larger and smaller cylinder. The larger, or *main cylinder,* is covered with sheet cards, and moves at a considerable velocity; the lesser, or doffing cylinder, is covered with a spiral fillet of card, wound round it, and moves slowly. These cylinders revolve in opposite directions, and nearly in contact with each other. Over the main cylinder, is a kind of arch, covered with cards, at rest, called the *top-cards.* The cotton is fed by means of rollers into the main cylinder. The main cylinder lays it on the doffing cylinder, from which it is combed, and in an uniform fleece is wound round a cylinder, or sometimes, instead of it, on a perpetual cloth. After this cylinder or cloth has made a certain number of revolutions, and thereby plying or doubling, (the fourth elementary process,) the cotton is broken off, and is in that state, called a lap, ready to be carried to the finisher. The finisher is similar to the breaker, only that the fleece, instead of forming a lap, is gradually brought into a narrow band or sliver, and is compressed by a pair of rollers, which deliver it into a tin can, which is afterwards removed to the drawing frame.

The drawing frame. In this machine, drawing first occurs. Drawing is a curious contrivance, and is the ground-work or principle of Arkwright's patent, for it is used in the roving and spinning, as well as in the drawing frame. It is an imitation of what is done by the finger and thumb, in spinning by hand, and is performed by means of two pair of rollers. The upper roller of the first pair is covered by leather, which being an elastic substance, is pressed, by means of a spring or weight. The lower roller, made of metal, is fluted, in order to keep a firm hold of the fibres of the cotton. Another similar pair of rollers are placed near to those we have been describing. The second pair moving at a greater velocity, pull the fibres of the cotton from the first pair of rollers. If the surface of the last pair move at twice or thrice the velocity of the first pair, the cotton will be drawn twice or thrice finer than it was. This relative velocity is called the *draught* of the machine. This mechanism being understood, it will be easy to conceive the nature of the operation of the drawing-frame. Several of the narrow ribands or slivers from the cards, (or as they are sometimes termed, card ends,) by being passed through a system of rollers, are thereby reduced in size. By means of a detached single pair of rollers, the reduced ribands are united into one sliver. These operations of drawing and plying serve to equalise the body of cotton, and to bring its fibres more on end, which, in the card ends, were crossed in all directions. These slivers are again combined and drawn out, so that one sliver of the finisher's drawing contains many plies of card-ends. Hitherto the cotton has got no twist, but is received into moveable tin cans or canisters, similar to those used for receiving the cotton from the cards ; sometimes, however, it does receive a small degree of twist in the finishing drawing.

Roving. The roving is a process similar to the drawing, only that it always communicates a degree of twist to the cotton. The roves are wound up on bobbins, and are then ready to be spun. The operation of winding is in some cases performed by hand, and in others by power. The bobbins containing the rove are placed on the back part of the spinning frame. The spinning is little more than a repetition of the process gone through in making the rovings. The spinning frame contains rollers similar to those of the drawing and roving frames, which serve to extend the rove, and reduce it to the required fineness ; at the same time it is twisted by means of a spindle, but of a different kind from that of the common jenny.

Previously to the year 1767, spinning was performed on the domestic one-thread wheel, of which there were two kinds. The first, which had a simple spindle, required the material to be previously carded ; and, as we have seen, the common jenny was founded upon 'this simple machine. The second, was the flax-wheel, which was used for other substances that, from their nature, but more particularly for the length of staple, did not admit of carding, but were prepared by an operation resembling combing.

The spindle of this machine had a bobbin and fly, which served to wind up the yarn as fast as it was spun. This last kind of spindle is that which was adopted by Arkwright in his mode of spinning. When the bobbins are full, they are taken off the spindles in order to be reeled.

The reeling is performed on a machine consisting of six wooden rails, parallel to the axis, which winds a considerable number of threads at once from the bobbins. It is one yard and a half in circumference, and is of such a length as to give room for the skeins without danger of the threads getting foul of each other. At one end of the axis is wheel-work, constructed to strike a check at every eighty revolutions of the reel. These eighty revolutions form a *lay* or *rap*, of 120 yards in length, and seven of these lays constitute a skein, which measures 840 yards. *Water-twist* is generally spun hard, and in that case is used for purposes requiring much strength, such as the warps of fustians, calicoes, &c. A softer kind of water-twist, which is very uniform and even in its thread, is used, when doubled and slightly turned, for making stockings, and is denominated stocking-yarn. The lower numbers are sometimes used single, and are called double-spun. Water-twist is used of all sizes, from No. 6. to No. 60. The above description answers precisely to the state of Arkwright and Strutt's mills in England, in 1790, and describes exactly the machinery which Mr. Slater constructed in Pawtucket, during that year.

It is known, that Mr. Peel, as early as the year 1762, with the assistance of Hargreaves, erected a carding engine with cylinders, at Blackburn, which differed very little from the one now used, except that it had no mechanism for detaching the cotton from the cards, an operation which was performed by women with hand-cards. Afterwards, this was done by the application of a roller with tin plates, like the floats of a water-wheel, which, revolving with a quick motion, scraped the cotton off the cards. The first inventor of the cylinder cards, or the carding engine, was probably Mr. Wyatt. But the carding engine was greatly improved by Arkwright; in place of the roller with tin plates, he substituted a metal plate toothed at the edge like a comb, which, instead of being made to revolve like the other, was moved rapidly in a perpendicular direction, by a crank, and with slight, but reiterated strokes, detached the cotton from the cards in a uniform fleece. In place of the sheet cards, with which the doffing cylinder had hitherto been covered, he employed narrow fillet cards, wound round it in a spiral form; by this contrivance a continuity of the fleece was produced, which, as it left the card, was gradually contracted by the conductor, and delivered by rollers into the can, in the form of a continued carding, or rowan, called a card end. The taking off the cotton from the cards, in this manner, is one of the most beautiful and curious operations in the whole process of cotton spinning, and renders the carding engine one of the most important machines employed in the process. Carding engines have sometimes been made to consist of one large cylinder, and a number of smaller ones, called urchins, disposed of at proper distances over above the main cylinder, and revolving in opposite directions to it, but nearly in contact; by which means the cotton was delivered from cylinder to cylinder, until it came to the finishing cylinder, called the doffer—from which it was taken off by the comb.

At present, carding engines are generally made to consist of only two cylinders; sometimes three—one at the feeding rollers. But the main cylinder is covered with a kind of arch, composed of several pieces of wood called tops, which have no motion, having sheet cards fixed on them, and nearly in contact with the main cylinder. If any machine in the whole process of cotton spinning be of more use and importance than another, it is the carding engine, nor do I see how its use can at all be dispensed with; and in fact it may be said, that the process of cotton spinning, (properly speaking) begins only at the carding; for all the previous departments of the process are merely preparatory to this, and consist, chiefly, in mixing, cleaning and opening the cotton, so as that the cards may take the best effect upon it; and therefore are called the preparation. Previous to the cotton being put through the cards, the fibres may be lying in every direction into which they may accidentally be thrown; but the use of the carding engine is to draw out the fibres of the cotton, to straighten and lay them side by side, and form them into a thread commonly called an end; and this is the first formation of the thread of yarn. It is first begun in the cards, and advanced onward, step by step, through each successive machine in its order, until it is completed. When the fibres are properly straightened, and the end equally formed at the cards, there is good reason to expect a superior quality of yarn, but failing this, an inferior quality is unavoidable; for no skill or attention applied to any subsequent department of the process, can altogether remedy the injuries the cotton may have sustained in this: hence it is an object of the highest importance in cotton spinning, to have the cards always properly set, and adjusted to suit the particular kind of cotton used, and the quality of the yarn required.

In the adjusting and fitting up of cards, great care should be taken to have all their parts properly leveled; the bite of the feeding rollers should especially be on a perfect level with the centre of the main cylinder, and both cylinders should be turned to the perfect truth, and always kept so if possible; but, through the influence of the variations of the temperature, &c., the cylinders are frequently found to go off the truth, notwithstanding all the care that may be taken to prevent it; when this takes place, the only remedy is to strip them of their sheets, and turn them anew, until they are perfectly just; for to work with card cylinders off the truth is attended with the most injurious effects upon the cotton. Seeing it is an object of some importance to keep card cylinders from going off the truth, to which they have a great tendency, particular care should be taken to have the wood well seasoned before it is made into cylinders. New carding engines should also be allowed to stand at least two months in their place, exposed to the heat of the mill, before they commence operations, during which they should be turned and adjusted several times.

The following letter refers to the first yarn that Mr. Slater made on his machinery : it is rather singular that Moses Brown should not name him, but speak of him " as an English workman from Arkwright's works," when at the time he was proprietor of one half of the machinery, while Almy and Brown had only a quarter each :—

PROVIDENCE, 19th of 4th mo. 1791.

Esteemed Friend,—I have for some time thought of addressing the Beverly manufacturers on the subject of an application to Congress for some encouragement to the cotton manufactory, by an additional duty on the cotton goods imported, and the applying such duty as a bounty, partly for raising and saving of cotton in the southern states, of a quality and cleanness suitable to be wrought with machines, and partly as a bounty on cotton goods of the same kind manufactured in the United States, or in some other manner, as may be thought advisable. It is thought that the interest of all the cotton manufacturers who work with carding and other machines, united, would effect such encouragement as would effectually prevent the English manufacturers from sending in such increased or large quantities as has been of late, and establish the business advantageously to this country. Thy sentiments, with those of the concerned, would be acceptable, and it is the desire of those concerned, this way, that you, being the first and largest, would take the lead, and devise such plan as may be most eligible to effect the purpose.

My son-in-law, William Almy, has handed me three sizes of cotton yarn : a lay of each I enclose for your inspecton. Almy and Brown, who conduct the business of the cotton manufactory, with an English workman from Arkwright's works, have often fourteen labourers of the various mechanics necessary, completed the water spinning machines to the perfection as to make the inclosed yarn,—the former mills which I had purchased, made from the state's model at Bridgewater, proving not to answer. The weavers inform me the yarn works better than any linen they have had, and takes less trouble to warp and weave it. As the doubling and twisting mill, by water, is not yet ready, Almy & Brown have had a number of pieces of thicksets and fancy goods, made of single warps, which appear much superior to any linen warp. The two coarsest enclosed answer this purpose,—the finest would answer for cords, velvets, &c., when doubled and twisted. If you should incline to try some warps, they can supply you with almost any size, weekly, monthly, or quarterly ; that of about 12 skeins to the pound at 6d per skein, of 1200 yards. Coarser or finer, will vary some. As we find that warps cannot be made equally as good on jennies, and apprehending that you wish to perfect the cotton manufactures, so as to preclude foreign importation, induces us to make the offer of supplying you in preference to any other works. Thy or the company's answer will be attended to by Almy & Brown, and by thy friend,

MOSES BROWN.

P. S. I have heard that I was censured by some of the concerned, as being suspected of having enticed away your workmen, but as I knew myself clear, I did not write you. But if any thing of that kind remains, and I could know what it is, I doubt not I can remove every suspicion to your satisfaction, and will endeavour to do it on notice; as I went to Beverly disapproving such conduct, I acted on the same principles, and now disavow any such conduct. I mention this, as I wish to live in harmony with all men, and especially with those in the same line of business.

Moses Brown,
   To be communicated to the proprietors of the Beverly Factory.

In a letter to John Dexter, Moses Brown gives the following account, October 15, 1791:—

"In the spring of the year 1789, some persons in Providence had procured to be made a carding machine, a jenny and a spinning frame, to work by hand after the manner of Arkwright's invention, taken principally from models belonging to the state of Massachusetts, which were made at their expense, by two persons from Scotland, who took their ideas from observation, and not from experience in the business. These machines made here not answering the purpose and expectation of the proprietors, and I being desirous of perfecting them, if possible, and the business of the cotton manufactures, so as to be useful to the country, I purchased them; and, by great alterations, the carding machine and jenny were made to answer. The frame, with one other on nearly the same construction, made from the same model, and tried without success at East Greenwich, which I also purchased, I attempted to set to work by water, and made a little yarn, so as to answer for warps ; but being so imperfect, both as to the quality and quantity of the yarn, that their progress was suspended till I could procure a person who had wrought or seen them wrought in Europe, *for as yet we had not.* Late in the fall I received a letter from a young man, then lately arrived at New York, from Arkwright's works in England, informing me, his situation, that he could hear of no perpetual spinning mills on the continent but mine, and proposed to come and work them. I wrote him and he came accordingly ; *but on viewing the mills he declined doing any thing with them,* and proposed making a new one, using such parts of the old as would answer. We had by this time got several jennies, and some weavers at work on linen warps, but had not been able to get cotton warps to a useful degree of perfection on the jennies; and although I had found the undertaking much more arduous than I expected, both as to the attention necessary, and the expense, being necessitated to employ workmen of the most transient kind, and on whom little dependence could be placed, and to collect materials to complete the various machines from distant parts of the continent. However, we (I say we, because I had committed the immediate management of the business to my son-in-law William Almy, and kinsman Smith Brown, under the firm of Almy & Brown), contracted with the young man from England, to direct and make a mill in his own way, which he did, and it answered a much better purpose than the former; but still imperfect, for want of other machines; *such as cards of a different construction* from those already made and re-made over; *with various other machines preparatory to the spinning.* All which, with the necessary appendages, the mechanics skilled in working of wood, iron, brass, &c. &c., were more than a twelve-month completing, before we could get a single warp of cotton perfected. During this time, linen warps were wove, and the jenny spinning was performed in different cellars of dwelling houses. But finding the inconvenience of this, we have now a factory house and dye shop erected, and occupy other buildings for the singeing, callendering, and other machines. There being a variety of branches in the perfecting of the cotton business, as the picking, soaping, stoning or dyeing the cotton: roping it, by hand or on machines, spinning, bobbin winding, weaving, cutting for velvets or other cut goods, singeing or dressing, bleaching, dyeing, and finishing, renders it more difficult, and requires longer time to perfect than many other branches of business, in a country where there are very few acquainted with it; but when each branch is learned, it may be extended to any length necessary, by means of the great advantage of the machines, in the saving of labour. There are also several other persons who manufacture cotton and linen by the carding machines and jennies, but when they make all cotton goods, they have the warps from Almy & Brown's mills,—*Samuel Slater, the young man from England, being also concerned therein.*"

To this advantage, arising from the introduction of the Arkwright Patent, Alexander Hamilton refers, in his report, as secretary of the treasury, made December 5, 1791, on the subject of manufactures :—" The manufactory at Providence *has the merit of being the first in introducing into the United States the celebrated cotton mill* (meaning Arkwright's patent) which, not only furnishes materials for that manufactory itself, but for the supply of private families, for household manufacture."

In allusion to this notice, Mr. Hunter, in his address before the Rhode Island Agricultural Society, speaks very eloquently :—" On an altar raised in decoration of manufactures, we would transfer one from a fact recorded on a more imperishable monument than the altar and temple itself,—Hamilton's report on manufactures, in 1791, in which the introduction of the first cotton mill (meaning the series of machines patented in England) in this country is mentioned, and the introducer was—*Slater.*" The claim, which

I have therefore made, is only an echo of public acclamation, issuing from the first secretary of the treasury of the United States.*

Hamilton recommends, "the encouragement of new inventions and discoveries at home, and the *introduction* into the United States of such as may have been made in other countries, particularly those which relate to machinery. This is among the most useful and unexceptionable of the aids which can be given to manufactures. The usual means of that encouragement are pecuniary rewards, and, for a time, exclusive privileges. The first must be employed according to the occasion, and the utility of the invention or discovery. For the last, so far as respects 'authors and inventors,' provision has been made by law. But it is desirable, in regard to improvements and secrets of extraordinary value, to be able to extend the same benefit to *introducers*, as well as authors and inventors, a policy which has been practised with advantage in other countries. If the legislature of the Union cannot do all the good that might be wished, it is at least desirable that all may be done which is practicable. Means for promoting the introduction of foreign improvements, though less efficaciously

---

* The spinning machines of Arkwright and others had not been long in operation in England, until they attracted the notice of traders in Scotland, who soon attempted what was then, to many, a most lucrative branch of manufacture. But it is difficult to plant a manufacture in a new country, even where there is no secret in the process; and the difficulty was still greater in this instance, where pains were taken to keep the business involved in mystery. Many, who had been employed in the works of Arkwright, left his service, pretending to a knowledge of the business, which they did not possess; and those men were eagerly sought after by new adventurers in both kingdoms. But, in most cases, those adventurers were no gainers by the acquisition. This may easily be conceived, when we consider how very little a great proportion of the people now employed in cotton mills know, and how much less they can communicate of the construction of the machinery, or the general system of the business; and, if such be the case at present, what must it have been at the period and place of which we are speaking. It is supposed that the first cotton spun by water, in Scotland, was in the island of Bute, in what had been a lint mill, and was afterwards, for some time, the corn mill of Rothsay. But this was only by way of trial, and before the completion of the larger cotton mill.

In the year 1782 a large mill, of six stories, was erected at Johnson; there is reason to suppose this was the first in Scotland that was productive of much profit to the proprietors. Originally, it was managed by people from England, but they proved of the description alluded to above; and the proprietors were indebted to the discernment, perseverance, and mechanical genius of Mr. Robert Burns, for rescuing the concern from ruin, and rendering the business a source of affluence.

than might be accomplished with more adequate authority, will form a plan intended to be submitted in the close of this report. It is customary with manufacturing nations to prohibit, under severe penalties, the exportation of implements and machines, which they have either invented or improved. There is something in the texture of cotton, which adapts it in a peculiar degree to the application of machines. The *cotton mill* (the Arkwright patent) invented in England, within the last twenty years, is a signal illustration of the general proposition which has just been advanced. In consequence of it all the different processes for spinning cotton are performed by means of machines, which are put in motion by water, and attended chiefly by women and children, and by a smaller number of persons, in the whole, than are necessary in the ordinary mode of spinning. This very important circumstance recommends the fabrics of cotton, in a more particular manner, to a country in which a defect of hands constitutes the greatest obstacle to success. Among the most useful and unexceptionable of the aids which can be given to manufactures, is the encouragement of new inventions and discoveries at home, and of the introduction into the United States of such as may have been made in other countries, particularly those which relate to machinery.

" Manufactories of cotton goods, not long since established at Beverly, in Massachusetts, and at Providence in the state of Rhode Island, and conducted with a perseverance corresponding with the patriotic motives which began them, seem to have overcome the first obstacles to success, producing corduroys, velverets, fustians, jeans, and other similar articles, of a quality which will bear a comparison with the like articles brought from Manchester. Other manufactories of the same material, as regular business, have also been begun at different places in the state of Connecticut, but all upon a smaller scale than those above mentioned. Some essays are also making in the printing and staining of cotton goods. There are several small establishments of this kind already on foot. The printing and staining of cotton goods is known to be a distinct business from the fabrication of them. It is one easily accomplished, and which, as it adds materially to the value of the article in its white state, and prepares it for a variety of new uses, is of importance to be promoted."

Connected with the above report, Moses Brown states :—" The public spirit of the Massachusetts legislature on this subject, as well as Pennsylvania, are to be applauded, and in justice to the latter I mention this circumstance :—The publication of their grant to a certain person for a certain machine in this manufactory, reaching England, and coming to the knowledge of the workmen at Arkwright's mills, occasioned the young man, Slater, before mentioned, privately coming to America, and perfecting the first water-spinning in the United States that I have heard of,—though I am informed a company from England are about to erect mills near New York, for which the machinery is making at New Haven. It is an undoubted fact, authenticated to me by divers persons from England, that the king has frequently made proclamation against any tradesmen leaving the kingdom, and called on his officers for their most vigilant watch against it, as well as against any draft of machinery being carried out. This, also, should excite our attention to those advantages, which they find of so much consequence to that country."

These remarks of Moses Brown show that he was a man of enlarged and sagacious views of the importance of the cotton manufacture, and in his joining with the introducer in his endeavours to establish it, as appears also by his further remarks :—" I have been lengthy on this subject, not only because my family have engaged in it, but because I conceive from the advantage of the mills, and other machines, and the raising of the raw materials among ourselves, this country may avail itself of one of the most valuable manufactories, from which every part of the Union may be supplied. I apprehend this subject would have been laid before congress, by the united representation of the cotton manufacturers, had not some states liberally contributed to the promotion of it, particularly Massachusetts, and the incorporated company at Beverly have partaken largely of their bounty, in proportion to what they have done. Whether under an idea that the assistance they had received would have enabled them to go on, while others would be under a necessity of discontinuing the business, (as some have in fact, which they would not have done but for want of that assistance in the same government, namely, the factory at Worcester,) or whatever other reason the Beverly company may have, they have not come forward as expected. I have mentioned yarn, as the importation of that article from India has been suggested by the late manufacturing committee in Philadelphia, at which time, no good yarn had been made fit for warps. But, as the manufactory of the mill yarn (meaning the Arkwright patent) is done by children from eight to fourteen years old, it is as nearly a total saving of labour to the country as perhaps any other that can be named, and therefore no importation of the yarn ought to be admitted without a large impost, if at all—as the secretary may be assured that mills and machines may be erected in different places, in one year, sufficient to make all the cotton yarn that may be wanted in the United States, both for warps and for knitting and weaving stockings, were encouragement given to protect the manufactures from being intercepted in the sale, by foreign importation." Such was the confidence that Moses Brown had in the skill and enterprise of Samuel Slater, in July 1791, that he believed he would cause to be erected sufficient machinery to supply the whole continent with yarn, in a year from that time. "There are also cotton and linen goods manufactured at East Greenwich; their cotton warps are made at the aforesaid mills, (meaning by Almy, Brown and Slater) the quantities manufactured by those several persons, and others, in the common way of family work, I expect will be given an account of by themselves, or collected by the mechanical and manufacturing society of this town; I therefore refer to them. For the degree of maturity our cotton manufacture has obtained, and their different qualities, I refer to the patterns of the mill yarn, and goods made from warps of it herewith sent; the prices sold at are also marked."

Some of Mr. Slater's first yarn, and some of the first cotton cloth made in America, from the same warp, was sent to the secretary of the treasury, the 15th October, 1791, and may possibly be preserved in the secretary's office, as Mr. Clay says he has some of the first yarn, which is said to be as fine as No. 40. As to the impediments under which this business laboured, Moses Brown observes,—" No encouragement has been given by any laws of this state, nor by any donations of any society or individuals, but wholly begun, carried on, and thus far perfected, at private expense." I have never heard of any premium or advantage conferred on Mr. Slater, for his introducing the cotton manufacture, or for his establishing it on a permanent basis; but his own money and time were pledged to the object. "The manufacture of iron into blistered steel, equal in quality to English, has been begun, within about a year, in North Providence, and is carried on by Oziel Wilkinson, who informed me he can make a good business at ten per cent. for the steel in blister, returning weight for weight with the iron manufactured; the drawing into bars of any shape, being an additional charge. I thought of speaking, also, of pig and bar iron, slitting it into nail rods, rolling into hoops and plates, making it into spades and shovels, hot and cold nails, anchors, &c. all in this district."

Little more than sixty years since, every thread used in the manufacture of cotton, wool, worsted, and flax, throughout the world, was spun singly, by the fingers of the spinner, with the aid of that *classical* instrument, the domestic spinning-wheel. In 1767 an *eight-handed* spinster sprung from the genius of Hargreaves ; and the *jenny*, with still increasing power, made its way into common use, in spite of all opposition. Two years afterwards, the more wonderful invention of Wyatt, which claims a much earlier origin, but which had disappeared, like a river that sinks into a subterraneous channel, and now rose again under the fortunate star of Arkwright, claimed yet higher admiration, as founded on principles of more extensive application. Five years later, the happy thought of combining the principles of these two inventions, to produce a third, much more efficient than either, struck the mind of Crompton, who, by a perfectly original contrivance, effected the union. From twenty spindles, this machine was brought, by more finished mechanism, to admit of a hundred spindles, and thus to exercise a Briarean power. Kelly relinquished the toilsome method of turning the machine by hand, and yoked to it the strength of the rapid Clyde. Watt, with the subtler and more potent agency of steam, moved an iron arm that never slackens or tires, which whirls round two thousand spindles in a single machine. Finally, to consummate the wonder, Roberts dismisses the spinner, and leaves the machine to its own infallible guidance. So that, in the year 1834, several thousand spindles may be seen in a single room, revolving with inconceivable rapidity, with no hand to urge their progress or to guide their operations,—drawing out, twisting, and winding up, as many thousand threads, with unfailing precision, and indefatigable patience and strength; a scene as magical to the eye which is not familiarised with it, as the effects have beeen marvelous in augmenting the wealth and population of the country. If the thought should cross any mind, that, after all, the so much vaunted genius of our mechanics has been expended in the insignificant object of enabling men better to pick out, arrange, and twist together the fibres of a vegetable wool,— that it is for the performance of this minute operation that so many energies have been exhausted, so much capital employed, such stupendous structures reared, and so vast a population trained up ; we reply—an object is not insignificant because the operation by which it is effected is *minute*. The first want of men in this life, after food, is *clothing ;* and as this art enables them to supply it far more easily and cheaply than the old methods of manufacturing, and to bring cloths of great elegance and durability within the use of the humble classes, it is an art whose utility is inferior only to that of agriculture. It contributes directly, and most materially, to the comforts of life, among all nations where manufacturers exist, or to which the products of manufacturing industry are conveyed ; it ministers to the comfort and decency of the poor, as well as to the taste and luxury of the rich. By supplying one of the great wants of life, with a much less expenditure of labour than was formerly needed, it sets at liberty a large proportion of the population, to cultivate literature, science, and the fine arts. To England, the new inventions have brought a material accession of wealth and power. When it is also remembered that the inventions, whose origin I have endeavoured carefully to trace, are not confined, in their application, to one manufacture, however extensive, but that they have given nearly the same facilities to the woollen, the worsted, the linen, the stocking, and the lace manufactures, as to the cotton ; and that they have spread from England to the whole of Europe, to America, and to parts of Africa and Asia ; it must be admitted that the mechanical improvements, in the art of spinning, have an importance which it is difficult to over-estimate. By the Greeks, their authors would have been thought worthy of deification ; nor will the enlightened judgment of moderns deny that the men, to whom we owe such inventions, deserve to rank among the chief benefactors of mankind.

It is not a little remarkable that Watt's patent, " for lessening the consumption of steam and fuel, in fire engines," should have been taken out in the same year as Arkwright's patent for spinning with rollers, namely, 1769,—one of the most brilliant eras in the annals of British genius ;—when Black and Priestley were making their great discoveries in science ; when Hargreaves, Arkwright, and Watt revolutionised the processes of manufactures ; when Smeaton and Brindley executed prodigies of engineering art ; when the senate was illuminated by Burke and Fox, Chatham and Mansfield ; when Johnson and Goldsmith, Reid and Beattie, Hume, Gibbon, and Adam Smith, adorned the walks of philosophy and letters ; and Whitfield, Hervey, and Cowper, reformed the protestant churches of Christendom.

To turn from these high names to the subject of our memoir. The Rhode Island society for the encouragement of domestic industry always treated Mr. Slater very respectfully, and the following letter was filed among his papers :—

Samuel Slater, Esq., Pawtucket.

PROVIDENCE, 28th Feb. 1820.

Sir,—By the primary laws and list of the officers of the Rhode Island Society for the Encouragement of Domestic Industry, herewith forwarded, you will observe, that you are elected one of the vice presidents thereof.

The society will deem themselves highly honoured in enrolling, among their chief officers, one of the earliest pupils of Arkwright, one who has done so much for the promotion of domestic industry, peace and comfort, and one whose private character is so deservedly and universally respected by the whole community.

I perform a pleasing duty while I respectfully solicit in behalf of the society your acceptance of the office to which you have been chosen. I am with sincere respect, your obedient servant,

WM. E. RICHMOND.

The state of Rhode Island justly claims the honour of being one of the earliest seats of the mechanic arts and of manufactures, on this side of the Atlantic. It has sustained, through the successive periods of its history, the character of a manufacturing and agricultural district.

A correspondent writes, in reference to the fact that Mr. Slater's mind was first directed to Philadelphia, some reflections on the supposition that he had taken that course, instead of wending his way to Providence :—" Can there be any doubt that if Mr. Slater had turned his steps towards Philadelphia, as he had thought, that his undertaking would then have been attended with success ? In such an event what would have been the relative position of Pennsylvania and Rhode Island at the end of twenty years from that time, compared with their actual state at the close of that period, in regard to manufactures of cotton ? Is it not seen that almost the entire business of the country, which had become considerable at that time, was made up of different ramifications from the original stock imported from Belper, and planted at Pawtucket? Would the flood of labourers coming into the country and enriching it with their skill, have been directed to the village of Pawtucket ? Or would it not have rather set in the direction of Philadelphia ? And would not the result of all this have been a very different state of things, even to this day, than exists now ? These reflections, or similar, may aid in determining who was the *principal*, and who aided and abetted only.

" It is certain, that an individual in a distant land, with the definite and well matured design of establishing the cotton manufacture in this country, on a plan the best then existing, did, after months spent in perfecting himself at the fountain head in all the various knowledge necessary to render success certain, leave bright prospects, and an eligible situation in his native land, and bidding adieu to his home, embarked for this country, with a spirit which it cannot be doubted, with his means, must with certainty, his life being spared, have gained for him the merit, whatever it might be, of first establishing on a firm basis the cotton business in this country, without the aid of any *one* patron in particular; what the result was is pretty well known. You are aware that before the introduction of the Arkwright process of manufacturing cotton, there had been attempts made by Mr. Brown to prepare yarns from cotton, on certain machines, to which he alludes in his letters of that period, for the purpose of filling upon linen warps. That these machines (for spinning only, for the carding was done in families, by hand) did not answer the purpose, appears from Moses Brown's own letter, as also that there were no persons who had seen the operation of the Arkwright machinery, and that all the machines which an attempt had unsuccessfully been made to operate previous to the year 1790, at Pawtucket, or elsewhere in the United States, could not have been profitably carried on with the greatest degree of skill, and must therefore have been abandoned, must be obvious to those who are acquainted with their utter worthlessness compared with the Arkwright machinery. I am very much gratified at the aspect of testimony in relation to the moral influence of manufacturing establishments, and think that the facts of the case cannot fail to weigh favourably upon the public mind."

Mr. Slater's connection with the Wilkinson family, as mentioned by Moses Brown and Tristram Burgess, was certainly a circumstance which led greatly to the promotion of business in Pawtucket. David Wilkinson became a machinist of great skill, and carried on the business in an extensive manner. He is a man of great enterprise and judgment, and his failure in 1829 was very much regretted. The capitalists of Rhode Island ought not to have allowed David Wilkinson to leave the state. But he is now planted at Caboose Falls, and that place has already felt the benefit of his business talents, and his ardent zeal in internal improvement.

Perhaps nothing will show more clearly the part which Moses Brown took in early life, than the following letter :—

To Moses Brown, Esq.

PROVIDENCE, July 7th, 1791.

Sir,—I take the liberty to send you the enclosed, being the copy of a letter which I received a day or two since, from the secretary of the treasury, and to request you to give me, as soon as convenient, in writing, such information as you may possess, (and which the secretary is solicitous to obtain,) on the subjects stated in his letter. You will readily conceive that a transmission of the information requested, to the secretary, may involve consequences favourable to the manufacturing interest in this state. I address myself to you on this subject with the more confidence from a full conviction, that as no one in the state has more at heart the encouragement of our infant manufactures—has been more indefatigable and liberal in the establishment, improvement and use of them than yourself, so no one can possibly possess a more competent knowledge of their commencement, progress, and present state. I am, sir, your obedient servant,

JNO. S. DEXTER.

In connecting the name of Slater, with the first successful introduction of manufacturing machinery into this country, it will not be amiss to draw on the eloquence of a distinguished statesman of Rhode Island. Mr. Burgess remarks:—

" A circumstance worthy of the attention of the whole nation, and worthy also, of a fair page in her history, is the art and mystery of making cloth with machinery moved by water power. This was introduced into Rhode Island, and commenced in Pawtucket, four miles from Providence, about the same time that the American system was established, by the impost law of July 4th, 1789. Samuel Slater, an English mechanic of the first order of mental ability, brought this invention to Pawtucket. He could not bring out from England, models, draughts, or specifications. The whole art was treasured in his own mind; that alone, which could not be rummaged and pillaged by any custom-house regulation. He, on his arrival, addressed himself to Oziel Wilkinson and sons. They were blacksmiths, whose hands were as skilful as their minds were intelligent and persevering. I have often thought Divine Providence directed *Slater*, and brought him to lay his project before the Wilkinsons; because he had not fitted any other men in this country, with minds and abilities, either to see, and at once comprehend the immense benefit of it; or to understand and perform, what must be understood and performed, to bring this scheme into full and perfect operation. I will not detain the house to enumerate or even mention any benefits resulting to those who have, from that time to this, engaged in the cotton trade. What was the condition then, and what is now the condition, of the consumption of cotton cloths in your country? A yard of cloth, then, made by the wheel and loom, cost fifty, and never less than forty cents. It may now be had for nine or ten cents. A trade so productive of public benefit will be duty appreciated by all patriots. The law of July 4, 1789, was enacted by the almost unanimous voice of the whole nation. By this law the great scheme was commenced. The law of protection, enacted in 1816, was equally national; men from the east, the north, the south, and the west, equally supported the measure. The bill was laid before the house by the lamented Lowndes, of South Carolina. It was advocated, in every stage of its progress, by another distinguished individual of the same state. When it passed this house, Hall and Lumpkin of Georgia, Cannon and Powell of Tennessee, Basset and Barbour of Virginia, voted in favour of its passage. So far as the bill related to the cotton trade, it was enacted with the sole view to the protection of that great and increasing interest. It was then known and acknowledged, though it seems now to be forgotten, that this law for the protection of the cotton trade, was founded on a most able, luminous, and statesman-like report, made to that congress, by the chairman of the committee on commerce, another distinguished gentleman from Virginia, Mr. Newton."

In repeating the evidence, in relation to the foregoing facts, it appears that previous to 1790, the year in which Samuel Slater arrived in this country, there had been introduced into the United States, at Providence, New York, Beverly, Worcester, &c. "jennies," and "billies," with cards, for the spinning of cotton filling, to be wove into velverets, jeans, fustians, &c., with linen warps, chiefly by Scotish and Irish spinners and weavers; and the history of these times declares the imperfection of the above machinery to be such as to preclude the manufacture of cotton cloth, or cotton yarn for warps, and that there was a desire to import cotton yarn from India : that it was even inadequate and its operations deficient and expensive in its immediate application ; and further, that under such difficulties and perplexities, it was entirely beyond the power of American manufacturers to compete with foreign goods introduced by British agents and American merchants, even when they received legislative aid, as they did at Beverly.

The citizens of Massachusetts—perplexed and involved in their incipient and imperfect attempts at the manufacturing of cotton goods, and fully aware of the importance of introducing a better system of machinery, which they knew to be in successful operation in England—exerted themselves to obtain a model of the Arkwright patent. But finding no person able to construct that series of machines, and unable to obtain one from England, in consequence of the heavy and severe penalties imposed by the British government on the exportation of mechanism, they entirely failed in their first attempts. In this downcast period of American manufactures, Samuel Slater, then in the employ of Strutt & Arkwright, having seen a premium offered by the Pennsylvania Society, for a certain machine to spin cotton, was induced to leave his native country and come to America. On his arrival, being informed that Moses Brown had made attempts in water spinning at Providence, he immediately repaired thither. On viewing Moses Brown's machinery, he pronounced it worthless, and induced him to lay it aside. At this period, without the aid of a single individual skilled in making machinery, Samuel Slater constructed the whole series of machines on the Arkwright plan, and put it in operation so perfectly, as to supply all the establishments with cotton warps, superior to linen—and in fourteen months, Moses Brown informed the secretary of the treasury that machinery and mills could be erected within one year to supply the whole United States with yarn, and render its importation unnecessary. Such is the amount of evidence of the introduction of the Arkwright machinery into this country. If the manufacturing establishments are in reality a benefit and blessing to the Union, as Mr. Clay observes, the name of Slater must ever be held in grateful remembrance by the American people.

Mr. Slater began his machinery under every disadvantage; for though he had full confidence in his own remembrance of every part and pattern, and in his ability to perfect the work, according to his agreement, he found it difficult to get mechanics who could make any thing like his models.

His greatest perplexity was in making the cards; for which purpose he employed Phinney Earl, of Leicester, who had never before made any machine cards of that description. This circumstance gave rise to the published anecdote of his dream, by which it was said he had been extricated from his embarrassment. There is no wish to deny the possibility of such an occurrence, if such had been the fact; but I enquired of Mr. Slater, two years previous to his decease, and he assured me such was not the case. He related to me the reality of his obstructions :—after his frames were ready for operation, he prepared the cotton, and started his cards; the cotton rolled up, on the top cards, instead of passing through the small cylinder. This was a great perplexity to him, and he was for several days in great agitation. The family in whose house he boarded have since described his trial to me. When leaning his head over the fireplace, they heard him utter deep sighs, and frequently saw the tears roll from his eyes. The family had become interested in his favour. He said but little of his fears and apprehensions; but Mrs. Wilkinson perceived his distress, when she said to him, " art thou sick, Samuel ?" When he explained to the family the nature of his trial, he showed the point on which he was most tender :—" If I am frustrated in my carding machine, they will think me an impostor." He was apprehensive that no suitable cards could be obtained, short of England—and from thence none were allowed to be exported.

After advising with Mr. Earl, and pointing out to him the defect, he perceived that the teeth of the cards were not crooked enough, as they had no good card leather, and were pricked by hand, the puncture was too large, which caused the teeth to fall back from their proper place. They beat the teeth with a piece of grindstone, which gave them a proper crook, and the machinery moved in order, to his great relief—and to the joy of his friends. Moses Brown told me, that the machinery was so much longer in preparation than he expected, that he was discouraged. Mr. Slater, knowing this anxiety, and that he was liable to lose the confidence of his partners by the complete failure on his first trial of the cards, and knowing that he could appeal to no one, who could judge of the correctness of the machinery, it was no wonder that he was distressed, or that it occupied his thoughts day and night—his sleeping and waking hours. This circumstance gave rise to the report of the dream.

Another rumour which has spread far and wide, calls for contradiction and explanation. It has been positively asserted, that the British government employed a person to assassinate Mr. Slater, by means of an infernal machine; similar, it is said, in its operation, to the one employed to attempt the life of Napoleon. I never believed this story worthy of any attention, till Mr. and Mrs. Slater made us a visit in Canterbury in 1827. His coachman told it as an undoubted truth among the inhabitants of the village; it received implicit credit, on account of the supposed knowledge of his driver, and it was spread as a Canterbury tale. I therefore applied to my friend for a correct exposition of the circumstance :—he assured me there was no ground whatever for such a representation. It arose from the circumstance of a box of clothes being sent him from England, and it was stopped in the custom-house in New York, which the following letter to Moses Brown, Providence, and endorsed by him will show.

PAWTUCKET, July 1st, 1790.

Sir—I have received letters from England that there is a box at New York with some clothes, which the officers have stopt, the impost not being paid. The clothes are new, but made for my use, and I supposed they would be free of duty. Should be glad if you would use such means as you think best, to get them with little or no duty, and oblige yours, &c.

SAMUEL SLATER.

N.B. I suppose there is more than a hundred dollars of clothes in the box.

As a box actually came from England, which was directed to Mr. Slater, and as there was a correspondence with the officers of the customs, relative to the detention of the box ; with some remaining jealousies at that time towards old England, it was no wonder under all the circumstances of the case, that such an evil surmise should have arisen, and spread as a true report.

The public are assured that I have the fullest authority for the above explanation. The tailor's bill of these very clothes is now in possession of the family, and some of the buttons of the coat. The tailor, at Belper, occupied a store of Mr. Slater's, which was given him by his father, and these clothes were sent to pay the rent.

As it has been observed, Mr. Slater started his cards in the water-wheel belonging to the clothier's shop, which was so exposed that it was frozen every night. He could get none to expose themselves to break the ice, in order to start the wheel in the morning. Those who can well remember the fact, informed me, that he spent two or three hours breaking the ice, before breakfast, till he was wet and cold, and his limbs benumbed, which affected him very much. This exposure laid the foundation of those chronic disorders, from which he suffered so much in the latter part of his life.

He took care to have his water-wheel, when he built his first mill, under cover, having experienced the bad effects of a frozen wheel. The first winter he spun on his frames, he endured great hardships : and when he had produced an excellent yarn, there was but little sale for it.

He had to instruct the boys who assisted in the mill, and commence the factory regulations ; as nothing of the kind was known here.* The following is his first account of time and wages with his workpeople.

---

* The wise and active conquer difficulties,
  By daring to attempt them ; sloth and folly
  Shiver and shrink at sight of toil and danger,
  And make the impossibility they fear.

CARDERS AND SPINNERS' TIME LIST.

Decemb. 1790.	M 20	T 21	W 22	T 23	F 24	S 25	No.	NAMES.	TIME. D.	WAGES. S.	MONEY PAID. £. s. d.
							1	Arnold, Torpen,	6		
							2	Do. Charles,	6		
							3	Wilkinson, Smith,	6		
							4	Jenks, Jabez,	6		
	27	28	29	30	31	1					
							1	Arnold, Torpen,	6		
							2	Do. Charles,	6		
							3	Do. Eunise,	6		
							4	Jenks, Jabez,	6		
	4	4	4				5	Do. Jno.	3		
	4	4	4				6	Do. Varnus,	3		
	4	4					7	Borrows, Otis,	4		
							8	Wilkinson, Smith,	6		
January 1791.	3	4	5	6	7	8					
							1	Arnold, Torpen,	6		
							2	Do. Charles,	6		
							3	Do. Eunise,	6		
							4	Do. Ann,	6		
							5	Jenks, Jabez,	6		
							6	Do. John,	6		
							7	Do. Varnus,	6		
							8	Wilkinson, Smith,	6		
							9	Borrows, Otis,	6		
	10	11	12	13 2	14	15 2					
							1	Arnold, Torpen,	5		
							2	Do. Charles,	6		
							3	Do. Eunise,	6		
							4	Do. Ann,	6		
							5	Jenks, Jabez,	6		
							6	Do. John,	6		
						4	7	Do. Varnus,	6		
							8	Wilkinson, Smith,	5		
							9	Borrows, Otis,	6		

The factory system in England takes its rise from the period of the trial concerning the validity of the patent, by Arkwright, in 1785. Hitherto the cotton manufacture had been carried on almost entirely in the houses of the workmen, the hand or stock cards, the spinning wheel, and the loom, required no larger apartment than that of a cottage. A spinning jenny of small size might also be used in a cottage, and in many instances was so used; when the number of spindles was considerably increased, adjacent work-shops were used. But the water-frame, the carding engine, and the other machines which Arkwright brought out in a finished state, required both more space than could be found in a cottage, and more power than could be applied by the human arm. Their weight also rendered it necessary to place them in strongly built mills, and they could not be advantageously turned by any power then known, but that of water. The use of machinery was accompanied by a greater division of labour than existed in the primitive state of the manufacture; the material went through many more processes, and of course, the loss of time, and the risk of waste, would have been much increased, if its removal from house to house at every stage of the manufacture, had been necessary. It became obvious that there were several important advantages in carrying on the numerous operations of an extensive manufacture in the same building. Where water power was required, it was economy to build one mill, and put up one water-wheel, rather than several. This arrangement also enabled the master spinner himself to superintend every stage of the manufacture; it gave him a greater security against the wasteful or fraudulent consumption of the material—it saved time in the transference of the work from hand to hand, and it prevented the extreme inconvenience which would have resulted from the failure of one class of workmen to perform their part, when several other classes of workmen were dependent upon them. Another circumstance which made it advantageous to have a large number of machines in one manufactory, was, that mechanics must be employed on the spot, to construct and repair the machinery, and that their time could not be fully occupied with only a few machines. All these considerations drove the cotton spinners to that important change in the economy of English manufactures— the introduction of the factory system; and when that system had once been adopted, such were its pecuniary advantages, that mercantile competition would have rendered it impossible, even had it been desirable, to abandon it. The enquiry into the moral and social effects of the factory system, will deserve our attention. Though Arkwright, by his series of machines, was the means of giving the most wonderful extension to the system, yet he did not absolutely originate it. Mills for the throwing of silk had existed in England, though not in any great number, from the time of Sir Thomas Lombe, who in 1719 erected a mill on the river Derwent, at Derby, on the model of those he had seen in Italy. Wyatt's first machines, at Birmingham, were turned by asses, and his establishment at Northampton by water; so Arkwright's first mill, at Nottingham, was moved by horses; his second, at Cromford, by water. During a period of ten or fifteen years after Mr. Arkwright's first mill was built (in 1771) at Cromford, all the principal works were erected on the falls of considerable rivers; no other power than water having then been found practically useful.

Those who have not taken the trouble to witness, or to enquire into, the process by which they are surrounded with the conveniences and comforts of civilised life, can have no idea of the infinite variety of ways in which invention is at work to lessen the cost of production. The people of India, who spin their cotton wholly by hand, and weave their cloth in a rude loom, would doubtless be astonished when they first saw the effects of machinery in the calico which is returned to their own shores, made from the material brought from their own shores, cheaper than they themselves could make it. But their indolent habits would not permit them to enquire how machinery produced this wonder. There are many amongst us who only know that the wool grows on the sheep's back, and that it is converted into a coat by labour and machinery. They do not estimate the prodigious power of thought—the patient labour—the unceasing watchfulness—the frequent disappointment—the uncertain profit—which many have had to encounter in bringing this machinery to perfection. How few, even of the best informed, know that in the cotton manufacture, which from its immense amount, possesses the means of rewarding the smallest improvement, invention has been at work, and most successfully, to make machines that make the cotton thread. There is a part of the machinery used in cotton-spinning called a reed. It consists of a number of pieces of wire, set side by side in a frame, resembling, as far as such things admit of comparison, a comb with two backs. These reeds are of various lengths and degrees of fineness, but they all consist of cross pieces of wire, fastened at regular intervals between longitudinal pieces of split cane, into which they are tied with waxed thread, and the machine cuts the wire, places each small piece with unfailing regularity between the canes, twists the thread round the cane with a knot that cannot slip, every time a piece of wire is put in, and does several yards of this extraordinary work in almost as little time as it takes to read this description.

The most marked traits in the character of Arkwright were his wonderful ardour, energy, and perseverance. He commonly laboured in his multifarious concerns, from five o'clock in the morning till nine at night; and when considerably more than fifty years of age,—feeling that the defects of his education placed him under great difficulty and inconvenience in conducting his correspondence, and in the general management of his business,— he encroached upon his sleep, in order to gain an hour each day to learn English grammar, and another hour to improve his writing and orthography. He was impatient of whatever interfered with his favourite pursuits; and the fact is too strikingly characteristic not to be mentioned, that he separated from his wife not many years after their marriage, because she, convinced that he would starve his family by scheming when he should have been shaving, broke some of his experimental models of machinery.

Arkwright was a severe economist of time, and, that he might not waste a moment, he generally traveled with four horses, and at a very rapid speed. His concerns in Derbyshire, Lancashire, and Scotland, were so extensive and numerous, as to show at once his astonishing power of transacting business, and his all-grasping spirit. In many of these he had partners, but he generally managed in such a way, that, whoever lost, he himself was a gainer. So unbounded was his confidence in the success of his machinery, and in the national wealth to be produced by it, that he would make light of discussions on taxation, and say that *he* would pay the national debt! His speculative schemes were vast and daring; he contemplated entering into the most extensive mercantile transactions, and buying up all the cotton in the world, in order to make an enormous profit by the monopoly; and from the extravagance of some of these designs, his judicious friends were of opinion, that if he had lived to put them in practice, he might have overset the whole fabric of his prosperity.

Moses Brown introduced Mr. Slater to Oziel Wilkinson of Pawtucket, R. I., as a suitable place for him to board; as the stranger came into the house, the two daughters, as is not uncommon, ran out of sight; but Hannah lingered with curiosity, and looked through an opening in the door: Samuel saw her eyes, and was interested in her favour. He loved at first sight, but it was sincere, it was permanent, nothing but death could have severed the ties which endeared him to Hannah Wilkinson. He was happy in fixing his affections so soon on one who loved him, and on one so worthy; that loadstone served to bind him to Pawtucket, when every thing else appeared dreary and discouraging. The parents of Hannah being Friends, they could not consistently give consent to her marriage out of the society, and talked of sending her away some distance to school; which occasioned Mr. Slater to say,—"You may send her where you please, but I will follow her to the ends of the earth."

Though absorbed in perplexing business, his hours of relaxation were cheering; he spent them in telling Hannah and her sister the story of his early life, the tales of his home, of his family connections, and of his father-land.

This introduction was one of the favourable circumstances that finally secured his success. In Oziel Wilkinson's family, he found a father and mother, who were kind to him as their own son. He was not distrustful of his ability to support a family—did not wait to grow rich before marriage, but was willing to take his bride for better and for worse, and she received the young Englishman as the man of her choice, and the object of her first love. This connection wlth Oziel Wilkinson was of great service to him, as a stranger, inexperienced in the world beyond his peculiar sphere. Besides, it is well known, that sixty years since, the contrast of character of New England men and manners, in men of business, and other peculiarities, were very great between the two countries. He found consolation in that family, he found a *home*. Those who have left their native country, know something of what Slater felt when he was "home-sick." On seeing the old and worthless machinery, as Moses Brown expressed it, "Samuel felt *down-hearted*." No one knows the heart of a stranger but he who has been from home in a strange land, without an old acquaintance, without a tried friend to whom he could unbosom his anxieties—without confidence in those around him, and others without confidence towards him. These are sorrows only known to the sufferer who knows the heart of a stranger, and no sympathies can be expected but from those who have trodden in the same path. Mr. Slater always treated the numerous strangers who flocked to him for advice, assistance, or employment, with marked attention, without partiality and without hypocrisy.

It is easy to conceive that his correspondence with his old schoolmaster must have been highly gratifying to his feelings. In that way he heard of what they were doing in Belper, and proved the truth of the assertion, how valuable is good news from a far country.

BELPER, 11th Jan. 1792.

My dear friend,—I am much obliged to you for the favour of your letter, and with pleasure embrace this opportunity of answering it; though the Atlantic rolls between us, I hope our friendship will remain undiminished. I wish you every felicity which the honourable state you have entered into can afford—may you enjoy a long life of domestic comfort and prosperous fortunes, is my sincere wish. I myself have ventured to put on the shackles of matrimony, and find in it those charms which I in vain sought for in the idle and dissipated pursuits of a single life—though I am willing to hope I never materially trespassed against the laws of decorum.

I have delayed writing, some weeks, in order to be able to answer some of your enquiries more decidedly than I am at present able to do. This is the most important era which the history of the world has ever furnished. All is agitation and confusion; what the event will be, God only knows.

You have no doubt heard of the fate of the combined armies against France, and the success of the French commanders, Dumourier, Castine, &c., in Brabant and Germany. They have carried all before them; but I fear the French, elated with victory, are now aiming at too much. They seem, contrary to their former declarations, to be actuated by the desire of conquest. They have added Savoy to the republic as an 84th department. I am a warm admirer of the French revolution, as it is likely to establish the liberty of twenty-six millions of my species; but I lament, grievously lament, the many disorders with which it has been attended. The fate of the king I cannot send you, though it will finally be decided in a few days; they are now trying him, his defence has been heard by counsel; Deseze, his first counsel, dealt long and ably on the acts of the new constitution, which declares the inviolability of the king's person. I believe the business will be finally decided by the people at large, in their primary assemblies; and I believe that perpetual banishment will be the sentence. At least I hope this, for if they touch his life, there is not a state in Europe but what will join the detestable crusade against them. Indeed, there is something in the fate of monarchs which is interesting to the mind; I know it is a remain of the doctrine of divine right, which was formerly so prevalent in all countries. I own I shall feel hurt if they touch Louis's life, though I think him guilty. Much, very much, depends on the event, not only to France, but the world. France, I believe, is pretty free from internal commotions at present; but various preparations are making for the next campaign, in Germany, Prussia, Russia, &c. *Britain* and Holland, too, are arming to fall upon her next spring. They have given umbrage to their high mightinesses by attempting to open the river Scheldt. We, you know, are in alliance with Holland and Prussia; we, that is, our government, must assist them for that reason, but perhaps more for others, which will readily occur to you. A republic like France, cannot be a pleasant thing to a certain description of men, and I believe all that can be done will be done to crush it. But an armament is nothing with us; it is but an annual advertisement; we have had four in as many years, yet no war. However, I believe we have now a pretext for a war with France. Yesterday's papers inform us that an English sloop of war received a shot from the batteries at Brest,—quere, did not she go to provoke them? I believe the people in general of this country do not wish for war. Every thinking man knows we have a flourishing trade, which war must very much injure; he knows, too, that we have a public debt of upwards of two hundred and seventy millions, and a revenue to raise in these times of peace of seventeen mllions annually, yet we are purse proud. As to the stadtholder, I cannot suppose he has forgotten the disturbances of his people four years since. Does he think they have forgotten it? If he puts his finger in this fire, I am much mistaken if he will not have to call in Prussia and us to quell them again. Spain has declared her intention of neutrality in case the king's life is spared. I would here ask you what part America will take in case Britain does declare war against France. I think I can see it. I believe America will not overtly assist her by declaring formal war; but your ports will be open to France; you will fit out privateers under French colours. I fear, my friend, this will be the case, and that harmony which exists between this country and you will be suspended, perhaps to the inconvenience of both. It is rumoured that Turkey is arming against Russia, but of the truth of this I can say nothing. This country, with respect to politics, never stood in so precarious a situation. Societies have been formed in various places for the discussion of constitutional subjects for the purpose of promoting a reform of parliament. Government has taken the alarm, and loyal meetings are calling in every considerable town in the kingdom to testify their adherence to the present government. Much difference of opinion prevails in parliament, and the business is discussed in a very intemperate manner, every night in every inn and alehouse in the kingdom. I am a friend to reform, because our representation is unequal, and dislike the conduct of both of the parties, because I think them both wrong. I am well assured that our present government, a mild and good constitution compared with others, is best for us; but many things call loudly for amendment. A few persons have avowed republican principles, and insisted too much for the introduction of French politics to this country. For America, I am sensible a republican (that is, the representative) form of government is best. But for Britain, a limited monarchy, certain. I have no room to give you my reasons for this. —— made an able and manly speech at the opening of parliament. It will find its way to America, and is well worth perusal; it has been published some time. Burke rants against reformers and the "swinish multitude," as usual. Thomas Paine is one of the members of the French convention; he has been tried for treason. Rights of Man, parts 1 and 2, and Common Sense, condemned as a libel on our constitution. Many other persons are in prison, and in the courts of justice, for publishing what are termed seditious writings. French refugees are so numerous, and government is so alarmed, that a bill is now in the house of commons and will soon be passed, entitled the "Alien Bill," which will empower officers to search all foreigners who may arrive in Britain, and scrutinise them as to their means of living here, and their business. How will your independent republican merchants like this? From this you will see that this is not the happiest of countries. Happy America, thou hast no such foes—thou art free; and thy sons and daughters are not harassed by political arts. I have said nothing on local subjects, as I supposed your other friends would supply that. John Spencer, senr. was lately drowned. Sir R. Arkwright is *dead*. James Liggit is at Canterbury—I believe doing well. Messrs. Strutts go on swimmingly—they are erecting a very large mill at Belper; and Mr. George is beginning to build himself a noble house on the bridge hill, just above the watering troughs. Present my respects to Mrs. Slater, and believe me yours very sincerely,

T. J.

To Samuel Slater, North Providence, North America.

This letter from Mr. Jackson, shows that he was an intelligent man; and he appears to have continued his correspondence with his pupil.

Smith Wilkinson, Esq., the principal owner of that fine estate, called the Pomfret factory, Connecticut, has favoured me with his early recollections in relation to the commencement of the business in Pawtucket, as the following extract will evince :—

"Mr. Slater boarded in my father's family, at which time there were only a few houses, while building his first machinery, and in the course of the year was married to my sister Hannah, who died in 1812, leaving six sons quite young, having buried four children. When the manufacturing business first commenced in Pawtucket, it may be very naturally supposed that it was frequently a subject of conversation, especially in a family so immediately connected with it. I recollect to have heard frequent conversations on the subject, in which the state and progress of the business was discussed.

"An attempt to manufacture cotton was made at Derby, in Connecticut, under the patronage of Colonel Humphreys, late minister to Spain. One at or near Hurlgate, New York, under the patronage of Mr. Livingston, was commenced, but failed, and was abandoned. I believe nearly all the cotton factories in this country, from 1791 to 1805, were built under the direction of men who had learned the art or skill of building machinery, in Mr. Slater's employ. Mr. Slater used to spin both warp and filling on the water-frame up to 1803. The operations of manufactories up to 1817, were confined to spinning yarn only, which was put out in webs, and wove by hand-loom weavers. Mules for spinning filling had not then been introduced. The cotton used to be put out to poor families in the country, and whipped on cords, stretched on a small frame about three feet square, and the motes and specks were picked out by hand, at four to six cents per pound, as it might be, for cleanness."

From the above, it appears, that at the commencement of the manufacturing business, Mr. Slater was under the necessity of hiring mechanics, or workmen, in iron and wood, of the then common trades of the country, and teaching them the trade of building machinery; in consequence of which, he made very slow progress, in erecting his first and second establishments; it being the custom then, and for many years after, not only by him, but of all who went into the business, to erect machine shops; generally in the basement or first story of the building, where all the machinery was constructed. In 1798, Mr. Slater entered into company with Oziel Wilkinson, Timothy Green, and William Wilkinson, the two latter, as well as himself, having married daughters of Oziel Wilkinson. He built the second mill, on the east side of Pawtucket river, the firm being Samuel Slater & Co., himself holding one half of the stock.

A short time afterwards, his hands in this mill revolted; five or six of them went to Cumberland, and erected a small mill, owned by Elisha Waters, and some others named Walcot. From these men and their connections, several factories were commenced in various parts of the country, and in fact most of the establishments erected from 1790 to 1809, were built by men who had, either directly or indirectly, drawn their knowledge of the business from Pawtucket, the cradle of the cotton business. Mr. Slater used to work cotton from Cayenne, Surinam, and Hispaniola, and made first quality of yarn. Some time after, when short cotton began to be used, he mixed about one third—he called the yarn of such, second quality, making fifteen cents per lb. difference. Thus while No. 12 was eighty-four cents of second quality, No. 12 of first quality was ninety-nine cents per lb.

Mr. Samuel Slater, on the establishment of the old mill, introduced among the labourers therein such regulations, as his previous observations of cotton mills in Derbyshire had shown to be useful and applicable to the circumstances of an American population. Amongst these, that which every philanthropist will deem the most important, was the system of *Sunday-school instruction**— which had been for some time in full operation, at all the mills of Messrs. Strutt and Arkwright, when Mr. Slater left England.

These schools, the first of the kind in America, are still continued at the present day. They have been copied, and extended with the extension of the cotton manufacture through this country; and they have prompted the establishment of similar schools in our seaport towns and in foreign countries. It was from Pawtucket that they were introduced into Providence in 1815, by the young men of the latter place, one of whom, William Jenkins, had been a clerk with Mr. Slater. These institutions were at first considered

---

* Twelve hundred persons are employed in the cotton factories of Mr. Thomas Ashton, of Hide, England. This gentleman has erected commodious dwellings for his work-people, with each of which he has connected every convenience that can minister to comfort. He resides in the immediate vicinity, and has frequent opportunities of maintaining a cordial association with his operatives. Their houses are well furnished, clean, and their tenants exhibit every indication of health and happiness. Mr. Ashton has also built a school, where 640 children, chiefly belonging to his establishment, are instructed on Tuesdays, in reading, writing, arithmetic, &c. A library, connected with this school, is eagerly resorted to, and the people frequently read after the hours of labour have expired. An infant school is, during the week, attended by 280 children, and in the evenings others are instructed by masters selected for the purpose. The factories themselves are certainly excellent examples of the cleanliness and order which may be attained, by a systematic and persevering attention to the habits of the artisans.

as charity schools only ; and the teachers paid by the young men. They were subsequently taken under the care and patronage of the different religious societies, by whom they have been made to serve the purpose of biblical instruction.   In addition to these schools for Sunday instruction, the establishment and support of common day schools was promoted at all the manufactories in which Mr. Slater was interested ; and in some cases, the teachers were wholly paid by himself. Regular and stated public worship, also, was liberally supported at those points where the people could be most conveniently assembled. A strict, though mild and paternal scrutiny of the conduct of the workpeople was maintained ; and prudent and effectual regulations against disorderly and immoral behaviour secured the peace, harmony, and quiet, of the mill companies.   The introduction of manufacturing was thus, in every place, a harbinger of moral and intellectual improvement, to the inhabitants of the vicinage, and the numerous operatives from remote and secluded parts of the country, attracted to the manufacturing villages by the employment, comforts, and conveniences which they afforded.   Hundreds of families of the latter description, originally from places where the general poverty had precluded schools and public worship, brought up illiterate and without religious instruction, and disorderly and vicious in consequence of their lack of regular employment, have been transplanted to these new creations of skill and enterprise ; and by the ameliorating effects of study, industry, and instruction, have been reclaimed, civilised, Christianised. Not a few of them have accumulated and saved, by close application and moderate economy, very handsome estates.   Indeed, such have been the blessed results of concentrating and giving employment to a population formerly considered almost useless to the community, that there is among our manufacturing population at this moment, a greater number of males, of from twenty to thirty years old, who are worth from $300 to $1000 each, and of marriageable females worth from $100 to $800 each, than can be found in any population, out of the manufacturing villages.

The impulse given to industry and production by the cotton manufacture has not been confined to one branch of business alone ; but has been felt in every sort of employment, useful to the community. We need not, in this place, enlarge upon the close affinity and mutual dependence of these various employments ; they are obvious to every mind which has acquired the habit of tracing results to their causes in the endless relations of society. As a general fact, it is undoubtedly true, that the advance of our country, in the production and manufacture of wool and iron, has been greatly accelerated by the cotton manufacture; and that *those* branches of industry have always been deeply affected by the temporary reverses which *this* branch has experienced. Mr. Slater was, for many years, and at the time of his death, concerned in woollen and iron, as well as cotton manufactories; and his observation and sagacity never suffered him to question the identity of their interests.*

There was another point on which his views and sentiments, though decried by some, as too disinterested and liberal in any matter of business, were truly wise and sagacious, and fully concurred in by his partners. He always maintained that legislative protection would be beneficial to himself as well as others,—to those already established in business and having an ample capital, as to those who were just beginning, and with little or no capital. This opinion, maugre all the huckstering calculations and short-sighted views of would-be-monopolists, was certainly the best for himself. Monopoly, in this country, and by any man or set of men subject to our laws, is unattainable, either by legislation or combination. It is, or ought to be, excluded from all the calculations of a sober and practical business mind. There was, therefore, nothing in their preoccupation of the cotton business that gave them an advantage over other manufacturers, except their skill and capital. Of these advantages, legislation could not or would not deprive them; and *with them on their side*, they could extend their investments as fast, certainly with as much profit, as those who were without them, or with capital only. Events have fully sustained these views. The fostering protection of the government, up to the election of the president who now is, brought forward and established many adventurers who had begun without money or skill, but have since acquired both; whilst those

---

* Their subsequent business, up to the year 1806, turned their thoughts upon a more extended investment in spinning. John Slater, brother of Samuel, had arrived from England, and had, most probably, brought with him a knowledge of the recent improvements of the English spinners. The now flourishing village of Slatersville, in Smithfield, was then projected; and John Slater embarked as a partner, and in June of the same year, removed to Smithfield as superintendent of the concern. In the spring of 1807, the works were sufficiently advanced for spinning; and they have been, up to the present time, under the very prosperous management of that gentleman, in an uninterrupted state of improvement. This fine estate was first owned, in equal quarters, by the four original partners, but now wholly belongs to John Slater and the heirs of his late brother.

who preceded them in the business are, generally, as far in advance of them as they were before. In the measures adopted by the manufacturing districts of our country to obtain this protection, Mr. Slater was ever a prominent and efficient man; and his name was affixed to the memorials from the people of this vicinity, from time to time presented in the two houses of congress.*

The impression, that Mr. Slater was " *an obscure, humble emigrant*," was a sentiment more general than correct. Few young men were better situated for advancement in life in his own coun-

---

* A question has been made concerning the constitutional right of the government of the United States to apply this species of encouragement; but there is certainly no good foundation for such a question. The national legislature has express authority " To lay and collect taxes, duties, imposts, and excises, to pay the debts and provide for the common defence and general welfare," with no other qualifications than that "all duties, imposts, and excises, shall be *uniform* throughout the United States: that no capitation or other direct tax shall be laid unless in proportion to numbers ascertained by a census or enumeration taken on the principles prescribed in the constitution;" and that "no tax or duty shall be laid on articles exported from any state." These three qualifications excepted, the power to raise money is plenary and indefinite; and the objects to which it may be appropriated are no less comprehensive, than the payment of the public debts, and the providing for the common defence and general welfare. The terms "general welfare" were, doubtless, intended to signify more than was expressed or imported in those which preceded; otherwise numerous exigencies, incident to the affairs of a nation, would have been left without a provision.

The phrase is as comprehensive as any that could have been used; because it was not fit that the constitutional authority of the Union, to appropriate its revenues, should have been restricted within narrower limits than the "general welfare;" and because this necessarily embraces a vast variety of particulars, which are susceptible neither of specification nor of definition. It is therefore of necessity left to the discretion of the national legislature, to pronounce upon the objects, which concern the "general welfare," and for which, under that description, an appropriation of money is requisite and proper. And there seems to be no room for a doubt, that whatever concerns the general interests of learning, of agriculture, of manufactures, and of commerce, are within the sphere of the national councils, *as far as regards an application of money.* The only qualification of the generality of the phrase in question, which seems to be admissible, is this,—that the object, to which an appropriation of money is to be made, be *general* and not *local;* its operation extending, in fact, or by possibility, throughout the Union, and not being confined to a particular spot. No objection ought to arise to this construction, from a supposition that it should imply a power to do whatever else should appear to congress conducive to the general welfare. A power to appropriate money with this latitude, which is granted in express terms, would not carry a power to do any other thing, not authorised in the constitution, either expressly or by fair implication.—*Hamilton's Report.*

PAWTUCKET.

Drawn by

try ; and few in this had more resources at his age than he. Moses Brown's plain manner of speaking of the partner of his son-in-law, led, in some measure, to this mistake ; and Mr. Slater, if he knew it, would never take the pains to explain his condition, or do any thing to disabuse public opinion with regard to his personal affairs ; for he was never known to boast of any thing relating to himself, whether of property or abilities, being ever acknowledged a modest, unassuming man. Capital alone is not worthy of credit, unless associated with moral qualities in the tradesman ; for a prudent man of great industry, integrity, and knowledge in his business, is more worthy of credit without capital, than a rich man, ignorant of his business. Persons who begin with large capitals do not succeed, generally speaking, so well as those who begin with small ones cautiously administered.

It is proper, perhaps, to close this chapter with an extract from a "Short Sketch of the Life of Slater," in the Providence Journal:

"Such are the outlines of the business life of a man, whose skill and knowledge of detail, in a business which, up to the time of his appearance among us, was unknown to this community, were unrivaled, whose commercial views were of the most liberal and enlightened character,—whose energy, perseverance, and untiring diligence, aided in his early efforts by the money and countenance of those who justly appreciated his merits and confidently antici- pated his eminence, have triumphed over obstacles which would have discouraged others ; have given a new direction to the indus- try of his adopted country, and opened a new and boundless field to its enterprise. It has rarely fallen to the lot of any single indi- vidual to be made an instrument, under Providence, of so much and such widely diffused benefit to his fellow-men, as this man has conferred upon them, without any pretension to high-wrought philanthropy, in the ordinary, unostentatious pursuit of that pro- fession to which he had been educated, as a means of honest and creditable living. Yet, unpretending as he was, and noiseless in that sublimated charity, which is now so fashionable and predomi- nant, his sympathy for the distressed, and his kindness and good will for all, were ever warm, active, practical, and efficient sentiments ; based upon steadfast principles, and aiming at the greatest attainable measure of good. In the relief of immediate and pressing want he was prompt and liberal. In the measures which he adopted for its prevention in future, he evinced paternal feeling and judicious forecast. Employment and liberal pay to the able-bodied promoted regularity and cheerfulness in the house, and drove the wolf from its door. ' Direct charity,' he has been heard to say, 'places its recipient under a sense of obligation which trenches upon that independent spirit that all should maintain. It breaks his pride, and he soon learns to beg and eat the bread of idleness without a blush. But employ and pay him, and he receives and enjoys, with honest pride, that which he knows he has earned, and could have received for the same amount of labour from any other employer.' It would be well for all communities if such views, on the subject of pauperism, were generally adopted and carried into practice. It is hardly necessary to state, concerning one who has done so much business, and with so great success, that his business habits and *morals* were of the highest character. The punctual performance of every engagement, in its true spirit and meaning, was, with him, a point of honour, from which no consideration of temporary or prospective advantage would induce him to depart; from which no sacrifice of money or feeling were sufficient to deter him. There was a method and arrangement in his transactions by which every thing was duly, and at the proper time attended to. Nothing was hurried from its proper place, nothing was postponed beyond its proper time. It was thus that transactions the most varied, intricate, and extensive, deeply affecting, and affected by, the general business of three adjoining states, and extending their influence to thousands of individuals, proceeded from their first inception to their final consummation, with an order, a regularity and certainty, truly admirable and instructive. The master's mind was equally present and apparent in every thing; from the imposing mass of the total to the most minute particular of its component parts."

CHAPTER IV.

MORAL INFLUENCE OF MANUFACTURING ESTABLISHMENTS.

" There is no artist, or man of industry, who mixeth judgment with his practice, but findeth in the travail of his labour, better and nearer courses to make perfect the beauty of his work, than were at first presented to the eye of his knowledge."

We have already seen that manufacturing establishments exert a powerful and permanent influence in their immediate neighbourhoods, and time, if not already, will teach the lesson, that they will stamp indelible traits upon our moral and national character. Evidences abound, wherever man exists, that his character is modified by localities, by a diversity of pursuits, by a facility of acquiring a living, by the quality and fashion of the living itself, by a restrained or free exercise of his rational powers, and by restraint on the enjoyment of liberty. Different climates and different countries produce indelible peculiarities. In the same climate and in the same country similar changes appear, from the effects of immoral habits, and from what may be termed artificial or mechanical causes. The effects of immoral habits are well known to all observers of human nature.

Those pursuing different occupations are aware that these exert an influence upon character, producing moral, no less than physical, varieties. For example, butchers become hard-hearted and cruel, and in England are excluded from the jury-box ; those who are confined to a particular routine against their will, peevish and discontented ; those who are always ordered or driven, and expect to be so, exercise little control or discernment for themselves.

Manufacturing establishments become a blessing or a curse according to the facilities which they create for acquiring a living, to the necessary articles which they provide, and the general character which they produce. To set up and encourage the manufacturing of such articles, the use and demand of which produces no immoral tendency, is one of the best and most moral uses which can be made of capital. The moral manufacturer, without the power or disposition to overreach, is in reality a benefactor. The acquisition of wealth in this way, is the most laudable. In point of benevolence and real worth of character, it claims a decided advantage over the cent per cent. process of accumulation.

Some have not the requisite ability to carry on manufacturing establishments; capital, then, with great propriety is loaned to those who have. The moral influence of a community is not promoted by creating or submitting to a manufacturing, or any other aristocracy, solely in the pursuit of interest, in which selfishness is wont to predominate.

The manufacturing interest, in a flourishing state, naturally creates power and wealth. The value of labour and the value of money are then at his disposal; but, in this free country, there is a sufficient counteracting influence to keep up the price of labour and to equalise the prices of their commodities with the value of the products of the earth. Without such a resisting power, a few would abound in wealth and influence, while the multitude would be in poverty and reduced to servitude. But there always exists a counteracting influence in the rival establishments, and the general spirit of enterprise. On the supposition that the manufacturing interest was strictly benevolent and moral, dispensing its favours according to merit and precisely as they are needed, the community might not be losers by such a state of things. This must be always the case where a people are left free to use and purchase according to their free choice. With the common experience of mankind, it could not be expected so. Only a few look beyond their own interest; when that is provided for, the employed who have assisted in the provision, are left to shift for themselves. Benevolence is not so general among mankind as to expect it uniformly. But in the progress of manufactures among us, every department becomes interested in its prosperity, the operatives receive a greater emolument for their services than in any other part of the world, whilst capital receives but a small interest, compared with other branches of industry. With such a power established merely by selfishness, morality is promoted so far and no further, than interest; but the promotion of morals becomes their interest. And if religion appears something in name or in sectarianism, more than in reality, still its promotion is for the interest of the whole community. It is said, on the presumption that the capitalists are aiming at their personal wealth, the facility for acquiring a fair compensation becomes less and less at every pressure. A rise of wages is then adapted to convenience or pleasure. But it must be remembered, that the pressure bears as heavy on the employer as the employed, and renders him liable to lose all the earnings of many years of labour, and the savings of much self-denial, and render him poor and dependent. There are two sides to this question, and the operatives in good times ought to lay up for time of need. Then they would not be obliged to bring their labour into market the best way they can, to obtain their daily bread. To take advantage of such a position, is one of the greatest immoralities. The liability of its consequences are as bad in creating discord and producing civil commotions. But the owners of factories are not known to stop their mills till obliged by dire necessity : they generally run them till they become bankrupt. The real power belongs to the labouring class ; no one ought to expect to employ this without paying for it, and no one does expect it. It is power when rightly used, and most often ceases to be so when abused. Those who are so thoughtless, negligent, or squandering, as to trust wholly to the present occasion for a bare subsistence, can hardly be thought powerful compared with what they would be did not necessity compel them to take what they can get for the present occasion. It is a mistaken notion to suppose the manufacturing interest promoted by creating poverty, or, in the end, by heavy reduction of wages. The articles manufactured very soon sink in like proportion, and the profits are swallowed up in the payment of the operative. Besides these consequences, the ability to purchase does not exist, a consideration which more or less affects the value of every article brought into market.

Our day has witnessed the surprising effects of the ingenuity of man, in calling into existence and putting in operation labour-saving machinery. If it would be, in reality, promoting human existence and human happiness in our present character and condition, that our food should come to us ready made, our habitations ready built, our conveyances already in motion, and our understandings already improved—the nearer we approach such a state of things the better.

But if not—if the desires and pursuits of objects be no less blessings than their possessions—if human nature be bettered, and the grand object of existence benefited by employment—there must be a point beyond which to obtain food and clothing and other things, without application, would be objectionable. To be moral and desirable, labour-saving machinery must bring along with it some particular benefit to the community, as well as to individuals.

This may be such as more than compensates for the many losses which are sustained in some countries, in consequence of the improvement. When it was proposed to introduce printing into the Prussian dominions, the king objected by saying, it would throw forty thousand amanuenses out of employment. After printing went into operation, to ameliorate the condition of those who were thrown out of employment, the Prussian government made a law that the initial letters should be omitted by the printers, in order that they might be executed by the amanuensis at a high compensation.   That they performed these letters with great ingenuity, and in a manner difficult to be imitated, may be seen from a copy of a bible now in possession of the antiquarian society at Worcester, Mass.   It must have been a calamity for so many to be thrown from their pursuits, and be deprived of the means of getting a livelihood.   The benefit resulting from the introduction compensated for this loss, more than ten-fold.   This is one, among many instances of human invention, which wonderfully adds to the dignity and happiness of mankind.

The first introduction of Hargreaves' and of Arkwright's machinery into England, was not only met with objections, but with popular vengeance.   It threatened a speedy destruction to every jenny and water-frame in England, and so in appearance carried in its motions frightful evils.   The anticipated evils actually happened; hand spinning met with a speedy overthrow, and those who had earned a few pence per day in following it, were compelled to resort to other employments, and perhaps to be employed in manufacturing on the new plan which they had laboured to oppose.

Similar feelings and similar consequences have happened and are still happening in America.   Manufacturing, instead of going on quietly and single-handed in private families, with immense labour, grows into large establishments, which employ and bring into association, masses of population.

This position is moral or immoral according as it furnishes proper stimulants for industry and for exertion, and for improving and directing the mental powers and principles.   With little or no inducements or expectation of emerging from a state of ignorance, with no schools, no moral or religious instruction, the liability is great for an introduction of all the evils which the opposers of manufacturing establishments have often predicted.

It is well known that vice grows worse by contact with its kind. If it can be proved that manufacturing establishments tend to accumulate, consolidate, and perpetuate, vicious propensities, and their consequences, on the community, this will serve as no inconsiderable drawback upon the apparent prosperity which is indicated in their immediate vicinity.   If found so, the condition must be charged directly to the establishments or to their consequences and abuses.   It is evidently an abuse to collect a mass of vicious population, and keep them in a state of ignorance and irreligion. When this is done, the whole community have a right to complain. If it can be shown that such things are frequently done—it is contended that they are not necessary consequences of manufacturing establishments. The owners of such establishments have it in their power to change the current of vice from its filthy and offensive channel, and make peace, order, and comfort among those they employ.

The dependence between the employed and employers should be mutual. But by employing vicious, improvident, and indigent characters, the dependence falls mostly on one side—yet it is a benefit to the community that such a class should find employment and support. Though in some countries, oppression ensues, poverty and vice show their dismal and disorderly features, and then the honest, upright, and intelligent, are driven from the establishment, and perhaps from the employment; better things can be spoken of this country, where the honest, upright, and intelligent, have always a preference. Such are leaving the old world, they are disappearing, and many of them are in the west, engaged in other employments. Pursuing such a policy, by and by, only the dregs are left, and then without looking for the causes, it appears that factories have been the immediate cause of all the mischief. On a candid enquiry, it is seen to be the abuse, and therefore not chargeable to a proper use.

Slater, the founder of the cotton manufacture in America, abundantly demonstrated, that under right management, they had no immoral tendency. On the contrary, he made it appear, that they might be serviceable to the most moral purposes. Following the plan instituted by Arkwright & Strutt in England, taking the oversight of the instruction and morals of those he employed, and instituting and keeping up sabbath schools, he successfully combated the natural tendency of accumulating vice, ignorance and poverty. Such remedies not only prevented their occurrence, but had a tendency to remove them, when they actually existed.

Industry, directed by honest and intelligent views in moral pursuits, and honourably rewarded, holds a very high rank among moral causes. To maintain good order and sound government, it is more efficient than the sword or bayonet. At the anniversary dinner of the public schools in Boston, the following toast was given by Edward Everett—"Education—A better safeguard for liberty, than a standing army. If we retrench the wages of the schoolmaster, we must raise the wages of the recruiting sergeant." So far as manufacturing establishments have promoted industry, and furnished means for an honest livelihood, thus far they have exerted a salutary influence on the character of those who have been employed. Multitudes of women and children have been kept out of vice, simply by being employed, and instead of being destitute, provided with an abundance for a comfortable subsistence.

Those who are furnished with an opportunity, and are trained up to lay by in store—moderate and regular returning means, to be used at some future day—are invariably superior in point of character to those who have not. It is not so when means flow excessive and irregular. Many a youth has been ruined by beginning with large wages, and having in prospect plenty of money.

It is believed that there may be found more young men and women, who have laid up a few hundred dollars, or even a few thousands, by being employed in manufacturing establishments, than among those who have followed other employments.

On the score of employment, manufacturing establishments have done much to support the best interests of society. It appears also, at the present time, that they have done so by their improvements. On the supposition that one or a few individuals, by the invention of labour-saving machinery, succeed, so as to furnish any particular article much cheaper than it could be done in the ordinary way, in this country where it deprives no one of a living, and goes to forward and hasten the general improvement, it cannot fail to be a benefit to the community. The diminution of price in the articles has been such, that the people have been doubly paid for all the protection granted; and commerce has been benefited by the opening of a foreign market. The failures and fluctuations in the manufacturing establishments have arisen from their weak and incipient state, and the competition of European fabrics. This cause appears greater than want of management and calculation, for the same men have alternately succeeded and failed on the same ground.

Fluctuations, whatever may be the cause, and whether they relate to business, morality, or religion, exert a wide influence on individual and national character. Those to which we are here attending, give currency to monstrous species of swindling, and form a most suitable juncture for unprincipled and unfeeling knavery to grasp with an unsparing hand, while industry and honesty are thrown into the back ground, or kicked out of doors. When such occurrences happen, and the intriguer goes off rewarded and applauded, while the honest man is stripped, despised and neglected, they give a turn to the whole character of the community. The flooding our cities with foreign importations has had this kind of tendency, and produced those evil effects.

Shrewdness and over-reaching are common events. Morality, however much respected in principle, is extremely liable to be set aside in practice. These are some of the bad tendencies of seeking out many useless inventions, and too eager a grasp after traffic and exchange of property, or what is technically called *speculation*. The acquisition and possession of property, are made the main objects of existence, whether it be needed or not. On the other hand, it will be granted, that every objection vanishes, when mechanical inventions acquire permanency, and can be subjected to the regularity of calculations. It may dignify and exalt man to triumph over the known laws of nature, and bring out the hidden treasures of air, earth, and water, in tame submission to his use. For aught we can discern, it would have no injurious effect upon his character, could he extend his journeys and researches further than this globe. One thing is certain, the more he studies and understands the works of nature and Providence, the greater will be his admiration of the display and application of wisdom and goodness. If applied as intended, the more of the resources which have been provided he brings into action, the more he adds to his true dignity and happiness.

Contrivances to favour selfish views and selfish ends are common to the animal creation. The human family are distinguished from the infinity of being, only by a greater possession and cultivation of moral and intellectual faculties. Unlike the most of the animal creation, man is left to provide for himself. Strength and powers are given him, objects are placed before him, and the strongest conceivable motives presented to use this world as not abusing it.

There must be a limit, beyond which refinement will be objectionable. When excessive it is a precursor of a relapse in civilisation.

When wealth and its appearance abound, children are most often brought up in idleness, and indulged in extravagance. Supposing labour a burden, and retrenchment the ruin of happiness, they are made liable to be overtaken by poverty, and with their last energies and ruined characters to be plunged in real misery. Individual calamities of this description, as they accumulate, become national calamities, and foment domestic dissentions. Suffering pride is all the while meditating revenge. It has nothing to lose and will endure any thing to regain what it has lost. Appearances and extravagances are prominent causes of dissention, when a part are rioting, and a part are suffering. Distinctions of rank are introduced. Individuals and nations who have run into excesses in making and maintaining such distinctions, sooner or later, are wont to be caught in their own snares. Poverty feels the burden of degradation when the power is lost to remove it.

In the present happy condition of the manufacturing districts, there are no advantages enjoyed by the rich, that are not reciprocated with the poor. Labour was never better paid, and the labourer more respected, at any period, or in any part of the world, than it is at present among us. And that man is not a friend to the poor who endeavours to make those dissatisfied with their present condition, who cannot hope, by any possibility of circumstances, to be bettered by a change. This is emphatically *the poor man's country.**

MORAL EFFECTS OF INTERNAL IMPROVEMENT.

In all the efforts that have hitherto been made for the improvement of the country, by means of rail roads and canals, reference has been made to their physical advantage only. In executive recommendations, and the application for chartered companies to construct these works, the enhanced value of lands through which they pass; the importance of establishing communications between commercial cities; the facilities they afford for conveyance of produce to market; the securing the trade of distant regions, to the ports of our own states, are the principal reasons which are urged

* The philanthropist and the political philosopher will enquire, what is the physical and moral condition of the vast population employed in manufactures? The workmen who construct or attend upon all these machines are not to be confounded with the machines themselves, or their wear and tear regarded as a mere arithmetical question. They are men, reasonable, accountable men; they are citizens; they constitute no mean part of the support and strength of the state; on their intelligence and virtue, or their vices and degradation, depend in a considerable measure not only the character of the present age, but of posterity; their interests are as valuable in the eyes of the moralist as those of the classes who occupy higher stations, yet the enquiry should be, not if the manufacturing population are subject to the ills common to humanity, not if there is not much to be lamented, but what is their condition compared with others. It is the destiny of man to earn his bread by the sweat of his brow; idleness, improvidence, and dissoluteness, are found in our large cities, and are invariably the parents of wretchedness; every where, people of all ages and conditions are liable to disease and death. The principal considerations are, the command which the working classes have over the necessaries and comforts of life, their health, their intelligence, and their morals.

upon us why they should be constructed. These indeed are sufficient, if no other could be given, to justify all the expenditures already made to establish such communications, and many more, as soon as the country can bear it. But their moral effects on the community must not be lost sight of by the philanthropist. The effect of an extensive internal commerce, in as large a country as this, on morals and the arts, science and literature, as subservient to morals and religion, are too obvious and important long to escape the notice of an attentive observer. All experience proves that good morals never did, and never can exist, among an indolent people, and people who are poor in consequence of their indolence. "Idleness is the parent of many vices," says an old proverb, and none more true was ever spoken. But in districts far from convenient markets, idleness is inevitable. Never will men labour in any employment if they can avoid it, unless they can foresee some pecuniary advantages sufficient to reward them for their pains-taking. On the contrary, they are too apt, for want of due encouragement to industrious habits, to throw away their time in worse than useless idleness and dissipation. Whoever has experienced the difficulties attendant on almost all efforts for the moral advancement of a poor and scattered population, without this encouragement, and compares them with the facilities afforded by thriving towns and villages, inhabited and surrounded by an industrious and happy people, will see at once that whatever tends to improve the physical condition of man, must, as it renders him more comfortable, conduce, in no small degree, to the improvement of his morals; and that (whatever some may have dreamed otherwise), in real life, poverty, from want of encouragement to industry, is a condition very unfavourable to the practice of virtue. If a people, under these circumstances, are ever moral in their deportment, no credit is due to their condition for it. Let our legislators be assured, that while they are extending towards its completion that system of improvement planned and hitherto carried forward with so much wisdom, they are putting into operation a moral machine which, in proportion as it facilitates a constant and rapid communication between all parts of our land, tends most effectually to perfect the civilisation, and elevate the moral character, of the people.

The general amelioration in the moral condition of communities, by the healthful encouragement of internal industry, and by affording proper aids to the development of national resources, is well worthy of the serious attention of legislators. An idle population is ever vicious and degraded; and perhaps the perpetuity of free institutions and with them a sound state of public morals, cannot exist among a people whose energies are not kept constantly in play by the pursuit of some incessant productive employment. Let us look at the contrast given in the following sketch by a North American resident in South America:—

"It is impossible to look at the present state of our neighbouring republics without a mingled feeling of pity for the weakness, and of contempt for the inefficiency, of their governments. The first out-breaking of the revolution there was hailed by the people of this country with enthusiastic joy, as the grand step towards the formation of other governments equally happy with our own ; because based upon like principles, and aspiring to like ends. The success of their undertaking we confidently predicted, for, for them it was not reserved to try the first grand experiment,—that trial had been ours ; and when the potentates of Europe, following our example, had come forward and acknowledged the independence of those republics, we felt that we, as a nation, were not alone,— that another, as promising, had risen up to prove the practicability of a new and a distrusted form of government ;—we felt that a new light had dawned upon the hitherto benighted half of the great western world, which was to guide them to freedom and happiness, and we exulted in the prospect of the noble contrast about to be presented to the tyranny and despotism of the East. But the day-star of their liberty was the brightest at its dawn. Instead of increasing in splendour as it rose, its rays beamed fainter and fainter, till at length, it is now almost totally obscured in the mists of error, discord, and confusion.

" And we are naturally led to enquire, in view of these facts, into the cause of this. We are at a loss to account for this lamentable failure of reaching that high stand which the world was led to believe the new republics would take,—we compare their first efforts with ours, and we find them equal ; indeed, more than equal. While ours were furthered and sustained by petition and remonstrance, and partook more of the character of mild persuasion than of determined opposition, *their* first efforts were accompanied with the heat and the fury of sanguinary conflict; and *their* hopes of redress were founded solely on the extermination of their oppressors.

" How sad is the prospect which, to-day, is presented to our view, in sight of all the nobleness of enterprise and undertaking which characterised the first efforts of our sister republics ! There can be no hope of their stability, under their present forms of government. The people have shown themselves unequal to the task of supporting it ; they do not understand, neither can they practise upon, the principles of self-government.   And the grand secret of all this inability lies in the universal propensity of the people to indolence, in their want of enterprise, and in the listlessness which must infallibly spring from such propensity.   All the better feelings of that people were called into action in the moment of rebellion ; they were kept alive and nurtured by a constant series of almost unhoped for successes in the grand struggle ; and, at such a time, the men who weighed the most in the scale of popularity, and who were looked up to, by the lower orders, with reverence and respect, were military men,—men who had risen by their valour, or their patriotism, or their zeal in the common cause, to a comparatively high and dignified station.   While the struggle lasted, there was no want of energy, or stability, or perseverance among them; the confusion and turmoil of the revolutionary era seemed admirably calculated to give to each and every man an opportunity to display himself in the sphere peculiarly adapted to his powers; and thus all were occupied and satisfied.

" But the contention at last ceased, and the time came when it was found necessary to re-organise the government, and establish it upon the principles for which they had fought.   With that moment commenced the troubles and internal divisons which have since brought the country to the verge of ruin.   Intriguing and ambitious men had grown up in the midst of them,—hundreds of young officers, whose education had been purely military, and whose views and ambitions were limited to one point, were stopped short in their career, and left, without a single resource in themselves, to plot and plan the means of their own advancement in the sphere of action to which they had so fondly looked forward, and for which they believed themselves solely fitted.   Among the more advanced in age and acquirements,—those who had taken a more immediate and active part in the strife just finished,—patriotism, love of country, zeal in the advancement of the national interests, all were buried and forgotten in the all-absorbing consideration of how they might secure to themselves, against the pretensions of the less experienced, those temporary advantages and emoluments of station which were theirs at the close of the revolution.

" Agriculture, commerce, manufactures, and domestic industry, although never much attended to, were now less thought of than ever.   They depended entirely upon Europe and North America for the ordinary supplies of the most essential necessaries of life.   With a soil the most fertile, and an extent of country sufficient to furnish a supply to half the world, they are still dependent upon

North America for the flour they consume. With their prairies teeming with millions of cattle, they are still dependent, in a great measure, upon foreign countries for their butter and cheese. The mechanic and higher arts are attended to almost exclusively by foreigners; indeed, wherever energy, or enterprise, or industry, is requisite, the native plays but a poor part in competition with the foreigner. This can be easily accounted for: in the first place by their excessive indolence, and in the second by a sort of hereditary pride and loftiness of feeling, which will not suffer them to follow any acknowledged trade or occupation; and which feeling, so far from rendering them superior, either in attainments or appearance, places them actually far below the ordinary standard of mediocrity. Many or most of their young men are living, and must continue to live, upon the scanty resources of their impoverished parents, some of whom, from a state of high affluence, have been reduced to comparative poverty by the destructive internal dissensions, which have laid waste and ravaged the country, and shaken, to their basis, her institutions since the revolution.

"How striking the contrast that our own land, or at least New England, presents! Where, among us, is found the youth, affluent or not, high-bred or low, who acknowledges neither occupation or profession? It is, among us, as deep a stigma as exists, that cast upon him who neglects to adopt *some* means of rendering his natural faculties subservient to one grand end of our being—that of usefulness and assistance to our fellow-men,—and who refuses to occupy that station among them to which he seems called by the particular circumstances and wants of the age, and for which his Creator has fully endowed him, with peculiar faculties and advantages.

"What a striking difference do we perceive in the morals, the feelings, and the habits, of the two people! While the billiard-rooms and the gaming-houses of the one are overflowing with the flower of her young men, and fitting them for any thing save for the performance of their duty in the approaching struggle of life, the workshops and colleges of the other are giving birth to men who are to supply the places and walk in the paths their fathers trod,—who are to further the interests and contribute to the respectability and importance of the nation,—young men who are eminently fitted to enlarge upon and improve the present system of things,—to give force and influence to the virtues, and reform the abuses of those who have gone before them.

"National grandeur and elevation of standing are founded, we may say solely, on the industry and enterprise of the people. The wealth and power of a nation have their existence in them, and the hopes of a nation's prosperity, advancement, and continuance, are, and can be, founded on nothing else. How all-important, then, in view of this, is that great branch of national industry, its manufactures! How evident is the fact that, without them, the noble fabric of our national hopes, and happiness, and freedom, would want, perhaps, the most efficient pillar of its support! The contrast that exists between the moral condition of our own country and that of the South American republics, is too striking to fail of attracting the attention of any one at all conversant with the facts of the case; and we have dwelt thus far on the subject, from the consideration, that thus might be afforded a fresh proof of the superiority, in every point of view, of a nation whose principal resources are in the industry, energy, and enterprise of its people."

DOCUMENTARY TESTIMONY ON THE MORAL INFLUENCE OF MANUFACTURING ESTABLISHMENTS IN NEW ENGLAND.

The following circular was addressed to several heads of manufacturing establishments :—

1. Are there any laws existing in the New England states by which the manufacturers of cotton and wool are prevented from the too constant employment of children? Or from the employment of those of too tender age? Would not such laws prove very salutary?

2. How old are the youngest children usually employed? Are children under fifteen years of age often deprived of opportunities of schooling, by unremitted employment in cotton or woollen factories?

3. Are there not many cotton establishments in which no children under fifteen years are employed? And is this the case with woollen establishments?

4. Are there not many establishments where the proprietors have adopted a regulation, by which children are allowed to work only a portion of the time, with a view that opportunity for schooling may be enjoyed by them? And to what age does this regulation apply?

5. What is the probable proportion of children under fifteen years, to those over fifteen, and adults, employed in cotton factories? What is the proportion in woollen?

6. Are there any factories in New England in which the proprietors employ one set of hands by day and another during the night?

7. How many hours are the operatives employed? Please to specify them. Is there an entire conformity in all the factories?

8. Do the females employed generally live with their parents, or at boarding-houses? And what are the disadvantages attending the system of boarding houses? Are they well regulated, or too large to admit of careful supervision?

9. Are instances of immorality in consequence of the employment of both sexes together, frequent, or otherwise?

10. Do the females employed in these factories generally lay up their earnings, or spend the amount in dress? Are savings banks used by the operatives for depositing their surplus gains?

11. Are first-day or Sunday schools generally established in manufacturing villages, and attended by the children?

12. Are there auxiliary tract societies established generally in these villages, for the purpose of disseminating, at a cheap rate, the excellent moral and religious publications of the American Tract Society? Could not individuals undertake so laudable a work singly?

13. Is it supposed that those persons employed in cotton and woollen manufactories are equally healthy with such as pursue agriculture? If so, can you mention any facts in corroboration?

14. What proportion of the operatives accumulate property? and what classes are generally improvident? Do you not suppose that some of the families who find employment in factories, would, if it were not for such employment, be chargeable to town as paupers?

15. Will you enumerate some of the most striking advantages which have resulted to your town or neighbourhood, by the introduction of manufactures? And also name the prominent disadvantages, if any.

16. What remedies would you propose for those evils which do exist?

17. Do you know of any cotton or woollen factories in which any improved system, or any peculiarly beneficial management, prevails? And will you specify the establishment and give a sketch of its regulations?

18. Are there existing in some manufacturing villages, libraries of useful books which circulate among the operatives?

19. Do you consider the mass of the manufacturing population, equally well educated and intelligent as the mass of agriculturists?

20. Do you know of many instances where families who were in poverty have by their successful industry in the manufactories, made themselves independent? And have you often witnessed the effect of such success in improving their habits and general characters?

21. Is it not the practice in many of the manufacturing villages, for the head of such families as are employed in the mills, to cultivate a small lot of ground, to raise corn, potatoes, and garden vegetables generally and to keep a cow? And is not this productive of much comfort to such families?

From Smith Wilkinson, Esq., Pomfret, Conn. to the author.

" You ask my opinion as to the tendency of manufacturing establishments on the morals of the people. I answer, that my settled opinion is that the natural or consequent influence of all well conducted establishments, is favourable to the promotion of good morals, for the following reasons:—
The helps are required to labour all the time, which people can sustain in regular service through the year, consistent with what is necessary to attend to their personal wants,—for meals, sleep and necessary relaxation, and a proper observance of the sabbath. The usual working hours, being twelve, exclusive of meals, six days in the week,—the workmen and children being thus employed, have no time to spend in idleness or vicious amusements. In our village there is not a public house or grog-shop, nor is gaming allowed in any private house, if known by the agent, and very few instances have

occurred in twenty-nine years, to my knowledge. In collecting our help, we are obliged to employ poor families, and generally those having the greatest number of children, those who have lived in retired situations on small and poor farms, or in hired houses, where their only means of living has been the labour of the father and the earnings of the mother, while the children spent their time mostly at play. These families are often very ignorant, and too often vicious; but being brought together into a compact village, often into the families, and placed under the restraining influence of example, must conform to the habits and customs of their neighbours, or be despised and neglected by them. Thus it happens sometimes that when it becomes generally known that a family are noted for any vice, they are neglected by the rest, and no person, male or female, will visit or be seen keeping company with them, who is at all concerned to sustain a good name. Another reason is, by being in a way to earn the means, they almost invariably clothe better; and it is a fact of common notoriety, that the females employed in factories clothe better or more expensively than others in similar circumstances as to property, or even than the daughters of our respectable farmers. But this disposition to dress extravagantly soon abates, and the helps contract habits of economy, and lay up their wages by loaning the money at interest.

"I have known a great many, who have laid aside $200 to $300, in from three to four years, and were enabled to fit themselves out decently, when married, for housekeepers. Others, who remained single, laid by four, five, and some seven and eight hundred dollars, and now have it out on interest. As public opinion goes far in regulating the moral habits and behaviour of cities and towns, so it does in manufacturing villages,—by this influence, it is an established fact, that if a female is introduced into a factory of bad or loose character, she must be discharged as soon as her character is fully known, or the rest of the female help will quit the mill. Perhaps I cannot furnish better proof of the practical tendency and effect on female character, than to state, that in twenty-nine years, during which term I have had the sole agency of Pomfret cotton manufacturing establishment, I can assert that but two cases of seduction and bastardy have occurred. One of these was by means which have often proved fatal—where the object was placed in the most disadvantageous circumstances to withstand them.

"The company of the Pomfret establishment, was formed, January 1st, 1806, consisting of,—James Rhodes, Esq., Christie Rhodes, Wm. Rhodes, brothers, all of Pawtucket, R. I.; Oziel Wilkinson, and sons-in-law; Timothy Green, Wm. Wilkinson, of Providence; Abraham Wilkinson, Isaac Wilkinson. David Wilkinson, Daniel Wilkinson, Smith Wilkinson, all of Pawtucket or North Providence, five sons of Oziel Wilkinson.

"The capital stock invested from April 1st, 1806, to October 1808, was sixty thousand dollars—of which, five twelfths was invested in real estate—it was then known by the name of Conger's mills, in Pomfret, Connecticut, on the Quinebaug river, and includes about one thousand acres of land, lying partly in three adjoining towns, namely, Pomfret, Thomson, and Killingly. There was at this time on said lands, a grist mill, saw mill, and blacksmith's shop; two houses, an old gin distillery, then just abandoned; three houses, and some other small buildings of little value. A leading object of this company in buying so much land, was to prevent the introduction of taverns and grog shops, with their usually corrupting, demoralising tendency. Another object was, to be able to give the men employ on the lands, while the children were employed in the factory. The company very early exerted their influence in establishing schools, and introducing public worship on the sabbath. In 1812, they erected a convenient brick building, to answer as a school house, and a place for holding meetings; which is now occupied for those purposes, and has been ever since its first erection."

M—— B——, Esq.

TROY, Dec. 26, 1827.

Dear Sir—I fear I have neglected too long to answer your interesting enquiries on the subjects of manufacturing and manufactories; but will now make the attempt, though on several points I have not been enabled to collect the information required. Supposing that you have a copy of the several questions, I will answer them in the order they are put, without repeating them.—(See page 125.)

1. I know of no such restrictive laws in the northern or eastern states, nor can I see any occasion for them. Public opinion, with the independent feelings of the parents and guardians of children, would prevent such abuse should it be attempted; but I never heard of such a practice in our country among manufacturers. Young children are unprofitable in almost every branch of our labour, and so much so, that it is the practice to keep them out of factories as long as the importunities of parents can be resisted.

2. Children under ten years are generally unprofitable at any price, and it is very seldom they are employed, unless their parents work in the mill, and they are brought in to do light chores, or some very light work, such as setting spools in the frame, or piecing rolls. As far as I am acquainted, there is more attention paid to schooling children in manufacturing villages, than in districts of other employments.

3. I do not know of any works where the age is positively limited, nor do I think that it could well be done. There are many boys at fourteen years, who are able, in most employments, to do the work of men; they only want the skill. The heavy work is mostly done by machinery; and there are many girls at fourteen years who are as steady and discreet, as others at sixteen or over. I have no doubt that it would be more profitable to employ young women in our factories generally, except for overseers, if they could be obtained.

4. I do not know of any thing exactly in that shape; it is not consistent with the operations of a mill, that any part of the help should leave their place to spend certain hours in school; but the child is refused employment until it has had its necessary schooling.

5. I have never heard fifteen years referred to, as an age below which employment would be wrong or unprofitable. I should say the proportion might be 10 per cent. There is less young help employed in the woollen than in the cotton manufactures.

6. I never heard of such an instance in our country, though I believe there are those who practise and pursue such a system in England. I do not think it would be tolerated here: public opinion would not suffer it, nor could workmen be procured.

7. An average through the year of twelve hours, is every where under-

stood as factory hours; this is by common consent, nor have I heard of any attempt to increase the number, as a rule of employment.

8. It is customary, in commencing a manufacturing village, to build a boarding-house to begin with: and this is necessary from the nature of the case in most instances; but as soon as families are brought in, the help employed is generally distributed. The custom in most places is, to allow and require every hand to provide for themselves. This is found more satisfactory and best; in this way the price of board is regulated by competition, and labourers choose their associates, and the females in this distribution in families are better protected, and more pleasantly situated.

9. As far as I am acquainted, unfrequent beyond the expectations of any one.

10. There is a disposition to dress among the unmarried females, though many do lay up something, and many help their parents in supporting the younger members of a family. Our factory villages have many widows, who resort there to bring up their families, and are thus enabled to keep them together, and provide for them very comfortably; and here the young women are the stay and support of their mothers, while they receive counsel and protection.

11. Sabbath schools are common to a considerable extent, and are becoming more so in manufacturing villages.

12. In many villages there are tract societies, where from funds of their own, they purchase of the larger institutions, and in others there are auxiliary societies. Something is done, and much more might be done.

13. I have no doubt of the healthiness of the employment. I have been engaged in a cotton factory since 1813, and have employed from sixty to one hundred hands, men, women and children, and do not believe there is a more healthy village any where to be found; and can speak confidently in saying that the farmers in the immediate neighbourhood are not more hardy, nor do I believe they can undergo the same fatigue, because not so accustomed to such constant and regular labour.

14. I cannot say how far they accumulate property; I know that many do, and very many live comfortably and independently, who but for such employment would be paupers. Many families begin in debt and embarrassment, who soon pay their debts, and support their families, and gain property afterwards.

15. This would be to write a volume. The property in the neighbourhood is greatly advanced. It is quite a market for vegetables, fruits, meats, to the farmers around. Industry, education, and morals, are greatly improved. The farmers and mechanics look for the money paid out at the factory store as an unfailing resource for their circulating medium; and depend on furnishing their necessaries, as a sure means of getting money. I not know of, nor can I conceive of, any disadvantages. Our manufactures have greatly increased the commerce of our city, in bringing the raw material and distributing the articles manufactured, and furnish a large market for the product of the farmer. I paid for the last four months $758.63 for the single article of flour for our families.

16. I know of no evils which exist in manufacturing villages as such, which are not increased, and more or less aggravated in other villages, or

which are not to be found in every society. I think any evil is easier re-
medied in such places than in different society.

17. I will give you our regulations at the close in general terms.

18. I am not acquainted with any where libraries are established, but have
no doubt it would be beneficial.

19. I consider them decidedly better educated, more intelligent, of better
cultivated manners, higher notions of character, more enterprise, and every
way more improved citizens, than the mass of agriculturists. When the
latter change to the former there is generally a marked improvement, and
when the former to the latter, a deterioration and running down.

20. I do know of many instances where those quite poor have, by their industry and economy, become comparatively independent, and the character
of the whole family changed for the better.

21. There are many whose families work in the factories, when the man
takes a piece of land on shares, and raises corn and potatoes; but this is a
more common practice in the New England states, than with us. When the
man cannot be employed to advantage, this may do well, but the leisure hours
such an one would have, would be a bad example for the factory hands, and
I would prefer giving constant employment at some sacrifice, to having a man
of the village seen in the streets or shops on a rainy day at leisure.

M—— B——, Esq.

TROY, Dec. 27, 1827.

Respected Friend—I said, in answering your 17th query, that I would give
you our general regulations in our manufacturing establishment. In 1812,
five individuals, one of whom was myself, built the establishment which I
think you visited with me when at Troy. We were all ignorant of our
undertaking, but had very great expectations from what we had been told. I
had the principal agency in erecting the buildings, and procuring machinery
&c.—but we had one partner who was superintendent, and who professed
much, but knew very little. We commenced work in the spring of 1813,
but every thing went bad, and we found our superintendent a man of loose,
bad notions, bad principles, and he had brought together a bad set of workmen. We dismissed him, and after some time persuaded my brother to
come and take charge of it. He was a merchant, and knew nothing of the
manufacturing business. Things still went bad; the workmen were de-
ceivers, and my brother had a difficult place to fill; but we dragged along
until the peace, and found ourselves very much in debt, and embarrassed,
and stopped our works in the fall of 1816. Thus the works remained until
the spring of 1817. I then bought eight of the ten shares in which the factory was owned. We had kept a store of groceries, and sold rum to our
hands as freely as they required. I have never brought any spirituous liquors
to our village since—the hands were all poor and most of them in debt. I
bought cotton in April, and started the mill—the hands that chose to stay,
and were willing to live without the use of ardent spirits, I kept, and divided
their debts into small sums, which they agreed to deduct from their wages
weekly—their rents were all payable weekly, that no debts might be suffered
to accumulate against the hands, and no one was to ask or expect credit,
unless at the beginning of a week, when they could anticipate half the
wages of the week if necessary. If they could not live under these regula-

tions, they were at liberty to go; but if they stayed, their old debts must be paid, they must live without spirits, and they were not at liberty to get in debt any where—no liquors could be brought into any workshop under any pretence whatever. Thus I began, now nearly eleven years ago; many of the families are now with me, or those that were young men and girls are now married and have families; they were all poor without exception. I will mention the condition of some of the hands—one young man, an apprentice in the machine shop, is now out of my employ as a steady hand, but does job work for me—he has a large family, but owns a good house, has considerable money at interest, has two buildings for rent, is worth three thousand dollars. Another has two thousand dollars at interest. Another has bought him 100 acres of good land, owns a house in the village, and has money at interest. Another has $1000 at interest—several others have three or four hundred dollars beforehand. Families all above board, with one or two exceptions; we keep a district school the year round, with a competent man teacher—through the season of working in nights, a school goes in at eight o'clock, and out at ten o'clock, which all the young men and women calculate to attend—here are taught writing, arithmetic, and grammar, geography, and history—this is very much encouraged and is a very popular school; we have a very prosperous Sunday school; there is a small house for worship in the village, and one a mile east, and many come into Troy to meeting, it being only about two miles. In order to keep out tippling and grog shops, I have a clause inserted in all the leases given for building lots, that any one selling ardent spirits on the same, forfeits the premises.

A large proportion of our families are hopefully pious, have family prayers daily, and are members of churches in good standing, and a majority of our young people belonging to the cotton factory are professors of religion. Since 1815, there have been three revivals of religion. We have there a bible society, tract society, and domestic missionary society. There are a large number of newspapers taken, and some reviews and quarterlies : and I think a state of society which would be gratifying to the patriot and philanthropist—and the Christian. We have all our hands by the year, which commences on the first of May. We inventory every March, and then engage our help for the year. We seldom have any hands leave us, that we wish to retain. Our young people marry and settle in the same village in many instances. Our contracts are to pay as fast as the individual or family need to live upon, and the balance at the end of the year. To those who will let their balances remain in book we pay interest, but will not give notes, because the advisory influence is in some measure lost if you give notes which can be negotiated; but on our plan, our books become a savings' bank for the hands. If they want a note we pay the balance. We have over five hundred inhabitants, and in 1812 the ground was cleared where our village now stands. Our establishment is very small compared with many of the eastern works, and our buildings and machinery are not after the modern improvements, but we cannot afford to throw them by. We have built a very firm excellent building for the woollen business, and have it well filled with the best machinery that could be procured, and have commenced operation, but it will take time to get such a set of hands as we have at the cotton mill; yet I see no difficulty. The wool business requires more man labour, and this we study to avoid. Women are much more ready to follow good regulations, and are not captious, and do not clan as the men do against their overseers; but I can afford to give a religious man or woman higher wages, than I can one who has no fixed principles of action and government for themselves. It should be the first object of our manufacturing establishments, to have their superintendents, and overseers, and agents, men of religious principles, and let it be felt by the owners that it is always for their interest to support religion, schools, and all those institutions which promote good morals, and diffuse information among the operatives and their families. I feel confident that we have made a sufficient experiment, in the manufacturing business, to see its effect upon those employed and the state of society which it produces, and the influence it has upon a neighbourhood of farmers, and others in the district round about, and have no hesitation in saying, that in every particular it is favourable. It grows up a healthy population, is favourable to early schooling and good education, and early habits of industry; stimulants to enterprise, economy, and frugality in living, and saving the products of their labour—and at the same time the organisation of these establishments in villages, being necessary for their success, they are placed in a more favourable situation for the cultivation of moral and religious character, without which, civilised man is still a savage, and a very limited degree of human happiness attained.

I am, respectfully, your friend and obedient servant,

JEDEDIAH TRACY.

The following remarks are from a correspondent who has paid attention to this subject, and who sincerely wishes well to every branch of useful industry which shall benefit the country :—

" I noted that the legislature of Massachusetts instituted an enquiry some nine or ten years ago, to ascertain the moral influence of manufacturing establishments, which resulted in a favourable report—never published.

" In pursuing thy enquiries upon this deeply interesting subject, I sincerely hope thou wilt state the whole case fairly, so that those points where danger is to be apprehended may be seasonably guarded by the conservators of public morals. The employment of young children of too tender age, should be freely and warmly discouraged; and if at the present moment there should appear to be any increase of this evil, our legislatures should timely adopt such wise and prudent measures as would cure the evil. No patriot could advocate the extension of any branch of national industry which would necessarily bring along with it an ignorant and consequently vicious population.

" We find many men of philanthropic minds who view with alarm the rapid extension in our country of manufacturing industry, under a conviction that it stands opposed to the progress of religion and sound morals—in a word that it is essentially repugnant to the general well being of the community; nor is this surprising, since those whose interests stand opposed to the increase of manufactures on a large scale, have long and vehemently insisted upon its demoralising tendency. A great deal has been said about the sad change this mischievous system has produced among our neighbours of the eastern states—it has been described as a Pandora's box that has filled the land with all sorts of moral plagues. It must be obvious that the subject has been presented to us through a medium somewhat distorted by wrong prejudices, and even the interesting columns of 'The Friend' may have contributed to strengthen these prejudices by the revival of the somewhat trite sentimentality of Goldsmith and Southey—I allude to an article in the second number. I am, however, as little disposed to call in question the motives of our philanthropists in opposing the manufacturing system, as I am to extenuate or defraud any abuses to which it is liable. That abuses do exist, even in this country, I am well aware, and I would be the last person to discourage any well directed effort to remdy them.

"It is certainly an interesting enquiry, whether, as manufactures have advanced in our country, the general character of the operative classes has deteriorated? Have these occupations had an unfavourable influence upon the *intelligence*, the *morals*,* or the *health*, of those engaged in them?

---

* With reference to this point, we have great satisfaction in adducing the following conclusive testimony :—

WATERFORD, R. I. May 23d, 1835.

Dear Sir,—In reply to yours of 7th inst. will observe, that many persons can give you better views than I can, respecting the condition of the cotton manufacture business in its various stages and fluctuations, since its establishment in this country, and the effect of the tariff laws upon it. Our business has always been seven eighths woollen, and is now exclusively so. We have a woollen mill, eighty feet by thirty-six, and one, three hundred and fifty feet by fifty, both five stories high; for broadcloth principally.

As regards the effects of manufacturing villages on the morals of the people, there can be but one opinion among those who know any thing about the subject. They certainly tend very powerfully to the improvement of morals. In our village, with a population of three hundred to four hundred, not an intemperate person lives. Nearly one hundred females are in the village, and since its establishment, a term of ten years, not a case of illegitimacy has occurred, nor has a rumour of such a nature ever been in the village. No person who has ever resided in the village, has ever become chargeable to the town in any manner. On the first of April last, the people who work in our mills had $10,000 due to them in cash. We have an excellent free school through the year, of about fifty scholars. Yours truly,

WELCOME FARNUM.

"Having had access to authentic information upon this subject, I answer as follows :—

"The cotton manufacture may now be considered permanently established; it is prosperous and rapidly increasing in the New England states, which must remain, as they are at this time, the principal seat of it. For the present, my remarks will be confined to this branch of manufactures.

"A great change has taken place within the last few years, in regard to the proportion of children employed in these factories; the proprietors having found that their interest is promoted by dispensing almost entirely with the labour of children under fifteen years.

"In the factories at Newmarket, N. H., which have been in operation about four years, there are employed, 250 girls, five boys and twenty overseers and assistants—twelve of the overseers have families. Nine only of the girls are under fifteen years of age, six of whom are fourteen. Three of the boys are under fifteen, two of whom are fourteen. In every instance the children under fifteen reside with their parents or guardians in the village, and are admitted into the factories on account of the peculiar circumstances of the families; they are allowed to work only six months in the year—during the other six months, they attend a public school in the village. Besides the operatives mentioned, there are thirty machinists, twenty of whom have families; these, however, are employed in a separate workshop. The relative number of children employed in this establishment, it is believed, will correspond, without much variation, with the proportion to be found in most of the factories east of Providence and its vicinity; in the latter district, the manufactories were established at an earlier period, and still give employment to a larger proportion of children.

"In cases of newly formed villages, it is found necessary to erect at the commencement several boarding-houses, sufficiently spacious to accommodate a large number of the workpeople in each; to this arrangement there are powerful objections. At Newmarket it has been entirely abandoned, and is superseded by the increased number of private families, which have taken up their residence in the village; and not being inconveniently large, are kept under good regulation. A part of the girls whose parents do not live in the village, are distributed as boarders with those families which are disposed to receive them.

"Nearly all of the manufacturing villages are small, and there is very generally attached to each dwelling a lot of ground, which is appropriated to the culture of garden vegetables, and food for a cow and swine; these are considered very essential comforts, and are rarely dispensed with by the industrious operatives.

" It should be borne in mind, that in this country *water-power* is almost exclusively used in manufactures, and, on account of its greater cheapness, the day must be far distant indeed, when steam power will be extensively used; the consequence is, that the manufacturing population must be scattered. We can have no Manchesters on this side the Atlantic, while our thousand rivers and streams afford an inexhaustible supply of unimproved power."

Dr. Ure says:—" The present is distinguished from every preceding age by an universal ardour of enterprise in arts and manufactures. Nations, convinced at length, that war is always a losing game, have converted their swords and muskets into factory implements, and now contend with each other in the bloodless, but still formidable, strife of trade. They no longer send troops to fight on distant fields, but fabrics to drive before them those of their old adversaries in arms, and to take possession of a foreign mart. To impair the resources of a rival at home, by underselling his wares abroad, is the new belligerent system, in pursuance of which every nerve and sinew of the people are put upon the strain." Dr. Ure continues in another place :—

" Great Britain may certainly continue to uphold her envied supremacy, sustained by her coal, iron, capital, and skill, if, acting on the Baconian axiom, 'knowledge is power,' she shall dilligently promote moral and professional culture among all ranks of her productive population. Were the principles of the manufactures exactly analysed, and expounded in a simple manner, they would diffuse a steady light to conduct the masters, managers, and operatives, in the straight paths of improvement, and prevent them from pursuing such dangerous phantoms as flit along in the monthly patent-lists. Each department of our useful arts stands in need of a guide-book to facilitate its study, to indicate its imperfections, and to suggest the most probable means of correcting them. It is known that the manufactures of France have derived great advantage from the illustrated systems of instruction published under the auspices of its government and patriotic societies. Manufacture is a word which, in the vicissitude of language, has come to signify the reverse of its intrinsic meaning: for it now denotes every extensive product of art, which is made by machinery, with little or no aid of the human hand; so that the most perfect manufacture is that which dispenses entirely with manual labour. The philosophy of manufactures is to modify the texture, form, or composition of natural objects by mechanical or chemical forces, acting either separately, combined, or in succession.

" The blessings which physico-mechanical science has bestowed on society, and the means it has still in store for ameliorating the lot of mankind, have been too little dwelt upon; while on the other hand, it has been accused of lending itself to rich capitalists, as an instrument for harassing the poor, and of exacting from the operative an accelerated rate of work. It has been said, for example, that the steam-engine now drives the power-looms with such velocity as to urge on their attendant weavers at the same rapid pace. But the truth is, that every member of the loom is so adjusted, that the driving force leaves the attendant little to do, certainly no muscular fatigue to sustain, while it procures for him good, unfailing wages.

" The constant aim and effect of scientific improvement in manufactures are philanthropic ; as they tend to relieve the workman, either from niceties of adjustment, which exhaust his mind and fatigue his eyes, or from painful repetition of effort, which distort or wear out his frame. At every step of each manufacturing process, the humanity of science will be manifest.

" The title of factory, in its strictest sense, involves the idea of an opera-tion composed of various mechanical and intellectual organs, acting in unin-terrupted concert for the production of a common object,—all of them being subordinated to a self-regulated moving force.

" In its precise acceptation, the factory system is of recent origin, and may claim England for its birth-place. The mills for throwing silk, or making organzine, which were mounted centuries ago, in several of the Italian states, and transferred to England, by Sir Thomas Lombe, in 1718, contained indeed some elements of a factory, and probably suggested some hints of those grander and more complex combinations of self-acting machines, which were first embodied, half a century later, in the cotton manufacture, by Richard Arkwright, assisted by gentlemen of Derby, well acquainted with its celebrated silk establishment. But the spinning of an entangled flock of fibres into a smooth thread, which constitutes the main operation with cotton, is, in silk, superfluous; being already performed by the unerring instinct of a worm, which leaves to human art the simple task of doubling and twisting its regular filaments. The apparatus requisite for this purpose is more elementary, and calls for few of those gradations of machinery which are needed in the carding, drawing, roving, and spinning processes of a cotton mill. When the first water-frames, for spinning cot-ton, were erected at Cromford, in the romantic valley of the Derwent, about sixty years ago, mankind were little aware of the mighty revolution which the new system of labour was destined by Providence to achieve, not only in the structure of British society, but in the fortunes of the world at large. Arkwright alone had the sagacity to discern, and the boldness to predict, in glowing language, how vastly productive human industry would become, when no longer proportioned in its results to muscular effort, which is by its nature fitful and capricious, but when made to consist in the task of guiding the work of mechanical fingers and arms, regularly impelled, with great ve-locity, by some indefatigable physical power. What his judgment so clearly led him to perceive, his energy of will enabled him to realise with such rapidity and success, as would have done honour to the most influential individuals, but were truly wonderful in that obscure and indigent artisan. The main difficulty did not, to my apprehension, lie so much in the inven-tion of a proper self-acting mechanism, for drawing out and twisting cotton into a continuous thread, as in the distribution of the different members of the apparatus into one co-operative body, in impelling each organ with its appropriate delicacy and speed, and above all, in training human beings to renounce their desultory habits of work, and to identify themselves with the unvarying regularity of the complex automaton. To devise and administer a successful code of factory diligence, was the Herculean enterprise, the noble achievement of Arkwright. Even at the present day, when the system is perfectly organised, and its labour lightened to the utmost, it is found nearly impossible to convert persons past the age of puberty, whether drawn from rural or from handicraft occupations, into useful factory hands. After struggling for a while to conquer their listless or restive habits, they either renounce the employment spontaneously, or are dismissed on account of inattention. If the factory Briareus could have been created by mechanical genius alone, it should have come into being thirty years sooner; for upwards of ninety years have now elapsed since John Wyatt, of Birmingham, not only invented the series of fluted rollers, (the spinning fingers usually ascribed to Arkwright,) but obtained a patent for the invention, and erected 'a spinning engine without hands,' in his native town.

" The details of this remarkable circumstance, recently snatched from oblivion, are given in Baines's History of the Cotton Manufacture. Wyatt was a man of good education, in a respectable walk of life, much esteemed by his superiors, and therefore favourably placed, in a mechanical point of view, for maturing his admirable scheme. But he was of a gentle and passive spirit; little qualified to cope with the hardships of a new manufacturing enterprise. It required, in fact, a man of a Napoleon nerve and ambition, to subdue the refractory tempers of workpeople, accustomed to irregular paroxysms of diligence, and to urge on his multifarious and intricate constructions, in the face of prejudice, passion, and envy. Such was Arkwright, who, suffering nothing to stay or turn aside his progress, arrived gloriously at the goal, and has for ever affixed his name to a great era in the annals of mankind: an era which has laid open unbounded prospects of wealth and comfort to the industrious, however much they may have been, occasionally, clouded by ignorance and folly.

" Prior to this period, manufactures were every where feeble and fluctuating in their development ; shooting forth luxuriantly for a season, and again withering almost to the roots, like annual plants. Their perennial growth now began in England, and attracted capital in copious streams to irrigate the rich domains of industry. When this new career commenced, about the year 1770, the annual consumption of cotton, in British manufactures, was under four millions of pounds weight, and that of the whole of Christendom was, probably, not more than ten millions. Last year, 1835, the consumption in Great Britain and Ireland was about two hundred and seventy millions of pounds, and that of Europe and the United States, together, four hundred and eighty millions. This prodigious increase is, without doubt, almost entirely due to the factory system, founded and upreared by the intrepid native of Preston.

" If, then, this system be not merely an inevitable step in the social progression of the world, but the one which gives a commanding station and influence to the people who most resolutely take it, it does not become any man, far less a denizen of England, to vilify the author of a benefaction, which, wisely administered, may become the best temporal gift of Providence to the poor,—a blessing destined to mitigate, and, in some measure, to repeal, the primeval curse pronounced on the labour of man, 'in the sweat of thy face shalt thou eat bread.' Arkwright well deserves to live in honoured remembrance among those ancient master-spirits, who persuaded their roaming companions to exchange the precarious toils of the chase for the settled comforts of agriculture.

"Under the auspices, and in obedience to Arkwright's polity, magnificent edifices, surpassing far in number, value, usefulness, and ingenuity of construction, the boasted monuments of Asiatic, Egyptian, and Roman despotism, have, within the short period of fifty years, risen in England, to show to what extent capital, industry and science, may augment the resources of a state, while they meliorate the condition of its citizens. Such is the factory system, replete with prodigies in mechanics and political economy, which promises, in its future growth, to become the great minister of civilisation to the terraqueous globe. As to exact mechanical science, no school can compete with a modern cotton-mill.

"There are five distinct classes of factories; first, the cotton factories; second, the woollen; third, the worsted; fourth, the flax, hempen, or linen; and fifth, the silk. These five factories have each peculiarities, of its raw material and of its fabrics; but they all possess certain family features, for they all employ torsion to convert the loose slender fibres of vegetable or animal.origin, into firm, coherent threads, and, with the exception of silk, they all employ extension, also, to attenuate and equalise these threads, technically styled yarn. Even one kind of silk which occurs in entangled tufts, called floss, is spun like cotton, by the simultaneous action of stretching and twisting. The above named five orders of factories are set in motion by steam engines or water-wheels; they all give employment to multitudes of children or adolescents. Mr. Anthony Strutt, who conducts the mechanical department of the great cotton factories of Belper and Milford, has so thoroughly departed from the old routine of the schools, that he will employ no man who has learned his craft by regular apprenticeship; but in contempt, as it were, of the division of labour principle, he sets a plough-boy to turn a shaft of perhaps several tons weight, and never has reason to repent his preference, because he infuses into the turning apparatus a precision of action, equal, if not superior, to the skill of the most experienced journeyman. It was indeed a subject of regret, to observe how frequently the workman's eminence, in any craft, had to be purchased by the sacrifice of his health and comfort. To one unvaried operation, which required unremitting dexterity and diligence, his hand and eye were constantly on the strain, or if they were suffered to swerve from their task for a time, considerable loss ensued, either to the employer or the operative, according as the work was done by the day or by the piece. But on the equalisation plan of self-acting machines, the operative needs to call his faculties only into agreeable exercise; he is seldom harassed with anxiety or fatigue, and may find many leisure moments for either amusement or meditation, without detriment to his master's interests or his own.* As his business consists in tending the

---

* " It has been heretofore stated, that a portion of mankind laboured for others, as well as for themselves. They are a respectable portion, and perform an essential part in the business of life. We have seen that the two classes are useful to each other. They are not the less so, because one is not as rich as the other, or labours in a subordinate station. They are co-workers for their own and the common good. He that

work of a well regulated mechanism, he can learn it in a short period ; and when he transfers his services from one machine to another, he varies his task, and enlarges his views by thinking on those general combinations which result from his and his companion's labours. Thus, that cramping

would set one at variance with the others, is justly reprehensible, as a disorganiser, an enemy to the public family, and its individual members. The man who would oppress or depress either, deserves the indignation of the community, and until better disposed, should be left to help himself.

"But the evil most to be deprecated, is not that one man is poor and another rich, it is not that the poor are oppressed by the rich—the evil has a foundation deeper and broader than has yet been suggested. The condition of society would be much improved, men would be made more equal and more respected, by a more general diffusion of that information which is useful in all situations, by encouraging habits of industry and temperance, by raising the moral character above the vices which disgrace and degrade men. There is poverty, want and wretchedness everywhere ; more or less of these are in all families and in all places. And why is it so ? The fault is our own ; every man is chargeable with a portion of it. The remedy is as near home as the disease. The evil is so common the cause is overlooked.

"It is ignorance. The want of that knowledge of men and things, necessary to a due estimation of the rights and duties belonging to the various situations in life. People will neither read, think, or reflect as they ought. They neglect the mind, which distinguishes them from the beasts of burden ; and they care as little for their children as for themselves.—There is no want of schools. The means of instruction are furnished, and they are accessible to every child at the public expense. Add to this the teachings which may and ought to be acquired at home, and at church, with a due improvement of all, and the evils which originate in ignorance will cease; the poor boy by habitual industry, will ' become a philosopher, a statesman, or a divine ;' and shed around him the benign influence of his great and good works, enjoy the honour and confidence of the public, and the high satisfaction of having acted his part well, which is the best of all rewards. But ' poverty and shame shall be to him that refuseth instruction.'

"It is idleness. The parent of a thousand evils and as many vices. The legitimate progenitor of poverty—many will not work. Some that are most busy do nothing— what they acquire they waste, and with it waste themselves. The idler not only injures himself, but others come within his baneful influence. It requires many hands to do the idler's work. ' The sluggard will not plough by reason of the cold, therefore he shall beg in the harvest and have nothing.'

"It is extravagance. Mankind are deluded by fashion. Dress, show, and equipage, hold too high a place among their household gods. They live beyond their income. The luxuries of life are its bane,—the canker worms that eat up a man's substance and turn him out of his house, and send his children begging.

"It is intemperance—a near relation to the preceding. The morning, noon, and evening dram, and the rum bottle at home, will finish the mischief and consume all that is left of body and mind. Of the reward of these, others may speak; of their degradation none can doubt. Such evils are more or less prevalent among all classes and ranks, sinking, destroying, and brutalising man. The remedy is for each one to reform himself. It is the moral courage and determined energy of the philanthropist who would make men happier, by making them better ; and not the doubtful dogmas of the mere politician, or the cold philosophy and metaphysical reasonings of a cloistered ' book-worm.'

"Moral evils are the real and alarming cause of complaint. Remove them, and there will be more equality, less poverty, less murmuring, and less discontent. The well directed power of moral influence, will effect the surest cure ; it will do for society, what the lever of Archimedes would in mechanics, move the world and overturn the reservoirs of vice.

"New legislation cannot reach the source of the evil, or heal the disease which is weakening and wasting the energies of our political and social relations."

"Operatives in England.—The idea most prominent in the minds of most people in relation to the great manufacturing establishments of Great Britain is, that they are sources of immense individual and national wealth ; and the next is, that they enclose within their walls a demoralised and over-worked population. The Edinburgh Review,

of the faculties, that narrowing of the mind, that stunting of the frame, which were ascribed, and not unjustly, by moral writers, to the division of labour, cannot, in common circumstances, occur under the equable distribution of industry. How superior in vigour and intelligence are the factory mechanics in Lancashire, where the latter system of labour prevails, to the handicraft artisans of London, who to a great extent continue slaves to the former. The one set is familiar with almost every physico-mechanical combination, while the other seldom knows any thing beyond the pin-head sphere of his daily task."

Copy of a letter from Benjamin Hawkins, accompanying the President's communication to Congress, December 8, 1801.

" The present spring, the agent has delivered to Indian women, 100 pair of cotton cards, and 80 spinning wheels; there are eight looms in the nation, four of them wrought by Indian or half breed women, and the remainder by white women. There is a woman employed as an assistant, to teach the

to which we recur for the purpose of saying a few words on this interesting point, strongly contradicts the statements that have been circulated, chiefly, it says, by Mr. Sadler's famous factory report, in regard to the ruinous effects of factory labour. The publication of Mr. Sadler's report and the discussion consequent hereupon, led to the appointment by the British government of a commission to enquire on the spot into the actual condition of the labourers, which enquiry resulted in proving, says the Edinburgh Review, that the representations in regard to the pernicious influence of this kind of labour have been grossly exaggerated. Instances of abuses are declared to be rare, and it is asserted that, speaking generally, factory work people, including children, are as healthy and contented as any class of the community obliged to earn their bread by the sweat of their brow.

" Mr. Tufnel, one of the commissioners who went through Lancashire, makes statements which appear conclusive as to the condition of labourers employed in factories. Of all the common prejudices with regard to factory labour, none, says this gentleman, is more unfounded than that which ascribes to it excessive tedium and irksomeness above all other occupations, owing to its being carried on in conjunction with the ' unceasing motion of the steam engine.' This erroneous opinion proceeds from the belief that because the motion of the steam engine is incessant, the labour accompanying it is incessant also. But the reverse of this is the fact. The way to prevent an employment being incessant is to introduce a steam engine. Three fourths of the children employed in cotton mills are not actively at work for more than four hours out of the twelve. The English speak always of steam, because with them it has, for all kinds of large factories, superseded almost entirely the use of water power. In this country, water power continues to be used in nearly all our large manufacturing establishments. The result, of course, is precisely the same as regards the human labour required in conjunction.

" The stories as to the immorality of persons employed in factories, are declared to be utterly false. The evidence of various clergymen of Manchester intimately acquainted with the factory proprietors, goes to show that the morals of the persons engaged in mills are quite as good as those of any other class of people. This account coincides with what is known to be the fact in this country as to this important part of the factory system. From gentlemen connected with the large manufactories in the neighbourhood of this city, we have heard an equally good report. The manufacturing population of Lowell, Massachusetts, five thousand of whom are females, is as moral as any in the world. Nay, we doubt whether in any community in the United States, or any where else, in town or country, comprising the same number of inhabitants, there is so little vice as in Lowell, a town which has grown up to sudden prosperity solely through manufacturing industry.

" In regard to the effects on health, enquiries resulted in the conclusion, that ' factory labour is decidedly not injurious to health or longevity, compared with other employments.' "

women how to spin and weave ; and the agent has appointed as a temporary assistant, a young Englishman, from a manufactory in Stockport, England, who can make looms and spinning wheels, and every thing appertaining to them, and he understands weaving. He will in a few days have a ninth loom set up at the residence of the agent. The women have this spring adopted this part of the plan with spirit, and have promised to follow the directions of the agent with exactitude. These Indian women, of one family, have been spinning for two years only, have clothed themselves well, are proud of the exertions they have made, and are, by their conduct, a stimulus to their countrywomen. One of the looms and two of the spinning wheels in use, were made by an Indian chief, for his own family.

" The chiefs, who were apprehensive at first, that if their women could clothe and find themselves by their own exertions, they would become independent of the degraded connection between them, have had proofs that the link is more firm, in proportion as the women are more useful, and occupied in domestic concerns."

" Perhaps," says Babbage, " to the sober eye of inductive philosophy, these anticipations of the future may appear too faintly connected with the history of the past. When time shall have revealed the future progress of our race, those laws which are now obscurely indicated, will then become distinctly apparent ; and it may possibly be found that the dominion of mind over the material world advances with an ever accelerating force.

" Even now, the imprisoned winds which the earliest poet made the Grecian warrior bear for the protection of his fragile bark ; or those which, in more modern times, the Lapland wizards sold to the deluded sailors ; these, the unreal creations of fancy or of fraud, called, at the command of science, from their shadowy existence, obey a holier spell : and the unruly masters of the poet and the seer become the obedient slaves of civilised man.

" Nor has the wild imagination of the satirist been quite unrivaled by the realities of after years: as if in mockery of the college of Laputa, light almost solar has been extracted from the refuse of fish ; fire has been sifted by the lamp of Davy; and machinery has been taught arithmetic instead of poetry.

" In whatever light we examine the triumphs and achievements of our species over the creation submitted to its power, we explore new sources of wonder. But if science has called into real existence the visions of the poet—if the accumulating knowledge of ages has blunted the sharpest and distanced the loftiest of the shafts of the satirist, the philosopher has conferred on the moralist an obligation of surpassing weight. In unveiling to him the living miracles which teem in rich exuberance around the minutest atom, as well as throughout the largest masses of ever-active matter, he has placed before him resistless evidence of immeasurable design. Surrounded by every form of animate and inanimate existence, the sun of science has yet penetrated but through the outer fold of nature's majestic robe; but if the philosopher were required to separate, from among those countless evidences of creative power, one being, the masterpiece of its skill; and from that being to select one gift, the choicest of all the attributes of life;—turning within his own breast and conscious of those powers which have subjugated to his race the external world, and of those higher powers by which he has subjugated to himself that creative faculty which aids his faltering conceptions of a Deity, —the humble worshipper at the altar of truth would pronounce that being,—man; that endowment,—human reason.

" But however large the interval that separates the lowest from the highest of those sentient beings which inhabit our planet, all the results of observation, enlightened by all the reasonings of the philosopher, combine to render it probable that, in the vast extent of creation, the proudest attribute of our race is but, perchance, the lowest step in the gradation of intellectual existence. For, since every portion of our own material globe, and every animated being it supports, afford, on more scrutinising enquiry, more perfect evidence of design, it would indeed be most unphilosophical to believe that those sister spheres, glowing with light and heat radiant from the same central source—and that the members of those kindred systems, almost lost in the remoteness of space, and perceptible only from the countless multitude of their congregated globes—should each be no more than a floating chaos of unformed matter; or, being all the work of the same Almighty Architect, that no living eye should be gladdened by their forms of beauty, that no intellectual being should expand its faculties in deciphering their laws."

CHAPTER V.

THE VALUE AND USES OF PROPERTY.

" The sense to value riches, with the art
    To enjoy them, and the virtue to impart,—
    To balance fortune by a just expense,
    Join with economy, magnificence."

" Alas! for the sordid propensities of modern days, when every thing is coined into gold, and this once holy-day planet of ours is turned into a ' mere working-day world.' "

IRVING.

It cannot be concealed, that there have been apprehensions of the evil effects of manufacturing establishments in this country, but these forebodings have been chiefly prospective. It is not pretended that they have yet been productive of evil; indeed, the evidence is positive, that much good has been produced. With regard to the state of Rhode Island, I had an opportunity of knowing its moral condition previous to 1812; and I have since traveled in nearly every part of the state, and the change for the better, especially in the manufacturing districts, is incredible. No one but an eye witness could believe that such a favourable change of society could have taken place, in the short period of twenty-five years. It is true, that the abuse of these institutions may produce bad results, but the abuse is no argument against the thing itself. I am persuaded, that wherever a village is under good regulations, that the tendency is altogether favourable to morals and intelligence. There is, therefore, no more evil to be dreaded, in prospective, from the system of manufacturing for ourselves, than there is from the system of self-government; they may be turned to an evil purpose; and what blessing of heaven may not? But while a love of virtue and liberty remains, these institutions will be cherished with confidence and advantage to the whole community. Sufficient testimony has been adduced to prove that the present state of American manufactures is superior to any in the world, as it respects the rate of wages, the means of intellectual improvement, and their moral condition. If the introduction of labour-saving machinery, and of the whole manufacturing system, with all its accompaniments, had proved detrimental to the good order of society; if it had endangered the liberties of the people, or infringed on any principle of our free institutions; if it had reared a degraded, impoverished, or debilitated race of beings; if, in fact, ignorance and vice had marked these districts, as the victims of corruption and pollution, their destruction would have been inevitable : no laws could have saved a single establishment. All this and more was apprehended; and if these things had followed in the train of manufactories, I hope I should have been the last to have recorded their progress with approbation. I have eight *powerful* arguments to prevent such a course; but on the contrary, I trust I should have been the first to have stamped their features, in all their hideous forms, that they might justly receive the reprobation of mankind. No increase of wealth, or of strength, would have compensated for a destitution of virtue and intelligence. It was the circumstance, that I had witnessed the moral aspect of New England, decidedly improved, that induced me to attempt a survey of the subject.

I agree that, if the threatened deleterious effects had followed the making of our own clothing, instead of importing it from Europe; I would say, indeed, it would be better to drain the country of every dollar of specie than to have laid the foundation of impunity and slavery. With the loss of truth, virtue, and liberty, wealth is inadequate to give happiness to man.

The value of property is manifest, because it is the reward of the virtues of order, diligence, and temperance; and these are essential to the acquisition of it : for the industrious nations are elevated above all the people of the earth.*

---

* Mr. Burke, one of the greatest and best friends of our liberty, speaking, in the house of commons, of the wealth which the people of New England had drawn from their fisheries, pronounced that eulogium upon their genius and enterprise, which should be indelibly engraven upon the memory of every New England youth, in honour of his father-land.

In speaking of the manner in which the whale fishery had been carried on, he says :—" And pray, sir, what in the world is equal to it ?—Pass by the other parts, and look at the manner in which the people of New England have, of late, carried on the whale fishery. Whilst we follow them among the tumbling mountains of ice, and behold them penetrating into the deepest frozen recesses of Hudson's Bay, and Davies' Straits; whilst we are looking for them beneath the arctic circle, we hear that they have pierced into the opposite region of polar cold; that they are at the antipodes, and engaged under the frozen serpent of the south. Falkland Island, which seemed too remote and romantic an object for the grasp of national ambition, is but a stage, and resting-place in the progress of their victorious industry. Nor is the equinoctial heat more discouraging to them, than the accumulated winter at both the poles. We know that whilst some of them draw the line and strike

Mr. Webster's eulogy of Hamilton accords with my own views, and it will serve to introduce another extract from his report on manufactures, which I consider the true American doctrine on wealth.

" Hamilton felt the full importance of the crisis ; and the reports of his speeches are yet lasting monuments to his genius and patriotism. He saw, at last, his hopes fulfilled ; he saw the constitution adopted, and the government under it, established and organised. The discerning eye of Washington immediately called him to that post, which was infinitely the most important in the administration of the new system. He was made secretary of the treasury, and how he fulfilled the duties of such a place, at such a time, the whole country perceived with delight, and the whole world saw with admiration. He smote the rock of the national resources, and abundant streams of revenue gushed forth. He touched the dead corpse of the public credit, and it sprung upon its feet. The fabled birth of Minerva, from the brain of Jove, was hardly more sudden or more perfect, than the financial system of the United States burst forth from the conceptions of Hamilton."

The following extract exhibits some of those lucid principles of national wealth :—

" That which seems to be the principal argument offered for the superior productiveness of agricultural labour, turns upon the allegation, that labour employed in manufactures yields nothing equivalent to the rent of land ; or to that net surplus as it is called, which accrues to the proprietor of the soil. But this distinction, important as it has been deemed, appears rather verbal than substantial. It is easily discernible, that what in the first instance is divided into two parts, under the denominations of the ordinary profit of the stock of the farmer, and rent to the landlord, is in the second instance united under the general appellation of the ordinary profit on the stock of the undertaker ; and that this formal or verbal distribution constitutes the whole difference in the two cases. It seems to have been overlooked, that the land itself is a stock or capital, advanced or lent by its owner, to the occupier or

the harpoon, on the coast of Africa, others run the longitude, and pursue the gigantic game along the coast of Brazil. No sea but what is vexed by their fisheries,—no climate that is not witness to their toils. Neither the perseverance of Holland, nor the activity of France, nor the dexterous and firm sagacity of English enterprise, ever carried this most perilous mode of hardy industry, to the extent to which it has been pushed by this recent people, a people who are still, as it were, but in the gristle, and not yet hardened into the bone of manhood."

tenant; and the rent he receives is only the ordinary profit of a certain stock in land, not managed by the proprietor himself, but by another to whom he lends or lets it, and who, on his part, advances a second capital to stock and improve the land, upon which he also receives the usual profit. The rent of the landlord and the profit of the farmer are therefore nothing more than the ordinary profits of two capitals belonging to two different persons, and united in the cultivation of a farm. As in the other case, the surplus which arises upon any manufactory, after replacing the expenses of carrying it on, answers to the ordinary profits of one or more capitals engaged in the prosecution of such manufactory. It is said one or more capitals; because, in fact, the same thing which is contemplated in the case of the farm, sometimes happens in that of a manufactory. There is one who furnishes a part of the capital, or lends a part of the money, by which it is carried on; and another, who carries it on, with the addition of his own capital. Out of the surplus which remains, after defraying expenses, an interest is paid to the money lender for the portion of the capital furnished by him, which exactly agrees with the rent paid to the landlord; and the residue of that surplus constitutes the profit of the undertaker, or manufacturer, and agrees with what is denominated the ordinary profits of two capitals employed in a manufactory; as, in the other case, the rent of the landlord and the revenue of the farmer compose the ordinary profits of two capitals, employed in the cultivation of a farm. The rent, therefore, accruing to the proprietor of the land, far from being a criterion of exclusive productiveness, as has been argued, is no criterion even of superior productiveness. The question must still be, whether the surplus, after defraying expenses, of a given capital, employed in the purchase and improvement of a piece of land, is greater or less, than that of a like capital employed in the prosecution of a manufactory; or whether the whole value produced from a given capital and a given quantity of labour, employed in the other way; or, rather, perhaps, whether the business of agriculture or that of manufactures will yield the greatest product, according to a compound ratio of the quantity of the capital and the quantity of labour, which are employed in the one or in the other. The solution of either of these questions is not easy. It involves numerous and complicated details depending on an accurate knowledge of the objects to be compared. It is not known that the comparison has ever yet been made upon sufficient data, properly ascertained and analysed. To be able to make it on the present occasion with satisfactory precision, would demand more previous enquiry and investigation, than there has been hitherto leisure or opportunity to accomplish. Some essays, however, have been made towards acquiring the requisite information; which have rather served to throw doubt upon, than to confirm, the hypothesis under examination. But it ought to be acknowledged, that they have been too little diversified, and are too imperfect to authorise a definitive conclusion either way; leading rather to probable conjecture than to certain deduction. They render it probable, that there are various branches of manufactures, in which a given capital will yield a greater total product, and a considerably greater net product, than an equal capital invested in the purchase and improvements of lands; and that there are also some branches, in which both the gross and the net produce will exceed that of agricultural industry; according to a compound ratio of capital and labour. But it is on this last point that there appears to be the greatest room for doubt. It is far less difficult to infer generally, that the net produce of capital engaged in manufacturing enterprises is greater than that of capital engaged in agriculture. In stating these results, the purchase and improvement of lands, under previous cultivation, are alone contemplated. The comparison is more in favour of agriculture, when it is made with reference to the settlement of new and waste lands; but an argument drawn from so temporary a circumstance could have no weight in determining the general question concerning the permanent relative productiveness of the two species of industry. How far it ought to influence the policy of the United States, on the score of particular situation, will be adverted to in another place. The foregoing suggestions are not designed to inculcate an opinion that manufacturing industry is more productive than that of agriculture. They are intended rather to show that the reverse of this proposition is not ascertained; that the general arguments which are brought to establish it, are not satisfactory; and consequently that a supposition of the superior productiveness of tillage ought to be no obstacle to listening to any substantial inducements to the encouragement of manufactures, which may be otherwise perceived to exist, through an apprehension, that they may have a tendency to divert labour from a more to a less profitable employment. It is extremely probable, that on a full and accurate development of the matter, on the ground of fact and calculation, it would be discovered that there is no material difference between the aggregate productiveness of the one, and of the other kind of industry; and that the propriety of the encouragements, which may in any case be proposed to be given to either, ought to be determined upon considerations irrelative to any comparison of that nature. But without contending for the superior productiveness of manufacturing industry, it may conduce to a better judgment of the policy, which ought to be pursued respecting its encouragement, to contemplate the subject under some additional aspects, tending not only to confirm the idea, that this kind of industry has been improperly represented as unproductive in itself; but to evince in addition that the establishment and diffusion of manufactures have the effect of rendering the total mass of useful and productive labour, in a community, greater than it would otherwise be.

"In prosecuting this discussion, it may be necessary briefly to resume and review some of the topics which have been already touched. To affirm that the labour of the manufacturer is unproductive because he consumes as much of the produce of land as he adds value to the raw materials which he manufactures, is not better founded, than it would be to affirm, that the labour of the farmer, which furnishes materials to the manufacturer, is unproductive, because he consumes an equal value of manufactured articles. Each furnishes a certain portion of the produce of his labour to the other. In the meantime the maintenance of two citizens instead of one, is going on ; the state has two members instead of one ; and they together consume twice the value of what is produced from the land. If instead of a farmer and artificer, there were a farmer only, he would be under the necessity of devoting a part of his labour to the fabrication of clothing and other articles which he would procure of the artificer, in the case of there being such a person ; and of course he would be able to devote less labour to the cultivation of his farm, and would draw from it a proportionably less product. The whole quantity of production, in this state of things, in provisions, raw materials, and manufactures, would certainly not exceed in value the amount of what would be produced in provisions and raw materials only, if there were an artificer as well as a farmer. Again—If there were both an artificer and a farmer, the latter would be left at liberty to pursue exclusively the cultivation of his farm. A greater quantity of provisions and raw materials would of course be produced, equal, at least, as has been already observed, to the amount of the provisions, raw materials, and manufactures, which would exist on a contrary supposition. The artificer, at the same time, would be going on in the production of manufactured commodities; to an amount sufficient not only to repay the farmer, in those commodities, for the provisions and materials which were procured from him, but to furnish the artificer himself with a supply of similar commodities for his own use. Thus then, there would be two quantities of values in existence instead of one; and the revenue and consumption would be double in one case, what it would be in the other. If, in place of both these suppositions, there were supposed to be two farmers and no artificer, each of whom applied a part of his labour to the culture of land, and another part to the fabrication of manufactures; in this case, the portion of the labour of both bestowed upon land, would produce the same quantity of provisions and raw materials only, as would be produced by the entire sum of the labour of one applied in the same manner, and the portion of the labour of both bestowed upon manufactures, would produce the same quantities only, as would be produced by the entire sum of the labour of one applied in the same manner. Hence the produce of the labour of the two farmers would not be greater than the produce of the labour of the farmer and artificer; and hence it results that the labour of the artificer is as positively productive as that of the farmer, and as positively augments the revenue of the society. The labour of the artificer replaces to the farmer that portion of his labour with which he provides the materials of exchange with the artificer, and which he would otherwise have been compelled to apply to manufactures; and while the artificer thus enables the farmer to enlarge his stock of agricultural industry, a portion of which he purchases for his own use, he also supplies himself with the manufactured articles of which he stands in need. He does still more.—Besides this equivalent which he gives for the portion of agricultural labour consumed by him, and this supply of manufactured commodities for his own consumption; he furnishes still a surplus, which compensates for the use of the capital advanced either by himself or some other person, for carrying on the business. This is the ordinary profit of the stock employed in the manufactory, and is, in every sense, as effective an addition to the income of the society as the rent of land. The produce of the labour of the artificer, consequently, may be regarded as composed of three parts ; one by which the provisions for his subsistence and the materials for his work are purchased of the farmer; one by which he supplies himself with manufactured necessaries ; and a third which constitutes the profit on the stock employed. The two last portions seem to have been overlooked in the system, which represents manufacturing industry as barren and unproductive. In the course of the preceding illustrations, the products of equal quantities of the labour of the farmer and artificer, have been treated as if

equal to each other. But this is not to be understood as intending
to assert any such precise equality. It is merely a manner of expression adopted for the sake of simplicity and perspicuity.
Whether the value of the produce of the labour of the farmer be
somewhat more or less than that of the artificer, is not material to
the main scope of the argument, which hitherto has only aimed
at showing that the one, as well as the other, occasions a positive
augmentation of the total produce and revenue of the society. It
is now proper to proceed a step further, and to enumerate the
principal circumstances from which it may be inferred, that
manufacturing establishments not only occasion a positive augmentation of the produce and revenue of the society, but that they
contribute essentially to rendering them greater than they could
possibly be without such establishments. These circumstances
are, 1. The division of labour. 2. The extension of the use of
machinery. 3. Additional employment to classes of the community not ordinarily engaged in the business. 4. The promotion of
emigration from foreign countries. 5. The furnishing greater
scope for the diversity of talents and dispositions, which discriminate men from each other."

" This report on manufactures is perhaps the most elaborate performance he left on the files of his office. It is distinguished for
extensive research, judicious application of the knowledge attained,
and an accurate estimate of the policy of encouraging the manufacturing interest, as an essential feature in the independence of
the nation. This report adopts the principles of the mercantile
system, in opposition to Adam Smith and the French economists.
They attacked the combined manufacturing and mercantile interests of Great Britain, as founded upon oppressive monopoly ; and
contended for entire freedom of commerce and industry, undiverted
and unimpeded by government, as the best means of advancing
nations to prosperity and greatness. The secretary combated
with the greatest ability some of the dogmas of these philosophers,
and maintained his favourite system as much by the power of his
logic, as by illustrative and pertinent reference to the experience of
those nations, at once successful in commerce and great in the
productions of art. It is now more than forty years since his
report on manufactures was made to congress. Now his opinions
on that great branch of natural economy are become popular in
the United States. For the last fifteen years societies have been
formed in every part of the country, composed of gentlemen in all
the various pursuits of life, expressly to procure and disseminate
information tending to encourage the manufacturing interests of

the nation.   Memorials of most interesting and impressive character for eloquence, correct principles, and patriotic devotion, have
been published to the people ; and committees appointed to stimulate the federal government to a particular patronage of that
branch of industry and political strength.   These memorials and
committees espouse the sentiments which were assumed by Secretary Hamilton.   The Hon. John Holmes delivered, in the senate
of the United States, a synopsis of this report, as a speech on the
tariff, observing that nothing new could be added.   In this particular, as on the subjects of the funded debt and national bank,
the experience of the last half century has clearly proved that he
was, in his time, more correctly impressed as to the true interests
and policy of the United States, and better understood their political and domestic economy, than any other statesman who has
been at all prominent in their public affairs.   All his official reports
are remarkable for wide research, profound thought, close logic,
and precision of expression.   His labours in the treasury department, united with the integrity with which he conducted it, and
which the most penetrating inquisition into all the avenues of his
office could never bring into question, will form with posterity the
fairest monument of his fame.   In organising the federal government, in 1789, every man of either sense or candour will allow, the
difficulties seemed greater than the first rate abilities could sur-
mount.   The event has shown that his abilities were greater than
those difficulties.   He surmounted them, and Washington's administration was the most wise and beneficent, the most prosperous,
and ought to be the most popular, that ever was entrusted with
the affairs of a nation.   Great as was Washington's merit, much
of it in plan, much in execution, was due to the talents, and ought
to enhance the memory, of his minister.   As a statesman, he was
not more distinguished by the great extent of his views, than by
the caution with which he provided against impediments, and the
watchfulness of his care over the rights and liberty of the subject.
In none of the many revenue bills which he framed, is there to
be found a single clause that savours of despotic power ; not one
that the sagest champions of law and liberty would, on that
ground, hesitate to approve and adopt.   It is rare that a man who
owes so much to nature descends to seek more from industry ; but
he seemed to depend on industry, as if nature had done nothing
for him.   His habits of investigation were very remarkable, his
mind seemed to cling to his subject till he had exhausted it.
Hence the uncommon superiority of his reasoning powers, a superiority that seemed to be augmented from every source, and to be

fortified by every auxiliary—learning, taste, wit, imagination, and eloquence. These were embellished and enforced by his temper and manners, by his fame and his virtues. It is difficult, in the midst of such various excellence, to say in what particular the effect of his greatness was most manifest. No man more promptly discerned truth. No man more clearly displayed it. It is not merely made visible. It seemed to come bright with illumination from his lips. For the truth, which his researches so distinctly presented to the understanding of others, was rendered almost irresistibly commanding and impressive, by the love and reverence which, it was ever apparent, he profoundly cherished for it in his own. While patriotism glowed in his heart, wisdom blended in his speech her authority with her charms. Such, also, is the character of his writings. Judiciously collected, they will be a public treasure.

" The most substantial glory of a country is in its virtuous great men. Its prosperity will depend on its docility to learn from their example. That nation is fated to ignominy and servitude, for which such men lived in vain. Power may be seized by a nation that is yet barbarous, and wealth may be enjoyed by one that it finds or renders sordid. The one is a gift and the sport of acci- dent, and the other is the sport of power. Both are mutable, and have passed away, without leaving behind them any other memo- rial, than ruins that offend taste, and traditions that baffle con- jecture.

" But the glory of Greece is imperishable, or will last as long as learning itself, which is its monument. It strikes an everlasting root, and bears perennial blossoms on its grave. The name of *Hamilton* would not have dishonoured Greece in the age of *Aristides*."*

* M. Carey, the author of the Olive Branch, in his disinterested exertions to promote the American system, was the means of circulating the report of Hamilton, more than any other individual ; and, indeed, Mr. Carey's patriotic exertions are deserving of high praise.

" Believing that Alexander Hamilton was the real father of the American system—that therefore the manufacturers were very deeply indebted to him —that they ought to hold his memory sacred—and that they would of course rejoice in an opportunity of showing their gratitude, I projected the striking of a medal to his honour; and made a conditional arrangement with Mr. Gobrecht, a celebrated die sinker, for the execution. The expense of the die, and some small items, would have been two hundred and seventy dollars. The subscription was to be five dollars each, for fifty-four persons, to be divided equally between Boston, New York, and Philadelphia, eighteen to each place. But trifling as was the contribution, economy prevailed over

That timidity which causes young men to remain in idleness, and distrust the bounties of Providence, is a vice which ought to be fought against on its first approaches. The earth bringeth forth abundantly, the young ravens, the cattle upon a thousand hills, are fed; and shall He not feed you, O ye of little faith! Ambition to prosper in business, in the first place, fired Slater to leave the home of his parents—to separate from his kindred—to leave his country—to cross the Atlantic, then a more formidable voyage than at present. This enabled him to come among strangers, and suffer their suspicions and neglect, to endure every hardship in his first attempts; so it never left him—he gained his purpose. A fortune raised in that spirit ought to be cherished, and managed in an honourable manner, out of respect to its founder. Ambition operates in various ways; in Slater, I think, it led to a desire to leave his children in a permanent and lucrative business, as his old master, Strutt, left his sons, whose posterity are now enjoying their inheritance. Nor can I see any evil in the exercise of such ambition, if it does not interfere with other and more important duties. There is no evil in the accumulation of property, if it be done honestly and honourably, without infringeing on the rights and privileges of others. This being with Slater a strong passion, he could not be easily diverted from it, but met every obstacle with fortitude, before which mountains became plains, and hills were removed. This courage when properly used, is virtuous and praiseworthy, and ought to be imitated.

" To do good, with the property which we have saved by our

gratitude. I sent the prospectus to two very extensive and influential manufacturers in Boston and New York, neither of whom procured a subscriber. I hired a person in Philadelphia at a dollar per day, to go among the manufacturers to procure signatures. In five days he procured eleven! I need not add that the project was abandoned.

" The subscribers, desirous of transmitting to posterity a lasting testimonial of their high sense of the profound and wealth-producing system of political economy displayed in the admirable report on manufactures, by Alexander Hamilton, secretary of the treasury, under the administration of General Washington—a report, which, considering the previous uncongenial habits of the illustrious writer, may be placed among the proudest monuments of the human intellect; and, considering his political and anti-manufacturing associations, as a decisive proof of the most sterling patriotism, have agreed to subscribe each five dollars for the purpose of procuring a die for striking medals to commemorate the memory of a statesman, who, by the work in question, has had a beneficent influence in promoting the national prosperity, which it would be scarcely possible to appreciate too highly."

honesty, economy, temperance, and industry, is one great end of our existence; it is the perfection of the Christian character, and should be the first lesson in all education. The selfish and hard-hearted, who strive, by monopoly and every unfair advantage, to obtain unequal privileges, to get all they can, to accept all that is given, and to give nothing, never dream of that, which is so true, that the giver is the happiest man. But to enable us to give we must have something, and this again shows us the value of pro-perty. Those who have nothing, may be kind-hearted, generous, and naturally noble-minded; they may for ever be thinking to do good, and hoping that the time will come, when they shall be able to bring something about; but very little, comparatively, is ever in their power.

" Property provides for the body, clothes and feeds us; it builds our houses, supplies them with furniture, provides all the tools for our work on our farms, and every where else, and settles our wild lands; for a poor man connot even move from the old to the new states unless he has made some provision for that purpose. It builds the manufactories, supplies them with stock, and pays the wages of the hands. If indigent people come to us from Europe, there must be more property than just enough for us to live upon, or we cannot set them to work, and they must starve.

" If the destitute English, Scots, and Irish, were to emigrate to the poor countries of Europe, they would perish; they therefore, are as much interested in increasing the property of this country, as the natives are. It is the increasing property of the United States which is now employing these poor people in the building of canals and railroads. Nothing but our *superfluous* wealth can feed the hungry or clothe the naked.

" All progress and improvements in the arts, in the engines, tools, and labour-saving machines of the mechanic, farmer, and manu-facturer, are to be attributed mainly to the increasing property of the people."—*Sedgwick.*

" When a poor man wants food or drink, and must have it, the first thing he does is to work; this is the price he pays, and at night he receives his recompense, in a bushel of wheat, or rye, or money, or some other thing. The reason why he must pay in his own labour immediately, is, that he has no labour stored or laid up: in other words, he has none of the products of labour, such as money, or other property. But suppose a good farmer, whose farm is not mortgaged, and whose cattle and goods are neither pledged for debt, nor under a sheriff's execution, desires to buy; he also pays in labour; ·but it is not the labour of that day, but of some former period. He has been a man of prudence ; he has stored up labour, which now consists of wheat, corn, rye, cattle, &c. ; these are the things that he worked for last year ; these he exchanges for what he wants. A rich man, who never wrought a day in his life, he may not have wheat, corn, or rye, with which to pay, but he has money, which is as completely labour laid up, as the farmer's stores. It is not the result of his own labour, but that of his father, grandfather, or some other industrious man. Some one has given labour for it ; for there is no other way, as an almost universal rule, by which money can be obtained, in the first instance, but by being worked for. It is obtained from the mines by labour, as before stated ; and the labourer who gets it, is paid for his work, as all other labourers are. The merit of this rich man, then, is that, he has saved, and not foolishly thrown away, his hoarded labour,—that which he is sure has cost the sweat and toil of industrious people."—*Ibid.*

" New England has not been a leader in this policy. On the contrary, she held back herself, and tried to hold others back from it, from the adoption of the constitution of 1824. Up to this time, she was accused of sinister and selfish designs, *because she discountenanced the progress of this policy.* It was laid to her charge, then, that having established her manufactures herself, she wished that others should not have the power of rivaling her ; and for that reason, opposed all legislative encouragement. Under this angry denunciation against her, the act of 1824 passed. Now, (1828) the imputation is precisely of an opposite character. The present measure is pronounced to be exclusively for the benefit of New England ; to be brought forward by her agency, and designed to gratify the cupidity of her wealthy establishments. Both charges are equally without the slightest foundation. The opinion of New England, up to 1824, was founded in the conviction that, on the whole, it was wisest and best, both for herself and others, that manufactures should make haste slowly. She felt a reluctance to trust great interests on the foundation of government patronage ; for who could tell how long such patronage would last, or with what steadiness, skill, or perseverance, it would continue to be granted ? Fifteen years ago, I ventured to express a serious doubt, whether this government was fitted, by its construction, to administer aid and protection to particular pursuits ; whether, having called such pursuits into being, by indications of its favour, it would not afterwards desert them, when troubles came upon them, and leave them to their fate. Whether this prediction, the result, certainly, of chance, and not of sagacity, will be fulfilled, remains to be seen. At the same time it is true, that from the very first commencement of the government, those who have administered its concerns have held a tone of encouragement and invitation towards those who should embark in manufactures. All the presidents, without exception, have concurred in this general sentiment; and the very first act of congress, laying duties of import, adopted the then unusual expedient of a preamble, apparently for little other purpose than that of declaring, that the duties which it imposed, were imposed for the encouragement and protection of manufactures. When, at the commencement of the late war, duties were doubled, we were told that we should find a mitigation of the weight of taxation, in the new aid and succour which would be thus afforded to our own manufacturing labour. Like arguments were urged, and prevailed, but not by the aid of New England votes, when the tariff was afterwards arranged, at the close of the war, in 1816. The act of 1824 received the sanction of both houses of congress, and settled the policy of the country. What then was New England to do? She was fitted for manufacturing operations, by the amount and character of her population, by her capital, by the vigour and energy of her free labour, by the skill, economy, enterprise, and perseverance of her people. Nothing was left to New England, after the act of 1824, but to conform herself to the will of others. Nothing was left to her, but to consider that the government had fixed and determined its own policy; and that policy was protection.

" New England, poor in some respects, in others is as wealthy as her neighbours. Her soil would be held in low estimation by those who are acquainted with the valley of the Mississippi, and some of the meadows of the south. But in industry, in habits of labour, skill, and in accumulated capital, the fruit of two centuries of industry, she may be said to be rich. She had foreseen, that if the system of protecting manufactures should be adopted, she must go largely into them: a vast increase of investment in manufacturing establishments was the consequence. Those who made such investments, probably entertained not the slightest doubt that as much as was promised would be effectually granted ; and that if, owing to any unforeseen occurrence, or untoward event, the benefit designed by the law, to any branch of manufactures, should not be realised, it would furnish a fair case for the consideration of government. Certainly, they could not expect, after what had passed, that interests of great magnitude would be left at the mercy of the very first change of circumstances which might occur."—*Webster on the Tariff.*

A comparative view of the weekly and yearly expenditure of an English and an American family, will show that the advantage, with regard to the price of labour, is not so great as many have represented.

The English labourer must be supported in a country where rent and provisions are much higher than in the United States. It may be asked, how does the English labourer get the money to purchase this expenditure? His expenditure has but one element, it is work, his daily toil. He can neither beg nor steal. His labour, or wages, must meet the whole expenditure. No matter who pays it, in the first instance. He consumes so much value; whether his employer or the public advance this amount, is immaterial. It costs as much to support the population of manufacturing establishments in England, as it does in America. He who employs this labour, receives directly the product, and must ultimately pay the cost of it. Pauperism is a part of the English system, and it is known, that almost all labourers are, to some amount, one quarter, one half, three quarters, or all, supported by enormous poor rates. These are paid by the employers of labour and capital, and must, like wages paid directly to the labourer, be charged on production, and paid by consumption. How different the condition of American labourers! Each family may lay up two thirds of their wages, and still be in comfort and accommodation. They can do this, because the produce of land is so cheap. Those who allege that we cannot manufacture so cheap as the English, because we pay so much higher wages, should consider that this is true in appearance only. If such apparent difference resulted in that effect, how is it true that England can compete with France? Labour is much higher, in its apparent price, in England, than the same labour is in France. In America, machinery is moved by water, the English by steam, and 150 in 151 manufacturing *labourers* are machines. Proximity to our market is a great advantage: the cost to carry the raw material abroad, and to return the finished fabrics, are items of some consequence. British manufacturing labour affords no surplus saving, over and above consumption; and can add nothing to national capital. American labour can save one third of its wages, whereby to augment national capital.

Any day of the year, since 1824, the true Leeds and Manchester prices current, of cotton and woollen cloths, have quoted them at an equal, or higher price, than goods of the same quality, on the same days, were sold on the same terms, at Providence. We do not yet export much amount of woollens, but in cottons we undersell the English, in South American markets. In 1827 we paid a duty of 15 per cent. ad valorem, and then sold our cottons, in the Canadas, cheaper than the English, paying no duty, sell their fabrics of like quality.

The English have been at pains and cost, to obtain samples and marks, of cloths made in Cumberland, Smithfield, N. Providence, and Coventry, in Rhode Island; and imitating these cloths, and forging their marks, they have sent their fabrics to South America. The American domestics are still distinguishable; and, because of a firmer fabric, sell more readily, and at better prices, than these fraudulent imitations.

When manufactures began in this country, they began with little skill, less capital, and imperfect machinery. They took shelter under impost for encouragement. Aided by that, they came into the market, and selling their products at, or nearly at, the price of the English fabrics, with added importation and impost, they were able to meet the augmented expenditures incident to incipient establishments, want of capital, want of skill, and want of perfected machinery. Mr. Burgess said, in 1828 :—" The system is your great system of impost; the vital principle of your government, together with its acknowledged and inseparable concomitants,—breathed into this legislative, judicial, and executive body, by the spirit of wisdom itself; this body then, and thereafter, became a living, active, and efficient being. You would have revenue 'to support this government, pay the national debt, provide for the common defence and secure the general welfare.' The constitution directed, and the laws have provided, that you should raise it by impost. Unless you confine impost to such products as your country does not, nor ever can produce, your impost will, of necessity, by increasing the price of foreign, encourage the production of domestic products of the same kind. As that impost, by encouraging, increases the supply of domestic, the amount of impost to sustain revenue must be increased. This reciprocal increase of impost and encouragement, will finally have called labour, skill, machinery, and capital, in such abundance, to the aid of domestic production, that your market must be supplied with whatever class of domestic products may thus have fallen within the influence of impost. So soon as your market is supplied from domestic production, *impost* must cease to be *productive* of revenue; because, when the market is supplied with the domestic, there can be, for no fair purpose of purchase and sale, any further importation of foreign products. Was it not, therefore, just, when it was, of necessity, true, that the law of impost should have announced that all impost for revenue, on all articles within the productive capabilities of our country, was also impost for encouragement ? If it was just, and of necessity true, *then*, to make that announcement to this nation, is it not *just*, and of necessity true, *now*, when it has been re-enacted and solemnly repeated, in the same manner, during a course of legislation, for the term of almost forty years ? If, stimulated by that impost, operating that encouragement, millions of men, with millions of property, have been labouring after skill, perfecting machinery, and collecting capital, will you now, when they can supply the nation at a less expense, and with as good a fabric,—will you, I say, *now* announce, that all you said *then*, of encouragement, was fabled and false ; a stratagem to lure money into your coffers, and men into ruin ? You published a system of impost for revenue, encouragement and protection. You knew that, when you had received the last cent of your revenue, you would have been perfectly paid for protection. The people of this nation have paid the full and stipulated consideration to their government for her full protection, on every item of domestic production. They do not claim protection on this ground ; but they respectfully petition to be protected on those products only, which they can, and demonstrate that they can, supply at a cost *much less* than foreign labour and capital can supply them."

In reflecting on the value and uses of property, I am aware there are many conflicting opinions on this subject ; a great variety of theories are proposed, many of them founded on the idea, that the same principles will operate in relation to capital now, as it would in the origin of society. It must be remembered, that the state of society is formed, fashions and customs are fixed, and with the present situation, it becomes us to ask, what are the value and uses of property ? To lay up in store in those years of plenty, in order to provide for years of scarcity, was considered in Joseph a maxim of profound wisdom, and practically was of immense benefit to mankind. Where this power of accumulation exists without infringing on the rights and necessities of others, it is performing a work of public benefit ; filling store houses, as our security against sudden emergencies and times of scarcity. These are the value and uses of property, and in the present situation of the United States, the capitalists form an important part of the community ; they do not receive exorbitant interest in the general works of improvement, but on the contrary, suffer great risks and losses. Why should prejudices exist against individuals who are willing to employ their money in works of public utility, which afford means of wealth to others ?

On the subject of wages there is much said that to me is not easily to be understood, much intricacy and such theories as are impracticable, and that will not bear on the present state of society. My simple idea has always been, that wages must be regulated according to the demand, and according to the state of business. It is liable to depression, like the interest of money, or any other article of commerce—it is far best to let it alone, it will regulate itself; nothing like coercion can be allowed in a free country, every individual must be left to act for himself; and this has answered well, in its practical operation in every age of the world. I read Mr. Carey with the hope of getting something definite on a subject on which I do not profess to be a very proficient student. I was, however, somewhat disappointed in my examination of the Essay on Wages,* but will let the author speak for himself.

" We may safely trust that population will limit itself, and that the wisdom of the arrangements of the Deity in regard to man, will be as evident as it is in every other part of the creation. At the time Mr. Malthus formed his theory, he had but few facts

---

* This subject is attracting general notice, and it must necessarily become more interesting, as the population and business transactions of the country increase.   As it is closely connected with the well being of the community, the discussion ought to be conducted in a calm and dispassionate manner, and every thing relating to it weighed with justice and judgment; without partiality and without hypocrisy ; without respect either to the poor or to the rich.

Something can be learned from the past experience of mankind, for like causes will produce like effects in every age and section of the world.   Every thing will find its level, and it is impossible to press it beyond its natural course ; you may impede its regular progress, by artificial contrivances, but it will burst through every obstruction, and break down every barrier in its way.   The less we legislate on this subject the better ; labour must and will be paid according to the demand ; and you cannot raise wages upon the large scale, no more than you can raise the price of gold.   However precious and important it may be to the country's prosperity, still there must be a price, and that will be varied by circumstances, like the value of any other article.   Nothing can be ultimately gained by combinations and opposition of one class to the other, because such things are always met with counteracting influences.

The state of business and of capital in the United States, prevents any monopoly or advantage to the injury of the operatives, and nothing should be done to discourage investments for the promotion of business and improvement; for without such arrangement of property, a stagnation must ensue, and in such a case the labourers are the first who feel the effects, especially those of them who do not save from their earnings to help them in time of need.

in regard to *civilised* man, upon which it could be based.* The experience of this country had been too short to enable him to use

---

* Since making the above extract, I have examined Malthus's "Essay on the Principle of Population ; or, a view of its past and present effects on Human Happiness ; with an enquiry into our prospects respecting the future removal or mitigation of the evils which it occasions,"—2 vols. 8vo, third edition,— and I cannot agree with Mr. Carey, that the author had not the facts of the case before him, for in this respect he is very full and overpowering in his argument.

His proposed remedy is self-denial, founded on purity and chastity ; he recommends prudence, temperance, industry, and economy, and the exercise of these is certainly a remedy against vice and misery. These virtues would render it unnecessary to restrict population ; they would richly provide for such a population, however numerous. It is but justice to let Malthus define what he terms a moral restraint on population ; he says,—" By *moral* restraint, I would be understood to mean, a restraint from marriage from prudential motives, with a conduct strictly moral during the period of this restraint, and I have never intentionally deviated from this sense. When I wished to consider the restraint from marriage unconnected with its conse-quences, I have either called it prudential restraint, or a part of the preven-tive check, of which it forms the principal branch. Tacitus describes the inhabitants of ancient Germany, as not living in cities, or even admitting of contiguous settlements. Every person surrounds his house with a vacant space, a circumstance, which, besides its beneficial effect as a security from fire, is strongly calculated to prevent the generation, and check the ravages, of epidemics. They content themselves almost universally with one wife. Their matrimonial bond is strict and severe, and their manners in this respect deserving the highest praise. They live in a state of well-guarded chastity, corrupted by no seducing spectacles, or convivial incitements. Adultery is extremely rare, and no indulgence is shown to a prostitute. Neither beauty, youth, nor riches, can procure her a husband ; for none there look on vice with a smile, or call mutual seduction the way of the world. To limit the increase of children, or put to death any of the husband's blood, is accounted infamous, and virtuous manners have there more efficacy than good laws elsewhere. Every mother suckles her own children, and does not deliver them into the hands of servants and nurses. The youths partake late of the sexual intercourse, and hence pass the age of puberty unexhausted. Nor are the virgins brought forward. The same maturity, the same full growth is required ; the sexes unite equally matched and robust, and the children inherit the vigour of their parents. The more numerous are a man's kinsmen and relations, the more comfortable is his old age, nor is it any advantage to be childless.

" With these manners, and a habit of enterprise and emigration, which would naturally remove all fears about providing for a family, it is difficult to conceive a society with a stronger principle of increase in it ; and we see at once that prolific source of successive armies and colonies against which the force or the Roman empire so long struggled with difficulty, and under which it ultimately sunk."—*Malthus.*

it with any advantage, and he was obliged to argue from the state of man as he exists in the eastern hemisphere, 'checked like a bondman,' fettered by laws and regulations, and oppressed by claims for the support of government and of individuals. To argue from facts thus obtained, is like constructing a theory of the tides from a collection of observations on mill-dams. I am not aware of a fact in his book in regard to man in a state of civilisation, that goes to support his theory, or that is not much better evidence that man has been misgoverned, and his increase repressed thereby, than that it has been repressed by inability of the earth to afford him support.

" *High wages*, or a large ' fund for the support of the labouring class, in proportion to the extent of that class,' are an infallible evidence of prosperity.

" National prosperity does not depend nearly so much on advantageous situations, salubrity of climate, or fertility of soil, as in the adopting of measures fitted to excite the inventive powers of genius, and to give perseverance and activity to industry. The establishment of a wise system of public economy can compensate for every other deficiency. It can render regions naturally inhospitable, barren and unproductive, the comfortable abodes of an elegant and refined, or crowded and wealthy, population. But where it is wanting, the best gifts of nature are of no value ; and countries possessed of the greatest capacities of improvement, and abounding in all the materials necessary for the production of wealth, with difficulty furnish a miserable subsistence to hordes distinguished only by their ignorance, barbarism, and wretchedness.

" As yet we know nothing of the productive powers of the earth. In an article on America, in the Encyclopedia Britannica, it is stated, that notwithstanding the difference in size between the eastern and western continent, the proportion of the former that is unfit for cultivation, in consequence of sterility, or absence of water communications, is so much greater that the latter is capable of subsisting an equal population.

" The most fertile soils, miserably tilled, according to the prescriptive rule of ' follow my leader,' are every where found contiguous to examples of skill and industry, which raise abundant crops ; and the contented boor sits down to his starved returns, quite satisfied with what rude implements, wasteful defects, and ignorant blindness, have permitted him to gather like his predecessors.

" How different would it be, were the opposite course pursued! were all the British empire, for instance, as ably and intelligently cultivated as the Lothians and lowlands of Scotland. Were Mr. Lowe's practical lessons universally acted upon, we should then hear no more of a surplus population beyond the supply of food ; of the necessity of exporting our hearty peasantry to Australian or other colonies; of the dreadful sufferings of the labouring poor. The honest toils of the field would largely supersede the depraving employment of the workhouse ; and the reward of those toils would be plenty of wholesome food to sustain the humblest classes of our fellow-creatures. Such is the fact in the United States, pauperism and the workhouse in an evil sense is unknown among us.

"Having done all in our power to make man poor and miserable,—to prevent the growth of capital or any improvement in his situation, and finding that there is a great deal of poverty in the world, we enquire the cause, and find it arises out of a mistake in the Deity, who fitted man to increase in a geometrical ratio, while he permitted the fruits of the earth to increase in an arithmetical ratio only, thus making poverty and misery inseparable accompaniments of the human race. This result is highly satisfactory to us, as it transfers to the Deity what should rest upon our own shoulders, and we then invent the starvation check ; discourage matrimony that we may promote profligacy, and thus check population ; while the earth is as yet, in a great measure, untouched, and is capable of supporting thousands of millions, in those parts where cultivation is almost unknown.

" The people of the United States have corn, and provisions generally, very cheap. Tea and coffee are imported free of duty, and are sold at a very small advance upon their cost at the places of production. Sugar is at much smaller duty than in France and England. Fuel is cheap. Most descriptions of manufactured goods are higher than in England, particularly those of wool and iron ; and, the rate of interest being higher, house rent is also higher. Making allowances for these differences, it is probable that the English labourer would be required to work sixteen days to obtain the same amount of commodities that would be obtained by the American labourer in eleven days.

" In the United States, the situation of the labouring classes is confessedly better than in any other nation whatever.

" Until within a very recent period, France has known little of the benefit of security, either of person or of property.

" Fettered and oppressed in every way, as France was, under her despotic kings, the spirit of invention and enterprise could never rise to those high conceptions, which of late years have brought England and America to the summit of prosperity. Manufacturers, placed under the severe control of men who purchased their offices from government, and who, therefore, exercised them with rapacity, could not hazard any improvement, without infringing the established regulations, and running the risk of having their goods destroyed, burned, or confiscated. In every trade, official regulations prescribed to workmen the methods of working, and forbade deviation from them, under pain of the most severe punishments. Ridiculous to say, the framer of these statutes fancied he understood better how to sort and prepare wool, silk, or cotton, to spin threads, to twist and throw them, than workmen brought up to the trade, and whose livelihood depended on their talent. Habits of industry constitute a very important item in the consideration of the causes which tend to increase or diminish the product of labour, and, of course, the fund out of which it is to be paid. In the United States, every inducement is held out to industry. The people have the confidence that they will have the enjoyment of almost the whole product of their labour undiminished by taxation, and that moderate exertion, with economy, will lead to independence. As no people ever had stronger inducements, so none ever pursued their avocations with more earnestness.

"Nothing so nurtures virtue as the spirit of independence. The poor should be assisted in providing for themselves.

"In Holland, the truths of political economy were first acted upon, and they brought with them a copious harvest of wealth. Security and freedom and economy were looked to as the sources of riches, as may be seen by the following passages from a description of the policy of the republic, written nearly a century since, in answer to inquiries respecting the state of trade, addressed to the merchants of Holland by the stadtholder William IV. To sum up all, amongst the moral and political causes of the same flourishing state of trade, may be likewise placed the wisdom and prudence of the administration; the intrepid firmness of the councils; the faithfulness with which treaties and engagements were wont to be fulfilled and ratified; and particularly the care and caution practised to preserve tranquillity and peace, and to decline instead of entering on a scene of war, merely to gratify the ambitious views of gaining fruitless or imaginary conquests. By these moral and political maxims was the glory and the reputation of the republic so far spread, and foreigners animated to place so great a confidence in the steady determinations of a state so wisely and prudently conducted, that a concourse of them stocked this country with an augmentation of inhabitants and useful hands, whereby its trade and opulence were from time to time increased.

" The above observations are at present applicable to the United States. It has been seen that the United States are comparatively free from those disturbing causes which impede the growth of capital. With a vast body of land ; with mines of gold, lead, iron, copper, and coal, abounding in every direction ; circulating capital alone was wanting to bring them into activity, and the system has tended to promote its rapid growth. Secure in person and property, comparatively free from taxation, unrestrained in action, comparatively so in all matters of trade, and very industrious, the people of this country, applying their labour in the way which they think will produce the largest reward, find their capital rapidly augmented ; the consequence of which is, that mines are opened in all directions, new lands are brought into cultivation, rail-roads and canals are constructed, and machinery is applied in every way to increase the produce of labour. Capital flows from all quarters to this country, where it can be best paid for, and, increasing the demand for labour, finds employment, not only for the vast natural increase of population, but for great numbers who are led to seek here an improvement of their condition. The fund out of which the labourer is paid, is larger, and his wages are consequently greater, than in any other country. It is in a very high degree satisfactory to see that this arises out of circumstances peculiar to the United States, and that there is no reason to believe that any increase which may take place in the extent of their population, can make it otherwise, while adhering to the present system.

" By the following statements the reader will be enabled to compare the rate of money wages of England and the United States.

" The number of persons employed in the cotton manufacture of the United States, is thus stated in the memorial of the New York convention, 1832:—males, 18,539 ; females, 38,927 ; children, 4,691 ; hand weavers, 4,760; in all, 66,917 ; total wages, $10,294,944, equal to $3 or 12s. 6d. per week. In the History of the Cotton Manufacture, by Mr. Baines, (p. 511,) the above amount of wages is taken, but the children and hand weavers are omitted, by which the number of operatives is reduced to 57,466, and the wages are thereby made to appear to be 14s. 11d. per week. Mr. Baines's reasoning in relation to the comparative wages of the United States and England, is thereby vitiated.

" It is to be regretted, that the gentleman by whom the report was drawn up, did not give the average wages of men, women, and

children.   As they have not done so, we must endeavour to estimate them.

		$.
18,539 men, at $5 per week, would be		92,695
38,927 women, at $2 per week,		77,854
4,691 children, at $1,75 per do.		8,211
4,760 hand weavers, at $4 per do.		19,040
		$197,800

52 weeks, at $197,800 each, would be $10,285,600, being nearly
the amount given in the report.

" In the above it will be observed that only about seven per
cent. are termed children, and even those are much above the age
at which children are employed in England.   At Lowell, the
number employed below sixteen is very small, and none below
twelve.   In the Lawrence factory at that place, out of 1000 females,
only 129 are below seventeen, and of the males, there are twenty-
eight below that age, or who may properly be styled children, cannot exceed eight per cent. of the whole number employed, which
is 1160.

" In a summary of the returns to the questions of the factory
commissioners, of 151 owners of cotton mills, in Lancashire,
Cheshire, and Derbyshire, for five weeks, ending May 1833, it is
stated, that out of 48,645 persons employed, 20,084 are under
eighteen years of age.   The average wages in these mills, are
10s. 5d. (*Baines*, p. 371.)

" In an estimate of the number of persons employed in the cotton mills of England, the total number is given at 212,800, of
whom 43,703 are under fourteen years of age, and 39,554 between
fourteen and eighteen.   One half of the latter being deducted, the
total number employed below sixteen years, would be 63,480, or
30 per cent. of the whole quantity.   Notwithstanding the vastly
greater quantity of inferior labour thus used, wages are estimated
at 10s. 6d. per week, or within two shillings of what was paid in
the United States in 1832.

Dr. James Mitchell was employed under the factory commissioners to draw out tables, showing the wages, health, &c., of the
factory operatives, and the results of some of the principal cotton
mills, embracing 7614 operatives, are as follow :—(*Baines*, p. 437).
1415 males below 16, 2355 males above 16, giving above 35 per
cent. below the age at which children are usually employed here.
As wages differ very much with age, and as it is to be supposed

that the efficiency of the labourer is in proportion to the wages received, the only fair mode of comparing those of the United States and England, is to strike of all whose ages are below that at which they are here employed. The average wages of persons above sixteen, in those factories, as given by Dr. Mitchell, are as follows:

> 2355 males, 16s. 3d.
> 2566 females, 8s.
> _____
> 4921—general average 12s.

or within 6d. as much as the average of the estimate furnished by the New York convention. It may be said, that seven per cent. of the labourers employed in the United States being below sixteen, there should be some allowance made therefor, but they are generally so little below that age, that any allowance would have small effect upon the result.

" The great disproportion that exists between the two countries, in the employment of male and female labour, cannot fail to strike the reader. In England, the females exceed the males by only about 9 per cent., while in the United States they exceeded them, agreeably to the above statement, by above 110 per cent. Since that time, great improvements have taken place in machinery, increasing the proportion of females very greatly. At first sight, it might be supposed that this should cause wages to be lower here, the labour of men being generally more productive than that of women, and that this would be an offset to the number of children employed in England. Such is not, however, the case, women being employed *here*, because every thing is done to render labour productive, while *there* a large portion of the power of the male operatives is wasted. By the above statement, it is shown that in the United States, there were only 4760 hand weavers in the year 1832, and the number can hardly be supposed to have increased. From the great influx of emigrants from Ireland, it is probable that there will be, for a long time to come, an equal number ; but the modes of employment are so numerous, that a large number must be annually absorbed. On the 1st January, 1835, there were in the town of Lowell 5051 power looms, or more, by nearly 300, than the whole number of hand looms in this country.

" The whole number of power looms in Great Britain is estimated by Baines, p. 238, to be 100,000.

" I think it must be evident to the reader, that any difference in wages that may exist between England and the United States, must arise out of its better application in the latter. The perfection to which machinery has been brought, enables the proprietor to avail himself much more extensively of female labour than is the case in Europe. The labour of the females, as shown, is much more productive, and they consequently receive higher wages. The males, not being compelled to compete with machinery, are enabled to apply their powers in other ways that are more productive, and as a consequence, when they marry, the necessity for the employment of their wives and young children in factories is unknown. A further consequence is, that all parents have it in their power to obtain education for their children, and the children have time to receive it. A still further consequence is, that the state of morals at Lowell, Dover, Providence, and its vicinity, and other places where extensive factories exist, is such, as is almost utterly unknown in any other parts of the world, and constitutes a phenomenon in the moral, equal to that of Niagara in the natural world.

"Of one thousand females in the Lawrence factory at Lowell, there are but eleven who are married. There are nineteen widows. The following passage from a statement furnished by a gentleman who has charge of one of the principal establishments in Lowell, shows a very gratifying state of things. 'There have only occurred three instances in which any apparently improper connection or intimacy had taken place, and in all those cases the parties were married on the discovery, and several months prior to the birth of their children; so that in a legal point of view, no illegitimate birth has taken place among the females employed in the mills under my direction. Nor have I known of but one case among all the females employed in Lowell. I have said known— I should say heard of one case. I am just informed that this was a case where the female had been employed but a few days in any mill, and was forthwith rejected from the corporation, and sent to her friends. In point of female chastity, I believe that Lowell is as free from reproach as any place of an equal population in the United States or the world. At the great establishment at Dover, New Hampshire, I have been assured there has never been a case of bastardy. Let this be compared with the statements of the poor law commissioners, and it will go far to show that the means which tend to promote the increase of wealth, tend also to the promotion of morality, and, as a necessary consequence, of happiness. There can be no doubt, that with a different system, there would in time arise, in the factories of England, a similar state of things. There are, even now, some similar cases to be found in England, proving how much good may be done, where the owners are disposed to do what is in their power to promote the cause of morality; and that can be done most effectually by being moral ourselves.

" Amongst the great numbers of factory operatives employed under William Grant, Esq., at Ramsbottom, England, only one case of female misconduct has occurred in the space of twenty years, and that was a farmer's daughter.

" The necessity for the passage of 'Factory Bills,' does not exist in this country. In England, by interferences of all kinds, the parents are oppressed and reduced to the necessity of sending their children to work at the earliest possible age; and then it becomes necessary to interfere anew, to prevent the children from bearing too much of the burden. In the United States, on the contrary, it is so desirable to have efficient hands, that the owners are not disposed to employ children at too young an age, and thus, while the excellent situation of the labourer renders it unnecessary, the interest of the employer would tend to prevent it, should idleness or dissipation lead the parent to desire it."—*Carey's Essay on Wages.*

Those who desire a wise and fair distribution of property must conspire to be economical; to save their wages; to produce the most useful kinds of property; to create something that will last, and may be beneficially distributed; instead of working for trash, and where no work is wanted; being servants where no servants are required; grinding where there is nothing to grind; drawing for water where there is no water. They must cease to produce or use that immense amount of trinkets, finery, fashionable trifles,* dainties, and poisonous drinks, with which our persons are decorated, our groceries, stores, cellars, kitchens, pantries, and houses, are now too often crammed. This is not the kind of property that wise people wish to be distributed; nor is it property at all in their eyes; so far as this kind of property is imported from foreign nations, and paid for by our products, it is certain that we may substitute the more useful productions of those nations for this trash.

But how can the farmers, mechanics, labourers in manufacto-

---

* During the war of the revolution, General Lafayette, being at Baltimore, was invited to a ball; he went as requested, but instead of joining in the amusements, as might be expected of a young Frenchman, he addressed the ladies,—" You are very handsome; you dance very prettily; your ball is very fine; but my soldiers have no *shirts*." The appeal was irresistible; the ball ceased, the ladies ran home and went to work, and in a few days, a large number of shirts were prepared, by the fairest hands in Baltimore, for the gallant defenders of their country.

ries, and other common labourers, help working to produce this
kind of property ? They say that they must have employment,
must earn wages ; and if the rich merchant, capitalist, and manufacturer, chooses to manufacture it, or import it from foreign countries, what means of prevention have they ?

The answer is plain. They can cease to use it, to buy it, to
pay their wages and earnings for it to the rich capitalist and manufacturer. As they are the consumers of nine tenths of it, they
would soon put an end to the production, if they ceased to be customers for it. It is by not combining and using their power in
this way, as they certainly can, that they defeat the just distribution of property, and keep themselves down. Thus they make
the rich richer than they should be, and the poor poorer than they
need be; thus we see the poor playing into the hands of the rich,
and throwing their solitary hard earned sixpences and shillings
into others' heaps, where there are already thousands. Thus we
see them running from tavern to tavern, from store to store,
emptying their pockets into those of men who are ten times richer
than themselves. All the legislatures in the world cannot prevent
this ; the people alone can do it.

It is plain, that as wealth is created by labour, it can only be
increased by saving and economy. By the same means that one
man becomes independent, a hundred and a thousand do, and the
same is true of a nation ; that is, by keeping on hand for future
use, what has already been acquired, or some portion of it ; because
all cannot be preserved ; a part must be daily eaten, drank, worn
out, or consumed in some way or other.

It is in the nature of wealth to increase, and this is plainly
proved by showing what the uses of capital are. One animal
breeds many, one seed produces a hundred or a thousand. Our
own experience in this country, shows an increase of wealth
beyond what the world ever saw under the like circumstances,
and commands us to go forward. We see, every year, new
sources of wealth opened, labour-saving machines invented ; new
substances or combinations of them brought to light, and turned
to some useful account, never before thought of. Steam, gas-light,
granite, anthracite coal, India rubber, soap stone, railroads, canals,
&c. furnish new employments, and of course increased wealth, to
thousands who but a few years since did not dream of deriving
advantage from any of them, and perhaps did not know of their
existence.

If these things are the means by which people are fed and
clothed, and get good farms, and houses and cattle, and after

obtaining a reasonable independence for themselves, are able, out of their superfluous riches, to get leisure and money to enable them to carry light, knowledge, and comfort, to their poor neighbours, and to the miserable nations, how unwise and unthinking to declaim against the increase of wealth ! It would be as childish to talk against too much good land, too many good houses, too many fine cattle. It is the perversion of wealth from the uses designed for it, that we have to deplore ; it is the heaping up of our meagre stores by monopoly and every kind of oppression, in the laps of a few, thus causing poverty and universal nakedness among the multitude, that the world ought to be ashamed of. It is the vanity, pride, selfishness, gluttony, intemperance, of both rich and poor, that we are to withstand. Wealth can never be an evil but by being turned to unnatural purposes, and an ancient philosopher says with truth, "that it is not the liquor but the vessel which is corrupted."

These subjects are no longer mysteries, when people give their thoughts to them; people are more puzzled about words than things ; they are often acquainted with the things, but do not understand the signs.—*Sedgwick.*

True religion lies at the foundation of all wholesome and permanent increase of wealth. Political economy professes to point out *all* the principles by which wealth is gained, the surest of all is the observance of moral precepts. The divine rule of doing to others as we would be done by, forbids all oppression, all cruelty to the poor, all unlawful taxes to support the pride, vanity, and luxury of the rich. Nothing is more striking in the scriptures, than the constant condemnation of all injustice to, and robbery of, the poor, who are the labourers for small wages. The Christian religion equally forbids, on the part of the poor, all hatred of the rich—all wanton destruction of property. There always have been rich and poor—there must be rich and poor. The people have been most miserable in those countries where there are no rich. The first duty of the rich to the poor, then, is, not to give them bread —for it is better that they should earn it—but the same legal advantages of getting bread that they themselves have. To attempt to teach economy without reference to our religious duty, is like taking the picture of a man from a corpse. Do the people of the United States desire to bring forth the magnificent riches which are to be found in the natural advantages of their country and free government; to elevate themselves to an eminence which nations have never yet thought of; do they long for the pleasures and glories of science, the delights of charity to their own poor and uninstructed, and to the wretched of other countries ; a better and more equal education for their children ; to increase their hospitality and social pleasures; to save their paternal houses and estates from a decay and ruin so common and so disgraceful in the old states ; do those whose interest it is to emigrate to the new, wish for the means of making such a change; do the men, women, and children, desire more rest and time for a proper improvement of their minds,—then both rich and poor must first unite, discard their jealousies and feuds, get what good they can out of the old world, turn their backs upon the stupid fashions and follies imported by nearly every packet, and study the proper economy of their own country—of the new world.   Those especially who live upon wages, as journeymen mechanics, labourers in factories, and day labourers of every description, must learn to save their wages, and thus preserve property, which is the true and common sense way of changing their condition for the better, and which can never be done, as long as they are slaves of fashion.

" There is an abundant increase of intelligence and moral sentiment springing up among the factories in England: the fruits of Sunday-schools and other philanthropic establishments,—planted and upreared chiefly by the workpeople themselves, unaided by opulence, and unpatronised by power.   It is a sublime spectacle to witness crowds of factory children arranged in a Sunday school. I would exhort the friends of humanity, who may chance to pass through Cheshire or Lancashire, not to miss a Sunday's visit to the busy town of Stockport, which joins these two counties.   It contains 67 factories, in which 21,489 operatives, of all ages, are employed comfortably for their families.   The Sunday-school of this place was erected by the voluntary contributions, chiefly, of mill owners, in the year 1805.   It is a large, plain, lofty building, which cost 10,000*l.*, having a magnificent hall for general examinations and public worship on the uppermost story, capable of accommodating nearly 3,000 persons, besides upwards of forty comfortable apartments for the male and female schools, committee and library rooms on the other floors.   On the 16th of June in the above year, the committee, teachers, and children, of the existing Sunday schools, assembled on the elevated site of the new building to celebrate, in a solemn manner, the commencement of this noble enterprise ; the foundation stone having been laid the evening before.   Many thousand inhabitants of the town and neighbourhood having joined them, the whole multitude raised their voices in a hymn of praise to the Father of light and life, in which they were accompanied by a full band of music.   The treasurer then pronounced a solemn prayer, dedicating the intended edifice to God, and imploring his blessing on its objects. In a concluding address he said :—' Our meeting together this day, on this spot, has nothing in it of parade or show ; nothing that can allure the eye by its splendour, or beguile the imagination by its pomp. It is, nevertheless, of the highest importance to the rising generation, to the town of Stockport, and as far as its influence extends, to the nation. We meet to erect a perpetual standard against ignorance and vice, to confirm, and render permanent, an establishment intended to train up the children of this town in knowledge and virtue. We expect thousands of children will here be taught not only the grounds of human science, but the first principles of the Christian religion ; that religion which is the true source of all sound morality, of all public and private virtue. This building is to be erected and maintained on the principle of pure and genu- ine benevolence, and is intended to consecrate as much of the piety and charity of this town as will supply a succession of gratuitous teachers. I feel happy to declare, thus publicly, the sentiments of the committee, that this building is not to be confined to any sect or party ; nor to be under any exclusive direction or influence. Learning is intended to be put in its proper place, as the hand- maid of religion ; and whatever human science is taught, is to be rendered subservient to this important purpose.'

" In the annual report of this admirable institution for 1833, the committee state, ' that, since its commencement, the names of 40,850 scholars have been inscribed on our registers, a consider- able part of whom have received a moral and religious education within our walls. Part of the fruit of these pious labours is already reaped in a temporal point of view, in the general decorum that pervades this town and neighbourhood, and the regard for the liberties, lives, and properties of others, evinced by the Stock- port population, at a period of political excitement, in which they were too much disregarded at other places. The well-judged liberality of the public has now made Sunday schools so numerous in our borders, that it is hardly possible to approach the town of Stockport, in any direction, without encountering one or more of these quiet fortresses, which a wise benevolence has erected against the encroachments of vice and ignorance. The advocates of general education hear no more of the danger of educating the lowest classes ; on the contrary, the necessity of doing so is gene- rally insisted upon. The people are extravagantly complimented upon the proficiency they have already made, and appear to be in as much danger of suffering from the effects of artful and injudicious

flattery, as they have done, in times past, from the unnatural
neglect with which they have been treated.'

" In 1835 there were from 4,000 to 5,000 young people profiting
by the instructions administered by 400 teachers, distributed into
proper classes, and arranged in upwards of forty school rooms,
besides the grand hall in the top of the building.   It was pleasing
to see 1500 boys, and as many girls, regularly seated upon separate benches : the one sit on the right side, and the other on the
left.   They were becomingly attired, decorous in deportment, and
of healthy, even blooming, complexions.   Their hymn-singing
thrilled through the heart like the festival chorus of Westminster.
The organ, which was excellent, was well played, by a young man
who had lately been a piecer, in the spinning factory of the gentleman."—*Ure's Philosophy of Manufactures.*

A collection of facts, evincing the benefactions of the arts
and manufactures to agriculture, commerce, navigation and the
fisheries, and their subserviency to the public defence, with an
indication of certain existing modes of conducting them, peculiarly
important to the United States, may be found in a communication
to Mr. Gallatin, by Tench Coxe.

" The resolution of Congress, 19th March, 1812, is formed with
a view so comprehensive as to include all pertinent information
of an authentic character, while it allows the most convenient
latitude, as to the form and manner ; requiring only, that the statement shall so exhibit the matter as to be most conducive to the
interests of the United States.   It is considered as a very interesting and fundamental truth, that manufactures facilitate the first
struggles of the American settlers, for decent comforts, thrifty
profits, and farming establishments.

" On examination into the state of manufactures, in four several
sparsely settled districts of our country, which, in 1810, had been
recently laid out, according to the nature of the places, for future
establishments as counties, the inconsiderable population within
these four intended counties exhibits the infantine condition of
their respective settlements in that year.   In these new and widely
scattered settlements, where foreign consumers have no agents, the
presence of flax, and of sheep and cattle, supplying wool, hides,
skins, horns and tallow, with other materials for manufactures,
that is to say, the *presence* of the *raw materials*, occasions the corresponding manufactures.   In such places, profit, comfort and
necessity appear to invite, or rather to compel, the farmers and
their families to that mode of industry.

" In these new and widely scattered settlements, it is observed, that the surplus industry of these new settlements is applied to the manufacture of cotton, from the Atlantic, Ohio, and Mississippi."

" A material error seems to have prevailed, on the subject of manufactures, in southern scenes. It has been supposed, that manufactures could not arise or exist in the southern states of America, and this, it is believed, has produced some local prejudice. Catalonia, Biscay, Valencia, Segovia and Guadalaxara, in Spain; the district of Lyons, and Languedoc, in France; Genoa, Venice, the principality of Tuscany, and Italy in general; the peninsula of India in particular, and the southern moiety and warm districts of China, were more early distinguished in manufactures than the districts in the latitude of the centre of Europe, and north of that centre. It was an exemption from the rigours and terrors of the inquisition and other ecclesiastical evils, in the south of Europe, which drew the objects of those fears and persecutions into Silesia, Saxony, Prussia, Westphalia, the Hanse towns, Holland and England. In Asia, where ecclesiastical terrors and persecutions have not occasioned such a dispersion of the manufacturers, they remain in and near the district which produces the cotton and silk that employ them. The numerous holidays of the church of Rome, which prevail in Italy, Spain, Portugal, Austria and France, have been unfavourable to general and manufacturing industry in the southern parts of Europe; where the useful arts early appeared and flourished. Where industry is free, it is believed that the manufacturers will gather at the sources of raw materials, food, forage, fuel, and building materials. The British interruption of our coasting trade is forcing these principles into operation, in a manner peculiarly injurious to the eastern and northern manufacturers of southern cotton, tobacco, iron, wood, hemp and wool. Southern produce, capable of manufacture, obstructed in its way to the European and northern United States' markets, will prove to be a southern manufacturing capital; forcing itself into employment upon the estates, and in the vicinities of the planters and farmers. The columns of ' looms—value of all kinds of cloths and stuffs—stockings, bagging for cotton, spinning wheels, hatteries, furnaces, forges, bloomeries, naileries, blacksmitheries, tanneries, spirits, beer, cabinet wares, tobacco and snuff, cables and cordage, gunpowder and salt,' demand a careful inspection and consideration, in order to ascertain the extent and proportionate importance, in A. D. 1810, of manufactures, in those states which are inhabited, in part by blacks, and which lie on the south side of the common line of Pennsylvania on the one part, and Delaware, Maryland, and Virginia on the other."

" It is a manifest truth, to which we ought most seriously to advert, that besides the proper or corporal powers, industry and skill of the people of the United States, we have attained, by water, steam, cattle, labour-saving machinery, and power and skill, a great variety and number of manufacturing operations. These wonderful machines, working as if they were animated beings, endowed with all the talents of their inventors, labouring with organs that never tire, and subject to no expense of food, or bed, or raiment, or dwelling, may be justly considered as equivalent to an immense body of manufacturing recruits, suddenly enlisted in the service of the country.

" Machinery and processes to effect manufactures, so as to leave manual industry for other employments, are of a degree of importance to the United States, proportioned to the smallness of the average population on a square mile. This is an interesting fact to a nation enjoying an extensive territory. As we possess innumerable contrivances, put into operation by horse power, to turn up and break the soil and cover the seed grain, under the names of the plough, the harrow, and the roller, to our incalculable profit, some have water-mills, wind-mills, and steam engines, in numerous instances and of diversified forms, to manufacture boards, bark, powder, flour, bar and sheet iron, nails, wire, carded wool and cotton, yarn and thread, metal plates of every kind, hair powder, snuff, gunpowder, paper, cannon, muskets, scythes, bolts, stocking web, various cloths and printed and other goods. These and many other machines have been obtained from abroad, or derived from the actual and very considerable talents of our own citizens. The complicated silk mill, the earliest invention for making yarn or thread, the fulling mill and various other mechanical constructions, were acquired by the British, the greatest manufacturing nation at this time in Europe, from their neighbours of Italy. The wisdom of the world has been and is as fairly attainable by us, as by other industrious and qualified nations, and the inventive genius of the people of the United States has produced a great number of curious and valuable instruments and machines."

" The fine arts, particularly painting and sculpture, have beautified the manufactures of alabaster, marble, clay, plaster and metals, and of wool, linen, cotton and leather. The fine porcelain of France and Saxony, the statues and paintings of Greece and Rome, the modern imitations of them in paintings, statues and casts, the elegant miniatures of alabaster, its various flowers and ornaments, the improvements in composition and in the pottery of Wedgwood, the imitations of the antique vases and figures in various gold and silver ornaments and utensils, and indeed of brass, the tapestry of the Gobelins, embroidery, dyeing, engraving and the printing of linen, cotton and silken cloths, are among the numerous examples that crowd upon the mind. The fluctuations and disorders of the old world have occasioned innumerable transfers of the instruments, the libraries, the models, the works, the welcome agents and the lovers of the fine arts from thence to the United States, and the manufacturers of fine wool from their proper original countries. The effect of such transfers, of much that was foreign, and all that was necessary for the interesting cultivation of the fine arts, either in their distinct and separate character and form, or as pleasing and beneficial auxiliaries to the useful arts and manufactures, are manifest to the attentive observer. The works of human genius and cultivation, which belong to the elegant and magnificent class of the arts, have a very considerable effect upon the convenience, utility, and profits of those things, which are usually called manufactures. A knowledge of architecture is necessary even to the cheapness of construction."*

* This work was so far arranged and limited, before I came to Philadelphia, that I find it difficult to use much valuable matter that I have since obtained; which also includes notices of individuals whose praise ought to be in history. The writings and indefatigable life of *Tench Coxe*, would require and richly deserve a volume to do justice to his memory. The notice that I have given, is far too scanty to afford even a slight view of his important services, in the establishment of manufactories; and his exertions to promote the growth of cotton, both of which objects he lived to see in a flourishing degree of progress. In an enlarged edition, a more extended view of the services of this eminent statesman shall be given; and I very much regret the obligations, which prevent my enriching the work, in this impression, with a review of his publications, containing extracts from his writings, which not only fulfilled valuable purposes at the time, receiving the approbation of Washington, Hamilton, Jefferson, Jay, Ames, and indeed of the whole community; but they contain principles, on national economy, that will live for ever, and their author will be had in respectful remembrance. I find no author on American statistics, but what is deeply indebted to Tench Coxe. I have no doubt but that the chartered company of Paterson, New Jersey, though the plan is generally attributed to Hamilton, originated with the assistant secretary of the treasury; this is proved by the letter of Fisher Ames.

For the following statement I am indebted to Dr. James Mease, of Philadelphia.

"In order to make an experiment in manufactures, and to ascertain whether this could be carried on to profit, a company was formed, with a capital of $ 200,000, in the year 1791, under the name of " The Society for the Establishment of Useful Manufactures;" and received a charter bearing

The following correspondence will show, what I have before stated, that the administration of Washington was greatly indebted to the assistant secretary of the treasury, for important and extensive views of commercial affairs, as well as for a correct digest of all the great resources of the country; also for statistics of the operations of manufactures: in short, for all that kind of information, which are the foundation principles of the wealth of nations. The services of Tench Coxe were viewed in this light by Washington, Hamilton, and Jefferson, and they will be held in high respect by posterity.

—

PHILADELPHIA, November 30, 1789.

Dear Sir,—It was my wish to have forwarded to you sooner, the enclosed paper, No. 6, by way of answer to the queries I had the honour to receive from you, the 26th of last month, but I could not revise the facts with sufficient care, till this time.

You will observe, I have pursued a mode different from that which the form of the queries pointed out, thinking that " *a present state of the navigation of Pennsylvania,*" which should comprehend the information you desired, would be more useful than short answers, going merely to the points specified. I have, besides, this private reason, that I wish by these investigations and statements, as they occur, to extend or digest my own knowledge, and, as far as I am able, to place the several subjects in my own mind on their true principles.

As the gentlemen in the senate, for Pennsylvania, and some of those in the house of representatives, have been pleased to request my communications

---

date 22d November, of that year, from the state of New Jersey, from which the company purchased the title to the falls of Passaic river, and were invested with the sole power over, and possession of, the waters of that stream, for mills or manufactures. The society soon after established the first cotton factory and printing house, in that state; but in a short time found that a loss attended their business, and it is more than probable that from this circumstance, a cessation would soon have taken place of their operations, had they not been forced to give them up, from the following cause. As there were no native workmen to be had, the company were obliged to employ foreigners, who were either expressly sent for, or, more probably, found in New York. Without any assignable cause, the foreman expressed to the manager of the concern, his determination to leave the establishment, when fully employed: and as no persuasion appeared to have the least effect in altering his determination, he was desired to pack up the machinery. This he did, but filled the vacant spaces with quick-lime, so that when they were examined, the iron work, and particularly the cards, were found entirely destroyed.

" This fact I had many years since, from the late Hon. Elias Boudinot, a representative in congress, from New Jersey, who was a stockholder in the company."

on the subjects that from time to time arise in the legislature, I have taken the liberty to show this paper to one or two of them; and indeed it seems to be a matter, both of propriety and prudence, as I am a citizen of Pennsylvania, and they are the guardians of her interests. I anxiously desire the detection of any errors in either the facts or reasonings, which I may bring forward; and in order completely to guard against their ill effects, I wish them unreservedly subjected, as well to the examination of these well informed judges, as to gentlemen of similar character and stations from the other states. As I may, in future, avail myself of the permission you have given me, to communicate with you as I shall see occasion, I apply these wishes to all such communications, leaving it in your discretion to determine to whose eye observations on points that require secresy may be safely confided.

I have the honour to be, with great respect, dear sir, your most obedient servant,   TENCH COXE.

P.S. As it may throw some light upon the subject, I have enclosed a paper of mine, (No. 1,) which you have seen before. To this copy, I have added some manuscript notes; also a paper, (No. 2), to which I have likewise added some notes. The latter is not immediately interesting to your present enquiry, but may be thrown among your documents belonging to the subject.

To the Honourable Alexander Hamilton, Esq. New York.

—

PHILADELPHIA, December 16th, 1789.

Dear Sir,—A few days ago I forwarded to you, per post, a " state of our navigation," which I presume you have received. I have the honour to transmit you in this inclosure some notes upon two subjects, one of them of great importance, that may be useful when arranging our affairs with France and Spain. The rough draughts of these papers were made a few weeks before I received your letter, and I then intended to have given them to Mr. Madison in his way to New York, for the purpose of submitting them to Mr. Jefferson, in whose department I thought they might be of use. The general request at the conclusion of your letter justifies me, I hope, in troubling you with them, and in requesting that you will dispose of them as you see fit.

On No. 7, I beg leave to suggest, it may be useful to converse with Col. J. Wadsworth, whose opportunities in the branch it concerns are greater than those of any other person among us.

Of the subject of No. 8 it may be truly said, that it is one of the most important objects of business in all our affairs. The calculations you will find are all within the truth, and of course the result on paper might have been rendered much greater.

I congratulate you most sincerely on the adoption of the constitution by North Carolina, which almost completes this wonderful revolution. The law of New Jersey abolishing the tender of their paper money, in cases wherein gold and silver have been specified in the contract, occasions a further subtraction from the objects, and of course a new inducement to the acquiescence of the opposition. The federal cause has received a fresh confirmation by our convention, for I think it may be justly said, that every recognition of the principles of the general constitution, and every step towards an efficient and well balanced government by any member of the Union, is a furtherance of the object. It has been determined,—

1. That the legislative power ought not to be in a single house.

2. That the judges, in addition to their former independence from fixed salaries, should be appointed during good behaviour—with some provisions for removal in case of a decay of talents, or of private virtue. This important and difficult clause is not yet digested.

3. That the executive power should be in a single person.

4. That the chief executive officer should have a qualified negative upon the proceedings of the legislature.

Messrs. Finlay, Smiley, and M'Lene, who led the opposition to the federal constitution, have been in the majority which passed these resolutions. It is, therefore, almost certain that the constitution of Pennsylvania, which was *the great cause of our opposition* to the proceedings of the general convention, will be altered in these important particulars. How near to the standard of propriety, which the gentlemen have formed for themselves, they will be able to arrive, is uncertain, for so very democratic have been our former ideas, and so much does a jealousy of the city prevail in the counties, that it must be expected they will influence in some particulars.

I beg your pardon for this digression from the original design of my letter, but the proceedings of each state even in its own arrangements are of so much importance to the order of the whole, that I thought the information I have given would not appear impertinent to the business of your office.

I have the honour to be, very respectfully, sir, your most obedient humble servant,   TENCH COXE.

The Hon. A. Hamilton, Esq.

—

NEW YORK, December 24th, 1789.

Dear Sir,—Your obliging favours of the 30th of November, and 16th instant, with the communications accompanying them, have been duly received.

Accept my best acknowledgments for the attention you have paid to my request; and believe that I mean not a mere compliment, when I say that your compliance with it has procured me much useful information, and many valuable observations.

I have not leisure to add more, than that I am, with sincere esteem and regard, dear sir, your obedient servant,   A. HAMILTON.

Tench Coxe, Esq.

—

NEW YORK, May 1st, 1790.

Dear Sir,—I have just received your letter of the 27th of April. Yours of the 6th of the same month also came to hand in due time; though peculiar reasons prevented an earlier acknowledgment of it.

The appointment of his assistant is, by the act establishing the treasury department, vested in the secretary himself. The conviction I have of your usefulness in that station, and my personal regard for you, have determined me to avail myself of the offer of service which the last mentioned letter contains.

The state of the public business under my care, is such as to make me desire to see you as soon as may consist with the dispositions which your change of situation will render necessary.

I am, with great regard and esteem, dear sir, your obedient servant,

A. HAMILTON.

Tench Coxe, Esq.

———

Mr. Coxe, Assistant Secretary of the Treasury.   At the Treasury Office.
DECEMBER 14, 1791.

Dear Sir,—Not having distinguished between the furs, ginseng, coffee, mahogany, wine, and sugars, carried to Great Britain and Ireland, and to other countries, at the time we were extracting those articles from your large tables, I find myself unable to proceed in making the deductions from our whole exports to Great Britain, which should be made for that proportion of those articles which go there.   The extract I made, for instance, tells me how much furs we send to all the world, but not how much of them go to England and Ireland, but your tables would tell this.   I must, therefore, ask the favour of the loan of them to have this distinction made, unless it would be more agreeable to you to let some one state the *amount in value* of the furs which we send to Great Britain and Ireland.

Ginseng do. coffee do. mahogany do. wine do. sugars do.   Having this amount, I can deduct it with precision from that of our whole exports to Great Britain and Ireland.

I am, with great esteem, dear sir, your most obedient humble servant.

TH. JEFFERSON.

———

From Thos. M'Kean, Governor of Pennsylvania, to Tench Coxe.
PHILADELPHIA, June 14th, 1801.

Sir,—As secretary of the land office, you may probably be acquainted with Mr. John M'Kissick, the principal clerk in the office of receiver general; he has been well recommended to me by several respectable characters in public as well as private stations, as a suitable person to succeed Mr. Muhlenberg as principal officer.   There will certainly be a difference between the speaker of the house of representatives of the United States, and of this state, as to rank and services, and Mr. M'Kissick, a writing clerk in the office; but I wish to promote modest merit, and from recommendations of him by members of our public councils, I think favourably of his talents and integrity for the ordinary duties of the office, but is he qualified to act as a judge of the board of property?   Please to give me your sentiments, for I wish for something more than "a successor in form."   This leads me to ask you also, whether you think the appointment of Mr. Andrew Ellicot as your successor would meet with general approbation.   I would wish your answer as soon as is convenient, that I may be prepared to fill both stations immediately on your coming to town; which I suppose will be the latter end of this, or the beginning of next week, as the revenue offices, of all others, must not be many days vacant.   Though our official connection may for some time be suspended, yet I shall always expect to see you as a friend, and hope to see you in a day or two at farthest, after you shall have entered on the duties of your new appointments.   The nature of this communication is such, as to render it unnecessary to request it may be confined to yourself.   I am, sir, with esteem, your friend and humble servant.

To Tench Coxe, greeting:

Reposing especial trust and confidence in your integrity, diligence, and abilities, I, Alexander Hamilton, secretary of the treasury of the United States, in virtue of the power to me given, by the act entitled "An act to establish the treasury department," do constitute and appoint you assistant to the said secretary: To hold and exercise the said office during the pleasure of the secretary of the treasury of the United States for the time being.

In witness whereof, I have hereunto set my hand, and affixed the seal of the treasury, the tenth day of May, in the year of our Lord one thousand seven hundred and ninety.

ALEXANDER HAMILTON.
Secretary of the Treasury.

George Washington, President of the United States of America:—to all who shall see these presents, greeting:

Know ye, that reposing special trust and confidence in the integrity, diligence, and ability of Tench Coxe of Pennsylvania, I have nominated, and by and with the advice and consent of the senate, do appoint him commissioner of the revenue, and do authorise and empower him to execute and fulfil the duties of that office according to law; and to have and to hold the said office with all the rights and emoluments thereunto legally appertaining unto him, the said Tench Coxe, during the pleasure of the president of the United States for the time being.

In testimony whereof, I have caused these letters to be made patent, and the seal of the United States to be hereunto affixed. Given under my hand, at the city of Philadelphia, this ninth day of May, in the year of our Lord one thousand seven hundred and ninety-two, and of the independence of the United States of America the sixteenth.

G. WASHINGTON.

By the president, Th: Jefferson.

Lincoln del.

WEBSTER

R.Kimberly Sc.

CHAPTER VI.

THE EXTENSION OF THE COTTON BUSINESS.

> " The echoing hills repeat
> The stroke of axe and hammer; scaffolds rise,
> And growing edifices; heaps of stone
> Beneath the chisel beauteous shapes assume
> Of frieze and column; some with even line,
> New streets are marking in the neighbouring fields,
> And sacred domes of worship."
>
> DYER'S FLEECE.

" All men naturally think themselves equally wise; and, therefore, as any ship that sails faster than another is said in sea phrase to wrong it, so men are apt to think themselves wronged by those who, with better talents than they, or greater skill in their use, get beyond them."

The workmen employed by Mr. Slater, in Pawtucket, took advantage of their opportunity to steal patterns and models of his machines; and in this way, attempts were made to extend the business, in a short time after its commencement at Pawtucket by the firm of Almy, Brown & Slater. Those attempts were generally so weak and ineffective, that they proved ruinous to the adventurers.

Wm. Pollard, Philadelphia, obtained a patent for cotton spinning Dec. 30, 1791, which was the first water-frame put in motion; whether he obtained his patterns direct from England, or by the way of Pawtucket, is not certain; but it is indubitable that he could have no claim as the original inventor, nor as the first introducer of the machinery; because it has been shown in the previous chapter that the whole of the machinery was in full operation in Rhode Island, a year previous to the date of his patent.

Mr. Pollard's mill was a very early attempt at water-spinning, and I am sorry to have to record, that his business failed in his hands; which retarded the progress of cotton spinning in Philadelphia. Respect and pity are due to the character of a projector —respect, because society owes to it many obligations, and much of the progress of the useful arts must be ascribed to its existence;

and pity, because it is unfriendly to the interests of the individual, and generally plunge him from affluence into ruin.*

An outline of a plan to encourage industry, is a part of the report of the secretary of the treasury in 1791.

" Let a certain annual sum be set apart, and placed under the management of commissioners, not less than three ; let these commissioners be empowered to apply the fund confided to them, to defray the expenses of the emigration of artists and manufacturers in particular branches of extraordinary importance—to induce the prosecution and introduction of useful discoveries, inventions, and improvements, by proportionate rewards, judiciously held out and applied—to encourage by premiums, both honourable and lucrative, the exertions of individuals, and of classes, in relation to the several objects they are charged with promoting—and to afford such other aids to those objects, as may be generally designated by law. The commissioners to render to the legislature an annual account of the transactions and disbursements ; and all such sums as have not been applied to the purposes of their trust at the end of every three years, to revert to the treasury. It may also be enjoined upon them, not to draw out the money, but for the purpose of some specific disbursement. It may, however be of use, to authorise them to receive voluntary contributions ; making it their duty to apply them to the particular objects for which they may have been made, if any shall have been designated by the donors. There is reason to believe, that the progress of particular manufactures has been much retarded by the want of skilful workmen. And it often happens, that the capitals employed are not equal to the purposes of bringing from abroad workmen of a superior kind. Here, in cases worthy of it, the auxiliary agency of government would, in all probability, be useful. There are also valuable workmen, in every branch, who are prevented from

---

* The project for a manufacturing company with joint stock, incorporated and privileged by the state of Maryland, was very much opposed ; and the doctrine that it was better to buy of Europe and India, was widely spread. And it is said, that the Paterson company suffered from treachery and bribery ; it however failed of accomplishing the fond hopes of the projectors—of introducing the best machinery and the best workmen from England, which if accomplished, and such companies had been protected, we should ere now have been entirely independent of foreign fabrics.

At this time, a joint stock company might introduce fine goods, in cotton, linen, or woollen—or in cutlery. It is not too late to adopt the plan which Hamilton proposed. It only requires a patriotic spirit to arise among the people, and a preference for our own goods, and any thing can be done.

emigrating solely by want of the means. Occasional aids to such persons, properly administered, might be a source of valuable acquisitions to the country. The propriety of stimulating by rewards, the invention and introduction of useful improvements, is admitted without difficulty. But the success of attempts in this way must evidently depend much on the manner of conducting them. It is probable that the placing of the dispensation of those rewards under some proper discretionary direction, where they may be accompanied by collateral expedients, will serve to give them the surest efficacy.

" It seems impracticable to apportion, by general rules, specific compensations for discoveries unknown and of disproportionate utility. The great use which may be made of a fund of this nature, to procure and import foreign improvements, is particularly obvious. Among these, the article of machines would form a most important item. The operation and utility of premiums have been adverted to, together with the advantages which have resulted from their dispensation, under the direction of certain public and private societies. Of this, some experience has been had in the instance of the Pennsylvania Society for the promotion of manufactures and the useful arts ; but the funds of that association have been too contracted to produce more than a very small portion of the good to which the principles of it would have led.* It may confidently be affirmed, that there is scarcely any thing which has been devised better calculated to excite a general spirit of improvement, than the institutions of this nature. They are truly invaluable. In countries where there is great private wealth, much may be effected by the voluntary contributions of patriotic individuals ; but in a community situated like that of the United States, in 1790, the public purse must supply the deficiency

* *Amount of Domestic Goods sold in Philadelphia, the produce of New England ; 1804 to 1806 inclusive.*

In 1804, cotton yarn,		$2388	
"	wove goods,	$1526	
			——3914
1805, cotton yarn,		$3805	
"	wove goods,	$1581	
			——5386
1806, cotton yarn,		$6185	
"	wove goods,	$2185	
			——8370

Total for three years, $17670

of private resources.   In what can it be so useful, as in prompting and improving the efforts of industry ?"

The last war with Great Britain taught the Americans one most excellent lesson, viz. to rely upon their own *resources for support*, and the results of this one lesson have been far more useful to us than would have been ten thousand of the most brilliant victories over the mother country.* It has resulted in the erection of manufacturing establishments in almost every nook and corner of the middle and northern states—affording sure markets for the produce of the flocks and fields of the northern farmer, and increasing the demand for the staple of the southern planter.   The mechanical genius, the industry, and the resources of the country, have been drawn out and put in successful competition with those of the old world—and now, at a period of about twenty years since setting up for ourselves and manufacturing our own articles, we find ourselves amply able to supply our own demand for the most important fabrics necessary for our comfort, and even carry the war of commerce and manufactures into the country of the enemy.   In cottons and broadcloths we have succeeded admirably ; what genius and perseverance have done for

---

* The power of cultivation has been variously exerted by individuals, as well as by nations; and the earth has been, and now is, clothed with appearances exceedingly various, under those several operations.   It is not the husbandman possessing the richest lands, who always shows the best conditioned fields.   If his acres might yield sixty measures each, he will, at times, take his ease ; nor labour throughout the whole of any day, or fill up the round year with none but days of toil.   His fields may be found without the refreshment of artificial fertility, and are seldom relieved by skilful rotations. Lands, on the contrary, yielding but thirty measures, are cultivated by their owner with untiring and ceaseless diligence and skill.   Instead of exhausting, he enriches, his fields ; and what may be wanting in fertility, is more than supplied by increased labour and judicious management.   As the traveller goes by them, over whose cornfields, pastures, meadows, and orchards, does his eye wander with most delight, or linger and gaze longest ? In different quarters of the globe, labour and cultivation have produced effects more obviously different.   Asia was originally equal to Europe, both in soil and climate ; but what is Asia now compared to Europe ?   The plain of Shinar, once the richest, and most productive region of the East, what can be found upon it to equal much, very much, of Great Britain ?   When Cæsar invaded that island, as he tells us, "most of the people in the interior sow no corn, but feed on milk and flesh ; and clothe themselves in the skins of beasts."   What has wrought this mighty change ?   What has removed and transplanted the oriental paradise from the banks of the Euphrates to those of the Thames ?   Labour and cultivation, the incessant toil of almost two thousand years.—*Burgess.*

us in these departments of manufactures, they will do for us in other departments. Why not try silk, then? Have we forgotten the great lesson which the last war taught us? Must we wait for a rupture with France, and a consequent failure in the supply of silks, to teach us the lesson again? Silk has become a common, if not a necessary, article of consumption. The wealthy and the poor use it more or less; in robes, veils, handkerchiefs, and ribbons, and thread, it is used, perhaps, by every man, woman, and child, in the country; not a *button-hole* can be made well without it. We are paying France more than *six millions of money a year*, for this very article; and yet it can be as well cultivated and manufactured in the United States as in France. The valleys, and the hills even, of the Green Mountain state can be made to produce silk—and they should be made to do it. Some enterprising citizens of Vermont have commenced cultivating the mulberry, upon the leaves of which the silk-worms are fed, and we doubt not, with a little care and labour, they will soon find this a source of pleasure and of profit. Let those individuals persevere, let them impart to their neighbours and to their brother farmers, the result of their experiments. By so doing we doubt not they will satisfy the most incredulous of the practicability of raising silk in New England, and thus introduce the cultivation of it as a regular and profitable branch of agriculture.

The following statistical accounts, show the progress* of manufactures at the beginning of the last war :—

* Small factories spread in Rhode Island about the year 1807, and improvements began to be introduced; Hines, Dexter & Co., tried a picker to pick cotton by water; this was superseded by a picker made by a Scotsman, which answered a good purpose at that time, but there have been greater improvements made in pickers. As early as 1808, $80,000 was invested in the Globe factory, Philadelphia, in which Dr. Redman Coxe was concerned. The Arkwright machinery was introduced very early at Copp's creek Delaware, by Goodfellow. Also at Kirkmill, Delaware, near Wilmington. Those early attempts in Pennsylvania, were not continued with much success. The mill in Warwick, which Mr. Potter left, was owned by Brown & Almy. Cumberland and Blackstone were early seats of the cotton manufacture; also Smithfield. David Wilkinson established a machine shop in Pawtucket. Jeremiah Wilkinson commenced cutting nails, in which Mr. Slater was concerned.

Record of Plainfield Union Manufacturing Co. Jan. 7, 1809. At the house of John Dunlap; 70 feet by 33—3 stories.

The following persons composed this company :—Anthony Bradford, James Gorden, Jr., Christopher Dean, Walter Palmer, Lemuel Dorrance, Jer. Kinsman, Vine Robinson, John Lester.

Cotton mills within thirty miles of Providence in 1812.

Towns.	Factories.	Spindles in operation.	No. of spindles which might run in the buildings.
Providence, R. I.	1	540	1250
North Providence,	5	3592	6700
Johnson,	2	1382	2700
Cranston,	4	1100	2988
Cumberland,	2	412	412
Smithfield,	3	4188	5800
Scituate,	3	2688	4000
Gloucester,	2	72	432
Warwick,	9	10757	17856
Coventry,	5	5124	12800
Exeter,	1	400	800
South Kingston,	1	408	408
	——33	——30663	——56246

Massachusetts, within thirty miles of Providence.

Rehoboth,	8	5250	9438
Attleborough,	4	1200	4469
Taunton,	1	800	1000
Dighton,	4	2775	7000
Wrentham,	1	260	260
Merton,	2	480	2400
Mansfield,	2	360	1600
Medway,	2	1000	1500
Franklin,	1	200	400
Mendon	1	3392	11000
Dedham,	1	654	1200
Walpole,	1	——	800
Canton,	2	1000	2400
	——20	——17371	——45438

Each spindle would then produce yarn enough weekly, to make two and a half yards of cloth, of the value of 30 cents per yard. The number of spindles then in operation produced, therefore, sufficient yarn when wove, to make in each week 128635 yards of cloth, worth $96,476. What an immense importance does this attach to the introduction of this manufacture previous to the war!

As the following letter of Wm. Almy to Samuel Slater is probably the only one I shall be able to obtain from his first partner, I will insert it. It will be read as a curiosity.

Samuel Slater, Pawtucket.

PROVIDENCE, 18th 9th month, 1795.

Inclosed is ten dollars—We have made enquiry about corn, have not found any ; shall continue to look out, and as soon as we can find any, will purchase it and send it up.   We are to have a load of meal, which we expect to-day or to-morrow ; if we don't light of any corn, will send part of it to Pawtucket. I have desired my brother to get the bristles &c. this morning and send them.

Having been a housekeeper myself, these two days, with a specimen of the dysentery, which is pretty prevalent. I showed the candle-wick to Thos. Hazard Jr. who liked it much, supposed it nearly the size they use ; they use about four or five hundred pounds a year. He took the skein with him to compare with theirs, which as far as I could find, at present cost them about 4s. —he says they are obliged to have it wound in balls.   *Quere,* what would be the additional expense of winding it into balls off the spools, five threads together?   He says if they take it in skeins, they will have to get it wound, as the method we talked of reeling it, and lee winding it with the number of threads suitable for a wick, he thought would not answer so well. I think the price thou puts upon Sampson's wick is as high most probably as he will give, and perhaps is about right.   Should be glad of thy opinion respecting the bag of cotton last sent, it cost 1s. 8d., we have another between three and four hundred weight of the same quality.   Georgia cotton seems growing rather more plenty.   We have received several invitations from Newport to purchase a quantity that is there, which they say is good, and they will sell very cheap. Will endeavour to send thee a little more cash, beginning of the week, if possible.   WM. ALMY.

The increase of business was probably the reason of Mr. Slater's sending for his brother.   His wife's brothers were employed by him ; Smith Wilkinson spun for him, David wrought on machinery, and the whole family were engaged in some way connected with the business.   He built, in company with his father-in-law, Oziel Wilkinson, the *New Mill,* on the Massachusetts side, and which was the first cotton-mill in that state on the Arkwright improvement.   Samuel Slater superintended both the old and the new mills, for which he was allowed one dollar and fifty cents a day for each mill ; which gave him three dollars a day for his personal services.   He was very laborious, and incessant in his attention to business.   So that Samuel Slater did not get his property without hard work, anxiety, and severe application : few persons ever laboured more for his age.   He went forward unassured that even common prosperity would attend his enterprise, but he faced the difficulties and encountered them.   An event of real magnitude in human history, is never seen in all its grandeur and importance, till some time after its occurrence has elapsed. In proportion as the memory of small men and small things is lost, that of the truly great becomes more bright.   The cotemporary aspect of things is often confused and indistinct. The eye which is placed too near the canvass, beholds too distinctly the separate touches of the pencil, and is perplexed with a cloud of seemingly discordant tints. It is only at a distance, that they melt into a harmonious living picture. The inhabitants of Pawtucket, who saw Slater labouring day and night, and sometimes beheld him loaded with a bale of cotton on his back, little supposed what abilities he possessed, or the importance of his enterprise.

The war of 1812 decided the success of Mr. Slater's business, by that time* he had got so far under way, and all the operations and preparations he had previously made, now gave him a great advantage. Cotton cloth sold at forty cents per yard, and the demand was unlimited. While his business was thus increasing and he was making money rapidly, he suffered a severe domestic affliction, in the loss of his beloved wife, in the thirty-seventh year of her age, soon after the birth of her last child.

Thus he was left with a helpless family, when his business demanded every moment of his attention. Of course the care of his family was left to persons hired for the purpose, and they sometimes suffered for the common and necessary attentions, suitable to their age and infirmities. At that time it was extremely

---

* Writers on the progress of the mechanic arts, during the last century, refer almost exclusively to Europe'; the nineteenth century will claim a notice of American improvements. Less than seventy years ago, the only machine much used for reducing cotton into yarn, was the *one-thread-wheel*. Other methods had been thought of, and proposed, for making a more easy and expeditious process; but without any extensive or permanent success. About the year 1767, James Hargreave, an English weaver, constructed a machine, by means of which any number of threads, from twenty to eighty, might be spun at once, and for which he obtained a patent; and soon after a new method of *carding cotton*, more easy and expeditious than the old way of carding by the hand, which was now found inadequate to the rapid progress and large demands of the improved mode of spinning. The first calicoes were made in Lancashire, about 1772; muslins, 1781; previously, chiefly confined to India. In 1789, a machine was invented in Massachusetts, by either Foster, or M'Clinch, for cutting and bending wire in a state completely prepared for sticking cards; before this they were imported. In 1797, Amos Whittemore, of Cambridge, Mass. invented a machine which by a simple operation, bends, cuts, and sticks card teeth; 1799, Wm. Whittemore & Co. commenced the manufacture of cards with this machine, in Cambridge, and were able very soon to furnish two hundred dozen pairs of cards on an average every week. Steam-engines were scarcely at all known, prior to the eighteenth century. To the honour of inventing and perfecting this kind of machinery, the artists of Great Britain are entitled.

difficult to obtain suitable persons to help in families—no money could secure them. Under no circumstances can you fill the place of a mother. I visited my friend while he was a widower, and could not help observing how great a chasm was made in his family, by the loss of his beloved Hannah ; her loss was felt by all her friends, and the poor lamented her whose charities and kindness they had experienced.

The company formed in Smithfield, were Almy, Brown & Slaters; a large establishment was erected under the superintendence of John Slater, Esq., who understood the business, and managed the concern to great advantage. Notwithstanding some favourable circumstances, such as the non-importation, non-intercourse, and finally the war, helped to raise the prices of home manufactures, a great deal depended on economy. Mr. Slater's personal expenses were comparatively small ; he paid nothing for show, or parade, or ostentation; or as they say in England, which proverb he was apt to repeat, "he did not keep more cats than caught mice." He probably learned the art of saving, from Mr. Strutt, who gave him lessons to save the waste cotton, and this led much to his careful habits and self-denial.

Another anecdote was in circulation, respecting the first interview which Mr. Slater had with his brother John, after his arrival in this country. It was stated that Samuel Slater saw his brother John in the streets of Providence, as he was riding through, and that he instantly jumped out of the chaise, and left the horse to take his own course, while he embraced his brother. This story was incorrect ; Wm. Wilkinson, of Providence, saw John Slater on his landing on the wharf, and took him to the house, and told him he was acquainted with his brother, and that he would take him out to Pawtucket. When Mr. Wilkinson arrived at Mr. Slater's house, he found him within, and said to him,—" I have brought one of your countrymen to see you, and can you find any thing for him to do ?" He desired them to be seated and he would be with them in a few minutes. He soon came up to his countryman, and asked what part of England he came from ? From Derbyshire.—What part of Desbyshire ?—Belper.—Ah, the town of Belper, I am acquainted with that place ; what may I call your name ?—*John Slater.*—When Samuel left, John was a boy, and he had changed so much that he did not recognise him. My readers need not be told that the interview was a joyful one to the two brothers.—Is my mother yet alive ? How are all my brothers and sisters ? How is my old master, Strutt ? How is my old schoolmaster, Jackson ? How is the old " Holly-House"

farm getting along?—With innumerable other questions, were
rapidly put and answered between the brothers ; and Mr. Wilkinson told me he enjoyed the scene of their meeting and greetings ;
it was like Joseph's seeing his brother Benjamin after so long an
absence.

John came to America in consequence of his brother's invitation
and persuasion, and they always maintained an affectionate intercourse, and were a long time connected in business with each
other.

" *June* 14, 1817. The American society for the encouragement
of American manufactures, met last evening, in the assembly room
at city hotel.—Daniel D. Tomkins, president of the society, took
the chair, supported by the vice-presidents, Col. Few, and John
Ferguson, Esq. The society being organised, James Monroe, president of the United States, was proposed as a member, whereon,
the presiding officer suggested that the usual form of ballot be
dispensed with, and that James Monroe be received as a member ;
a motion to this effect was then made, and carried unanimously.
Messrs. Morris, Colden, and Pierson, were appointed a committee
to wait on the president of the United States, to inform him of his
being elected, and to solicit the honour of his attendance at the
meeting ; to which he politely assented, and being inducted by the
committee, took his seat on the right of the presiding officer, who
immediately rose, and in an extempore and eloquent address, assured
his excellency of the high sense entertained by the society of the
honour he conferred, by assenting to become one of its members,
which created a confidence that he would do all, which he consistently could, to promote the views with which the society was
instituted. To which his excellency replied, with much eloquence
and force, that he duly appreciated the objects of the institution,
which were particularly dear to him, from their being intimately
connected with the *real* independence of our country, and closed
with an assurance that he would use his efforts as far as the general interests of the country would permit, to promote the patriotic
and laudable objects of the society. James Madison, Thomas
Jefferson, * and John Adams, were then separately proposed as

* The American society for the encouragement of domestic manufactures,
in New York, on the 13th of June 1817, unanimously elected John Adams,
Thomas Jefferson, and James Madison, members thereof, and directed their
secretary to apprise them of the circumstance by letter. The following is a
copy of the secretary's letter, and the answers thereto.

                                    NEW YORK, 14th June, 1817.
Sir—The American society for the encouragement of domestic manufac-

members, and admitted unanimously; the usual form of ballot being, on motion, dispensed with.

tures, instituted in this city, sensible of the zeal you have uniformly displayed, in the promotion of every object connected with the welfare and independence of our country, had the honour to elect you a member at their last meeting, convened on the 13th inst., for the purpose of initiating into the society, James Monroe, president of the United States. It would afford me the highest gratification to announce to the society your assent to become one of its members.

I have the honour to be, sir, with respect and consideration, your obedient servant,   D. LYNCH, Jr.

QUINCY, June 23, 1817.

Sir,—I have received the letter you did me the honour of writing to me, on the 14th of this month, announcing to me my election by the American Society for the encouragement of Domestic Manufactures, instituted in New York, as a member, an honour made more illustrious by the presence of the president of the United States. Be pleased, sir, to present my respects to the society, and my thanks for the honour they have done me, and to assure them, if the best wishes of a man at eighty-one years of age can promote the wise purposes of their institution, I shall be a useful member. For, according to my superficial view of political economy in civilised society, next to agriculture, which is the first and most splendid, manufactures are the second, and navigation the third. With agriculture, manufactures, and navigation, all the commerce which can be necessary or useful to the happiness of a nation will be secured. Accept my thanks for the civility with which you have communicated the vote of the society to their and your friend,

JOHN ADAMS.

D. Lynch, Jr., Secretary of the American Society for the
        encouragement of Domestic Manufactures.

MONTICELLO, June 26, 1817.

Sir,—I am thankful for the honour done me, by an association with the American Society for the encouragement of Domestic Manufactures, instituted in New York. The history of the last twenty years has been a sufficient lesson for us all to depend for necessaries on ourselves alone : and I hope that twenty years more will place the American hemisphere under a system of its own essentially peaceable and industrious, and not needing to extract its comforts out of the eternal fires raging in the old world. The efforts of the members of your institution being necessarily engaged in their respective vicinages, I consider myself, by their choice, as but a link of union between the promoters there and here of the same patriotic objects. Praying you to present to the society my just acknowledgments for this mark of attention, I tender to yourself the assurance of my great respect and consideration.

TH : JEFFERSON.

Mr. Lynch.

MONTPELIER, June 27, 1817.

Sir,—I have received your letter of the 18th inst, informing me that the American Society for the encouragement of Domestic Manufactures, had

" The corresponding committee offered the following report, with an address from the pen of C. D. Colden Esq., which were severally read—After which, the president of the United States withdrew, and the society adjourned.

Report of the corresponding committee of the Society for the encouragement of Domestic Manufactures.

" The corresponding committee, elected in pursuance of the third article of the constitution, for the current year, respectfully report—

" That immediately after the meeting of the society, held on the 31st of December 1816, they took the speediest measures for carrying into effect the resolutions, respecting the printing and publishing the address then reported and adopted. They accordingly caused to be printed 5000 copies ; one of which was presented to the president of the United States, and one to each of the members of congress and heads of departments of the general government, and to the governors and members of the legislatures of the states

been pleased to elect me one of its members. Although I approve the policy of leaving to the sagacity of individuals, and to the impulse of private interest, the application of industry and capital, I am equally persuaded that in this as in other cases, there are exceptions to the general rule, which do not impair the principle of it. Among these exceptions, is the policy of encouraging domestic manufactures, within certain limits, and in reference to certain articles. Without entering into a detailed view of the subject, it may be remarked, that every prudent nation will wish to be independent of other nations, for the necessary articles of food, of raiment, and of defence —and particular considerations applicable to the United States, seem to strengthen the motives to this independence. Besides the articles falling under this description, there may be others, for manufacturing which, natural advantages exist, which require temporary interpositions of bringing them into regular and successful activity. Where the fund of industry is acquired from abroad, and not withdrawn nor withheld from other domestic employments, the case speaks for itself. I will only add, that among the articles of consumption and use, the preference, in many cases, is decided merely by fashion or habit. As far as equality, and still more, where a real superiority is found in the articles manufactured at home, all must be sensible, that it is politic and patriotic to encourage a preference of them as affording a more certain source of supply for every class, and a more certain market for the surplus products of the agricultural class. With these sentiments, I beg you to make my acknowledgments for the mark of distinction conferred on me ; and which I accept from respect for the society, and for its objects, rather than from any hope of being useful as a member. To yourself, I tender my friendly respects.   JAMES MADISON.

respectively, as far as the same was practicable. Your committee, in further pursuance of the duties delegated to them, caused a memorial to be drawn up on behalf of the society, addressed to the congress of the United States, praying for the permanency of the duties imposed by the tariff; the prohibition of cotton goods, manufactured beyond the Cape of Good Hope; such revision and modification of the revenue laws, as might prevent smuggling, false invoices, and other frauds; for a duty of ten per cent. on auction sales, with the exceptions therein stated; for a recommendation to the officers of the army and navy, and to all civil officers, to be clothed in American fabrics; that all public supplies for the army and navy might be of American manufacture; and for such other protection as might place our mercantile and manufacturing interests beyond the reach of foreign influence. It is with pleasure and gratitude your committee have learned, that the war department has given an entire preference to domestic manufacture, and as much is confidently hoped from the department of the navy. Your committee elected a delegate to proceed with the same to the seat of government. Memorials of similar import, were drawn up by the merchants of this city, and by the citizens at large, respectively : and another member of your committee was deputed by the merchants, who also appointed a citizen of New York, then in the city of Washington, to co-operate with the delegates of this society, and cause the above named memorials to be laid before congress, with instruction to solicit and promote the objects of them by their best endeavours. The delegates, on their way to the seat of government, took occasion to explain to certain respectable and influential citizens of Philadelphia and Baltimore, the objects, views, and motives of this society and the nature of their mission; and had the satisfaction, during the short period of one day in each of these cities, to witness the formation of kindred associations, whose proceedings have been long since made public, and which by their intelligence, patriotism, capital, and character, have proved an inappreciable acquisition to the cause of domestic industry. During their residence in the city of Washington, the said delegates, with the aid and co-operation of their colleagues, made a similar and no less successful appeal to the citizens of Washington, Georgetown, and Alexandria; who at a meeting convened by public notice, instituted and organised an association, entitled the Metropolitan Society—the proceedings of which association have also been made public, and their zeal, influence, and respectability, have done much in rousing the spirit of enquiry and promoting the true interests of their country.

The delegates were heard with much attention by the committee of commerce and manufactures of the house of representatives, to whom the above memorials were referred, and that committee reported, in part, by a bill for a continuance of the existing duties upon importation as prayed : and referred the other matters more immediately connected with the revenue to the secretary of the treasury ; whose opinions, we think ourselves authorised to state, were in unison with the prayer of the memorialists. And although the lateness of the session, and the mass of unfinished business, prevented the immediate attainment of the objects desired, yet the wisest and most experienced in and out of congress, (the enlightened members of the committee of the house included,) were of opinion that nothing would be lost by the delay, as every day would offer new manifestations of the public sentiment, and the circumstances of the times be more fully developed, and operate as a law of necessity. It may be important also to state the friendly intimation of the committee itself, that nothing would more conduce to future success, than an authentic collection of facts, tending to show the value of the property embarked in domestic manufactures, the great portion of which was jeopardised by the causes set forth, and the loss and irreparable injury the community must suffer from neglect and indifference to so essential an interest. As that information could be best collected and embodied by the active industry of this and other societies, we mention it as an additional stimulus to exertion, and efforts well combined ; and we trust that all citizens, who prize the lasting independence of their country, who rejoice in its general and individual prospects, will take pride and pleasure in sharing so generous a task., The two delegates who proceeded together from this city, were gratified in returning through the town of Lancaster, in Pennsylvania, to witness the formation of an association of citizens, possessed of every qualification to be useful ; talent, influence, and capital. They were there, as on a former occasion, invited to explain the views and tendency of their mission, and had the pleasure to find the principles of this institution approved, adopted, and promptly acted upon, by their respective fellow-citizens.

" Numerous societies have cotemporaneously, and in rapid succession, arisen throughout the Union ; many have announced themselves by publications full of energy, and *marked* with intelligence. Regular communications have been transmitted to us from the society of Wilmington, in the state of Delaware; Middletown, Hartford and Hatfield, in Connecticut ; Rome and other places, in the state of New York; and we have full authority to say that

Ohio, Kentucky, New Jersey, Virginia and Mississippi, will soon add their strength and weight to the common stock. The most eminent journalists, without regard to political or party relations, have lent their unbought talents; and essays have appeared in their columns, which would do honour to any country or to any cause. The periodical publications, of most acknowledged merit and extensive circulation, have likewise appropriated their labours to the service of their country, and as far as their sphere extended, have put prejudice to flight and ignorance to shame. A pamphlet has been compiled by a judicious and masterly hand in the city of Philadelphia, from the report of the celebrated Alexander Hamilton, made by that statesman in the year 1790, when secretary of the treasury, by order of the house of representatives: this paper has been eminently serviceable, inasmuch as it brings back the judgment of the reader to the natural order of things, before the distorted and disjointed relations of the civilised world had habituated mankind to disturbed and crooked views, and fallacious reliances upon ephemeral hopes and transient speculations. It establishes principles pure and unerring, and has the merit, not only of sage predictions, but of prophecies fulfilled. It is impossible to notice *all* the valuable tracts that patriotic excitement has given birth to, within the short period since *our* institution led the way,—the address of the society of Middletown, in Connecticut, and the report of the committee of Pittsburgh, are documents deserving much attention; and it is to be wished, that a collection of the most of these valuable tracts should be embodied and preserved,—they are so many pledges to the public, of the faith and loyalty of the citizen. The address of the society has been reprinted and circulated in abundance, in so many different forms, and noticed with so much favour, that it is impossible to retire from the *front* of the battle, where we first appeared, without some loss of character. It is our turn *now*, to take the next step in the field of generous emulation, and we should meet more than half way, every overture to correspondence and co-operation. We should acknowledge our obligations for the confidence reposed in us, and for the light of instruction reflected on us. So far your committee have traced their progress in the execution of their trust; so far our bark has adventured with a favouring gale; for although we lament that some of our fabrics must suffer, within this year, irreparable loss, yet we trust that the certainty with which they may count upon the fostering care of the government, will, in general, restore courage, confidence, and credit; and enable the greater part to ride out the storm. The immense losses, at which our markets are glutted, cannot endure for many years; and little can he see, who does not read the rising prosperity of our manufactures, at no distant day, and with it, the power, happiness, and security of this highly favoured land. Your committee, considering the interests of commerce and manufactures as inseparable and identical, cannot close this report without noticing an evil which has grown to an enormous and alarming extent. The present system of auction sales of recent date, in this country, and an anomaly in the history of commerce, has nearly exploded all regular business; and the auctioneer, whose office was formerly subordinate to that of the merchant, is now nearly the only seller; and if *subordinate* to any, merely to a foreign principal. If any sales are now made by the regular trader, they are occasional and supplementary. Commercial education, orderly habits and sober pursuits, honour and good faith, too fatally yield to gambling speculations and fraudulent contrivances. The benefits, if any, that result from this extraordinary monopoly, are daily paid for by the ruin of a class, whose industry was the life of the community, and through them, in a greater or less degree, of the various and numerous descriptions of persons, who without being commercial, depend upon commerce for their support. And if once the merchant disappears from the scene; if the source is once destroyed, the thousand channels which it occupies become dry and fruitless; the proprietor, the mechanic, the artist, the labourer, follow in the train, and must seek elsewhere for subsistence. Already has the public feeling remonstrated against this abuse, but the practice has still prevailed. The established merchant, it has been shown, must ever be unable to compete with the stranger who is charged with no contribution to the public service, subjected to no rent or household expenditure, none of the costs and charges of a commercial establishment, nor taxes, nor impositions, for the support of government. Your committee therefore, refer this subject to the most serious attention of the society, that the most suitable means of investigation may be adopted to substantiate its truth and secure its relief."

The following is an abstract of the address delivered at this meeting:—All who believe that the happiness and independence of our country are connected with the prosperity of our manufactures, must rejoice to see the chief magistrate of the nation honouring with his presence, a society instituted for their protection and encouragement. Knowing that the manufactures of the United States cannot, in their infant state, resist the rivalship of foreign nations without the *patronage* of the government, it is consoling to find, that *he*, to whom the unanimous voice of a free people has committed the highest office, has not only consented to become a *member* of our institution, but that he avails himself of the first opportunity of giving it the countenance and support of his attendance. An incident like this may form a new era in the history of society. In other countries, the influence of the magistrate is felt *only* from the operation of his laws, or through the instrumentality of his subordinate agents: while on the other hand, he derives his information through intermediate channels; but our happy constitution places the people and their officers in such relations to each other that they may have a mutual and direct intercourse; and we now behold the first magistrate of a great nation seeking, at its source, the information which will enable him to know the *wants* and *wishes* of the country. A life devoted to the good of his country, gives us assurance, that it is only necessary to make him *acquainted* with what will promote its happiness, to insure *all* the support which may be derived from his high station. It is now too late to question the advantages of manufactures; all history shows us how much they have contributed to the prosperity of every state where they have been encouraged. Indeed, we find that, in some instances, they have been the source of all the wealth and power of a people. As they have prospered or *declined*, nations have *risen* or *sunk*. Even *wealth*, without manufactures and commerce, has only served to *degrade* a great community, by the introduction of that luxury which was purchased with the produce of inexhaustible mines of gold.

But it is not as they are sources of wealth, that an American must feel the deepest interest in the fate of our manufactures; they more nearly concern us, as they are connected with our independence. For how shall we avoid the influence of foreign nations, while we suffer ourselves to be dependent on them, not only for the luxuries but the necessaries of life? Can that nation feel independent, which has no reliance, but upon foreign lands, for the fabrics which are to clothe her citizens? For manufactured materials which are necessary for the construction of their dwellings, and for the tools with which they are to cultivate their soil? But such has been our situation, (unknown almost to ourselves,) until a jealousy of our prosperity provoked a war, which barred us from the workshops of England; and then we found we were in some measure obliged to rely on a treasonable trade to clothe the armies which met her in the field of battle. The very powder which generated the thunder of our cannon was sometimes British manufacture, and the " striped bunting" may often have been from the same loom with the "cross of St. George," over which it so frequently waved with triumph. Such a state of things could not but awaken the spirit and enterprise of Americans. Amidst the agitation of war, while one part of the population was ranging itself under the military banners of our country, another devoted itself to her interest in another form. Manufactures arose as if by enchantment—on every stream she formed for herself spacious dwellings, and collected in them many thousands who in no other way could contribute to the general weal. Those too young or too old to bear arms, who had no strength for agricultural labours—the female, whose domestic services could be dispensed with in her family, found here a means of individual gain, and of adding to the public prosperity. In a short three years, the produce of our looms rivaled foreign productions, and the nation with which we were contending felt more alarm from the progress of our manufactures, than she did from the success of our arms. But peace came,—while we were at war, the warehouses of England were filled with the produce of the labour, which a loss of market had enabled her to purchase at a depreciated price. The moment intercourse between the two countries was opened, her hoarded stores were thrown upon us, and we were deluged with the manufactures which had been waiting the event. They could be sold without profit, because the foreign manufacturer thought himself fortunate if he could realise the capital which he had been obliged to expend, to support his establishment while there was no sale for his wares. But he was content to bear a loss, because, in the words of an English statesman, "It was well worth while to incur a loss upon the first exportation, in order, by the glut to stifle in the cradle those rising manufactures in the United States, which the war had forced into existence." It would have been surprising indeed, if our infant manufactures, the establishment of which had generally exhausted the capitals of those who embarked in them, could have sustained themselves under such circumstances, without any aid or support from the government, without any means of countervailing the effects of the sacrifices which foreigners were willing to make for their destruction. How were they to maintain themselves? It was impossible,—many of them sunk—but, we hope, to rise again. The attention of the government was too ardently directed, during the war, to other objects, to perceive the policy or necessity of that protection which the manufacturing interest did not then appear to want. But now, that peace will leave our legislators free to consider and provide for the real independence, and perma-

nent prosperity of our country ; now, when we have at the head
of our administration, a citizen, whose presence here this evening
assures us of the interest he takes in the objects of our institution,
we may hope, that American manufactures will receive all the
countenance and support that can be derived from the power of
the government.   Let that power be exerted only so far as to
counteract the policy of foreign nations, and every American may
be gratified in the pride of wearing the produce of the American
soil, manufactured by American hands.   Again shall the surplus
population of our great cities, and the feeble powers of women and
children, find that means of useful and profitable employment
which manufactures alone can afford them.   Again shall the
patriotic and enterprising capitalist find advantage in devoting his
means and mind to objects so calculated to promote the prosperity
and happiness of his country.   And again shall foreign nations
dread to see us rising to that real independence, which we never
can in truth enjoy, while we depend upon any but ourselves for
the first necessaries of life.   The society beg leave to testify to the
chief magistrate of the nation, the high sense they entertain of the
honour he has conferred upon them by his presence at this time,
and sincerely participate in the feelings, which have been so universally manifested on his visit to our city, and most cordially
tender him their best wishes for his health and happiness."

A very favourable impression, in favour of domestic manufactures, was every where manifested at the conclusion of the war of
1812.   Mr. Jefferson had changed his views on the subject, and
expressed himself as follows :—" To be independent for the comforts of life, we must fabricate them ourselves.   We must now
place the manufacturer by the side of the agriculturist.   Experience has taught me that manufactures are as necessary to our
independence as to our comfort."   And Mr. Monroe's message of
December 30th, 1821, was much to the point :—" It cannot be
doubted, that the more complete our internal resources, and the
less dependent we are on foreign powers, for every national as
well as domestic purpose, the greater and more stable will be the
public felicity.   By the increase of domestic manufactures will
the demand for the rude materials at home be increased ; and thus
will the dependence of the several parts of the Union, and the
strength of the Union itself, be proportionably augmented."   It is
said that Mr. Monroe's tour to New England made a very favourable impression on his own mind, with regard to the resources of
the country, for manufacturing operations ; the population of the

eastern section of the Union struck him as altogether adapted to the object.

When the President of the United States arrived at Providence,[*] a committee of arrangements was chosen at Pawtucket, who met Mr. Monroe and his suite, and escorted him to the " Old Mill," where Mr. Slater received him, and exhibited to him his first frames, by which he had spun his first cotton ; explaining to him the present progress of the business, with which the president was highly delighted, and it was considered a proud day for Pawtucket, and more particularly to the individual who had been the means of raising that obscure hamlet to such a flourishing town. The change was remarkable, and it took place during a severe contest with Great Britain. Providence and Rhode Island, in general, received an impetus which has continued to raise that comparatively small state to wealth and importance.[†]

---

[*] *Mr. Monroe's answer to the Providence Address, previous to his visit to Pawtucket.*

TO THE COMMITTEE OF THE TOWN OF PROVIDENCE.

Gentlemen,—I received, with great satisfaction, the address which the citizens of Providence, through their committee, have been pleased to communicate to me. The pleasure of my journey has been greatly enhanced by the uniform kindness and promptitude with which the objects of my visit have been seconded by my fellow citizens. Every where in our country the reflecting mind cannot fail to observe the blessings of a free government. Living under a constitution which secures equal, civil, religious, and political rights to all, it is a great consolation in administering it, that the people have formed so just an estimate of its value ; and from rational conviction, and not from blind prejudices, are sincerely devoted to its preservation. I hope that this just confidence in the stability of our government may continue to increase; and if it does, it cannot fail to produce the happiest effects, by encouraging a love of our country, and an honest zeal to promote its best and permanent interests. Happy shall I be, if my exertions in the public service shall be so far successful, that they may assist the industry and enterprise of my fellow citizens, in increasing the general prosperity.

JAMES MONROE.

The next morning he received all that wished to be presented to him, and then proceeded to view the town, and visit the neighbouring cotton mills, &c. At Pawtucket, he was shown the first frame upon the Arkwright plan, put into operation in this country ; it has been running 27 years, and was erected by Mr. Slater, the present owner of the establishment. After which he took a polite leave of his Rhode Island friends, and passed into Massachusetts.—*Niles's Register.*

[†] While Rhode Island was a colony of Great Britain, Newport was, by far, the place of the greatest importance in the state. Delightfully situated

The North American Review, July 1823, attempts to account for the failures previous to that time, on other grounds than want of protection from government :—" All manufactures, to be prosecuted to great extent and with great profit, require a very complicated and perfect machinery, not to be had without a great disbursement, nor easily for that. Accordingly, the factories which were so imprudently set up at every waterfall in our country, ill provided with machinery, possessed of none of its most costly improvements, and furnished with nothing but of the cheapest and most ordinary construction, though they might be able, during the total exclusion of foreign trade in time of war, or under a system of prohibitory duties, to continue in operation, must necessarily stop under any competition. Many accordingly did stop ; and who that sees them, and knows how they were furnished, and how managed, but rather wonders how they got on? Another cause of the failure of our manufactures was the want of experience. A vast accumulation of individual and traditional observation, of dexterity acquired in practice, and often a secret skill, is necessary to the successful conduct of a factory. More or less of it is necessary in every pursuit. A capitalist who knows nothing of trade, would commit a great error in buying cargoes, chartering ships, and making voyages. We much fear, that, without any depression of manufactures, he would soon become a bankrupt. But yet it is much easier to conduct a voyage than a factory. Good ships can be bought to your hands, cargoes judiciously laid in by the brokers, and experienced captains sent to sea. But to command all the skill, ingenuity, and experience, requisite to erect and conduct a factory, is a far different affair. Hundreds were

for commerce, it received its share of commercial trade, and the *Island* was cultivated as a garden, compared with other parts of New England. The Naragansett country and the greater part of the state was then a mere wilderness. It possessed, however, natural advantages in water falls, not surpassed by any other portion of America, of the same extent of territory. These attracted the capital of manufactures, and a dense population, in beautiful villages and hamlets, now spreads over the greatest part of the country ; the whole scene is changed : schools are introduced, places of worship erected, and the state of improvement is quite equal, if not superior, to any other state or section of the country.

Rhode Island is no longer despised, by her sister states, as ignorant and irreligious, but they are as zealous and devoted to science and literature, and especially the mechanic arts, as either Connecticut or Massachusetts, or any other state in the Union.

erected without a particle of either, and stand the mournful monuments of the improvidence of their undertakers.*"

* The following remarks are in substance the words of Mr. T. Burgess, in his address before the Rhode Island Agricultural Society :—" Forty years ago there was not a spindle wrought by water on this side the Atlantic. Since then, how immense the capital by which spinning and weaving machinery are moved ! How many, how great, how various, the improvements ! The farmers of Flanders erected a statue in honour of him who introduced into their country the culture of the potatoe. What shall the people of New England do for him who first brought us the knowledge of manufacturing cloth, by machinery moved by water ? In England, he would in life, be ornamented with a peerage, in death, lamented by a monument in Westminster Abbey. The name of *Slater* will be remembered as one of our greatest public benefactors. Let not the rich, in his adopted country, envy the products of his labour—his extensive opulence—his fair and elevated character. Let the poor rise up and call him blessed ; for he has introduced a species of industry into our country, which furnishes them with labour, food, clothing, and habitation ; and that, too, when the long and hungry winters of our climate lock up all other employment from them. It may be said, I think, without any fair imputation of national vanity, that the United States have, during the last forty years, made a more respectable progress in manufactures than any other nation or people.

" It is within the personal knowledge of every merchant conversant with the importation of foreign goods, that there was scarcely such a thing heard of as British cotton sheeting before the manufacture of them was attempted in this country. In the year 1787, the cotton used in England was for the following purposes :—Candlewicks, hosiery, silk and linen mixtures, fustians, calicoes, and muslins. Neither sheetings nor shirtings are mentioned in this enumeration.

" The progress of the United States in this manufacture stands unrivaled. It may be attributed to the enterprising spirit, to the industry and ingenuity of our countrymen, aided by the immense advantage of producing the staple at home. This advantage has enabled us to apply the finer kinds of cotton to heavier fabrics than had before been attempted.

" The committee of 1832 have turned their attention with great interest to the influence of the cotton manufacture upon the moral habits and character of the operatives. No class of the working population in this country is more respectable and intelligent or better educated. In the United States, manufactures are dispersed through the country. The operatives are, to a considerable extent, females, who come into the factories, after having acquired their education, who stay there but a few years, and whose liberal wages enable them during those few years to lay up considerable sums of money. In many factories, the proprietors have instituted savings banks, to encourage the economy of the operatives, by enabling them to deposit such portions, however small, of their earnings as they could spare, the proprietors allowing a moderate rate of interest, and being responsible for the safety of the capital. One factory has made a return on this subject to the committee, where the wages amount to about sixty thousand dollars per annum ;

In order to appreciate the value and importance of the extension of the cotton business, it will be necessary to take a retrospective view of the condition the country was found in, at the commencement of the last war with Great Britain.   The abstract which follows was selected from memorials which had reference to this state of things, and to the distresses which followed the peace, in consequence of the influx of foreign goods.   This refers to a most serious state of affairs, connected with manufacturing establishments ; and before we proceed to their progress, it will be proper to revert to that disastrous period of bankruptcy and ruin.   It cannot be better expressed than in the language used by persons who deeply felt the pressure of the calamity.

It is said that hundreds of our ill-fated soldiers perished for want of comfortable clothing in the early part of the war of 1812, when exposed to the inhospitable climate of Canada.   The war found us destitute of the means of supplying ourselves, not merely with blankets for our soldiers, but a vast variety of other articles necessary for our ease and comfort.   Our citizens entered on the business of manufactures with great energy and enterprise ; invested in them many millions of capital—and having, during the thirty months while the war continued, the domestic market secured to them, they succeeded wonderfully.   Never was there a prouder display of the power of industry, than was afforded on this occasion.   Unaided by the expenditure of a single dollar by our government, they attained, in two or three years, a degree of maturity in manufactures, which required centuries in England, France, Prussia, &c.—and cost their governments enormous sums, in the shape of bounties, premiums, drawbacks, with the fostering aid of privileges and immunities bestowed on the undertakers. The supply became commensurate with the demand ; and full confidence was entertained that the government and nation, to whose aid they came forward in time of need, would not abandon

the fund thus laid by has accumulated, in four years, to the sum of twenty six thousand and four hundred dollars, or about eleven per cent. on the whole amount of wages paid.

" It will be observed, that no less than thirty-nine thousand females find employment in the cotton factories of the United States, whose aggregate wages amount to upwards of four millions of dollars anuually. This immense sum, paid for the wages of females, may be considered as so much clear gain to the country. Daughters are emphatically a blessing to the farmer. Many instances have occurred within the personal knowledge of this committee, in which the earnings of daughters have been scrupulously hoarded, to enable them to pay off mortgages on the paternal farm."

them to destruction. Previous to the revolution, they had no competitors in the markets of their country but their fellow-subjects of Great Britain. Now they have competitors from almost every part of Europe, and from the East Indies. The case of the paper-makers in 1818, affords proof of this disadvantage. One half of them in the middle states were ruined—not by the importation of British paper, of which little came to this market, but by French and Italian, with which our markets were deluged for two or three years after the last war. By an investigation ordered in 1819, by the citizens of Philadelphia, it appears so great was the decay of manufacturing industry that, in only thirty out of fifty-six branches of business, there were actually 7728 persons less employed in 1819 than in 1816.

It was reported, "That embarrassment is universal; that the sordid and avaricious are acquiring the sacrificed property of the liberal and industrious; that so much property is exposed to sale under execution, that buyers cannot be had to pay more for it than the fees of office."

All nations and communities have fallen to decay, in proportion as they abandoned, and have prospered in proportion as they protected, the industry of their people. There are great advantages to agriculture from the vicinity of manufacturing establishments. The settlement at Harmony, in the state of Pennsylvania, was begun in 1804, and is probably the only settlement ever made in America in which, from the outset, agriculture and manufactures proceeded hand in hand together. The progress to wealth and prosperity, therefore, has been far beyond any previous example in this country. In 1809, they built a fulling mill, which does a great deal of business for the country, a hemp mill, an oil mill, a grist mill, a brick warehouse, 46 by 36 feet, having a wine cellar completely arched over; and another brick building of the same dimensions. A considerable quantity of land was cleared. The produce of this year was 6000 bushels of Indian corn; 4500 bushels of wheat; and they distilled 1600 bushels of rye. In 1810, a wool-carding machine and two spinning jennies were erected, for the fabrication of broad cloth from the wool of merino sheep. A frame barn was built, 100 feet long, and a brick house built, to accommodate 20 weavers' looms. In the wool loft, eight or ten women were employed in teazing and sorting the wool for the carding machine, which is at a distance on the creek. From thence the roves are brought to the spinning house in the town, where we found two roving billies and six spinning jennies at work. They were principally wrought by young girls, and they appeared perfectly happy, singing church music most melodiously. In the weaving house, sixteen looms were at work, besides several warpers and winders. We there saw the soap and candle works; the dye works; shearing and dressing works; the turners, carpenters, and machine makers; and we were conducted through the warehouses, which we found plentifully stored with commodities;— among others 450 pieces of broad and narrow cloth, part of it merino wool, and of as good a fabric as any that ever was made in England. In 1813 they could sell the best broad cloth, as fast as made, at ten dollars per yard. The society in 1811 consisted of about 800 persons, and the operative members as follows :— one hundred farmers, three shepherds, ten masons, three stonecutters, three brick-makers, ten carpenters, two sawyers, ten smiths, two wagon makers, three turners, two nailers, seven coopers, three rope makers, ten shoemakers, two saddlers, three tanners, seven tailors, one soap boiler, one brewer, four distillers, one gardener, two grist millers, two oil millers, one butcher, six joiners, six dyers, dressers, shearers, &c., one fuller, two hatters, two potters, two warpers, seventeen weavers, two carders, eight spinners, one rover, one minister of religion, one schoolmaster, one doctor, one storekeeper with two assistants, and one tavern keeper with one assistant. The original stock in 1804, was $20,000, which was expended in the purchase of land, and in supporting themselves till they commenced their operations. And in 1811, their property amounted to the sum of $220,000. To this delightful picture of the effects of a judicious distribution of industry, the statesman ought to direct his eyes steadily. It holds out a most instructive lesson on the true policy to promote human happiness, and to advance the wealth, power, and resources of nations. Hundreds of places might be mentioned, where the establishment of manufactories, by affording an extensive and advantageous market to the farmer, doubled and trebled the price of the lands in their neighbourhood—and increased in an equal degree the comforts and prosperity of the farmers.

A nation peopled only by farmers, must be a region of indolence and misery. If the soil is naturally fertile, little labour will produce abundance; but for want of exercise even that little labour will be burdensome and often neglected. Want will be felt in the midst of abundance; and the human mind be abased nearly to the same degree with the beasts that graze in the field. If the region is more barren, the inhabitants will be obliged to become somewhat more industrious, and therefore more happy. Those therefore who wish to make agriculture flourish in any country, can have no hope of succeeding in the attempt but by bringing commerce and manufactures to her aid; which by taking from the farmer his superfluous produce, gives spirit to his operations, and life and activity to his mind. Without this stimulus to activity, in vain do we use arguments to rouse the sluggish inhabit· ants. In vain do we discover that the earth is capable of producing the most luxuriant harvests with little labour. Our own abundant crops are produced as undeniable proofs of this in vain. But place a manufacturer in the neighbourhood, who will buy every little article that the farmer can bring to market, and he will soon become industrious—the most barren fields will become covered with some useful produce. Instead of listless vagabonds, unfit for any service, the country will abound with a hardy and robust race of men. When one nation receives only luxuries from another, and pays for them in the necessaries of life, or specie, or in raw materials which would find employment for its own people, commerce is pernicious; but when conducted on fair and reciprocal terms, it tends to civilise, and increase the comforts of the great family of mankind. Suppose that England were to furnish France with her raw wool, lead, tin, iron, flax and hemp, and to receive in return merino shawls, silks, satins, pearl necklaces, diamond watches, &c.—the most devoted advocate for commerce would allow this species of it to be extremely pernicious. And it is as absurd as impolitic, and as cruel to our citizens, who can manufacture cotton goods for us, to export raw cotton and receive cambrics and muslins in return, as it would be for England to export her wool, and import her woollen manufactures.

The war of 1812 was closed under the most favourable auspices. The country was every where prosperous. Inestimable manufacturing establishments, in which probably 60,000,000 of dollars were invested, were spread over the face of the land, and diffusing happiness among thousands of industrious people. No man, woman, or child, able and willing to work, was unemployed. With almost every possible variety of soil and climate—and likewise with the three greatest staples in the world—cotton, wool, and iron; the first, to an extent commensurate with our utmost wants, and a capacity to produce the other two—a sound policy would have rendered us more independent, probably, of foreign supplies, for all the comforts of life, than any other nation whatever.

Peace, nevertheless, was fraught with destruction to the hopes and happiness of a considerable portion of the manufacturers. The double duties had been imposed with a limitation to one year after the close of the war. And a tariff as a substitute was prepared by the secretary of the treasury, with duties fixed at the minimum rates which he thought calculated to afford them protection. On many of them, these rates were insufficient. Yet had his tariff been adopted, it would probably have saved the country forty or fifty millions of dollars, and prevented a large portion of the deep distress that pervaded the land, and which drove legislative bodies to the desperate measure of suspending the course of justice. But a deep-rooted jealousy of manufacturers was entertained by many members of congress, on the ground of imputed extortion during the war; and the old hacknied themes of " taxing the many for the benefit of the few,"—the country not being ripe for manufactures—wages being too high—the immensity of our back lands, &c. were still regarded as unanswerable arguments. In consequence of the combined operation of these causes, the rates were reduced on most of the leading articles, ten, fifteen, and in some cases, thirty per cent. Every per cent. reduced was regarded, by many of the members of congress, as so much clear gain to the country. Some of them appeared to consider manufactures as a sort of common enemy, with whom no terms ought to be observed. Some of them held the broad doctrine, that every dollar paid as duty or bounty to encourage manufactures, is a dollar robbed out of the pockets of the farmers and planters.

From year to year since that time, ruin spread among the manufacturers. A large portion of them have been reduced to bankruptcy, from ease and affluence. Most of them had entered into the business during the war, under an impression, as I have already stated, that there was a sort of implied engagement on the part of the government that, having been found so useful in time of need, they would not be allowed to be crushed afterwards. To what extent there was any foundation for this idea, I am unable to decide. Suffice it to say, that all the calculations predicted on it were wholly and lamentably disappointed. The strong arm of government, which alone could save them from the overwhelming influx of foreign manufactures, by which they were destroyed, was not interposed in their behalf. Noble establishments, the pride and ornament of the country, which might have been rendered sources of incalculable public and private wealth, and which Edward III., Henry IV., Frederic the Great, and Catherine II. would have saved at the expense of millions, if necessary, were mouldering to ruins. And to crown the whole, millions of capital which had every claim to the protection of government, had become a dead and heavy loss to the proprietors. At every stage of this awful progress, the devoted sufferers not only appealed to the justice, but threw themselves on the mercy, of their representatives. The utmost powers of eloquence were exhausted in those appeals, some of which may be ranked among the proudest monuments of human talents. In the second session of the fourteenth congress, 1816–17, there were above forty memorials presented to the house of representatives from manufacturers in different parts of the United States, and some of them, particularly that from Pittsburg, fraught with tales of ruin and destruction, that would have softened the heart of a Herod. *Not one of them was ever read in the house!* The following are a few short specimens of the facts and reasonings they placed before the eyes of congress :—

The Philadelphia memorial holds this language :—" We regard with the most serious concern the critical and dangerous situation in which our manufactures are placed by the recent extravagant importations of rival articles, which, owing to the great surplus of them, and to the pressure of money, are in many cases sold at such reduced prices, as to render it impossible for our manufactures to compete with them. We believe that with the interests of the manufacturers are connected the best interests of the nation—and that if the manufactures of the country are deprived of that support from the legislature of the United States, to which we think they are fairly entitled, the evil will be felt not by us merely, but by the whole nation; as it will produce the inevitable consequence of an unfavourable balance of trade, whereby our country will be impoverished, and rendered tributary to foreign powers, whose interest are in direct hostility with ours."

The Pittsburg memorial says :—" The committee have found that the manufacture of cottons, woollens, flint, glass, and the finer articles of iron, has lately suffered the most alarming depression. Some branches which have been several years in operation, have been destroyed or partially suspended; and others, of a more recent growth, annihilated before they were completely in operation. The tide of importation has inundated our country with foreign goods. Some of the most valuable and enterprising citizens have been subjected to enormous losses, and others overwhelmed with bankruptcy and ruin. The pressure of war was less fatal to the hopes of enterprise and industry, than a general peace with the calamities arising from the present state of our foreign trade. It was confidently believed, that the destinies of the United States would no longer depend on the jealousy and caprice of foreign governments, and that our national freedom

and welfare were fixed on the solid basis of our intrinsic means
and energies.   But these were ' airy dreams;' a peace was concluded with England, and in a few months we were prostrate at
her feet.   The manufacturers appealed to the general government
for the adoption of measures that might enable them to resist the
torrent that was sweeping away the fruits of their capital and
industry.   Their complaints were heard with a concern which
seemed a pledge for the return of better days.   The tariff of duties,
established at the last session of congress, and the history of the
present year, will demonstrate the falsity of their expectations.
England never suffered a foreign government, or a combination
of foreign capitalists, by glutting her own market, to crush in the
cradle any branch of her domestic industry.   She never regarded
with a cold indifference the ruin of thousands of her industrious
people, by the competition of foreigners.   The bare avowal of
such an attempt would have incurred the indignant resistance of
the whole body of the nation, and met the frowns, if not the
instant vengeance of the government.   The consequences of this
policy in England are well known ; her manufactures have
become a source of wealth incalculable; the treasures of Spanish
America are poured into her lap ; her commerce is spread over
every ocean, and, with a population comparatively small, she is
the terror and the spoiler of Europe.   Take from England her
manufactures, and the fountains of her wealth would be broken
up ; her pre-eminence among nations would be lost for ever.   For
a speedy redress of such pressing evils, we look to the government
of the Union.   Will they uphold the sinking manufactures of the
country, or will they not ?   Are their late assurances of aid and
protection forgotten with the crisis that gave them birth ?   Let
them realise the hopes of the country, and act with decision
before it be too late.   In the United States we have the knowledge of the labour-saving machinery, the raw material, and provisions cheaper than in Britain ; but the overgrown capital of the
British manufacturer, and the dexterity acquired by long experience, make a considerable time and heavy duties necessary for
our protection.   We have beaten England out of our markets in
hats, boots, and all manufactures of leather ; we are very much
her superior in ship-building ; these are all the work of the hands,
where labour-saving machinery gives no aid ; so that her superiority over us, in manufactures, consists more in the excellence
and nicety of the labour-saving machinery, than in the wages of
of labour.   With all their jealousy and restrictions upon the
emigration of workmen, the distresses and misfortunes of Eng-

land will, by due encouragement, send much of her skill and knowledge to our shores; let us be ready to take full benefit of such events, as England herself did when despotic laws in Germany, and other parts of Europe, drove their manufacturers into Britain, which laid the foundation of her present eminence. That the cotton trade and manufacture is a concern of vast importance, and even of leading interest to the country is a truth, your memorialists conceive, too palpable to be denied or doubted. Were not our own constant observation and daily experience sufficient to establish it, the prodigious exertions of our ever-vigilant and indefatigable rival, directed against this particular interest, would place the matter beyond a question. For where a judicious and enterprising opponent (as England undoubtedly is in this respect) directs her strongest engines of hostility, we have reason to conclude there lies our vital and most important concerns.

" This consideration is coming home to us with more and more force; and the cotton planter, as well as the manufacturer, must have before this time discovered the alarming fact, that our great rival has become possessed of both our plants and seeds of cotton, which she is employing all her vast means to propagate in the East Indies and other British possessions, with an energy and success which threaten the most alarming consequences. When your memorialists consider that the article thus jeoparded is the great staple of the country, they cannot but hope the people and their representatives will be generally convinced that it is not the interest of individuals alone that is at stake, but that of the whole community. An appeal is made to the equity, to the patriotism of the southern statesman; his aid and co-operation is invoked for the relief of the suffering manufactures of the northern and middle states. In the interior of the United States, few articles can be raised which will bear a distant transportation; products much more valuable, when the grower and consumer are near each other, are therefore excluded from cultivation. A dependence on foreign markets, in the most prosperous times, necessarily restricts the labours of agriculture to a very few objects; a careless, decrepit, and unprofitable cultivation is the known result. The propriety of these observatione may, in some degree, be illustrated by the difference in value between the land in the vicinity of a large town, and at a greater distance from it. The labour which produces the greatest quantity of subsistence is bestowed in the culture of articles too cumbrous for transportation; and in general, a farm which will subsist fifty persons in its vicinity, would not subsist the fifth of that number three hundred miles off. If the value of land be so much enhanced by the proximity of a market, and so rapidly diminished by the distance of transportation, the introduction of manufactories, and the creation of an interior market, ought to be regarded as peculiarly auspicious to the interests of agriculturists.   Confining our views to the western country, we might emphatically ask, with what exportable commodities shall we restore the balance of trade, now fast accumulating against us?   How arrest the incessant drain of capital? Our manufactures are perishing around us, and already millions have escaped never to return."

The Oneida Memorial says :—" That the above county contains a greater number of manufacturing establishments, of cotton and woollen, than any other county in the state, there being invested in said establishments at least $ 600,000.   That although the utmost efforts have been made by the proprietors to sustain those establishments, their efforts have proved fruitless, and more than three fourths of the factories remain, necessarily, closed ; some of the proprietors being wholly ruined, and others struggling under the greatest embarrassment.   In this alarming situation, we beg leave to make a last appeal to the congress of the United States.   While we make this appeal, our present and extensive embarrassments in most of the great departments of industry, as well as the peculiar difficulty in affording immediate relief to manufacturers, are fully seen and appreciated ; yet your petitioners cannot believe that the legislature of the Union will remain an indifferent spectator of the wide-spread ruin of their fellow citizens, and look on and see a great branch of industry, of the utmost importance in every community, prostrated under circumstances fatal to all future attempts at revival, without a further effort for relief.   We would not magnify the subject which we now present to congress, beyond its just merits, when we state it to be one of the utmost importance to the future interests and welfare of the United States.   It is objected that the entire industry of the country may be most profitably exerted in clearing and cultivating our extended vacant lands.   But what does it avail the farmer, when neither in the nation from which he purchases his goods, or elsewhere, can he find a market for his abundant crops !   Besides, the diversion of labour from agriculture to manufactures, is scarcely perceptible.   Five or six adults, with the aid of children, will manage a cotton manufactory of two thousand spindles."

I have found but few letters of Mr. Slater's, and these are chiefly to his agents on business ; extracts from some of them will serve to show his views of punctuality and correctness in all his concerns; some of them evince also a shrewdness of observation, and a dry humour, which were characteristic of the man, and of his communications. It was a peculiar trait in him to dislike change, either in his agents or any persons in his employment. He knew when he was well served, and, when persons did his business well, no flattering inducement would cause him to employ new persons. Some of his agents in Salem, Boston, New York, Philadelphia and Baltimore, became the first houses in those cities. And some, who had been clerks in his employment, became first rate men of business. Whether as president of the bank in Pawtucket, or in the payment of a labourer, there was the same exactness and integrity. Few men ever conducted so much business, with so much ease, and with so much good-will from those connected with him, as Mr. Slater. He had no tricks, no double dealing, all was open, fair and honourable.*

Mr. Elijah Waring.

N. PROVIDENCE, February 23d, 1814.

Dear Sir,—Your esteemed favour, under date of December 29th last, and the contents of which, were duly received. I have delayed answering it some time in order to more fully make up my mind relative to some parts of the subject under consideration. Your observations respecting a permanent agent fully coincides with my ideas and wishes in that part, although not suggested to you in mine of the 25th. Placing full reliance on your extensive experience and knowledge in that point, I did not then, or now, conceive it necessary to enter into a specification of the permanency of an agent, &c. &c. In regard to the amount I shall have for the Philadelphia market, from the Oxford factory, I presume, during one year from this time, I shall have about one hundred thousand dollars for sale, more than half of which I should wish to send to Philadelphia. At times, Almy and Brown, and myself, have conversation on the subject of my vending one third part

---

* His connection with Almy and Brown, who were of the Society of Friends, fastened him in the principles of economy and utility. Few men, except those who have been personally engaged in business, know the trials and perplexities which men of business endure; and there is not always sufficient allowance made for their irritable feelings, and for the difficulties in which they are involved. Mr. Slater, in early life, was sometimes severe in his expressions. He was always silent with regard to his business, and disliked that his men should speak of where he was going, or of what he was about; he also disliked any one who was inquisitive or prying about his affairs, and he never interfered with other people's matters. Some of his men had mentioned in the village, that Mr. Slater was going to Boston next morning; he found that they had spoken of it: he went to the mill, in some anger, and asked them if they could not keep their insides from dropping out; alluding to the old woman, who parted with a secret entrusted to her, for fear of losing more important parts of her existence.

of the yarn and goods made here, and my quarter part of the yarn and goods at Smithfield factories. In that case an agent may reasonably calculate on being supplied with more than a hundred thousand dollars annually, besides an additional amount arising from an increase of machinery. But in case of an alteration in sales of goods made here, and at Smithfield factories, I conceive you would claim a right of selling what were sent to the Philadelphia market, and I should not feel justified in curtailing your present supplies, &c. Samuel Haydock is now selling goods for four or five companies. Do Almy & Brown fully supply you with goods to meet all the calls for them ? From your last orders to them, I fear they will not be competent to meet the whole of them this year.

Provided you cannot, without taking too much trouble, meet with an agent that will undertake the agency for me, who is likely to continue in the business for me, during *storms* and *calms*, I shall be induced to consign the goods to Messrs. Gilman & Annison, who have strongly solicited an agency of my business. They are doubtless good men, but I fear they will desert from selling American goods, (should commerce revive) to selling English, which desertion would not be a pleasant thing to me. On the receipt of this, I will thank you to give me your candid opinion on the foregoing points ; and any new idea that may occur to you, you will have the goodness to communicate it, which will be gratefully received by yours, &c.   SAMUEL SLATER.

———

To Jeremiah Brown, Philadelphia.

The cotton business now appears very gloomy and I fear will continue. Many establishments are stopped. And many have already done it of their own accord, and many are daily stopping from mere necessity, they being indebted to a much larger amount, than every thing they possessed would bring under the *hammer.* I hope you will do the best you can for the Oxford companies, in obtaining fair prices for them, as to keep them from being daily harassed with sheriffs, who have stripped many of every thing they were possessed of.*

———

* The annexed schedule of Mr. Slater's estate in 1817, will serve to show the progress of his business.

"I own the house, &c., in which I live in Pawtucket, one other house, and six house lots, one house and land in Seekonk, and third part of the old factory, so called, counting fifteen hundred spindles, water privilege, stores, and five dwelling houses ; and one third part of three farms in Attleborough and Saybrook. One house and lots near Hartford, also one quarter part of several buildings and lots in Providence. One quarter of a brick house in Boston, one quarter of the estate in Smithfield, containing two cotton factories, with between five and six thousand spindles, together with three water privileges, about thirty-five good houses and twelve hundred acres of land. My estate in Oxford, Mass., consisting of one cotton factory of two thousand spindles, one woollen establishment, grist and saw mill, sixteeen dwelling houses and seven hundred acres of land. Also one handsome farm in Pelham, and a right in six mortgaged estates, to the amount of ten thousand dollars, which I shall have to hold."

Almost every manufacturer is now shivering in the wind, and when and where the present distress among them all will stop, time alone will unfold.

Flour will pay the exchange.

A great many of the establishments for spinning cotton in this section of the country are stopping, either all or a part. I hope goods will command a higher price next month than they now do.

NEW PROVIDENCE, August 14th, 1816.

J. & M. Brown.

Gentlemen,—Your favour under date of the 8th inst. was duly received, covering a bill of $2100 in specie, per the sloop Dove, which arrived to day about noon.

The Lively has not yet made her appearance here. I wish she had the *wings* of the *Dove.* I told the owners yesterday, that if she was my vessel I would change her name. Several persons to-day, on seeing the Dove arrive, and learning that she had not seen or heard any thing from the Lively, were induced to insure. However, I hope she will still arrive safe and sound.

N. B. Please give me, in your next, a price current of specie and cotton goods.*

June 11*th*, 1816.—The box of specie has arrived, and on counting it there was twenty-five cents over.

In consequence of almost all the cotton factories being stopped in this country, the general idea is, that cotton goods, and yarn, too, will soon advance; under these considerations, will it be advisable to force sales?

Will thank you to make an arrangement with some of your merchant tailors, to supply the Oxford mills with a few thousand yards good listing, and less than one inch wide; the general price when money was plenty, and also when the rope-makers wanted many of them, was about a cent per yard, hope they are no higher now. As many of the tailors have them wound into large balls (the inside of which are very poor,) I fear it will not answer to take them in that state without examining them, unless your tailors are much honester than ours here.

December 3*d*, 1817.—I left New York on Friday morning last, and arrived here in about thirty-five hours with my family all in good health. Request Daniel Large to send me five tons of his best pig iron, on trial, that is suitable to make soft iron in an air furnace.

Feb. 7*th*, 1816.—As soon as you can procure some specie or *good* drafts,

---

* *Extract of a letter from Moses Brown at Providence, to Jeremiah Brown of Philadelphia.*

Dear Brother,—I have already seen several of our friends, and last evening had the pleasure of introducing to friend Samuel Slater, his brother, whom he had not seen for thirty years. He arrived four days ago at New York, from Liverpool, and accidentally we both met in the packet. Samuel did not recognise his brother, as I introduced him as a person recently arrived from Derbyshire, England, and who knew his friends there. He does not resemble Samuel, but has a very striking resemblance to John. [This meeting was like the one formerly noticed.]

at a fair discount, you will forward either, so as to enable us to keep our *chins above water.*

Nov. 5th, 1817.—My brother and I have agreed to weigh our sheet anchor to-morrow for Philadelphia and Baltimore. Accommodate Mr. Dean with $300.

June 6th, 1816. The box of specie has not arrived. The copperas has arrived, and on examining it, find a part of it *real good English* copperas, and a part of it very poor American. One of the casks was entirely new, which I condemned before it was opened, and it turned out to be poor. Business is very poor here; how is it in Philadelphia?

March 30th, 1818.—I am extremely sorry that the mother bank is under the necessity of suspending giving drafts on the branches, especially to those who make their deposits with her. The alteration will seriously affect many of the manufacturers in New England. In short, I do not see how I shall get along, unless you obtain the specie for me, as post notes will be shortly one or two per cent. below par, at least, if I am under the necessity of going to a broker to get them transmuted into our money.

May 8th, 1818.—Mr. Tyson wrote you a few days past of my serious disaster; my many pains and bruises round my head and body are rather subsiding; so that I think I can truly say that my shattered leg is the most painful. *By S. Slater, Jun.*

April 21st, 1818.—The Providence iron foundry is greatly in want of pig iron. Hope the first lot is under way. If you can obtain them for something less than forty-five dollars, you will add ten tons more.

March 19th, 1816.—As respects goods, I sincerely hope that a very considerable quantity will be sent you from Oxford this season, notwithstanding a part of the spindles are motionless, as is the case almost every where. Goods cannot be made now from the high priced cotton, without a loss to the manufacturers, therefore it behoves every consignee to sell the goods for as much as they will possibly command. I wrote to S. & T. about 10 days past, to forward you every piece of coloured goods they had on hand. If you can purchase one or two tons of good English copperas at $2,75 or nearly that, you will forward it.

April 27, 1818.—A Providence friend of mine showed me a letter to day which he had recently received from his correspondent in Philadelphia, stating that you, he, and others, could not obtain more than about thirty cents for good ginghams, on a credit of from four to six months. If the advice is correct, I fear we shall all be bankrupted in a heap. Do advise me in your next whether or not your market is so squally.

Sept. 17, 1816.—With respect to crediting western merchants, in lieu of an acceptance in the city of Philadelphia—If some of them should appear to buy goods on credit, on note or book account, and you are fully satisfied from personal knowledge of them, or, 'from *good* references, that they are actually trustworthy, then I conceive it would be advisable to credit some of them, but, still, don't lose sight of obtaining acceptances in your city when practicable. As almost every one here is of opinion that Philadelphia money will still improve, therefore, you will purchase only about 1500 dollars specie until further advised, which you will forward by first packet. As respects the Lively being a dull sailer, I have been of the opinion, that the old captain of her was a duller sailor than she. Now there being a new captain, probably she will get along somewhat faster. In regard to sending you some coarse twist from here, (Pawtucket,) it is not practicable, having scarcely a pound on hand. I hope you will receive some of it from Oxford before long. Can you obtain a good, neat thermometer for me in Philadelphia, for about four dollars? if you can, please forward one.

Dec. 23, 1817.—Four cases of goods from Oxford arrived in Providence, the middle of last week, and my young man wrote he should send down two more cases in a day or two—all of which I have engaged to go by way of New York, so that they may be in Philadelphia seasonably for the spring sales. The household goods arrived in Providence per the Dove, on Friday last, in excellent order, which I attribute to your particular care in having them well packed, for which, and many other like favours, I consider myself greatly indebted to you, which I hope a long life will enable me to discharge, and in the interim, remain with every respect your assured friend.

May 19, 1818.—In consequence of Sea Island cotton being seventy-five cents per pound, Almy & Brown and myself have concluded that threads, and all first quality yarns, must command higher prices, or it will not be wisdom in us to make them. I am sorry that your J. B. is going into the western states this summer, because, I fear, it will deprive me of seeing either of you in New England this season. With respect to my own bodily infirmities, I ought to rejoice and be thankful, that I am getting along, beyond all human calculations. You will please to remit as usual, money still being a cash article and in demand.

May 14, 1818.—I received yours of the 8th inst. this day, it took a trip by the way of Taunton.

I remain still flat on my back, day and night, attended with considerable pain, but am thankful I am still favoured to remain in the land of the living. I have been blessed with good medical aid, and also with a kind and very attentive nurse, (Mrs. Slater,) which tends very much to mitigate pain.

I hope a few more solitary weeks will favour me with a peep at the sun at least. It is a sad misfortune to me, as it would be to any other person. However, I hope I bear it with all the resignation and fortitude a rational man ought to do. Hoping I may contine to be favoured, gaining slowly, until I am once more restored, &c.   *By Samuel Slater, Jr.*

Taking a retrospective view of the state of society, previous to the American revolution, with regard to English manufactures, will enable us to form a better estimate of the progress which we have made here. Sixty years since, the cotton establishments in England were but in embryo. Their commencement was small and imperfect, and the use of linen was so prevalent, and so esteemed, that it retarded the consumption of the cotton article, especially at *home ;* where habits and fashion are not very easily withstood or overcome. Arkwright did for Old England, in a certain degree, what Slater has done for America, in a much more extensive, and vastly more important situation.*

* As soon as the business increased, new difficulties arose; the operatives began by demanding exorbitant wages, which Mr. Slater resisted, against

A memoir of Slater must necessarily include a history of the rise and progress of our manufacturing establishments: for it is with them that his whole life has been connected. He embarked himself, body, soul, and spirit, in this enterprise; and he was so absorbed in his object that every other consideration was comparatively neglected. The extent of Mr. Slater's business, and the fact that he attended to so much of it himself, rendered it impossible to divide his time for other considerations.

This devotion to business prevented much attention being paid to literature or politics. The Romans held trade in a very low estimation; they prohibited men of birth and rank from engaging in commerce, of which the code speaks contemptuously; and Cicero says, it was not fitting that the same people should be both the *porters* and the masters of the world. This kind of contempt was common in this country previous to 1812. We had better have our "*workshops*" in Europe, was the language of some of our wiseacres: forgetting that wealth consists of the savings of industry, after supplying immediate demands. An instinct, prompting the human being, after his appetites of hunger and thirst are appeased, and his person protected against the elements of heaven, to labour from the mere delight of accumulating; and to the ceaseless industry which this instinct produces, is to be ascribed the wealth with which civilised man is every where surrounded. It prompts the husbandman, the artisan, the manufacturer, the merchant, to activity in their several vocations; it is one of the sources, when properly directed, of the comforts and elegances of life. The prodigal spends his last shilling and leaves no trace behind him. The laborious artisan, who consumes only half the produce of his labour, leaves the other half as a contribution to the stock of national capital, to maintain and set in motion the industry of generations yet unborn.   These, if animated by the same spirit, will leave it with new accessions, and so keep increasing.[*]

He spent nothing for show and appearance in his buildings;

the advice of others; and in this he was right, for by submitting to unreasonable demands, he would only have given them occasion to call for still greater. He therefore took his stand, and risked the consequences. They stole his patterns and models, and set up for themselves, but generally failed.

In the management of help, and establishing order and discipline, Mr. Slater showed great abilities, and he could arrange his affairs easier than any other person.

[*] "You have heard of the hills of Berkshire, (Mass.); you have heard of the beautiful and classic stream of the Housatonic; of the Hoosac, studded

utility and durability he considered all-important. The enlargement of his business called forth all his business talents. His
commanding and penetrating eye was formed, by nature, for the
best of government; and it is astonishing what effect even his look
had, on those who waited his orders and direction. It was not
the look of pride, contempt, or disdain : he never appeared to feel
above the poorest of his help. It was the indication of a superior
judgment and experience, in whatever business he undertook :
this caused every one to be obedient to his directions. No one
could be conceited enough to suppose that they knew better than
he did ; for every one had been taught by him : this was what
commanded respect, and enabled him to carry on his affairs
without difficulties and tumults. His dislike of all ostentation
and extravagance was excessive ; and he was always severe and
sarcastic upon the young men in his employment who spent all
their earnings in dress and follies.

Those who were beginning in business, he cautioned against
building before they had counted the cost ; and the idea of failure
impressed him with horror. He therefore disapproved of a loose
way of doing business ; and foretold the consequences which, unhappily, proved not to be mere groundless forebodings, for nearly
all failed round him. Young Lord Bolingbroke and Mr. Sheldon,
two English gentlemen, who were in Providence about this time,
visited Mr. Slater, and recognised in him the son of one of
the respectable yeomanry of Derbyshire. These young men
brought with them a purse of gold, of *ten thousand guineas* each,
and spent the whole in a few years ; while Slater, by his persevering industry, realised a fortune.

It is of all things, that which most effectually conduces to a
flourishing state of agriculture. The uniform appearance of an
abundance of specie, as the concomitant of a flourishing state of
manufactures, and of the reverse, where they do not prevail,
afford a strong presumption of their favourable operation upon the
wealth of a country. Not only the wealth, but the independence
and security of a country, appear to be materially connected with

with thriving manufacturing villages. There was a time, not long since,
when the temptations of more fertile regions appeared so great, that it
seemed that those hills must be deserted; that those streams must be left to
flow on in solitude; but then came the beneficial influence of the policy of
protection to American industry, and then was developed, along our beautiful
streams, and among our wild waterfalls, a power which, by the application
of native industry, has clothed our hills with plenty, and placed our young
men beyond the reach of the temptations of the fertile west."—*Rockwell.*

the prosperity of manufactures. Every nation, with a view to these great objects, ought to endeavour to possess within itself all the essentials of national supply. These comprise the means of subsistence, habitation, clothing and defence. Considering a monopoly of the domestic market to its own manufactures as the reigning policy of manufacturing nations, a similar policy on the part of the United States, in every proper instance, is dictated, it might almost be said by the principles of distributive justice— certainly by the duty of securing to their own citizens a reciprocity of advantages. Whatever this country has suffered or may suffer, by a contrary policy, is justly attributable to a disregard of these maxims, which comprise the fundamental principles of political economy. " If Europe will not take from us the products of our soil, on terms consistent with our interest, the natural remedy is, to contract as fast as possible our wants of her."[*]

In order to estimate correctly the progress of American manufactures, we must keep in mind the state of the English, only sixty years since. Their progress was slow for many centuries, and it is only within the last fifty years, that they have arisen to such perfection. A reference to their history will not be misplaced, but will be read with much interest.

The following is from Baines's History of the Cotton Manufacture :—

" The cotton manufacture arose in this country at a critical period of our history. England had just lost her American colonies, but that loss was more than compensated by this new source of prosperity springing up at home. The genius of our mechanics repaired the errors of our statesmen. In the long and fearful struggle which followed the French revolution, this country was mainly supported by its commerce ; and the largest, though the newest branch of that commerce, was furnished by the cotton manufacture. To Arkwright and Watt England is far more indebted for her triumphs, than to Nelson and Wellington. Without the means supplied by her flourishing manufactures and trade,

* Paterson, in New Jersey, at the close of the war, exhibited an appearance of prosperity and happiness scarcely exceeded in the world. But in 1822, it was said, there was not a single cotton establishment in the place, then in the possession of the original proprietors, as they had been almost universally ruined ! This is a fact, the force of which fifty columns of newspaper essays and paragraphs, and fifty speeches of ten hours each, could not obviate. One manufactory in that town, which cost $100,000, has been sold for $19,000. What masses of misery, therefore, followed the want of sufficient protection !

the country could not have borne up under a conflict so prolonged and exhausting.   In the article of cottons alone, the exports
amounted, between 1793 and 1815, to £250,000,000. From 1816
to 1833 inclusive, the declared value of the cotton exports was
£306,167,518. Within the last half century, cottons to the enormous
value of £570,000,000 have been sent from this country to foreign
markets.   It is obvious that a trade of this magnitude must have
contributed largely to sustain the revenue, to prevent the national
resources from being intolerably oppressed by taxation.   The
question has been much canvassed, whether England is likely to
maintain the superiority she has gained among the nations of the
world, in regard to the cotton manufacture. There are those who
prognosticate that she has already reached the highest point, and
is destined rapidly to decline from it.   These individuals apprehend a competition too formidable to be withstood, on the part of
several foreign nations :—from the United States of America,
where the spinning machinery is equal to that of England, where
there are thousands of English workmen, where ingenuity and
enterprise eminently mark the national character, and where the
finest cotton is grown within the States themselves; from Belgium,
Switzerland, and other countries of Europe, where the manufacture exists, and is rapidly extending, and where labour is lower
priced than in England ; and from the East Indies, where one or
two spinning mills have been established, and where in weaving,
if not in spinning, the natives are supposed to have a great advantage, from their having so long been habituated to the employment,
and from the excessively low rate of wages they require.

  " It is true, that each of these countries has, in some respects, an
advantage over England.   It is true that the cotton manufacture
has acquired a great extent in the United States, and is advancing
rapidly in Germany and Switzerland.   It would be infatuation to
trifle with the safety of a manufacture which affords subsistence
to a million and a half of our population. Yet we see no ground
for apprehending that England will lose her present manufacturing pre-eminence. All the natural and political causes which
originally made this a great manufacturing and commercial nation remain unimpaired.   There are advantages derived from the
established ascendency of our manufacturers, the importance of
which it would be difficult to over-estimate. Our master manufacturers, engineers, and artisans, are more intelligent, skilful and
enterprising than those of any other country ; and the extraordinary inventions they have already made, and their familiarity with
all the principles and details of the business, will not only enable

them to perfect the processes already in use, but can hardly fail to lead to the discovery of others. Our establishments for spinning, weaving, printing, bleaching, &c., are infinitely more complete and perfect than any that exist elsewhere ; the division of labour in them is carried to an incomparably greater extent ; the work-men are trained from infancy to industrious habits, and have attained that peculiar dexterity and sleight of hand in the perform-ance of their separate tasks, that can only be acquired by long and unremitting application to the same employment. Another ad-vantage consists in the almost unlimited amount of capital at the disposal of the English manufacturer and merchant. The course of mechanical and chemical improvement is not stopped. In each of the countries mentioned as likely to compete successfully with England, there are circumstances unfavourable to such competi-tion.

" One of the original emporiums of the cotton manufacture is the establishment of the Messrs. Strutt situated in the fine valley of the Derwent, a few miles below Cromford, the primitive seat of the water-spinning-frames. The cotton factories of this eminent family have for half a century furnished steady employment and comfortable subsistence to a population of many thousand indivi-duals. During this long period, the skill, prudence, and capital of the proprietors have maintained their business in a state of pro-gressive improvement, and nearly exempt from those fluctuations which have so often, in that interval, spread seasons of distress among agricultural labourers. So high is the character of their stocking-yarns and threads for uniform excellence, that the stamp of their firm on the great bale is a passport to their ready sale without examination in every market of the world. Under their auspices the handsome town of Belper has uprisen, built of hewn stone, with streets flagged with the same, in regular houses on the most commodious plans, where the operatives with their families pass the tranquil tenor of their lives. The mills there, plainly elegant, built also of stone, as well as their other mills at Millford, three miles lower down the river, are driven altogether by eighteen magnificent water-wheels possessing the power of 600 horses. A self-acting governor attached to each wheel adjusts its velocity to the purposes of the factory, and is never in a state of repose, but is seen incessantly tightening or slackening the reins of the mill-geering, so to speak, according to the number of machines moving within, and the force of the stream acting without. As no steam-engines are employed, this manufacturing village has quite the picturesque air of an Italian scene, with its river, overhanging woods, and distant range of hills. A neat refectory is fitted up within the works, where any of the work-people, who choose, may have a comfortable pint of hot tea or coffee, including sugar and milk, for one halfpenny. The persons who regularly join in this refreshment, become entitled to medical attendance gratis."

A dancing-room for the recreation of the young is also provided.

Dr. Ure says, "What I have myself witnessed at several times, both on Sundays and working days, has convinced me that the population of Belper is, in reference to health, domestic comfort, and religious culture, in a truly enviable state, compared with the average of our agricultural villages. The factory rooms are well aired, and as clean as any gentleman's parlour. The children are well complexioned, and work with cheerful dexterity at their respective occupations. Not one of Messrs. Strutt's work-people at Belper was attacked with cholera, while the neighbouring handicraft people and farmers were falling victims to the pestilence."

Mr. Kempton, a respectable manufacturer in New England, assured our central board, that factory labour for twelve or fourteen hours is not found to be injurious to the health or growth of the children of ten years of age and upwards in the States, because they are well fed, their board being paid out of their wages by the proprietors—an excellent practice, which would not, however, be permitted by the pauper parents in England, who live too much upon their children's earnings. In their manufacturing districts, principally in New England, upwards of 4000 children are employed under twelve years of age.

The evidence collected in England proves, that under such a diet as the wages could afford, the young inmates of our factories would thrive equally well with the American. And as to the charge which has been made of the injury done to their constitutions by entering a factory in early life, the following refutation of it is most decisive. There is one thing I feel convinced of from observation—that young persons, especially females, who have begun mill-work at from ten to twelve, independently of their becoming much more expert artists, preserve their health better, and possess sounder feet and legs at twenty-five, than those who have commenced from thirteen to sixteen and upwards.

I have drawn freely upon Dr. Ure, as a fund of genuine information.

It appears that the artisans of the United States are treated on this principle; and they are accordingly declared to be more moral than the agricultural population. "At our establishment," says our authority, Mr. Kempton, "the proprietors, deeply sensible of the value of religious nurture, paid the greater part of the minister's salary after building a meeting-house; and they frequently officiated themselves at the evening meetings, which were well attended. We would not keep any workers that would drink spirits, nor did they at other establishments. Almost all of them belong to the temperance societies. In the New England states, no man will get employment who is known to drink to excess. In America, the employer is viewed rather as a tradesman to whom the workpeople dispose of their labour, than as a person having a hostile interest. The manufacturers are always anxious that the children should be well educated, as they find them so much the more useful and trustworthy. "I hope the mother country," says Dr. Ure, "will not disdain to take a word of advice from her meritorious daughter, and that the mill owners of Old England will study to discourage, by the effectual means above mentioned, the sin of drunkenness, the peculiar opprobrium of our people both at home and abroad. There are no jealousies between the American workmen and their employers, of the nature of those which appear to prevail between the English workman and his master."

BELPER.

The rapid improvements, made in almost every branch of the manufactures of England, during the last sixty years, are not more conspicuous in the increased wealth of the nation at large, than in the rising eminence of those places which before were hardly known. The most populous of the present manufacturing towns in Great Britain, were, at the beginning of the last century, either of little importance or not known at all. Such was Belper, which now holds a high rank in point of population among the towns in Derbyshire: it was, prior to 1776, as low in population as it was backward in civility; and considered as the insignificant residence of a few uncivilised nailers. In the year 1801, the population of Belper amounted to 4,500, and in 1809, to 5,635. This increase is owing to the extensive cotton mills erected there, belonging to the Messrs. Strutt; where in 1811, 1,300 persons found employment. These mills are four in number, the first of which was erected in 1776 by Jedediah Strutt, and rebuilt in 1810. With its increase in extent and population, Belper has increased in civilisation and respectability. Immorality and ignorance, which were once thought the characteristics of the place, have, in a great measure, disappeared; and improved morals and more enlarged views, supply their places. About the centre of the town, is the mansion of Jedediah Strutt, and a little above the bridge, pleasantly situated, is Bridge-Hill, the seat of G. B. Strutt. The wear above the bridge is well worth attention ; and the fine expanse of water extending for a considerable way off the river, interspersed with islands covered with young trees, has a pleasing effect. A little to the north of the mills, is a handsome stone bridge of three arches, erected over the Derwent at the expense of the county. In 1811, four hundred children were taught at the Sunday-school, supported by Mr. Strutt; who, at that time, adopted several of the plans of education recommended by Lancaster.*

The principal mill, as seen in the print, is 200 feet long, 30 feet wide, and six stories high; and its floors being constructed of brick arches, and paved with brick, it is considered absolutely indestructible by fire, and therefore proof against the havoc of that dreadful element. This mill has three water-wheels attached to it ; the largest one, which is used in floods only, is remarkable, as well for its magnitude, as for its singular construction. It is upwards of 40 feet long, and 18 feet in diameter. It being impossible to procure timber sufficiently large to form the axle, or shaft, of this wheel in the usual mode of structure, it is made circular and hollow, of a great number of pieces, hooped together like a cask ; the shaft is between five and six feet in diameter. The other two, which are used when the water is at a common height, are composed principally of iron, and are remarkable for their simplicity, strength, and lightness of appearance. Their diameters are 21 feet 6 inches, and length 15 feet. Each shaft is of cast iron, and the arms which connect them with the sole, or that part of the wheel to which the buckles or ladles are attached, are simply round rods of wrought iron, an inch and a half in diameter. Each wheel has eight of these arms, and they are supported, in the direction of the shaft or axis, by eight diagonal rods of the above dimensions.

*" At the period of the discovery of America, 1492, the great mass of the common people of Europe were little better than slaves; of that which we call liberty, they scarcely knew the name. They had no absolute property in the land, and they were so wretchedly indigent, as to have little property of any kind. Their political privileges corresponded with this state of their property; they had no elections; officers from the highest to the lowest were placed over them. Those who then cultivated the earth, were: First slaves, these slaves were generally some portion of a conquered nation, white like ourselves. Second, villeins, who were said to be fixed to the soil, and were transferred with the land. Third, there were a small number of freemen who held property absolutely as their own. But such was the

There do not exist in America, in the same degree, those circumstances of a dense and degraded population which occasion, in the old nations of Europe, such an infinite difference of knowledge and ignorance, of wealth the most exuberant and indigence the most horrible.* No man in America need be poor if he has an axe and arms to use it. The wilderness is to him the same retreat which the world afforded to our first parents. His family, if he has one, is wealth ; if he is unencumbered with wife or children, he is the more easily provided for. An immense proportion of the population of the United States consists of agriculturists, who live upon their own property, which is generally of moderate extent, and cultivate it by their own labour. Such a situation is peculiarly favourable to republican habits. The man who feels himself really independent,—and so must every American who can use a hoe or an axe,—will please himself with the mere exertion of his free will, and form a strong contrast to the hallooing, bawling, blustering rabble of a city, where a dram of liquor, or the money to buy a meal, is sure to purchase the acclamation

wretched condition of the times, and such the violence and outrage to which men were exposed in those barbarous ages, that this latter class made a formal surrender of this independent property, and became slaves, that they might enjoy the protection of the lords. The first dawn of liberty arose from the fact that many of the slave peasants were enabled, by their economy and wise savings, to purchase their liberty. As their property procured them liberty, liberty made them profitable labourers to their former masters, whose revenues were thereby so much augmented, and the value of their lands so much increased, and so many saw the advantages accruing to themselves from the liberty of their slaves, that innumerable serfs were every where enfranchised. It is related by Robertson, that in the progress of time and of public improvement, charters of manumission were granted. These concessions were—first, that the right of sale of the person should be relinquished ; second, power was given to convey property by will or deed ; third, the taxes and services, which before were at the will of the lord, were now rendered certain and fixed ; fourth, marriage was allowed without the lord's permission. Little do we think of the condition of our English ancestors, when we look back to the period long after the discovery of this continent, and find Queen Elizabeth, in 1574, granting manumissions to certain slaves of her own. The labouring people were governed and legislated for more like animals than human beings ; what they should eat, what they should wear, and what they should earn, being prescribed by law. Even the dress of merchants and artificers, who were inferior to the lords and landholders, was provided for by law."—*Sedgwick.*

* As you walk along our streams you may hear the merry notes of the bell mingling with the sounds of our water-falls, calling not the lazy, lounging monastic, to yawn over his matins; but the vigorous and active mechanic to the conduct of the spindle and loom.

of thousands, whose situation in the scale of society is too low to permit their thinking of their political right as a thing more valuable than to be bartered against the degree of advantage they may procure, or of license which they may exercise, by placing it at the disposal of one candidate or another.*

* *Extracts from the Prospectus of the Emporium, a periodical work edited by Judge Cooper, of Pennsylvania, now President of Columbia College, in South Carolina.*

"Our agriculturists want a home market. Manufactures would supply it. Agriculture, at a great distance from seaports, languishes for want of this. Great Britain exhibits an instance of unexampled power and wealth by means of an agriculture greatly dependent on a system of manufactures— and her agriculture, thus situated, is the best in the world, though still capable of great improvement.

"We are too much dependent upon Great Britain for articles that habit has converted into necessaries. A state of war demands privations that a large portion of our citizens reluctantly submit to. Home manufactures would greatly lessen the evil.

"By means of debts incurred for foreign manufactures, we are almost again become colonists—we are too much under the influence, indirectly, of British merchants and British agents. We are not an independent people. Manufactures among us would tend to correct this, and give a stronger tone of nationality at home. I greatly value the intercourse with that country of pre-eminent knowledge and energy ; but our dependence upon it is often so great, as to be oppressive to ourselves.

"The state of agriculture would improve with the improvement of manufactures, by means of the general spirit of energy and exertion, which no where exists in so high a degree as in a manufacturing country ; and by the general improvement of machinery, and the demand for raw materials.

"The home trade, consisting in the exchange of agricultural surpluses for articles of manufacture, produced in our own country, will, for a long time to come, furnish the safest and the least dangerous, the least expensive and the least immoral—the most productive and the most patriotic employment of surplus capital, however raised and accumulated. The safest, because it requires no navies exclusively for its protection ; the least dangerous, because it furnishes no excitement for the prevailing madness of commercial wars ; the least expensive, for the same reason that it is the safest and the least dangerous ; the least immoral, because it furnishes no temptation to the breach or evasion of the laws ; to the multiplication of oaths and perjuries ; and to the consequent prostration of all religious feeling, and all social duty ; the most productive, because the capital admits of quicker return ; because the whole of the capital is permanently invested and employed at home ; because it contributes, directly, immediately, and wholly, to the internal wealth and resources of the nation ; because the credits given are more easily watched and more effectually protected by our own laws, well known, easily resorted to, and speedily executed, than if exposed in distant and in foreign countries, controlled by foreign laws, and foreign customs, and at the mercy of foreign agents ; the most patriotic,

The most noticeable peculiarity in Rhode Island scenery, is the great number of cotton and woollen factories which are seen peeping from every valley where water power can be employed. Villages have grown up in this way in regions the most sterile and uninviting, and a large population are there fed, where without wealth, which they may almost be said to create, fewer families could subsist than the number of thriving and flourishing villages which now meet the eye on every side. " What the moral influence upon society will be, to have such masses of population collected together, without schools and without churches to counteract the tendency to corruption which all promiscuous assemblages of population have, it cannot be difficult to anticipate." Such were the reflections of the "National Ægis," in 1825. But we are happy to say that, in 1835, the grounds of those fears and apprehensions are removed; schools and churches have been introduced, and are producing the most happy effects. For, to promote the best good of our fellow men, we must aim, not only to make them industrious and wise in their occupations, but upright in their conduct and virtuous in their lives. Let the arts of life be carried to the greatest possible perfection ; multiply the means of wealth ever so much—still, unless men are moral, virtuous and good, these improvements are lost, and worse than lost upon them. You may make every farm in our country a garden,

because it binds the persons employed in it, by all the ties of habit and of interest, to their own country ; while foreign trade tends to demoralise the affections of those whose property is dispersed in foreign countries, whose interests are connected with foreign interests, whose capital is but partially invested at the place of their domicile, and who can remove with comparative facility from one country to another. The wise man observed of old, that, 'where the treasure is, there will the heart be also.' And time has not detracted from the truth of the remark.

" We have a decided superiority in the raw materials of cotton, hemp, and flax ; in our alkalies for glass-works ; in the hides and the tanning materials of the leather manufactory ; and we can easily procure that advantage, so far at least, as our own consumption requires it, in the woollen manufactory. Other branches might be enumerated wherein our advantages of internal resource are undeniable; but I cannot see why we should neglect or despise these. Nothing but a stimulus is wanted to induce and enable us to make a proper use of our domestic riches. But men of skill and men of capital fear to begin; lest on the return of peace they should be exposed, in the weakness and infancy of their undertaking, to contend with the overwhelming capital and skill of the European powers, particularly of Great Britain.

" THOMAS COOPER.

" *Carlisle, Feb.* 1813."

and the country around a paradise; yet if good institutions are trampled in the dust; if vice and moral corruption pollute and curse the soil; it is not a paradise; it is not an Eden; it is a *hell*.*

The advancement of this country, in manufacturing industry, is perhaps unexampled in history. In the year 1805, the total consumption of cotton, by the manufactories of the United States, was a little more than 1000 bales. Now, Rhode Island uses 30,000. In 1805, our woollen factories could not furnish the army with 6000 blankets. During the last war, capital was taken from commerce and invested in manufactures. This was the first impulse. In 1816, a report made to Congress showed that forty millions of dollars capital were invested in cotton manufactures, and *twelve millions* in woollen. In that year we manufactured 90,000 bales of cotton. In 1816, it was estimated that the whole amount of goods manufactured in the United States, was equal to fifty or sixty millions of dollars. It is now believed that we manufacture, of all kinds, to the amount of two hundred and fifty millions in a year, about twenty-five millions of which are exported, and the rest consumed in the country. The internal or domestic trade of every country is, perhaps, more permanent and useful than the foreign. It is not subject to the fluctuations of the commercial world, which frequently break out and spread desolation around.

The Missouri Advocate states, that copper is found from

---

* There are two sorts of labour, working for profit and working for nothing. Persons who have nothing to do, generally have hard work to live. A late distinguished senator said in the parliament of England, "man is born to *labour*, as the sparks fly upwards." This observation is founded on a thorough knowledge of the destiny from which none can escape. The idle are always unhappy, nor can mental vigour be preserved without bodily exercise. Neither he who has attained to inordinate wealth, nor he who has reached the greatest heights of human intellect, is exempt from the decree, that every man must "work for his living." If the "gentleman" does not work to maintain his family, he must to maintain his life; hence, he walks, rides, hunts, shoots, and travels, and occupies his limbs as well as his mind; hence noblemen amuse themselves at the turning-lathe, and the workman's bench, or become their own coachmen. Hence kings sometimes play at being workmen, or, what is worse, at the game of war. Without exercise, the body becomes enfeebled, and the mind loses its tension. Corporeal inactivity cannot be persisted in, even with the aid of medicine, without symptoms of an asthenic state. From this deliquium the patient must be relieved in spite of his perverseness, or he becomes a maniac or a corpse. Partial remedies render him "a nervous man;" his only effectual relief is bodily exercise.

Ouisconsin and the falls of St. Anthony, to the shores of Lake Superior, in such abundance and purity, that the Indians make hatchets and ornaments of it; and that it is easily worked, into any form, without any other instrument than the hammer. The whole region of the upper Mississippi is mineral, abounding in lead and copper. The lead mines are in the hands of the United States, but the copper, in 1826, was retained by the Indians.

Mr. Shirreff, an English farmer, who visited this country with a view to decide upon allowing a younger brother to emigrate hither, thus speaks of Lowell :—

" The females engaged in manufacturing, amount to nearly 5000 ; and as we arrived at Lowell on the afternoon of Saturday, we had an opportunity of seeing those connected with some of the largest cotton factories, retiring from labour. All were clean, neat, and fashionably attired, with reticules hanging on their arms, and calashes on their heads. They commonly walked arm in arm, without levity. Their general appearance and deportment was such, that few British gentlemen, in the middle ranks of life, need have been ashamed of leading any of them to a tea party. Next day, being Sunday, we saw the young females belonging to the factories going to church, in their best attire, when the favourable impressions of the preceding evening were not effaced. They lodge, generally, in boarding houses, and earn 8s. 6d. sterling, per week, independent of board; sewing girls earn about 4s. 6d. The recent introduction of large manufacturing establishments, this population, and ample reward of labour, account for the apparent comfort and propriety of the Lowell young women. The situation of the manufacturing class in Britain is very different; nurtured amidst poverty and vice, they toil in crowded and unwholesome factories from infancy, often disregarded by parents and employers, and attaining maturity ruined in constitution, and with few of the sympathies of humanity.

" This village may be taken as an instance of the great strides by which the United States are advancing to greatness, and the immeasurable water power nature has lavished upon them. The canal supplies more water than the present machinery requires; and after inspecting the surplus in the canal and rivers, I am of opinion there is water enough to propel nearly one hundred times the machinery at present employed, and which might employ a population of above one hundred thousand more. Britain is said to owe much of her greatness to the supply of coal, with which she has been blessed ; but however extensive and available it may be, the water power of the United States will excel it in cheapness and magnitude. The price of labour is, and will likely continue, much cheaper in Britain than in the United States, which seems the only circumstance that can ultimately give a superiority to the former.*

Depression of Manufactures in 1815.—Antecedent to the period of the restrictive system, the great mass of manufactures consumed in the United States, was derived from great Britain. During that period, and the consequent war, foreign goods were attainable only in insufficient quantities, and at high prices. The inconvenience of depending on a foreign supply, being severely felt, led to the investment of much unemployed capital in manufacturing establishments. The facility with which water power, sufficient for these purposes, was attainable in various sections of the country, strongly invited to this object. During the war this capital was very productive; but at its close, the British manufacturers, having large quantities of goods on hand, adapted and originally destined for the American market, poured them into this country, to an amount far beyond the wants of the people, or their ability to pay, with a double view of vending their goods, and ruining the rival establishments of the United States. Many of these goods, after being warehoused a considerable time, were sold at auction at less than first cost, and often at little more than to pay the freight and duties. Improvident people, allured by the apparent cheapness of goods, were induced to make unnecessary purchases. The goods destined to the American auctions were

---

* The attempt to introduce females into other employments, and especially into the printing office, is very properly reprobated; and the following note from the manuscript of an operative, is very expressive of a just indignation against it :—

" To woman belongs the service of the domestic temple; there she is nature's priestess,—to minister in peace, far from the turmoil and pollution of busy life,—offering up the incense of pure affection, on the altar of innocence. Wo unto him, or to them, who would degrade the shrine, or stain its hallowed censer with ' strange fire.' Much of her bland power to bind up the wounded spirit, proceeds from her happy ignorance of the vicissitudes of public life, to which the tougher sex is doomed, and, while shielded from the bitter truth, she hopes the best, and her sanguine faith is often contagious. It is certainly a most curious trait of civilisation that drives woman from the ease and independence which the most enlightened policy of all former ages awarded her. Those who are really anxious for the welfare of females, let their exertions be directed towards procuring for their natural providers and protectors a sufficiently *just* amount of wages as shall serve to retain, in comfort, the sister, and wife, and daughter of the workingman, in her proper sphere."—*Remarks on an attempt to introduce females into printing offices.*

handsomely finished, but of the cheapest materials and texture. The operation had, in a great degree, its designed effect; most of the considerable manufacturing establishments were obliged to stop, and many of the proprietors failed. This state of things commenced in 1815; its effects were more severely felt in the two succeeding years, and continued until congress, by a judicious arrangement of the tariff, in some measure relieved the manufacturing interest; and the people, learning wisdom by experience, relieved their circumstances, by substituting a prudent use of domestic articles, for an extravagant consumption of foreign.— *Perkins's Historical Sketches.*

The history of Fall River, a place which is becoming of so much importance in the manufacturing world, cannot but be acceptable. Situated on a rather abrupt elevation of land rising from the northeast side of Mount Hope bay, distant about eighteen miles from Newport, and nine from Bristol, R. I., stands the beautiful and flourishing village of Fall River, so called from the river, which, taking its rise about four miles east, runs through the place, and after many a fantastic turn, is hurried to the bay over beds of rocks, where, before the scene was changed by the hand of cultivation and improvement, it formed several beautiful cascades, and had a fine and imposing effect. The village is now only picturesque from the variety of delightful landscape by which it is surrounded; the back ground presenting a variety in rural scenery—where neat farms and fertile fields show themselves here and there between hill and dale, and rock and wood. The soil, though for the most part fertile, is in some places exceedingly rocky, and often in the midst of such places some little verdant spot shows itself to much advantage.

But Fall River is chiefly inviting as a place of residence, from the salubrity of the air, and the vicinity of Mount Hope bay, which spreads before it like a mirror, and extends easterly until it meets the waters of Taunton river, forming on each side numerous little creeks and coves, which add to the charms of the landscape materially; while on the southwest it takes a bold sweep, and passing round through Howland's ferry, where it is compressed through the narrow channel of a drawbridge, having the island of Rhode Island on one hand and the town of Tiverton on the other, again expands and flows on to meet the ocean. Howland's ferry is not visible from the village of Fall River, though it is from the bay, when at the distance of three or four miles. Vessels do sometimes pass and repass through the drawbridge at Howland's ferry to and from Fall River and Taunton; but the most usual way of access to the former is through Bristol ferry, two miles south of Bristol port. It requires no great effort of imagination to go back a few years, and imagine the Indian with his light canoe sailing about in these waters, or dodging about among the rocks and trees.

The neighbourhood of Fall River has been the scene of frequent skirmishes among the Picknets, the tribe of King Philip, and the Pequods and Narragansetts. Uncas, too, with the last of the Mohicans, and the best, has set his princely foot upon its strand. Fall River, which in 1812 contained less than one hundred inhabitants, owes its growth and importance principally, indeed almost wholly, to its manufacturing establishments; which, though not splendid in appearance, are very numerous, and employ several thousand persons, collected from different parts of the country, as well as many foreigners; the immense fall of water here being now nearly covered by establishments of various kinds. There are more than forty thousand spindles in operation, and it is only twenty-one years since the erection of the first cotton manufactory. Previous to this the land in this vicinity belonged principally to the families of Borden, Bowen, and Durfee; three families from whom the principal part of the stationary inhabitants sprung. The land now divided among the different manufacturing establishments, is principally held in shares, that is, in the neighbourhood of the establishments. So flourishing has business been there, that there is scarce a mechanic, trader, or even labourer, who has been there for any length of time, who has not acquired an estate of his own. In 1812, the first cotton manufactory was erected by a company incorporated by the name of the Fall River Company. In the same year, another company was incorporated called the Troy Manufacturing Company, and another factory built. There were, in 1833, thirteen manufactories, viz. two cotton manufactories of the Troy Company; Pocasset, one woollen, do.; New Pocasset, Massasoit, Olney's mill, Calico Works, Fall River Company's mills, three in number; Annawan iron works and nail manufactory. The calico works alone, which cover a large area of ground, employ nearly three hundred hands; its state of improvement is not exceeded by any establishment of the kind in the country. There are besides a number of machine shops, &c., which, stuck about on the jutting rocks, many of them in the very bed of the stream, have a most singular appearance. The fall originally was through a deep black gulf, with high rocky sides. Across this gulf most of the manufactories are built. There is an appearance of active industry and a spirit of enterprise, as well as of cheerfulness and contentment, that at once strikes a stranger.   It is evident, too, from the number of houses of worship, schools, &c., that the moral and religious education of the rising generation is not neglected.   There are eight houses of worship, and a number of free-schools here, towards which the inhabitants themselves voluntarily contribute twenty-five hundred dollars per annum.   The number of inhabitants in 1833, exceeded five thousand.   It is to be supposed, that among the heterogeneous materials which form the community in this place, there is a great variety of character, as well as of creeds; occasionally some differences of opinion as well as clashing of interests; yet for the most part crime has been unknown there.   It has often been the boast among the inhabitants that, living as they do, on the borders of two states, (part, and by far the greater part, is in Troy, Mass., the other in Tiverton, R. I.) the laws of either were seldom called to punish any thing except venial transgressions.

Fall River, too, can boast of its prowess in battle, of its revolutionary characters, in " the times that tried men's souls."   For although their humble attempts to resist invasion have not yet found a place on the pages of history, yet certain it is, the tide of war has once rolled its threatening waves as far up as to reach the shores of Mount Hope bay.   The character for bravery, generosity, and independence of mind, manifested at that period, seems to have become a part of their inheritance.   Among all the changes which the increase of population causes, the primitive virtues of simplicity and hospitality are still eminently conspicuous.   Whoever goes to reside there seems to adopt readily the manners of the inhabitants.   Even the labouring part of the community in the manufactories, at well as in other departments, are positively distinguished by a degree of refinement and courtesy of manners, which serve to leave the most favourable impressions in relation to manufacturing villages.   I shall always recollect with pleasure one little incident in one of the weaving rooms of the manufactory, where the noise was very distracting, arising from a vast number of looms going at once.   The machinery suddenly stopped, and a strain of music arose simultaneously from every part of the room, in such perfect concord that I at first thought it a chime of bells. My conductor smiled when I asked him if it was not, and pointed to the girls, who each kept their station until they had sung the tune through.

At the time Newport was in possession of the British, there was an attempt made to destroy their mills at this place, consisting of saw mills, grist mills, and a fulling mill; which the bravery of the few inhabitants, men, women, and boys, prevented.

The growth of Fall River, from the period of the revolution to the year 1812, must have been very slow; and ever since that time, until 1822: when there was but four stores in the place, of any description, and not exceeding four hundred inhabitants. The third manufactory was erected in 1821, and two more the ensuing year. In 1833, a lage and elegant one was built. There is now one hundred shops and stores of various descriptions; but, excepting two or three on the Tiverton side of the village, scarcely any where spirituous liquors are retailed, and not a single distillery in the place. The roads north and south of the village lead through a delightful country. The view of the island of Rhode Island on the south one is beautiful,—while that leading to Taunton is scarcely less picturesque. On this road lies the little village of Assonet, where there is considerable commerce carried on. It is a singular sight to see vessels coming up to the very doors of the cottages, sheltered and shut in by the little woody point that encloses the tiny harbour,—and music to hear the voices and loud laughter of numerous little urchins, who are frequently seen playing on the hull of some old vessel on the grassy strand. These fairy landscapes on the one hand, are strangely contrasted by the wildness and sterility of that on the east, which resembles a newly settled country. The land lying between Fall River and New Bedford, a distance of sixteen miles, is a perfect desert; being only diversified by bogs, rocky pastures, and forests of scrub oak and wild poplar.—*History of Fall River.*

The annexed report to the "Society for Establishing Useful Manufactures in New Jersey," shows the progress and extension of the cotton business in Paterson, from 1791 to 1827 :—

" Your records show, that soon after the American revolution, when the United States had just established that form of national government which provides for commerce and its protection; when agriculture, the primary interest and pursuit, began to extend and flourish, and it was foreseen would become redundant and out of proportion to all other branches of industry, a number of men whose patriotism had been long conspicuous in public affairs, conceived that the prosperity and happiness of their country would be essentially promoted by the introduction of those manufactures known to be sources of benefit in Europe. It seemed to them *then*, as the later history of our country has proved, that it would be more for the common good, that the useful arts should share in the growing physical and financial ability of the people, and the expense to convert the raw materials, abundantly produced among us, might as well be saved to the industry of our country. It appears, in the preamble of the charter they were presented with by the legislature of New Jersey, that a contribution of capital was made for this object, to the amount of more than two hundred thousand dollars. The great falls of the Passaic were ascertained to have an elevation, above tide, of 104 feet, and were calculated to be capable, by their elevation and the volume of water, of driving two hundred and forty-seven undershot water wheels; and at Little Falls, four miles higher up, thirty-six feet fall was deemed capable of driving seventy-eight water wheels; that this river was navigable for thirty miles above the falls, with boats drawing five feet, to Chatham, and beyond, with a few locks, fifty miles. Becoming, from various sources of intelligence, thus satisfied of the superiority of this situation, the associated contributors of capital bought the right of the falls, the title to which was originally derived from the state itself, and were granted their charter, under the name and style of ' The Society for the Establishment of Useful Manufactures,' 22d November, 1791, vesting them with power over, and possession of, the waters of the Passaic.

" In consequence of the general war in Europe, the neutral commerce of the United States was soon found to be exceedingly advantageous; and it is well known that, for ten or twelve years succeeding the year 1791, it attracted most of the active capital of our country into its operations, and had so much effect upon our agriculture as to raise the price of provisions.

" By this accidental state of things, the society was retarded, but its purpose was not defeated, nor scarcely suspended. It was well known that the time could not be remote when every interest would seek its proper level,—a reflux of capital be expected to our shores, and the original occasion for such an example as the society proposed to itself to be, would recur with tenfold reason— the accumulated wealth of our country act and display itself, not only in great establishments of manufactories, but in opening the mines and the avenues of internal commerce and profit. The society, soon after the purchase of the Passaic, and the grant of its charter, proceeded to establish the first cotton factory and printing house : this was attended with loss. The society invited and encouraged skill, by leasing privileges, and aiding manufacturers with capital. This system was well calculated to draw numbers to share in the use of this great water power. Experienced mill owners have been induced hither, bringing wealth even from

England.   Numerous artisans have sought and found employment coming from abroad, and from the adjoining states.   The wages of the supernumerary hands of the surrounding counties, together with the sale of their surplus provisions, have enriched Bergen, Essex, and Morris.

" In July 1827, there were in Paterson, New Jersey, 6,236 inhabitants, 1,046 heads of families, 7 houses of public worship, 17 schools, a philosophical society,—(it is evident that these establishments do collect around them, in due proportion, every art and profession) ;—15 cotton factories, in which 24,000 spindles operate ; 2 factories of canvass, 1,644 spindles, employing 1,453 persons, whose wages are $224,123 a year ; extensive machine shops, and iron works, flax, 620,000 lbs. annually, 6000 bales of cotton, 1,630,000 lbs. cotton yarn spun annually, 430,000 lbs. of linen yarn, cotton and linen duck made, annually, 630,000 yards, cotton cloth, 3,354,500 yards, yarn exported, 796,000 yards, and new factories then building.

" This is but the beginning of what Paterson must be, if not disturbed in its well planned career of usefulness.

" Perhaps the time has nearly arrived, contemplated by the legislature, when it may be expedient and necessary to organise the corporate government as provided for by the act.   For in every populous place, where a great amount of property is concentrated in business, a preventive police, a united local magistracy, a prompt administration of justice, the preservation of health, by the cleanliness of markets and streets, and the establishment of a hospital, where the accidentally injured may have the best medical aid and care, and the sick be better taken care of than in the midst of a busy multitude,—the preservation of morals, too, by affording an opportunity to every one to save, and not expend their earnings, beyond the sum necessary to subsistence, laying up the surplus in a savings bank, at interest, open to receive and secure any sum, however small, placed to the owner's credit, as often as it should be brought ; thus accumulating a sum competent to an establishment in business, or in a home, and thus avoiding temptations to dissipation and extravagance, were among the objects of the legislature.

" The advantages of doing business in a well regulated town, are considerations which interest all, and promote harmony, order, union, and good will ; and all know that, *thus*, accessions of numbers will lead to the increased value of property.   Foreigners are enabled to hold real estate in Paterson."

The improvement of roads and canals leading towards Massachusetts, Connecticut, and Rhode Island, from the surrounding districts of greater extent and production, are manifestly of the utmost importance, as they facilitate and cheapen the introduction of raw materials, grain, and other productions of the soil of less populous or more fertile districts. This was a subject of great interest with Mr. Slater, who was a principal agent in promoting the famous road from Pawtucket to Providence, also what is called the Gore turnpike, to Webster, and the Worcester and Norwich turnpike. He was always in favour of the project of the Worcester and Norwich railroad, now so happily commenced, which will pass through Webster.

Indeed Mr. Slater is said to have owned forty thousand dollars, in turnpike road stock, little of which was available ; but he considered the importance of good roads as a necessary appendage to the manufacturing interest. When he commenced business, Rhode Island and Massachusetts were very defective in roads and canals.*

* The momentous fact is satisfactorily established, that the American manufacturers' demand has greatly surpassed, in 1812, all the abilities of the planters, farmers, land-holders, and miners, to supply those five descriptions of raw materials. It is certain, that neither in commerce, nor in navigation, nor in the fisheries, nor even in agriculture itself, do we find a truth so vast and stupendous, as that which is exhibited to our eyes in the case of labour-saving machinery. Taking the advantage, in favour of the cotton carding and spinning, at the ascertained rate of two hundred to one above manual labour, we are astonished to find that the industry of four millions of persons, operating with water and steam machinery, would be able to execute as much work as eight hundred millions of persons could perform in the old mode of manual industry. We do not expect to accomplish miracles, nor to engross manufactures. But the United States of America, sincerely regarding and thoroughly respecting the rights and interests of the rest of mankind, are able and authorised to participate with all the sister nations of the world, in this wonderful object of human industry, to which they have actually contributed so many valuable inventions.

Of all the discoveries and inventions yet accomplished, the machinery which saves labour, incidental to manufactures in the greatest degree, is that of Whitney, for ginning cotton wool.

The richest object of commercial enterprise, (continues Tench Coxe) for the merchants of the United States is the trade of those countries which do not manufacture. Of this, the trade of our American brethren, from Texas and Mexico to the Straits of Magellan, is a very interesting instance. We can import their raw materials and export our manufactures to an immense amount, with substantial benefit. Their rich products will not often be received in the ports of Europe in our vessels foreign to them. Their copper, crude sugar, peculiar cotton and woods, their various dyeing materials, drugs and medicines, their wool, hides, and tallow, and their gold and

The following is a specimen of Mr. Slater's business letters, they are full of information and close calculations ; in short, his opinion did much to regulate rules of interest, commissions, &c., with the agents of manufactured articles.

Messrs. ——, ——, & Co.

Gentlemen,—Your letter under date of 7th ult. by way of Oxford, is at hand, covering your last quarter's sales, discounts, commissions, and a check on New York for $1500, which is at your credit.   I was much mortified to see your account come on in the old style, notwithstanding so much has been said at times on the subject.   You have charged bad debts back, but no deductions for commissions and interest thereon.   As respects these bad debts, and others previous, the law is considered very plain on that point, unless proper diligence is exercised when the debt is due, the commission merchant has no right to charge the debt back.   However, this is a subject which the manufacturers are taking into serious consideration.   You have also charged four per cent. on case and bale goods ; amount of which, in your last quarter's sales, $5,268 75 difference between that and what others generally charge, and what I can have a single barrel of flour or a quintal of salt fish sold for, amounts to $79 04.   Then comes a more serious item, which is, no interest account.   How shall we get along with for time past.   Two individual houses, the year past, have credited me nearly $1000 interest, whose balances at the end of the last year was only about fifty per cent. more than the balance from you.   My sons, and I too, think it necessary to go fully into an interest account.   Many of my good friends, who dispose of my goods, keep no interest account; but when they send in their quarterly account of sales, they stipulate, when due, by average, which I consider is the best mode.   I have to request of you to give me your mind on the foregoing subjects, as well as on what terms you will agree to receive and dispose of my goods in future.   The cotton business in now in such a deplorable state, that no manufacturer can live, if he gives about seven per cent. in commission and interest.   Respectfully your obedient servant,

SAMUEL SLATER.

Mr. Slater's second marriage,* was with the widow of Robert Parkinson, who had entrusted his affairs with Mr. S. and who had

silver, will be exchanged for cabinet wares, plate and jewelry, pottery, iron manufactures, mill-work, cooper's utensils, machinery, types, gunpowder, arms, ships, and other vessels, boats, &c.   As our manufactures progress, the trade with that new und interesting country, and with St. Domingo, and all the countries similarly circumstanced, cannot fail to increase.

* This is to certify whom it may concern, that on Friday, the 21st day of November, Anno Domini 1817, Samuel Slater and Esther Parkinson were lawfully joined in holy matrimony, and pronounced man and wife together, according to the rites of the protestant episcopal church, as witness my hand,   JOSEPH PILMORE,

Rector of St. Paul's Church in Philadelphia.

been an acquaintance many years in the Slater family. In this way Mrs. Parkinson had known the former wife of Mr. Slater, and had very much esteemed her as a friend. Mr. Slater's letter on that occasion, a copy of which was found among his papers, is written with so much propriety, that there can be no objection to its publication.

Mrs. Robert Parkinson, widow, Philadelphia.

NORTH PROVIDENCE, R. I. Sep. 23d, 1817.

Dear madam,—As the wise disposer of all events has seen fit in his wisdom to place you and me in a single state—notwithstanding, I presume none of his decrees have gone forth which compels either of us to remain in a state of widowhood. Therefore, under these and other circumstances, I now take the liberty to address you on a momentous subject. I have been inclined for some time past to change my situation in life, and have at times named you to my brother and sister for a partner, who have invariably recommended you as suitable, and have fully acquiesced with my ideas on the subject. Now if you are under no obligation to any one, and on weighing the subject fully, you should think that you can spend the remainder of your days with me, I hope you will not feel reluctant, in writing me soon to that effect. You need not be abashed, in any degree, to express your mind on this business, for I trust years have taught me to receive your reply favourably, if my understanding has not. I have six sons to comfort you with the oldest is about fifteen years, he has been at Oxford about a year, (not Oxford in Great Britain), the youngest is in his sixth year, I believe they are all compos mentis, and they are as active as any six boys, although they are mine. Cousin Mary is now down from Ludlow on a visit; she has a noble corpulent son about six months old. I should have divulged my intentions to you months past had not my brother given me to understand that he expected you daily on this way on a visit. Probably you may consider me rather blunt in this business, hope you will attribute that to the country that gave me birth. I consider myself a plain candid Englishman, and hope and trust, you will be candid enough to write me a short answer, at least, whether it be in the affirmative or negative; and should it be in the negative, I stand ready and willing to render you all the advice and assistance in my power relative to settling your worldly matters.

With due respect, as a friend and countryman, I am, dear madam, your well wisher,   SAMUEL SLATER.

N.B.—Hope you are a freemason as respects keeping secrets.

The death of Mr. Slater's eldest son,* at a time when he became useful in his business and a pleasing companion to his

---

* The following register from the town clerk, will show the number and ages of Mr. Slater's children:—

Samuel Slater and Hannah Wilkinson, married Oct. 2d, A. D. 1791.

William Slater, son of Samuel Slater and Hannah his wife, born August 31st, A. D. 1796.

father, was a severe trial; I find the following letter written to him during his sickness:—

Samuel Slater, Jr.

NORTH PROVIDENCE, Nov, 18th, 1820.

Dear Son,—Herewith you will receive, per John Sims, your shirts, stockings, &c., which I thought you would be in want of, before I should probably again be at Oxford, therefore I send the bearer up on purpose with them, and in order to ascertain the state of your health; which you will get Mr. Tyson to inform me of. Probably it will be some weeks before we again have sleighing, therefore, if you should wish to return home before we have sleighing again, I will have the carriage sent up any hour you may see fit to say. Now, as your life and health depend entirely on your strict attention to every thing appertaining thereto, do let me entreat you to be very particular in all your food, &c., and see that you keep yourself free from the inclemency of the weather, and above all things, keep your feet warm and dry. I had a letter from John this week; he says if that vessel which was coming to Providence after nails, &c., does not come, he will send your trunk by mail. He sent your grammar by Captain Cooke, whom A. and B. and I sent to Cheshire to look at Mr. Granger's farm. I saw Mr. Johnson of Providence respecting soldering those dye tubs; who says, the upright parts cannot be soldered without being turned partly down, observing that there was no way to keep the solder in its place, after melting it with the soldering iron, until it became cold. Shall write Mr. Tyson on the subject. I have been in Providence this afternoon to attend the funeral of Mr. Wheelock's little daughter, Eliza Slater Wheelock; from all accounts she was almost a perfect being; the heavy loss is almost insurmountable to her parents. My dear son, do let me entreat you to be very careful of your health, and spare

---

Elizabeth Slater, daughter of Samuel Slater and Hannah, born November 15th, A. D. 1798.

Mary Slater, daughter of Samuel and Hannah, born Sept. 28th, A. D. 1801.

Samuel Slater, son of Samuel and Hannah, born Sept. 28th, A. D. 1802.

George Basset Slater, son of Samuel and Hannah, born February 12th, A. D. 1804.

John Slater, son of Samuel and Hannah, born May 23d, A. D. 1805.

Horatio Nelson Slater, son of Samuel and Hannah, born March 5th, A. D. 1808.

William Slater, son of Samuel and Hannah, born October the 15th, A. D. 1809.

A true extract, as appears of record, &c.

Witness, H. ANGELL, T. Clerk.

November 5th, A. D. 1814.

Thomas Graham Slater, son of Samuel and Hannah Slater, was born Sept. 19th, 1812.

Mrs. Slater died a short time after her last child, and left her husband, overwhelmed in business which was daily increasing, with a family of small children. Perhaps a mother's loss was never more severely felt.

no pains to get restored to your former health, and believe me your affectionate father, SAMUEL SLATER.

N.B. I forgot the title of the book which you requested me to get when last at Oxford. Do send me word per J. Sims what it is, and I will get it without delay and forward it.

———

George Benson Strutt, Esq.

NORTH PROVIDENCE, June 4th, 1821.

Dear Sir,—At the special request of G. Sullivan Esq. counsellor, and many of my friends in this section of the country, I now take the liberty to address you principally in their behalf. The object is merely this: A certain cotton manufacturing company in this country, who have been in the cotton business a few years only, still, they have pretended to be the inventors of almost every thing, and have taken out patents accordingly; but as it is so well known, that, before they commenced business, one of their brightest partners was in England, for some time, (cloaked as a merchant,) obtaining information and workmen, which induces the public here to believe, that they claim that which belongs to the public, &c. The greatest question is concerning the double speeder, now much used in this country, which is said to be on a much improved plan to any thing in Great Britain. Mr. Sullivan will forward this letter to one of his friends in England, who will wait on you in order to ask you some questions, but not with a view of obtaining any information, as respects any new improvements with you. If the questions asked appear pertinent you will have the goodness to answer them accordingly. We have a very recent new plan of machinery, just set in operation, only yet nicknamed the treble speeder, for roving and winding, which, from all appearance, far exceeds the double speeder; as it will not cost more than one third per spindle, will be abundantly more durable, and perform double the work. The front roller must make at least 400 revolutions per minute, or the machine will not perform the work to best advantage. I contemplate having some of the kind in operation shortly, and should the plan far exceed the double speeder, on a full experiment, I will send you a draught of it with pleasure. I am told the inventor, a country boy about twenty years of age, is now spinning on the same principle, as fine as one hundred skeins to the pound, and running the front roller about as fast as for roving.

I am, dear sir, your most obedient servant,

SAMUEL SLATER.

———

WEBSTER, Jan. 31, 1835.

Most honoured friend, Moses Brown—Your esteemed favour under date of the 26th ult., was duly received, which I should have answered without delay, had not I been deprived of holding my pen, owing to a lame hand and wrist. However, I immediately sent word to my son John, instructing him to see you on the subject of your letter, and to render every assistance in my behalf. It is very unpleasant to me that the lodge and chapter should attempt to violate their sacred contract, made with the owners of Union Block. I was not over friendly to putting on the additional story, but my two partners (who were both masons) stated the masons would take a lease of it for forty or fifty years, and pledge thirty shares which they owned in the Manufacturer's bank as security for payment of the rent, but some years after, I learned the shares had not been pledged, for some reason or other. Some of the candid masons have frequently observed to me, that it was the intent and meaning to pledge that stock, and although it had not been done, still it ought to be. I have no surplus cash to spend in the law, but still I, for one, consider a part of my duty to my fellow beings to aid and assist in trying to make people to be honest and upright in all their contracts. Hoping the many years which have passed over your honourable head, still permit you to enjoy your usual state of health and activity, I remain with every respect, your obedient servant,

SAMUEL SLATER.

Mr. Slater's business, up to the year 1829, had progressed, and was established on a permanent basis. And such was the snug and punctual manner in which he managed his concerns, that he did not owe, in all his purchases and debts, one thousand dollars; while he had fifty thousand dollars in mortgages on real estate. No one could justly accuse him of want of prudence and foresight in his loans or responsibilities. It, however, appeared, when the village of Pawtucket was shaken to its foundation, that Mr. Slater's endorsements were very heavy and extensive; and during the panic which followed, he was unable to take up all his endorsed paper, without great sacrifice, yet he knew that, with some accommodation, and with perfect safety, he could meet all demands and save much property from destruction. It was with these views that he applied to William Almy, one of his first partners in his business, and who was then a partner in Pawtucket and in Smithfield, but his application did not receive that prompt and cheerful attention which Mr. Slater had reason to expect; but was considered as a refusal.

This circumstance increased the alarm and shook credit, in Rhode Island, to its centre. All confidence was lost, when Mr. Slater said that, without some accommodation, to gain time, to meet his endorsed paper, he should stop his mills, till he could turn himself round. There was something strange, passing strange, that Wil m Almy should not have fully entered into Mr. Slater's views; having known his circumstances, and being convinced, as he must have been, of his immense property. A meeting of wealthy men was held in Providence, at which meeting Mr. Slater gave a schedule of his property, when Cyrus Butler, Brown & Ives, Moses Brown, and others, expressed a wish for an arrangement, that Mr. Slater should go on with his business. He finally sold out his third in the " *Old Mill*" in Pawtucket, and his fourth of the Smithfield property; and Wm. Almy became the purchaser of those places.

Mr. Slater was concerned in the new steam mill, in Providence, and it was found necessary to take the whole of that into his hands; so that he weathered the storm and settled his affairs in a much shorter time than was expected. Not without a considerable loss of property, and what was of more consequence, a loss of confidence in men of business in general. It was very evident that his mind and feelings were very essentially affected, and, with his poor state of health, he never fully recovered his tone of assurance.

Some of his letters, about this time, discover a sensibility that was never observable before; for he was remarkably free of all remarks on those with whom he was connected in business. This was, however, a rebuff that he little expected, and a kind of trial that he was unaccustomed to ; he never before knew what it was to be unable to meet every demand, and could generally anticipate such calls. He said to me : "I felt the more, because I had never been used to it." He felt his dignity, as a business man, hurt, when his proposition did not meet with prompt and cheerful attention and acquiescence.

About this time I find, on some of his papers, the following passages copied. "As the partridge sitteth on eggs, and hatches them not, so he that getteth riches, and not by right, shall leave them in the midst of his days, and at his end shall be a fool."— Jer. xvii. 11.

"Bread of deceit is sweet to a man, but afterward his mouth shall be filled with gravel."

———

Messrs. ———

NORTH PROVIDENCE, Feb. 3, 1829.

Gentlemen,—S. Slater & Sons have come to a determination to place that *ignoble* establishment in Dudley, called Slater & Howard's woollen factory, in a state of respectability. Whether or not it was got up in iniquity I cannot say ; but I fear some things, during the life of it, are mysterious. It is the united wish of S. Slater & Sons to sink into oblivion the past inroads that have been made, one way or another, on that establishment. They are very anxious to place the business, in future, on a fair mutual ground, so as to pay about six thousand dollars a year for extra *stock*, raising the wind, bad debts, and too liberal commissions. Perhaps you may think that I am rather severe in my remarks; but I think I can say, as the Earl of Essex said, when Queen Elizabeth boxed his ears. A noble lord told him to submit. His reply was: You are only a looker on, *but I feel it.* However, waiving the allegory, I would just observe to you that, in the course of this month, I contemplate remitting to you from twelve to sixteen thousand dollars, in bills on the south, and bank bills on Slater & Sons' account, providing the negotiations can be made on as favourable terms in your city (where neither Jew nor Quaker has an abiding place,) as can be done elsewhere. I should like your reply on the subject, both as it respects bills of exchange, and Providence and current bank bills. Yours, &c.

SAMUEL SLATER.

Messrs. ———

N. PROVIDENCE, Jan. 7th, 1829.

Gentlemen,—In my last, under date of the 31st ult., I wrote you that I had drawn on you, for ten thousand dollars, on four months, in favour of the Steam Cotton Manufacturing Company, in order to meet a demand nearly due in Philadelphia, since which, have altered a five thousand draft into three, two of $1500 each, and one of $2000, all payable at the same time.

It is rather a pinching time here for money ; though many of the money borrowers say times are becoming more easy. Since the failure of Mr. Hurd, money-jobbers and anti-tariff folks have propounded almost every one, who has seen, or at least touched of late a cotton or woollen factory, that he must go down stream, and amongst them, some whose chins are barely above water, are (friendly) afraid that I have a very heavy load on my back, &c. It is true, I am on two neighbours' paper, but am partially secure, and hope in a day or two, to be fully secured against an eventual loss, providing Mount Etna should not extend its lava much beyond the usual limits. Last week, my sons George, John, and Nelson, bought out my old friend Edward Howard, in the woollen business, which relieves my mind considerably. The business in future will be transacted by myself and sons ; and as it respects the Amoskeage and Steam Cotton Manufacturing Company, including the woollen factory and all my private concerns, (which I consider very trivial,) I think I can boldly say, after the whole company debts are paid, (all of which I have to meet,) there will be left from 800,000 to 1,000,000 of dollars to all concerned. I barely mention these circumstances to in some measure rebut any flying reports that may reach your city, and of course will not retard your acceptance of my paper so long as you have my funds in your hands to make you perfectly secure : I shall probably spend (at least) several weeks here, therefore, if you have not already forwarded your last quarter's sale and account current to Oxford, you will send it to Pawtucket. In great haste, your obedient servant,

SAMUEL SLATER.

N.B. It is a general time of health in my family. Hope you and all connections are well. S. S.

To the same.

NORTH PROVIDENCE, June 15th, 1829.

Gentlemen,—Since I wrote you under date of the 12th inst., there has been a dreadful storm in and about Pawtucket. I believe on Friday last, Samuel B. Harris made an assignment of his property without even consulting his endorsers, A. I. & W. On Saturday A. & I. W. made an assignment of their property, and as a great amount of paper was lying over, both of their own, and that which they had endorsed for W. Harris & S. B. Harris, as soon as the alarm was given in Providence, the Providence people, with their lawyers and sheriffs, were busy enough here until midnight on Saturday night, but the conjecture is, they were too late. It will not be necessary for you to make known the name of your informant of the above. Yours, &c.

S. SLATER.

To the same.

July 29th, 1829.

Gentlemen,—On the 22d inst., I drew on you in favour of B. & C. Dyer & Co. at four months, for $1000 to take up my son Nelson's draft on A. & I. Wilkinson, which was by them dishonoured. Nelson received the draft in part payment of his legacy. Since I wrote you last, D. W. has gone down the falls. His failure is a serious one, and it affects my mind and body seriously, and purse too for the present, but hope eventually to meet with but little loss.*

Nelson started the Kennedy factory on my account last Monday, I hope shortly to have some goods for you. To-day Jonathan Congdon & Sons, Charles Hadwin, and others, made assignments; so we slide along. I should write you oftener would my health and spirits permit. Yours, &c.

SAMUEL SLATER.

N.B. Kennedy's debts amount to $115,000, which greatly surprised me and every other person it is about double what I expected.

I exposed myself very much and got cold in my left arm, so that, now, I may almost say, that I am armless. As soon as the humble-bee makes his appearance, I hope my infirmities will leave me.

I hope the great scarcity of money at this time, 1828, will have some effect on those dealers in negroes, who are so opposed to the woollen and other bills before congress.

As the great-gun of the brokers has made an assignment, and failed, it creates a fear in me that they are not so safe to place funds with as many of the state banks. Notwithstanding I own forty shares in the United States Bank, Slater, Wardwell & Co, who have made use of my name as a stockholder, have in no one solitary instance been able to get one cent of the best paper discounted at that bank. I wish the mother bank would take a peep into the business.

1829.—You may rely on one thing, that, if you do, or are obliged to sell cotton goods much lower, you will bankrupt a number of poor cotton spinners. I am not very partial to this mode of drawing, but money is extremely scarce in Providence and its vicinity, that if people do not resort to some stratagem or other, (who can,) nothing but a general bankruptcy would ensue. I have the unpleasant news to give you, that J. Green & Son and John Gardner made an assignment last night, (June 18th 1829,) and their mills are motionless to-day.

---

* This was the most trying time in Mr. Slater's life, he was unable to sustain those who relied on him for assistance any longer; he found himself responsible for $300,000, when the pressure of money was so great as to shake the confidence of the capitalists of New England, and the community in general.

June 11th, 1829.—My health has been at a very low ebb, I have suffered almost every thing from a violent distress at my stomach, which produced indigestion, and nearly a total loss of appetite; and in addition to other afflictions, about three weeks past, I was violently attacked in my old emaciated knee, with the rheumatism, to that degree, which deprived me of motion. I am now rather creeping up hill, and make out with the assistance of my crutches to hobble about my room two or three times a day.

Connoisseurs say, that the steam factory is now making the best goods in the country.

To the same.
N. PROVIDENCE, August 3, 1829.

Gentlemen,—Your two letters under dates of the 27th and 28th ult. are at hand. In regard to my endorsements for D. Wilkinson, they are heavy without doubt, but I am secured for the whole eventually. The steam mill is in debt to a large amount, but as $70,000 have been paid in, and as the *whole* establishment is holden for her debts, I conceive, taking all things into view, that the depreciation will not exceed the amount paid in. As I have to look up entire new friends to aid me in my unexpected liabilities, makes my task more arduous.

There is coming due at different periods, at the Merchant's bank, Providence, on'D. W. and J. K.'s account, about $62,000, which some of the directors say I can have my own time to pay. Brown & Ives and C. Butler sent me out word, that they wished to have an interview with me; they say I must be carried through, and I doubt not they will do it,

My brother is down here, and he and Mr. Sayles made out a sketch of my real and personal property, valued in their judgment, at what they consider it worth now, at $690,000, leaving out the Dudley woollen establishment. As respects your observations relative to your fears not being unreasonable, I make every allowance, after taking into view your informant, whom I for years have thought was a *near-ox*, but now I have reason to believe the *off-side* is more congenial to his feelings. It is contemplated to make some arrangements to-morrow, so as to put my affairs in a proper train. When I see any of you face to face, I will give you a history of *human* or *inhuman* generosity. Two of my consignees have already offered to loan me $10,000 each, over and above the amount of invoices, whom I have not been acquainted with forty years. The failures round here are pretty frequent, the names, no doubt, you have already heard. I shall endeavour to advise you frequently of what is going on here. Respectfully your obedient servant,
SAMUEL SLATER.

Samuel Slater, Esq. Oxford, Massachusetts.
NEW YORK, 10th mo. 21, 1831.

We take the liberty of writing to thee on a subject which has been discussed by our mutual friend John B. Toulmin and ourselves. In the course of every year we receive a great many letters of recommendation with emigrants from Europe, who come out here to seek employment, as labourers, manufacturers, servants, &c. and we are frequently at a loss to procure situations for them. This city is such a general resort for emigrants, there are always more applicants than places to fill, and consequently much misery is endured by those who are without employment, many of whom return to their native country in despair. J. B. Toulmin has told us of thy kindness in assisting poor people to find employment, and he recommended us to address thee on the subject. We shall feel much obliged to thee if thou wilt permit us occasionally to recommend poor emigrants to thy notice, and also if thou wilt let us know whenever thou or any of thy friends are in want of men, women or children, who have testimonials with them. In this way we may both be the means of serving our country people who cross the Atlantic to obtain a livelihood.

We remain respectfully thy assured friends,   A. BELL & Co.

—

Samuel Slater, Esq.

NEW YORK, 21st Oct. 1831.

Dear sir,—I was at Providence a few weeks ago, and much regretted to hear of the sickness of your son, H. Nelson, and of your own indisposition. I had not time to visit you at Oxford, but it will afford me much satisfaction to attend to your orders at Mobile, to which place I return on the 1st November, per ship "Splendid." The crop of cotton, state of Alabama, is represented to be much better this year than last, and prices will probably open at six to eight and a half cents. Such cottons as will spin No. 16 and 18, I think will be bought at seven and a half to eight cents, perhaps lower. Freights are also likely to be lower this year than last. I now beg to call your particular attention to the annexed letter from my most respectable friends, A. Bell & Co. I think aid may be rendered to respectable emigrants, that may be useful to manufacturers in want of hands, as well as to them. I am fully aware of your disposition to be useful, and feel assured you will excuse the liberty now taken.

I am, sir, very truly, your obedient servant,   J. B. TOULMIN.

—

The above letters afford me an opportunity of introducing the usefulness and benevolence of Mr. Slater, in a point of view in which his character has not been duly appreciated.

From the first establishment of the old mill in Pawtucket, it was the resort of every English mechanic who reached our shores; whether by the way of Nova Scotia or New York, you would meet them steering for Rhode Island, with enquiries for Slater's Mills. It is easy to conceive that this continual drain on his attention not only taxed his purse but his patience. But in Samuel Slater they always found a friend who would find them immediate employment if possible, or direction to the most probable places, where they would fulfil their wishes. He knew well how to advise, they looked up to him as a father, and had undoubted confidence in his directions. Many thousands applied to him in this way; he sent none empty away, and it is not easy to conceive of the amount of money which he presented, as well as the amount of joy afforded, to strangers. This was his fort of charity, it was thrown in his way, and he exercised his benevolence for upwards of forty years in a retired unostentatious manner. He treated none with contempt or reproach, but assured them all that with sobriety and industry they would be able to live in plenty and peace. He warned the idle and intemperate of their danger, reminding such that no country could sustain vice from misery. This was the sphere of Mr. Slater's charities, in which situation few were ever situated to do so much good, and few would have availed themselves of the opportunity to the extent that he did.

Messrs. George B. & John Slater.

NORTH PROVIDENCE, Feb. 8th, 1832.

Dear sons,—I wrote John on the 28th ult. that I thought it would be advisable for one of you to come down and see your sick brother, hoping it might in some degree revive his drooping spirits, since which time have not decidedly heard from either of you, only circuitously, that you were in Boston. I hope your brother Nelson is rather more comfortable. He is placed in a disagreeable situation, his nurse is sick, and his uncle has a large family, which must very much interfere with their comfort, &c. He has pretty much made up his mind to move out here in the course of a few days, providing it can be done without endangering his existence. Probably the presence of one of you might make his journey out here rather more agreeable. As the Rev. J. Fletcher once wrote to his friend who had omittted writing for some time, he asks, "Are you alive, paralytic, gouty, slothful, or too busy to write a line to your friend?" Your affectionate father,   SAMUEL SLATER.

—

Mrs. Esther Slater, Pawtucket, R. I.

WILKINSONVILLE, April 9th, 1832.

Dear wife,—I arrived at Webster the day I left Pawtucket, at about five o'clock, pretty comfortable, though somewhat fatigued. I found all my sons and grandsons in good health. Yesterday, son John, wife and son, and I, too, left Webster for this place, where part of us tended church fore and after noon, although very cold. They have not completed repairing the breach in the flume but expect to go to work in two or three days. When I arrived at Webster, daughter Sarah having no help but Harriet, she sent for Fanny, who came over that night. I had a little conversation with her on the subject of going to Pawtucket. She said she would not live with Miss R.; otherwise should be glad to live with us at Pawtucket. Do write me how Nelson gets along, as well as the other invalids. I do not expect to return any earlier, at least, than the last of this week. In haste, yours, &c.

SAMUEL SLATER.

N.B.—Send me all the news you can.

—

Mrs. Samuel Slater, Pawtucket, R. I.

WEBSTER, February 25th, 1833.

Dear wife,—I left Wilkinsonville the same day which you left there sick. Son Nelson informed me that your health was measureably restored. Indeed I was, in some degree, satisfied that the salubrious air of Pawtucket would soon reanimate you. I have been tolerably well since I arrived here, until a few days past. On Thursday last I traveled round on foot to view some house lots, in the snow broth, and got my feet at least a little damp, if not perfectly wet. The night following was very cold and froze very hard. The next morning after *breakfast,* not in the afternoon, I recommenced my pursuits, and as I was so much older and more clumsy than I thought I really was, that while I was going up a steep frozen hill, and being not sure-footed, I happened, accidentally, to fall prostrate on the ice, to the annoyance of my hip and shoulder. I am now some better, but am severely afflicted with a cold, probably partly from sleeping alone. Last Wednesday morning, about 5 o'clock, a little grand-daughter came to town: she and her mother (as the old woman's sayings are,) *are as well as can be expected.* Son John arrived here last Saturday night, and, no doubt, before this time, has kissed the baby, &c. &c.

I shall endeavour to leave here as soon as the sleighing will permit, so as to get clear of the old maids (both white and black,) who are daily soliciting me for a chance to go to Pawtucket; also a black, or coloured, man wants to live with us. This looks a little like what I have often told you, that there are people to be got for money.

A certain hook which has been baited with shiners, for some time past, will not induce a certain mackerel to bite, or at least swallow the bait. Further particulars when I see you. Respectfully yours, &c.

SAMUEL SLATER.

N. B. How does your old maid do? If Wm. Bliss should want a few dollars, towards cutting wood, you will let him have some.

—

Mrs. Esther Slater, Pawtucket, R. I.   Favoured by Miss M. Turner.

WEBSTER, September 28th, 1833.

Dear wife,—The bearer, Miss Mary Turner, would have gone down to Pawtucket, some days past, had I not deferred it on account of seeing my son Thomas, who promised, on Tuesday last, since which time I have not seen and scarcely heard from him, excepting by way of a teamster or tin pedlar, verbally. Mrs. Turner expects to recruit you up in the course of a week or ten days, and then bring you up into the county of Worcester, where you can see, among other curiosities, a noble stone dam, built after the architectural skill of Sir C. Wren. It is a very heavy job, and you may rely on it, I pay good attention to it. I generally eat my breakfast in season, so that I get over there by sunrise, and remain, either sitting or standing on rocks or stones, until sunset; and then during the night I sleep from two to six hours. I enjoy tolerable good health, and my limbs are daily gaining their wonted activity, &c. You will endeavour to find some employment for my new driver, Silvester Davy, during his stay at Pawtucket. If you should come up shortly, I wish you to send up a little good West India, which I want for a *medicine.* I should like to hear how you and all your invalids get along. I would say many things, but having about forty *eye servants* under pay, on out door jobs, all whom I find it necessary to watch as close as a cat does a mouse, therefore I must close.

With due respect, yours, &c. &c. SAMUEL SLATER.

N. B. It is a general time of health here.

To the Assessors of the Town of Sutton, Mass.

WEBSTER, August 23d, 1834.

Gentlemen,—Ever since I have owned the estate at Wilkinsonville I have felt injured at the high tax that has been assessed on that property. I have understood that after scaling down the real value, from one quarter to one third, you have then estimated the property at fifty-six thousand dollars, until last year, when you reduced the tax some. Now, in order to give you some light respecting the actual value of it, I will take forty-seven thousand dollars for all the real estate and machinery I own in the town of Sutton ; and if you require it, I stand ready to make oath of it. If any one of you will find a purchaser at the above price, I will cheerfully make him a present of fifty dollars. Yours, &c.

SAMUEL SLATER.

Mathew Carey, Esq., of Philadelphia, in 1827 visited the village of Lowell, and desirous of laying before the public a correct statement of its progress and present condition, proposed a number of queries to Mr. Boott, from whom he received the following answer, and communicated it to the public ·through the medium of the United States Gazette.

———

LOWELL, October 25, 1827.

Dear sir,—I believe the following brief statement embraces all the objects specified in your letter of the 22d. If, however, I have, in my haste, omitted any thing, I will cheerfully supply it. With regard to Mr. Hurd's works, I am very imperfectly informed, and should prefer you to draw your information from some other source.

There are now in full operation, at Lowell,* six cotton mills, four stories

———

* " About fifteen years ago the now territory of Lowell, being about four square miles, and bearing upon it fifteen thousand inhabitants, was owned by a few honest farmers, who obtained subsistence for themselves and families by the cultivation of this comparatively barren spot, and the fish they caught in the Merrimac and Concord rivers. It comprised the northeasterly part of Chelmsford, and bounded easterly by the Concord river, which separated it from Tewksbury, and northerly by the Merrimac that divided it from Dracut ; and from the fact of its situation at the confluence of these rivers, was called Chelmsford Neck, and originally by the Indians, *Wamaset.*

" Thus for centuries it lay with the vast resources, which we now see developed, slumbering in its bosom, unsuspected and unknown. But the spirit of enterprise and improvement came, and its touch, like that of the magic wand, has turned this seeming wilderness, not simply into a fruitful field, but into a busy, enterprising, and prosperous city.

" In 1819, Kirk Boott, Esq. a wealthy merchant of Boston, in the habit of a hunter, explored this place. He discovered its resources, and immediately, in company with several other rich merchants of that city, purchased the land and water privileges. They were incorporated by the name of the

high, 155 feet by 44, containing 25,000 spindles, and about 150 looms; in which were made, the last year, 5,042,408 yards of cloth, weighing 1,045,386 pounds, from 1,176,082 pounds of raw cotton. The numbers of yarn, 22, 26, 30, and 40. Two mills for twilled and four for plain goods. Three other mills are covered in; the first will be started in January, and the other two in July and January following. There are now employed 1200 persons in

---

'Proprietors of the Locks and Canals on Merrimac river,' and commenced operations by digging a canal from the Pawtucket Falls, easterly, one mile and a half, where it emptied into the Concord river. This canal is sixty feet wide, and carries in depth eight feet of water. This is their grand canal; lateral branches are cut, which carry the water to the several manufacturing mills, and then discharge into the Merrimac or Concord rivers. They then erected a large brick machine shop, and commenced building machinery. This company sell out the privileges to manufacturing companies, dig the canal, erect the mills and build the machinery, and put the whole into operation;—they do it cheaper than any body else would do it; and these are the only terms on which they will sell the privileges. The company has a capital of $600,000, and employs, constantly, about 200 workmen in their machine shop. A part of their lands they have sold out to individuals at an enormous advance on the original price. Land for which they paid $20 or $30 per acre, they have sold for one dollar per square foot. They have still a considerable portion of it on hand and unsold. Kirk Boott, Esq. is their agent.

"Lowell contains, as we have before remarked, about 15,000 inhabitants, and was incorporated in 1824 into a town distinct from Chelmsford, and received its name from Francis C. Lowell, Esq. who early introduced manufactures into this country. There are now about twenty-five factories in operation, and there yet remain unoccupied privileges for nearly as many more. When these shall be taken up, as they, in all probability, will, they will probably afford means of subsistence to another 15,000 inhabitants, making in the whole 30,000.

"A new canal is now being dug, which will furnish sites for about a dozen mills, of the size already built. A company has recently been incorporated by the name of 'Boott Cotton Mills,' which have purchased four of these sites, and upon them are immediately to erect four large brick mills. The railroad from this place to Boston is now complete. It will be, we apprehend, of mutual advantage to both places, and especially to Lowell. It is said to be more permanently built than any other in the country. There are to be two tracks. It will greatly facilitate the immense transportation between these places. A steamboat, owned by Messrs. Bradley & Simpson, has commenced running, between Lowell and Nashua, a distance of fourteen miles. It is to co-operate with the railroad. A spacious market house, 166 feet long, is to be built this season,—$40,000 have been appropriated for the purpose. Our town is deficient in public buildings. A town house, school houses, and poor house, are all, we believe. Our streets are not paved, but will be ere long. And on the whole, notwithstanding its present imperfections and deficiencies, which time, we trust, will remedy, it yet presents, as we believe, much to interest the curious traveller."—*Lowell Journal.*

the mills; nine tenths of whom are females, 20 of whom are from 12 to 14 years of age. Adjoining the mills of the Merrimack Manufacturing Company, are their bleach and print shops, covering more ground, but equal in capacity to two mills; something over a hundred are here employed, about one fifth females, and one fifth boys. None are taken under 12. Apprentices are taken at 14 to 16, until 21; receiving for the first year, including board, $125, and $25 in addition, each succeeding year. Except in the print works, there are no foreigners, and there exceed not one quarter part. Daily wages would perhaps average 50 cents, the minimum being 37½, and the maximum $2 00. At present about 2,500,000 yards are printed, the residue are sold bleached. The average value of the prints is about 18 cents, of the bleached goods 12 to 13 cents. The foundation of the first mill was laid in 1822, and the first return of cloth, November 1823. Belonging to the mills and print works, and in their immediate vicinity, are 130 tenements, about 24 by 36 feet, which rent from $60 to $100 per annum.

The machine shop is of the same dimensions as the mills, and gives employment to about 1,800 machinists; average wages about ninety cents: but as a large portion of the work is by contract, and done by the apprentices, many of them earn from four to six dollars per day. There are 20 tenements attached to the shops; the rent of each of which is about $90 per annum. The cast iron is furnished from Gen. Heach's furnace, about four miles above: consumption averages a ton daily.

The company to whom the machine shop belongs, have a large tract of land and an immense water power, and are prepared to furnish machinery of all descriptions at short notice, and erect the necessary buildings. They have lately contracted to erect two mills, 155 by 44, near the same, and furnish the machinery capable of making 3,000,000 of yards of cloth, yard wide, of No. 14 yarn, per annum,—to build thirty three-story brick tenements, agent's house, and out buildings,—to furnish eight acres of land, and ample water power, and to put the same in operation for about $300,000.

Besides those steadily employed in the mills, about 150 mechanics, such as masons, carpenters, &c., find constant work. The amount of capital actually invested is $2,400,000, viz:

Merrimack Manufacturing Company, - - -	$1,200,000
Proprietors of Land and Canals, - - - - -	600,000
Hamilton Manufacturing Company, - - - -	600,000

With respect to the appropriation of land, I will mention a fact. I purchased, in 1822, nine tenths, undivided, of a farm of 110 acres, for $1,800. The owner of the other one tenth had agreed to convey it for $200, but dying, suddenly, insolvent, it was sold by order of the court, and I gave, for seven and a half tenths of his one tenth, upwards of $3,000. All his debts being satisfied the remainder was sold, a year afterwards, for the benefit of minor children, for nearly $5,000.

Land favourably situated is worth fifteen cents a foot, and there are a few spots that would command fifty. In 1822, the whole population of that part of Chelmsford which now constitutes Lowell, did not, exclusive of Mr. Hurd's mill, exceed 100; it is now probably 5,000.

The solitary storekeeper of 1822, is now surrounded by numerous rivals; and there are few luxuries, and no necessaries, that sharp competition among the dealers does not enable the consumer to purchase as cheap in Lowell as in Boston.

Lowell is situated 25 miles northwest of Boston, on the Merrimack river, and is divided from Tewksbury by the Concord, which here falls into the Merrimack. Middlesex canal empties into the Merrimack, a mile above Lowell, and furnishes a cheap conveyance for heavy articles. At present no manufactured goods are conveyed by this channel to Boston, there being no suitable boats. And indeed, if there were, unless the tolls were considerably lower, there would be little saving. Teaming is done low, and the goods carried to any point. The canal terminating in Charles's River, trucking would be necessary, and the expense would thus very nearly equal teaming.

The consumption of foreign articles, in Lowell, such as madder, sumac, indigo, &c., gives employment to far more tons of shipping than would be required to bring the manufactured goods from abroad; and at the same time furnishes to our own coasters an immense increase of freight, by its steady demand for the products of the other states of the Union, such as quercitron bark, flour, starch, copperas, lime, &c. Were this subject actually examined it would be found to exceed the belief of even those most favourable to the American system.

There is a branch of manufactures rapidly increasing, (and in which there is still great room for improvement,) that owes much of its progress to the establishment of print works. I allude to chemical works; many articles are imported from abroad that can be made full as well at home, and which I have no doubt soon will be. Trusting that the present duties will not be abated for some years, we shall go on building two mills a year; and while we hope to reap a reasonable return, I am sure we are benefiting our country, in at least an equal degree. Yours, truly,

KIRK BOOTT.

—

Extract of a letter, dated Lowell, April 20, 1835.

Gentlemen:—As you have considered the brief sketch which I gave of the business of Fall River, worthy of a place in your columns, the annexed account of Lowell, Mass., which has been obtained at some pains and expense, I think cannot be less so.

The total amount of capital employed in the incorporated companies of this place is $6,650,000. They are at present *nine* in number. The first is the

Locks and Canals Co.—Capital $600,000, for supplying water power to the various manufacturing establishments. The company have an extensive machine shop, for the manufacture of cotton and woollen machinery, railroad cars, engines, &c. They employ 200 men, at good wages.

The Merrimack Co.—Capital $1,500,000,—have an extensive print works, and five cotton mills. They run 34,432 spindles, 1,253 looms, give employment to 1321 females, and 437 males, and make 172,000 yards per week.

The Hamilton Co.—Capital $900,000, have a large printing establishment and three cotton mills. They run about 19,000 spindles, 600 looms—employ about 800 females and 200 males; and make 78,000 yards of prints and drillings per week.

The Appleton Co.—Capital $500,000, run two mills, between 10 and 11,000 spindles, 350 looms—employ 475 females, 70 males, and make 80,000 yards of No. 14 sheetings and shirtings per week.

The Lowell Co.—Capital $500,000, manufacture cotton, carpets, rugs, negro cloths, &c., of a very superior quality. They run 4,500 or 5,000 spindles in their cotton mills—140 cotton and 68 carpet looms—employ 330 females, 150 males, and manufacture in the aggregate about 43,000 yards per week.

The Suffolk Co.—Capital $450,000—run two mills in the manufacture of No. 14 drillings, with 10,240 spindles, 350 looms, give employment to 460 females, 70 males, and makes 90,000 yards per week.

The Tremont Co.—Capital $500,000,—run two mills, 11,000 spindles, 400 looms, employs 450 females and 80 males, and makes 120,000 yards of No. 14 sheetings and shirtings per week.

The Lawrence Co.—Capital $1,200,000, went into operation since either of the above. They run at present four cotton mills, for the manufacture of sheetings and shirtings, No. 14 to 30, 37 to 41 inch wide ; another large mill and a bleaching establishment is soon to be in operation.

The Middlesex Co.—Capital $500,000, is a very fine establishment; the superior character of their goods is too well established to require notice here. They manufacture broadcloths and cassimeres, in which they consume 470,000 lbs. of wool and 1,500,000 teasels annually. They run two mills, 3120 spindles, 98 looms—give employment to 240 females, and 145 males—making about 6000 yards of cloth per week. In a few weeks this company will manufacture 500 yards of satinet per day, in addition to their present business.—They will then work up 2000 lbs. of wool per day !

The above establishments consume yearly 11,239 tons anthracite coal ; 4750 cords of wood, and 50,549 gallons of oil. The total amount of cloth made is 39,170,000 yards per annum, which requires in the manufacture about 12,256,400 pounds of cotton. In the bleacheries &c. they use 310,000 lbs. of starch, 380 barrels of flour, and 500,000 bushels of coal per annum.

The average sum of money paid to the persons in these establishments, is $89,000 per month.

Besides the above, there are in this place, a flannel factory ; the extensive powder mills belonging to O. M. Whipple, card and whip factory, glass works, furnace, &c. employing from 300 to 400 hands.

I believe it is decided on to commence shortly the erection of *four* new mills (*not thirteen*, as has been published) on a canal now cutting for the purpose. There will still be room and water in the place for *five* more, but I have not learned that it will be likely to be occupied soon. *Belvidere* is now a part of Lowell, by an act of the legislature : taken together, they present the most thriving and business-like appearance ; and will rank in population with Newark, in New Jersey, or indeed, with any inland town in the United States.

North Providence was incorporated 1767. It is now distinguished for its manufactures, particularly those of cotton, which form an important interest. There are ten cotton mills, one of which is the first that was built in America, and in Pawtucket, S. Slater erected the first water-frame spinning machinery. The extent of this business having concentrated a large capital, and an immense aggregate of industry, has, within the last thirty years, given rise to a large and flourishing village. The village of Pawtucket is situated in the north-east section of the town, four miles north-east of Providence, on the border of the Seekonk river; its site being principally the declivity of a hill, and it is highly romantic and picturesque. The river here affords numerous natural sites for manufacturing establishments, mills and hydraulic works of almost every description; which are occupied to a great extent. The rapid march of manufacturing and mechanical industry, which the short annals of this place disclose, has few examples in our country, and has produced one of the most considerable and flourishing manufacturing places in the United States, and the village is built upon both sides of it, being partly in Rhode Island and partly in Massachusetts. That part of the village which is in Rhode Island, is principally built on four streets; and comprises eighty-three dwelling-houses, and twelve mercantile stores. There are six shops engaged in the manufacturing of machinery, having the advantage of water-power; and various other mechanical establishments, affording extensive employment and supporting a dense population. Upon the Massachusetts side of the river, there is a village of nearly equal size and consequence, for its manufacturing and other interests. Besides the cotton business, there are in the town two furnaces for casting, one slitting mill, two anchor shops, two screw manufactories, three grain mills, one clothier's works, &c. fourteen stores, three places of worship, two academies, and eight schools.

Here the first Sunday-school was taught in New England.

Pawtucket had advanced with uninterrupted prosperity; in consequence of the superior road to Providence, it was viewed as a suburb of the city, and the intercourse was a continual stream of carriages, and conveyances of cotton, returning with cloth and other manufactured goods.

Iron works, machinery, nail manufactory, flour mills, as well as the cotton manufacture, were carried on in the first style; till such a demand for houses, tenements, &c. obliged the inhabitants to build in a rapid manner, so that its appearance as a place of business surpassed any other of its size and dimensions; all its water was fully occupied. This was the cradle of the cotton business, and the consequence of Slater's spinning frame.

Previous to 1829, Pawtucket presented a village of steady and increasing prosperity; every man, woman, and child, found full employment, at the highest rate of wages. Those who knew the place in 1790,* were astonished at the rapidity with which buildings of every description arose. And though in the vicinity of Providence, every article of commerce was kept for sale in elegant shops and stores. The cotton mills never ceased to operate their thousands of spindles which had been erected, and produced a quantity of cloth almost incredible to those unacquainted with the power and speed of the water frame and power loom, of the latest improvement. Here, machinery was manufactured for other parts

---

* In Benedict's history, 1813, is the following notice :—" The manufacturing of cotton on Arkwright's plan was begun in Pawtucket, in 1790, by Samuel Slater, Esq. from England. There are now in this village, and near, almost 7000 spindles in operation, and within a mile and a quarter of it, including both sides of the river, are buildings erected, capable of containing about 12,000 more. In 1810, according to an account taken by John K. Pitman of Providence, in the state of Rhode Island, only, were thirty-nine factories, in which over 30,000 spindles were running, and the same factories were capable of containing about as many more. The number of spindles in this state only is, in 1813, probably not far from 50,000. In 1810, the gentleman above mentioned ascertained, that within thirty miles of Providence, which includes a considerable territory in Massachusetts, and a small portion of Connecticut, there were seventy-six factories, capable of containing 111,000 spindles. The number of spindles now in actual operation within this circumference are said to be 120,000. The amount of yarn spun each week is not far from 110,000 pounds, or 5,500,000 a year. This side of the river Delaware, the number of cotton factories of different dimensions, built and building, are estimated at five hundred. We may add to the account of places of worship in Rhode Island, that there are many new commodious school houses, in the neighbourhood of the factories, built by their owners on purpose for public worship, as well as schools.

" In 1809, seventeen cotton mills were in operation within the town of Providence and its vicinity, working 14,296 spindles, and using 640,000 pounds of cotton, which yielded 510,000 pounds of yarn. About 1000 looms were employed in weaving. At that time seven additional mills were erecting in the vicinity of the town. One was in operation in East Greenwich with five hundred spindles. The cloths manufactured were bed-ticking, stripes and checks, ginghams, shirting, and counterpanes. They are superior to imported goods of the same kind. There was then a woollen manufactory in Warwick and another at Portsmouth. About 50,000 hats were then made annually, worth $5 each, exclusive of felt hats. A number of paper mills are established. Linen and tow cloth are made extensively, as well as rum, cards, chocolate, and the coarser manufactures of iron. At North Providence, in 1795, there were erected on the Pawtucket, three anchor forges, one slitting mill, two machines for cutting nails, one tanning mill, one oil mill, three snuff mills, one grist mill, one cotton manufactory, one clothier's works, and three fulling mills; they all go by water. Their number in 1812 was much increased."

of the country, and the very best mechanics from Europe found ready employment. There was a time when wheat was brought from the west to the flour mills. These, together with nail factories and other iron works, caused Pawtucket to be a place of business. The road from Pawtucket to Providence was equal to any in the world, and was the admiration of travellers; it connected North Providence with the city, and the intercourse was incessant. Churches and schools were created in sufficient numbers to educate the youth, and accommodate the whole of the inhabitants in their different modes of worship.

The cotton manufactories of Smithfield, R. I. (1819) are important and extensive. There are nine factories, all of which contain more than 11,000 spindles. About one half of these belong to one establishment, owned by Almy, Brown and Slaters. This mill is situated upon the aforesaid branch of the Pawtucket river, about one mile and a half from its junction, being an excellent site for hydraulic works. At this place, there is a large and flourishing village called Slatersville, comprising from six to eight hundred inhabitants. This village is of recent date, having grown up with the manufacturing business, which may be considered as the parent of it. It is impossible to contemplate such a village as this, without the most pleasing sensations and reflections. What a seat of wealth, a focus of activity, and a nursery of industry! What a display of mechanical ingenuity, and what a developement of the importance and influence of the useful arts! What a combination and variety of operations, what diversity of employment, and what a number of distinct and curious processes are comprised in the manufacture of those fabrics requisite to supply the wants which the refinements of society occasion! Who can look upon such manufacturing villages as this, without regarding them as the germs of the future Manchesters of America? In addition to the cotton factories which have been noticed, there is another establishment, containing 8000 spindles, which is supposed to be within the bounds of this town, owned by Butler, Wheaton, & Co. of Providence.

Smithfield is well supplied with schools, there being twenty regular ones, which are provided with suitable houses, and are maintained through the year, and several private schools; three incorporated academies; four social libraries; and four places of worship. There is a remarkable fall of water upon the Pawtucket river, called Woonsocket Falls, which is a curiosity. The fall is about twenty feet; it is not perpendicular, but over a precipice of rocks for some distance. The fall of the water upon these rocks,

through a succession of ages, has occasioned numerous excava-
tions, all of which are smooth and circular, and some of them
very large, being sufficient to contain several hogsheads.

CHEPACHET, (Gloucester, R. I.) Nov. 1831.

Dear sir,—This village is sixteen miles north west of Providence, and
contains about six hundred inhabitants, a church, a school house, and a fire
engine ; it is on a branch of the Blackstone.   Here are three cotton factories,
two of them belong to H. B. Lymon & Co., who run 1452 spindles, 41
looms, employ 60 hands, consume 125 bales of New Orleans cotton of 400
pounds each, or 50,000 lbs. a year, and make 270,000 yards of No. 30 printing
goods ; the other one belongs to Arnold & Wood, who run 1000 spindles, 23
looms, employ about 20 hands, and work up 800lbs. a week, or 40,000lbs. a
year—they make 3000 yards a week, or 150,000 yards a year, of shirting.

About eight miles from this settlement, I struck upon a small stream,
called the Woonsocket.   There is no stream that I have yet seen, for
its size, that sustains so many manufacturing establishments as this little
river does.   There are on its banks twenty-five mills of various kinds,
giving support and employment to about thirteen hundred persons.   On this
stream the first power looms in Rhode Island were put into operation.   It is
indeed a little river, but it is more valuable to the country from the efficient
industry that it sustains, than if its waters flowed over a bed of auriferous
lands.

On this stream there are, also, two reservoirs, belonging to the several
mill proprietors, who are united into a company for the purpose, under an
act of incorporation—the first ever constructed under the authority of this
state for use of mills.   The reservoirs contain 200 acres, with an average
depth of eight feet, and to be drawn off in seasons of drought.   My leisure
did not admit of my visiting the mills on this stream: I therefore commenced
at the Georgia Manufacturing Mills.   Their main building is of stone, four
stories high, and 180 feet long; they run 3700 spindles, 104 looms, employ
150 hands, and work up 3000lbs. of cotton a week, or 156,000lbs. a year.
They manufacture printing goods, and turn out 13,500 yards a week, or
675,000 in a year.   Samuel Nightingale, Esq., is the agent at Providence,
and Israel Saunders at the factories.

Half a mile below, is another large establishment, belonging to Philip
Allen, Esq.   There is a stone building 125 feet long, with several ramifications of brick and wood, all painted white, which gives it an aspect of neatness and beauty : 4300 spindles and 100 looms are run, giving employment
to 130 operatives.   Here are made only fine goods, from No. 45 to 50.
H. Holden, agent.

Another half a mile below this, Richard Anthony & Son have a cotton
mill of 768 spindles, 22 looms, giving employment to 30 hands ; they work
up 80 bales of cotton, and make 2200 yards of sheetings a week, or 111,000
in a year.   A short distance from here, the Centre Manufacturing Company
have a stone mill of 2475 spindles, 60 looms, and employ 75 hands.   They
make sheetings.   They use 2500lbs. of cotton a week, or 125,000lbs. in a
year, and turn out 7500 yards a week, or 375,000 a year.   James Anthony
is the agent of both these establishments.

Something short of a mile from the last mill, you come to Zachariah Allen, Esq.'s woollen manufactory. It is of stone, 60 feet by 40, four stories high, with out buildings for dyeing, &c. There are 600 spindles, 21 broadcloth looms, which give employment to 60 hands. He works up 50,000lbs. of wool, and makes 65 yards a day, or 22,500 yards a year, of broadcloth, valued at from three to four dollars a yard. John Wait, agent.

Mr. Allen's mill is about four miles from Providence. As you proceed down the stream you come to the Lyman Manufacturing Company's establishment. They have two mills, and run 2200 spindles, 60 looms, and employ 75 hands. They make 11,000 yards a week, or 550,000 yards a year of printing goods. Three quarters of a mile below, Manton & Kelley run 800 spindles, 26 looms—employ about 30 hands, and make 5,500 yards a week of printing goods, equal to 275,000 yards in a year. The Marino mills are three miles from Providence, and belong to Franklin & Waterman. They run 1656 spindles, 78 looms, and employ 80 hands: they make 7000 yards a week, or 350,000 a year. Two miles from Providence, in the village of Johnston, Ephraim Talbot and others, have 1500 spindles, 40 looms, and employ 65 hands. They make 5,500 yards a week of seven-eighth sheetings, which is equal to 275,000 yards in a year. Half a mile below, R. Waterman has two mills—one for the making of oil, the other for brown paper. The last establishment on the Woonsocket, and to me the most interesting, is Salmon Townsend & Co.'s manufactory of hat bodies. Mr. Joseph Grant is the company and the inventor of machinery. He is a native of Rhode Island, and has been possessed of his patent for ten years. They work up 200lbs. of wool a day, and make in the same time 1000 hat bodies, or 300,000 in a year. I should like to give you a description of the machinery, but it requires more technicalites than I am possessed of to do it justice—beside, although simple in itself, it should be seen in operation to form a just estimate of the genius that invented it, and of the great value it is to the country.

WOONSOCKET FALLS.

The following article is from the pen of a correspondent of the New York Transcript, under date, " Smithfield, R. I., April 12." The writer ought to have said Woonsocket Falls may be denominated the " capital of Smithfield and Cumberland." The Blackstone river is the dividing line between the towns, at this place, and the principal part of the village lies in Cumberland. The writer says—

This is a delightful town. It is the "bordershire" of the state, and joins the county of Worcester, one of the richest, most healthful, and enterprising sections of country to be found on the face of the globe.—The town of Smithfield, for many years had devoted itself exclusively to agricultural pursuits, but of late has become the very focus of " American industry." The Blackstone river and canal runs through it, and the almost endless variety of scenery with which it abounds, gives it many advantages over the ordinary inland towns of New England. It largely participates in the industry of the day, and probably operates a greater number of spindles than any town or village this side of the Potomac.

The village of Woonsocket, which may be denominated the "capital of Smithfield," is at the fall of the Blackstone river, and drives a very heavy as well as a profitable business. I am informed that upwards of fifty thousand spindles are operated at this place, to say nothing of an immense quantity of other machinery. The village partakes of all the variety of pastoral beauty, and its cliffs and waterfalls, and bubbling rivulets, are preeminently calculated to give inspiration to the poet.

The mill sites at Woonsocket are very valuable; it is said they could not be purchased for half a million of dollars, and yet the whole village was sold twenty years ago for twenty thousand dollars. The price given for it at that time was considered exorbitant; and its former proprietor, James Arnold, Esq., has, I believe, made some legal attempts to get the estates back again. In all this he has been unsuccessful; and the consequence has been, tedious and vexatious litigation, without the attainment of a single object.

The village and most of its "dependencies" belong to capitalists of Providence, and in their operations they give employment to some hundreds if not thousands. Although I am not an advocate of the "factory system," and know that it is full of abuses, I must confess that the appearance of the operatives of Woonsocket goes in no small degree to repel and repudiate the objections that have been so often and forcibly urged against manufacturing establishments. The whole body of spinners have the appearance of comfort and domestic happiness, and if they do not enjoy these rich and desirable blessings, I am deceived in my calculations.

———

SOUTH OXFORD, Slaterville, Nov. 1831.

Dear sir,—The town of Douglas is about an equal distance from Uxbridge and this place, being about six miles from each. The source of the Mumford river, which I have heretofore named to you, is within four miles of Douglas, and is from Manchoug, Wallace, and Badluck Ponds. On this stream and in the east part of the town, the Douglas Manufacturing Company have two mills—one of stone, and both five stories high. They have 4,000 spindles, 119 looms, and employ 200 hands. They work up 275,000lbs. of cotton into 1,000,000 of yards of printing goods. They have, also, a small woollen concern for making *bockings*; but it is to be relinquished, as it does not answer their expectations—Samuel Lovett, agent. Douglas contains 2,000 inhabitants, and three places of public worship.

Slaterville embraces a part of Dudley, as well as of this town, and an effort is to be made, I understand, to have it set off as a separate and independent town. Here resides Samuel Slater, Esq. the patriarch of manufactures in this country. It is only known to a few that the world is indebted to this gentleman for the discovery of cotton thread. In 1794, while spinning a quantity of Sea Island cotton, the evenness and beauty of the yarn attracted the attention of Mrs. Slater. The question arose, if this is doubled and twisted, why will it not make good sewing thread? The experiment was made, and in order to be fully satisfied of the result, a sheet was made with one half of linen thread and the other half with the cotton. It was immediately put into use, and the first thread that gave way was the linen! From this period, he commenced the manufacture of thread, and it soon spread into England, France, and other European countries, where it is generally supposed to be of English origin.

Mr. Slater is also the author of Sunday schools in this country, the good effects of which will be more durable than monuments of marble. He is now in his 64th year. His benevolence and philanthropy have been co-extensive with his means; and few have done more to bring young and enterprising men into business than Samuel Slater. He has, probably, now a larger amount employed in manufactures than any single individual in the United States. The firm here is Samuel Slater & Sons.

They have seven mills—two of stone, three of brick, and two of wood. Five of these derive their power from French river; the other two are in the centre of the village, and obtain their power from Slater's lake; the Indian of which is *Chorgoggaggoggmanchogga*. It is a large pond more than four miles long, and is a never failing source of supply. They use 6,000 spindles, and 90 looms, employ 180 hands, and work up 1,000 bales of cotton, which produces 15,000 yards a week, beside large quantities of satinet warps, and sewing thread. They manufacture, also, broad cloths, cassimeres, and satinets. In this branch of their business, they use 600lbs. of wool a day, or 180,000lbs. a year.

GENERAL JACKSON'S VISIT TO PAWTUCKET.

The present chief magistrate of the Union, in company with the vice president, waited on Mr. Slater, at his house, to thank him, and congratulate him, as the representative of this great republic, as a friend and benefactor of the country, by introducing among them valuable machinery, before unknown, which has changed the whole policy of the nation. In particular, it has promoted the growth of cotton at the south, and changed the whole face of New England, and thereby made the solitary places literally glad. It has raised amidst rocks and barren land the most beautiful villages, teaming with joy and gladness. Forming a numerous population, not ignorant and vicious, not ragged and oppressed, but paid, fed, and dressed, with the best the country affords; not sunken in profligacy and dissipation, but raised in intelligence, and morals, as well as religious feeling, beyond the other parts of the States. When the president witnessed these scenes of honest industry, of happiness and plenty, of order and decorum, examples of sobriety and morals—he expressed the highest satisfaction. When he was told, that the man who introduced the foundation of this prosperity resided in the village, but was confined to his house by a rheumatic disorder, the consequence of his early exposure in operating his first machinery, President Jackson, with his suite, repaired to the house to pay his respects to the man who had thus benefited our common country. With the affability and complaisance so peculiar to General Jackson, he addressed Mr. Slater as the father of the American manufactures, as the man who had erected the first valuable machinery, and who had spun yarn to make the first *cotton-cloth* in America ; and who had, by his superintendence and direction, as well as by intense personal labour, erected the first *cotton-mill* in Rhode Island ; which was first in the land of the pilgrims.   General Jackson, who had been informed of these particulars, entered into familiar conversation on the subject. " I understand," said the president, " you taught us how to spin, so as to rival Great Britain in her manufactures ; you set all these thousands of spindles at work, which I have been delighted in viewing, and which have made so many happy, by a lucrative employment." " Yes, sir," said Slater, " I suppose that I gave out the psalm, and they have been singing to the tune ever since."   " We are glad to hear also, that you have realised something for yourself and family," said the vice president. " Yes, sir, I have obtained a competency."   " We are all glad to hear that." " So am I glad to know it," said Slater ; " for I should not like to be a pauper, in this country, where they are put up at auction to the lowest bidder."

After this social talk with the president and his suite, General Jackson observed in parting—" It must give you great pleasure to see health and prosperity spread all around you, and to see the progress which has been made, since you first came amongst us ; the change is very great, I am told that cotton cloth is lower than was ever known before.   I trust you will persevere and go on to perfection."   " Cotton cloth is rather too low for profit, but I suppose it is as good as raising corn for fifty cents per bushel, so that we must not complain."

I visited the present Mrs. Slater, at her house in Pawtucket, R. I. for the purpose of conversing with her on the last sickness of her deceased husband ; and nothing could exceed the reverence and affection with which she spoke of him ; his firmness and forbearance in conducting his business ; his abilities to regulate his numerous concerns ; how he always relied on his own resources ; his deep sense of gratitude for the care and goodness of a benignant Providence over him, from his youth up ; when, left in early life without a father's watchful eye to guide him, he bound himself to Mr. Strutt ; when he left his native land, and visited a land of strangers, without introduction or a single acquaintance, in raising him up friends, especially a father in Oziel Wilkinson, and beloved companion ; and in affording him opportunities to prosecute his enterprise ; for these mercies, and others innumerable, I have great cause for gratitude. He bore his various pains and sicknesses with great patience, though he disliked that any one should have the particular care of him but Mrs. Slater, who was constantly at his call, and watching over his wishes, to alleviate his complaints, and afford him all that a tender and affectionate female can afford her best friend in distress.   These consolations he had to the last ; she watched over his dying moments, and his dying breathings, and heard the last word he uttered, "*Farewell.*"* That final word closed all his communications with man on earth ; whereby he bade adieu to his wife and children and to all his concerns. Mrs. Slater has endeared herself to his children, for her constant and unwearied care to them when young, and to those of them who died after her marriage to Mr. Slater.

The writer of this memoir can give testimony with what fidelity and judgment she took the charge of Mr. Slater's domestic concerns—the whole care of his family ; which she conducted in a style becoming their situation ; and though the last seventeen years were in a great measure years of sorrow and affliction, yet his situation was greatly alleviated by a faithful friend and a partner of his griefs. Our deceased friend was sensible of her value to him ; he arranged her property, and adjusted his will in all respects satisfactorily and agreeable to the wishes of his widow, according to their mutual agreements. Mrs. Slater knew him and lived with him when his mental powers were fully developed; he had improved himself by much reading of the best authors in the English language. His perceptions were quick and his observations of mankind very extensive and penetrating. He knew the depth of every person he conversed with ; his particular dislike was to *falsehood, deception, and dishonesty;* other faults he appeared readily to forgive, these he never passed over without severe censure. It was no wonder that so indefatigable a man as he was himself, should dislike listlessness and idleness ; he used to say, "I will help those who will try to help themselves ; but

---

* Found in Mr. Slater's bible, written on a small piece of paper, a short time before his death; his mind had been depressed by some afflictive circumstances which weighed on him. Also the passage in Judges, chap. X. 15th verse, was marked by a leaf being turned down.

Psalms, chap. XLII. 11th verse,—" Why art thou cast down, O my soul, and why art thou disquieted within me? Hope thou in God, for I shall yet praise him who is the health of my countenance and my God."

Prov. chap. XVII. 28th verse,—" Even a fool when he holdeth his peace is counted wise, and he that shutteth his lips is esteemed."

those who will not, I do not see it my duty; such ought to suffer the consequences of their indolence;" this was a fixed principle with him. His tenderness to animals, and every thing under his care, whether cat or dog, horse or cow, sheep or oxen, showed that he was of a merciful disposition. He was not cruel and morose, though he was frequently silent and reserved, especially to persons with whom he was not intimate. It took some time for him to unbend and become easy and talkative; but when he did, his conversation was worth hearing; and his sons hung on his lips, and all his people treasured up his sayings and observations as so many oracles of wisdom.

With Obadiah Brown (his partner, mentioned in the note below) * he formed a close and sincere friendship, and always spoke of his loss with sincere regret. In the year 1829, he observed to me, " I should not have been so tried, if Obadiah Brown had been living." This affection was reciprocal; for there was no one in whom the son of Moses Brown placed more confidence, than in Samuel Slater, whom he named as his executor in his will; and showed, to his last moments, how highly he esteemed his valuable partner at the " Old Mill."

* Whereas there are acts unsettled between William Almy and Obadiah Brown, under the firm of Almy & Brown, and Samuel Slater, commencing from the year one thousand eight hundred and three, and continuing to the present time, and whereas they being desirous to bring them to a close, have in order thereto mutually and hereby fully agree that the following terms shall be the final close thereof up to the first day in the present year, viz. that Almy & Brown pay to Samuel Slater the sum of five thousand dollars, and that the stock in the mill, and in the hands of Almy & Brown, and Samuel Slater, or in the hands of their agents, as well as all debts due to them as owners of the cotton mill at Pawtucket, shall continue and belong to them in the several proportions which they hold in the said mill, say one third to each person; and that all their acts with each other of every name be considered as settled up to the said first day of the present year; and that the said acts, whether in the mill books, or in the books of either Almy & Brown, or Samuel Slater, be entered balanced up to the first day of the said present year, excepting so far as relates to the balances of stock and outstanding debts, which at that time was in the hands of the said Almy & Brown, and the said Samuel Slater or their agents, which stock and debts belonged to them as owners of the said cotton mill at Pawtucket, shall, as beforesaid, continue to belong to them as heretofore. It is also understood that all the notes and mortgages which they hold together as owners of the cotton mill aforesaid, shall be considered as belonging to them the same as the balances of stock and outstanding debts of any other description. It is also agreed that all notes which they have of each other, that is to say against each other, shall be given up as included in this settlement; and that this agreement and conclusion shall be binding upon them, the said

CABOTSVILLE.

This pleasant village is growing up with astonishing rapidity, and bids fair to become, at no very distant day, a second Lowell. A few weeks produce changes here that almost destroy the identity of the place, and give to the visiter new objects of admiration on every repetition of his visit. Streets are cut in every direction, and dwellings and shops going up as if by some magic influence ; yet, notwithstanding the changes that are wrought from week to week by the spirited enterprise of its citizens, the influx of population and the increase of business ; its growth seems to be that of health, and warranted by its extremely favourable location and business facilities. The water power at this place is immense ; and as yet, scarcely begun to be occupied. There is a neatness, too, and good taste in the location of the streets and the arrangement of buildings, which is not common in manufacturing villages, and which reflects great credit upon those who have superintended the arrangement. The cotton factories are extensive, and in appearance resembling those at Lowell. We were politely conducted through the different establishments at this place a few days since, by a friend connected with one of them, and were highly pleased with the perfect good order which prevailed in every department—every one apparently understanding and discharging his duties with a promptness and ease which showed familiarity with the occupation. From the cotton factories and machine shops we proceeded to the sword establishment of N. P. Ames. This is well worth a visit from every one who has a taste for finished cutlery. Mr. Ames is a contractor under government for the manufacturing of swords for the officers of the army and navy of the United States.

The flourishing village of Willimantic is situated in Windham county, Connecticut, on the Willimantic river, near its confluence with another small river called the Natchaug. It extends about a mile along the former stream. Twelve years ago, there were less than a dozen houses, and those very indifferent ones, on the site

Almy & Brown, and the said Samuel Slater, their heirs, executors, and administrators. Agreed to and signed, this nineteenth day of second month, called February, in the year of our Lord one thousand eight hundred and nineteen.   ALMY & BROWN.
                                                        SAMUEL SLATER.
          Witnesses, *Samuel Slater, Jun., John Slater.*
   Obadiah Brown, named in this agreement, took the place of Smith Brown, and continued in the business till his death.

of the present village.* Now there are four manufacturing establishments here, (running twelve thousand eight hundred spindles,
and making annually two millions nine hundred and fifteen thousand yards of cotton cloth,) besides a very superior paper mill
lately erected, where printing paper of the best quality is made in
great quantities, and there is also a small sattinet manufactory.
There are three houses for public worship in the village,—two
free and three private schools, a public library, six stores where
goods are retailed, and one hundred dwelling houses, containing,
many of them, from two to four families each. I have resided
three years in Willimantic, and have no hesitation in asserting,
from personal experience and observation, that the schools are as
well attended here, the scholars, generally, as forward in their
education, and the inhabitants as moral in their conversation and
conduct, as the people of the neighbouring towns where the *manufacturing system* has not yet been introduced.

A great proportion of the inhabitants of this place, before they
came here, were possessed of little or no property. Many of them
were in a state of abject poverty. Not owning land for cultivation,
and having been educated to no trade, they had no regular employment for themselves or for their families, nor means of supporting
them. To them the manufacturing system has indeed proved a
blessing. It has furnished them and their children with steady
employment, enabled them to clothe their families and obtain for
them a regular and comfortable subsistence, and to give their
children a decent education.

The *system*, therefore, as it respects the classes above mentioned,
(and they constitute three fourths of the population of all the
manufacturing villages,) works well; and no objections can be
offered against it which cannot, in my opinion, be readily and
satisfactorily answered.

GREENEVILLE.

This beautiful village, situated on the west bank of Shetucket
river, a little below its junction with the Quinebaug, and five

---

* No chapter in the history of national manners would illustrate so well
the progress of social life, as that dedicated to domestic architecture. The
fashions of dress and of amusement are generally capricious and irreducible
to rule, but every change in the dwellings of mankind, from the log house to
the stately mansion, has been dictated by some principle of convenience,
neatness, comfort or magnificence.

hundred rods above steam and packet navigation, has had almost as rapid a growth as the villages of the west. In the year 1828, the general assembly of Connecticut granted a charter to a company of individuals under the name of the "Norwich Water Power Company," the object of which was the construction of works to bring into use the immense water power then wholly unoccupied at this place. The capital of the company was $40,000; and having purchased a large tract of land lying on both sides of the river, they proceeded to erect a dam and dig a canal, through which the water of the river, necessary for manufacturing purposes, might flow.

These works required much skill and labour. The river at this place is much larger than any other in this section of the country across which a dam had ever been erected for manufacturing purposes, and there are perhaps few if any larger in the United States. It was doubted by many whether a dam could be made to stand permanently against so powerful a stream, and one subject also to great annual freshets. It was built of stone, in length 280 feet, and of a character so solid and substantial, as when finished there seemed little reason to apprehend that it would be carried away. Experience thus far has strengthened this opinion. The abutments of this dam are certainly very handsome and durable specimens of stone masonry. The canal is about one mile (4620 feet) in length, 46 in width at the surface, and 10 feet deep. These works were completed in 1830.

It will be recollected that the manufacturing business was in a state of great depression about this period of time; so great indeed that many persons entertained the belief that it would never revive again in New England. The prospect was gloomy indeed, but the work had been commenced and was vigorously prosecuted. The growth of the village, as has been remarked, has been most rapid. It already contains about sixty dwelling houses, one church, two stores, one tavern, three firms of carpenters engaged in building, one firm of masons, one shoemaker's establishment, one tailor's, two milliner's, and one blacksmith's, (besides a blacksmithery establishment connected with each manufactory). Population about 850.

Of the manufacturing establishments, it may be proper to speak more in detail.

The largest is that of the Thames Company, for the manufacture of cotton cloth. It is one of the finest edifices of the kind in New England, being built of brick, five stories high, 138 in length by 44 in width. There are employed in it about 180 persons of different ages and sexes ; about 42,000 lbs. of cotton are worked up in it per month, and about 132,000 yards of cloth manufactured in the same space of time.

The mill of Messrs. Kennedy & Tillinghast, the Shetucket Tick Factory, for the manufacture of bed ticking, contains 1650 spindles, and employs about 70 persons. About 14,000lbs. of cotton are worked, and 28,000 yards of cloth manufactured each month.

The Greeneville Manufacturing Co. employs about 50 persons, and turns out about 12,000 yards of flannel per month, using for that purpose about 4800lbs. of wool.

The Chelsea Manufacturing Company employs about 20 persons in the manufacture of paper. About 2800lbs. of rags are worked up each day. Some idea of the amount of business done by this company may be inferred from the fact, that the paper sold to a single newspaper establishment in the city of New York, amounts to about $20,000 per annum.

In addition to these establishments there are two manufactories of carpets, one of which is just getting into operation, and which together employ about 30 persons ; a machine shop which employs about 20 men ; a manufactory of wood-screws which employs a similar number ; a window sash and blind manufactory which employs about a dozen ; and a manufactory of mould buttons which employs about 20 persons. The place is still increasing, numerous dwelling houses and stores now being in progress. A number of very eligible sites for manufacturing establishments of any description are yet unoccupied, and there is a large amount of water power unemployed. No ardent spirits are sold at any place within the limits originally purchased by the Water Power Company, and in all deeds or grants of land made by them, is a clause requiring the observance of that regulation, the penalty for the violation of which, if persisted in, after thirty days' notice in writing given to discontinue the same, is a forfeiture of the building where the offence shall have been committed, with the land annexed to the same, to the granters, their successors and assigns.

The village is situated in a delightful tract of country, and is very neat and attractive in its appearance. The dwellings, though not large, contain generally from two to four families, most of which take boarders. Being all painted white, they have a uniform and handsome appearance, and seem to be the abode of industry and contentment. The place derives its name from William P. Greene, Esq. formerly of Boston, now of this city, to whose capital and public spirit, not merely this village, but this town and vicinity are very largely indebted for their prosperity.

The theme we have selected would seem to afford little room for the exercise of the fancy or the imagination. Still, the scene where our article is laid, is by no means barren of poetical associations. The brave and warlike Miantonimo, the sachem of the Narragansets, lies buried on the estate of the Water Power Company, all unconscious of the buzzing wheels and whirring spindles which are revolving so rapidly around his last resting place. We may as well add that the grave of Uncas, the sachem of the Mohicans, is also in the vicinity, near the residence of the Hon. Calvin Goddard. Miantonimo, it will be remembered, was defeated and taken prisoner by Uncas, and subsequently put to death. Life's fitful fever being over, the victorious and the vanquished, the captive and the conqueror, sleep quietly and peacefully together.

There are a number of cotton and woollen factories established in the towns along the Ohio. Cincinnati is a rival of Pittsburg, in manufactures of iron, &c. There are a number of furnaces for smelting iron ore, in the counties along the Ohio, particularly in the region of Hocking River. Glass is manufactured in several towns in the same part of the state. Iron is also made in some of the counties bordering on Lake Erie. On the Muskingum, below Zanesville, salt is manufactured at various places, for about thirty miles,—260,000 bushels are made annually. Considerable quantities are also made on Yellow Creek, about fourteen or fifteen miles above Steubenville. In 1830, there were, in this state, $334,672 invested in the manufacture of salt, and 446,350 bushels were made. In every town and village in the state, all the ordinary manufactures, such as hats, cabinet ware, &c., are made to an extent proportioned to the demand. And almost every farmer is the manufacturer of a large part of the articles of wearing apparel, &c. which his family need. It is impossible to make any estimate of these things ; if it could be done, it would exhibit a very great amount of manufactures of this sort, and of immense value.

Cincinnati is the great commercial emporium of Ohio,—and, next to New Orleans, the largest city in the valley of the Mississippi. It was founded in 1789. There have been built, at this city, no less than *one hundred and fifty steamboats !* The value of the manufactures of this city is very great ; exceeding $2,500,000 annually ! Vast quantities of cabinet work, hats, &c., are here made for exportation.

1. There are ten foundries, including a brass and bell foundry,

and one for casting type. 2. There are three or four cotton factories, and fifteen rolling mills, and steam engine factories and shops. 3. There are five breweries. 4. There is a button factory, and a steam coopering establishment, where several thousand barrels are made, annually, by machinery, propelled by steam. 5. Two steam flour mills, and five or six steam saw mills. 6. There is one chemical laboratory. There are not less than forty different manufacturing establishments driven by steam power.

"We had the pleasure," says a traveller, "a few days since, of visiting the works of this company, situated on the north bank of the Appomattox, about four miles from Petersburgh, and were no less gratified by the beauty and substantial appearance of the buildings than surprised at the expedition with which they have been erected. They consist of two cotton mills, three stories high, a machine shop and sizing house, built of granite of a superior quality, obtained from a quarry on the company's land. The principal mill is 118 feet long by 44 feet wide ; the other 90 feet long by 40 feet wide. They will contain about 4,000 spindles and 170 looms ; a large portion of which have been set up and ready for use. In addition to these buildings, the company have erected a granite house for a store, and fifteen or twenty frame tenements, as residences for the workmen, each to contain two families ; and preparations have been made to erect as many more as the establishment may require. When the whole shall be completed, and the mills in full operation, it is estimated that Matoaca will contain between four and five hundred inhabitants. It had already assumed the appearance of a village, and will, in a short time, vie with any manufacturing establishment in the country, for beauty of situation, the substantial construction of its buildings, and the care and attention bestowed on the comfortable accommodation of the workmen.

"It is expected to put the works in operation early in the next month, and we understand that it is the intention of the company to manufacture all the cotton spun in their mills, into cloth. Matoaca furnishes another gratifying evidence of the enterprise of our fellow citizens, and of the increasing prosperity of Petersburgh. We have now, in addition to the several well known flour mills, five cotton, and two cotton seed oil mills ; and there remains a large unemployed water power on the Appomattox."

"It gives me great pleasure," says Webster, "on occasion of so large an assembly of the city of Buffalo, to express my thanks for the kindness and hospitality with which I have been received in this young, but growing and interesting town.   The launching of another vessel on these inland seas, is but a fresh occasion of gratulation on the rapid growth, the great active prosperity, and the exciting future prospects of this town.   Eight years ago, fellow citizens, I enjoyed the pleasure of a short visit to this place : there was then but one steamboat on Lake Erie ; it made its passage once in ten or fifteen days only ; and I remember that persons in my own vicinity, intending to travel to the far west, by that conveyance, wrote to friends to learn the day of the commencement of the contemplated voyage.   I understand that there are now eighteen steamboats plying on the lake, all finding full employment; and that a boat leaves Buffalo, thrice every day, for Detroit and the ports in Ohio.   The population of Buffalo, now four times as large as it was then, has kept pace with the augmentation of its commercial business.   This rapid progress is a sample, but certainly is not to be regarded as the measure, of the future advancement of the city.   It will probably not be long before the products of the fisheries of the east, the importations of the Atlantic frontier, the productions, mineral and vegetable, of all the northwestern states, and the sugars of Louisiana, will find their way hither by inland water communication.   Much of this, indeed, has already taken place, and is of daily occurrence.   Many who remember the competition between Buffalo and Black Rock, for the site of the city, will doubtless live to see the city spread over both.

" Desiring always to avoid extremes, and to observe a prudent moderation in regard to the protective system, I yet hold steadiness and perseverance, in maintaining what has been established, to be essential to the public prosperity.   Nothing can be worse than that that which concerns the daily labour and the daily bread of whole classes of people should be subject to frequent and violent changes. It were far better not to move at all, than to move forward and then fall back again.   A just and leading object in the whole tariff system, is the encouragement and protection of American manual labour.   I confess, that every day's experience convinces me more and more of the high propriety of regarding this object.   Our government is made for all, not for a few.   Its object is to promote the greatest good of the whole ; and this ought to be kept constantly in view in its administration.   The far greater number of those who maintain the government belong to what may be called the industrious or productive classes of the community.   With us labour is not depressed, ignorant and unintelligent.   On the contrary, it is active, spirited, enterprising ; seeking its own rewards, and laying up for its own competence and its own support. The motive to labour is the great stimulus to our whole society; and no system is wise or just which does not afford this stimulus, as far as it may. The protection of American labour, against the injurious competition of foreign labour, so far, at least, as respects general handicraft productions, is known, historically, to have been one end designed to be obtained by establishing the constitution; and this object, and the constitutional power to accomplish it, ought never to be surrendered or compromised in any degree. The interest of labour has an importance in our system, beyond what belongs to it as a mere question of political economy. It is connected with our forms of government, and our whole social system. The activity and prosperity which at present prevail among us, as every one must notice, are produced by the excitement of compensating prices of labour; and it is fervently to be hoped that no unpropitious circumstances, and no unwise policy, may counteract this efficient cause of general competency and public happiness." Again, when at

Pittsburg, July 5th, 1833. " The chief magistrate of Pittsburg has been kind enough to express sentiments favourable to myself, as a friend to domestic industry. Domestic industry! How much of national power and opulence, how much of individual comfort and respectability, that phrase implies! And with what force does it strike us, as we are here, at the confluence of the two rivers whose united currents constitute the Ohio, and in the midst of one of the most flourishing and distinguished manufacturing cities in the Union! Many thousand miles of inland navigation, running through a new and rapidly improving country, stretch away below. Internal communications, completed or in progress, connect the city with the Atlantic and the lakes. A hundred steam-engines are in daily operation, and nature has supplied the fuel which feeds their incessant flames, on the spot itself, in exhaustless abundance. Standing here, in the midst of such a population, and with such a scene around us, how great is the import of these words, ' domestic industry !' Next to the preservation of the government itself, there can hardly be a more vital question, to such a community as this, than that which regards their own employments, and the preservation of that policy which the government has adopted and cherished, for the encouragement and protection of those employments. This is not, in a society like this, a matter which affects the interest of a particular class, but one which affects the interest of all classes. It runs through the whole chain of human occupation and employ-

ment, and touches the means of living and the comfort of all.
New England has conformed herself to the settled policy of the
country, and has given to her capital and her labour a corresponding direction.   She has now become vitally interested in the preservation of the system.   Her prosperity is identified, not perhaps
with any particular degree of protection, but with the preservation of the principle ; and she is not likely to consent to yield the
principle, under any circumstance whatever.   And who would
dare to yield it ?   Who, standing here, and looking round on this
community and its interests, would be bold enough to touch the
spring, which moves so much industry, and produces so much
happiness ?   Who would shut up the mouths of these vast coal
pits ?   Who stay the cargoes of manufactured goods, now floating
down a river, one of the noblest in the world, and stretching
through territories almost boundless in extent, and unequalled in
fertility ?   Who would quench the fires of so many steam engines,
or stay the operations of so much well employed labour ?   I cannot
conceive how any subversion of that policy, which has hitherto
been pursued, can take place, without great public embarrassment,
and great private distress.   I have said, that I am in favour of
protecting American manual labour ; and, after the best reflection
I can give the subject, and from the lights which I can derive from
the experience of ourselves and others, I have come to the conclusion that such protection is just and proper ; and that to leave
American labour to sustain a competition with that of the over-
peopled countries of Europe, would lead to a state of things to
which the people could never submit.   This is the great reason
why I am for maintaining what has been established.   I see at
home, I see here, I see wherever I go, that the stimulus, which has
excited the existing activity, and is producing the existing prosperity of the country, is nothing else than the stimulus held out
to labour by compensating prices.   I think this effect is visible
every where, from Penobscot to New Orleans, and manifest in the
condition and circumstances of the great body of the people : for
nine tenths of the whole people belong to the laborious, industrious,
and productive classes ; and on these classes the stimulus acts.
We perceive that the price of labour is high, and we know that
the means of living are low ; and these two truths speak volumes
in favour of the general prosperity of the country.   Is it not true,
that sobriety, and industry, and good character, can do more for a
man here than in any other part of the world ?   And is not this
truth, which is so obvious that none can deny it, founded in this
plain reason, that labour, in this country, earns a better reward

than any where else, and so gives more comfort, more individual independence, and more elevation of character."

—

MASSILLON, Ohio, 1825.

"Neither the limits of my time or paper would allow me, in my last, to say one word in relation to the beautiful and hospitable village in which it is my happiness at present to sojourn. Six years ago the place where it stands contained only such houses as were occupied by the tillers of the soil. Within that time a place of extensive business has grown up, as by the stroke of a magician's wand. I do not mean, however, to be understood that Massillon has yet attained the dimensions of a very considerable town. It is, on the contrary, not more than one quarter as large as most towns in the country which have not a greater amount of trade. But so far as it has been built, the buildings give the strongest evidence of its prosperity, and foretell the rapid growth which it will experience for many years. Its stores, warehouses, and dwellings, are large and neatly built, and almost uniformly of brick. There is not a single ordinary building in the place, except two or three that stood here before the village was laid out. The streets are arranged in the most convenient order, and the grounds laid out with an uncommon degree of taste.—Nature seems to have indulged her fancy in preparing for the approach of art, and art has by no means rendered to nature an ungrateful return. All things considered, I think it is one of the most pleasant villages I have ever seen, and, located as it is, in the midst of numerous water-mill sites, beds of coal, limestone, and iron ore, all on the very banks of the Ohio and Erie canal, and all, too, near at hand and in possession of its enterprising citizens; situated in the centre of one of the largest and most fertile districts of Ohio, a district inhabited by a very numerous and industrious population, it cannot fail of becoming, in a few years, one of the most important places of the great west. In addition to its communication by water with New York, New Orleans, and Philadelphia, a rail road, of which Massillon will constitute the western terminus, will doubtless be constructed in the course of two or three years, to connect with the Pennsylvania rail road, which is to be extended to Pittsburg. The necessary charter has already been obtained from the legislature of this state, and persons ready to build the road are only waiting for a similar act from the next session of the legislature of Pennsylvania.

"Before the construction of the Ohio and Erie canal the vast resources of this country were comparatively little known, and were of little value. By means of that great work the value of wheat, the staple commodity of the country, has appreciated from twelve and a half to eighty seven and a half cents per bushel, and the cost of supplies from the cities has been diminished in an equal ratio. Of course the inducements for the farmer to grow crops to any greater extent than was necessary for his own consumption was very slight. Some idea of the change which has supervened since the completion of the canal may be gathered from the fact, that this day, while the harvest is yet unfinished, there have been purchased, at the warehouses in this village, upwards of *fifteen hundred* bushels of wheat. And I am assured by one of the most respectable dealers here, that, during the business season, from three to four hundred bushels in a day is not an unusual quantity to be received at the warehouses and mills.

"With this trade, then, very rapidly increasing, you will not doubt that, when all other resources are brought into action, Massillon will become an important town.

"The crops of all descriptions, throughout this whole country, are this year unusually abundant, but as they flow into granaries entirely empty, present prices are likely to be maintained. The farmers upon this exuberant soil are all growing rich, and the industry of every man reaps a liberal reward."

—

"I wonder not," says an English writer, "that the first settlers in Virginia, with the bold Captain Smith of chivalrous memory at their head, should have fought so stoutly to dispossess the valiant father of Pocahontas of his fair domain, for I certainly never saw a more tempting territory. Stonington is about two miles from the most romantic point of the Potomac river, and Virginia spreads her wild, but beautiful and most fertile paradise on the opposite shore. The Maryland side partakes of the same character, and perfectly astonished us by the profusion of her wild fruits and flowers. We had not been long within reach of the great falls of the Potomac, before a party was made for us to visit them; the walk from Stonington to these falls, is through scenery that can hardly be called forest, park or garden; but which partakes of all three. A little English girl accompanied us, who had but lately left her home, 'Oh how many English ladies would glory in such a garden as this!' and in truth they might; cedars, tulip-trees, sumacs, junipers, and oaks of various kinds, most of them new to us, shaded our path. Wild vines with their rich expansive leaves, and their sweet blossom, rivaling the mignionette in fragrance, clustered round their branches, strawberries in full bloom, violets, anemones, heart's-ease, and wild pinks, with many other and still lovelier flowers, literally covered the ground. The arbor judeæ, the dog-wood, in its fullest glory of star-like flowers, azalias, and wild roses, dazzled our eyes whichever way we turned them. It was the most flowery two miles I ever walked. The sound of the falls is heard at Stonington, and the gradual increase of this sound is one of the agreeable features of this delicious walk; I know not why the rush of water is so delightful to the ear; all other monotonous sounds are wearying, and harass the spirits, but I never met any one who did not love to listen to a waterfall."

"The manufactures of Virginia, like her coal mines, are but just beginning to rise into importance. But recently the attention of her citizens has been directed to the subject, and few out of the state are aware how far she has already advanced, and how rapidly she continues to advance in this branch of industry. I make no reference to the manufacture of tobacco, for in this she has long been engaged, with celebrity and success. I would observe, however, while mentioning it, that this branch has increased immensely within a few years, and now gives employment, in Richmond and Petersburg alone, to not less than 1,500 persons. This business is also extensively carried on in Lynchburg. But the manufactories to which I particularly allude, are such as are carried on elsewhere, in manufacturing the raw materials common to the United States, and in which the question of competition may be considered as involved.

" In Richmond, and Manchester, on the south bank of the river, during the last year, a large cotton manufactory, a large paper mill, and an extensive iron foundry, all went into operation. They are all owned by chartered companies, have adequate capitals, and the buildings are of the most substantial kind, and in the finest order. There are now in full operation here, two cotton manufactories, three iron foundries, to one of which a steam engine manufactory is attached, one cotton seed oil mill, one paper mill, one screw manufactory, two cut nail works, and an extensive puddling furnace and iron making and manufacturing establishment is nearly completed. A number of other companies have been chartered by the legislature, for the purpose of carrying on various other branches of manufacturing, all of which will, no doubt, soon be in operation. Besides the manufactories above mentioned in the vicinity of Richmond, few places can boast of so large or superior flour mills. The Galego mill, which is perhaps the largest in the world, alone runs 22 pair of stones, and makes five hundred barrels of flour daily. Haxal's mill is but little inferior to this, and Rutherford's and Clark's, though less than the others, are considerable mills. The Richmond city mills' flour is the finest bread flour in the United States, and commands in the foreign markets the highest prices. There are also in this vicinity at least six corn mills.

" The water power at and near Richmond is immense, and easily available ; it is the entire James River, which is nearly half a mile wide, and falls more than a hundred feet in a few miles. The advantages of its position for manufacturing purposes, are many and great. Situated at the head of good navigation,—open nearly all the year,—adjacent to a rich coal field,—connected with the interior, as it soon will be, by a canal leading through a fine iron district,—with a healthy and pleasant climate, surrounded by a good soil, nothing can prevent its becoming one of the greatest manufacturing cities in the Union.

" Next to Richmond in importance, and in some respects in advance of it, is Petersburg, at the head of the tide water of the Appomattox. Here cotton manufactories grow up and flourish, as if by magic. They have five or six here now, all of them extensive establishments, and some of them with numerous out buildings. One of them, a short distance from Petersburg, called by an Indian name that I have forgotten, is an establishment inferior to few, if any, in the northern states, and with its houses built for the workmen, forms quite a village. All these manufactories employ white labourers. The experiment, however, of negro or slave labour, has been made in one of the manufactories at Richmond, and has proved fully successful. Other manufactories are about to be erected near Petersburg, in some of which it is expected that negro labour will be introduced generally, if not exclusively. Indeed, there is every reason to believe that it is better adapted to the manufactory than to the field, and that the negro character is susceptible of a high degree of manufacturing cultivation. Should this kind of labour be found to succeed, of which I think, from some years' acquaintance with it, there can be no doubt,—it will give a decided advantage to the southern over the northern or European manufacturer. This kind of labour will be much cheaper, and far more certain and controllable. He will have nothing to do with 'strikes' or other interruptions, that frequently produce serious delay and loss to the employer. Before the present year the average expense for a good negro man per year, might be estimated at one hundred dollars, for field labour. Some superior hands, well acquainted with tobacco manufacturing, or good mechanics, would perhaps go to one hundred and fifty dollars. These prices include hire, food, clothing, &c. This year, in consequence of the great demand for labourers on the railroads, they are at least twenty dollars higher.

"The water power of Petersburg, though inferior in magnitude to that of Richmond, is yet very considerable. It is also without the advantages of an immediate connexion with the coal and iron regions; nor has it so good a navigation as the latter, as vessels only of six feet draught of water can come to it, while those drawing eleven may go to Richmond; yet is Petersburg as well, if not better, situated for the cotton manufacturing than Richmond. A railroad of sixty miles in length connects it with the Roanoke, and brings to it daily large quantities of cotton, from which it can have the first and best selection. This, together with the cheapness of water power, building materials, and all the articles that enter into the consumption of those who labour, give to it great advantages. Besides its cotton manufactories, it has a cotton seed oil mill, and several flour mills.

"Besides these two prominent places, many others may be found in Eastern Virginia, but little less favourably situated for manufactories. At Fredericksburg, on the Rappahannock, is a considerable water power, and on nearly all the rivers that empty into the Chesapeake, there are more or less sites. On the James River, between Richmond and the mountains, they are almost innumerable, and when the state improvements will have been completed, they will all be in good location. Manufacturing is carried on at Wheeling, on the Ohio, but Western Virginia is identified with the great valley of the Mississippi, the future greatness or prosperity of which no imagination can reach,—it is a world in itself, and the world beyond it cannot change its destinies.

"Heretofore the cheapness and superior productiveness of land in the new states, has operated to retard the prosperity of Eastern Virginia; and those causes, to which has recently been added the high price of cotton, are now seriously checking her advancement, by withdrawing much of her money capital, and many of her citizens and labourers to those states, attracted by the prospects there offered, in the cultivation of the soil, a pursuit more congenial to the habits and feelings of Virginians than commercial or manufacturing enterprises. If Virginians had remained on her own soil, and retained, for her own use, the labourers she has grown, and the capital they have earned, instead of building up other states, she would be a giant in these days. It may be better, however, for her sons, herself, and the Union, that she has peopled Kentucky, Tennessee, Mississippi, and Alabama, than that she should be the first state of the Union, or that the banks of her rivers should be covered with towns and manufactories.

"A new day is dawning in this part of the Old Dominion. She has found that boasting of her past greatness and glory will add nothing to her present prosperity. The active and regenerating spirit of the west has infused new life into her veins, and that same spirit makes her less metaphysical and more rational. The spirit of improvement is abroad, and within a year or two has worked wonders. Every where, railroads, canals, mines, and manu-factories, are the subjects of discussion and action. Enterprising citizens of other states and countries are directing their attention to the many in-ducements she offers for the profitable employment of their skill, their labour, or their capital. Her own enterprising citizens have asked for and will doubtless obtain additional capital by the establishment of new banks. Old habits and feelings may, for a while, check her onward progress, by denying to her the facilities necessary to the full development of her vast resources ; yet must the genius of the age triumph ; and when the old lion fairly shakes the dew from his mane, and the cobwebs are cleared from her halls of legis-lation, the manufacturers of the northern states and of the old world will have to look well to their spinning jennies."—*Pennsylvanian.*

" Wisdom and knowledge, as well as virtue, diffused generally among the body of the people, being necessary for the preserva-tion of their rights and liberties ; and as these depend on spreading the opportunities and advantages of education in the various parts of the country, and among the different orders of the people, it shall be the duty of legislatures and magistrates, in all future periods of this commonwealth (Massachusetts), to cherish the interest of literature and the sciences, and all seminaries of them ; public schools, and grammar schools in the towns ; to encourage private societies, and public institutions, rewards and immunities, for the promotion of agriculture, arts, sciences, commerce, trades, manufactures, and a natural history of the country, to countenance and inculcate the principles of humanity and general benevolence, public and pri-vate charity, industry and frugality, honesty and punctuality in their dealings ; sincerity, good humour, and all social affections, and generous sentiments among the people." It is not saying too much, when we assert that Slater's opinions and conduct coincided with the above sentiments : and that we have reason to be thankful that his footsteps were directed to America ; that it was put into his heart to visit these shores, for the purpose of introducing the cotton spinning into the United States ; without which we never could have maintained our independence, but should have relied on foreign supplies. Its establishment is therefore one of the greatest events that has yet taken place in the whole world, and will in the end be the means of revolutionising the whole inhabitable globe.

Though I was the personal friend of Mr. Slater, and had a better opportunity, than any other individual, of knowing his opinions and views on all subjects connected with business, politics, and religion; yet it is not my intention to press any of his peculiarities, nor did I design to become his eulogist. It was my duty to record the fair fame that had gathered round his successful life. In consequence of his being the introducer of the carding, drawing, roving, and spinning by water, in the improved state as used by Mr. Strutt at Belper, both for stocking yarn and twist; it was not thought improper to connect his memoir with an Essay on Manufactures; so that this circumstance may be noted by future historians of the cotton business in the United States. In this account it was important that a correct statement should be preserved, which would have been difficult to obtain, if the present opportunity had been lost. I am only anxious for the authenticity of my statements, for which I feel myself responsible, and liable to correction. My own views of the character of Samuel Slater are expressed in two words—*the Arkwright of America.*

Mr. Slater no sooner found that his business collected children and young people, who were destitute of the means of instruction, and knowing the plan of his old master, Strutt, at Belper, in establishing a Sunday school, than he followed his example, and opened a school in his own house, sometimes teaching the scholars himself, but generally hired a person to perform that duty. One young man from Providence college was deterred by his father, who was a minister of the standing order in Connecticut, who considered it a profanation of the Sabbath. But Mr. Slater persevered, and he was assisted by his father-in-law Oziel Wilkinson, and Obadiah Brown—and I am acquainted with persons who are indebted to that institution for all the early instruction they ever received. There are several living who attended this school at Pawtucket. Mr. Slater told me, that he claimed to have commenced the first Sunday school in New England, and I promised him that it should not be forgotten.

These schools have followed almost every manufacturing establishment that I am acquainted with; and there are no places where they are of so much importance. I observe in the History of Derbyshire, England, that the school which Mr. Strutt established in 1782 is still in existence at Belper, and endowed so that four hundred children are taught, in the common rudiments of English instruction. This gave rise to Sunday schools in Britain, and the same cause led to their establishment in New England. There may be different opinions respecting what kind of education shall be afforded at Sunday schools, but there can be but one opinion upon their general utility, more especially in manufacturing towns and villages. They have had a very happy effect in the state of Rhode Island, and they have led to the formation of other schools in different parts where instruction had been much neglected.

I conversed with the Rev. Wm. Collier, now engaged in the City Mission in Boston. He stated to me at his house, corner of Chambers and Green street, that he remembers perfectly well in the spring of 1796 that, while at Providence college, President Maxcy informed him that he had received an application from Mr. Slater of Pawtucket, to send him one of the students to instruct a Sunday school, and that he would compensate them for their services. The reason of the president's giving Mr. Collier the first offer was, that he was not able to pay his college expenses. Mr. Collier said, that the compensation would have been a great benefit to him, but he doubted the propriety of teaching a school on Sunday, as he was religiously disposed, and was associated with those who had received their early impressions from the preaching and writings of Mr. Whitfield, and the idea struck him as a profanation of the Sabbath. The president reasoned with him on the opportunity he would have to do good in Pawtucket; stating that there had never been a school of any description there, and no place of worship, and probably no religious or moral instruction, certainly not of a public nature. There was no restriction as to the course of instruction, and he could conduct it, so as to be most useful to the children. These considerations caused him to accept the offer, and he began his labours in the Sunday school on the following Sabbath. He does not recollect that there was any particular form of religious instruction introduced by him, but has no doubt that he did so in a conversational manner with the young people, as he was at that time very religious and disposed to converse with people on the subject.

Mr. Allen succeeded him in teaching the school.

—

At a fine water privilege in Athens, Georgia, there was established a cotton mill with machinery from England, by Dearing & Co.; it is still in operation, and one also in Columbus. Mills are erecting in Tennessee on a small scale; and in Kentucky they are anxious to obtain persons who understand the business. The time is approaching when there will be factories at the south and far-west: New England must send out her sons to superintend their operations.

CHAPTER VII.

MISCELLANEOUS DOCUMENTS.

" Seal up the mouth of outrage for a while,
Till we can clear these ambiguities
And know their spring, their head, their true descent."

This chapter is designed to preserve important information which came too late to be arranged in the first part of the work, to which it more properly belongs. The pieces by Tench Coxe are those referred to by Fisher Ames, and which were published under his patronage. They are characteristic of the writer, who was constantly adapting the energies of the people to the natural resources of their country, congenial with their habits, their soil, and their climate.

———

" *A Plan for encouraging Agriculture, and increasing the value of Farms in the Midland and more Western counties of Pennsylvania, by means of Manufactures applicable to several other parts of that State, and to many parts of the United States.**

"In a country, the people, the soil and the climate of which are well suited to agriculture, and which has immense natural treasures in the bowels and on the surface of the earth, *the creation of a ready, near, and stable market for its spontaneous and agricultural productions, by the introduction and increase of internal trade and manufactures, is the most effectual method to promote husbandry, and to advance the interests of the proprietors and cultivators of the earth.* This position has been assumed by *one* and maintained and relied upon afterwards by others of the most informed and sound minds in Great Britain, in relation to the internal trade, manufactures, and landed interests of that kingdom, although it is an island, possessing uncommon advantages in its artificial roads, canals, rivers, and bays, which, altogether, afford the inhabitants a *peculiar* facility in transporting their surplus produce, with very little expense, to foreign markets.

" To a nation inhabiting a great continent, not yet traversed by artificial roads and canals, the rivers of which, above their natural navigation, have been hitherto very little improved, many of

* See Fisher Ames's Letters, pp. 51, 52.

whose people are at this moment closely settled upon lands which actually sink from one fifth to one half the value of their crops, in the mere charges of transporting them to the seaport towns, and others of whose inhabitants cannot at present send their pro-duce to a seaport for its *whole* value, a thorough sense of the truth of the position is a matter of unequaled magnitude and import-ance.

" The state of things in most of the counties of Pennsylvania which are contiguous to or in the vicinity of the river Susquehan-nah, and its extensive branches, is considered to be really and precisely that which has been described ; and the object of this paper is, to suggest hints for a plan of relief from the great expense and inconvenience they at present sustain, by creating a market town for their produce, on the main body of that river, at some proper place between the confluence of its eastern and western branches, and the lower end of its present navigation.

" It is proposed that the sum of five hundred thousand dollars, to be applied as hereinafter mentioned, be raised in either of the three following methods—that is to say, either by five thousand subscriptions of one hundred dollars each, to the capital stock of a company, to be temporarily associated for that purpose, without any exclusive privileges. Or, by the sale of one hundred thou-sand lottery tickets at five dollars each, or fifty thousand tickets at ten dollars each ; the whole enhanced amount of which is to be redrawn in prizes, agreeably to a scheme which will be herein-after exhibited. Or, by the application of five hundred thousand dollars of the moneys in the treasury (or otherwise in the command) of the state of Pennsylvania. The inducements to the operation, either to the states, to the adventurers in the lottery, or to the sub-scribers of the stock of the associated company, will appear in the sequel to be an augmentation of about one hundred per cent. in the value of the property to be embraced ; that is, in a profit of about one hundred per cent. on the moneys to be raised or advanced for the purchase of the lands, and the erection of the buildings.

" The application of the above sum of five hundred thousand dollars, might be as follows :—

" 1st. In the purchase of land on the western bank of Susque-hannah, as a town seat, to be regularly laid off in a town or city for inland trade and manufactures, with streets sixty feet wide, in oblongs of five hundred feet, fronting the southwestern or preva-lent summer winds, by two hundred and twenty feet ; each oblong to be intersected by a twenty foot alley, running lengthwise, or from the northwest to southeast, so as to give all the lots southwest front exposures, or southwest exposures and outlets in the rear."

Here follows a detail of particulars which are too local and unimportant to be followed minutely. The above sum is therein appropriated to the purchases of land, the erection of houses, mills, rope-walks, tan-yards, bake-houses, steel-furnaces, soap-boilers, tallow-chandlers, blacksmiths, coopers, wheelwrights, coppersmiths, brass-founders, turners, skin-dressers, gunsmiths, and plumbers' shops; malt houses, breweries, distilleries, printing office, bleach-yards, fulling-mills, potteries, water forges, tobacco and snuff manufactories, lumber yards, boat-builders' yards, school houses, churches, taverns, sail-cloth manufactory, brick-kilns, twine and cord factories, starch works, and dwelling houses, public library, parchment and glue manufactories, pump maker's shed and yard, &c.

" The buildings above mentioned will form a town of one thousand houses, useful work shops and factories by water, fire, or hand, all of stone or brick, which is larger by near one half than the borough of Lancaster. Being on the river Susquehannah, a very great and extensive natural canal, which, with its branches, flows through a country of fifteen millions of acres, and will be connected with the lakes, the position for a town must be considered as warranting a presumption that the lots would be more valuable. In order to extend this advantage, the buildings should be erected on every second or perhaps every third lot, whereby a number of interval lots would be left, which would be nearly of the same value. A further advantage would result from such a disposition of the houses, as the vacant lots could be usefully applied to garden purposes until they should be built upon. As the proposed houses and workshops would be of stone and brick, the possibility of the progress of fire would be less, if the owners of the interval lots should build wooden houses hereafter, than if they were to erect such houses in a compact separate quarter.

" The lots, without the scene which should be first built on, would cost, after throwing out the streets and alleys, about five dollars, and might be moderately estimated, were such a town erected, at the medium value of ten dollars.

" This town being contemplated as such an auxiliary to Philadelphia, as Manchester, Leeds, Birmingham, and Sheffield, &c. are to the seaports of Great Britain, it would be necessary to connect it with the city immediately and effectually by opening a good road to the Lancaster turnpike, by whatever might be necessary to give it the benefit of the communication with Philadelphia through the Swatara and Tulpohocken canal, through the Brandywine canal, and through the Newport and Wilmington roads, and by all other means which can be devised. It would also be proper to connect it with the borough of Reading, Lancaster, York, Carlisle, &c., and with the western and north-western, northern, and other great roads. Thus circumstanced, with the supplies of wood fuel, coal, bark, iron, grain, cotton, hemp, flax, wool, timber, stone, lime, forage, &c., which those roads and the Susquehannah and its branches, would certainly and permanently afford, this plan could not fail to become of very great profit to the subscribers or prize-holders, or the state, and to the landed interest, both tenants and owners. The expense of transportation from the nearest navigable part of the Susquehannah by way of Newport, is nine dollars per ton; from Middletown it is twelve dollars per ton to sixteen dollars per ton ; and as four-fifths of the state are on or westward of that river, the immense saving that would be made by a great and stable market like that contemplated, is equally manifest and desirable. It may be asked, whether the owners of the houses, shops, and works, would receive application from tenants ? The answer is, that they would themselves be induced to occupy some of them, that the boroughs in the vicinity have been greatly extended by the settlement of tradesmen, manufacturers and others, who depend upon them and upon the farmer; and that unless their inhabitants open canals to the Susquehannah, or discover coal in their vicinity, those boroughs which are not on that river cannot grow much larger, though the demand for manufactures is steadily increasing with our population. It is regretted that the latter increase of Lancaster has been inconsiderable. But the water works, and the works by fire, which are proposed to be erected, will attract and support tradesmen and the workmen requisite to proceed with the goods they have now begun ; as is constantly the case in Europe.

" It may be safely affirmed, that no part of the United States at present half as fully populated as the five counties on the Susquehannah, offers so encouraging or so certain a prospect for an inland town. It is as it were the bottom of a great bag or sack, into the upper parts of which natural and agricultural produce are poured from the northeast, from the north, and from the west.

" It will be observed, that many water works, and objects requiring the moving power of water, are particularised in the plan. For which reason, and in order to procure all the public and private advantages which are attainable, it is proposed to take some position where the river can be so drawn out of its natural bed, as to create those mills seats and falls. It is confidently affirmed, and is not at all doubted, that there are not wanting places of that great and valuable natural capacity.

" Doubts may arise about the expediency of erecting some of the works. It is therefore observed, that those which are mentioned are merely offered for consideration. None of them are intended to be urged : but it is believed that most of them would prove, on examination, eligible.

" The greater part of the private emolument would be realised, it is supposed, by the erection of nine hundred dwelling houses of various sizes (in any of which various kinds of manufactories could be pursued,) and one hundred shops for such branches as, by reason of their producing loud noises, or unpleasant smells, or of their requiring greater room, could not be carried on among women and children, infirm, aged, or sick persons, or within the compass of an apartment in a common dwelling-house. In that case, however, it would be manifestly prudent to bring the unimproved mill seats into view, that they might be in the way of early use and improvement.

" The reasons of extending a view to the immediate erection of those water mills and other works, is, that by their very great consumption of the raw materials and produce which may be drawn by purchase from the farmers, they will as early and materially increase the benefits of the proposed town to the landholder and cultivator, without taking any hands from agriculture, or preventing any from going to it.

" It will be proper to ascertain, with precision and certainty, what would be a reasonable value of two thousand acres of land, thus purchased, and thus built upon, that the inducements to the operation may be duly exhibited.

" The borough of Lancaster will appear to afford a means of comparison not too favourable, when it is remembered, that a position on the west side of the Susquehannah would give the proposed town a most extensive and fertile back country for its supplies by land, free from the expense and risk of any ferry ; and that it would acquire building materials, provisions, raw materials, and the infinitely important article, pit coal, the very important articles timber and bark, in the greatest abundance, and on the cheapest terms, by means of the navigable waters of the Susquehannah ; and that its traders and artisans could transport produce and manufactures to and receive supplies from Philadelphia, through the canal of Swatara, without any the least expense of carting.

" An estimate of a town, consisting of the lands and number of
buildings particularised above, may be reasonably made as follows :

" The actual first cost of all the various buildings above mentioned, is stated to be $500,000

" From these deduct the value of the four schools and the church,
seven thousand two hundred dollars, which would be public, and
would be of no value to the owners of the town, as such, but as they
might reflect value upon the houses, manufactories, and lots. Also
deduct the sum of five thousand dollars, allowed for the charges of
superintendence.   12,200

" Remains as the actual cost and real value of all the private build- ———
ings.   487,800

" The value of one hundred lots to be given for twenty churches,
and thirty-two for the market, court house, and jail; nothing, but as
they reflect value on the other property in the town.   000,000

" The value of one thousand and ninety nine lots, of the size of
twenty by one hundred feet, on which the above private buildings
and works are to be erected when they shall be completed, at one
hundred dollars each on a medium.   109,9000

" The value of two thousand one hundred and ninety eight interval lots, (lying between and among the private and public buildings,
and exclusively of those without that part of the town plot proposed
to be built upon, with the fund of five hundred thousand dollars,) at
eighty dollars each on an average.   175,480

" The value of one hundred and twenty feet lots, making twenty
large lots equal to one hundred feet square, suitable for erecting
twenty other mills, with the requisite share of water right, at five
hundred dollars for each mill seat.   10,000

" N.B.   These will make with the improved mill seats about forty,
and will not require the height of water, or command of a fall to be
kept for more than a quarter of a mile.

" It is believed much more might be placed against this item.

" The value of the exclusive privilege of keeping ferries, arising
out of the ownership of the grounds, to constitute prizes.   5,000

" The value of twenty two thousand lots, accommodated with
streets and alleys, not within the part built upon as above, with the
wood on them, and on the streets and alleys, for fuel and timber, the
stone, lime, clay, &c. for building, at ten dollars per lot, to constitute
prizes.   220,000
                                                                      ————————
                                                                     $1,008,540

" The several objects in the foregoing estimate of one million
eight thousand five hundred and forty dollars, to constitute prizes
to be drawn by the purchasers of five hundred thousand dollars
worth of tickets : a scheme of a lottery more profitable than
most which have been exhibited, and which will moreover yield

great advantages to every proprietor and tenant of lands within the sphere of trade belonging to the town.

" Although such calculations and estimates as these ought always to be received with the utmost caution, and to be examined with strictness, yet there are circumstances, which, it is conceived, insure success to a well devised and well executed plan in the scene already mentioned.

" A very great and increasing supply of all those things which can create, maintain, and extend a town ; which can attract, cheaply support, and certainly and thoroughly employ, an industrious community, forced by the nature of the river and country into this singular scene—justify an affirmation that no such spot for a town of inland trade and manufactures of native productions exists in the populated parts of the United States. To estimate the value of the river, and the water works, and their permanent influence upon the prosperity and growth of such a town, let us for a moment suppose, that twenty similar mills, twenty unimproved mill seats, and a copious canal leading to the Susquehanna, were superadded to the present advantages of the borough of Lancaster.

" It cannot but be perceived, that most of the American inland towns have been commenced without due attention to the powers of water, the advantages of interior navigation, and a copious and certain supply of other fuel, when wood shall become scarce and dear. The whole number of the houses in the towns of some of the states is very inconsiderable, which is principally owing to their produce having passed on, without any natural stoppage or heavy expense of transportation, from their farms to their export market ; or to a scarcity of fuel, which has been created, and will be increased by their growth.

" There will be a peculiar certainty and stability in the value of property, in such a place as that contemplated, because its trade and manufactures, depending on our own laws, and upon our productions, will not be subjected to the injuries and vicissitudes which often arise from foreign restrictions and prohibitions, and from the defalcations of the imports of foreign, precarious and tropical productions. On the other hand, every new discovery of a mineral or fossil, every addition to the articles of cultivation in the great landed scene, on which it will depend, whether for food or manufactures, will yield fresh nourishment and employment to its inhabitants.

" In addition to the reasons already suggested for placing the town upon the western side of the Susquehanna, it ought to be

added, with a view to the present and all other plans of establishing towns, in this climate, that the eastern and northern sides of
all waters in the United States (the elevation, dryness of the soil,
and other things being equal) are less healthy than the southern
and western sides.   As it further regards that great concern, the
health and comfort of the citizens, it also merits repetition, that by
the plan proposed, no inadvertent or uninformed man will be able
to build his house or place of business in such a manner as to
deprive himself of the blessing of the summer winds.

"Although great stress has been laid upon a particular scene in
the course of this paper, from a thorough conviction of its fitness
and value, it is manifest, that many of the ideas will apply to such
of the existing towns in the state of Pennsylvania and elsewhere,
as have a capacity to command, by due exertion, and at a moderate expense, water falls, coal or inland navigation.   A diligent
examination of their respective capacities, in those particulars,
ought, upon the general principles suggested, to be made.*   It is
also clear, that a very large part of those advantages may be gained
at Harrisburg, Middletown, the falls of the Delaware, at the lower
end of the Schuylkill canal, and most of the other canals in the
United States, by such a power of water as has been mentioned
above.   In the states of Vermont and Kentucky, in the western
parts of Pennsylvania and New York, in the northwestern and
southern governments, and in general, at those places on the east-
ernmost, or nearest parts of all the western waters, and the southern, or nearest parts of all the northern waters, where the internal
navigation terminates, the whole of the above plan, in a maturer
state of their population, will apply, with the most solid and
extensive benefits, to the cultivators and proprietors of the soil."†

* *T. Coxe, Esq.*

SATURDAY.
Dear sir,—I mentioned one or two things yesterday, which were urgent.
One was the papers for the enquiry. You will see by the enclosed, that
they are to go to the house of representatives. Will you be so good as to
have a letter prepared this morning. I stay at home to-day, to look over
petitions. Let the warrants, &c., be sent me. Yours, affectionately.
                                        A. HAMILTON.

† The grounds around the lower falls of many of the rivers emptying into
the Atlantic Ocean, are also very suitable for such a plan, because provisions, wood, coal, and raw materials may be transported to them coastwise
and from foreign countries.

MULE SPINNING.

Reflections on the affairs of the United States, occasioned by the present war in Europe. (Recommended to the particular attention of the Owners of Coal and Water falls in the Western country.)*

" It is highly prudent in every nation, seriously to consider the effects which great events in other countries may have produced on their affairs, and to anticipate, in time, the consequences in regard to their interests, to which such events may possibly give

* *Tench Coxe, Esq.*

NEW YORK, January 7, 1792.

Dear sir,—I lately received, and read with pleasure and profit, the enlarged copy of the examination of Lord Sheffield's publications: and yesterday I was favoured with your letter, enclosing Secretary Hamilton's interesting and able report on the subject of manufactures, for both of which accept my thanks.

No better way can, in my opinion, be devised, for negotiating treaties of commerce, than that of augmenting the national respectability, and exhibiting successive and unequivocal proofs of the resources and union of the states, and of the stability and wisdom and energy of the national government.

With sentiments of esteem and regard, I have the honour to be, dear sir, your most obedient humble servant,

JOHN JAY.

Tench Coxe, Esq., Philadelphia.

LONDON, December 18, 1794.

Dear sir,—Accept my thanks for your obliging letter of the 8th of last month, and for the book which accompanied it. As yet, I have not had time and leisure to give it that regular and attentive perusal which it appears to merit. It certainly contains much useful information; and from your accuracy, I presume that the facts and statements in it are correct. It will naturally lead both our own people and foreigners to form a favourable and just estimate of the United States, and show, in a strong light, the policy of maintaining that respect for our government and laws, without which, our local and other advantages can neither be enjoyed nor improved.

The manner in which the insurrection has been dissipated, gives me pleasure ; and there is reason to hope, that the arts and counsels which produced it, will not be able to operate such another. Our affairs, relative to this country, have a promising aspect : the best disposition towards us prevails here, and indications and proofs of it daily increase. I do really believe that this government mean to give conciliatory measures with the United States a full and fair trial. It never can be wise to cast ourselves into the arms and influence of any nation ; but certainly it is wise and proper to cherish the good will of those who wish to be on terms of friendship and cordiality with us. It may seem strange, and yet I am convinced that, next to the king, our president is more popular, in this country, than any man in it.

With the best wishes, and with sentiments of esteem and regard, I am dear sir, your most obedient servant, JOHN JAY.

rise. The enhancement of the cost of our manufactured supplies, by the demand for the immense armaments, by land and sea, now making in Europe, and the impediments to the cheap transportation of our produce by the recent deduction of a large proportion of the vessels which lately carried them at peace freights, with the impossibility of building, in time, a sufficient number of ships to perform the service, and to supply the purchases, by foreign nations, render it a matter of most comfortable reflection that we have made such frequent and full examinations of our capacities in the business of manufactures, and that we have made so great progress in the establishment of many of the most useful and necessary branches. There seems nothing to warrant a belief, that we shall cease to pursue our course in peace. But it is manifest that, even in that desirable situation, the inducements to pursue manufactures are not a little increased by the advanced cost of our supplies, and the diminution of our carriers at peace freights, already mentioned. It will be wise, then, to devise more methods of increasing our manufactures, in order to cheapen and multiply supplies, and to extend the home market for our agricultural productions. It is, moreover, well worthy of remark, that in consequence of the war in Europe, many articles of great importance, in the building of houses, improving new plantations, and supplying the settled country, and the industrious poor, are said to be prohibited to be exported from Great Britain, because they can be applied to military purposes, or may be wanted for themselves. However reasonable or customary, in similar circumstances, this may be, our citizens must actually be subjected thereby to great additional expense, and the charges of improving and cultivating real estates of every description, must be considerably increased. Manufacturers of these prohibited kinds of goods, are therefore rendered indispensable, by the situation of that country which is the principal foreign source of our supplies.

"However improbable or impossible war may appear, in the judgment of many, or most of us, it can do no injury to remark, that the cost of our supplies would be so excessively increased, by that worst of all possible events, and the vessels to carry our produce at peace freights, would be so extremely diminished, if our own should be involved, that nothing but such great and vigorous efforts as that suggested for consideration, could save our cultivators from a very inconvenient expense, in procuring supplies, and the most distressing reduction of the market prices of many articles of their produce.

"It will be perceived that the plan is laid upon a scale which is not likely, at this time, to be carried into execution in any one place. It is necessary, therefore, to remark, that it is not intended in any view, but to exemplify what might be done with a given capital. The owners, however, of certain great water situations might, safely and advantageously, lay out their circumjacent grounds in a town plot, with such views, and they might sell or let, on ground rents, such ordinary building lots, or such situations for water works, as purchasers or tenants might apply for, leaving the plan to mature by time and the natural attractions and advantages of the several scenes ; or improvements might be commenced upon a scale of 5,000, 10,000, 15,000, or 20,000 dollars, as capital might be obtainable, and prudence might appear to justify. In all events, it is conceived, that a profitable attention to our situation may be promoted, and possibly some reflections, favourable to the United States, and to the proprietors of particular estates, and many vicinities, may be suggested, by the publication of the plan at the present very interesting crisis."*—*Federal Gazette.*

* *Tench Coxe, Esq., Lancaster.*

WASHINGTON, February 11, 1801.

Dear sir,—Your favour, of January 25th, came to hand some days ago, and yesterday a gentleman put into my hand, at the door of the senate chamber, the volume of the American Museum for 1798. As no letter accompanied it, I took it for granted it was to bring under my eye some of its contents.

I have gone over it with satisfaction. This is the morning of the election by the house of representatives. For some time past, a single individual had declared he would, by his vote, make up the ninth state. On Saturday last he changed, and it stands at present, eight one way, six the other, and two divided. Which of the two will be elected, and whether either, I deem perfectly problematical : and my mind has long been equally made up for either of the three events. If I can find out the person who brought me the volume from you, I shall return it by him, because I presume it makes one of a set. If not by him, I will find some other person who may carry it to Philadelphia if not to Lancaster. Very possibly it may go by a different conveyance from this letter. Very probably you will learn, before the receipt of either, the result, or the progress at least, of the election. We see already, at the threshold, that if it falls on me, I shall be embarrassed, by finding the offices vacant, which cannot be even temporarily filled, but with the advice of the senate ; and that body is called on the 4th of March, when it is impossible for the new members of Kentucky, Georgia, and South Carolina, to receive notice in time to be here.

The summons for Kentucky, dated, as all were, January 31st, could not go hence till the 5th, and that for Georgia did not go till the 6th. If the difficulties of the election are got over, there are more and more behind. Until new elections shall have regenerated the constituted authorities, the defects of our constitution, under circumstances like the present, appear very great. Accept assurances of the esteem and respect, dear sir, of your most obedient servant,   TH: JEFFERSON.

COMMONWEALTH OF MASSACHUSETTS.—*In the House of Representatives.*
                                                Oct. 25, 1786.

Ordered, that Mr. Clarke and Mr. Bowdoin with such as the honourable senate may join, be a committee to view any new invented machines that are making within this commonwealth for the purpose of manufacturing sheep's and cotton wool, and report what measures are proper for the legislature to take to encourage the same.

Sent up for concurrence,
ARTEMAS WARD, Speaker.

In Senate, Oct. 25, 1786.—Read and concurred, and Richard Cranch, Esq. is joined.

SAMUEL PHILLIPS, JUN. President.

COMMONWEALTH OF MASSACHUSETTS, Nov. 1786.

The committee of both houses appointed to view any new invented machines that are making within this commonwealth for the purpose of manufacturing cotton and sheep's wool, have attended that service, and examined three very curious and useful machines, made by Robert and Alexander Barr, for the purpose of carding and spinning of cotton, and ask leave to report the following resolve, which is submitted.

RICHARD CRANCH, per order.

Resolved, that there be granted and paid out of the public treasury of this commonwealth, to the said Robert and Alexander Barr, the sum of two hundred pounds, to enable them to complete the said three machines and also a roping machine, and to construct such other machines (connected with those already exhibited) as are necessary for the purpose of carding, roping, and spinning of sheep's wool, as well as of cotton wool ; they to be accountable for the expenditure of the same, and to lay their accounts of the whole expense of those several machines before the general court for allowance. And it is also

Resolved, that all those machines before-mentioned, when finished, shall be delivered by the said Robert and Alexander Barr to a committee of the general court to be hereafter appointed ; to be disposed of as the legislature shall think meet, for the purpose of promoting, extending, and encouraging the manufacture of woollens and cottons within this commonwealth. And it is further

Resolved, that a gratuity, such as the general court may hereafter agree upon (when a full trial shall have been made of the utility and public advantage of those machines) shall be given to the said Robert and Alexander Barr, as a reward of their ingenuity, and as an inducement to other ingenious artists and manufacturers to bring their arts also into this commonwealth.

In Senate, Nov. 16, 1786.—Read and accepted. Sent down for concurrence.   SAMUEL PHILLIPS, JUN. *President.*

In the House of Representatives, Nov. 16. 1787—Read and concurred.
ARTEMAS WARD, Speaker.

Approved—JAMES BOWDOIN.

The committee of both houses appointed to examine the machines for carding, roping, and spinning cotton and sheep's wool, lately made at Bridgewater, under the patronage of the general court, by Robert and Alexander Barr, have attended that service, and on the most critical examination of those machines, your committee find them to be constructed on such true mechanical principles, and executed with such accuracy, as reflects honour on the genius and ability of those young artists; and that in the opinion of your committee they are well adapted to promote several very valuable branches of manufacture within this commonwealth, and therefore ask leave to report the following resolves, which are submitted.

RICHARD CRANCH, *per order.*

COMMONWEALTH OF MASSACHUSETTS.

Whereas by a resolve of the general court passed the 16th of November, 1786, the sum of two hundred pounds was directed to be paid out of the public treasury of this commonwealth to Robert and Alexander Barr, to enable them to complete certain machines for carding, roping, and spinning cotton and sheep's wool.

And whereas the said Robert and Alexander Barr have exhibited to this court an account of the expenditure of one hundred and eighty-nine pounds and twelve shillings of the sum aforesaid, which account appears to be just and reasonable. And whereas by the resolve of the general court passed the 16th of November aforesaid, it is further resolved, " That a gratuity, such as the general court may hereafter agree upon, (when a full trial shall have been made of the utility and public advantage of these machines) shall be given to the said Robert and Alexander Barr as a reward of their ingenuity, and as an inducement to other ingenious artists and manufacturers to bring their arts also into this commonwealth," therefore resolved that the said Robert and Alexander Barr be and they hereby are discharged from the whole of the said sum of two hundred pounds granted as aforesaid, and also that six tickets in the land lottery established by an act passed the 14th of November, A. D. 1786, be given by this commonwealth to the said Robert and Alexander Barr, "as a reward for their ingenuity in forming those machines, and for their public spirit in making them known to this commonwealth." And the managers of the said lottery are hereby directed to deliver to the said Robert and Alexander Barr six lottery tickets accordingly, taking duplicate receipts for the same, one of which to be lodged in the secretary's office. And it is further resolved, that the said machines be left under the care of the Hon. Hugh Orr, Esq. until the further order of the general court, and that public notice be given for three weeks successively in Adams and Nourse's newspaper, that the said machines may be seen and examined at the house of the Hon. Hugh Orr, Esq. in Bridgewater, and that the manner of working them will be there explained to those who may wish to be more particularly informed of their great use and advantage in carrying on the woollen and cotton manufactures. And the said Hon. Hugh Orr, Esq. is hereby requested to explain to such citizens as may apply for the same, the principles on which the said machines are constructed, and the advantages arising from their use, both by verbal explanations, and by letting them see the machines at work. And it is further resolved, that the said Hon. Hugh Orr, Esq. be, and he hereby is, permitted and allowed to make use of the said machines during the whole time of his having the care of them, as aforesaid, as some recompense for his own time and trouble in showing them and explaining their use to the citizens of the commonwealth at large.

In Senate, May 2d, 1787.—Read and accepted. Sent down for concurrence.   SAMUEL PHILLIPS, JUN. *President.*

In the House of Representatives, May 2d, 1787.—Read and concurred.
                                        ARTEMAS WARD, *Speaker.*

Approved—JAMES BOWDOIN.

COMMONWEALTH OF MASSACHUSETTS.—*In Senate, March* 8, 1787.

Resolved that Richard Cranch, Esq., with such as the honourable house shall join, be a committee to examine the machines now making at Bridgewater by Robert and Alexander Barr, under the patronage of the general court, for the purpose of carding and spinning cotton and sheep's wool, which machines are now nearly completed. And the said committee are hereby empowered and directed, as soon as may be, to examine the accounts of the said Robert and Alexander Barr, respecting the expense they have been at in making those machines, and to allow the same, or so much thereof as to them shall appear reasonable ; and also to report to the next general court what gratuity, in their opinion, the said Robert and Alexander justly deserve, as a reward for their ingenuity in forming those machines, and as an encouragement for their public spirit in making them known to this commonwealth.

And the said committee are further directed to report their opinion, in what manner those machines may be disposed of, so as to make them most universally known, and generally useful to this commonwealth.

                                        Sent down for concurrence,
                                        SAMUEL PHILLIPS, JR.

In the House of Representatives, March 8, 1787.—Read and concurred, and Mr. Clarke and Mr. Howard are joined.

                                        ARTEMAS WARD, *Speaker.*

Approved—JAMES BOWDOIN.

—

Commonwealth of Massachusetts to Robert and Alexander Barr,   Dr.

To sundry materials, &c. for making and completing the several machines for the purpose of carding, roping, and spinning cotton and sheep's wool, viz :—   £.   s.

	£.	s.
To leather, ...	2	00
To card teeth, ...	3	19
To cash paid Ezekiel Reed, for altering his machine, and pricking the leaves, and setting the card teeth, .	9	
To 36lb. of brass at 10d. per lb.	1	10
To card tacks, 4m.		5
To cash paid for files, crucibles, &c.	4	
To 8 months labour of two men, each at £6 10 per mo.	104	
To 8 months board of do. at 9s. per week, ...	28	16
To wood for fuel, ...		14

                                Carried forward,   £154   4

	£.	s.
Brought forward,	£154	4
To 261 different pieces of iron work	36	12
To coals for melting brass, and timber for the machines,	1	
To expenses in transporting the machines to and from Boston.	1	4
	£187	
To cash paid for passages and expenses on the road to Bridgewater, omitted in the above account. . .	2	12
	£189	12

ROBERT BARR.
ALEXANDER BARR.

To the Honourable Senate and House of Representatives of the common-wealth of Massachusetts, in general court assembled. The petition of Thomas Somers humbly showeth,

That in the fall of the year 1785, the tradesmen and manufacturers of Baltimore in Maryland, having formed themselves into an association, in order to apply to the legislature in behalf of American manufactures, being stimulated thereto by a circular letter received from a committee of the tradesmen and manufacturers of the town of Boston. Your petitioner then, residing in Baltimore, (having been formerly brought up to the cotton manu-factory, and willing to contribute what lay in his power to introduce said manufacture in America,) did, at his own risk and expense, go to England, in order to prepare the machines for carding and spinning cotton. That after much difficulty, your petitioner found that he could only take descrip-tions and models of said engines; with which he returned to Baltimore last summer. Soon after his arrival he found that they were very dilatory about encouraging the matter, and with the advice of some friends he resolved to try what might be done in Boston. That on his way to Boston, the sloop was driven ashore by the late storms, on Cape Cod, by which misfortune your petitioner lost almost one half of the small property he had to subsist on until he could get into business. Your petitioner therefore humbly prays for such assistance to begin the manufactory as shall seem most agreeable to your honours, and as in duty bound shall ever pray, &c.

THOMAS SOMERS.

N.B. Your petitioner is perfect master of the weaving in the speediest manner, and of adapting to advantage the different kinds of yarn for mar-seilles quilting, dimity, muslins plain, striped or checked, calico, cotton and linen jeans, jeannettes, handkerchiefs, checks, drabs, and many other kinds in that line, and understands the management of cotton, and how the spinning should be performed. T. S.

COMMONWEALTH OF MASSACHUSETTS.—*In the House of Representatives, March 2, 1787.*

On the petition of Thomas Somers, setting forth his being possessed of certain descriptions and models of machines, for the facilitating labour in the carding, roping, and spinning of cotton wool; and also, his knowledge of adapting the thread for, and of weaving dimities, plain, striped and checked muslins, calicoes, jeans, jeannettes, and other cotton manufactures; and praying that he may receive some encouragement for the establishing the cotton manufacture within this commonwealth:

With a view to encourage the aforesaid manufacture, and to give the said Somers an opportunity to give specimens of his abilities to perfect the manufactures set forth in his said petition, *Resolved*, That there be paid out of the public treasury, by warrant from the governor and council, twenty pounds lawful money to be applied to the purposes aforesaid, which sum shall be deposited in the hands of Hugh Orr, Esq. of Bridgewater, who shall be a committee to superintend the application of the same.

Sent up for concurrence,
Artemas Ward, Speaker.

In Senate, March 8, 1787.—Read and concurred,

Samuel Phillips, Jr. President.

Approved—James Bowdoin.

—

It has been observed that Mr. Slater introduced stocking yarn and sewing thread. It is not easy to estimate the value of these articles to this country in 1790; the following remarks will show that these yarns required superior skill and experiment.

Stockings are made of only one thread, entwined so as to form a species of tissue, extremely elastic, and readily adapting itself to the part it is employed to cover. The tissue cannot be called cloth, for it has neither warp nor woof, but approaches it closely, and for the purposes to which it is applied, is much superior. It is well known that the ancient Romans had no particular covering for the legs; but during the middle ages, hose or leggings made of cloth came into use; and at a later period, the art of knitting stockings was invented. Very different accounts are given of the time and country of this important invention, some attributing it to the Scots, and others deriving it from Spain. Woven stockings are manufactured by the machine called *stocking-frame*, which is exceedingly ingenious, but too complex to be described without plates. It was invented by William Lee, of Nottinghamshire, England, in 1589. He met with little encouragement in his attempts to set up an establishment in England, but was invited into France by Henry IV. and received with great favour. Henry's assassination, soon after, interrupted his prospects, and he died in Paris in great poverty. A knowledge of his machine was carried back to England by some of his workmen, who established themselves in Nottinghamshire, which has since continued to be the principal seat of the manufacture. For near two hundred years, few improvements were made on Lee's invention, and two men were usually employed on one frame; but it has been much improved, and adapted also to the manufacture of *ribbed* stockings.

The yarn for the stocking-frame is required to be particularly smooth and equal, and it is therefore spun in a manner different from other yarn, two roves being united to form the thread; on this account it is called double-spun twist.

The making of sewing-thread, by firmly twisting together two three, or more threads of cotton yarn by machinery, is a considerable branch of business, carried on both at Manchester and in Scotland, and in which Mr. David Holt, of the former place, has made great improvements. The beauty of this article, and its remarkable utility and cheapness, are universally known, as it is used in every house, and in the making of almost every kind of clothing. Several shops in the principal streets of London sell this article only. It is also extensively exported; the quantity sent abroad in 1833, was 1,187,601lbs. Cotton hosiery is chiefly made throughout the counties of Nottingham and Derby, at Hinckley, and at Tewkesbury. The number of persons employed in the cotton branch of the hosiery trade, will probably amount to nearly 40,000, in Great Britain.

The following notices of Brindley and Crompton are too interesting to be omitted in this work.

James Brindley, a native of Tunsted, near Wormhill, Derbyshire, an eminent engineer and mechanic, was born in 1716. The poverty of his family prevented his receiving more than the rudiments of education, and at seventeen he became apprentice to a millwright. On the expiration of his indenture he commenced business as an engineer, and, in 1752, displayed great talent in contriving a water engine for draining a coal mine. A mill, which he constructed on a new plan, and other works of the same description, introduced him to the patronage of the Duke of Bridgewater, then occupied in planning a communication between his estate at Worsley and the towns of Manchester and Liverpool, by water. This immense work, the idea of which was ridiculed by most of the scientific men of the period as impracticable, Brindley undertook, and by means of an aqueduct over valleys, rivers, &c. completed so as to form a junction with the Mersey. This success caused him to be employed in 1766, to unite the Trent and Mersey, upon which he commenced the "grand trunk navigation canal," but dying before its completion, the work was finished in 1777 by his brother-in-law, Mr. Henshaw. From this main branch Brindley also cut another canal near Haywood in Staffordshire, uniting it with the Severn in the vicinity of Bewdley, and finished it in 1772. From this period scarcely any work of the kind in the kingdom was entered upon without his superintendence or advice. Among other designs, he prepared one for draining the fens in Lincolnshire and the Isle of Ely, and another for clearing the Liverpool docks of mud, which was especially successful. The variety of his inventions, and the fertility of his resources, were only equaled by the simplicity of the means with which he carried his expedients into effect. He seldom used any model or drawing, but when any material difficulty intervened, generally retired to bed, and there meditated on the best mode of overcoming it. On such occasions, he has been known to seclude himself for days; and so partial was he to inland navigation, that he is said, to a question humorously put to him on his examination before the house of commons, "For what purpose did he consider rivers to have been created," at once to have replied, "Undoubtedly to feed navigable canals." The intensity of his application to business brought on a hectic fever of which he died in 1772.

CROMPTON.—The "short and simple annals" of the life of this worthy man,—so much resembling the history of many other sons of genius,—are thus recorded by Mr. Kennedy, in his "brief memoir":—

"About the year 1802, Mr. G. A. Lee and myself set on foot a subscription for Mr. Crompton, which amounted to about £500; and with this he was enabled to increase his little manufacturing establishment, in Bolton, namely, of spinning and weaving. He was prevailed upon also, to sit to a London artist, for his portrait, which is now in my possession. He was left a widower when his children were very young, and his only daughter kept his little cottage, in King street, Bolton, where he died, and where she lived in 1829. Being a weaver, he erected several looms for the fancy work of that town, in which he displayed great ingenuity. Though his means were but small, his economy in living made him always in easy circumstances. In 1812, he made a survey of all the cotton districts in England, Scotland, and Ireland, and obtained an estimate of the number of spindles then at work upon his principle, which amounted to between four and five millions; in 1829 about seven millions. On his return, he laid the result of his enquiries before Mr. Lee and myself, with a suggestion, that parliament might grant him something. With these data before him, Mr. Lee, who was a warm friend to genius of every kind, with his usual energy entered fully into his merits, and made an appointment with the late George Duckworth, Esq. of Manchester, who also took a lively interest in the scheme, and gratuitously offered to draw up a memorial to parliament in behalf of Mr. Crompton. This was signed by most of the principal manufacturers in the kingdom who were acquainted with his merits. He went to London himself with the memorial, and obtained an interview with one of the members for the county of Lancaster. He remained there during the session, and was in the house on the evening that Mr. Perceval was shot, and witnessed the catastrophe. A short time before this disastrous occurrence, Mr. Perceval had given him a promise to interest himself in his behalf; and, in accordance with this assurance, had brought in a bill, which was passed, for a grant of £5000, in full, without fees or charges. Mr. Crompton was now anxious to place his sons in some business, and fixed upon that of bleaching: but the unfavourable state of the times, the inexperience and mismanagement of his sons, a bad situation, and a misunderstanding with his landlord, which occasioned a tedious law-suit, conspired in a very short time to put an end to this establishment. His sons then dispersed, and he and his daughter were reduced to poverty. Messrs. Hicks and Rothwell, of Bolton, myself and some others, in that neighbourhood and in Manchester, had, in 1824, recourse to a second subscription, to purchase a life annuity for him, which produced £63 per annum. The amount raised for this purpose was collected in small sums, from one to ten pounds; some of which were contributed by the Swiss and French spinners, who acknowledged his merits, and pitied his misfortunes. At the same time his portrait was engraved for his benefit, and a few impressions were disposed of: he enjoyed this small annuity only two years. He died January 26th, 1827, leaving his daughter, his affectionate housekeeper, in poverty."

Mill Ponds and Reservoirs.—A large mill pond is very advantageous on small rivers, the natural currents of which are not sufficiently abundant at all seasons to furnish the requisite supply of water. It serves as a reservoir, to collect and retain the water which flows into it during the night, for use the subsequent day; in effect, as before observed, doubling the power of the stream. Each acre of a mill pond, one foot in depth, contains 43,560 cubic feet of water, weighing 62½ lbs. to the foot = 2,722,500 lbs. of water; which, with a fall of ten feet, give available force equal to 567 horse power. If the water were all applied in the course of one minute to the water wheels, or $567 \div 720$, the number of minutes in a day of 12 hours, gives .787 or very nearly three fourths of a horse power for each acre of water one foot deep, used with a fall of ten feet, for one day. With this fall, a mill pond containing 20 acres, and susceptible of retaining a quantity of water of the same extent, and one foot in depth, will give to the proprietor of the mill a command of a 15 horse power, for one day, independent of the ordinary supply of the stream. The depth of pond will not compensate for a deficiency in extent of surface; because, in proportion as the surface of the water subsides, or is drawn down, the height of the fall, and consequently the power, is diminished in an equal ratio. On this account reservoirs, constructed entirely above the level of the mill pond, are peculiarly serviceable; a small extent of ground, covered to a considerable depth with water, being thus rendered equal to a great extent of ground covered with a shallow sheet of water. Where large natural ponds or swamps can be converted into reservoirs, for retaining the flood waters of winter, for use during the droughts of summer, the water power of small streams may be surprisingly augmented. During nine or ten months of the year, inconsiderable brooks yield sufficient water for important hydraulic operations. If, then, by means of artificial reservoirs, the deficiency in the supply of water, during the two or three months of summer, can be obviated, and the winter torrents be made to swell the current of the summer brook, the stream at once becomes as important and effective as one much larger without these artificial resources. The expense of constructing a reservoir may be rendered comparatively light should all the proprietors of the mill seats benefited by it unite to defray them. Even the amount of the very costs of litigation in some cases, relating to water privileges, would be sufficient, if judiciously expended in this way, to place at the control of both parties a greater additional water power than that for which they may be contending.

In the town of Providence, which has been termed the Manchester of America, from having been the centre of the most extensive manufacturing operations, there was, in 1826, only one cotton mill of less than a thousand spindles, whilst several hundred thousand were in operation on the mill streams in the country adjacent. A cotton mill, intended for operating seven or eight thousand mule spindles, with the preparation and looms, was erected in 1827, as an experiment of the practicability of employing *steam power*. Anthracite coal, from the Schuylkill, is successfully used in the furnace of the steam engine of this cotton mill. Mr. Slater was concerned in the above experiment, and has owned the whole of it since 1829. At present, it produces yarn No. 80, and the cloth is said to be the finest and best in the country. It has more than answered the expectations of the proprietor.

Zec. Allen says :—" By an experiment made with a large high pressure steam engine, in Rhode Island, it appeared that when the throttle valve was thrown open, and the machinery of the mill disconnected with the engine, it required 25 lbs. to the inch on the safety valve, to cause the steam engine to make its regular number of working strokes, and to maintain its proper speed. Without having its friction at all increased by being loaded, it thus required about 17 horse power, equal to one third of the whole estimated power of this engine, to move the beam, piston and fly wheel."

Calculating Machine.—Of all the machines which have been constructed in modern times, the calculating machine is doubtless the most extraordinary. Pieces of mechanism, for performing particular arithmetical operations, have been long ago constructed; but these bear no comparison, either in ingenuity or in magnitude, to the grand design conceived and executed by Mr. Babbage, for the British government.

Great as the power of mechanism is known to be, yet few will scarcely admit it to be possible, that astronomical and navigation tables can be accurately computed by machinery; that the machine can itself correct the errors which it may commit; and that the results of its calculations, when absolutely free from error, can be printed off without the aid of human hands, or the operation of human intelligence. All this, however, Mr. Babbage's machine can do. The calculating machine, constructed under the superintendence of the inventor, has been executed at the expense of the British government, and is, of course, their property. It consists, essentially, of two parts,—a calculating part and a printing part; both of which are necessary to the fulfilment of Mr. Babbage's views: for the whole advantage would be lost if the computations made by the machine were copied by human hands, and transferred to types by the common process. The calculating machinery exhibits workmanship of such extraordinary skill and beauty, that nothing approaching to it has been witnessed. In order to execute it, particularly those parts of the apparatus which are dissimilar to any used in ordinary mechanical constructions, tools and machinery of great expense and complexity have been invented and constructed; and, in many instances, contrivances of singular ingenuity have been resorted to, which cannot fail to prove extensively useful in various branches of the mechanical arts. The drawings of this machinery, which form a large part of the work, and on which all the contrivance has been bestowed, and all the alterations made, cover upwards of 400 square feet of surface, and are executed with extraordinary care and precision. In so complex a piece of mechanism, in which interrupted motions are propagated, simultaneously, along a great variety of trains of mechanism, it might have been supposed that obstructions would arise, or even incompatibilities occur, from the impracticability of foreseeing all the possible combinations of the parts; but this doubt has been entirely removed by the constant employment of a system of mechanical notation, invented by Mr. Babbage, which places distinctly in view, at every instant, the progress of motion through all the parts of this or any other machine; and, by writing down in tables the times required for all the movements, this method renders it easy to avoid all risk of two opposite actions arriving at the same instant, at any part of the engine. In the printing part of the machine, less progress has been made in the actual execution, than in the calculating part. The cause of this is the greater difficulty of its contrivance, not for transferring the computations from the calculating part to the copper or other plate, destined to receive it, but for giving to the plate itself that number and variey of movements which the forms adopted in printed tables may call for in practice.

The practical object of the calculating engine is to compute and print a great variety and extent of astronomical and navigation tables, which could not be done without enormous intellectual and manual labour; and which, even if executed by such labour, could not be calculated with the requisite accuracy. Mathematicians, astronomers, and navigators, do not require to be informed of the real value of such tables; but it may be proper to state, for the information of others, that seventeen large folio volumes of logarithmic tables alone were calculated, at an enormous expense, by the French government, and that the British government regarded these tables to be of such national value, that they proposed to the French board of longitude to print an abridgment of them, at the joint expense of the two nations, and offered to advance £5000 for that purpose. Besides logarithmic tables, Mr. Babbage's machine will calculate tables of the powers and products of numbers, and all astronomical tables for determining the positions of the sun, moon, and planets; and the same mechanical principles have enabled him to integrate innumerable equations of finite differences; that is, when the equation of differences is given, he can, by setting an engine, produce, at the end of a given time, any distant term which may be required.

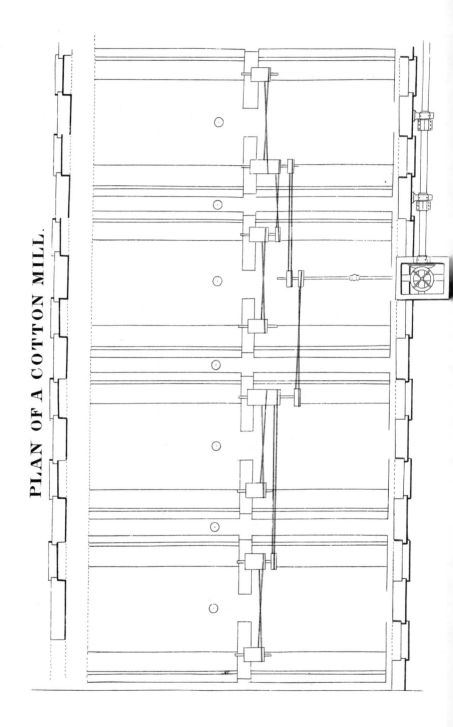

PLAN OF A COTTON MILL.

CHAPTER VIII.

EXTRACTS FROM THE SPINNING MASTER'S ASSISTANT.

" To complete the wonder, this manufacture is the creation of the genius of a few humble mechanics; it has sprung up from insignificance to its present magnitude within little more than half a century ; and it is still advancing with a rapidity of increase that defies all calculation of what it shall be in future ages."—*Baines.*

Previous to the above work, published in Glasgow, 1832, nothing ever appeared in Europe on the art of cotton spinning, fitted to assist the master, manager, or artisan, in acquiring a correct and systematic knowledge of the *real* principles of the business. So that the manager of a cotton spinning factory could only acquire a proper knowledge of his business by long experience and application in the practical department of the manufacture, and it depended upon the situation in which he was placed, and the advantages he enjoyed, if he ever obtained that correct knowledge of all its details which is essentially necessary to render him fully qualified for managing a large establishment with satisfaction or profit to the proprietors.

It is only when *theory* and *practice* are combined, that efficiency can be attained in effecting improvements.

In all factories where there is a variety of machinery employed in the manufacturing of any particular kind of goods, it has always been found that the manner in which the machinery is placed, together with the arrangement of the different departments has a very prominent influence in either retarding or accelerating the progress of the work. But in no place is this influence more sensibly observed than in a cotton spinning factory. It is obvious, however, that the manner in which the machinery is placed, and the arrangement of all its different departments, will entirely depend upon the plan of the house, or the form in which it is built ; hence the propriety and advantage of having a mill built on such a plan, or form, as to admit of having all the machinery placed, and the various departments arranged, in the manner best adapted for facilitating the progress of the work as a whole.

The situation of the ground, or space upon which the mill is to be erected, must always be taken into consideration in laying down the plan or fixing upon the particular form in which the house is to be built; and in some cases this plan must just be made to suit the situation or place in which it must stand. But when the situation and extent of the premises are such as to afford ample scope for the proprietors to build their mill on any plan or form which they may think proper; in these circumstances, the house may be built in a form that will admit of having the machinery and the various departments and offices of the establishment, arranged in such a manner as to afford the greatest facility for accelerating the progress of the work in all the different stages or departments. They ought to be so situated as to prevent all unnecessary going to and from any of the different departments of the work, by the workers employed about the establishment. All the different offices, such as ware-room, picking-room, mechanic's shop, &c. ought to be contained within the walls of the mill, if possible, because there is always a continued communication with these different offices.

A good ground plan of a *cotton-mill*, is 145 feet long, and 37 feet wide within the walls; with a wing attached to one end, 64 feet by twenty. A house of these dimensions would cover a space of about 7461 square feet, besides the stair-case and water-closets. A house 37 feet wide affords ample space for machines of 300 spindles each. A wing attaches to the body of the building, the various departments of which should be occupied for all the different offices, or separate apartments necessarily required about a cotton spinning factory. The body of the mill is supposed to be 145 feet long and 37 feet wide within the walls; and supposing it to be six stories high, a house of these dimensions would be capable of containing 23,000 spindles, with all the necessary preparation for average numbers. If steam was needed it would require an engine of between 40 and 50 horses' power to drive a mill of this extent. Every spinning factory ought to have a little more power than is merely necessary to drive it, because the weight of the machinery will often vary with the weather, the quality of the oil used, &c.; consequently, when there is barely a sufficiency of power, the engine will frequently be so overburthened, as to render it incapable of driving the machinery at a regular speed, thus requiring more trouble and expense for fuel, &c. This is worthy of attention where steam is used.

The breadth of the mill being 37 feet, affords ample room for arranging all the different machines in the carding department in the best order, both for promoting the progress of the work, and allowing the different workers that are employed in this department to attend to their employments, without being in the least incommoded for want of sufficient room.

The length of the mill being 145 feet, would afford sufficient space for the spinning machines. Two upright shafts would be quite sufficient for driving all the machinery contained in a mill of this length. The cotton and waste cellars should be a detached building to lessen the risk. As the raw material is prepared in the carding room for all the spinning departments, the cards ought to be placed as near the centre of the mill as possible. A factory of the dimensions recommended above, six stories, would require two preparation rooms; these might be placed on the same floor with the picking-rooms. As there is always a constant communication between these two departments, if they are placed at a distance from each other, a great deal of time must unavoidably be lost in passing to and from the one to the other; but by this arrangement very little time will be lost; for the laps can be carried direct from the spreading machines to the back of the breaker cards, and the tops, strips, or other waste returned in the same way. An easy method for conveying the rove from the carding to the spinning room, should be adopted to save time and labour. The staircase ought always to be placed on the outside of the mill, and the outer door always kept shut during working hours. As it is obvious that the particular arrangement of the different departments, and the order in which the machinery is placed will always have a prominent influence upon the productive capabilities of large establishments, the advantage of having them arranged in the best manner which practical wisdom and experience can suggest, is so apparent as to require no force of language to prove it. And if such arrangements depend upon the particular form or plan upon which the factory is built, then the importance of having the different departments arranged in the most approved manner, is so obvious as to need no further comment.

The Method of calculating the Speed of the different Shafts and Machines.

In calculating the speed of the various shafts, the first thing to be done is to find the revolutions per minute of the first or main shaft; and when this is known, the principle upon which to proceed in tracing out the speed per minute of all the other shafts throughout the whole establishment, is both simple and easy to be understood.

Suppose the first moving power to be a water wheel; find how many revolutions it makes per minute, then, how many teeth are in the spur or bevel wheel. Multiply this number by the revolutions of the wheel per minute, and divide the last product by the number of teeth in the pinion acting in the same, and the result will be the revolutions of the first shaft per minute.

But if the first moving power should be an engine, the first thing to be done is to find the number of strokes the engine makes per minute ; and if the engine crank be attached to the wheel, then every double stroke of the engine will make one revolution of this wheel, and it will be the first driving wheel. Multiply the number of teeth which it contains by its revolutions per minute, and divide the product by the number of teeth in the pinion which is fixed on the end of the first shaft, and the result thus obtained will be the revolutions per minute of the shaft. And when the speed of the first shaft is thus found, the process of tracing out the speed of all the others, will be comparatively easy. Suppose an engine of 50 horses' power, and making 40 single strokes per minute, equal to 20 revolutions of the first shaft ; therefore this shaft revolves 20 times per minute. Upon the end of the first shaft there is a large driving wheel, containing 96 teeth, driving the second shafts. Upon one end of the second shafts are two pinions containing 48 teeth each, driven by the large wheel. Upon the other end are two wheels, containing 56 teeth each, driving the upright shafts, upon the foot of which are the pinions, containing 32 teeth ; upon the top of the upright shafts are the wheels, containing 54 teeth each ; these wheels drive the cross shafts. The pinions upon the ends of the cross shafts (which receive the motion from the upright shafts) contain 42 teeth each. Required the revolutions per minute of each shaft.

RULE.—Multiply the speed per minute of the first shaft, by the number of teeth in the first driving wheel, and divide the product by the number of teeth in the pinion, which is fixed upon one end of the second shaft, and the result will be the speed per minute of the second shaft. In like manner, the speed of the upright shaft may be obtained by multiplying the speed per minute of the second shaft, by the teeth in the driving wheel, which is fixed upon the other end of the second shaft, and dividing the product by the number of teeth in the pinion which is on the foot of the upright shaft. And to find the speed of the cross shafts, multiply the speed per minute of the upright shaft by the teeth in the wheel on the top of the upright shaft, and divide the product by the teeth in the pinion on the cross shaft ; and so by the same process, the speed of any shaft may be traced out, however remote, or at whatever distance it may be situated from the first moving power.

EXAMPLES.

Speed per minute of the first shaft, 20 revolutions.
Number of teeth on the first driving wheel, 96.
Number of teeth in the pinion   48)1920(40   speed per minute of
                                  192   second shaft.
                                  ——

Speed of second shaft per minute,   40 revolutions.
Number of teeth in the wheel,   56
                                    ——

Number of teeth on the pinion 32)2240(70 speed of upright shaft.
                                 ——

Speed of upright shafts per minute,   70
Teeth in the wheel on the top of upright shaft, 54
                                           ——
                        42)3780(90 speed of cross
                           ——   shaft.

To find the speed per minute of any given shaft.

RULE.—Begin at the first moving power, and trace out all the
driving and all the driven wheels separately. Multiply all the
driving wheels together, and their product by the speed per minute
of the first shaft; then multiply all the driven wheels together,
including the first driven wheel on the given shaft, (the speed of
which we wish to ascertain;) divide the product of the drivers by
the produce of the driven, and the result thus obtained will be the
speed of the given shaft. Required the speed of cross shafts.

EXAMPLE.

Driving wheels.		*Driven wheels or pinions.*	
First wheel,	96	Second pinion,	48
Third wheel,	56	Fourth pinion,	32
Fifth wheel,	54	Sixth pinion,	42

                96
                56
                ——
               576
               480
               ——
              5376
                54
              ——
             21504
             26880
             ——
            290304
Speed of shaft   20
            ——
64512)5806080(90 speed of the cross shafts.
      580608
      ——

The preceding examples sufficiently illustrate the process of tracing out the speed of all the different shafts ; for by the same ⁎process we can trace the speed of any number of shafts throughout all their windings, even to the remotest department of any factory. The speed per minute of the cross shafts, which give motion to all the machinery in both the carding and spinning rooms, should always range from 88 to 90 revolutions. By the preceding examples the speed of the cross shafts will be found to be 90 revolutions per minute. When the speed of the cross shafts is known, the speed of all the different machines in either the carding or spinning departments, may be easily ascertained. Commence with the spinning department.

To find the speed per minute of the fly on the jenny.

RULE.—Begin first at the cross shaft, and trace out all the driving and driven pulleys and drums separately, from the large driving pulleys, on the cross shaft, to the fast and loose belt pulleys on the axle of the fly on the jenny. Multiply the diameters of all the driving pulleys and drums together, and their product by the speed of the cross shaft.⁎ Then multiply the diameters of all driven pulleys and drums together, and with their product divide the product of the drivers as found above ; the result will be the revolutions of the fly per minute.

Say the large driving pulleys, upon the cross shaft, are 20 inches in diameter ; likewise suppose that all the belt drums, and belt pulleys, are all the same diameter, viz. 18 inches. Required the revolutions of the fly or rim per minute.

EXAMPLE.

Driving drums and pulleys.	Driven drums and pulleys.
Pulleys on cross shaft, 20 inches.	Top speed pulleys, 18 inches.
Belt drums, 18 do.	Belt pulleys, 18 do.
Speed of cross shaft per minute, 90	
Diameter of pulleys, 20	

Diameter of top speed pulley 18)1800(100 revolutions per minute
                             18   of the belt.

Say the wheel, on the same shaft with the pulleys, contains 74

⁎ In all calculations of this kind where the drivers and driven are separated and multiplied together with a view to ascertain their relative speed, should wheels, containing the same number of teeth or drums, or pulleys of the same diameter, occur on both sides, these may be omitted in the operation. In these examples such are therefore omitted in the operation.

FLY FRAME.

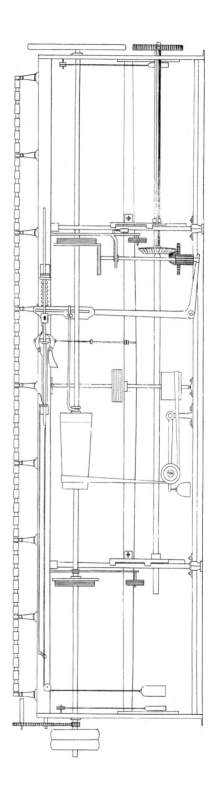

teeth, and working into the wheel, of 84 teeth, on the axle of the fly.

Speed per minute of belt pulleys, 100
Teeth in the wheel,   74

84)7400(88.09 revolutions of the fly per minute on the first speed.

Say the wheel, on the same shaft with the pulleys, contains 84 teeth, and working into the wheel, of 74 teeth, on the axle of the fly.

Speed per minute of belt pulleys, 100
Teeth in the wheel,   84

Teeth in the wheel,   74)8400(113.5 revolutions of the fly per minute on the second speed.

The revolutions of the fly being known—to find the revolutions of the front roller of the jenny per minute.

RULE.—Begin at the bevel wheel, on the axle of the fly, and trace out the driving and driven wheels from it to the wheel on the front roller. Multiply the number of teeth in the drivers together, and their product by the revolutions of the fly, and multiply the number of teeth in the driven together. Divide the product of the former by the product of the latter, and the result will be the revolutions of the front roller per minute.

EXAMPLE.

Drivers.		Driven.	
Wheel on axle of fly,	50	Wheel on top of bevel shaft,	50
Wheel on under end of bevel shaft,	34	Wheel on front roller,	50
Revolutions of the fly per minute,	88.09	or first speed.	
Teeth in the wheel on under end of bevel shaft,	34		

35236
26427

Wheel on top of bevel shaft,   50)2995.06(59.90 revolutions of the front roller per minute.

To find the revolutions of the spindle for one of the fly, and of the spindle per minute.

RULE.—When the wharves are one inch diameter, multiply the diameter of the fly by the diameter of the drum-band groove in the twist pulley, and divide by the diameter of the fly-band groove.

Suppose the diameter of the fly to be 40 inches, fly-band groove in twist pulley 14½, and drum-band groove 16 inches. Required the revolutions of the spindle for one of the fly.

EXAMPLE.

Diameter of fly,   40 inches.
Do. of drum-band groove,   16
———

Do. of fly-band groove, 14.5)640.0(44 revolutions of the spin-
                          580   dle, for one of the fly.
                        ———
                        600
                        580
                        ———
                        20

The revolutions of the spindle for one of the fly being 44, this multiplied by the revolutions of the fly per minute, gives the revolutions of the spindle per minute.

Revolutions of fly on the first speed, $88.09 \times 44 = 3875.96$ revolutions of spindle per minute on first speed.

Revolutions of fly on the second speed, $113.5 \times 44 = 4994$ revolutions of spindle per minute on second speed.

Note.—It is difficult to find any general rule by which the revolutions of the spindle for one of the fly or rim can be exactly ascertained by calculation, because these are often found to vary according to the thickness of the drum and fly-bands, the diameter of the wharves, &c. The older these bands are, they become smaller and sink deeper into the grooves ; hence the variations of the spindle in proportion to the fly. The above rule, will be found to come as near the truth as any which has hitherto been suggested.

Say the cross shafts which give motion to the various machines in the carding and picking rooms, revolve 90 times per minute. Required the speed of the different machines in these departments.

To find the speed of the cards per minute.

RULE.—Begin at the cross shaft, and multiply its revolutions per minute, by the number of teeth in the wheel, and divide the product by the teeth in the pinion on the card-drum shaft; this will give the revolutions of the shaft per minute. Multiply this by the diameter of the card drums, and divide the product by the diameter of the belt pulleys, on the axle of the card cylinder ; the result thus obtained, will be the revolutions of the card cylinder per minute.

EXAMPLE.

Teeth in the wheel,	40	Teeth in the pinion,	36
Diameter of card drums in.	18	Diameter of belt pulleys,	16
Speed of cross shaft,	90		
Teeth in driving wheel on do.	40		

Teeth in driven pinion, 36)3600(100*revolutions per minute of
36   the card drum shaft.
Revolutions of shaft per minute, 100
Diameter of card drums,   18 inches
Diameter of belt pulleys on axle ———
    of card,   16)1800(112.5+ revolutions of card
           cylinder per minute.

To find the revolutions per minute of the delivering shaft in the card.

RULE.—Begin at the pinion on the main axle of the card cylinder, and trace out the driving and driven wheels, or pinions separately, from it to the pinion on the end of the delivering shaft.*

Multiply all the drivers together, and their product by the revolutions of the cylinder per minute ; then multiply all the driven together, and with their product divide the product of the former.

EXAMPLE.

Drivers.		*Driven.*	
Teeth in pinion on main axle,	20	Teeth in wheel,	144
Teeth in pinion,	48	Teeth in pinion,	22
Revolutions of cylinder per minute,	112.5	Teeth in wheel,	144
Teeth in pinion on main axle,	20	Teeth in pinion,	22
	2250.0		288
Teeth in pinion,	48		288
	180000		3168
	90000		

3168)108000.0(34.99+ revolutions
of delivering shaft per minute.

* The revolutions of the feeding roller is found by the same method as the delivering shaft.† Intermediate wheels or drums are never taken into the operation of calculating the speed or draught of any kind of machinery.

† The shafts in carding and picking rooms, revolving at the rate of 100 times per minute, the speed of all the different machines in these departments may be calculated from this.

The revolutions of the delivering shaft per minute being 34.09, multiplying it by the circumference of the delivering ball, gives the length produced per minute.

To find the speed of the cylinder shaft in the drawing-frame.

RULE.—Multiply the diameters of the drums together, and their product by the speed per minute of the shaft, and multiply the diameters of the driven pulleys together. Divide the product of the former by the product of the latter; the result is the speed per minute of the cylinder shaft.

EXAMPLE.

Driving drums.		*Driven pulleys.*	
Speed of shaft,	100	Diameter of pulley,	16.75
Diameter of drum,	18	Diameter of pulley,	16
	14400		10050
	1800		1675

268.00)32400.00(120.89+ revolutions   268.00
of cylinder shaft per minute.

To find the speed of the fly or tube frames per minute.

RULE.—Multiply the diameters of the driving drums together, and their product by the speed of the shaft; and multiply the diameters of the speed pulley, and the belt pulley, on the end of the frame shaft, together. Divide the product of the former by the product of the latter, and the result is the speed per minute of the frame shaft.

EXAMPLE.

Speed per minute of shaft	100	Diameter of speed pulley,	$13\frac{3}{4}$
Diameter of drum, inches,	18	Diameter of belt-pulley,	$11\frac{1}{2}$
Diameter of drum, do.	18		
Speed of shaft,	100	Diameter of pulley, 13.75	
Diameter of drum,	18	Diameter of pulley,	11.5
	1800		6875
Diameter of drum,	18		1375
	14400		1375
	1800		158.125

158.125)32400.000(204.90 speed of fly or tube frame
shaft per minute.

To find the speed per minute of the scutching machine.

RULE.—Multiply the speed per minute of the shaft in the picking room, by the diameter of the main drum, and the product by

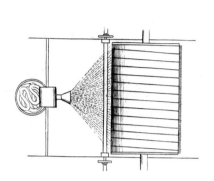

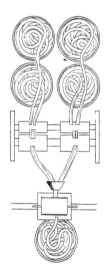

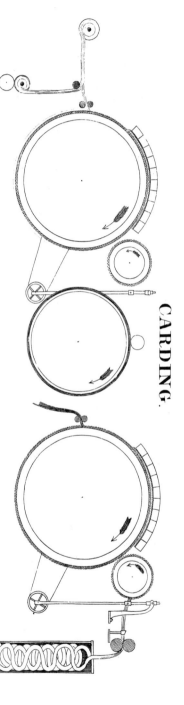

CARDING.

the diameter of the drum ; then multiply the diameter of the drum by the diameter of the belt pulleys, on the shaft, on the machine. Divide the product of the former by the product of the latter ; the result will be the speed per minute of the shaft.

EXAMPLE.

Speed of shaft per minute,	100	Diameter of drum,	18
Diameter of drum,	24	Diameter of belt pulleys,	$10\frac{1}{2}$
Diameter of drum,	22		

$$\underline{180}$$
$$9$$
$$\overline{189}$$

Speed of shaft,   100
Diameter of drum   24
$$\overline{}$$
2400
Diameter of drum   22
$$\overline{}$$
4800
4800
$$\overline{}$$

189)52800(279.36+ revolutions per minute of shaft in scutching machine.

The preceding calculations are merely intended to exemplify the method of tracing out the motions of the various shafts and machines, from the power which gives the first motion, to the remotest movement in the whole establishment.

The plan of the shafts and other gearing, in some of the old establishments, will be found much more complicated ; yet still the principles upon which their various speeds are calculated are always the same ; and if once these are properly understood, the method of tracing out the speed of every shaft throughout the ramifications of even the most complicated establishments, will then be comparatively easy.

If there are different kinds of cotton used, it is important that they should be properly and regularly mixed together ; and unless this be particularly attended to, a regular and uniform quality of yarn cannot be produced.

The cotton is weighed previous to being put into the spreading machine, and when spread into a given length and thickness, is called a feed ; a number of these follow each other ; so that a continuous web of cotton passes through the machine, and is rolled on a wooden roller, until it be of sufficient size, when it is carried to the cards, in which state it is called a breaker lap.

If any machine, in the whole process of cotton spinning, be of more use and importance than another, it is the carding engine ;

nor can it be dispensed with, the process of cotton spinning, (properly speaking,) begins only at the carding ; for all the previous departments of the process are merely preparatory to this, and consist chiefly in mixing, cleaning, and opening the cotton, so as that the cards may take the best effect upon it.

That much depends upon a proper system of doubling and drawing for making a superior quality of yarn, is generally admitted. And as I believe that it is owing to the particular management of this essential part of the process that enables one spinner to excel another in the quality of the yarns they produce, too much importance, therefore, cannot be attached to this subject. For whatever be the quality of the cotton that is used, or the yarn required, the whole doubling and drawing must be regulated accordingly. And unless the one be adjusted to suit the other, it is vain to expect a superior quality of yarn.

To find the twists per inch on the yarn, suppose No. 36.

RULE.—Multiply the revolutions of the front roller by its circumference, and divide the revolutions of the spindle per minute by the product.

EXAMPLE.

Revolutions per minute of the front roller, 58.72
Circumference of do. $3\frac{1}{8}$ inches.

$$\frac{17616}{734}$$

$$183.50)4000.00(21.70+ \text{ twists}$$
per inch in the yarn.

Spinning masters who have occasion to be frequently changing the sizes of yarn, may sometimes be at a loss to know the precise quantity of twist that particular numbers will require, unless they have some rule to direct them how to find what twist will suit any given numbers of either weft or warps.

The following rules for finding this are considered to be the most correct. RULE 1. If for warp yarn, allow 25 twists to the inch, or 25 revolutions of the spindle for the inch of yarn of No. 50, and the same for No. 60 wefts. Taking the above for the data upon which to proceed. To find the twists per inch that any given size of yarn will require. RULE 2. If for warp yarn, as No. 50 is to the square of 25 so is the given size, to the square of the twists per inch which the given size requires.

EXAMPLE.

How many twists per inch will No. 64 warp yarn require?
As No. 50 : 25×25=625 : : 64

$$\begin{array}{r} 64 \\ \hline 2500 \\ 3750 \\ \hline \end{array}$$

50)40000

800(28⅓ twist required for No. 64 warps.

$$\begin{array}{r} 4 \\ \hline \end{array}$$

48)400
384

$$\begin{array}{r} \hline 16 \\ 16)\overline{}=\tfrac{1}{3} \\ 48 \end{array}$$

RULE 3.—If for weft yarn, as No. 60 is to the square of **25** so is the given size to the twists per inch, which the given size of yarn requires.

EXAMPLE.

How many twists per inch will No. 80 wefts require?
As No. 60 : 25×25=625 : : 80

$$\begin{array}{r} 80 \\ \hline \end{array}$$

60)50000

Find the square root of   823.33(28.69 twists per inch re-
                 4   quired for No. 80 wefts.

48)423
8 384

566)3933
6 3396

5729)53700
51561

2139

There is another short and simple rule, approved of by some managers, for finding the twists per inch, which any given size may require, which may be shortly stated without exemplifying it.

RULE.—Multiply the square root of the given size by 3¾ if for warp yarn, and by $3\frac{1}{4}$ if for wefts ; the result of either will be the twists per inch which the given size of yarn requires.

Managers of spinning factories do not seem yet to be agreed upon what is the most proper dimensions of a mule jenny. Some contend, that mules containing from 264 to 280 spindles, are the most profitable, because they generally turn off a much greater quantity of yarn in proportion to their spindles, than those of a larger size ; and, besides, they are easier to work or manage, and not so destructive to the drum and fly bands, having less weight to drive. Others, again, suppose, that as all mules, of whatever size, require the same gearing, as well as drums and belts, to move them, the larger the better : as a factory filled with mules of a large size will require less power to drive it, having less gearing, it will require fewer belts, &c. &c.

Young carding and spinning masters, who have newly entered into a charge in any of the departments, or for operatives and mechanics, who may be looking forward to such a situation, it is of the utmost importance that they exercise themselves in performing all kinds of calculations connected with the business, and thereby acquire expertness in performing them, when necessary, as it will be the means of saving much trouble and uncertainty afterwards.

Velocity of Wheels.—Wheels are for conveying motion to the different parts of a machine, at the same, or at greater or less velocity, as may be required. When two wheels are in motion their teeth act on one another alternately ; and, consequently, if one of these wheels has 40 teeth, and the other 20 teeth, the one with 20 will turn twice upon its axis for one revolution of the wheel with 40 teeth. From this the rule is taken, which is :—As the velocity required is to the number of teeth in the driver, so is the velocity of the driver to the number of teeth in the driven.

Note. To find the proportion that the velocities of the wheels, in a train, should bear to one another, subtract the less velocity from the greater, and divide the remainder by the number of one less than the wheels in the train ; the quotient will be the number rising in arithmetical progression, from the least to the greatest velocity of the train of wheels.

EXAMPLE.

What is the number of teeth in each of three wheels, to produce 17 revolutions per minute ; the driver having 107 teeth, and making 3 revolutions per minute ?

$$\frac{17-3=14}{3-1=\ 2}=7, \text{ therefore 3, 10, 17, are the velocities of the}$$

three wheels.

By the rule,

$$10 : 107 : : 3 : 32 = \frac{107 \times 3}{10} = 32 \text{ teeth.}$$

$$17 : 32 : : 10 : 19 = \frac{32 \times 10}{17} = 19 \text{ teeth.}$$

THE COMMUNICATION OF POWER.

There are no prime movers of machinery from which power is taken in a greater variety of forms than the water-wheel, and among such a number there cannot fail to be many bad applications. Suffice it here to mention one of the worst, and most generally adopted. For driving a cotton mill, there is a water-wheel about twelve feet broad, and twenty feet diameter; there is a division in the middle of the buckets upon which the segments are bolted round the wheel, and the power is taken from the vertex: from this erroneous application, a great part of the power is lost; for the weight of water upon the wheel presses against the axle in proportion to the resistance it has to overcome, and if the axle was not a large mass of wood, with very strong iron journals, it could not stand the great strain which is upon it.

The most advantageous part of the wheel, from which the power can be taken, is that point in the circle of gyration horizontal to the centre of the axle; because, taking the power from this part, the whole weight of water in the buckets acts upon the teeth of the wheels; and the axle of the water wheel suffers no strain. The proper connection of machinery to water wheels is of the first importance, and mismanagement in this particular point is often the cause of the journals and axles giving way, besides a considerable loss of power. To find the radius of the circle of gyration in a water wheel is therefore of advantage to the saving of power, and the following example will show the rule by which it is found.

EXAMPLE.

Required the radius of the circle of gyration in a water-wheel, 30 feet diameter; the weight of the arms being 12 tons, shrouding 20 tons, and water 15 tons.

30 feet diameter, radius=15 feet.

S. $20 \times 15^2 = 4500 \times 2 = $ 9000 } The opposite side of the water-
A. $12 \times 15^2 = 900 \times 2 = $ 1800 } wheel must be taken.
W. $15 \times 15^2 = 3375 = $ 3375
$2 \times 20 + 12 = 64$
W.15   14175

$$\frac{W.15}{79} \qquad \frac{14175}{79} = 179 \text{ the square root of which is } 13\tfrac{4}{10} \text{ feet, the radius of the circle of gyration.}$$

The preceding examples sufficiently illustrate the process of tracing out the speed of all the different shafts : for by the same process we can trace the speed of any number of shafts throughout all their windings, even to the remotest department of any factory. The speed per minute of the cross shafts, which give motion to all the machinery in both the carding and spinning-rooms, should always range from 88 to 70 revolutions. By the preceding examples the speed of the cross shafts will be found to be 90 revolutions per minute. When the speed of the cross shafts is known, the speed of all the different machines in either the carding or spinning departments, may be easily ascertained.

On the opposite page will be found a table condensed from Newton's machinist's table, showing the proportional radii of wheels to their pitch.

Extract from Baines's History of the Cotton Manufacture in England.

	Prices of machinery in England, 1834.		Prices of machinery in the United States, 1834		Actual prices sold in U.S.
Card'g engines,	£30 to 40	$144 to 192	£40 to 50	$192.00 to 240	$100 to 250
Throstles, per spindle,	8s. to 9s.	2.91 to 1.92	1.4. to 1.6	$ 5.76 to 6.22	$4.25 to 6
Mules per do.	4s.6 to 5s.	1.08 to 1.20	13s to 14s	$ 3.12 to 3.36	$2.12 to 2.25
Dressing Machines,	£30 to 35	$144 to 168	£80 to 90	$ 384 to 432	$400
Power Looms,	£7½ to 8½	36 to 40.80	£12 to 16	57.60 to 76.80	$ 50 to 75

Mr. White.

I have obtained the actual sale prices of the above named machinery from one of the principal machine makers in this city, Mr. Stanford Newell, which I believe to be correct.   Yours, very respectfully,   Z. ALLEN.

The fact respecting the higher prices of American machinery, arises from their ornamental work, which the English think unnecessary ; as they regard only the utility and durability of the machine. This circumstance may be worthy the attention of our machinists ; whether it is best to expend so much for polishing the appearance of the works.

No. of Teeth.	¼	½	¾	1	1¼	1½	1¾	2	2¼	2½	3
10	0.405	0.809	1.214	1.618	2.023	2.427	2.832	3.236	3.641	4.045	4.854
11	0.444	0.887	1.331	1.775	2.218	2.662	3.106	3.549	3.993	4.437	5.324
12	0.483	0.966	1.449	1.932	2.415	2.898	3.381	3.864	4.347	4.830	5.795
13	0.522	1.045	1.567	2.089	2.612	3.134	3.656	4.179	4.701	5.223	6.268
14	0.562	1.123	1.685	2.247	2.809	3.370	3.932	4.494	5.056	5.617	6.741
15	0.601	1.202	1.804	2.405	3.006	3.607	4.209	4.810	5.411	6.012	7.215
16	0.641	1.281	1.922	2.563	3.204	3.844	4.485	5.126	5.767	6.407	7.689
17	0.680	1.361	2.041	2.721	3.401	4.082	4.762	5.442	6.122	6.803	8.163
18	0.720	1.440	2.160	2.879	3.599	4.319	5.039	5.759	6.479	7.198	8.638
19	0.759	1.519	2.278	3.038	3.797	4.557	5.316	6.076	6.835	7.594	9.113
20	0.799	1.598	2.397	3.196	3.995	4.794	5.593	6.392	7.192	7.991	9.589
30	1.196	2.392	3.588	4.783	5.979	7.175	8.371	9.567	10.763	11.958	14.350
40	1.593	3.186	4.780	6.373	7.966	9.559	11.152	12.746	14.339	15.932	19.118
50	1.991	3.982	5.972	7.963	9.954	11.945	13.935	15.926	17.917	19.908	23.889
60	2.388	4.777	7.165	9.554	11.942	14.330	16.719	19.107	21.496	23.884	28.661
70	2.786	5.572	8.358	11.145	13.931	16.717	19.503	22.289	25.075	27.861	33.434
80	3.184	6.368	9.552	12.736	15.920	19.103	22.287	25.471	28.655	31.839	38.207
90	3.582	7.163	10.745	14.327	17.909	21.490	25.072	28.654	32.235	35.817	42.981
100	3.980	7.959	11.938	15.918	19.898	23.877	27.857	31.386	35.816	39.795	47.754
110	4.377	8.755	13.132	17.509	21.887	26.264	30.641	35.019	39.396	43.774	52.528
120	4.775	9.550	14.326	19.101	23.876	28.651	33.426	38.202	42.977	47.752	57.302
130	5.173	10.346	15.519	20.692	25.865	31.038	36.211	41.384	46.557	51.730	62.077
140	5.571	11.142	16.713	22.284	27.855	33.426	38.996	44.567	50.138	55.709	66.851
150	5.969	11.938	17.906	23.875	29.844	35.813	41.781	47.750	53.719	59.687	71.625
160	6.367	12.733	19.100	25.466	31.833	38.200	44.566	50.933	57.299	63.666	76.399
170	6.764	13.529	20.293	27.058	33.822	40.587	47.351	54.116	60.880	67.645	81.174
180	7.162	14.325	21.487	28.649	35.812	42.974	50.136	57.299	64.461	71.623	85.948
190	7.560	15.120	22.681	30.241	37.801	45.361	52.921	60.482	68.042	75.602	90.722
200	7.958	15.916	23.874	31.832	39.790	47.748	55.707	63.665	71.623	79.581	95.497
210	8.356	16.712	25.068	33.424	41.780	50.136	58.492	66.848	75.204	83.560	100.271
220	8.754	17.508	26.261	35.015	43.769	52.523	61.277	70.031	78.784	87.538	105.046
230	9.152	18.303	27.455	36.607	45.759	54.910	64.062	73.214	82.365	91.517	109.820
240	9.550	19.099	28.649	38.198	47.748	57.297	66.847	76.397	85.946	95.496	114.595
250	9.947	19.895	29.842	39.790	49.737	59.685	69.632	79.580	89.527	99.475	119.369
260	10.345	20.691	31.036	41.381	51.727	62.072	72.417	82.763	93.108	103.453	124.144
270	10.743	21.486	32.230	42.973	53.716	64.459	75.202	85.946	96.689	107.432	128.919
280	11.141	22.282	33.423	44.564	55.705	66.847	77.988	89.129	100.270	111.411	133.693
290	11.539	23.078	34.617	46.156	57.695	69.234	80.773	92.312	103.851	115.390	138.468
300	11.937	23.874	35.811	47.747	59.684	71.621	83.558	95.495	107.432	119.369	143.242
310	12.335	24.669	37.004	49.339	61.674	74.008	86.343	98.678	111.013	123.347	148.017
320	12.733	25.465	38.198	50.930	63.663	76.396	89.128	101.861	114.593	127.326	152.791
330	13.130	26.261	39.391	52.522	65.652	78.783	91.913	105.044	118.174	131.305	157.566
340	13.528	27.057	40.585	54.114	67.642	81.170	94.699	108.227	121.756	135.284	162.341
350	13.926	27.853	41.779	55.705	69.631	83.558	97.484	111.410	125.336	139.263	167.115
360	14.324	28.648	42.972	57.297	71.621	85.945	100.269	114.593	128.917	143.241	171.890
370	14.722	29.444	44.166	58.888	73.610	88.332	103.054	117.776	132.498	147.220	176.664
380	15.120	30.240	45.360	60.480	75.600	90.719	105.839	120.959	136.079	151.199	181.439
390	15.518	31.036	46.553	62.071	77.589	93.107	108.625	124.142	139.660	155.178	186.213
391	15.558	31.115	46.673	62.230	77.788	93.345	108.903	124.461	140.018	155.576	186.691
392	15.597	31.195	46.792	62.389	77.987	93.584	109.182	124.779	140.376	155.974	187.168
393	15.637	31.274	46.911	62.549	78.186	93.823	109.460	125.097	140.734	156.372	187.646
394	15.677	31.354	47.031	62.708	78.385	94.062	109.739	125.416	141.092	156.769	188.123
395	15.717	31.433	47.150	62.867	78.584	94.300	110.017	125.734	141.451	157.167	188.601
396	15.757	31.513	47.270	63.026	78.783	94.539	110.296	126.052	141.809	157.565	189.078
397	15.796	31.593	47.389	63.185	78.982	94.778	110.574	126.370	142.167	157.963	189.556
398	15.836	31.672	47.508	63.344	79.180	95.017	110.853	126.689	142.525	158.361	190.033
399	15.876	31.752	47.628	63.504	79.379	95.255	111.131	127.007	142.883	158.759	190.511
400	15.916	31.831	47.747	63.663	79.578	95.494	111.410	127.325	143.241	159.157	190.988

Motion, Resistance, and Effect of Machines.

Various as the modifications of machines are, and innumerable their different applications; still there are only three distinct objects to which their utility tends. The first is, in furnishing the means of giving to the moving force the most commodious direction; and, when it can be done, of causing its action to be applied immediately to the body to be moved. These can rarely be united, but the former can be accomplished in most cases. The second, in accommodating the velocity of the work to be performed, to the velocity with which alone a natural power can act. The third and most essential advantage of machines, is in augmenting, or rather in modifying, the energy of the moving power in such a manner, that it may produce effects of which it would have been otherwise incapable. For instance, a man might with exertion lift 400lbs.; but let him apply a lever, and he will lift many times that weight. The motions produced by machines are of three kinds, viz. accelerated, uniform, and alternate, *i. e.* accelerated and retarded. The first of these always takes place when the moving power is immediately applied; the second, after the machine has been in motion for a short time; the third, in intermitting machines, such as pendulum clocks, &c.; but though a seconds' pendulum is accelerated the first half second and retarded the next, still it produces a constant number of vibrations in a given time, and therefore may be considered as a machine of uniform motion. The grand object, in all practical cases, is to procure a uniform motion, because it produces the greatest. All irregularities of motion indicate that there is some point resisting the motion, and to overcome which a part of the propelling power is wasted, and the greatest varying velocity is only equal to that velocity by which the machine would move when its motion is uniform. If the machine moves with an accelerating velocity, it is certain that the power is greater than what balances the opposing resistance, and therefore cannot produce the greatest effect; because the whole resistance is not applied. In both these cases the machine has neither the power nor the effect which it would have if moving uniformly. When irregularity of motion takes place, particularly in a large heavy machine, it suffers a continual straining and jolting which must very soon destroy it. It is therefore of the greatest consequence, that, from all machines, every cause tending to produce irregularity of motion should be taken away.*

* Hydrodynamics, which signifies water and power or force, is that branch of natural philosophy which embraces the phenomena exhibited by water

Management and government of Spinning Factories, &c.

Cotton spinning factories, like all other establishments where a
large capital is invested for the purpose of manufacturing any par-

and other fluids, whether they are at rest or in motion. It treats of the pressure, the equilibrium, the cohesion, the motion, and the resistance of fluids;
and of the construction of the machines by which water is raised, and in
which it is the first mover or the primary agent. This science is generally
divided into *hydrostatics* and *hydraulics*, the former of which considers the
pressure, equilibrium, and cohesion of fluids; and the latter, their motion,
the resistance which they oppose to moving bodies, and the various machines
in which they are the principal agent. Although hydrodynamics is but a
modern science, and was studied by the ancients only in its most general
principles, yet many of the leading doctrines and phenomena upon which it
is founded are familiar to the rudest nations, and must have been well
known in the very earliest ages of society. Even at the remote period
when man first trusted himself to the waves, the pressure of fluids, and the
phenomena of floating bodies, were undoubtedly known to him; and in the
more advanced state of navigation, when the Phœnicians were able to colo-
nise the most distant regions of the globe, the directing power of the helm,
the force and management of the oars, the action of the wind upon the sail,
and the resistance opposed to the motion of the vessel, were well known
facts which implied practical acquaintance with some of the most important
doctrines of hydrodynamics. Notwithstanding, the doctrine of fluids may
still be considered as deriving its origin from the discoveries of Archimedes.
The history of these discoveries has been rendered ridiculous by vulgar
fables which have long been discredited; but it appears unquestionable, that
they originated in the detection of a fraud committed by the jeweller of
Hiero, King of Syracuse. Archimedes was applied to by the king to ascertain, without injuring the workmanship, whether or not a new crown, which
had been made for him, consisted of pure gold. The method of solving the
problem is said to have occurred to him when in the bath, and he applied it
successfully in detecting the fraud. The hydrostatical doctrines to which
Archimedes was thus conducted, were illustrated by him in two books. He
maintained that every particle of a fluid mass in equilibrio is pressed equally
in every direction. He examined the conditions in consequence of which
a floating body assumes and preserves its position of equilibrium, and he
applied to bodies that have a triangular, a conical, and a parabolic form.
He showed that every body plunged in a fluid, loses as much of its own
weight as the weight of the quantity of water which it displaces; and upon
this beautiful principle is founded the process which he employed for ascer-
taining the impurity of Hiero's crown. No one could deny the result of this
experiment. The screw of Archimedes, which is still used in modern times
for raising water, is said to have been invented by him when in Egypt, for
the purpose of enabling the inhabitants to free themselves of the stagnant
water which was left in the low grounds after the inundations of the Nile;
and Athenæus informs us, that navigators held the memory of Archimedes
in the highest honour, for having furnished them with means of carrying off
the water in the holds of their vessels.

ticular kind of goods upon an extensive scale, require to be very skilfully managed in order to make them profitable, either for producing a superior quality of yarn, or turning off a large quantity in proportion to the extent of the machinery. All the different departments may be arranged in the most judicious manner, and every machine made and adjusted on the most approved principles, and yet the establishment and the mode of government which generally prevails, may be greatly deficient in respect both to the quantity and quality of its produce.

Considering the amount of capital invested in these establishments, it might be expected that proprietors would be much more scrupulous, with respect to ability and merit, in the choice of those to whom they confide the charge of the different departments, than they frequently are; hence the reason why certain proprietors realise a high profit from their establishments, whilst others can scarcely secure the interest of the capital.

It is an erroneous opinion to suppose that any person, who may not have been early and long practised in the business, can, notwithstanding, acquire as much knowledge by their own experience in the course of a few months, as will qualify them for taking a full charge of a factory. It will be admitted, that those who have been brought up to the business, where they had many opportunities of seeing the methods of adapting the different machines to suit the various qualities of cotton, and sizes of yarn, and who know how to adjust machinery in the event of any little accidents or errors that frequently occur in practice, must possess a decided advantage over those who have not enjoyed so favourable opportunities. It would be advantageous for the agent or overseer of a cotton mill to have a thorough knowledge of the business *in all* its details, as without this he must sometimes leave much of the management of certain departments to others, and they, occupying only a subordinate station, are likely to feel a subordinate responsibility: hence may arise much mismanagement, attended with loss to the proprietors. The manager who knows his business, can both give directions to those that are under him, as well as discern whether they are qualified for the situations they occupy, and when they fail in their duty.

It is a most essential qualification on the part of the manager, that he be expert in performing *all kinds* of calculations connected with the business; in regulating the speed of the different machines; in adjusting the draughts of the various machines; and in making changes in the qualities of the cotton and sizes of the yarn. In regulating the speed of the various machines, particularly in the preparation department, it is important to have them, so that the one shall not be over driven, nor the other working at an under speed.

Let the carding engines be adjusted to such a speed as will suit the nature of the cotton and the quality of the yarn for which they are preparing it; the speed of the drawing frame should also be regulated to take up exactly what the cards bring forward, without any unnecessary loss of time on the part of either, and all the other machines should be regulated in the same manner. But it might be desirable to ascertain the most advantageous speed, at which the different machines should be driven for the various qualities of yarn. The number of carding engines that should be allowed to the drawing-frame is important; from No. 80, downwards, the carding engines may range from eight to ten.

The proper adjustment of the draughts on the different machines is also of equal importance to a proper arrangement of the speed. Excess of draught on any one machine, while there is less than necessary on another, should be uniformly avoided.

In working an inferior quality of cotton, there is always a less quantity of yarn produced in a given time, but a much greater quantity of waste; besides, the yarn being of an inferior quality, is likely to hurt the credit of the manufacturer; whereas a superior quality will always support his credit, command a fair price, and secure a sale, so that he will often have his money when others have their stock.

Another primary object in the management of a factory, that ought to be studied, is the avoiding all *unnecessary* expenses by alterations on the plan of the gearing, or arrangement of the machinery, especially such as might only be adapted to please the eye rather than improve the productive capabilities of the esta-blishment. To have the large gearing all fitted up on the most approved plan, and the machinery arranged in the manner best calculated to facilitate the progress of the work, are doubtless objects of the greatest importance, but when once the establishment has been filled with machinery, and all its arrangements completed, it is better to let it remain as it is, than try to improve it; and indeed, to begin then to make alterations, would be highly objectionable, because the money expended on these alterations might far exceed all the advantages arising from the supposed improvements. To keep all the machinery in good repair, and in the best working order, cannot be too highly recommended; as without doing so, it is impossible to produce a regular and uniform good quality of yarn; and to keep machinery in good order, by regular care and attention, is much easier than to repair it after it has been allowed to go out of repair from negligence and want of care.

MR. ORRELL'S MILL, NEAR STOCKPORT, ENGLAND.

1. Its two-fold heart, or twin steam engines, one of which makes its maximum effort, while the other makes its minimum, to secure perfect equability of impulsion through all the ramifications of its shafts, and to prevent arterial throbbing or tremor, formerly so common, and so injurious to the work of delicate machines.

2. The great bevel wheel gearing, which transmits the power of the engine in rectangular directions, either transversely or vertically, and with any modification of speed.

3. The horizontal and upright shafts, with their several pulleys.

4. The distribution of the straps, or belts, that convey the power from these revolving shafts and pulleys.

5. The respective positions of the various productive organs in their respective floors : such as the preparation machines, throstles, mules, power-looms, dressing machines, warping mills, &c. Dr. Ure has promised the whole anatomy of the mill in the above order.

The recent innovations in proportioning the sizes, regulating the connections, and adjusting the movements of the system of shaft gearing, form a fine feature in the philosophy of manufactures. Thus, not only an improvement has been made in the regularity of impulsion, but a considerable increase of power from the same prime mover has been obtained ; amounting, in some cases of old mills remounted by Messrs. Fairbairn and Lillie, to fully 20 per cent. The durability of shafts so exquisitely turned and polished, is another great advantage. The spinning factory of Messrs. Ashworth, at Egerton, which has been at work for several years, exhibits an elegant pattern of the engineering just described : for it has some subordinate shafts, hardly thicker than the human wrist, which convey the power of ten horses, and revolve with great speed, without the slightest noise or vibration. The prime mover of the whole is a gigantic water wheel, of sixty feet diameter, and one hundred horse power. I have frequently been at a loss, in walking through several of the millwright factories, to know whether the polished shafts that drive the automatic lathes and planing machines, were at rest or in motion, so truly and silently did they revolve.

The method of increased velocities in the driving arms or shafts of factories is, undoubtedly, one of the most remarkable improvements in practical dynamics. It diminishes greatly the inertia of the mass to be moved, by giving to much lighter shafts and wheels the same momentum; and it permits the pulleys or drums, which immediately impel the machines by straps, to be reduced to a size much nearer to that of the steam pulleys, fixed on the main axis of these machines. About thirty years ago the velocities of the main shafts, proceeding from the moving power, whether of steam or water, amounted to no more than from thirty to forty revolutions per minute, and of the smaller and remoter shafts, to only forty or fifty. At the same period the drums were heavy tubs, and from thirty to upwards of sixty inches in diameter. This improved system is under deep obligations for its actual state of perfection to the above named engineers; though it had commenced, as we have stated, before their time.

In the mills mounted by these gentlemen, it is interesting to see slender shafts, like small sinewy arms, rapidly transmitting vast power through all the ramifications of a great factory.

A mill, propelled by a steam engine of fifty horse power, was formerly geared with shafts, having an average transverse section of thirty-six square inches, or varying in size from four to eight inches square. An engine of like power at the present day, will, in consequence of the increased velocities above described, work with cylindrical shafts not exceeding five and a half, and often only three inches in diameter; possessing, therefore, an average area of only fifteen square inches, instead of thirty-six. The horizontal shafts that run under the ceilings of the different working rooms are two inches, and seldom exceed two and a quarter in diameter. Hence, the mass of gearing has been reduced fully one half. But the shafts now make from one hundred and twenty to one hundred and fifty revolutions in a minute; and, occasionally, as where throstles are turned, so many as two hundred in the same time. Thus we see the requisite momentum is gained with a light shaft, while the friction is proportionally diminished, and the driving drum revolves with a velocity in accordance with the accelerated pace of the modern machines.

The philosophy of manufactures investigates the most economical and energetic modes of applying the motive force to the various working organs; the carding engings, the drawing heads, the roving frames, the throstles, the mules, the power looms, the dressing machines, &c.

The dressing machine does, at present, two hundred pieces of thirty yards each, in a week, equaling six thousand yards; and costs in wages, to the dresser, fifty shillings. This branch of the trade having, in consequence of the high wages, been, like the mule spinning, continually disturbed by unions and strikes, has led to the invention of a self-acting machine, which will dress at least six thousand yards of warp in two days, under the superintendence of a labourer, at three shillings a day; that is at a cost, in wages, of six shillings. This mechanism is, at the same time, greatly simpler and cheaper than the former, and will soon come into general use for coarse calicoes.

Prodigious sums are wastefully expended every year, which would be saved by a more thorough acquaintance with true principles of science and art. Several individuals who have embarked vast fortunes in factories, are, to a very great extent, the victims at least, if not the dupes, of scheming managers, who are ever ready to display their perverse ingenuity, by the substitution of some intricate trap, for a simpler but less showy mechanism. There have been many cases where a complete system of good machines, capable of doing excellent work, has been capriciously turned out of a cotton factory, and replaced by another of greater expense, but of less productive powers, and less suited to the style of work than the old one, if skilfully managed. These substitutions are continual in many establishments. They interfere most essentially, and often unnecessarily, with the going of the mill, and are referable almost always to injudicious choice at first, and capricious alterations afterwards; circumstances over which the proprietor, from ignorance of the structure of a good machine, cannot always venture to exercise the proper control. There are, no doubt, many mill managers perfectly fitted, by judgment, knowledge, and integrity, to second the sound commercial views of the mill owner, and to advance the business with a profitable career. These practical men form the soul of the factory system. But with a wrong-headed, plausible manager, the proprietor is sure to be led such a mechanical dance as will bewilder him completely, unless he has acquired a clear insight into the *arcana* of the business, by deliberate study of the composition and performance of each machine in his factory. It may be supposed that this species of education can be most easily acquired in the midst of the machinery itself; but this is a mistake, which experience speedily proves.

The object of manufactures is to modify the productions of nature into articles of necessity, convenience, or luxury, by the most economical and unerring means. They have all three principles of action, or three organic systems : the mechanical, the moral, and the commercial; which may not unaptly be compared to the muscular, the nervous, and the sanguiferous systems of an animal. They have also three interests to subserve,—that of the operative, the master, and the state ; and must seek their perfection in the due development and administration of each. The mechanical being should always be subordinate to the moral constitution, and both should co-operate to the commercial efficiency. Three distinct powers concur to their vitality,—labour, science, capital ; the first destined to move, the second to direct, and the third to sustain. When the whole are in harmony, they form a body qualified to discharge its manifold functions by an intrinsic, self-governing agency, like those of organic life.

The drawing-frame is a most essential constituent of the spinning system, executing a task much too delicate and irksome for handicraft labour, and therefore does the highest honour to its inventor, Sir Richard Arkwright. It equalises the riband delivered from the finishing card, and reduces it to one of smaller dimensions, called a sliver, ·which it effects by uniting many ribands into one, at the same time that it lays the fibres in parallel lines, and attenuates the whole by a regular process of extension. The twin-roller mechanism, which was perfected at least, if not invented, by Arkwright, derives its best illustration from the drawing frame. This talented individual saw so clearly the great part which this machine played, in cotton spinning, that when bad yarn made its appearance, in any one of his mills, he swore a loud oath, according to the vile fashion of the time, and ordered his people to look to their drawings, convinced that if *they* were right, every thing else would go well. It is only those who have deliberately studied the intricate train of operations in a spinning factory, who are qualified to appreciate the merit of so admirable a systematist as Arkwright; and they know the value of his drawing-frame far better than his invidious detractors.

The drawing of the sliver into parallel lines of filaments is effected by the joint action of upper and under rollers ; the former being smooth and covered with leather, the latter being fluted lengthwise. Of such twin-rollers, there are usually three in the same horizontal plane, of which the three under rollers are driven by wheel work, with either two or three successive velocities, and carry round their incumbent weighted rollers by the effect of friction.

In silk establishments the machinery can be, and is often, employed from three to six hours after the hands have left work, to the advantage of the masters, (the number of hours depending on the quality and cost of the silk); therefore the imposing of a restriction on the moving power, in silk establishments, would have the effect of increasing the cost on the quantity of silk turned off. When water power is used, the portion of the silk machinery which contains the swifts, generally works all night without being tended.

It is in spinning the lower numbers, as forties, and in weaving, that the English manufacturers, some time ago, were most fearful of being hard pressed by foreign competition.* Switzerland has,

---

* The Danforth (or cap) Spinner was invented in 1828, by Charles Danforth, a native of Massachusetts, who had been employed for a number of years as an operator of cotton machinery. He, at the time, resided in Rockland county, New York. Having had experience on the common throstle as well as the Waltham dead spindle, he was aware that the two greatest difficulties in these modes of spinning were the flyer being out of balance, and the dragg of the bobbin by the strength of the thread. He thought if any plan could be contrived to wind the yarn on the bobbin without the use of the flyer, it would enable him to run the bobbin very fast. After some reflection, it occurred to him, that a bobbin revolving on a fixed spindle, and circumscribed by a smooth, stationary, polished ring, suspended from, or fixed to, the top of the spindle, would produce the desired result. He accordingly proceeded to make the experiment. He, first, permanently secured a throstle spindle in the frame to prevent its turning; he then, after cutting the curls from the ends of the flyer, riveted to them a smooth ring, which passed round the bobbin; he then turned a groove, in the lower head of the bobbin, for the driving band to run in, and having put all together, he pieced up his thread and filled the bobbin without any difficulty. It was perceived, in this first attempt, that the tension on the yarn, while spinning, was very light, and consequently the yarn wound quite soft on the bobbin. It was, therefore, very naturally, thought the principle would be good for spinning weft. He, therefore, constructed his first model for weft; and, after making various experiments, fixed on the present mode of making and supporting the stationary ring, which is a cap with a polished steel ring on the bottom, having a conical socket in the top, made to fit a small cone on the top of the spindle. It was also found, that the wooden bobbin, running at the rate of 7000 turns per minute, on a fixed spindle, was apt to get dry, make a loud noise, and wear the bobbins. To obviate this difficulty, a waive was made, having a tube on the top of sufficient length to pass through the bobbin, on which the bobbin is placed, and revolves with it. This waive takes the friction all off the bobbin, and as it is made of metal, is durable, and runs without noise. Mr. Danforth has patented his invention in this country, and caused patents to be taken in England and different European states. This mode of spinning has now been thoroughly tested, and is found to be capable of producing full 40 per cent. more yarn, on counts from No. 14 to 50, than any other plan heretofore known. It is generally approved of by the spinners who have tried it, and has gone into use, both in this country and

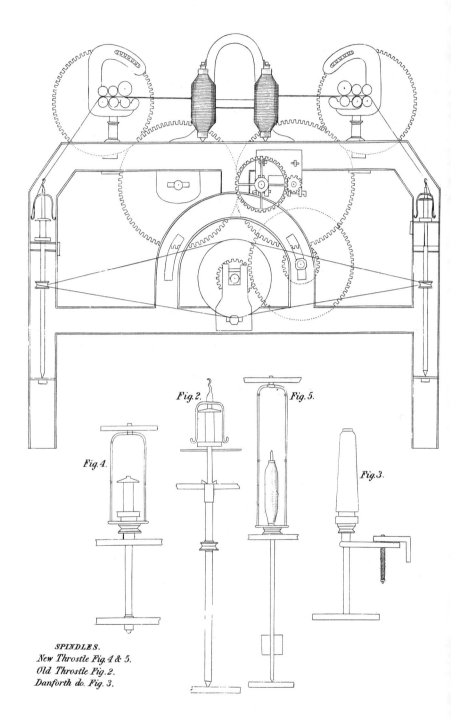

Fig.2.

Fig.5.

Fig.4.

Fig.3.

SPINDLES.
New Throstle Fig. 4 & 5.
Old Throstle Fig. 2.
Danforth do. Fig. 3.

for the last seven years, not only supplied herself, but her neighbours, to a considerable extent, with that mean quality which may be reckoned the staple of cotton yarns. It appears that the time of working cotton mills in Manchester is less, by about one hour daily, than that in any other part of the world, where the cotton manufacture is carried on to any extent.

It is my firm belief, that there is not a better or more certain mode of benefiting a country village than by establishing a cotton factory in it. The pure, unmixed effect of factory labour will be best and most easily found in the country,—where it affords regular employment, during a series of years, to the same families. The attendance at the Sunday schools, of such as are employed in factories, shows that that class of the operatives furnishes its full proportion of scholars.

Beset, as it now is, in the departments of cotton, wool, silk, linen, iron, and steel, by the industry of rival nations, it can maintain its place in the van of improvement only by the hearty co-operation among us, of heart and hand, of employer and employed. Once thrown out of the market, it would, ere long, be distanced in the race, by the more frugal and docile labour of the continent and United States.—*Ure.*

WAGES.

It was at my urgent request, that the writer of the following remarks on *Wages*, supplied me with his views upon the subject. His situation has enabled him to take a practical survey, and though I am surprised to find his ideas accord so materially with my own conceptions, yet his essay ought to have, and doubtless will have, more weight in the community than any thing that I could have produced, more from observation and reflection, than from the best opportunity of knowing the practical operations between the employer and the employed. I was very desirous of obtaining these observations for the chapter on the value and uses

Europe, more rapidly than any other improvement in spinning has before been known to do. The principle is such, that instead of making the thread drag the bobbin, the bobbin is made to drag the thread; and the resistance of the atmosphere and the slight friction of the thread, on the lower edge of the ring, produces that retardation necessary for winding the yarn on the bobbin. In consequence of which, the tension on all the threads, are perfectly uniform, and at the same time delicate, giving a great uniformity and elasticity to the yarn. The machine also takes much less power than the common throstle. They are made and sold by Messrs. Godwin, Clarke & Co., at their shop, in Paterson, New Jersey, who are the proprietors of the patent, and manufacturers of all kinds of cotton and woollen machinery.

of property, where they seem properly to belong ; but the mere circumstance of the place they occupy, will not prevent a due consideration of the arguments. To the writer, I feel deeply indebted, for the pains he has taken to fulfil my request, as well as for other assistance I have received in the progress of my work.

It has been my desire to derive from the best sources, such valuable information, as shall be useful to the operatives of this country, on whose welfare and respectability so much depends ; whether America will be able to maintain the high ground of liberty and self-government which she has assumed, and on which position the civilised world is looking with fear and reverence.

———

" Man is born to [labour, says a certain author,] as the sparks fly upward." We dispute not the authenticity of this text, no more than of the original. But why is he born to labour ? The simple reason is, that in the most spontaneous and fertile regions, the fruits of the earth drop not into his mouth. Were this the case, few would be found willing to give any extraordinary exertion to procure them in any other way : the necessity of exertion to procure, infers the right of possession and enjoyment when attained, and hence arises a notion of property, or right of using what has been obtained by the outlay of labour, and farther, what has luckily adverted to its possessor by discovery or chance. But in order to fully secure the possession of such acquirements, it is more than necessary that the use should be yielded to the reward of the exertion of achievement, it is requisite that full right should accrue to the individual to retain or dispose of such fruits of toil in any manner or direction that he may think proper, barring the direct injury or annoyance of his neighbour.

Hence the admitted right of bartering or devising it, either in his life time or at death, is essential to a perfect possession ; and we have no instances of a state of society in which one or both these rights were not believed inherent in individuals composing the community. Indeed the necessity of law or custom affording this guarantee, seems implied in the very nature of human association. Take away from man this motive to exertion, and you restrict his operations to the mere immediate exercise of those functions requisite to furnish the instant means of appeasing the stern demands of hunger and thirst. These satisfied for the moment, the uncertainty attending future possession would effectually preclude any desire to exercise the faculties that prompt to the accumulation of resources for consumption beyond the pressing necessities of the hour. It is the notion of a perfect property in whatever has accrued to him from the labour of his hands, that is the first inducement of man to any continued effort or exertion. For this he pursues the game on the hills, or casts his rude net into the waters; he spreads his snares in patience for the fowls of the air, or toils in anxious ex-pectation for the roots that nature has hidden in the earth ; or going one step further in the progress of civilisation and human improvement, he tames the more docile animals to domesticity, or returns to the earth a portion of the fruits wrested from its bosom, and awaits in full confidence the period of fruition, when he shall reap the reward of his toil and providence. It is plain that without this guarantee of possession of the proceeds of his industry and care, the first step in the amelioration of his condition could never be accomplished by man.

We are told of a race of men who were found, by strangers visiting their wretched island, grubbing with their fingers in the earth for roots, and stripping the bark from rotten logs in search of the insects and reptiles that harboured within its recesses, wherewith to satisfy the cravings of unappeased hunger. In such a herd, (for it would be preposterous to term this a community,) the notions of property and separate possession must have been very limited indeed, extending at most to a claim for the exclusive possession of a decayed bough, and probably not farther than to the loathsome grub just seized and about to be devoured. Tacitus describes the Fenni as " a savage race living in squalid poverty and misery ; with neither arms, nor horses, nor homes ;" and indeed whenever we hear of a nation deeply immersed in barbarism, we usually find as a concomitant, an utter disregard of the rights of property; almost all the savage nations of the South seas are reported by the first explorers to have been given to pilfering; not so much from any vicious or injurious feeling towards those they robbed, as from an imperfect notion of the right given the proprietor by previous possession.

These people are constantly represented by voyagers as idle and thriftless in no ordinary degree: living on the spontaneous fruits of the earth, and taking little or no care to hoard or increase the stock for subsistence spread out by the hand of nature before them. They were likewise found extremely unsusceptible of improvement or amelioration, and most probably would never have attained any portion of either, had not some notions of property and separate possession been infused into them by accidental intercourse with strangers.

The idea of property, then, is the earliest germ of civilisation—the first step in the improvement of the physical, intellectual, and moral condition of mankind ; and law and custom have found it necessary to recognise this idea, in every *really social* condition. In order that these ideas may be of any avail to the community, it is absolutely necessary that the guarantee should be of the most perfect and inviolable character. A restricted right or possession would be entirely nugatory. Being valueless to the individual, it could not result in any general benefit to the community, as all must hold under the same insecure tenure. The best laws have therefore secured possessions in the most limitless and unrestricted manner, only restraining the proprietor from such flagrant uses of them as would result in immediate injury to his fellows. Subject to this wholesome restraint, he is at liberty to use the fruits of his labour according to his own view of happiness to himself. He may barter one species of fruit for another, he may cast his surplus to the waves, or he may hoard it in granaries to meet his own future occasions, or to relieve the necessities of his brethren: but the same laws which accord these privileges to him for trifling emergencies afford the basis of more extended operations upon similar principles. If, having a tree, he may barter its fruits for the products of another's labour, there is no seeming reason why he may not reserve the fruits until he can purchase double the amount with the same quantity : if his own economy and foresight have secured him from the effects of a failure in the earth's product, is it consistent with the rights of property, as necessarily laid down, that he should part with his hard-earned store without an equivalent; and he, having acknowledged right over his own property, has also the right of dictating the terms on which he will part with it: and here sprouts out the germ of evil in that which is productive of so much good.

If the provident man has secured by his own unassisted endeavours sufficient for the sustenance of two for any specified time, it becomes as easy, he may make it more so, for another to procure subsistence by giving him his exertions for any specific objects as to seek it from other sources. It is easy to perceive that the efforts of two, directed by the sagacity of one, will speedily enable the chief to add another labourer on the same terms as the first, from whom a further profit will be derived; and the number of those employed at length swells to an extent that precludes any other employment for the director, than that of planning and apportioning the tasks of others. Herein arises the evil from a very necessary admission. Preponderance is given to one, and comparative subjection imposed on others, by the steady operation of that law, without which civil society could not hold together for an hour. Overgrown capitals, vested in the hands of particular individuals or families, control in some measure the destinies of large portions of their fellows, and particular cases of oppression consequent upon their predominance, grow into such common practice as to call down just obloquy upon the whole mass of those on whom it has devolved to furnish employment to fellows of their race.

It is probable that, in a primitive condition, a man, compelled to seek in the forest or the flood for the means of relieving his physical wants, would not stop short on the possession of what was enough for one meal or two, or for the supply of a single day. He would prefer an extra hour of labour, at successful seasons, in order to indulge his love of ease for a longer term after his present exertion should have ceased: he would therefore return from his toil with a surplus that might be hoarded for the wants of the morrow, or be bartered to advantage with his neighbour for products of another sort. If he has stripped a tree of its chestnuts, he may dispose of all or a part for the returns of the labour of him who has gathered shell-fish from the waters. The rate at which this exchange is made will depend on several contingencies, but chiefly on the facility or difficulty of procuring the different commodities. If, for example, the labour requisite for the gathering 100 chestnuts be about the same as that of securing a dozen mussels, the likelihood is that one will be reckoned a fair equivalent for the other. But on the other hand, should one or the other article be difficult of attainment, the rates would speedily change, and the one would rise and the other fall proportionably to the operation of the above causes. If in consequence of the higher value of either commodity any one should devote himself, and others his hired labourers, to the task of securing large portions with a view to reaping the benefits of the labours of those engaged in obtaining the other commodity, he would be speedily met by two other elements that enter into the relative value of productions—the present demand existing for them, and the perishable or enduring nature of the article. In the first case, if he discovers that his exertions are bringing more to the mart than there are mouths to consume or other articles to pay for, he may slacken his exertions by parting with a portion of his labourers, or he may turn their industry into a different channel. Should the nature of his products admit of their being preserved uninjured or with slight deterioration in value for some time, it may become a consideration with him whether to continue the production and hold back in the hope of a more advantageous disposal. If however, he decide on withdrawing some part of his labourers from the employment and dismiss them altogether, they, having probably consumed all their share of the gains from day to day, are compelled to resort to some other mode of industry or continue at their present toil on their own account. This they will be likely to do at a decrease of remuneration to themselves, and to the manifest disadvantage of all engaged in their particular occupation.

In proportion as the produce of their toil is perishable in its nature, will these, their difficulties, increase, and their wages fall; or, in other words, the amount of general commodities they can obtain for that produced by their particular occupation will decrease, until they will, by sheer necessity, be compelled to carry their toil into some other channel, or fail entirely in procuring subsistence.

Perhaps there is no other element, in the fixing of a standard of value, so prompt in its operation as the above, viz: the perishability of the article. The difference between the products of the mine and the garden are obvious at a glance. While all the metals, whether precious or base, maintain a steady determinate value, from year to year, and almost extending through centuries, the fruits of the surface of the earth, frequently many of those most necessary to man, vary in price from day to day, and even fluctuate in value in the same market-place within the hour. However inordinate and keen may be the demand, it cannot preserve the equality in the price of the most delicate and quickly injured fruits, or esculents, for a few hours together. The rapidity with which they waste enjoins a necessity for their speedy disposal; and in exact proportion to this, is their price fickle and transitory. As the prices of labour, or wages, must of necessity depend on the avails of that labour, at all events in the last resort, it is not at all to be wondered at,—indeed it would be marvellous were it otherwise,—that it should feel the influence of the same laws. Hence, as a general rule, there is no branch of human industry so poorly remunerated, or in which profits can be so little relied on, as agriculture ; the very branch that devotes itself to the most urgent necessities of the race. As if those who produce the "fund, out of which the labourer is supported,"* should draw less of it to their own behoof than any of the rest of their fellows.

That labour, the producing cause of all commodities, should follow the rule of the commodities themselves, is in strict accordance with general laws. That its price or wages should be regulated both by the demand and by the plentifulness of the commodity or fund wherewith it is to be paid, may be conceded to a limited extent. But there are some exceptions to the latter, which it may be necessary for the advocates of these (as exclusive) causes, to explain or account for. The miners in South America are the

---

* See " An Essay on wages," by H. C. Carey. Mr. C. has better conceived than explained his ideas. It were easy to show, were his book under review, that many or most of his views are fallacious. But we may safely trust him to the *Reviewers*. It seems, however, this notion belongs to Mr. Senior.

worst paid labourers in the universe, yet the fund from which they are sustained is in the utmost profusion around them. The labourers, in the new settlements of our own country, are better paid than any other at agricultural employments, and this in spite of an utter scarcity of the means of payment, and when the means of subsistence have to be brought, at great labour and expense, from a distance. In the first case, labour is carried to a very bad, and in the latter, to a very good market. Whatever may be the gross amount, even to profusion, of the fund from which labour is to be paid, the proportional quantity accorded to the labourer must ever be controlled by those who have the present possession or property of the means of payment: and to say that there is ample, nay, exuberant means of repaying the labour of the whole race, throughout the globe, and yet that there are numbers who cannot achieve a bare subsistence, by the utmost exertion, is but to describe the present, and almost every past, condition of humanity.

It would appear that those who have turned their attention to this somewhat obscure subject, have paid little attention to that depression in the price of wages which results from the ill choice or acceptance of the market, at the same time that they have overlooked, entirely, the material element that, more than all others, affects the produce of labour, in common with all other commodities, viz:—its extreme perishability.

When we consider that this quality or defect enters more largely into human labour than into any of its products,—that it is as evanescent as time itself,—and even perishes in the very operation of seeking a mart, we may cease to wonder at its being so severely subjected to the overbearing exactions of its employers. Capital may lie idle for a time,—the most that it can lose is the profit that might accrue from its active employment; or, should it be in the shape of articles liable to decay, from the necessary deterioration in quality that will result from their peculiar susceptibilities. But the time lost to the labourer is without compensation; the commodity is not lessening in value only, it is departing, departed, entirely from his grasp: and being that, on which alone he depends for existence, unless he is willing to perish himself, he must take the offers of the best bidder in the market. If, therefore, he shall have confined his acquirements, or capacity for employment, to any specific branch of industry, although by thus doing he may have increased the avails of his labour while his employment is marketable, he has yet thereby rendered himself more liable to a chance of failure at different seasons: yet it must be confessed, that the general rate of the highly skilled in one branch exceeds largely that of those who have no other capacities than those with which strong hands and willing hearts have invested them. The meanest handicraftsman, almost constantly, reaps more for his exertions than the strongest and most active day labourer.*

On the other hand, the more general employment afforded to the great mass more perfectly secures them from total inaction. The union of the two requisites of skill in peculiar and adaptation to general operations seems to furnish the conditions that would entirely place the disposal of his labour

---

* It must be confessed that, the terms we are compelled to use, very much tend to confuse our notions on subjects of this sort. The handicraft operative is equally a day labourer with him who understands no more than the wielding of a spade or a mattock : and as yet we have no terms whereby to distinguish, accurately, the two.

perfectly at the command of the labourer. If we add to this a proper restraint on the quantity brought into the market, and a careful economy in its expenditure, as well as in the use of its proceeds, we shall go far towards placing the amount of remuneration to the labourer within his own control.

But these objects are not to be effected by combinations to make specific rules for individuals or trades. All general unions of men to carry partial measures, must rebound with accumulated force against their operators. By the time that the Trades Union system shall have gone the round of the circle of the mechanic arts, its supporters will not be a little mortified to discover that they are precisely in the position whence they set out—viz: that the proceeds of their toil will not enable them to purchase one ounce more of meat, or one jot of additional gratification, beyond the prices already afforded them—while they will, in the mean time, have caused a great deal of individual misery and annoyance. The error lies in supposing that they may effect in mass what as individuals they are incompetent to perform. But the true statement would seem to be, that every community is strong in proportion to the strength of the individuals composing it. If their efforts were bent to the objects of making the individual labourer experter, wiser, more intelligent and economical than at present—could he depend more for his gratifications on sources within himself, and less on the trappings of the external world, if a proper self-denial could be imposed, and juster views cherished of the relations under which his Maker has permitted him to exist, the labouring man might speedily be placed in a condition to secure all the compensation that mere human toil is fairly entitled to.

These efforts must begin with the imposition of restraints on those appetites which exhaust his physical powers and drain his purse ; which impose on him the maintenance of a family before he has secured even the certainty of constant provision for himself alone ; and which, at the same time, tend directly to increase that stock of labour in the market which it is his manifest interest should be limited in supply. They must go farther than this: by making his source of enjoyment more intellectual, they must give the death blow to that infatuated affectation or vanity that impels the man of an income of one dollar to compete in external appearance with him of one hundred per day. A miserable vain glory, the offspring, but an illegitimate one, of our republican institutions ; but fruit utterly unworthy the sons of those mothers who substituted the hedge-thorn for pins in the dark days of our struggle for freedom.

The first question for the day labourer to solve is :—On how much less than my earnings can I satisfy my natural and wholesome wants—preserve or renew my powers for future operations, and defend myself against the inclemency of the weather. When this is satisfactorily ascertained, he may enquire : Is it prudent, is it honourable, is it just, that with the means within my power, I should invite another to share the proceeds of my labour, with the probability, almost certainty, of introducing other helpless beings into the world to draw upon the scanty and hard-pressed pittance. Should he not pause upon this consideration, and weigh well the different position in which the lapse of a single year may place him ? In one case hampered

---

* I use the word in its vulgar acceptation. There are none in this country who do not *labour*.

with cares for which he is unable to provide, and which subject him to labour as a stern necessity; in the other with surplus enough to enable him to oppose arrogant demands, and with a mind trained to examine and decide upon his best interests. We are aware that argument of this sort is met by the common cant, that the rich are not willing to permit the poor to indulge in the enjoyments so eagerly sought by themselves; and that the desire of employers is to restrict the happiness of the employed; but we are not to be deterred from the truth by such fallacies or false testimony. Were the accumulation of wealth the sole object of the already wealthy, their most direct means would be the encouragement of improvidence among the labourers: inasmuch as it would place these more directly and inevitably in their power. On the other hand, habits of providence and economy would put within the labourer's power the means of living in real independence of the capitalist's employment; or, in the event of a dispute, to engage in business on his own account. He would thus be really strong; and being in a position to withhold his labour for a time from the market he must of necessity be enabled to dispose of it to greater advantage to himself, without at all interfering with the rights or good order of the community.

But the agrarian spirit, unhappily too rife in this country, if it were permitted its sway, must speedily root up the foundations not alone of our prosperity, but of our whole system of liberty and laws; and to none could it prove more injurious than to those who imagine their great advantage lies to themselves in the change. That portion of freedom and property which is yielded in exchange for the protection of law and the preservation of order, redounds most forcibly to the advantage of those who apparently have the least at stake. The wealthy, and otherwise powerful, have or may create means of resistance to popular or individual rapacity; they may gather friends or hire mercenaries; but these means of protection are not within the compass of the small possessor. And in all turbulent or violent changes, the greatest miseries have been undergone by the poor and weak: while, on the other hand, under the steady operation of orderly systems, they have been gradually advancing in comfort and consideration.

That there are objections the other way, and in this country, it would be utterly vain to deny. That the improvidence and recklessness of labour have placed an inordinate amount of power in the hands of capitalists, ever too ready to accumulate in heavy masses; and that capital has made haste to swell its coffers, reckless of every other consideration, there is too much cause to fear; yet this furnishes no sufficient ground for any attempt to disturb the orderly operation of the system. The best counterpoise is in the hands of those who have most to dread; and if they would but use judiciously the means within their reach, they might essentially retard that too rapid march to excess and corruption so much opposed to "the greatest good of the greatest number."

It must be confessed, however, that there is small hope to cheer the true philanthropist, so long as the present defective and injurious education prevails; and especially while we continue the importation of foreign ignorance and agitation principles. Better views must be imparted to the labourer than he can obtain from Trades Union lectures, or the orations thundered forth at "strike" meetings. In place of considering the man who has husbanded the proceeds of his labour for himself or his children as a common robber of the human family, such must be considered as the true benefactors of the race; in as much as in no case could mankind have been in the enjoyment of the comforts by which they are now surrounded, were it not for the savings thus accumulated.

—

Upon the relative advantages possessed by England, France, and the United States of America, as manufacturing nations. By Z. Allen.

" The following table will give a comparative view of some of the most important advantages possessed by three of the principal manufacturing nations of the earth to manufacture at the cheapest rates. The price of labour forms the most important particular; but the superior skill of the labourers, and the improved machinery employed by them, must be taken into consideration, as well as the facilities of obtaining water or steam power. In respect to water power, the United States possess eminent advantages over most other countries. France abounds in fine mill streams; but in some of the principal manufacturing districts of that country, steam engines are from necessity frequently employed for operating machinery. In England the water power, although of inconsiderable amount compared to the steam power in use there, is highly improved wherever available in the manufacturing districts. It is probably attributable to the abundance and cheapness of water power, that the manufacturers of the United States are enabled to compete successfully with England and France in the production of such fabrics as require the application of a considerable moving force, notwithstanding the lower rates of labour in these two countries. With the several relative advantages possessed by England and by the United States, the rivalship between the two countries in manufactures is probably destined to continue long, and to be intensely interesting to the destinies of thousands of industrious artisans, when the manufacturers of the United States shall more generally extend their competition to supplying the markets of various foreign countries with some of the products of industry now furnished from England. Already has the competition been commenced and successfully maintained by the Americans, in supplying the markets of South America with coarse cottons, and with many other manufactured articles. Even the Hindoo labouring at his loom for a few cents per day, and subsisting upon a handful of rice for his daily fare, has been compelled to yield to the superior skill and machinery of the American manufacturers, whose fabrics have already been transported for sale to the distant markets of Calcutta and Canton.

" This table will also give an idea of the relative comforts which the labourers in these several countries can enjoy as the fruits of their toil. In France much less, and in the United States comparatively little, is exacted from the labourer by taxes upon the necessaries of life. For this reason a labourer in the United States, although he should receive only the same nominal amount of wages, possesses an advantage of more than twenty-five per cent. over a fellow labourer in England, from the circumstance of the comparative cheapness of almost every article which he requires for his own use or for that of his family.

Comparative Table of the average price of Labour in England, France, and the United States of America.

	ENGLAND s. d.	ENGLAND d. c.	FRANCE francs	FRANCE cts.	UNITED STATES dols.	UNITED STATES cts.
A common day labourer earns per day	3.0 stg.=	74	about 2.	37 to 40	about	1.00
A Carpenter	4.0 "	97	" 3 to 4.	55 " 75	"	1.45
A Mason	4.6 "	1.10	" 3½ to 4½	60 " 80	"	1.62
A Farm Labourer (per month and found)	27.0 "	6.50	"	400 " 600	"	8.00 to 10.00
A Servant maid (per week and found)	2.9 "	67			"	1.00 to 1.50
Best Machine Makers, Forgers, &c. per day	8.0 "	1.94	" 5.		"	1.50 to 1.75
Ordinary "	4.6 "	1.10			"	1.25 to 1.42
Common Mule Spinners in Cotton Mills	4.2 "	1.02	"	80 " 92	"	1.08 to 1.40
" Woollen Mills	3.10"	94	"	40 " 90	"	1.08
Weavers on hand looms	3.0 "	74	"	37 " 50	"	.90
Boys 10 or 12 years of age do. per week	5.6 "	1.30	"	85 " 100	"	1.50
Women in Cotton Mills per week, average	8.0 "	1.96	"	148 " 200	"	2.00 to 3.00
Do. Woollen Mills	8.0 "	1.96	"	" 150	"	2.50
In Holland a day labourer earns about 35 cents						
" Carpenters and Masons " 60 "						
" Ship Carpenters " 80 "						
					N. York.	Pittsburgh.
Average price of Wheat per bushel in 1827	7.4 "	1.79	" ‡	" 117	96 cts.	49 cts.
" price of good coals for steam engines per ton	9.0 "	2.20	"	600 " 700	700 "	106 "

[*] This table was formed with great care from the result of personal enquiries made in the most important manufacturing districts of England and France, and the prices are taken at an average, as nearly as practicable. Since the year 1825, at which period these notes were taken, there have been considerable fluctuations in the price of labour in England, resulting probably in a general depreciation of wages. The value of the Spanish dollar is estimated at about 4 shillings 1½ penny Stg. when the exchange between England and the United States is 10 per cent. in favour of the former country, making the shilling sterling about 24⅕ cents. The Spanish dollar is not a current circulating coin in England, and has no standard value in that country; but is bought and sold as bullion. By a statute law of the U. States the Spanish dollar was made a standard coin for the currency of the country, and was arbitrarily rated at the value of 4s. 6d. stg. for the purpose of assessing the duties upon all articles imported from England, and paying a certain impost upon the first cost. By thus underrating the value of the sterling currency, the American duties on English manufactures are in effect reduced about 10 per cent.

[†] In Manchester.   [‡] Near Louviers and Paris.

"From a view of the preceding table it appears that the average wages of persons engaged in manufacturing operations are nearly twenty per cent. cheaper in France than in England, and about eighteen or twenty per cent. cheaper in England than in the United States. Notwithstanding the difference in the prices paid for the same descriptions of labour in France and in England, judging from the observations which I have had opportunities of making, it would appear that the superior skill of the English operatives, and the improved machinery generally employed by them, yield so much greater products as nearly to equalise the difference in the cost of labour; and the two countries may be therefore considered as possessing nearly equal facilities for manufacturing cheaply, so far as labour is concerned. For instance, one man with the aid of two girls and a boy I have seen operating with the greatest apparent ease about seven hundred mule spindles in England; whilst in the same month I have seen in Lille, in France, two Frenchmen exerting their utmost force to turn by their manual labour the crank of a single mule of only two hundred spindles, with a boy to assist in piecing the threads. Very many of the French mills are operated by horses, which may be frequently observed traversing in their monotonous circle beneath the vaulted arches of old gothic cathedrals and monasteries, which have been converted into manufactories. The clustered pillars and sculptured stone work of these venerable structures form a strange contrast with the bright colours of the painted machinery, the perpetual din of which scarcely allows the spectator to muse upon the change that has taken place since the period when the silence that reigned within these walls was only broken by the chant of the matin and vesper anthem. Although the machinery of the French mills is generally put in motion by water or steam power, and the most improved English machines are introduced into them, yet there is a most apparent difference in the manufacturing enterprise of the inhabitants of the two countries. In the best cotton mills near Rouen and Paris, intelligent English mechanics are generally to be found aiding or directing the operations. In those branches of business in which the taste of the artist contributes to the value as much as his skill, the French appear to excel their English neighbours. This is particularly observable in the articles of jewelry exhibited at the glittering shop windows of the Palais Royal, and also in various branches of the silk manufacture.

"In respect to general information the French and Flemish mechanics appear to be deficient, their enterprise and industry having been for many years paralysed and interrupted by the continental wars of Europe. Since the arts of peace have gained the attention of the governments of Europe, and been sustained by them with fostering care, the mechanical arts have made more rapid advances. There still exists a languid indifference and want of information in relation to the progress of improvements made in other countries.*

* On my way from Brussels to Haerlem to view the national exhibition of the manufactures of Belgium, holden under the auspices of the king and honoured by his presiding at the distribution of the prizes, having accidentally fallen into company in a diligence with a Flemish artist on his way to the same place with some of his new machines, our conversation turned upon the subject of steam navigation, then lately introduced into that country. He enquired if there were any steamboats in America, and was surprised on being informed that they had been in successful operation there

" To the effects of a republican form of government existing in the United States it may be attributed (if the writer be not blinded by a partiality for the free institutions of his country) that a spirit of commercial enterprise and of manufacturing interest prevails, unequaled in any other country. There is in the United States no ennobled order of men, and lofty pride of ancestry, to render the manufacturer or merchant half ashamed of his profession ; and no burthensome system of taxation to depress the mechanic, and to circumscribe his scanty means to gaining a mere subsistence. From the habits of early life and the diffusion of knowledge by means of free schools, there exists generally among the mechanics of New England a vivacity in enquiring into the first principles of the science to which they are practically devoted. They thus frequently acquire a theoretical knowledge of the processes of the useful arts, which the English labourers may commonly be found to possess after a long apprenticeship and life of patient toil. For this reason the American mechanic appears generally more prone to invent new plans and machines than to operate upon old ones in the most perfect manner. The English mechanic, on the contrary, confining his attention simply to the immediate performance of the process of art to which he is habituated from early youth, acquires wonderful dexterity and skill. One of these labourers was pointed out to me by the proprietor of an English manufactory as having occupied for nearly thirty years the same spot by the side of his machine, or rather machines—the materials of brass and steel of a succession of them having failed and worn out under his inspection. The constant tread of his feet during this long period had channelled furrows in the very floors, and every motion of his body appeared almost as mechanical as if he had become a machine himself. Without information on any other branch of business, such a man, when thrown out of his accustomed employment by the vicissitudes which must at times attend the affairs of a manufacturing as well as of a commercial people, is usually left helpless and

nearly twenty years. I took occasion to describe to him several American inventions, among others the machine for cutting and heading nails, which were completely finished and fall off from the engine as fast as one can count them. The machine for making weavers' reeds or slaies seemed to strike attention as a wonderful invention, whereby the mechanism is made to draw in the flattened wire from a reel, to insert it between the side pieces, to cut it off at the proper length, and finally to bind each dent firmly in its place with tarred twine, accomplishing the whole operation without the assistance of the attendant, in a more perfect manner than can be performed by the most skilful hand. Although he possessed a good share of intelligence, the complicated operations of these machines, performing processes which he supposed could only be brought about by manual dexterity, appeared to him incomprehensible. But when I proceeded to describe Blanchard's lathe in which gun stocks and shoe lasts are turned exactly to a pattern, his belief seemed somewhat wavering, and on continuing to give him a description of Whitmore's celebrated card machine, which draws off the card wire from the reel, cuts it off at a proper length for the teeth, bends it into the form of a staple, punctures the holes in the leather, and inserts the staples of wire into the punctures, and finally crooks the teeth to the desired form—performing all these operations with regularity without the assistance of the human hand to guide or direct it, the credulity of my traveling companion in the diligence would extend no farther, and he evidently began to doubt all the statements I had been making to him, manifesting at the same time some little feeling of irritation at what he appeared to consider an attempt to impose upon him such marvellous accounts. Uttering an emphatic humph ! he threw himself back into the corner of the diligence, and declined further conversation during the remainder of our ride upon the subject of mechanics and of the improvements made in Flemish manufactures.

destitute, unable to turn his hand to other avocations. If a New England man does not succeed in one branch of business he may commonly be found readily essaying some other; even sometimes officiating in the profession of the law or of medicine, after commencing his career with the labours of the plane or anvil. It is undoubtedly true that in very many instances this versatility is attended with a profitless result, as in the present state of the arts and sciences a long period of assiduous labour is required to attain skill and experience in any branch of business. Although many valuable and ingenious inventions in the useful arts have originated in the United States, from which the old* as well as the new world have derived vast benefits, yet it cannot be denied that an incalculable loss of labour and expense in useless experiments has been the result to most of those who have been allured by the delusive search for new inventions and patent rights to deviate from the beaten path. These gropings in the dark for mechanical improvements can in no way be so successfully prevented as by opening the eyes of the mechanic, and causing him to view and examine his schemes more perfectly by the light of science. Some of the extensive manufacturers of Leeds, with a most commendable liberality, have formed small circulating libraries for the use of the persons engaged in their establishments, thus furnishing them with the means of becoming both more intelligent and more virtuous. For this purpose numerous mechanics' libraries have also been instituted throughout England, and the scholars and statesmen of that great and powerful country, with a philanthropy for which "ages yet unborn shall call them blessed," have lent the sanction of their names and the vigorous support of their talents for the general diffusion of useful knowledge. This has been effected, too, on terms so completely within the means of almost every labourer, that it can scarcely be said of the mechanics of the present day, in the words of Gray,

> " That knowledge to their eyes her ample page,
> Rich with the spoils of time, did ne'er unroll."

" England possesses a decided superiority over France and most of the United States in the abundance of coal, and in the consequent advantages afforded by steam power. Notwithstanding, however, the abundance of coal found in England, and the very general use of the steam engine, water power is highly valued in all the manufacturing districts, and mills are erected on streams, which in many instances are sufficient to turn the water wheels, and operate the machinery attached to them, during only a part of the year. Among the mountains of Scotland, however, I noticed numerous fine mill streams which remained unimproved. In Manchester, where coals are as cheap as in most of the manufacturing districts of England, the total cost of steam power, including all charges, amounts to about 20*l.* per year for each horse power, or at the current value of the Spanish dollar, to very near one hundred dollars per annum, as Mr. J. Dyer of Manchester stated to me. The opportunities of obtaining information on this subject possessed

---

* Of late years England has received more benefits from adopting improvements in the useful arts from the United States, than she has imparted; and the respectful attention of the inhabitants of that country, " illustrious in arts and arms," is now bestowed on the inventive genius of Americans.

by this enterprising American, from a long residence in Manchester, and from being engaged in an extensive branch of manufactures there, has probably enabled him to ascertain this fact with accuracy. The fuel forming the principal part of the expense of operating steam engines, by calculating the cost of coals in England and the United States, a comparative estimate may be formed of the expenses attending the operation of a steam engine in each of the two countries with a tolerable degree of correctness. In the manufacturing districts of France near Rouen, where the most extensive cotton and woollen mills are located, the coals used are brought principally from the mines at Charleroi, and are nearly as dear as in the United States. The coals exported from England to the United States are of a superior quality to those ordinarily consumed for manufacturing purposes, and sell at an advanced price in Liverpool of nearly four shillings per ton, or from fourteen to fifteen shillings sterling per ton. Virginia coal is about equal in quality to the common English coal for the purpose of operating steam engines, and costs on the seaboard of the northern and eastern states three times as much as the coals used in Manchester for steam engines. The daily wages of a fireman and good engineer is nearly as high in England as in the United States. The actual expense necessary for operating a steam engine in England, all other things being equal, may therefore be estimated at rather more than two fifths of what it is on the sea board of the middle and eastern states, when coals are used for fuel; while at Pittsburgh, on the contrary, from the wonderful abundance of coal, steam power is actually available at about three-fourths of the expense required in England. Pine wood seems to be preferred in the United States as fuel for steamboats, from producing a ready and intense heat without being attended with disagreeable sulphureous vapours during combustion.

CHAPTER IX.

GROWTH OF COTTON.

Cotton, as represented by Baines.

Sea Island cotton.

A statement of the Arts and Manufactures of the United States of America, for the year 1810. *Digested and prepared by Tench Coxe, Esquire, of Philadelphia,* 1817.

The capacity of the United States, in the country south of Annapolis, in Maryland, to produce cotton wool, in copious and extensive planters' crops, did not appear, in the year 1786, to have impressed the minds of the people of our own country, even from the thirty-first to the thirty-eighth degree of north latitude. Circumstances, in the family horticulture of the writer, arising among relations resident in Talbot county, had possessed him of the information, that cotton wool was constantly and familiarly raised there, in the little gardening of the children and domestics. It is distinctly remembered, that these impressions of early youth had matured, in the year 1785, into pleasing convictions, that the United States, in its extensive regions south of Anne Arundel and Talbot, would certainly become a great cotton producing country. This expectation was rendered the more deeply interesting, because European inventions of labour-saving machinery, for the carding and spinning of this raw material, were known to the writer to have occurred, though they were, at that time, very imperfectly understood, and not possessed in the United States.

An opportunity was taken, after the convention at Annapolis, in 1786, to examine into the opinions of persons of the highest qualifications, and the best opportunities to judge of the grounds of the suggested capacity for the cotton cultivation, and the connected prospects of those, who might become extensive planters. Mr. Madison was a member of the convention, and on an examination of the suggestion of our capacity, was immediately and decidedly of opinion, that our success would be certain and great.

The opinions of the best judges, and of those of the most frequent opportunities of observation, were decidedly favourable to the future success of the United States as a cotton producing country. In and before the year 1787, the United States had never exported one bale of domestic cotton to any country: no planter had adopted its cultivation as a crop: nor had we any of those numerous and *invaluable* labour-saving machines, which have been imported and adopted, to card, rove, spin, twist, colour, and print. Such was the real inadvertence, on the part of the intelligent cultivators of the south, to the natural advantages of our soil and climate: such the unacquaintance of the ingenious and energetic mechanicians of the whole Union with the form and value of labour-saving machinery.*

* Cotton has been known to the world, as an useful commmodity, ever since the days of Herodotus ; who, upwards of two thousand years ago, wrote that " Glossypium grew in India, which, instead of seed, produced wool." Cotton clothes more of mankind than either wool, flax, hemp, or silk. It has grown for many centuries in the East Indies. It had been declared by Dr. Hewat, in his account of South Carolina, printed in 1719, " that the climate and soil of the province were favourable to the culture of cotton." The first provincial congress in South Carolina, held in January, 1775, recommended to the inhabitants " to raise cotton," yet very little practical attention was paid to their recommendation. A small quantity only was raised for domestic manufactures. The labour-saving machines promoted, greatly promoted, the manufacture of cotton. In this culture the Georgians took the lead. They began to raise it, as an article of export, soon after the peace of 1783. Their success recommended it to their neighbours. The whole quantity exported from Carolina, in any one year, prior to 1795, was inconsiderable, but in that year it amounted to £1,109,653. The cultivation of it has been, ever since, increasing ; and in the first year of the present century, eight millions of pounds were exported from South Carolina. So much cotton is now (1809) made, in Carolina and Georgia, that if the whole was manufactured in the United States, it would go far in clothing a great proportion of the inhabitants of the Union ; for one labourer can raise as much of this commodity in one season as will afford the raw material for 1,500 yards of common cloth, or a sufficiency for covering 150 persons. It has trebled the price of land suitable to its growth ; and when the crop succeeds and the market is favourable, the annual income of those who plant it is double to what it was before the introduction of cotton. Nankeen cotton is cultivated, in the upper country, for domestic use. Mr. Whitney's saw-gin, for the separation of the wool from the seed, has facilitated that operation in the highest degree.

The presence of the raw material will provoke to, excite and produce the manufacture. American cotton will produce a home manufacture. The American will not be uncomfortable in his own cotton velvets, velverets, corduroys, swanskins, and cotton blankets.

Calicoes, or cotton cloths, (unmixed with linen) were first executed in England in 1772. British muslins were first made there in 1781.

Our vast and multiplied water power (1817) unfolds itself daily. A short canal of two miles, in the small county of Philadelphia, by taking the water out of the river Schuylkill, has given us new sites for 140 mills, equal to the turning of 280 mill-stones, to which sites there is good water carriage from the ocean! A packing machine, invented or introduced by Mr. Perkins, formerly of Massachusetts, is said, by the agency of a single person, to effect a pressure which requires the power of fifteen hundred men, and that it can be very much increased. The whole system and power of labour-saving machinery, used in cleaning and manufacturing to the extent of weaving and printing, may be considered as forming, by steam, by water, and by wooden and metallic machinery, a vast body of gigantic *automatons*, in aid of the labour of our people, and the draughts of our cattle. Of this Herculean corps of *automatons*, one of which may work 100,000 spindles, some of our women, our children, with a few men, and our acquired artists are required, as the *little* fingers. We can raise enough exportable surplus cotton for the world upon the fraction of five millions of acres of our sugar, rice, indigo, and cotton country. These strong assertions are no fictions. They are familiar and irrefragable truths.

——

ORIGIN OF THE SEA ISLAND COTTON.

Mr. Smith.

PHILADELPHIA, December 3, 1830.

Sir,—The original of the annexed letter has been many years in my possession, and was given to me by the gentleman to whom it was addressed. It settles the question as to the source of the Sea Island seed. For want of knowing the native country of the Sea Island cotton, the late Cæsar A. Rodney, upon his return from the mission to South America, by Mr. Monroe actually sent out one or two barrels of the seed to a friend there to improve the staple of the article. I am, respectfully,

JAMES MEASE.

——

John Cowper, Esq., St. Simon's, Georgia.

HAVANNA, February 2, 1805.

My dear sir,—Being informed by my friend, James Hamilton, of London, that you are the same John Cowper with whom I had the pleasure of being acquainted, many years ago, in St. Augustine, and for whom I have an interest which the lapse of time has not done away, I beg leave, now that I have drawn a little nearer to you, to revive our former friendship. It is pleasing to view the rising prosperity of the land you live in, and particularly so too when I reflect, that one of the present sources of her riches was, in a very great measure, derived from myself. In the year 1785, disgusted with the Bahama Islands, I settled in Kingston, Jamaica; where, finding my friend, Frank Levett, with his family and all his negroes, in a distressed situation, he applied to me for advice as to what steps he should take, having no employment for his slaves. I advised him to go to Georgia, and settle in some of the out islands and plant provisions, until something better turned up. Being well acquainted with Sapelo, I recommended that island. He could not, he said, bear to live in that country, but as many of his friends were settled in the Bahamas, he would attempt the planting of cotton among them. Being just from thence, I warned him against the attempt, but still he went, and planted cotton. At length, in a doleful letter, he acknowledged himself a convert to my opinion, having found things exactly as I had stated them, and resolved to go to the place I recommended, and there maintain his negroes, until he could look about him.

Early in the year 1786, I sent him a large quantity of various seeds of Jamaica, and as Mr. Moss and Col. Brown requested me to get some of the Pernambuco cotton seed, I also sent to Mr. Levett three large sacks, of which he made no use but by *accident.**

In a letter to me in the year 1789, he said, "being in want of the sacks, for gathering in my provisions, I shook their contents on the dung-hill, and it happening to be a very wet season, in the spring a multitude of plants covered the place. These I drew out, and transplanted them into two acres of ground, and was highly gratified to find an abundant crop." This encouraged me to plant more. I used all my strength in cleaning and planting, and have succeeded beyond my most sanguine expectations. This year I have every prospect of gathering twenty tons of clean cotton. I am, &c.

PATRICK WALSH.

—

Extract.—"*Savannah, Dec.* 11, 1788. I have been this year an adventurer, and the first that has attempted it on a large scale in the article of cotton. Several here as well as in Carolina have followed me, and tried the experiment : and it is likely to answer our most sanguine expectations, samples of which I beg leave now to send you, and request you to lay them before the Philadelphia society for encouraging manufactures, that the quality may be inspected into. I shall raise about 5000 pounds in the seed, from about eight acres of land, and next year I intend to plant from fifty to one hundred acres, if suitable encouragement is given ; the principal difficulty that arises to us is clearing it from the seed, which I am told they do with great dexterity and ease in Philadelphia with gins and machines made for that purpose. I shall now esteem it a singular favour your procuring me one of those gins, and I will thankfully pay whatever the cost of it may be. I

* Plaster of Paris was introduced near Philadelphia, and its effects discovered by accident.

am told they make them, that will clean from thirty to forty pounds clear cotton in a day, and upon a very simple construction. It would be the interest of the planter to sell it in the seed for the following reasons: in the winter we can employ our servants in cutting lumber, ditching and clearing land. Secondly, they are as handy and dexterous at any kind of machinery in cleaning it as white people. With you, labour is cheap, people are numerous, and ginning of cotton can be done within doors in winter when no other work can be done. I am directed by Captain Kerby to apply to Mr. Wetherill or General Mifflin of Philadelphia, who are members of the society for encouraging manufactures. But as I am unacquainted with those gentlemen, I beg leave to do it through you and request you to lay the samples of the cotton I send you before them. I shall be glad to know what quantity would sell and what price it will fetch in the seed, and what price clean. If suitable encouragement is given, I have not the smallest doubt but that this state will be able to furnish all that will be necessary for the manufactures of the northern states. The lands in the southern parts of this state are admirably adapted to the raising of this commodity. The climate is so mild so far to the south, scarce any winter to be felt, and another grand advantage, *whites can be employed.* The labour is not severe attending it, not more than raising Indian corn, it is planted on high land, and thrives the best near the salt water. I shall be glad to receive any information or instructions from time to time, and will cheerfully communicate any further discoveries or experiments I make in the planting or raising a *raw material* of so much magnitude to the manufacturing interests of America." [From Richard Teake, Savannah, to Thomas Proctor, Philadelphia.]

WHITNEY'S COTTON GIN.—(*See cut in next page.*)

ELI WHITNEY was born at Westborough, Worcester county, Mass. Dec. 8th, 1763. The paternal ancestors of Mr. Whitney emigrated from England among the early settlers of Massachusetts.

Indications of Whitney's mechanical genius were developed at a very early age. Of his passion for such employments, his sister gives the following account. Our father had a workshop and sometimes made wheels of different kinds, and chairs. He had a variety of tools and a lathe for turning posts. This gave my brother an opportunity for learning the use of tools when very young. He lost no time, but as he could handle tools he was always making something in the shop, and seemed not to like working on the farm.

His father once enquired what Eli had been doing, he being about twelve years of age; the answer was, " *He has been making a fiddle.*" "I fear," said his father, " he will have to take his portion in fiddles."

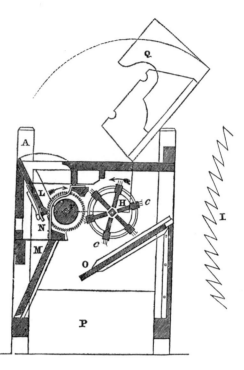

After this he was employed to repair violins, which he always did to the satisfaction of his employers. He took occasion once to take his father's watch to pieces, and put it together without being detected. He made knives or any thing he attempted; also nails. He manifested a fondness for figures and an uncommon aptitude for arithmetical calculations. By his own personal exertion he prepared himself for the freshman class in Yale college, which he entered in May, 1789. He finished his education with little expense to his father. The propensity of Mr. Whitney to mechanical inventions and occupations was frequently apparent during his residence at college. On a particular occasion, one of the tutors happening to mention some interesting philosophical experiment, regretted he could not exhibit it to his pupils, because the apparatus was out of order and must be sent abroad to be repaired. Mr. Whitney proposed to undertake the task, and performed it greatly to the satisfaction of the faculty of the college.

Soon after Mr. Whitney took his degree, in the autumn of 1792, he entered into an engagement with a Mr. B. of Georgia, to reside in his family as a private teacher. On his way hither he was so fortunate as to have the company of Mrs. Green, the widow of General Green, who with her family was returning to Savannah, after spending the summer at the north. Mr. Whitney had scarcely set his foot in Georgia before he was met by a disappointment, which was an earnest of that long series of events which, with scarcely an exception, attended all his future negociations in the same state. On his arrival he was informed that Mr. B. had employed another teacher, leaving Whitney entirely without resources or friends, except those he had made in the family of General Green. In these benevolent people, however, his case excited much interest, and Mrs. Green kindly said to him, " My young friend, make my house your home and pursue what studies you please." He accordingly commenced the study of the law under that hospitable roof.

Mr. Whitney made Mrs. Green a tambour frame ; not long after this incident, a party of gentlemen came from Augusta and the upper country to visit the family of General Green, principally officers who had served under the general in the revolutionary war.

Among the number were Major Beman, Major Forsyth, and Major Pendleton. They conversed on the state of agriculture among them and expressed great regret that there was no means of cleaning the green seed cotton, or separating it from its seed, since all the lands which were unsuitable for cultivation of rice, would yield large crops of cotton. But until ingenuity could devise a machine which would greatly facilitate the process of cleaning, it was in vain to think of raising cotton for market. Separating one pound of the clean staple from the seed was a day's work for a woman.

While the company were engaged in this conversation, " Gentlemen," said Mrs. Green, " apply to my young friend, Mr. Whitney, he can make any thing." Upon which she conducted them into another room and showed them her tambour frame, and a number of toys which Mr. Whitney had made or repaired for the children. She then introduced them to Mr. Whitney himself, extolling his genius, and commended him to their notice and friendship. He modestly disclaimed all pretensions to mechanical genius, and that he had never seen either cotton or cotton seed in his life. A new turn was now given to Whitney's views. It being out of season for cotton in the seed, he went to Savannah, and searched among the warehouses and boats until he found a small parcel of it. This he carried home and communicated his intentions to Mr. Miller, who warmly encouraged him, and assigned him a room in the basement of the house, where he set himself to work, with such rude materials and instruments as a Georgia plantation at that time afforded. With these resources he made tools better suited to his purpose, and drew his own wire, (of which the teeth of the early gins were made) an article which was not then to be found in the market of Savannah. Mrs. Green and Mr. Miller were the only persons who knew in what way he was employing himself. The many hours he spent in his mysterious pursuits afforded matter of great curiosity and often raillery, to the younger members of the family.

Near the close of the winter, the machine was so nearly complete as to leave no doubt of its success. Mrs. Green was eager to communicate to her numerous friends the knowledge of this important invention, peculiarly important, because then the market was glutted with all those articles which were suited to the climate of Georgia, and nothing could be found to give occupation to the negroes, and support of the white inhabitants. This opened suddenly to the planters boundless resources of wealth, and rendered the occupations of the slaves less unhealthy and less laborious than they were before.

Mrs. Green invited to her house gentlemen from different parts of the state, and on the next day after they had assembled, she conducted them to a temporary building, which had been erected for the machine, and they saw with astonishment and delight, that more cotton could be separated from the seed in one day by the labour of a single hand, than could be done in the former manner in the space of many months.

Mr. Whitney might now have indulged in bright reveries of fortune and fame, but his inventive genius was tempered with an unusual share of the calm considerate qualities of the financier. He felt reluctant even to apply for a patent, foreseeing many difficulties and expenses that must arise. Nor did he like to relinquish the profession of the law.

The individual who contributed much to incite him to persevere in the undertaking was Phineas Miller, Esq. Mr. Miller was a native of Connecticut and a graduate of Yale college. He married the widow of General Green. He had considerable funds at command, and proposed to Mr. Whitney to become his joint adventurer, and to be at the whole expense of maturing the machine until it should be patented.

If the machine should succeed in its operation, the parties agreed, under legal formalities, that the profits and advantages arising, as well as all privileges and emoluments to be derived from patenting, making, vending, and working the same, should be mutually and equally shared between them. This instrument bears date May 27, 1793, and immediately afterwards they commenced business under the firm of Miller & Whitney. An invention so important to the agricultural interests, (as it has proved to every department of human industry) could not long remain a secret. The knowledge of it soon spread through the state, and so great was the excitement on the subject that multitudes of persons came from all quarters of the state to see the machine ; but it was not deemed safe to gratify their curiosity until the patent right had been obtained.

But so determined were some of the people to obtain this treasure that neither law nor justice could restrain them, they broke open the building by night and carried away the machine. In this way the public became possessed of the invention ; and before Mr. Whitney could complete his model and secure his patent, a number of machines were in successful operation, constructed with some slight deviation from the original, with the hope of evading the penalty for violating the patent right. Mr. Whitney repaired to Connecticut, where as far as possible he was to perfect the machine, obtain a patent, and manufacture and ship for Georgia such a number of machines as would supply the demand.

On the 20th of June, 1793, Mr. Whitney presented his petition for a patent to Mr. Jefferson, then secretary of state ; but the prevalence of the yellow fever in Philadelphia, which was then the seat of government, prevented his conducting the business relative to the patent until several months afterwards. Mr. Whitney made oath to the invention, before the notary public of the city of New Haven, on the 20th of October, 1793. The importunity of Mr. Miller's letters urging Mr. Whitney to repair to Georgia, evinces how eager the Georgia planters were to enter the new field of enterprise which the genius of Whitney had laid open to them. In 1794, they borrowed money at 5 per cent. premium, besides the lawful interest ; but as they wanted more funds they could not obtain them short of 20 per cent. premium. Sickness and other casualties prevented the business from being profitable, besides the perplexities and anxieties which the inventor incurred.

In March, 1795, in the midst of perplexities and discouragements, with the fever and ague, Mr. Whitney went to New York on business, and was detained there three weeks by his sickness. As soon as he was able to leave the house, he embarked on board a packet for New Haven. On his arrival at this place, he was suffering under one of those chills which precede the fever. As was usual on the arrival of the packet, people came on board to welcome their friends and to exchange salutations, when Mr. Whitney was informed that on the preceding day *his shop with all his machines and papers had been consumed by fire!* Thus suddenly was he reduced to absolute bankruptcy, having debts to the amount of four thousand dollars without any means of making payment. Mr. Whitney, however, had not a spirit to despond under difficulties and disappointments, but was by them excited to still more vigorous efforts; Mr. Miller, also, on hearing of this catastrophe, manifested a kindred spirit. While struggling with these multiplied misfortunes, intelligence was received from England, which threatened to give a final blow to all their hopes. It was, that the English manufacturers condemned the cotton cleaned by their machines, on the ground that the staple was greatly injured. On the receipt of this intelligence, Mr. Miller writes as follows:—" This stroke of misfortune is much heavier than that of the fire, unless the impression is immediately removed. For, with that which now governs the public mind on this subject, our patent would be worth little or nothing. Every one is afraid of the cotton. Not a purchaser in Savannah will pay full price for it. Even the merchants with whom I have made a contract for purchasing, begin to part with their money reluctantly. The trespassers on our right begin to laugh at our suits, and several of the most active men are now putting up the *roller gin,* and what is to the last degree vexing, many prefer their cotton to ours."

In 1796, Miller and Whitney had thirty gins at eight different places in the state of Georgia, some of which were carried on by horses or oxen, and some by water. A number of these were standing still for the want of means of supplying them. The company had also invested about ten thousand dollars in real estate, which was suited only to the purposes of ginning cotton. All things now conspired to threaten them with deep insolvency. Mr. Miller writes : " A few moments are only allowed me to tell you that the industry of our opponents is daily increasing, and that prejudices appear to be rapidly extending themselves in London against our cotton. Hasten to London, if you return immediately; our fortune, our all, depends upon it. —The process of patent ginning is now quite at a stand. I hear nothing of it except the condolence of a few real friends, who express their regrets that so promising an invention should have entirely failed." Mr. Whitney was on the eve of departing for England, whither he was going with the view of learning the certainty of the prejudices which were so currently reported to be entertained in England against the cotton cleaned by the patent gin, and the rumour of which was so industriously circulated throughout the southern papers, and should he find those prejudices to exist, firmly believing, as the event has shown, that they were utterly unfounded, he hoped to be able to remove them, by challenging the most rigorous trials.

He had several times fixed on the day of his departure, and on one occasion had actually engaged his passage and taken leave of some of his friends.

But he was in each case thwarted by an unexpected disappointment in regard to the funds necessary to defray the expenses of the voyage.

However brighter prospects seemed now to be· opening upon them, from the more favourable reports that were made respecting the quality of their cotton. Respectable manufacturers both at home and abroad gave favourable certificates, and retailing merchants sought for the cotton cleaned by Whitney's gin, because it was greatly preferred by their customers, to any other in the market. This favourable turn in public opinion would have restored prosperity to the company had not the encroachments on their patent right become so extensive as almost to annihilate its value.

Mr. Miller writes May 11, 1797. "The event of our first patent suit after all our exertions made in such a variety of ways has gone against us. The preposterous custom of trying civil causes of this intricacy and magnitude by a common jury, together with the imperfection of the patent law, frustrated all our views, and disappointed expectations which had become very sanguine. Thus after four years of assiduous labour, fatigue, and difficulty, we are again set afloat by a new and unexpected obstacle."

Great efforts were made to obtain trial in a second suit in May 1798, when a great number of witnesses were called, from various parts of the country, one hundred miles from Savannah, at the regular session, but no judge appeared. In consequence of the failure of the first suit, and such a procrastination of the second, the encroachments on the patent right had been prodigiously multiplied, so as almost entirely to destroy the business of the patentees.

In April 1799, Mr. Miller writes. "The prospect of making any thing by the gin in this state, is at an end. Surreptitious gins are erected in every part of the country, and the jurymen at Augusta have come to an understanding among themselves, that they will never give a cause in our favour let the merits of the case be as they may."

Russel Goodrich, Esq. traveled through Georgia, for the purpose of collecting what was due Miller and Whitney for patent rights, but in consequence of evasions under different dishonourable pretences, he was unable to obtain money enough from all these claims to pay his travelling expenses.

The legislature of South Carolina, offered Messrs. Miller and Whitney fifty thousand dollars, which was accepted.

In Dec. 1802, Mr. Whitney negotiated a sale of his patent right with the state of North Carolina. The legislature laid a tax to be continued five years, to be collected by the sheriffs in the same manner as the public taxes, and after deducting the·expenses, the avails were faithfully paid over to the patentees. A similar negotiation was made with the state of Tennessee.

The importance of the machine began to be universally acknowledged in that state, and various public meetings of the citizens were held, in which were adopted resolutions strongly in favour of a public contract with Miller & Whitney. Of one of those meetings General Jackson was chairman. South Carolina annulled their contract under various pretences.

In consequence of extraordinary proceedings of the legislature of Georgia, Tennessee suspended the payment of their tax.

That Mr. Whitney felt very keenly in regard to the severities practised towards him, is evident from the remonstrance which he presented to the legislature.

The subscriber says "he respectfully solicits permission to represent to the legislature of South Carolina, that he conceives himself to have been treated with unreasonable severity, in the measures recently taken against him, by and under their immediate direction. He holds that to be seized and dragged to prison without being allowed to be heard in answer to the charge against, and indeed without the exhibition of any specific charge, is a direct violation of the common right of every citizen of a free government ; that the power in this case is all on one side, that whatever may be the issue of the process now instituted against him, he must in any case be subjected to great expense and extreme hardships, and that he considers the tribunal before which he is holden to appear to be wholly incompetent to decide, definitely, existing disputes between the state and Miller & Whitney. The subscriber avers that he has manifested no other than a disposition to fulfil all the stipulations entered into with the state of South Carolina with punctuality and good faith. And he begs leave to observe further, that to have industriously, laboriously, and exclusively, devoted many years of the prime of his life to the improvement of a machine, from which the citizens of South Carolina have already realised immense profits, which is worth to them millions, and from which their posterity to the latest generation must continue to derive the most important benefits ; and in return, to be treated as a felon, a swindler, and a villain, has stung him to the very soul. And when he considers that this cruel persecution is inflicted by the very persons who are enjoying these great benefits, and expressly for the purpose of preventing his ever deriving the least advantage from his own labour, the acuteness of his feelings is altogether inexpressible. This machine enables one man to perform the work of a thousand."

Mr. Whitney's application to congress to prolong the time of his patent was rejected.

In a correspondence with Robert Fulton, Mr. Whitney observes : " The difficulties with which I have to contend, have originated principally in the want of a disposition in mankind to do justice. It was not interference with any thing before known, and it can seldom happen that an invention or improvement is so strongly marked and can be so clearly and specifically identified, and I have always believed that I should have no difficulty in causing my right to be respected if it had been less valuable and been used only by a small portion of the community. But the use of this machine being immensely profitable to almost every planter in the cotton districts, all were interested in trespassing on the patent right, and each kept the other in countenance. Demagogues made themselves popular by misrepresentation and unfounded clamour both against the right and against the law made for its protection. Hence there arose associations and combinations to oppose both. At one time but few men in Georgia dared to come into court and testify to the most simple facts within their knowledge relative to the use of the new machine. In one instance, I had great difficulty in proving that the machine had been used in Georgia, although at the same moment, there were three separate sets of this machinery in motion within fifty yards of the building in which the court sat, and so near that the rattling of the wheel was distinctly heard on the steps of the court house."

The most remarkable trait in the character of Mr. Whitney, aside from his inventive powers, was his perseverance; and this is the more remarkable, because it is so common to find men of great powers of much actual invention deficient in this quality. One who knew him from early life says, "I have reflected often and much upon Mr. Whitney's character, and it has been a delightful study to me. I wish I had time to bring fully to view that particular excellence of mind, perseverance—in which he excelled all men that I have ever heard of."

The growing of cotton in the southern states was an original idea in the mind of Tench Coxe, who always said that the manufacture of a redundant staple must be the foundation of commerce and manufactures. Thus, laying agriculture in its proper place, as the basis for manufactures and commerce to build on; and not allowing it to be dependent on contingencies.

Mr. Coxe was an harbinger of light on this subject: he urged the subject with a force and energy peculiar to himself; always stating, most explicitly, that America was destitute of a redundant staple. England had long nursed their growth of wool; and it was their staple, the importance of which their Chancellor was ever to remember by his seat on the *woolsack*. America has now produced an article which has superseded the wool staple of England. Great Britain buys our cotton, manufactures it, and spreads her fabrics to all parts of the world. America, herself, needs no importation of cotton : she manufactures her own redundant staple, which no contingencies can deprive her of. Before a field of cotton was planted, and while we had nothing to manufacture, but were obliged to import even the raw material for their incipient measures in experiments of manufacture, Tench Coxe, with the eye of a political economist, who understood the true means of the wealth of nations, knew that the growth of cotton would enrich the south; that it would give vigour and energy to the north; and that both east and west would be mutually interested in the unity of agriculture, commerce, and manufactures. These unite all the vast resources which are combined in the vast capabilities of various climes, and of the immense variety of the industry, skill, and enterprise of mankind. These so operate as to work into each other's hands, so that no department of labour shall be lost, and that all the skill and mechanism, all the improvement in machinery and science shall be brought into full operation.

The writings now extant of Tench Coxe, prove, emphatically, that these were his great and enlightened views as a statesman, who was advocating principles that were to be the foundation of new empires; and of ameliorating the condition of mankind. It is not saying too much when we claim for him the appellation of the *Father of the growth of cotton in America.* It was his constant theme; there was an enthusiasm on this subject, that those inferior beings who were unacquainted with his sources of vision, were astonished at. His views reached into future prospects; he saw, in vision, from his enlarged principles and his correct calculations, what we now see in reality:—America increasing the number of her states; the federal government, loaded with surplus funds in the treasury; immense cities rising in every direction; peace and abundance enjoyed in the wide extended empire, and each department of enterprise, manifesting that each is beneficial to the other, and that the prosperity of agriculture adds to the increase of both manufactures and commerce. Legitimate objects of commerce are to transport the surplus produce of agriculture, and manufactured productions, to such parts of the world as present a market, and to bring back such articles as cannot be produced at home.

"Until the revolution in the cultivation of cotton, by which it was converted, through the strenuous excitements of the friend of manufactures, from a petty object in little fields and gardens, into an extensive cultivation among the planters and farmers, there was no redundant raw material for the manufacture of cloths and stuffs, for apparel and furniture, in the United States. There is at this time no other redundant raw material. The green seed cotton was the best adapted to the general quality and situation, and to the climate of the southern states. But its cultivation, though perfectly pleasant and easy, was very much restrained by the extraordinary difficulty of separating it from the seeds. This operation required so much manual industry as greatly to impede the manufacture; and, of course, for the time, to prevent an extensive cultivation. In the year 1793 the *invaluable saw gin* was invented by a citizen of the United States, Mr. Whitney, and was so improved and perfected as to render it easy to separate the seed from one hundred millions of pounds weight of cotton wool, by the employment of three or four hundred persons; although it is alleged that it would require three hundred thousand persons to effect the same by hand. Mr. Whitney states the difference between its operation in common hands, and the ordinary manual operation, at one thousand to one. By the employment of this machinery, every vicinity can easily and expeditiously prepare its cotton for the manufacturing cards, and that in the aggregate, to any extent that the world could require, were it to clothe itself entirely in cotton manufactures. Thus has there been added, by our own invention, to the machinery, to facilitate the manufacture of a staple production of our soil, a single improvement, moveable by water, steam, cattle, or hand ; which has let loose those immense powers of agriculture to produce cotton wool, that were before declined." The above remarks of Tench Coxe are only specimens of those enlightened and enlarged ideas which were original with him ; and as he knew them to be based upon unchangeable maxims, he indulged the discussion of them with an ardour and impetuosity of feeling, chastened with profound reasoning, that silenced those whose severity of feeling prevented their sound conviction. He never rested till the work was completed, and he lived to see the American staple preferred in the cotton markets, before the growth of any other country in the world. It has been proved, indubitably, that the adaptation of climate and soil was as decided as he declared it to be, before a bale of cotton had been shipped from Charleston.*

Tench Coxe appears to have inherited the talents and enterprise and even the peculiar turn of mind of his paternal grandfather, the first proprietor of Carolina, who in 1698, wrote of the natural capabilities of the south :†—" Cochineal is a commodity of

---

* The increase of the new staple is insured by the triumph of science and truth ; while the decay of the old is manifest, by the perversity of error and despotism. The former will be extended in its influence, while the latter will be confined within its contracted sphere.

If the " *wool-sack*" was a significant seat for the Chancellor of the British Peers, to remind him of what was the great staple of the empire, the " *cotton bag*," the staple of the new world, may well be held in equal remembrance by the legislators of the Union. Every member ought to wear it, as the girdle of his loins, emblematical of the bulwark of the agricultural, manufacturing, and commercial interests of the United Republics : every officer of the government should be clad in the productions of this superabundant article, from the crowns of their heads to the soles of their feet : and every citizen should be enrobed with it in life, and shrouded in it in death. It was protected, in its infancy, by the administration of Washington, and it has proved, in its *youth*, the defence of the " *beauty and booty*" of every section of the country.

† *The American branch of the family of* COXE.—The first ancestor of the Coxe family connected with America was Dr. Daniel Coxe, who was physician to the queen of Charles II., King of England, and also to Queen Anne. He was the principal proprietor of the soil of West Jersey, and sole proprietor of the government, he having held the office of governor, to him and his for ever. At the request of Queen Anne he surrendered the government to the crown retaining the other proprietory rights.† A member of the Coxe family was always appointed by the crown, while there was a resident member in the province, a member of the royal council of New Jersey until

---

† This document is extant in an old folio edition of Laws of New Jersey, which I saw some years since.

great value, very necessary as the world goes, and costs England great sums of money, which may all be saved, there being in the province sufficient to furnish both us and our neighbours.

" Silk is a commodity of great use in England for many manufactures, it being imported from France, Italy, Sicily, Turkey and the East Indies; and there is no foreign commodity which exhausts more of our treasure. This province abounds with forests of mulberry trees, both white and red ; a considerable quantity of silk may be here produced. It hath been tried in South Carolina, by Sir Nathaniel Johnson and others, and might be turned to great account. I would advise an imitation of the Chinese, who sow the mulberry seeds as we do pot-herbs, and to mow those of one year's growth for the young silk worms, the leaves being short and tender, fit food for them when first hatched ; and the second for them when in their infancy ; when grown strong they may be supplied with leaves from the trees, which method secures them from disease, which they are liable to when fed, from the beginning, with great rank leaves.

" Hemp and flax are very common in this country ; sufficient to supply the British market. Besides we have a silk grass, which makes very pretty stuffs, such as comes from the East Indies,

the revolution. (See Smith's History of New Jersey for an account of this gentleman, called the great proprietor, &c,: also of his son Colonel Daniel Coxe, the first ancestor who resided in America.)

Dr. Coxe was also sole proprietor of the extensive province of Carolana,* an account of which is extant, in an octavo volume, written by his son, Colonel Daniel Coxe, called the " History of Carolana ;" a copy of which will be found in the library of congress, the Philadelphia library, and the Athenæum of Philadelphia.

Colonel Coxe intermarried with Sarah, the only child of John Eckley, a Judge of the Supreme Court of Pennsylvania, and left issue : among others, William Coxe, who married Mary, the daughter of Tench Francis, Attorney General of the province of Pennsylvania. Tench Coxe was the son of this William and Mary Coxe, and was born in Philadelphia, 22d May, 1755, and died 17th July, 1824.

The charter was, in the extent of territory and powers, the most extensive ever granted by the crown to a subject, &c.: the family was, therefore, obliged to release it to the crown in consideration of a *mandamus* of the king conferring 100,000 acres of land in New York. Dr. Coxe was also a large proprietor in Pennsylvania, and nearly all the American provinces.

To his eldest son, Colonel Daniel Coxe, he gave all his American possessions, and this gentleman was the first of the family who resided in America. He arrived in America in 1709. (See Smith's History of New Jersey.

* *Carolana.*—This was the original name, and ought to have been so spelled in the previous mention of the province.

which they call *herba* stuffs, whereof a garment was made for Queen Elizabeth, whose ingredient came from Sir Walter Raleigh's colony, by him called Virginia, now North Carolina, a part of this province, which, to encourage colonies and plantations, she was pleased to wear for divers weeks. Excellent timber, turpentine, and every thing suitable for building ships. Iron, potash, materials for dyeing, such as logwood, campeachy wood, and many others, fusticks, &c. A valuable shrub called quassia, drank as a tea. Saltpetre, copper in abundance, lead in great quantities, with various metals and minerals, including both gold and silver."[*]

DIFFERENT GROWTHS OF COTTON.—FROM BAINES.

Cotton is now so extensively manufactured into a great variety of different qualities of cloth, that a short account of the various descriptions imported into the British market, with a few remarks

---

[*] " The plant of which indico is made, is very frequent in most of the southern parts of this country, and may possibly produce better than that made in our islands of Jamaica, &c. This province being in the same latitude with Agra and Byana, territories in the great mogul's country, whose indico is accounted the best of its kind in the world, and is double the price of ours. It is easily made, and the Indians may be assisting to us herein, if we think fit to undertake it. Besides, if we believe that judicious natural historian Hernando, there is in Mexico, and consequently here (being much the same climate) a plant or little shrub, which produces an indico abundantly more noble, and the colour more lively, than that which is the common indico. This the Spaniards call Azul, as being like Ultramarine.

" Ambergris or grey amber, is often found upon this coast from the cape of Florida to Mexico, which is of great value. The best, (for there are divers sorts,) is of equal worth to its weight in gold. This is agreed upon by the learned, to be a bitumen or naptha, which comes from certain springs or fountains, that empty themselves into the sea, and is coagulated by the salt water, as succinum commonly called amber, from another sort of bitumen or naptha, and in storms cast upon the coast. The same ambergris is also found upon the east side of the cape or peninsula of Florida, the Bahama islands, in the East Indies, and Brazil, and sometimes great lumps, even upon the coast of Cornwall and Ireland. And among others, I have read of a piece weighing eighty pounds, cast upon the coast of Cornwall, in the reign of King Charles I., which was bigger, till diminished by the countryman who found it, by greasing his cart wheels and boots, but discovered accidentally by an intelligent gentleman, who, riding by one of his carts, and perceiving a very grateful smell, enquired of the man whence it proceeded; he told him he had found a nasty grease upon the shore, which he hoped would have saved him the expense of kitchen stuff and tar for carts, harness, and boots, but it was of so poisonous a smell, that they were not able to endure it. The gentleman desiring to see the remainder, found it what he expected, purchased it at a very easy rate, presented it unto the queen, and was requited in places or employments far beyond the value of it.—*Coxe's Carolana.*'

upon their qualities,—the estimation in which they are generally
held by manufacturers,—the countries where they are cultivated,
&c., may, perhaps, not be uninteresting to managers, carding and
spinning masters, and to those interested in its manufacture.*

Cotton is generally distinguished by its colour, and the length,
strength, and fineness of its fibres. There are many varieties of

* Mr. Woodbury's letter on the culture and manufacture of cotton, is a
bright exposition of the present state of the business; it transcends all
possible conceptions of those who first conceived the project of raising cotton in the United States. Tench Coxe was ardent and sanguinary in his
hopes and prospects on this subject, but he lived to see his expectations more
than realised; we have lived to see what appeared incredible twenty years
ago. America, who imported all her cotton for manufacture in 1791, at
the present time raises and exports more than all the world besides; and the
manufacturing nations of Europe are absolutely dependent on America for
this staple. Not only is the business capable of an immense increase, but
of important improvements; a finer article can be produced, such as will
demand in Great Britain one dollar per pound.

The nankeen cotton can be raised of a finer fibre than in China; and a
fabric of the nankeen yarn, mixed with silk, can be manufactured superior
to any thing of the kind that has ever yet appeared either in Asia or Europe.
This new article is worthy of the nicest attention, and I must press the
subject, both on the growers of cotton, and the manufacturer, to cherish its
cultivation and its use; an article which will be purely American, and which
cannot be superseded in Europe for want of the raw material; nor in China,
because they are destitute of machinery.

The immense amount of capital invested in the growth and manufacture
of cotton, and the number of people employed in the business, renders it a
subject of great importance. It must proceed and it must increase, and
measures must be adopted to regulate the system, consistent with freedom
and good morals. We cannot neglect this with impunity; and the whole
community are interested in the course to be adopted and pursued, in relation
to this business. Industry and talent must be called into exercise to promote
the best possible order in the establishments and plantations, such as shall
be satisfactory to the parties concerned; for there must be no variance, no
discord, in an operation in which all are interested, and in which the prosperity of the whole of America is deeply involved.

Mr. Woodbury's letter has made a great impression; sixteen thousand
copies have been published by congress; and I presume few persons were
aware of the rapid and unparalleled increase of the exportation of cotton in
the short space of twenty years. The number of persons employed, both
in the culture and manufacture of cotton, calls for the consideration of the
wise and good, of the various communities concerned; and instead of re-
criminating each other, let both exert themselves to remove whatever positive evils exist.

The labour necessary for the culture of cotton, is attended with less
danger of affecting the health of the labourers, than either the culture of rice
or tobacco; the cotton plantations therefore produce an amelioration of the
condition of those employed; it is better than sugar, or any other article
raised in southern climates; and hopes may be raised, on those con-

cotton, their names being principally derived from the countries where they are cultivated. Also, under each general name, there are various denominations, distinguished by the particular province or district of the country where they are grown. In the following short account of the different descriptions, each kind is classed under the name of the country in which it is cultivated.

Smyrna Wool. The cotton wool known by the above name, was formerly imported from the Levant, in quantities proportioned to the then trifling demand. At one time, it was the only cotton wool to be met with, excepting a few bags occasionally imported from the West Indies. Although it has a soft silky appearance, yet it is neither well fitted to endure the necessary operations in being manufactured into yarn, nor does it, when finished, make an article either of strength, beauty or durability. Only a small quantity is now imported, and is used chiefly for making candlewick, being inflammable in a higher degree than any other kind of cotton.

East India Cotton includes Surat, Bengal, Madras, Bourbon, &c. The latter takes its name from the Isle of Bourbon, in the Indian ocean, where it is cultivated. It is generally a very superior cotton, both for strength and fineness, although short in the staple. For a number of years it was the only cotton used for spinning yarns of the finest quality, until superseded by Sea Island cotton, which is now found even superior to it. The other kinds of East India cotton are of very low quality. They have a fine glossy and silky appearance, yet are extremely short in the staple, and used only for spinning the lowest numbers of yarn. The imports have been on the increase for a number of years back, but especially since the partial opening of the trade to India; and it is supposed that the quantity cultivated might be greatly increased, and the quality improved, were it not for those impolitic regulations established under the East India monopoly

siderations, that an increase of happiness will be the consequence of the introduction of the cotton seed.

It is vain to expect to eradicate all evils from human society; circumstances must be adapted, so to contend with the evil, that good may have the pre-eminence; and where truth, justice, benevolence, and mercy, are predominant, ignorance, wretchedness, and vice, will be treated in a manner the most conducive to the peace and support of society. There must be an agreement of feeling on these subjects, as there is necessarily an accordance of interest.

This sensitiveness of feeling between the south and the north is very much to be regretted, and ought, seriously, to be avoided; and we trust every thing will be done to allay all excitement of this kind, which, without precaution, is liable to produce the most dangerous consequences to this confederacy.

for securing the revenue, &c. Hitherto East India cottons have generally been bought at the lowest prices in the British market, a proof of the low estimation in which they are held by manufacturers. But a new kind of cotton has lately been imported from Madras, said to have been raised from the same seed as the Sea Island. It is a fine white soft wool, having a silky or glossy appearance, very clean, and equal, if not superior in quality, to the Pernambuco, but rather short in the staple. It is much inferior to the Sea Island, but brings a much higher price than the common Madras cotton.

West India Cotton takes its name from those numerous islands, where it is still cultivated to a considerable extent, although the quantity imported into Great Britain is not now one fourth of what it was about fifteen or twenty years ago. In 1813 and 1814 the imports amounted to 73,219, and 74,800 packages; but since that period they have been gradually decreasing. In 1830 and 1831, the imports amounted only to 11,721 and 11,304; yet notwithstanding the great falling off in the quantity imported, in price, it ranks with Upland and the common and middling qualities of New Orleans. This wool is various in its qualities, but in general, it is a strong coarse article, irregular in the staple, and well adapted for the manufacture of the stouter fabrics of cloth to which it is mostly applied, but it is totally unfit for finer goods. It is said that the finest quality of cotton ever brought to the English market, or probably ever grown, was raised in one of the West India Islands, viz. Tobago, upon the estate of Mr. Bobley, between the years 1789 and 1792. That gentleman carried the cultivation of this article to some extent; but the price of cotton falling very low, and the growing of sugar becoming more profitable, in consequence of the destruction of the sugar plantations in the French islands, he was induced to convert his cotton plantation into a sugar one; and the production of cotton of this description was never attempted by any other person, though it is believed that the price it would command would amply repay the expense of growing it. The growth of cotton deserves attention so as to raise it in its greatest perfection, for lace and cambrics of the finest texture.

South American Cotton includes that imported from Brazils and Guiana. Brazil cottons are distinguished by the names of Pernambuco, Maranham, Bahia, Para, &c., according to the districts where they are grown. That which is known by the name of Pernambuco, is of a fine rich cream colour, and of superior quality. It long had the reputation of being superior to any imported, the Bourbon and Sea Island excepted. In quality, Pernambuco ranks with Egyptian; the latter is finer, but very irregular. Maranham, Bahia, and Para wools partake much of the same general description, but are inferior both in strength and cleanness to the Pernambuco. The imports of cotton wool from the Brazils have been remarkably steady for a long period. They seem, indeed, to have undergone little or no variation these twenty years past. In 1830 and 1831, the imports amounted to 191,468 and 168,288 packages, or 33,889,836 and 29,786,976lbs. The cotton imported from the coast of Guiana is distinguished by the the name of Demerara cotton, is a strong glossy wool, pretty long, though unequal in the fibre, and generally well cleaned and picked before it is packed. It makes a clean stout thread, and is frequently used for fine wefts, or warps of a moderate fineness; it is rather coarse, however, for the finest qualities of either. It is usually classed with the Berbice, but the latter is considered rather inferior. In price and quality they rank with Egyptian and Pernambuco wools. Essequibo is something similar to those mentioned, but inferior. Cayenne cotton is not much imported; it is like the Demerara, a clean wool, but very hard in the staple, which makes it difficult to card and spin.

Surinam resembles the Demerara and Berbice in appearance, but is inferior, both in strength and fineness, and similar to the Essequibo; both of them are considered to be pretty much on a level in quality with the West India wools. The imports, consumption, &c. of Demerara and Berbice, Surinam, and other cottons from Guiana, have been on the decrease for some years back. The imports in 1830 and 1831 amounted to 1263 and 811 packages or 395,319 and 253,843lbs.

The first cotton imported into the English market from Egypt was in the year 1823. Since that period it has been annually imported in considerable quantities, amounting, on an average, to about 6,593,073lbs. It is a very superior wool, of a yellowish colour, not so fine and silky as the Sea Island, but ranks next to it in price and quality. It is irregular in staple, and slovenly got up; but no description of cotton loses less after passing through the operation of carding, and it incorporates freely with cotton of a shorter staple, such as New Orleans, Maranham. Bahia, &c. The best qualities of this wool are generally used by manufacturers for yarn of superior quality.

Cotton from the United States. Previous to the year 1790, North America did not supply England with a single pound weight of cotton; it was only after the termination of the American war that cotton began to be cultivated in Carolina and Georgia, and it has succeeded so well, that it now forms one of the staple productions of the United States. But that which was first imported into the English market was very imperfectly cleaned, and, in consequence, was for some time used only for spinning low numbers. It was soon perceived, however, that the cotton grown upon the coast, termed Sea Island cotton, had a finer and longer staple than that which was produced farther up the country, and known by the name of Upland cotton. But some years elapsed before it was ascertained to be of a quality in every respect superior to that which was brought from the Isle of Bourbon, the only cotton then used for the finest qualities of yarn, but which now is entirely superseded by the former.

American cotton is generally distinguished by the names of Sea Island, Upland, New Orleans, Alabama, Tennessee, &c. Sea Island cotton is the finest that is imported into this country, or, indeed, that is known, and takes its name from being grown upon small sandy islands contiguous to the shores of Georgia and Carolina, and on the low grounds bordering on the sea. The principal of these islands are situated between Charleston and Savannah. It is a fine silky cotton, having a yellowish tinge, both long and strong in the staple, and used only for spinning the finest qualities of yarn, or for a superior quality of power loom warps. But its qualities differ so much, that the finest specimens are often more than double the price of the inferior sorts. Its close vicinity to the sea exposes it to the inclemencies of the weather, by which it is often injured, consequently that which is thus damaged sells at a much lower price than the better kinds of it. Upland cotton is a different species from Sea Island, and is grown in Virginia, North and South Carolina, and Georgia; and for a considerable time the cultivation was confined to these states. As the planting extended to the south, the quality varied in some respects, and the cotton received the name of its place of growth; hence, New Orleans cotton, Alabama, &c. &c.

That which is known in the market by the name of New Orleans is a very superior cotton, clean, soft, and of a glossy and silky appearance, rather short in the staple, and incorporates freely with other cottons of a longer staple. It is grown upon the banks of the Mississippi, and imported in great quantities into the English market, where it ranks in price and quality about equal to the common qualities of Brazil cottons. Alabama, Upland, &c. rank next to New Orleans, and are soft, short, and weak in staple. The cultivation of cotton wool is carried to a very great extent in the United States at present. The quantities imported into England is estimated at upwards of 230,000,000lbs. yearly, and apparently still increasing.

Various methods of cleaning cotton have been adopted at different periods. In the West Indies, and on the continent of America, what is called the roller-gin has been long used. It consists of a pair of fluted rollers, about five eighths of an inch in diameter, and nine or ten inches long; these are fitted up in a frame, and motion being communicated to them, the cotton is passed through between them, by which means it is separated from the seed, the diameter of the rollers being so small, that the gins, when whole, cannot be drawn in between them. This is but a slow method, and therefore expensive, consequently used only for the best qualities of cotton. Switching the cotton was tried, but disapproved of by manufacturers, as tending greatly to injure it.

The cotton, called Bowed Georgia, takes its name from a mode of cleaning cotton, long in use. This was performed by means of the bow-string, which, being raised by the hand and suddenly let go, struck upon the cotton with great force, and thereby served both to separate the gins and open the cotton, so as to render it more fit for the processes that follow. But this mode, whatever advantages it might possess in point of quality, has been abandoned for others better adapted for quantity; and what is called Bowed Georgia has, for a long time, in reality, been cleaned by a machine denominated a saw-gin. This machine consists of a cylinder about the size of a weaver's beam, and teeth cut out like a saw, at equal distances from each other, from which it derives its name. Instead of these saws, the machine originally had wires like card teeth, but these having been found to make what is called white naps upon the cotton, the former was substituted in their place. The saws pull the cotton through a grating which has its openings so narrow that the seeds cannot get through. The grating being a little inclined to the horizon, cotton is thrown upon it by the negro attending the machine, when the teeth of the saws take hold of it and pull it through the openings, whilst the gins, being pressed out, roll down the surface of the grating, and escape by an opening in the side of the machine. By the centrifugal force of the cylinder, the roller is thrown backwards, aided by another cylinder covered with brushes, for cleaning the teeth.

This machine, though not very injurious to the cotton of a short staple, yet is seldom used for the finest Sea Island, or any other that is very long in the fibres. It is worthy of remark, that when the Upland Georgia cotton was first brought to the English market, it yielded a higher price by about two pence per pound when it was cleaned by the roller-gin ; but contrary to all expectation, the saw-gin is found much better adapted for cleaning this species of cotton than the other, and what is done by it is preferred by those who understand spinning. The saws separate the gins more effectually than the rollers, and at the same time give it a kind of teaseling, which is found highly beneficial to it.

The cultivation of cotton is by no means a difficult operation.* It is planted very much as corn is planted, in March, and the early part of April, (depending of course upon the relative northern or southern situation of the land) and kept free from weeds through the summer, by constant ploughing and hoeing. In its early stage it resembles, when seen at a little distance, what are called *bunch beans*, growing in hills or rows. In the fall it is picked out of the opening pods by slaves, who go along with a basket and gather all that they can pick out. This is a tedious mode of getting the cotton from the husk or pod that contains it. When it is gathered into the cotton house, then comes the work of cleaning it of the seeds, by means of the gin. This is a simple operation. The cotton passes between a revolving cylinder (with teeth in

* *Extract from Moses Brown's letter to J. S. Dexter.*

PROVIDENCE, Nov. 15, 1791.

"When it is considered that cotton, the raw material, may be raised in the United States, it shows that legislative attention should be paid to this subject. The cotton raised at present, in the southern states, is as imperfect as our manufactured goods. This, I presume, is owing to the promiscuous gathering, and saving of the article, from the pods in which it grows, some of which, like fruit on a tree, are fair and full grown, while others are not. In the picking of these, and in taking the cotton out of the pods, care should be taken that it be kept separate, and the thin membrane, which lines the pod, and sometimes comes off with the cotton, should be separated, and the clean, full grown, preserved to work on the machines ; the other will answer to work by hand. But as the cotton must be clean before it works well on the card, the present production, in the mixed manner in which it is brought to market, does not answer a good purpose. The unripe, short, and dirty part, being enveloped with that which would be good, if separated properly at first, so spoils the whole as to discourage the use of it in the machines, and obliges the manufacturer to have his supply from the West Indies, under the charge of the impost, rather than work our own production. A circumstance truly mortifying to those, who from motives of promoting the produce and manufactures of our own country, as well as from interest, have been at much expense and trouble to promote so desirable an object. I, therefore, beg leave to suggest the idea of some encouragement to the raising and saving of cotton, clean and fit for the manufacturers."

Moses Brown told me that, for the above reasons, Mr. Slater could not be induced to use the American cotton.

circular rims of iron,) and a grate; by which the seeds are separated from the fine fibres of the cotton. It is next pressed into
bales by a machine somewhat like a cider-press, and is then ready
for market. A few good hands will cultivate several acres. From
one to two bales, sometimes three, is the produce of an acre of
good land in this state. The price of cotton lands is various,—
from $10 or $20 to $40 per acre; according to quality, situation,
buildings, and machinery on the premises. The above prices
refer to the state of Mississippi.

---

*To Whitemarsh B. Seabrook, Esq., Corresponding secretary of the
Agricultural Society of St. John's, Colleton.*

SULLLIVAN'S ISLAND, Sept. 1st, 1826.

Dear Sir,—Your useful circular has been received. I answer with pleasure your queries. Permit me to assure you, if I had the good fortune to
possess any information, not generally known, upon the culture of the cotton
plant or its preparation for market, nothing could afford me more satisfaction
than to disclose it for the benefit of others. A planter who would, from
interested motives, conceal any discoveries which might improve the culture
or the preparation for sale of any of our staple products, must certainly be
deficient in that patriotism and liberal feeling which, at least, are supposed
to govern every gentleman in this community.

Question 1. Is all your cotton equally fine? If not, what description of
your soil yields the most silky?

Ans. I consider that the most sandy parts of my soil produce the finest
cotton and the most silky.

Q. 2. What manure do you esteem the best to improve the fineness of
the staple?

Ans. I have never used any but the soft salt mud; it is taken out of the
creek during winter and spread in the old alleys with the back of the hoe,
about two inches thick in the lowest spots; and in the most sandy not more
than a quarter of an inch. The land is then listed over the mud before it
becomes hard. I have never manured more than eighty-five acres in one
winter.

Q. 3. Is your cotton which is so distinguished for one quality, remarkable
also for the length and strength of its staple, or both?

Ans. As machinery is the only test for fine cottons, allow me to give
you an extract of a letter, addressed to me from one of the most respectable
spinners in Manchester. "Although your cotton is second to no brand in
health and fineness, still it does not possess sufficiently the latter requisite
to spin our finest numbers."

Q. 4. What has been your average crop for the last five years, and what
quantity do you plant to the hand?

Ans. I have never made more than 150lbs. to the acre, and plant very
short to the hand, in consequence of not having a sufficient quantity of land.

Q. 5. Are you very particular in the selection of your seed, and which
kind do you prefer, the small or the large, the perfectly clean, or that which
is a little woolly.

Ans. I select that which has a little wool at the end, but am not satisfied as to the advantage of it.

Q. 6. Have you ever tested the experiment on the difference of the product and quality of cotton, from seed taken from the bottom, middle or top of the stalk?

Ans. Never.

Q. 7. How do you preserve your seed? Is it in a confined situation, or in a well ventilated room?

Ans. It is kept in a loft over my gin house, without any aperture to admit air.

Q. 8. In gathering your crop, do you ever pick the wool from those pods that from their immaturity are but imperfectly open?

Ans. Never.

Q. 9. Do you dry your cotton in the sun or in the shade? If in the sun, how long?

Ans. I always dry in the sun, and suffered it, until the last year, to remain on the cotton scaffold the greater part of the day.

Q. 10. What is your mode of preparation, and what quantity do you clean to the hand per day?

Ans. I require the cotton to be picked carefully from the pods, without leaves or dirt of any kind, and am very particular in the assorting before it goes to the gins. I give 28lbs. as a task in moting.

Q. 11. Are you in the habit of using the whipper before or after the cotton is ginned, or in both instances?

Ans. I use the whipper *only* for the cotton which is picked after frost, and for the stained; the operation is performed before it goes to the gins.

Q. 12. What is the character of your soil? Is your land high or low, indented with creeks, and how far from the ocean?

Ans. I have both high and low land in the same fields; white sand in the highest, and grey soil in the lowest. There are no creeks running into the fields; the distance from the ocean varies from a quarter to a half mile.

Yours respectfully,

E. VANDERHORST.

—

ST. HELENA, December 26, 1826.

Sir,—It would afford me much satisfaction could my limited experience enable me to throw a ray of light on the subject embraced in your queries. The replies to them you will accept more as matters of opinion than conclusions founded on definite practice.

Q. 1. Is all your cotton equally fine, &c.

Ans. I think not, but I have never heard purchasers remark any difference when I have separated the high from the low land. I prefer the cotton on the most sandy high hills, it being more productive and silky.

Q. 2. What manure do you esteem the best?

Ans. I have generally used the marsh mud taken from the creeks; sometimes green marsh.

Q. 3. Is your cotton so distinguished for one quality, remarkable for others, &c.

Ans. My cotton derives its character from its silkiness, strength, and evenness of fibre.

Q. 4. What has been your average crop for the last five years? and what quantity do you plant to the hand?

Ans. Caterpillars and storms have destroyed some of my most promising crops; but I think about 450lbs. per hand are about the average. I generally plant three and a half acres to the hand.

Q. 5. What kind of seed do you prefer?

Ans. I have generally preserved the seed from my earliest picking; sometimes I have planted seed exchanged with my friends both north and south. I think the cotton produced from the seed with a green tuft, the finest and most silky, though not the most productive. The finest I have seen, was from seed covered entirely with a green woolly coat.

Q. 6. Have you ever tested the experiment on the difference of the product and quality from seed taken from the bottom, middle, or top of the stalk?

Ans. I have not.

Q. 7. How do you preserve your seed?

Ans. I am not particular, so that it is kept dry.

Q. 8. Do you in gathering your crop pick those pods which, from their immaturity, are perfectly open?

Ans. My orders are to pass over defective pods, to save the trouble of selecting them when assorting; but, from the difficulty of seeing these executed, I presume they are much neglected, especially after a frost. We generally dry our cotton on a scaffold, unless it has been wet. I handle it as little as possible after it comes from the gin. We use the whipper, before the cotton goes to the gin, but not after.

Q. 9. What is your soil and situation?

Ans. High and low, mostly high; a yellow mixed sand on the hills, and black or grey in the narrow valleys, which run N.E. and S.W. through the extent of the island. I am on a neck of land, two sides of which are bounded by creeks, and one side by the ocean. I have *once* used a *machine-gin* from St. Simon's Island, to the rollers of which, made of hickory, I gave as many as six hundred revolutions in a minute. I ginned about twenty bales of cotton with this gin, and heard no complaint about the staple being injured; but my negroes continually putting it out of order, and my impelling power proving defective, I laid it aside. I introduce this remark, hoping that the want of a gin, as well adapted to the Sea Island cotton, as Whitney's saw gin is to the upland, may stimulate some of our planters in their exertions to procure one.   THOMAS ASTON COFFIN.

———

JOHN'S ISLAND, St. John's, Colleton, Oct. 4th, 1826.

If any thing I may communicate will add but one idea to the general stock of useful knowledge already possessed by the agricultural community, I shall be gratified in being instrumental in promoting that object.

Ist. The cotton raised by me is all fine, but not equally so. I apprehend some shade of difference in the cotton of every field will be a certain result where there is any diversity of soil; or, while any inequality of strength in the land exists. I have hitherto believed that high, light, rich soils produce the finest cotton; but I have not yet tested this opinion by repeated or satisfactory experiments to decide whether I am correct or not.

2d. In different parts of my fields, as most convenient, I have used fresh mud, salt mud, salt marsh, rushes, leaves, and rotten wood, and composts of the four latter with cow dung; applied in proportion to the natural strength of the land, and to the fertilising qualities of the manure; from twenty-one to eighty-four single horse cart loads per acre, so as to give health and vigour to the plants, and equalise their growth as nearly as possible. I am best pleased with the salt mud, salt marsh, and the compost of salt marsh and rushes, combined with animal manure. They improve the length, strength, and silky appearance of the staple in a great degree, but I am not certain that they increase the fineness of the fibre. I have noticed that cotton which has not arrived at full maturity from being injured by rust or frost, will be finer but of more tender fibre than cotton produced in the same field, fully matured, particularly on strong land.

3d. The length and strength of the staple depend chiefly on the natural strength of the soil; and on the application of fertilising manures, were necessary, in order to equalise the strength of the land as much as possible; when this is accomplished, the cotton produced will be nearly all alike.

4th. My average crops for the last five years, have been 98 pounds per acre; and two and a half to three acres are usually planted to the hand.

5th. I have generally been particular in selecting from the earliest ripe cotton, produced on the best land, the seed which has a small tuft at the point, and that which is clean and black; but neither of these will always produce the same kinds of seed only; they must be annually cleared of their degenerated woolly associates, which sometimes produce fine long cotton; but generally, the staple is short or of an uneven length. I have found it a good rule in saving all kinds of seed, to select that portion which is most perfect and comes to maturity first. The size of cotton seed varies like all other seeds, according to the strength or poverty of the soil in which it is produced. Its colour is also changed from black to brown, by exposure to the sun or frost. Seed may be kept close in a room, unless it be damp.

8th. My instructions to the gatherers are, to gather from the field, at every picking, all the cotton, good or bad, which is blown open sufficiently to enable them to extract the wool with ease. The reasons for being so particular are these: if the bad cotton be left to be gathered at a future period, before the gatherers return through the field it will have become so much bleached by the weather, that it cannot then be readily distinguished from the good, either by them or by the hands who afterwards sort it for the gins; and, if ginned with the good, the extreme weakness of its fibre will depreciate the value of the general crop in proportion to the quantity of it which may be mixed with the good.

9th. My directions given, are, to dry the cotton in the sun, only so much as will be necessary to prevent the seed being crushed by the rollers. This must be varied according to the state of the weather, and the condition in which the cotton is gathered from the field. When the weather is dry, if the gatherers go out after the dew has evaporated, the cotton is exposed to the sun on the sheets as fast as gathered, then spread in the house until the next day; then on the scaffold for five or six hours; and again spread in the house a few hours, to let the heat fly off, before it is packed away; I have found it sufficiently dry for the gins. If packed away damp, it will generate heat in a short time, ruin the fibre, and unfit the seed for planting. I prefer drying in the shade altogether, when practicable. One thing we are sure of, the less cotton is exposed to the air, and the closer it is packed, the better it is. We think that exposure to the air is prejudicial, by drying the natural moisture of the fibre. Cotton dried before the fire becomes brittle and tender, and we doubt whether if damped again, it ever regains its natural strength.

10th. The gatherers commence their labour after the exsiccation of the dew; at every emptying of their picking bags, the stained and rotten cotton is taken out, with any leaves that may have fallen in. If the cotton has been gathered with care from the field, one hundred weight to each labourer may be separated with ease for the gins. The cotton is then passed through a double drum whipper, and goes to the gins. Five to seven weight to each gin is ginned in the evenings, or twenty-five weight of clean cotton for a day's work. The ginners are directed not to screw more pressure on the rollers than is necessary, to prevent the seed being crushed, and the cotton should be as evenly spread to the rollers as possible, to prevent injury to the staple. The moters prepare twenty-five to thirty weight each, for the bag. One person searches for a bag of three hundred weight, if the cotton has been cleanly moted. The sorting of the seed cotton, moting of the ginned cotton, and searching for the packer, are all done on frames of wood, or on coarse wire sieves reversed. The sieves I have found very convenient.

11th. I have generally used the whipper for the seed cotton only; but latterly have used it for the ginned cotton also, I think with great advantage, before moting, and it does no injury to the fibre, if passed through but once. The less fatigue the fibres are exposed to, the better; switching, if done in moderation, and so as *not to string the cotton*, (which is to be apprehended in long fine staple) is a very harmless, and we think, effective operation. Ginning by means of rollers, if much pressure is applied, or if the cotton is not evenly spread, so as to distribute the pressure equally, is dangerous; since pressure completely destroys the fibre. A distinguished spinner says: "I send you a sample of cotton, which has undergone pressure between a pair of smooth iron rollers; the staple is perfectly destroyed." Iron rollers are now generally out of use in this part of the country; but too much pressure upon hard wood rollers will also do much injury.

12th. My soil is partly of a low heavy loam and sand, and partly high brown mould and sand, and clay indented with creeks, and situate on a large salt river, about six miles from the ocean.

KINSEY BURDEN.

———

In my experiments on the culture of this valuable staple, I have not been as particular as other gentlemen; relying too much on my soil and situation, and the advantage of manure. The cotton produced at my John's Island plantation is preferred to that of Edisto; and the cotton of the latter to that of Slarm's Island. My soil at John's Island is generally grey or dark; at Edisto, yellow: and at Slarm's Island, a tenacious loam. I am decidedly of opinion, that gray lands produce as fine cotton as any other soil: however, I believe it is the contiguity to the ocean that renders my cotton so fine at John's Island. Salt mud has the preference to all other manures.

My cotton at Edisto is longer and stronger than that raised on John's Island. At Edisto, I have averaged about 160lbs. per acre, and at John's island, about 120lbs. Three and a half acres to the hand. Change seed every second year. The seed kept in a loft or room, in which there is a free circulation of air. I do not pick the wool from those pods, that were but imperfectly open. I dry cotton in the sun one day, or until the seed can be cracked. When my cotton is well gathered from the field, each labourer assorts from 150 to 200lbs. in the seed. After the cotton has passed through the whipper, I never use it afterwards. The quantity of ginned cotton daily moted to the hand is 40lbs. In ginning, from 25 to 30lbs. is the task. My land, at John's Island, lies immediately on the ocean, with a bold creek running in the rear. At Edisto, it is much indented with creeks.

WM. SEABROOK, sen.

—

Previously to breaking the land, with plough or hoe, about 120 cart loads of *salt mud*, to the acre, are placed in convenient heaps at equal distances; a labourer then chops and scatters it, at the rate of about 50 cart loads per acre. The ground is then listed with a plough, drawn by a yoke of oxen, which partially turns in the mud under the list and covers the cow-pen manure; it is then bedded, either with the plough or hoe, in the usual manner. If the plough is used both for listing and bedding, a portion of the mud will be placed under the list, and another portion above it; which is the best mode of disposing of the manure, to give support to a needy soil. I commence planting about the 25th of March. The seed, without selection or preparation, is planted in hills, about twelve inches apart, or in the drill, as inclination suggests. The foregoing remarks apply to a tract of poor, high, light land, in which I reside, on Edisto Island. Four acres to the hand. I consider salt mud, as manure, highly valuable; it has a powerful tendency to increase the production of the cotton plant,—to hasten its maturity, and to make the fibre stronger and finer; it also gives consistency and strength to light, weak soils. On my plantations, we cautiously prevent the exposure of the seed to moisture. Best dried in the sun, before it is stowed in the cotton house. I finish thinning by the 15th of June, if possible, and hoeing about the 15th of July; between these dates, one hauling, or two at farthest, are fully sufficient. Cotton plants are much injured by too much nursing with the hoe. To keep down the grass, and thin early, are of primary importance. The bed should be kept very firm, to prevent, as much as possible, heavy rains from penetrating it, and to assist it in retaining moisture during a drought. Hauling gives the plant fresh growth, as often as repeated; and therefore, when resorted to late in the season, proper for hoeing, it has a tendency to cause disease in the fruit, or to make drop at each repetition. The bed should be hoed by drawing the hoe, obliquely, from the alley to the top, and the grass carefully shook off by hand. My cotton is not all equally fine, neither can any cottons, correctly, be deemed so. It is now ascertained that the finer qualities of this valuable article are fast disappearing from us. A spinner, in Manchester, says:—" Some years ago we readily found, in the cottons of different planters, a sufficient number of bags to spin all the fine yarns that were required: at the present period, when the consumption of fine yarns is doubled, we do not find, among all the cottons we examine, one bag per annum." This deterioration of our cottons appears natural, when we reflect, that the same effect is produced in our gardens and orchards.

Some of the finest cotton grew in Persia; its seed bears a strong resemblance to the green seed which produces our upland cotton, it being covered with a green wool, similar to that. Some foreign, coarse woolly seed, have, after 3 or 4 years' cultivation in this country, become clean black seed, and produced cotton of fine fibre, partially retaining its original nankeen colour. A superior cotton to any produced on our shores, is much wanted by English fine spinners: in 1826, a broker, in Liverpool, says :—"We have never regretted the purchase of really fine cotton ; and although competition renders it necessary for us to purchase our cotton as cheaply as possible, yet we shall always feel a pleasure in adequately remunerating the growers of a really superior article."

All dirt and extraneous matter should be separated from the cotton by fanning, both before and after ginning. My lands are surrounded by rivers and creeks, and are contiguous to the ocean. Of the soil planted in cotton, one portion is alluvial, and the other is light, high, and sandy. I use the *Virginia Cotton Planter.*

JOHN R. MATHEWES.

———

Answer to Question 1st.—There is a slight difference in its texture, the most fertile, sandy soil, producing the finest staple.

A. to Q. 2d.—The use of manures in Alabama, of any kind, are but seldom tried on lands cultivated in cotton. But I think half rotted cotton seed gives greater activity to the growth of vegetation, (for one or two years,) than any other manure that can generally be obtained ; and, consequently, produces an article of some superiority in texture. The third question I do not consider as applicable to any other than Sea Island.

A. to Q. 4th.—The average crop, through the state, might be set down at about 800 lbs. of seed cotton per acre ; but many make from 1500 to 1800 pounds. It is customary to plant from seven to twelve acres, in cotton, to the hand.

A. to Q. 5th.—We make no selection of the seed we grow, but are particular to change them from one section of country to another, every three or four years. The principal object of an Alabama planter, is to plant of that kind of seed of which he can gather the most in a day.

A. to Q. 6th.—I have not.

A. to Q. 7th.—The usual method of preserving seed is to have them thrown from before the gin into an adjacent room ; secure from moisture, though regardless of a confined, or free circulating air.

A. to Q. 8th.—Never.

A. to Q. 9th.—The cotton gathered in the first half of the day, is usually dried, from that time till night, on a scaffold, in the sun ; that in the latter seldom requires drying.

A. to Q. 10th.—We seldom or ever pick our cotton, but put it in the gin as it is taken from the field. Hands gather from one to three hundred pounds per day.

A. to Q. 11th.—In neither.

A. to Q. 12th.—The character of the soil in middle Alabama is various. There is the sandy soil, with oak and hickory growth ; and the sandy soil, with nothing but pine. The prairies have a mixture of lime with their soil ; some exceedingly stiff, and others more loose and sandy. Their growth is oak, hickory, ash, elm, blackjack, poplar, &c. &c.

What is known with us as the little green seed, furnishes the finest staple and is the most productive, but being more difficult to gather, was exchanged for the Mexican, it being found that the seed degenerates that is grown on the same land for a succession of four or five years, and that it becomes subject to the disease known as the rot in cotton; which often destroys from an eighth to a fourth of the crop. We now purchase our seed, every fourth year, from a section of country on the Red River, known as the Petit Gulf.

Z. WATKINS.

—

The following tables are prepared from a document of the Secretary of the Treasury, furnished by order of Congress:

Millions of Pounds of Cotton grown in various Parts.

YEARS.	The World.	United States.	Brazil.	West Indies.	Egypt.	Rest of Africa.	India.	Rest of Asia.	Mexico and S. Americ.	Other places.
1791	490	2	22	12	—	46	130	190	68	—
1801	520	48	36	10	—	45	160	160	56	15
1811	555	80	35	12	.085	44	170	146	57	11
1821	630	180	32	10	6	40	175	135	44	8
1831	820	385	38	9	18	36	180	115	35	4
1834	900	460	30	8	25½	34	185	110	35	4

THE FOLLOWING WERE THE RELATIVE PORTIONS GROWN IN OUR DIFFERENT STATES.

YEARS.	Virg.	N. Car.	S. Car.	Georgia	Florida.	Alab.	Tenn.	Missis.	Louisi.	Arkans.
1791	—	—	1½	0½	—	—	—	—	—	—
1801	5	4	20	20	—	—	1	—	—	—
1811	8	7	40	40	—	—	3	—	2	—
1821	12	10	50	50	—	20	20	10	10	—
1826	25	18	70	70	2	45	45	30	38	0¼
1833	13	10	73	73	15	50	65	70	55	0¼
1834	10	9½	65½	65½	20	45	85	85	62	0½

Statement of the number of pounds of Cotton exported from the U. States to other places than Great Britain and France, in the year ending September 30, 1821, to 1835, inclusive.

Years.	To Russia.	Holland and Belgium.	Spain.	Spanish W. I.	Trieste.	Hanse Towns.	Italy and Malta.	All other places.
1821	304,680	4,186,096	284,832	772,296	34,976	748,110	897,804	2,506,777
1822	713,789	1,970,258	-	445,964	210,138	2,955,581	1,956,253	450,762
1823	309,678	4,650,548	-	-	177,789	2,356,594	217,663	833,332
1824	501,645	432,976	-	3,853	-	292,852	-	227,529
1825	133,934	1,420,225	-	-	-	577,109	980	509,031
1826	15,262	4,592,439	-	-	33,311	2,012,679	-	1,820,116
1827	147,101	5,861,400	7,999	-	183,204	3,389,514	148,170	1,440,547
1828	649,791	3,780,988	-	-	980,354	3,386,108	407,068	1,072,448
1829	227,883	9,595,337	-	-	4,071,247	6,857,796	1,056,387	1,261,925
1830	111,376	8,561,193	32,210	-	2,814,477	4,123,047	235,565	638,877
1831	761,735	972,659	555,098	-	2,778,858	2,416,765	305,695	2,243,741
1832	838,951	3,920,016	2,283,875	-	1,654,775	4,075,122	580,974	2,250,190
1833	1,447,405	2,673,253	758,216	-	1,107,600	1,870,620	-	1,759,615
1834	1,260,494	6,096,462	892,967	-	3,805,312	6,612,895	190,842	1,153,382
1835	974,801	5,694,358	878,219	-	4,943,061	2,788,147	12,952	1,493,760

Amount of Cotton Manufactures, at different Periods.

	$ (1815)	$ (1828)	$ (1832)	$ (1835)
Yearly Value in England, . .	95,000,000	171,000,000	144,000,000	160,500,000
———————— France, ...		40,000,000	54,000,000	62,000,000
———————— United States,	24,000,000	. . . .	30,000,000	47,500,000
Capital employed in manufacturing by machinery in England, ...		309,000,000	160,000,000	185,000,000
Ditto, ditto, in France, ...			115,000,000	. . . . .
Ditto, ditto, in the United States,	40,000,000	. . . .	45,000,000	80,000,000

Capital. The capital employed in growing cotton, with the income it yields, is a question of much interest and importance. But very little can be found concerning it in books, and the information obtained on it from different correspondents in the United States is defective, and is founded on quite different data in different states and by different persons.

The elements of any computation must be, the average cost per acre of cotton lands, wild or cleared, and if the former, the expense of clearing them; the amount of labour necessary per acre to produce a given quantity of raw cotton; the cost of labour, whether in the form of wages or otherwise; the expense of tools, horses, &c., with salaries of overseers, taxes paid, &c. &c.

One mode of making the computation is as follows:—The average cost of cotton lands, when wild, in the old states, did not probably exceed often half a dollar per acre, including fees for patents, &c. In the new states it has generally ranged from $1 25 to $2 per acre, depending on its quality, location, and the price of cotton. The actual settlers, in purchasing of capitalists, have generally been compelled to give an advance from 50 to 100 per cent.: sometimes much more.

The expense of clearing wild land averages from ten to fifteen dollars per acre. Land in a condition to be cultivated, will, on an average, in the United States, yield from 250lbs. to 300lbs. of clean cotton. In the old states, 125lbs. clean, or 500lbs. in the seed, is an ordinary crop. (Cooper's Polit. Econ., p. 96.) Coxe, in 1810, estimated it at 138lbs. and others at 120lbs. (Rees's Cyclop. art. "United States.")

It is believed, that one field hand or labourer, with the aid hereafter named, can cultivate, on an average, eight acres. Some say five to seven, and others ten. He will at the same time assist in raising five to eight acres of corn.

It is usual to employ, in this business, slave labour, and the next element in the calculation must be the capital invested in slaves for this purpose, and the annual cost of their maintenance.

The price of field hands has nearly or quite doubled in ten years; and they now often cost eight hundred or one thousand dollars, when formerly four and five hundred dollars were the usual rate each.

The maintenance of them is another item very differently computed.— Sometimes it is done by the purchase of more land and cultivating it, putting stock on it, of cows, sheep, &c.; so as, with the aid of other slaves, kept partly for that purpose and partly for the culture of cotton, to raise corn, pork, &c., to feed, and other materials to clothe, the whole. In such case, the additional land put in cultivation, the additional slaves bought, and the stock on the plantation, &c., must be considered as so much more capital.

The additional slaves, in such case, being more youthful, or more aged ones, or infirm females, may be fairly computed at an equal number with the field hands, but costing only about one half the price. The additional land should be for cultivation, about twenty acres for each field hand. The capital, in oxen, horses, sheep, tools for husbandry, &c., about $30 to each slave on the plantation.

To these must be added the capital which may be deemed temporary, and not as a permanent investment, and hence is to be all yearly returned, such as expense for extra clothing not made on the plantation, for medicine, overseers, tools for labour, taxes, freight, &c., which may be forty-five dollars to each slave.

Differing from these last data, in some respects, in substance, and wholly unlike in form, is another mode of computing all the capital invested except that in the mere cotton lands. Instead of estimating the price of slaves, &c. it may be considered that slave labour could be hired, with food, clothing, medicine, &c., at a cost for each field hand from $100 to $120 per year. That from $30 to $40 each would defray the annual expense of overseers, tools, horses for each, and that the additional and equal number of slaves, not prime field hands, could be hired and supported for less than one half of annual cost of the others.

On these data the cotton crop, as estimated for 1835, at four hundred and eighty millions of pounds, would grow on 1,600,000 acres at 300 lbs. per acre, or 1,920,000 at 250lbs. each. Considering that some lands wear out quick and are changed, probably the whole quantity cultivated for cotton in the United States, at this time, should be estimated at two millions or more of acres.

From the above elements the whole capital invested in growing the cotton crop in the United States can be readily computed. On one hypothesis, converting the whole capital into that which is permanent, and partly invested in lands, slaves, and tools, as fixed capital, and partly invested in bank or other stocks, or in loans so as to yield an income, and not a capital sufficient to defray those kind of expenses which are usually deemed temporary, and are yearly remunerated, or require what is called a circulating or floating capital, and the whole will amount to more than $900,000,000. On another hypothesis, considering the capital, as it generally is, divided into fixed and circulating; the capital as fixed, which is invested in lands, slaves, stocks of horses, tools, &c., and only about $30,000,000 for other expenses, as circulating or temporary, and to be itself, and not its income or interest, used and repaid yearly, and the whole capital of both kinds will not quite equal $800,000,000.

This last amount accords nearly with a still different mode of testing the quantity of capital, by supposing that the whole crop of 480,000,000 lbs., at ten cents per pound, being $48,000,000, would yield six per cent. on all the money invested in any way in raising the crop. If the capital used was all permanently invested, it would, on this hypothesis, amount to near eight hundred millions of dollars; but as from twenty-five to thirty millions of dollars is temporarily invested, and must itself be repaid yearly, the whole may, in the usual mode of treating of capital employed in such business, be considered rather under than over $800,000,000.

That amount, however, has been assumed as about correct, in the table, and is near enough for the estimate and comparisons at different periods in this country, and at the same period between this and other countries. In others, as in India, Brazil, and Egypt, the cost of labour is less, and perhaps the amount of labour performed by each hand is believed to be less, independent of the failure there to use much the improved cotton gin.

Here, at 250 lbs. per acre as an average crop, and eight acres an average cultivation by one hand, the product would be 2,000 lbs. per hand, or at ten cents per pound, would be the average of $200 per field hand. All the planter obtains over ten cents per pound would yield him a large rate of interest above six per cent. to pay for the greater risk and uncertainty of capital invested in this species of property. The whole crop of 1834 was probably worth $75,000,000 at the actual market prices, though at ten cents per pound only $48,000,000.

It is difficult to institute any just comparison between the profits of capital invested here in the growing of cotton, and in the manufacture of it; as in the latter so much more in proportion is invested in temporary or circulating capital to pay for wages and stock, and the whole of which is to be annually repaid. Neither have I leisure for the details.

Indeed it might have comported better with the technical language of political economy to have divided the whole expenditures in raising cotton into three heads, viz: labour, capital, and land; to yield in return, wages for the labour, profit or interest on the capital, and rent for the land. (See Senior's Outline of Political Economy, page 165, from the Encyclopædia Metropolitana.) It will be easy, for those who prefer it, to throw the calculation into that form; but the results then, would not be such as accord best with the views proposed in this part of the table; which are, to present to the community here, in plain terms, and in a form as intelligible as possible to people at large, the amount of capital actually employed at different periods in growing the cotton crop in the United States; whether invested in the original purchase of lands, the clearing, or the culture of them; in the purchase of slaves, or in procuring an income for the payment, or in the actual payment of wages of free labour to raise the crop; for buying seed, tools, food, raiment, horses, &c., and for payment of taxes, overseers, or any other expense, incidental or direct, connected with the production of the crop.

Two brief statements of a very general character are subjoined, in illustration of some of the above remarks.

1st. The capital invested in cotton lands under cultivation, at two million acres, and worth, cleared, on an average, $20 per acre, is - $40,000,000

The capital in field hands, and in other lands, stock, labour, &c., to feed and clothe them, at $100 per year, on 340,000 in number, would require the interest or income of a capital, at six per cent. of - - - - - 554,000,000

The maintenance of 340,000 more assistants, &c., at $30 each per year, would require the income of a capital at six per cent. of - - - - - - 167,000,000

The capital to supply enough interest or income to pay for tools, horses for ploughing, taxes, medicines, overseers, &c., at $30, for the first 340,000, would be - - 167,000,000

Making in all a permanent capital, if so used, equal to $918,000,000

2d. The capital in cotton lands, as stated above   -   - $40,000,000

Capital in the purchase of 340,000 field hands, at $800 each,
on an average,   -   -   -   -   -   -   272,000,000

Capital in the other 340,000 to aid, and to raise food, clothing,
&c., at half price, -   -   -   -   -   -   136,000,000

Capital in horses, cattle, sheep, utensils, &c., for plantation,
about $30 to each person, to aid in making food and
clothing, &c.   -   -   -   -   -   -   20,400,000

Capital in other lands to support stock, raise corn, &c., at 20
acres to each of the 680,000, worth $20 per acre, cleared,   272,000,000

Capital, temporary or floating, to buy clothing not made on
plantation, pay taxes, overseers, freight, tools for cotton,
&c., $45 to each   -   -   -   -   -   -   30,600,000

$771,000,000

The increase of American cotton is such, as to create the utmost astonishment that our vast capacity to produce it had so long rested without notice. The export, by the last return, was about 24 millions. The late General Washington was a lover of agriculture, understood it well, and was not inattentive to fair profit in his patriotic pursuits and private business: yet he does not appear ever to have noticed our country's capacity to produce cotton. This is the more remarkable, because nearly all his landed property was in the *cotton district* of the United States. No circumstance can more strongly prove the universal inadvertency of America to her capacity to produce cotton.

One of the beneficial effects of our present active cultivation of cotton is, that, while it yields the greatest agricultural profit in proportion to the capital in land and stock, it has a sure tendency to diminish the quantities of rice, tobacco, indigo, grain, and cattle raised in the cotton district of America, and keeps up the price of those articles in a manner highly favourable to those who raise them. The moderate quantity of rice produced in 1801 and 1802 is a positive evidence of this profitable truth. The North American rice is of the *best class.* The body of our rice planters raise but three quarter crops or half crops, from their attention to cotton. Having so much less to sell, the market is not glutted. The price is consequently not low. It is favourable. The raisers of Indian corn in the southern states have also turned to cotton. Hence Indian corn and pork are every where better supported in price, to the general benefit of our farmers. Much corn will go from counties out of the cotton district to counties in the cotton district for sale and consumption. So of fish, and all eatables and drinkables.

From these circumstances it will appear, that we have an universal and deep interest to keep up the price of cotton. Home demand ought not to be neglected or overlooked. *The cotton manufacture* merits the earliest and best attention of the Union and of the states. Scotland cannot pursue that manufacture to as much advantage as the middle, northern and eastern states of America. The British duty of one penny sterling is nearly two cents per pound. The freight, insurance, storage, commissions, duty and other charges might be wholly or partly saved. We might use our own indigo, woad, madder, barks, and other dye stuffs, or those which we import and re-ship to Scotland, and other parts of Europe. The Scotish manufacturers are fed with our flour and that which they import, all the charges on which are saved so far as our own manufacturers consume our provisions. It appears to be expedient to give this great case of the *cotton manufacture* a complete examination and to make a luminous exhibition of it before our country. For which purpose it is respectfully suggested to the legislature of the United States, and those of the several states, to give the subject in charge (by an early reference) to the proper department of their respective executive governments, with instructions to enquire into, examine, consider and make report concerning the rise, progress, and present state of the cultivation of cotton, the course of the importation and exportation thereof since the 3d of March 1789, the course of the trade in cotton goods, since that day, the present state of the household and regular manufactory of cotton goods in the United States, and the measures which have been adopted by the Union and by the states to encourage the same, to the end of considering what further encouragement can and ought to be given by the governments to the cultivation, export, trade, and manufacture of cotton within the United States.—T. Coxe.

———

Circumstances connected with the cotton trade, chronologically arranged.

B.C. The cotton manufactures of India were taken notice of by the Greeks when Alexander overran Greece.

A.D. 1101. The measure of the ell fixed by Henry I.

1280. The manufacture of cotton introduced into China from India.

1500. The first attempt made to introduce cotton goods into England.

1560. Giuccardini records the Low Countries to be the depot of India goods and of cotton from the Levant.

1565. The first act of parliament relating to cotton goods.

1600. The first charter granted to the English East India company.

1631. Printed calicoes imported into England.

1640. Fustians made at Bolton.

1670. The Dutch loom first used in England.

1673. Blore in his History of Liverpool, speaks of great cotton manufactories in the adjacent parts.

1676. Calico printing first introduced into London.

1700. The manufacturing of muslins first attempted in Paisley.

1721. The weaving of India calicoes prohibited.

1725. Linens, lawns, and cambrics, first manufactured at Glasgow. Mr. James Monteith was the first manufacturer who warped a muslin web in Scotland.

1730. Cotton spinning attempted unsuccessfully by Mr. Wyat at Litchfield, who spun the first thread of cotton yarn ever produced without the intervention of the fingers.

1735. The cotton plant first cultivated in Surinam.

1738. Mr. Lewis Paul took out a patent for an improved mode of carding. The fly-shuttle invented by Mr. John Kay of Bury.

1742. The first mill for spinning cotton erected at Birmingham. It was moved by asses; but the machinery was sold in 1743.

1750. The fly-shuttle in general use.

1756. Cotton velvets and quiltings first made.

1760. Mr. James Hargreaves applies the stock card to the carding of cotton with some improvements.

1762. Cylinder cards invented. First used by the father of the late Sir Robert Peel.

1763. Rouen was the principal market for the sale of cotton wool.

1767. The spinning jenny invented by Mr. James Hargreaves.

1769. Mr. Arkwright, afterwards Sir Richard Arkwright, obtained his first patent for spinning with rollers, and built his first mill at Nottingham.

1770. 5521 bags of cotton imported into Liverpool from the West Indies, 3 from New York, 4 from Virginia and Maryland, and 3 barrels from North Carolina.

1774. Power Looms invented by the Rev. Dr. Cartwright.

1779. Cayenne, Surinam, Essequibo, Demerara, and St. Domingo cotton most in esteem.

Mule jenny invented by Samuel Crompton.

1781. Brazil cotton first imported from Maranham, but very dirty.

1782. James Watt obtains his patent for the steam engine.

1783. Surat, and also Bourbon cotton, first imported or known about this time.

1784. Arkwright's first patent expired.

Cotton manufactured in Great Britain this year was 11,280,238lbs., and valued at £3,950,000.

Cotton imported in small quantities from the United States.

1785. Mr. M'Intosh and Mr. Dale commenced dyeing turkey red in Glasgow.

1786. Bourbon cotton sold from 7s. 6d. to 10s. per lb.

1793. Cotton, the growth of the United States, first imported in large quantities, by way of the West Indies.

1797. Scutching machine, said to be invented by Mr. Snodgrass, and Mr. Cooper, first used at Johnstone.

About this time the saw-gin was invented.

1798. The Fame arrived with the first cargo of cotton from the East Indies.

1800 or 1801. The entire stock of American cotton in Liverpool one bag.

1803. Radcliff's dressing and warping machine invented.

1813. Trade to British India thrown open under certain restrictions.

1818. 105 millions of yards of cotton cloth manufacted in Glasgow, value £5,000,000.

1823. Cotton first imported from Egypt direct to Liverpool.

1825. Steam engines estimated at 893 horses' power, spinning cotton in and around Glasgow, in a space not more than two miles from the cross.

1830. The Danforth throstle frame introduced into England.

1832. Robert Montgomery of Johnstone (Scotland) obtained a patent for the three kingdoms for an improvement of the throstle frame, which it is considered will supersede all the machines hitherto used for spinning low numbers, also for making copes. The first entire machine was accidentally destroyed.   The second is now in full operation in the mill of John Miller, Esq. and giving entire satisfaction.

The value of cotton goods manufactured in 1832 in Great Britain estimated at £40,000,000 yearly, £20,000,000 of which are exported.

1834. Nankeen cotton raised in Georgia, manufactured at Lonsdale R. I.

The nankeen cotton of China has attained considerable celebrity, and it has been much disputed whether the nankeens are made from a cotton of their peculiar colour, or are dyed to that colour.   There is now no doubt that the cotton is naturally of the same yellow tinge which it preserves when spun and woven into cloth ; and it is of very fine quality.   The nankeen cloth requires no dye ; that raised by Mr. Forsyth in Georgia, is of a beautiful texture, and the cloth made from it surpasses any imported.   It seems to be a mistake, that the colour of the cotton depends on some peculiarity in the soil.   This new article of American produce promises to add much to the value of the staple, and to the increase of the manufacture.

———

PAWTUCKET, R. I. Sept. 1835.

Mrs. Williams, now living in this place, wove the first piece of cotton stripes, from yarn spun by S. Slater.

———

PRICE OF COTTON TWIST YARN.—BY S. SLATER.

1794—No. 12, 88 cts.; 16, 104 cts.; 20, 121 cts.
1795,6,7,8,9—Prices the same as above.
1800—No. 12, 103 cts.; 16, 119 cts.; 20, 136 cts.
1801,2—Prices the same as 1800.
1803—No. 12, 94 cts.; 16, 110 cts.; 50, 126 cts.
1804—The same as 1803.
1805—No. 12, 99 cts.; 16, 115 cts.; 20, 131 cts.

———

Copy of an original invoice of cotton yarn, in the year 1784, *and published by permission, to show the price of yarn at that period.*

" MANCHESTER, January 22, 1784.

Mr. Peter Heatley,

Bought of Richard Arkwright.

40 pounds of twist, No. 30, at 6s. 5d.	.	.	.	£12 16 9
20 „ „ „ 31, at 6s. 8d.	.	.	.	. 6 13 4

£19 10 0

Forwarded this day per Grundy."

N.B.—In the year 1784, the quantity of cotton imported into Great Britain, was 11,281,138lbs., consisting of West India, Surinam, and Berbice, no other sort being then imported: and the price of cotton during that year, fluctuated from one shilling to two shillings and one penny per lb.

———

Paterson, New Jersey, is one of the creations of the genius of Alexander Hamilton, the true father of the system of domestic industry, now cherished as the American system.   In the early part of the year 1791, on the recommendation, and by the active and influential exertions of this distinguished and patriotic statesman, a number of public spirited individuals of New York, New Jersey, and Pennsylvania, associated themselves for establishing useful manufactures, by the subscription of $200,000. The number of shares originally subscribed was 5000, at $100 the share; but 2267 shares only were fully paid up. A great emporium of manufactures was the general object of the company; their immediate object was the manufacture of cotton cloths; and the attempt is highly characteristic of the enterprising spirit of our countrymen. At this period, the improvements of Arkwright in cotton machinery, though perfected, were not much used, even in England, and were absolutely unknown in all other countries. In America no cotton had been spun by machinery, except in Pawtucket, Rhode Island. The act of incorporation is said to have been drawn or revised by Hamilton. The society was organised at New Brunswick; on the last Monday of November 1791, by the choice of the first board of directors, composed of Messrs. Duer, Dewhurst, Walker, Low, Flint, Boudinot, Bayard, Neilson, Mercer, Lowring, Lewis, Furman, and M'Comb. William Duer was chosen the first governor of the company. These names are illustrious by the present flourishing condition of the society, the result of their labours. Mr. Hamilton, who was not a stock-holder of the company, and whose disinterested exertions in its behalf were prompted by higher motives than pecuniary gratification, had, previously to the act of incorporation, at the request of the company, engaged English and Scotish artisans, and manufacturers of cotton machinery and cotton goods, to establish their business here. In May 1792, the society selected, with admirable judgment, the Passaic, as the principal site of their proposed operations; giving to their town the name of Paterson, after the governor who had signed their charter. At this period there were not more than ten houses here. At a meeting of the directors, at the Godwin hotel, on the 4th July 1792, appropriations were made for building factories, machine shops, and shops for calico printing and weaving; and a race-way was directed to be made, for bringing the water from above the falls to the proposed mills. Unfortunately, the direction was given to Major l'Enfant, a French engineer, whose projects commonly perished in the waste of means provided for their attainment. He commenced the race-way and canal, designing to unite the Upper Passaic with the lower, at the head of tide, near the present village of Acquackanonck, by a plan better adapted to the resources of a great empire, than to those of a private company. In January 1793, Peter Colt of Hartford, then comptroller of the state of Connecticut, was appointed general superintendent of the affairs of the company, with full powers to manage the concerns of the society, as if they were his own individual property. Mr. Colt completed the race-way, conducting the water to the first factory erected by the society. The canal to tide water had been abandoned, before the departure of the engineer. The factory, 90 feet long by 40 wide, and 4 stories high, was finished in 1794, when cotton yarn was spun in the mill; but yarn had been spun in the preceding year, by machinery moved by oxen. In 1794, calico shawls and other cotton goods were printed; the bleached and unbleached muslins being purchased in New York. In the same year the society gave their attention to the culture of the silk worm, and directed the superintendant to plant the mulberry tree for this purpose. In April of this year, the society employed a teacher to instruct, gratuitously, on the sabbath, the children employed in the factory. This was probably the first Sunday school established in New Jersey. Notwithstanding their untoward commencement, and the many discouragements attending their progress, the directors persevered in their enterprise, and during the years 1795 and 1796, much yarn of various sizes was spun, and several species of cotton fabrics were made. But, at length satisfied that it was hopeless to contend, successfully, longer with an adverse current, they resolved, July 1796, to abandon the manufacture, and discharged their workmen. This result was produced by a combination of causes. Nearly $50,000 had been lost, by the failure of the parties to certain bills of exchange purchased by the company, to buy in England plain cloths for printing : large sums had been wasted by the engineer ; and the machinists and manufacturers imported, were presumptuous, and ignorant of many branches of the business they engaged to conduct ; and more than all, a want of experience relative to the subject of the enterprise, and the country unprepared for manufactures. The cotton mill of the company was subsequently leased to individuals, who continued to spin candle-wick and coarse yarn until 1807, when it was accidentally burnt, and was never rebuilt. The admirable water-power of the company was not, however, wholly unemployed. In 1801, a mill seat was leased to Mr. Kinsey & Co.; in 1807 a second, and 1811, a third to other persons; and between 1812 and 1814, several others were sold or leased. In 1814, Mr. Colt purchased, at a depreciated price, a large proportion of the shares, and reanimated the association. From this date, the growth of Paterson has been steady, except during the three or four years that followed the peace of 1815. The advantages derivable from the great fall in the river, have been improved with much judgment. A dam of four and a half feet high, strongly framed and bolted to the rock in the bed of the river above the falls, turns the stream through a canal excavated in the trap rock of the bank, into a basin, whence, through strong guard-gates, it supplies in succession three canals on separate planes, each below the other; giving to the mills on each, a head and fall of about 22 feet. By means of the guard-gate, the volume of water is regulated at pleasure, and a uniform height preserved, avoiding the inconvenience of back-water ; $40,000 have been expended to perfect this privilege.

The advantages to be derived from opening a navigable communication between the Delaware and the Chesapeake, early attracted the attention of enlightened men in the colony of Pennsylvania. The American Philosophical Society, in 1769 and 1774, appointed committees to explore and survey the country between the Delaware and the Chesapeake ; and the legislature ordered similar explorations, some time later, of the country between the Delaware and the Susquehanna, with a view to opening an artificial communication between them. But the formidable nature of those objects, their novelty in this country, and, still more, the intervention of the revolutionary war, prevented the adoption, at that time, of any effectual measures for the attainment of those inestimable improvements. At length, in the year 1794, a number of public spirited citizens, and whom Robert Morris, the financier of the United States, to whom the nation was so largely indebted for procuring the ways and means, in "those times that tried men's souls," David Rittenhouse, Samuel Meredith, Walter Stewart, Benjamin R. Morgan, William Bingham, Rev. Dr. Smith, John Nicholson, Robert Hare, Levi Hollingsworth, Jonathan Bayard Smith, and James C. Fisher, entered with zeal on the business of internal improvement.

POWER LOOM WEAVING.

CHAPTER X.

ADVANCEMENT OF MACHINERY.

———————— " Art thrives most,
Where commerce has enriched the busy coast;
He catches all improvements in his flight,
Spreads foreign wonders in his country's sight,
Imports what others have invented well,
And stirs his own to match them, or excel."—*Cowper.*

POWER LOOM AND DRESSER.

In 1785 the Rev. Dr. Cartwright* of Hollander house, (brother of Major Cartwright, the well-known advocate of radical reform,) invented a power-loom, which may be regarded as the parent of that now in use. Dr. Cartwright was led by his invention to

* Edmund Cartwright was born in 1743, in Nottinghamshire, at Marnham, an estate which had long been in possession of his family. He was the youngest of three brothers, all of whom were remarkable men. His second brother, Captain William Cartwright, a man of great enterprise and energy of character, after a residence of sixteen years on the coast of Labrador, returned to England in 1792, and published his journal, which gave the first authentic account of the Esquimaux nations. His elder brother, Major John Cartwright, was forty years distinguished as an enthusiastic and persevering advocate for what is called parliamentary reform; and notwithstanding the many turbulent scenes in which he appeared in public, in domestic life he was exemplary as an amiable, affectionate and benevolent man; as a political leader he was truly consistent, and even his enemies have borne testimony to his being perfectly disinterested. Edmund, the younger brother, being destined for the church, was placed under Mr. Clarke of Wakefield, and the celebrated Dr. Langhorne. He afterwards studied at Oxford, where he was early distinguished for his literary attainments, and was elected fellow of Magdalen College. On entering the church, he retired to a small living in the gift of his family, where he discovered the application of yeast as a remedy in putrid fevers, and became known as a poet. His legendary tale of " Armine and Elvira," was greatly admired for its pathos and elegant simplicity. His " Prince of Peace," in a loftier style of composition, also excited much attention at its appearance. He married in 1772, and afterwards went to reside at Doncaster, but still assiduously continued his literary labours. Between 1774 and 1784, he was one of the principal contributors to the Monthly Review.

The origin of his invention of weaving by machinery instead of manual

undertake manufacturing with power-looms at Doncaster ; but the concern was unsuccessful, and he at length abandoned it. Though he had a handsome paternal fortune, his affairs became

labour has been minutely detailed by himself, in a letter written to Mr. Dugald Bannatyne, of Glasgow.

" Happening to be at Matlock in the summer of 1784, I fell in company with some gentlemen of Manchester, when the conversation turned on Arkwright's spinning machinery. One of the company observed, that as soon as Arkwright's patent expired, so many mills would be erected, and so much cotton spun, that hands never could be found to weave it. To this observation I replied, that Arkwright must then set his wits to work to invent a weaving machine. This brought on a conversation on the subject, in which the Manchester gentlemen unanimously agreed, that the thing was impracticable ; and in defence of their opinion they adduced arguments which I certainly was incompetent to answer, or even to comprehend, being totally ignorant of the subject, having never, at that time, seen a person weave. I controverted, however, the impracticability of the thing by remarking, that there had lately been exhibited in London an automaton figure which played at chess ; ' now you will not assert, gentlemen,' said I, ' that it is more difficult to construct a machine that shall weave, than one which shall make all the variety of moves which are required in that complicated game ?' Some little time afterwards a particular circumstance recalling this conversation to my mind, it struck me that, as in plain weaving, according to the conception I then had of the business, there could be only three movements, which were to follow each other in succession, there would be little difficulty in producing and repeating them. Full of these ideas, I immediately employed a carpenter and smith to carry them into effect. As soon as the machine was finished I got a weaver to put in the warp, which was of such materials as sail cloth is usually made of. To my great delight, a piece of cloth, such as it was, was the produce. As I had never before turned my thoughts to any thing mechanical, either in theory or practice, nor had ever seen a loom at work or knew any thing of its construction, it will readily be supposed that my first loom must have been a most rude piece of machinery. The warp was placed perpendicularly, the reed fell with a force of at least half a hundred weight, and the springs which threw the shuttle were strong enough to have thrown a Congreve rocket ; in short it required the power of two strong men to work the machine at a slow rate only for a short time. Conceiving, in my great simplicity, that I had accomplished all that was required, I then secured what I thought a most valuable property, by a patent, in April 1785. This being done, I then condescended to see how other people wove, and you will guess my astonishment when I compared their easy modes of operation with mine. Availing myself, however, of what I then saw, I made a loom, in its general principles, nearly as they are now made, but it was not until the year 1787 that I completed my invention, when I took out my last weaving patent in August in that year."—This also included the art of weaving checks, which the most skilful mechanics, even after they had seen his first machines in operation, deemed to be impossible by any except manual

inextricably embarrassed; but he was more fortunate than most inventors, in obtaining from parliament, in 1809, a grant of £10,000, as a reward for his ingenuity.

The great obstacle to the success of the power-loom, was, that it was necessary to stop the machine frequently, in order to dress the warp as it unrolled from the beam, which operation required a man to be employed for each loom, so that there was no saving of expense. This difficulty was happily removed, by the invention of an extremely ingenious and effectual mode of dressing the warp before it was placed in the loom.

The dressing-machine was produced by Messrs. Radcliffe & Ross, cotton manufacturers, of Stockport; but they took out the patent in the name of Thomas Johnson, of Bredbury, a weaver in their employment, to whose inventive talent the machine was chiefly owing.

Wm. Radcliffe justly thought, that the most effectual way of securing for the country the manufacturing of the yarn, was to enable the English to excel as much in weaving as they did in spinning. He saw the obstacles to the accomplishment of this object, but being a man of determined purpose, he shut himself up in his mill, on the 2d of January, 1802, with a number of weavers, joiners, turners, and other workmen, and resolved to produce some great improvement. Two years were spent in experiments. He had for his assistant, Thomas Johnson, an ingenious but dissipated young man, to whom he explained what he wanted, and whose fertile invention suggested a great variety of expedients, so that he obtained the name of the "conjuror" among his fellow-workmen. Johnson's genius, and Radcliffe's judgement and perseverance, at length produced the dressing machine; an admirable invention, without which the power-loom could scarcely have been rendered efficient.

The process is thus briefly described:—"The yarn is first wound from the top upon bobbins, by a winding machine, in which operation it is passed through water, to increase its tenacity.

---

means. The weaving factory which was erected at Doncaster by some of Cartwright's friends, with his license, was unsuccessful; and another establishment containing five hundred looms, built at Manchester, was destroyed by an exasperated mob, in 1790. The invention, however, has surmounted all opposition, and at the time of the doctor's death it was stated that steam looms had increased so rapidly, that they were then performing the labour of two hundred thousand men! Cartwright's next invention was a method to comb wool with machinery, which excited, if possible, a still greater ferment among the working classes than even the power loom.

The bobbins are then put upon the warping-mill, and the web warped from them upon a beam belonging to the dressing-frame. From this beam, placed now in the dressing-frame, the warp is wound upon the weaving-beam, but in its progress to it passes through a hot dressing of starch. It is then compressed between two rollers, to free it from the moisture it had imbibed with the dressing, and drawn over a succession of tin cylinders heated by steam, to dry it; during the whole of this last part of its progress being lightly brushed as it moves along, and fanned by rapidly revolving fanners. The dressing here spoken of is merely a size or paste made of flour and water, now generally used cold; and the use of it is to make the minute fibres, which, as it were, feather the yarn, adhere closely to it, so that the warp may be smooth like catgut. The brushes essentially aid in smoothing the yarn, and distributing the size equally over it; and by means of the fan and the heated cylinders the warp is so soon dried, that it is wound upon the beam for the loom within a very short space after passing through the trough of paste. This machine, from the regularity and neatness of its motions, and its perfect efficacy, is equally beautiful and valuable."

Radcliffe and his partner took out four patents in the years 1803 and 1804; two of them for a useful improvement in the loom, the taking up of the cloth by the motion of the lathe; and the other two for the new mode of warping and dressing. Johnson, in whose name they were taken out, received by deed the sum of £50 in consideration of his services, and continued in their employment. Radcliffe's unremitting devotion to the perfecting of this apparatus, and other unfortunate circumstances, caused the affairs of his concern to fall into derangement, and he failed. He wrote a book entitled, " Origin of the New System of Manufacture, commonly called Power-Loom Weaving," showing the purposes for which this system was invented.

Baines says, " The dressing machine itself has now in some establishments been superseded, and the warp is dressed in a shorter and simpler way by an improved sizing apparatus. By the aid of Johnson and Radcliffe's invention, the power-loom became available. A patent for another power-looom was taken out in 1803, by Mr. H. Horrocks, cotton manufacturer, of Stockport, which he further improved, and took out subsequent patents in 1805 and 1813. Horrocks' loom is the one which has now come into general use; it is constructed entirely of iron, and is a neat, compact, and simple machine, moving with great rapidity, and occupying so little space that several hundreds may be worked in a single room of a large factory. Horrocks, sharing the common destiny of inventors, failed and sunk into poverty. This retarded the adoption of the machine ; but independently of this, the power-loom and dressing machine came very slowly into favour. In 1813, there were not more than one hundred of the latter machines in England and Scotland, and 2400 of the former in use.

The introduction of the power loom and dresser formed a new era in the cotton business in America.

Previous to 1815, the whole of the weaving was done by hand looms ; in many of these looms great improvements had been made and a great quantity of cloth produced for home consumption. About the year 1814, Mr. Gilmore landed in Boston from England with patterns of the power loom and dresser ; and John Slater, Esq. invited him to Smithfield, Rhode Island, and made known his wishes to construct these important inventions ; but Mr. Slater could not prevail on the whole of his partners to engage him in the trial. He remained at Smithfield some time, employed as a machinist by that establishment. He introduced the hydrostatic press, and it proved of great advantage in pressing cloth, &c.

Judge Lyman of Providence had been endeavouring to obstruct the power-loom, but failed in the attempt ; and on hearing of Mr. Gilmore, he with some other gentlemen entered into a contract with him to build the power-loom and dresser, from the patterns which he brought with him from England. He accomplished all that he promised, and received a compensation of $1500, to the great satisfaction of his patrons. They were soon introduced into Pawtucket, and David Wilkinson made them as an article of sale. Mr. Gilmore, however, neglected to turn his talents and opportunities to the advantage of his family, and died leaving them poor in this country.

S. Green informed me, that Gilmore was a man of great mechanical genius ; he brought the first engineer's rule into Rhode Island, and Mr. Green obtained one from him, with a great deal of valuable information.

The hand-looms were immediately superseded, and now no one in the manufacturing districts thinks of using them any more than they do the one-thread wheel. Their introduction has enabled America to compete even with Great Britain in cotton cloths in South America and other foreign markets.

This is the crowning sequel in improvements in the cotton machinery, the addition of which has made a complete series, perhaps the most perfect which the world ever saw, whether with regard to the mechanical excellence of its operations or its results. I have said that the power-loom formed a *new era*, and it is not easy to conceive how this series can be much improved, as it now exists in England and America.

BLEACHING AND CALENDERING.*

After the manufacture of the cloth is complete, there is the important process of bleaching to be undergone by all cotton goods; this is a very extensive branch of the business; it is necessary to remove the dirt and grease contracted in the manufacture, and the dressing applied to the warp, and also to destroy all the colour belonging to the raw material, so as to make the cloth perfectly white. The bleaching process, as performed in the middle of the last century, occupied from six to eight months. " It consisted in steeping the cloth in alkaline leys for several days, washing it clean, and spreading it on the grass for some weeks. The steeping in alkaline leys, called *bucking*, and the bleaching on the grass, called *crofting*, were repeated alternately for five or six times. The cloth was then steeped for some days in sour milk, washed clean, and crofted. These processes were repeated, diminishing every time the strength of the alkaline ley, till the linen had acquired the requisite whiteness." The art of bleaching was at that time so little understood in Great Britain, that nearly all the linens manufactured in Scotland were sent to Holland to bleach, and were kept there more than half a year, undergoing, in the bleach-fields around Haarlem, the tedious processes just described.

The grand improvement in bleaching was, in the application of *chlorine* to the art. This acid was discovered in 1774, by Scheele, the Swedish philosopher, who observed its property of destroying vegetable colours, from its having bleached the cork of his phial. This observation having been recorded, suggested to the active mind of the French chemist, Berthollet, the thought of applying the acid to the bleaching of cloths made of vegetable fibres ; and, in 1785, having found by experiment that it answered the purpose, he made known this great discovery, which brings down the time

---

* Bleaching, calendering, &c. were introduced at a great expense, in Providence, by Dr. Bowen, where the water is well adapted, and there is now a bleaching and beetling establishment, called by his name. The bleaching business is now very extensive in the United States, and they are becoming more perfect in the process, as more attention is paid to every department in preparation for the calico printing.

Rhode Island appears to be in advance in the bleaching business, both for the quality and quantity of its work.

required for bleaching from months to days, or even to hours. James Watt learnt this at Paris, and introduced it into England in 1786.

Mr. Henry was one of the first persons to suggest the addition of lime, which takes away the noxious smell of the oxymuriatic acid without injuring its bleaching properties.

So great was the facility thus given to the process of bleaching, that it is recorded that a bleacher, in Lancashire, received fourteen hundred pieces of grey muslin on a Tuesday, which, on the Thursday immediately following, were returned, bleached, to the manufacturers, at the distance of sixteen miles; and they were packed up and sent off, that very day, to a foreign market. This is considered as not an extraordinary performance. Without this wonderful saving of time and capital, the quantity of cotton goods now manufactured could scarcely have been bleached.

Mr. Tennant, "after a great deal of most laborious and acute investigation," hit upon the method of making a saturated liquid of chloride of lime, which was found to answer perfectly all the purposes of the bleacher.

Mr. Tennant uses five and a half parts of black oxide of manganese, seven and a half parts of common salt, and twelve and a quarter parts of sulphuric acid, of the specific gravity of 1.843, diluted with an equal quantity of water to make the chlorine gas, with which he impregnates a layer of slacked lime, some inches thick, in a stone chamber. By recent improvements in the manufacture, he has doubled the value of the bleaching powder, whilst its price is reduced to one half; the present price is 3d. sterling per pound. By many bleachers this powder is used, mixed with a proper quantity of water; but the great bleachers use liquid chloride of lime, which they make in leaden stills; steam being used to expel the gas from the materials,—and the gas being received into a cream of lime, which becomes saturated with it.

The processes through which cottons pass in the hands of the bleacher, are as follows:—The cloth is first singed, by being drawn rapidly over a copper or iron cylinder heated to a red heat, which burns off the down and loose fibres on the surface, without injuring the fabric. It is next thrown, in loose folds, into a cistern of cold water, where it remains some time; and it is afterwards more effectually washed by being put into a large hollow wheel, called the dash-wheel, usually divided into four compartments; this is supplied with a jet of clear spring water, thrown in through a circular slit in the side, which revolves opposite the end of a flattened pipe, by which means the cloth is well washed, as it is

thrown backwards and forwards in the rapidly-revolving wheel.
By this means a considerable portion of the weaver's dressing
is removed. Next, the cloth is boiled with lime : the pieces of
calico are placed in a kier, or boiler having a false bottom, perfo-
rated with holes, and with layers of cream of lime between the
pieces ; one pound of lime being used for every thirty-five pounds
of the cloth. It is so contrived, that the boiling water is spouted
on the goods, filters through them and the lime into that part of
the boiler below the false bottom ; is again forced up a pipe in the
middle of the boiler, and falls again upon the goods : and this process is repeated for about eight hours. By this lime boiling the
dressing, dirt, and grease, are removed from the cloth ; and the
lime itself is removed by a careful washing in the dash-wheel.

The cloth is now subjected to the action of the bleaching liquid ;
that is, chloride of lime dissolved in water.

A solution of one pound of bleaching powder with one gallon
of water, has a specific gravity of 1.05 ; but water is added till the
solution is reduced to the specific gravity of 1.02.   The quantity
of this liquor used for 700lbs. of cloth is 971 gallons ; and 388lbs.
of the solid bleaching powder is required for 700lbs. of cloth. The
goods are left in the cold bleaching liquid about six hours, and
when taken out they are considerably whitened. Having been
washed, the cloth is next put into a very weak solution of sulphuric
acid, containing eight gallons of the acid in 200 gallons of water.
This is called the *souring* process, which lasts about four hours.
By this the oxide of iron, which, in the course of the operations,
has been deposited on the cloth, giving it a yellowish hue, and
the lime which it had imbibed, are removed, and the cloth becomes
much whiter. It is again washed in cold water, and then boiled
for eight hours more in an alkaline ley. Sixty-four pounds of
carbonate of soda are used to 2,100lbs. of unbleached cloth. After
this the cloth is steeped a second time in the bleaching liquid,
which is only two-thirds of the strength of the first, where it remains 5 or 6 hours ; and a second time in the mixture of sulphuric
acid and water, where it remains 4 hours. The last souring process
completes the bleaching of the cloth, which comes out of the acid solution perfectly white.   The cloth is then very carefully washed,
to remove all trace of the sulphuric acid and water : it is freed from
the greater part of the water by being squeezed between two rollers,
and is then straightened and mangled in the damp state. To
improve the appearance of the cloth, it is usually passed through
starch made of wheaten flour, often mixed with porcelain clay and
calcined sulphurate of lime ; by which the cloth is made stiffer,

and appears to have great substance. (It would be creditable to the trade to lay this aside, as having the appearance of fraud.) The cloth is dried by being passed through a drying machine, consisting of several copper cylinders heated by steam : it is then again damped, in order to fit it to receive the gloss which is imparted in the process of calendering.*

The calender consists of several wooden and iron rollers, placed above each other in a frame, and held together by levers and pulleys; the cloth, passing between these rollers, is strongly pressed; the surface becomes glossy, and sometimes it is made to assume a wiry appearance by two pieces being put through the calender together, in which case the threads of each are impressed on the face of the other. The goods are then folded up in pieces, stamped with marks varying according to the foreign or domestic markets for which they are intended, and pressed in a Bramah's press; after which they are packed up and sent to the merchant.

* On Mangling Cloths.—The business of smoothing cloths, as usually practised in the United States, is a very serious one in a warm day, and many females have laid the foundation for an attack of acute disease, and protracted ill-health, by fatigue and imprudent exposure to a current of air after being much heated by a hard day's duty. To remedy these evils, mangles have been invented. There are but few families in Europe without one of these useful machines, by which the numerous articles having plain, smooth surfaces, are smoothed with expedition, and acquire a gloss which cannot be given by flat irons. The following is the best.

Two horizontal cylindrical rollers form a bed for the roller on which the linen to be mangled is rolled. The axes of those rollers bear on brass, let into the wood frame, and have a wheel fixed to each, which works in a pinion on the axis of the fly-wheel: a moveable roller on which the linen to be mangled is rolled: a roller, the axis of which works in pieces of brass, which slide between iron, let into the inner side of the wood frame, to the bottom of which long pieces of iron are fixed, with hooks at their lower extremities, to which are attached the chains that support the scale or platform, where iron weights, or any other substance, are placed ; to the top of the brass in which the roller works, the engine chains are fastened, which pass through apertures at each end of the top of the wood frame, and are there again fastened on the pulleys of the shaft with a screw : there is a lever fixed to the end of the shaft. To use the machine, press the lever, and fasten it with the hook, which raises the roller with the platform and weights attached to it : then take out the roller, and roll the linen and mangling cloth round it, and replace it on the two bottom rollers, unhook the lever, and the weights on the platform will press the roller on the other ; give motion to the fly-wheel and also to all the rollers by turning the handle, which, in a short time, will make the linen beautifully smooth ; press down the lever, fasten it with the hook, and take the roller out: a spare roller is supplied, so that if two people are employed, one may be filling it with linen, while the other is mangling.

Such are the processes by which the rough, gray and dirty fabric brought in by the weaver, is converted into the smooth and snowy cloth ready for the hands of the seamstress. The processes vary a little in duration and frequency, according to the quality of the cloth to be bleached. Every thing is done by machinery or by chemical agents, and the large bleach-works require steam engines of considerable power. Human hands only convey the cloth from process to process. There is much beauty in many of the operations; and great skill is needed in the mere disposition of the several cisterns and machines, so that the goods may pass through the processes with the smallest expenditure of time. Large capital has been expended on many of the bleach-works; an extraordinary perfection has been attained in the machinery, and in all the details of the arrangements strict method and order prevail; the managers are men of science, who are eager to adopt every chemical and mechanical improvement that may occur to themselves or others. The processes above described can be performed in two or three days, at the cost of a half-penny per yard, on cloth bleached and finished.

A perfect understanding of the bleaching business is essential to success; great quantities of cloth were destroyed in the process, by those who first made the experiment in this country; and even now great care is necessary to prevent the fabrics being injured; but this, like every other branch of manufacture, is becoming more perfect, and is carried on with greater economy and order, and all which is essential to success. My limits forbid enlargement, which, for the importance of the subject, deserves a volume of itself, to explain all its branches and modifications.

CALICO PRINTING.

CHAPTER XI.

CALICO PRINTING.

" Truth is not local; God alike pervades
And fills the world of traffic and the shades,
And may be feared amidst the busiest scenes
Or scorn'd where business never intervenes."

COWPER.

We come now to treat of the important art of calico printing, which constitutes a very large branch of the cotton manufacture, and by means of which the value of calicoes, muslins, and other cotton fabrics, are greatly enhanced. Cotton cloth, when used for the outer garments of the female sex, the drapery of beds and windows, the coverings of furniture, and similar purposes, is ornamented with colours and patterns. Unlike silk and woollen fabrics, cottons are very rarely dyed of a uniform colour throughout; a variety of colours is fixed upon a single piece, and they are printed on the white cotton or muslin in an endless variety of patterns, thus giving a light and elegant effect to the print. The art of the calico printer, therefore, not only comprehends that of the dyer, which requires all the aid of chemical science, but also that of the artist, for the designing of tasteful and elegant patterns; that of the engraver, for transferring those patterns to the metal used to impress them on the cloth; and that of the mechanician, for the various mechanical processes of engraving and printing. Taste, chemistry, and mechanics, have been called the three legs of calico printing.

Calico printing is believed not to have been practised in Europe till the seventeenth century. In what country the art was first introduced is doubtful.

Calico printing has been the subject of modern improvements, which may be compared in importance with those in cotton spinning and bleaching. First was the block printing. But the grand improvement in the art was the invention of cylinder printing, which bears nearly the same relation in point of despatch to block printing by hand, as throstle or mule spinning bears to spinning by the one thread wheel.

This great invention is said to have been made by a Scotsman of the name of Bell, and it was first successfully applied in Lancashire, about the year 1785, at Morney, near Preston, by the house of Livesey, Hargreaves, Hull, & Co. ; celebrated for the extent of their concerns, and the magnitude of their failure in 1788, which gave a severe shock to the industry of that part of the country. This new mode of printing may be thus described :—A polished copper cylinder, several feet in length, (according to the width of the piece to be printed,) and three or four inches in diameter, is engraved with a pattern round its whole circumference, and from end to end. It is then placed horizontally in a press, and, as it revolves, the lower part of the circumference passes through the colouring matter, which is again removed from the whole surface of the cylinder, except the engraved pattern, by an elastic steel blade, placed in contact with the cylinder, and reduced to so fine and straight an edge as to take off the colour without scratching the copper. This blade has received the name of the doctor, which may be a workman's abbreviation of the word abductor, applied to it from the purpose which it answers ; or may have been given from a vulgar use of the word to doctor, meaning to set to rights. The colour being thus left only in the engraved pattern, the piece of calico or muslin is drawn lightly over the cylinder, which revolves in the same direction, and prints the cloth. After the piece is printed, it passes over several metallic boxes, six feet long, ten inches broad, and six inches deep, heated by steam, which dry it. A piece of cloth may be thus printed and dried in one or two minutes, which by the old method would require the application of the block 448 times. Nor is this all : two, three and even five cylinders may be used at the same time in one press ; each cylinder having engraved upon it a different portion of the pattern, and being supplied with a different colour. The piece passes over them successively, and receives the entire pattern almost at the same moment. To produce the same effect by hand block printing would have required 896, 1344, 1792, or 2240 applications of the blocks, according as two, three, four or five cylinders may have been employed. The saving of labour, therefore, is immense : one of the cylinder printing machines, attended by a man and a' boy, is actually capable of producing as much work as one hundred block printers and as many tear boys. But the course of improvement did not stop here. Another admirable invention, analogous to that just described, multiplied the advantage of cylinder printing.

The process of engraving itself, instead of being executed by the graver on the whole surface of the copper cylinder, is now performed by mechanical pressure, which transfers the pattern from a very small steel cylinder, only about three inches in length and one in diameter, to the copper cylinder three or four feet in length. The principle of this invention is the same which Mr. Jacob Perkins applied to the multiplication of plates for the printing of bank-notes, and Mr. Perkins has the reputation of being its inventor. Mr. Joseph Lockett, engraver for calico-printers in Manchester, introduced this system about the year 1808 : he may be consider-ed as at least one of the inventors, and he certainly did more than any other person to perfect it. The method of transferring is as follows :—The pattern intended to be engraved is so arranged in the first place by a drawing made to agree with the circumference of the copper cylinder, as that it will join and appear continuous when repeated. This is then carefully followed by the engraver, and cut or sunk on a small steel cylinder, about three inches long and one thick, so softened or decarbonised as to admit of being easily cut. The steel is then tempered or hardened, and by means of pressure against another cylinder of softened steel, a fac-simile is made in relief, that is, raised upon the surface. The second cylinder is then hardened in the same way, and it becomes hard enough to impress the whole engraving, even to the most delicate lines on the copper cylinder, when pressed against it in a machine. The small cylinder originally engraved is called the die ; the second cylinder, which is in relief, is called the mill. The latter is successively applied to the whole circumference of the copper cylinder, which is thus entirely covered with the pattern, as finely wrought as if it had been directly produced by the tool of the engraver. The surface of the die originally engraved is not more than about one-fiftieth part of the surface of the copper cylinder, and the engraving itself is therefore multiplied fifty-fold. By this means the most delicate designs, which would occupy an engraver as many months to effect by hand, can be completed in a few days ; of course the cylinders are produced at a much less price, and they may be executed in a very superior manner. Should the copper cylinder be so far worn as to require the pattern to be re-engraved, it can be done by the same process with amazing rapidity, and at a very trifling cost, as the mill is already prepared.

Other modes of transferring are practised. In some cases the die is cut on a flat surface, and the pattern transferred in relief to a cylinder, which again transfers it to the copper cylinder at proper distances on the surface. In other cases the die is cylin-drical, and the mill flat. When the design is very small, and requires to be repeated a great number of times on the copper cylinder, the pattern is engraved round the whole of the steel cylinder, so as to join or meet in the circumference, and at such equal distances that every repetition, or part forming the pattern, will fall into its fac-simile, like the teeth in a wheel. The mill is then placed in contact with and compressed into the copper cylinder, by means of machinery which is made to traverse by a spiral movement, until the whole of the copper cylinder is covered. By this means the most minute patterns are produced, such as human ingenuity could not accomplish by any other method. Sometimes the copper cylinders are etched, instead of being engraved,—a plan invented by Mr. John Bradbury of Manchester, extensively practised by Messrs. Joseph Lockett, jr. & Co.; and which is likely to prove of very great benefit to the printing business. The polished cylinder, having been heated, is covered with a thin coat of varnish, such as is used by historical engravers. The pattern is then traced on the cylinder with a diamond pointed tracer, by means of a most complicated and ingenious system of machinery, the invention of Mr. Lockett, sen.; and the varnish having been thus removed from the figure, the cylinder is immersed in aquafortis, and the parts exposed become corroded or engraved. The value of this process depends entirely on the beauty and novelty of the pattern. The tracing machinery is capable, like the kaleidoscope, of producing an endless variety of patterns, yet without being, like that instrument, dependent on mere accident for its changes. It has been so far perfected, that it will follow to a considerable extent designs made by persons perfectly unacquainted with its construction; and patterns may be produced by it which cannot be copied, or in many instances even imitated, by other means.

So great is the reputation acquired by the engravers of Manchester, from their skill and the perfection of their machinery, that orders are sent there for engraved cylinders from all parts of Europe and America where cylinder printing is practised; even though the cost and risk of getting them to their destination should treble or quadruple their original price.

The beautiful and admirable inventions we have described, do not complete éven the mechanical improvements in calico printing. It is still found necessary to execute parts of the patterns in fine goods with blocks, after the ground-work has been laid on by the cylinders; because different parts of the pattern, executed with different colours, cannot be made so exactly to fall into and fit with the other parts, by the cylinder as by the block. About the year 1802, an important improvement was made in the construction of blocks, for which the art is indebted to the workmen of London. Formerly all the blocks were cut in wood, like ordinary wood-cuts used in the prints of books, but the work was necessarily coarser, to endure the wear and tear of so many impressions; each piece of cloth, as has been stated, requires the application of the block 448 times, and, of course, 100 pieces would require its application 44,800 times. If the design, therefore, was fine and elaborate, the block would soon wear away. The improvement effected removes this objection. The pattern, instead of being cut in relief on the wood, is (in many cases), raised on the surface of a plain block, by pieces of flat copper, or brass wire, of various thicknesses and forms, produced by drawing the wire through dies of various shapes. These pieces of wire are set into the wood, and all stand exactly the same height, namely, about the eighth of an inch. The thicker parts of the pattern have merely the outline formed of copper, and they are filled up with felt. Blocks on this improved construction are ten-fold more durable than the old wooden blocks, and when the metal is worn down nearly to the surface of the wood, the last impression is as good as the first. The successful application of engraved copper cylinders to printing, was followed by that of cylindrical blocks, or engraved wooden rollers. This mode of printing, which is practised extensively in some establishments, is called surface-printing. The union of the two systems in the same machine, that is, of a wooden cylinder in relief with an engraved copper cylinder, forms what has been denominated the union or mule machine, and was the invention of Mr. James Burton, about the year 1805, whilst he was engineer in the establishment of Messrs. Peel & Co., of Church.

Many minor improvements have been made in the mechanical department of calico printing, but those which have been described are by far the greatest, and for ingenuity and beauty, as well as for productive power, they well deserve to rank with the more celebrated inventions in cotton spinning. The chemical department of printing has been not less rich in discoveries than the mechanical.

The proper use of mordants lies at the foundation of the dyer's art. The nature of mordants is thus explained by Dr. Thomson : " The term mordant is applied by dyers to certain substances with which the cloth to be dyed must be impregnated, otherwise the colouring matters would not adhere to the cloth, but would be removed by washing. Thus the red colour given to cotton by madder would not be fixed, unless the cloth were previously steeped in a solution of a salt of alumina. It has been ascertained that the cloth has the property of decomposing the salt of alumina. The red colouring principle of the madder has an affinity for this alumina, and combines with it. The consequence is that the alumina being firmly retained by the cloth, and the colouring matter by the alumina, the dye becomes fast, or cannot be removed by washing the cloth with water, even by the assistance of soap, though simple water is sufficient to remove the red colouring matter from the cloth, unless the alum mordant has been previously applied."

Mordant is also applied to certain substances, which have the property of altering the shade of colour, or of brightening the colour as it is called. The most valuable of all mordants is the acetated aluminous mordant, first employed by the calico-printers of England. By degrees they found out that sugar of lead and alum were the most important, and they discarded first one and then another of the ingredients they had been accustomed to mix with them, though without the aid of any chemical reasoning. The process of cylinder printing is very commonly employed to fix the mordant on the cloth, which is afterwards put into the dye-vat, when those parts only receive the colour which had previously been printed with the mordant, the other parts remaining white.

This was soon followed by the discovery of the process for producing what has been named resist-work, or neutral work. It consists in printing various mordants on those parts of the cloth intended to be coloured, and a paste or resist on such as are intended to remain white. It is the invention of a person named Grouse. It required the experience of a year or two to perfect this system, and make it practically useful. The house of Sir Robert Peel, of Bury, was the first to print by this plan so as to attract notice, 1802 : it is now one of the most beautiful and perfect of the operations of modern calico printing. The discovery of new facts, as well as the ingenious application of known ones, has enabled Mr. Mercer of Oakenshaw to make the bronze style his own, and literally to transmute the ores of manganese into ores of gold. This ingenious individual possesses a store of knowledge and facts unknown to scientific chemists, and sought for in vain in their latest works. It is to be hoped he will have both leisure and inclination at some time to present a portion of his labours to the world.

The large print-works of Lancashire are among the most interesting manufactories that can be visited. Several of the proprietors or managers are scientific men ; and being also persons of large capital, they have the most perfect machinery and the best furnished laboratories. All the processes through which the cloth has to pass, from the state in which it is left by the weaver, till it is made up a finished print ready for the foreign or home market, are performed in these extensive establishments. The bleaching, the block-printing, the cylinder-printing, the dyeing, the engraving, both of blocks and cylinders, the designing of patterns, and the preparation of colours, all go on within the same enclosure. Some of the print works employ as many as a thousand workpeople. The order and cleanliness of the works, and the remarkable beauty of most of the operations, impress the visitor with admiration and surprise. A printing establishment, like a cotton mill, is a wonderful triumph of modern science ; and when the mechanical and chemical improvements of both are viewed together, they form a splendid and matchless exhibition of science applied to the arts, and easily account for a rapidity of growth and a vastness of extension in the manufacture, which has no parallel in the records of industry.

Calico printing from cylinders.—Many of the patterns on printed calicoes are copies by printing from copper cylinders about four or five inches in diameter, on which the desired pattern has been previously engraved. One portion of the cylinders is exposed to the ink, whilst an elastic scraper of stuffed leather, by being pressed forcibly against another part, removes all superfluous ink from the surface previously to its reaching the cloth. A piece of calico twenty-eight yards in length rolls through this press, and is printed in four or five minutes.

Calico printing from blocks.—This is a mode of copying by surface-printing, from the ends of small pieces of copper wire, of various forms, fixed in a block of wood. They are all of one uniform height, about the eighth part of an inch above the surface of the wood, and are arranged by the maker into any required pattern. If the block be placed upon a piece of fine woollen cloth, on which ink of any colour has been uniformly spread, the projecting copper wires receive a portion which they give up when applied to the calico to be printed. By the former method of printing on calico, only one colour could be used ; but by this plan, after the flower of a rose, for example, has been printed with one set of blocks, the leaves may be printed of another colour by a different set.

The following account was sent me from Messrs. Marshall's establishment :—

STOCKPORT, January 20th, 1836.

The Hudson print works (Stockport) were first established in 1826 on a very small scale ; with one printing machine, small dye-house, and other necessary operations, such as bleaching, &c.; sufficient for printing about 3000 yards per day.   In the course of the year 1828 there were three printing machines imported from England, with all their necessary apparatus for dyeing the cloth by steam, and in the course of that and the two following years, the company were able to print 10,000 yards per day.   About this time a new bleaching house was requisite, as the first one was on too small a scale. And a new dye-house and other offices were needful to keep pace with the three printing machines.   In the year 1830 we had a severe fire, which burnt down the above bleaching house, and destroyed about 30,000 pieces of 30 yards each; say 900,000 yards.

At this time we erected other bleach works, competent to bleaching from four to five thousand pieces per week, and out of the ruins of the old bleaching house, which was a four story building, made a second dye-house.   This being accomplished we were able to finish regularly 2,000 pieces per week, of permanent madder colours, besides our navy blues, &c. making in all 2500 pieces, or 75,000 yards per week.   Our works now run much ahead of this. In our block shop we employ 42 block printers for printing by hand.   We have now increased our establishment to five printing machines, two of which print four colours at once and three of three colours each, of the very best models in England and lately imported.   With our present works, we can print an average of 120 pieces on each of these machines per day, making 600 pieces of 30 yards each, or 18,000 yards.   Or in one year of fifty weeks, 5,400,000 yards, worth on an average 18 cents per yard, equal to $972,000 per year in sales.   We employ about 250 hands, most of them men. We have every thing within ourselves for finishing the above in the first rate style of prints, either calicoes or furnitures.   From the above you will find that we have increased since 1826 to this time from 300 to 1800 yards per day, and those of as good and fast colours as can be made in either England, France, &c.

—

Hudson Calico Print Works, of Marshall, Carville, & Taylor.

The upper part of the calico works form a square; from the counting-house, which is at the entrance, we have a dry shed for drying the pieces, 200 feet long, running in a southerly direction; thence 200 feet east of the river, which supplies our water power.   From the office in a northerly direction is a space of 200 feet, in the middle of which runs one string of buildings, occupied as follows, measuring in all 500 feet in height :—

1. Blue dye-house,	90 feet long	4 stories.
2. Machine, &c. and making-up rooms,	100 do.	4 do.
3. Steaming and boiler rooms,	60 do.	4 do.
4. Drying and colour rooms,	80 do.	3 do.
5. Boiling and evaporating room,	70 do.	1 do.
6. Block cutting, engraving, and drawing rooms,	100 do.	2 do.

In a northerly direction there are 200 feet, which is taken up by a two story piazza of 130 feet, as a conveyance from the above string of buildings to the madder dye-house, runs in an easterly direction, making the square above mentioned.   In this square we have four other buildings: packing-room, where all our goods are packed for the market, our store-house for drugs, &c., one cloth room where all our printing cloths are stored secure from fire. The fourth is our block shop.

Besides the above buildings, we have our machine-shop, carpenter's shop, mills for grinding dye-woods, calenders for glazing, a dye-house, machine room, with three printing machine rooms, &c. for airing the goods after printing, with water power not half employed.

The madder dye house mentioned above, 286 feet long by 50 wide, I believe to be the largest ever built for that purpose; the main shaft frame water wheel being more than 300 feet long. Hoping this will give you some insight how far we have proceeded in calico printing, I remain your obedient servant, J. Taylor.

P.S. on the manufacturing of shirtings and fine printing cloths:—The two brothers, Joseph and Benjamin Marshall, having dissolved partnership, Benjamin Marshall at Troy has now all the factories; he makes the finest shirtings in the country, called the New York mills shirtings, besides the finest printing cloths.

Before the commencement of the printing bnsiness, the cotton manufacture was considered in a precarious condition; so that no one ventured on the finer fabrics, but since calico printing has been established, the cotton manufactures in the United States may safely be considered as built on a permanent basis.

The home consumption of cotton prints is immense; already the English and French articles have left our stores; and shortly printed goods will be sent to South America and other markets. Calico printing must therefore be considered of immense import- ance, both to the culture and manufacture of cotton. It is but yet in its infancy, and is capable of vast extension and improve- ment.

After the manufacture of the cloth is complete, there is the im- portant process of bleaching to be undergone by all cotton goods, by which the rough, gray, and dirty fabric brought in by the wea- ver, is converted into the smooth and snowy cloth ready for the hands of the sempstress. The processes vary a little in duration and frequency, according to the quality of the cloth to be bleached. Every thing is done by machinery or by chemical agents, and the large bleach works require steam engines of considerable power. Human hands only convey the cloth from process to process. There is much beauty in many of the operations; and great skill is needed in the mere disposition of the several cisterns and machines, so that the goods may pass through the processes with the smallest expenditure of time. Large capital has been expended in many of the bleach works in England; and extraordinary per- fection has been attained in the machinery and in all the details of the arrangements; strict method and order prevail; the managers are men of science, who are eager to adopt every chemical and mechanical improvement that may occur to themselves or to others. So greatly has bleaching been cheapened and quickened by the discoveries of modern science, that it costs only one cent a yard on the cloth bleached and finished.

Mr. Baines states that "the Americans print few of their cloths;" this must have referred to past information. From the calculations I have been able to make, one hundred and twenty millions of yards have been printed in the United States the last year, ending the 1st of April, 1836. And the prospect of an advance in quantity and quality is very great, as the demand justifies every exertion and improvement. In Rhode Island and Massachusetts the printing establishments are very considerable:—P. Allen, Providence; Sprague, Cranston; Crawford Allen, Pawtucket; one at Lowell, one at Taunton, and one at Fall River; one at Dover, New Hampshire; two at East Madden, Cheshire, two or three in New Jersey, and ten or twelve in Pennsylvania. The bleaching business is generally connected with the calico printing, as is the case of the Marshall's at Hudson.*

* The repeal of the print duty in England has proved highly beneficial, having given a stimulus both to production and to improvement. To the consumer it is a great relief, especially to the poor, as a woman can now buy a useful and respectable printed dress for *half-a-crown*, which before the repeal of the duty was a third more. A printed dress of good materials and a neat pattern, with fast colours, may now be bought for two shillings, or forty-seven cents. The large print works of Lancashire are among the most interesting manufactories that can be visited. Several of the proprietors or managers are scientific men; and being also persons of large capital, they have the most perfect machinery and the best furnished laboratories. All the proceeses through which the cloth has to pass, from the state in which it is left by the weaver, till it is made up a finished print ready for the foreign or home market, are performed in these extensive establishments. The bleaching, the block printing, the cylinder printing, the dyeing, the engraving both of blocks and cylinders, the designing of patterns, and the preparation of colours, all go on within the same enclosure. Some of the print-works employ as many as a thousand work-people. The order and cleanness of the works, and the remarkable beauty of most of the operations, impress the visiter with admiration and surprise.

Representation
of the different ages of the Silk worm

B. Chambers Engraver   City of Washington

CHAPTER XII.

SILK MACHINERY.

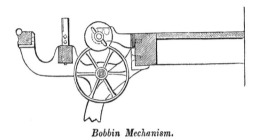

Bobbin Mechanism.

The plate annexed represents the series of changes from the formation of the egg to the death of the silk moth. We shall explain it with reference to the figures that are marked upon it.

1. The egg, or the development and birth of the silk-caterpillar.

2. The silk-worms, during the first age, till their first moulting.

3. Rearing of the worms in the second age.

4. The worms in their third age.

5. Rearing of the silk-worm in the fourth age.

6. The rearing of the silk-worms during the fifth age, until the completion of the cocoon.

7. A species of silk-worm of a dark gray colour, with singular marks.

8. The cocoons.

9. Two open cocoons, or cocoons with their grubs. The upper one contains only the shell of a developed chrysalis, but in the lower is seen the immature chrysalis, with the skin of the late moth.

10. A cocoon, from which the butterfly is near emerging.

11. A cocoon from which the butterfly has already escaped.

12. Two butterflies in the act of coupling.

13. The female moth laying eggs.

14. Raw silk, of a yellow or white colour.

15. Here is represented the excremental substance of the silk-worm, in its first and last age.

The silk-worm is a robust little animal, and its organisation is

simple ; but the rearing of it is often so defective, that, notwithstanding its sound constitution, it frequently perishes from the ill
management it experiences in its rearing.

It must not be concealed, that some antagonists of this industry
have maintained that it is injurious to the human constitution.
But this is a mere prejudice, or a vain pretence.   No human being
has yet suffered, bodily, from this cause.

Silk Engine or Swift

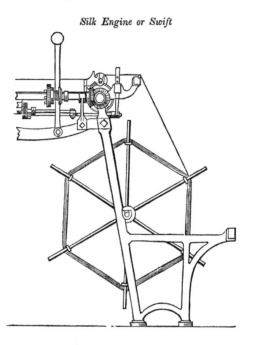

The machinery of the silk filature, from Dr. Ure.—These filatures
are very simple ; but the throwing-mills, for doubling and twisting silk, are most elaborate constructions.   Ever since they were
remodeled by Fairbairn, and upon the cotton-throstle plan, they
are incomparably superior in convenience, precision and speed of
performance, to what they formerly were in England, and still are
in other parts of Europe.   When these mechanicians took the
silk-mill in hand, the spindles moved at the rate of only 1,200
revolutions per minute : they forthwith raised it to 3,000,—a velocity since increased to 4,500 by Ritson, a cotton mill mechanic,
in whose favour they resigned this branch of engineering.   The
representations inserted are parts of a complete series of drawings
made, under my inspection, from the latest and most improved
silk-throwing machinery erected by him.   The first operation

which raw silk undergoes in the factory, is its transfer, from skeins upon bobbins, in diagonal lines; so that the ends of the threads may be readily found, in case of breakage. The bobbins are wooden cylinders of such thickness as not to injure the filaments by sudden flexure, which smaller cylinders would do, and to be able to receive a considerable length of thread without materially increasing their diameters; and, of course, their surface velocity in revolving.

The winding machine, called the engine, consists of a long wooden table, for laying out the skeins upon. These are called *swifts*, because, though they turn slowly round with the revolving bobbins, yet they do their work quickly, compared with hand-winding machines.

Doubling Engine.—In the doubling of silk, where two or three threads are wound, parallel together, upon one bobbin, an ingenious contrivance is employed to stop the winding whenever one of the threads happens to break.

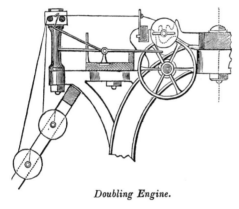

Doubling Engine.

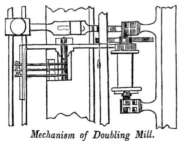

Mechanism of Doubling Mill.

The machine for twisting the single threads of silk, either before the doubling or after the doubling, is called the *spinning-mill*, sometimes also the throwing-mill; though the latter term often

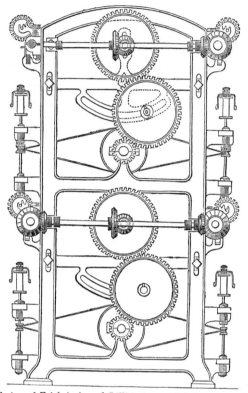

End view of Fairbairn's and Lillie's improved Silk Spinning Mill.

includes all the departments of a silk-mill. The section above, of
this apparatus, shows four equal working lines, namely, two on
each side of the frame, one tier being over the other. In some
spinning mills there are three tiers, but the uppermost is a little
troublesome to manage, as it requires the attendant to mount a
stool or steps.

Silk undergoes certain preparations. The hanks of the raw
silk are soaked in tepid soap-water in a tub; but the bobbins of the
spun silk are steamed by inclosing a basket full of them within a
wooden steam case, for about ten minutes. The bobbins are then
removed into a cistern of warm water, from which they are taken
to the doubling frame. It is probable that the power-loom will be
applied to the weaving of fancy, as well as plain goods; which
will give a great impulsion to the silk trade of England. Sharp
& Roberts will readily furnish the requisite machinery for producing any wished-for design, however complicated. What is to
prevent its introduction into America? In silk establishments, the

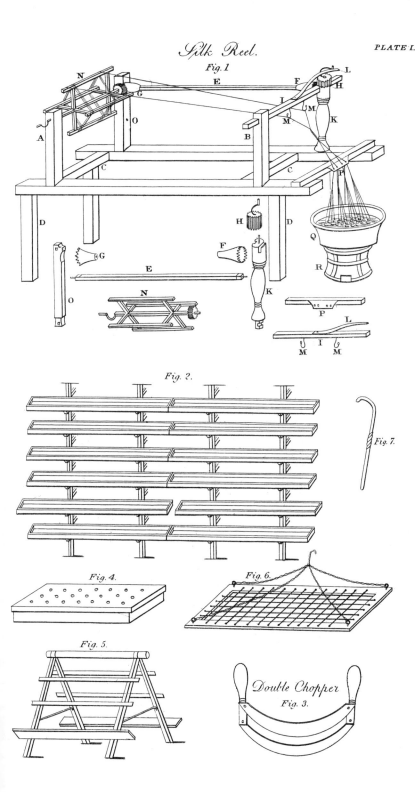

PLATE I.

Silk Reel.

Fig. 1

Fig. 2.

Fig. 7.

Fig. 4.

Fig. 6.

Fig. 5.

Double Chopper

Fig. 3.

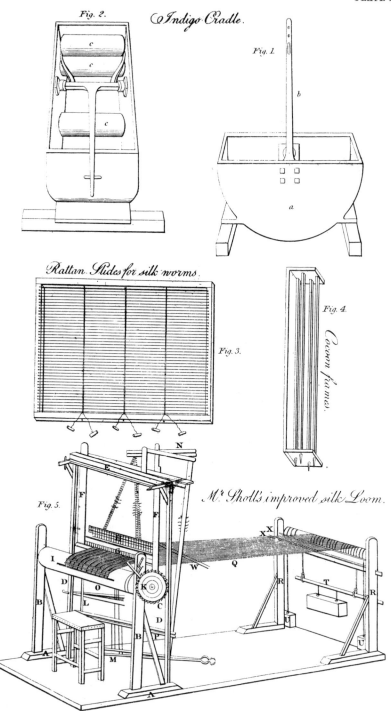

PLATE II.

Fig. 2.

Indigo Cradle.

Fig. 1.

Rattan Slides for silk worms.

Fig. 3.

Fig. 4.

Cocoon frames.

Fig. 5.

Mr. Sholl's improved silk Loom.

machinery can be, and often is, employed from three to six hours after the hands have left work. When water-power is used, the portion of the silk-machinery which contains the swifts, generally works all night without being tended.

NATURE AND OPERATIONS OF A SILK FACTORY.

The silk worm was first rendered serviceable to man in China, about 2700 years before the Christian era. From that country the art of rearing it passed into India and Persia. It was only at the beginning of the sixteenth century that two monks brought some eggs of the silk worm to Constantinople, and promulgated some information on the growth of the caterpillars. This knowledge became, under the emperor Justinian, productive of a new source of wealth to the European nations. In 1564, Traucat, a common gardener of Nismes, laid the first foundation of a nursery of white mulberry trees, with such success as to enable them to be propagated within a few years over all the southern provinces of France.

This insect is first an egg, which the warmth of spring brings forth : and this, as it enlarges, progressively casts its skin three or four times, according to the variety of the insect. This caterpillar at the end of twenty-five or thirty days having attained maturity of size, ceases to eat for the remainder of its life, merely discharges its excrementitious matter by spinning a cocoon, within which it is changed into a chrysalis. In fifteen or twenty days they come out, a couple of butterflies, male and female.

The eggs of the silk worm are covered with a liquid, which glues them to the piece of paper on which the female lays them ; and they may be freed from it by dipping them in cold water, and afterwards drying them. They should be preserved at the temperature of from 54° to 59° Farenheit. When the heats of April begin to be felt, they must not be suffered to act on the eggs, because they would bring on incubation before the first shoots of the mulberry have come forth to supply food to the young worms. This period should be kept back also, because it is proper to hatch almost all the eggs together, or at least in successive broods corresponding to the extent of the breeding establishment. The eggs may be laid in a stove room, and exposed to a warmth gradually increasing, till it reaches the temperature of 86° Fahrenheit, at which it must be kept stationary. Nature finishes the work of incubation in eight or ten days. The teeming seed is now covered with a sheet of paper pierced with holes, about one twelfth of an inch in diameter, through which the young worms creep upwards instinctively to get at the mulberry leaves previously placed above. Whenever the leaves become loaded with worms, they are transferred to plates of wicker work covered with grey paper. This transfer is repeated twice every day.

In the course of from forty-eight to seventy-two hours the whole of the eggs should be hatched. The nursery for breeding the worms ought to be a well aired apartment, free from damp, cold, and excess of heat, from rats and other destructive vermin. For breeding twenty-one ounces avoirdupois of seed, the chamber should be thirty-three feet wide by eighty feet long, and be provided with fire-places for heating and ventilating it; the window casements should be glazed. The temperature must not be allowed to fall under 66° Fahrenheit; it may be raised to 92° Fahrenheit, or even higher; but from 68° to 86° Fahrenheit, is the ordinary range. A current of air should be admitted to purify the atmosphere from the fetid emanations of the caterpillars, their excrements, and the decayed leaves. Light is nowise unfavourable; but may be regarded as in some respects advantageous. A spare room should be set apart for the diseased worms.

A few osier mats may suffice while the worms are young, but more are required in proportion as they grow larger, to prevent their getting piled on each other. The supply of leaves must be proportional to the age of the brood, and ought to be increased when nothing but their ribs are left. The very young should be fed with leaves minced small, and should not be troubled with the removal of the litter, which is trifling. At a future stage it must be removed with delicacy, to give the worms more air, on the new wicker frames, without parting them too far.

Before each moulting, the worm has a keen appetite, but during that process it loses it entirely, and falls into a languid state, from which it immediately revives on casting its skin. The pieces of paper are withdrawn from the bottom of the wicker-frames to permit a free transmission of air between their interstices, whenever the worms have become large enough not to fall through them. After the second moulting, they are half an inch long, and may then be transported from the smaller apartment, in which they are hatched, into the larger one, where they are to be reared to maturity. They must be well cleaned from the litter on this occasion, laid upon fresh leaves, and supplied with a succession of them, cut in pieces, every six hours. After the third moult, the worms may be fed with entire leaves; for they are then extremely voracious, and must not be stinted in their diet. The same remark is still more applicable to the period after the fourth moult. The heat should now be limited to 68° or 70° Fahrenheit. In every period of their existence, the silk worms are liable to a variety of diseases, under which they derive benefit from the exposure of portions of chloride of lime in their nurseries. When they have reached the fifth stage, they cease to eat ; they void their excrements, diminish in bulk, become somewhat semi-transparent, abandon the leaves, try to crawl on the upright posts, and to conceal themselves in corners. These symptoms indicate the development of the spinning instinct. Green oak twigs are to be laid in parallel rows on the wicker tablets in the form of little alleys, eighteen inches wide, with their little ramifications interwoven above. The worms of two tablets are to be collected on one, and freed from all their litter. Little coils of paper and of wood shavings are placed alongside of the diligent worms first, and, after a while, of the lazier ones. The creature sets itself to construct its cocoon, throwing about its thread in different directions, forming the floss, filoselle, or outer open net work. But it soon begins its regular operation of winding round about, in nearly parallel lines, a fine thread into an egg-shaped form, in the centre of which the caterpillar sits at work. The matter of the silk is liquid in the body of the worm, but it hardens in the air. The twin filaments, which the animal always spins through its double tubular mouth, are agglutinated by that liquid cement. The same matter may be extracted in a lump from the body of the worm, and drawn out artificially into a thin transparent web, or into threads of variable diameters. The cocoons are completed in the course of three or four days, after which they must be removed from the branches and sorted, the finest being reserved for seed worms. The cocoons which are to be unwound must not be allowed to remain with the worms ten or twelve days alive within them ; for if the chrysalis has time to come out, the cocoon would be cut through, and be useless. The animal must be killed by suffocation, which is effected either by exposing the cocoons for five days to the sunshine, by placing them in a hot oven, or in the steam of boiling water.

The erection of the first mill in England for the manufacture of silk was at Derby. The original mill, called the Silk Mill to denote its pre-eminence, being the first and largest of its kind ever erected in England, stands upon an island in the river Derwent. Its history remarkably denotes the power of genius, and the vast influence which even the enterprises of an individual has on the commerce of a country. The Italians were long in the exclusive possession of the art of silk throwing, and the merchants of other

nations were consequently dependent on that people for their participation in a very lucrative article of trade, and were frequently
deprived of their fair profits by exorbitant prices charged for the
original material.   This state of things continued till the commencement of the last century, when a person named Crotchet
erected a small mill near the present works, with an intention of
introducing the silk manufacture into England; but his machinery
being inadequate to the purpose, he quickly became insolvent, and
the design was for some time abandoned.   In the year 1715, a
similar idea began to expand in the mind of an excellent mechanic
and draughtsman, John Lombe, who though young, resolved on
the perilous task of traveling into Italy, to procure drawings or
models of the machines necessary for the undertaking.   In Italy
he remained some time, but as admission to the silk-works was
prohibited, he could only obtain access by corrupting two of the
workmen, through whose assistance he inspected the machinery in
private ; and whatever parts he obtained a knowledge of during
these visits, he recorded on paper before he slept.   By perseverance
in this mode of conduct, he made himself acquainted with the
whole ; and had just completed his plan, when his intention was
discovered, and his life being in extreme hazard, he flew with pre-
cipitation, and took refuge on ship-board.   The two Italians who
had favoured his scheme, and whose lives were in equal danger
with his own, accompanied him, and they all soon landed in safety
in England : this happened in 1717.   Fixing on Derby as a proper place for his purpose, he agreed with the corporation for an
island, or swamp, in the river, 500 feet long, and 52 wide, at a
rent somewhat below £8 yearly.   Here he established his silk-mill ;
but during the time employed in its construction, he erected temporary machines in the town-hall, and various other places; by
which means he not only reduced the prices of silk far below the
Italians, but was likewise enabled to proceed with his great undertaking, though the charges amounted to nearly £30,000.   In the
year 1718 he procured a patent to enable him to secure the profits
thus arising from his address and ingenuity, for the term of fourteen years; but his days verged to a close, and before half this
period had elapsed, treachery and poison had brought him to the
grave.   The Italians, whose trade rapidly decreased from the
success of the new establishment, were exasperated to vengeance,
and vowed the destruction of the man whose ingenuity had thus
turned the current of their business into another channel.

It is in the production of the patterns of silk goods, that the
French have a decided advantage over the British; they probably

have little or none after the design is put into the loom. The modes in which taste is cultivated at Lyons deserve particular study and imitation in this country. Among the weavers of the place, the children and every body connected with devising patterns, much attention is devoted to every thing any way connected with the beautiful either in figure or colour. Weavers may be seen in their holiday leisure gathering flowers, and grouping them in the most engaging combinations. They are continually suggesting new designs to their employers, and are thus the fruitful source of elegant patterns. There is hardly any considerable house in Lyons, in which there is not a partner who owes his place in it to his success as an artist. The town of Lyons is so conscious of the value of such studies, that it contributes 20,000 francs per annum to the government establishment of the school of arts, which takes charge of every youth who shows an aptitude for drawing, or imitative design of any kind, applicable to manufactures. Hence all the eminent painters, sculptors, even botanists and florists of Lyons, become eventually associated with the staple trade, and devote to it their happiest conceptions. The French manufacturer justly considers that his pattern is the principal element of his success in trade ; for the mere handiwork of weaving is a simple affair, with the improved Jacquard loom. He therefore visits the school, and picks out the boy who promises, by taste and invention, to suit his purpose the best. The French weaver prides himself upon his knowledge of design ; he will turn over several hundred patterns in his possession, and descant on their relative merits, seldom erring far in predicting the success of any new style. By this disposition the minds of the silk-weavers in France become elevated and refined. In flower patterns, their designs are remarkably free from incongruities, being copied from nature with scientific precision. They supply taste to the whole world in proportion to the extent of their exportations. There are also weaving schools; in these, a pattern being exhibited, they are required to exercise their invention as to the best means of producing the design on a piece of silk goods. Their superiority in art is turned to good account in many other manufactures.

England beheld, with no small degree of jealousy, the prodigious plantations of mulberry trees in France, the increasing production of silk, and the consequent multiplication of silk manufactures. James I. accordingly endeavoured to introduce this industry into his own kingdom; and, in 1608, a most earnest appeal was made to the British public, in regard to the advantages that might be derived from the plantation of mulberry trees; but nothing was done : and only as late as 1820, was this subject seriously taken up ; some inconsiderable experiments having sufficiently established the fact, that these trees, and the precious insects which feed upon them, thrive as well in England as in France. But long before that epoch, silk manufactures had flourished, to a considerable extent, in England ; the raw silk being imported from Italy. There existed already, in 1629, so many of these establishments in London, that the weavers of the city and of the environs were divided into corporations; and, in 1661, the individuals which composed them were more than 40,000 in number.

The revocation of the edict of Nantes, in 1685, contributed greatly to the future progress of this industry; the most skilful French weavers having taken refuge in England. Next to this cause of the rapid progress of this manufacture, must be mentioned the silk machine erected at Derby, in 1719. The reputation of the English fabrics increased at length to such a degree, that even in Italy English silk commanded a higher price than the Italian.

Silk has long been a profitable production of Georgia, and other parts of the United States ;* and may be increased, it is presumed, as fast as the demand will rise. This is the strongest of all raw materials, and the great empire of China, though abounding with cottton, finds it the cheapest clothing for her people.

Tench Coxe says, (1789):—" We have a large nursery of the white Italian mulberry established here this summer. Within ourselves, little can be expected ; but the idea of the nursery has been encouraged upon this principle, that it prepares things for an emigration from a silk country. This, perhaps, is refining, but the expense is small ; the trees are wanted to replace those destroyed by the British army; and the measure falls in with our plan, to foster and encourage, but not to force, manufactures."

* Extract from a description of Carolina, 1727. By Daniel Coxe, Esq. —" The father of Daniel Coxe was the first proprietor of the English province of Carolina. The vast trouble and expense of Governor Coxe, will scarcely be credited; for he not only, at his sole charge, for several years, established and kept up a correspondence with the governors, and chief Indian traders in all the English colonies, on the continent of America, employed many people on discoveries, by land, to the west, north and south of this vast extent of ground, but likewise, in the year 1698, he equipped and fitted out two ships, provided with above thirty great guns, sixteen patereroes, abundance of small arms, amunition, stoies and provisions of all sorts, not only for the use of those on board, and for discovery by sea, but also for building a fortification, and settling a colony by land; there being, in both vessels, besides sailors and common men, above thirty English and French

HISTORICAL SUMMARY OF THE ART OF DYEING.

The desire of attracting public admiration may be observed even in the least civilised state of society. Among the means of distinction which are eagerly laid hold of, the glare of colours is one of the most obvious. The art of dyeing, therefore, has unquestionably a very ancient origin; for when nature afforded colouring substances of easy application, there might arise, among people but slightly civilised, methods of dyeing which have been sought after by polished nations. Thus the Gauls prepared some dyes which were not disdained by the Romans. But for its enlargement and perfection, the art required to follow the progress of manufactures and luxury. The Egyptians had discovered a mode of dyeing analogous to that of our printed calicoes. Cloths, impregnated probably with different mordants, were plunged in a bath in which they assumed different colours.

It is to Greece that our attention turns when we wish to ascertain the progress which the human mind has made in antiquity.

volunteers, some noblemen, and all gentlemen. One of these vessels discovered the mouth of the great and famous river, Mississippi, entered and ascended it above one hundred miles, and would have had perfected a settlement therein, if the captain of the other ship had done his duty and not deserted them. They however took possession of this country in the king's name, and left, in several places, the arms of Great Britain affixed on boards and trees for a memorial thereof. This was the first ship that ever entered that river from the sea, or that perfectly discovered or described its several mouths, in opposition to the boasts and falsities of the French, who assume to themselves the honour of both; Providence seeming to reserve the glory, of succeeding in so noble an enterprise, to the zeal and industry of a private subject of England, which was twice, in vain, attempted by Louis XIV. of France, the most ambitious and powerful monarch of Europe. King William promised Governor Coxe to assist him in settling the province, but died before the accomplishment of his design.

" To the king's most excellent majesty,—' In obedience to your majesty's commands, signified to us by the right honourable Secretary Vernon, upon the petition of Dr. Coxe, in relation to the province of Carolina: We have considered his petition, and humbly crave leave to represent unto your Majesty, that your Majesty's Attorney General, upon the perusal of letters patent, and conveyances produced to him by Dr. Coxe, has reported to us his opinion, that Dr. Coxe has a good title, in law, to the said province of Carolina, extending from 31 to 36 degrees of north latitude, inclusive, on the continent of America, and to several adjacent islands.'

"Signed, STAMFORD, LEXINGTON, P. MEADOWS, WM. BLATHWAIT, JOHN POLLEXTREN, ABRAHAM HILL, GEORGE STEPNEY.

" *Whitehall*, December 21, 1699."

The petition was signed, D. COXE.

Ever since philosophy has taken observation for a guide, and, abandoning the illusions of systems, has adhered to the study of the phenomena of nature, and of the real properties to which they owe their origin, it has followed the chain of the numerous wonders which it has analysed, in subserviency to the welfare of society. It has recognised in manufacturing industry, as well as in commerce, the source of the prosperity of the nation, the germ of a great population, the principal support of agriculture. National industry is augmented and enlightened by a free communication of the processes it employs. India is the nursery of that knowledge and those arts which were subsequently diffused and improved among other nations.*

ON DYEING COTTON AND SILK.

To dye skein cotton yellow.—The same operations as those in the first common red dye are to be used here; to one pound of cotton four ounces of roche alum, and from one to four pounds of weld.

When dyed the cotton is to be worked in hot, but not boiling, liquor, consisting of four ounces of sulphate of copper to every pound of cotton; it is then to be boiled for three hours in a solution containing four ounces of soap to every pound of cotton.

When a dark or *jonquil colour* is wanted, no alum is used; of weld take two pounds and a half, very little verdegris, or a little alum in its stead, but nothing else. For brightening, however, boiling in a solution of soap is in all cases necessary.

On dyeing and re-dyeing cotton furniture yellow.—If the furniture, such as rough or finished cotton or cambric, intended for yellow linings for bed or window curtains, be in a perfect bleached state, which is now generally the case, according to the number of the pieces so must the size of the copper be to boil the weld in for the yellow dye. A small copper holding four or five pails would do for three pieces of twenty-eight yards each. The weld may be purchased by the half bundle, the bundle, or the load. Half a bundle would be enough for the above quantity of cotton, if a moderate yellow is wanted. The weld must be increased or decreased according as the pattern approaches a straw, a canary, a lemon, or towards a gold colour or orange.

The weld must be boiled about twenty minutes, the liquor then strained off

---

* Mr. John Wilson, of Ainsworth, near Manchester, an extremely ingenious dyer and manufacturer, who more than sixty years since gained both celebrity and wealth by the great improvements he introduced into the art of dyeing, had obtained from the Greeks of Smyrna the secret of dyeing Turkey red, which he described in two essays; but it is stated that he found this too tedious and expensive a process, less suited to manufactured goods than to cotton in the skein, nor even suited to that spun upon the single spindles then in use, though it might be applicable to that spun on machines.

PLATE III

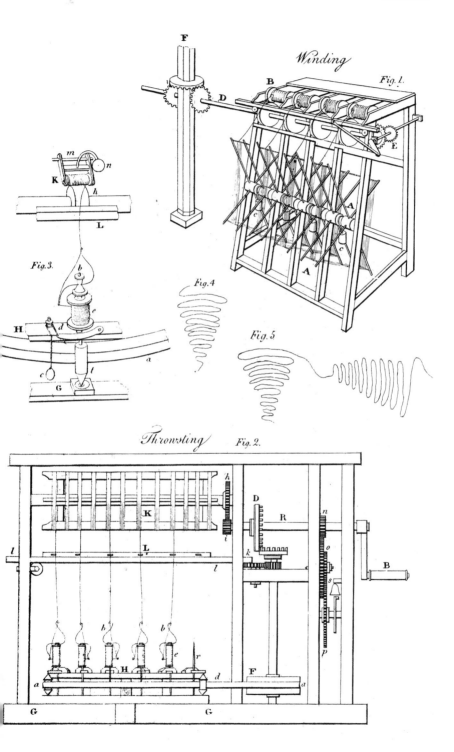

F

Winding

B

Fig. 1.

D

E

c

A

c

A

m

n

K

h

L

Fig. 3.

b

c

H

d

e

c

l

G

a

Fig. 4.

Fig. 5.

Throwsting *Fig. 2.*

h

D

R

n

K

o

l

L

l

k

B

s

b

b

e

r

p

H

d

F

a

a

G

G

Shenton's Tramming Engine.

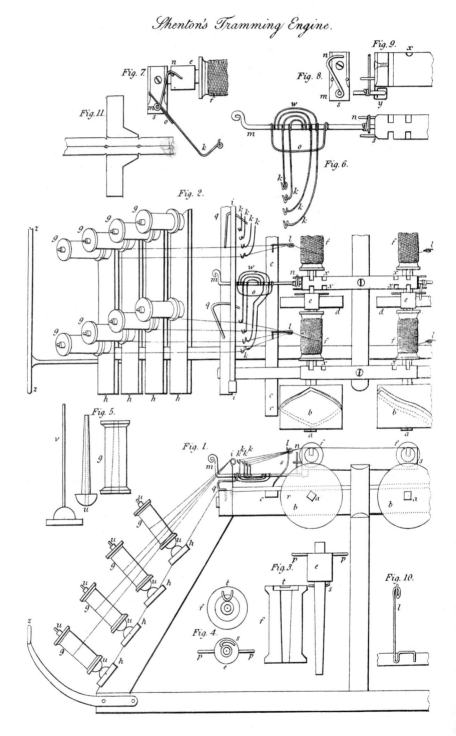

Fig. 9.

Fig. 7.

Fig. 8.

Fig. 11.

Fig. 6.

Fig. 2.

Fig. 5.

Fig. 1.

Fig. 3.

Fig. 4.

Fig. 10.

into a proper tub, and the weld boiled again. While the boilings are going on, three tubs, being wine pipes cut in two, must be got ready, and made particularly clean, being also previously seasoned for the work. One is to receive the boiled weld with some cold water to regulate it to the heat which the hand will bear; the other is for water, and as much alum liquor as will colour it and make it taste strong; and the third is to contain clear water to wash the furniture off.

Whatever yellow is in *fashion* (or indeed any fashionable colour,) has commonly a *fashionable name*. But if the dyer can, by his experience, proportion his drugs to the weakest, and from that to the strongest shade, let the name be what it may, after he has a set of patterns of his own dyeing, he will see, upon the first sight of any colour, how to set about it.

In the present instance let the pattern be a moderately pale colour of yellow ; then put all the first boiling of the weld in the first tub, and cool down as above directed. Two or three persons should then work the pieces quick from end to end by the selvages; that they may be even, two may do this ; one of whom must be an expeditious hand to work them and keep them even. When they have been edged over six or seven times, they are to be folded upon a board laid over the tub, and wrung as dry as possible by two persons. When they are all out, they are passed in the same manner through the tub of alum, and, after six or seven turns, they are to be taken out of the alum liquor, wrung as before, and then washed off.

By this time the second weld liquor will be boiled ; some of the first must be thrown away, and the second weld liquor added in its place. The goods are then passed through as before, and wrung out; the alum liquor being strengthened, they are passed through it, wrung out as before, and then washed off: the water in the wash tub having been changed.

In some instances verdegris is used instead of alum ; and in other cases it is used in addition to the alum. For some shades old fustic is used instead of weld, and sulphate of copper instead of verdegris.

The alum solution, and the sulphate of copper, and the verdegris, or acetate of copper, should be always ready. It is necessary to have a tub for each, in size proportioned to the work to be done; but larger for the alum than for the other two.

Sulphate of iron is also used in some dark grays, browns, slates, and in all blacks; this will require a tub as large or larger than that for alum.

When the yellows are dyed and wrung as dry as possible, they should be taken into a close room or stove to dry, particularly in London, because of the smoke, especially in winter. A German, or other stove, should be placed in the room, the size of which, as well as the number of the stoves, must be regulated by the quantity of work. When the goods are dry they must be sent to the calenderers, if directed to be calendered ; but the general and better way is to stiffen them with starch after they are dyed, and before they are dry ; and when dry they should be sent to the glaziers, instead of the calenderers, except when both branches are carried on by the same person.

When furniture, originally yellow, has become faded, it may be re-dyed thus: in this case it should be dyed rather of a fuller shade than the original. A large flat tub, such as described above, is to be filled three parts full of water, to which sufficient sulphuric acid must be added to make it taste strongly sour. After being well stirred, the pieces are to be put in, and worked in this sour liquor; and the yellow dye in consequence is stripped off. If the acid liquor be not strong enough, more acid must be added, with the precaution of well mixing it with the water, and the goods must be passed through the liquor again: by these means the yellow is discharged. They are then to be taken out on a board upon the tub and wrung by two persons; then to be washed off and wrung, washed and wrung again, when they are fit to be dyed.

It is still to be remembered that any faded or worn out colour, or that goods more or less decayed, seldom become so bright as the colour which a new piece of goods receives from the same dye.

Some cloths for re-dyeing require the application of oxymuriate or chloride of lime to discharge their colours, particularly when madder, galls, &c. form the constituent parts of the dye. In this case if a *bleacher* be near it might be best to let him perform the process with the oxymuriate of lime; not only from the pernicious nature, but also from the expense of it, which, unless the business be upon a large scale, will not pay the dyer for his trouble.

However, if the dyer thinks proper to perform this operation, then the oxymuriate of lime or bleacher's ashes, &c. may be obtained at the dry-salters and dissolved in a cask, and the clear liquor used in proportion to the quantity of goods, the colour of which is intended to be discharged, which, when done, should be washed off in two waters at least before they are dyed.

To dye cotton skein a duck's wing green and olive.—This is performed by a blue ground, next galling, dipping in the black vat, then in the weld dye, then in verdegris, remembering to wash off previously to performing each process.

Olive is to be performed with weld or old fustic, verdegris, and Brazil wood.

Of browns, marcons, coffee colours, &c.—It would answer little purpose to enlarge this treatise with a detail of all the possible methods of producing the various shades of these several colours, the whole consisting in the use of galls, verdegris, sulphate of copper, weld, and madder.

By welding a stuff previously maddered for *red* you may produce a *gold* colour; and by dipping the same red in a blue vat you obtain a *plum* colour.

Observations on silk.—Silk as it is obtained from the cocoons of the worm, is generally of an orange or yellow colour, more or less dark; in the south of France it is generally very dark: its natural shade is unfavourable to all other colours. It is also imbued with a kind of varnish or gum, which makes it stiff and hard; this stiffness is improper in the fabrication of most silk stuff, it is therefore *ungummed,* as it is called, by the following processes:—

On ungumming and boiling silk.—Observe, that throughout the following processes for silk *white* soap is directed to be used; and, generally speaking, we believe it will be found the best, more especially for the more delicate operations. Yet Mr. M'Kernan, in his process for ungumming silk, directs yellow soap and soft soap in equal parts, and of the same weight as the silk to be used: he adds, however, that different sorts of silk require more or less soap; the best rule he finds, nevertheless, is *the same weight of soap as of silk;* and he says also, that yellow soap and soft soap of the best quality he finds the best for this purpose.

The silk is divided into hanks, each hank is tied with a string, several of these are tied together (a handful of them) by putting a piece of string through each separate skein, and tying the piece of string in a long tie, to slip easily when they are wanted to be untied.

A liquor is prepared of thirty pounds of *white* soap to a hundred pounds of silk; the soap is cut into small pieces and boiled in water, when it is dissolved the fire is damped.

While the liquor is preparing, the skeins of silk are put on rods; as soon as the soap liquor becomes a little below boiling heat (for it should not boil, as boiling would tangle the silk) the silk is to be put into it in an oblong copper, being nearly full; it is to remain in the liquor till its gummy matter has left it, which will be seen by its whiteness and flexibility. It is then turned end for end on the rods, that the part above the liquor may undergo the same operation. As soon as this is accomplished the silk is taken out of the copper, the hanks which were first turned being soonest done.

The hanks are now to be taken from the rods to the peg, disentangled, and nine or ten of them put on one cord, this cord passing through the string that tied each hank. When the whole is corded it is put into pockets of coarse strong white linen, fifteen inches wide and five feet long, closed at each end and on one side; when the silk is put in, the pocket is sewed all along the other side with packthread, and fastened with a knot; four pockets will hold the whole hundred pounds.

The pockets being thus ready another liquor is prepared like the first. When ready, and the boiling checked with cold water, the pockets are put in and boiled well for a quarter of an hour, checking with cold water in order to prevent its boiling over; it is necessary also to turn the bags about often with a pole, or rather let two persons have a pole each for this purpose. This operation is called boiling.

In addition to the processes of boiling with soap, as above directed, Mr. M'Kernan recommends that the silk should be winched through a copper of water at the heat of 160°, having two pounds of soda (barilla) dissolved in it, then winch or wash in water, and wring and dry.

In the boiling of silks for common colours twenty pounds of soap will do for a hundred weight of silk; but, as in this case, the silk is not ungummed, it should boil for three hours and a half, adding water to supply the evaporation.

The silks intended for the greatest degree of white, either to remain white, or for the fabrication of white stuff, are boiled twice in soap and water; those that are to be dyed of different colours are boiled but once, and with a smaller quantity of soap, because the little remaining redness is by no means prejudicial to many colours. Different quantities of soap are, however, necessary for different colours.

Silk designed for blue, iron gray, brimstone, or any other colour requiring a very white ground, should be done according to the preceding process, and have thirty pounds of soap.

When the silk is boiled it is taken out of the copper by two men with poles, and placed in a clean barrow; they are then taken to a long shallow trough, from which the water may run away, the pockets are opened, and the silks examined; such as have yellow or lemon colour spots remaining are boiled again for some time, till the spots are removed. After unpocketing, the whole is dressed on the pegs.

Silk loses from twenty-five to twenty-eight per cent. of its weight in ungumming and whitening. The bags of silk should never be suffered to lie long together before they are emptied after being boiled, as their doing so would make the silk hard.

White silk, as before observed, is distinguished into five principal shades, namely, *China white, India white, thread* or *milk white, silver white,* and *azure white.*

The three first are prepared and boiled as has already been shown. Silver and azure white in the preparation or ungumming, thus: take fine powdered indigo, put it into water boiling hot, when settled the liquor is called *azure.*

To azure the silk it is taken from the ungumming copper after it is dressed and put into a trough of water; after it is worked, drained, and again dressed, it is ready for the whitening.

Whitening.—Put into a copper with thirty pails of water half a pound of soap; when it boils, and the soap dissolved, add for *China white* a little *prepared annatto.* The silk, being on rods, is now to be put into the copper, and kept turning end for end without intermission till the shade is uniform. For *India white* a little azure is added, to give the blue shade: for *thread white* and others a little azure is also to be added.

Observe, the liquor should be very hot, but not boiling; the turnings five times repeated, by which the shade is made even. When finished, it is taken out, wrung, spread on poles to dry, and that part of it required for sulphuring must be put upon rods or slight poles.

Sulphuring.—The hanks, being upon poles seven or eight feet from the ground, in an appropriate room, one pound and a half or two pounds of roll brimstone will sulphur a hundred weight of silk.

Put the brimstone, coarsely powdered, into an earthen pipkin with a little charcoal or small coal at bottom. Light one of the bits with a candle, which will kindle all the rest.

The room should be close, the chimney, if any, being closed up; the sulphur should burn under the silk all night. The next morning the windows should be opened to let out the smoke and admit the air, which, in summer, will be sufficient to dry the silk; but in winter, as soon as the sulphurous fumes are dissipated, the windows must be shut and a fire kindled in the stove or stoves to dry the silk.

Observe, if the room for sulphuring does not admit of openings sufficient for the dissipation of the sulphuric fumes, the work-people will be in danger of suffocation.

When the sulphur is consumed it leaves a black crust which will light the future sulphur like spirit of wine.

If, in dressing, the silk sticks together, it is not sufficiently dry.

Samuel Wetherill

**The First Manufacturer of Fustians and Jeans
in America.**

APPENDIX.

I visited the building where S. Wetherill carried on his manufactory of velverets, fustians, &c.; and by conversation with his descendants, I found that he was most enthusiastically engaged in producing goods, so as to render the colony independent of England. He was one of those worthy men, who entered, with all their souls, into the cause of liberty, and in consequence of the peculiar views of the Friends on the subject of war, he was disowned; as he maintained, in that particular exigence, the lawfulness of defensive operations. Nothing moved from his general religious principles, and being a decided advocate of civil and religious liberty, he commenced a society, still in existence in Philadelphia, called the Free Quakers.

From a perusal of his publications, I find him a faithful enquirer after truth and righteousness; swayed by no consideration, but a conviction of his own mind and the good influence of principles. He lived in a time which tried men's souls, and he bore the trial with firmness and patience; and manifested to the last an unwavering patriotic spirit, religiously maintained while his valuable life was spared. He lived to see the fruits of independence, in the extension of national prosperity; and in the progress of freedom, science, and truth. I was pleased to obtain the following original letter, which is characteristic of his kind feelings and liberal sentiments; and I regret that my limits will not allow me to give a fuller account of this pioneer in American industry.*

BALLSTON, July 26, 1809.

My dear Rebecca,

I wrote to thee from New York the next day after our arrival there, the second day of the week following we set off for Albany in the steam boat: the scenery all the way up the river is the most curious, grand, and beautiful I ever beheld; the shore being high mountains of rocks, little villages, and towns, and the remains of divers fortifications made in the late revolution, including the celebrated Stony Point, which General Arnold intended to betray into the hands of General Howe, and a great number of beautiful country seats and plantations. We left Albany the next day after our arrival, and came to Ballston the same day; we have had a great deal of company and a variety of amusements for such as have a relish for them. The evening before last there was a ball given in compliment to the governor of Mas-

---

* Mr. Wetherill also carried on the business of dyeing and fulling in South Alley; also chemical works. His ancestor, came to New Jersey before Wm. Penn's arrival in Pennsylvania, and before the war of the revolution he moved to Philadelphia, where he followed his trade as a carpenter, and was so decided a Friend to the cause of independence, that being disowned by the society of friends for asserting the lawfulness of defensive war, which he defended with his pen, he with others formed a new society; and being presented by the legislature with a lot at the corner of Mulberry and Fifth street, they erected a brick house of worship, which still remains.

sachusetts, who was here on a visit. The company are genteel people who have come far and near; from New York, Boston, Carolina, Georgia and Philadelphia. Great numbers are benefited by the waters together with the amusements combined. I suspect that the journey and amusements are a principal article in restoring health, the ball especially; but I have received no benefit from any or all of those means—simply trusting to the waters, which do not appear to have done me any good, my weakness still continuing much the same.

Farewell, my dear child, from thy grandfather; I have a most miserable pen, which, together with my weakness, makes it impossible to write intelligibly. Thy grandmother sends her love to you all.

(Signed)   SAMUEL WETHERILL.

———

From a review of "Colden's Life of Fulton," published in the New York Monthly Magazine, the following interesting extracts are made:—ROBERT FULTON was born, of Irish parents, in Little Britain, in the county of Lancaster, Pennsylvania, in 1765. His family is said to have been respectable but not rich. Mr. Colden says, that his peculiar genius manifested itself at an early age, and that his leisure hours in childhood were spent in mechanics' shops, or devoted to the pencil. The latter employment seems at that time to have possessed the greatest attractions, for, from the age of seventeen to twenty-one, he painted portraits and landscapes, at Philadelphia, for profit. He then purchased, with his little earnings, a little farm in Pennsylvania, upon which he established his mother. We rejoice to record this circumstance, as we can scarcely conceive one more honourable to the character of a young man. It proves early industry, frugality, and great strength of filial affection. In the same year he went to England to improve himself in his profession, as a painter, under the patronage of Mr. West. He was for some years an inmate in the family of that gentleman. After leaving it, he removed to Devonshire, and remained in that place, and in other parts of England for some years longer—it does not clearly appear how many—and then went to France. During the latter part of his stay in England, he seemed to have relinquished his profession, and to have busied himself about several projects relating chiefly to canal navigation. In 1793, he addressed (we presume from France) some general speculations on French politics, to Lord Stanhope, who appears to have been his friend, but though designed for the public, they attracted little of the public attention, as his biographer does not even know whether they were ever in fact

———

* The following letter has induced me to select the above notice.

ASHLAND, 4th July, 1835.

SIR:—I received your letter transmitting a copy of your prospectus, for the publication of a memoir of the late Mr. Samuel Slater. I have been highly interested by what I have heard from time to time, of his early and successful exertions to introduce the cotton manufacture in the United States; and I have now in my possession some cotton yarn spun by the first spindles which he put up, which I was informed were the first used in the United States. Without being able to contribute to the accomplishment of your undertaking, I shall be glad to hear of its successful execution. The names of Fulton, Evans, Whitney and Slater, should ever live in the grateful recollection of the people of the United States.   With great respect,
                                                        I am, your ob't servant,
Mr. George S. White, Canterbury, Connecticut.   HENRY CLAY.

published or not. In 1797, he took lodging at an hotel in Paris, with Mr. Joel Barlow, with whom he formed so strong a friendship, that when Mr. B. soon after removed to his own hotel, he invited Mr. F. to reside with him. For some years Fulton was a member of the family of Mr. Barlow. He projected a panorama, which proved successful and beneficial, and made some experiments upon the explosion of gunpowder under water. The French directory gave him hopes of patronising these attempts, but at length withdrew their support. He offered the project to the Dutch government, but it was declined. It was then offered to Bonaparte, who had become first consul, and he appointed a commissioner with funds and power to give the required assistance.

While in France, and probably about this period, he formed an intimate acquaintance with Chancellor Livingston, and at that period those gentlemen laboured conjointly in their attempts to introduce steam navigation, which was afterwards attended with such brilliant success. In 1801, he made several experiments with a plunging boat, designed for sub-marine warfare, with a degree of success which seems to have been satisfactory to himself.

The following very flattering account was given by St. Austin, a member of the tribunal :—The diving boat, in the construction of which he is now employed, will be capacious enough to contain eight men, and provision for twenty days, and will be of sufficient strength and power to enable him to plunge one hundred feet under water if necessary. He has contrived a reservoir of air, which will enable eight men to remain under water eight hours. When the boat is above water it has two sails, and looks just like a common boat ; when she is to dive, the mast and sails are struck. In making his experiments, Fulton not only remained a whole hour under water with three of his companions, but had the boat parallel to the horizon at any given distance. He proves that the compass points as correctly under the water as on the surface, and that, while under water, the boat made way at the rate of half a league an hour, by means contrived for that purpose. If we may judge of the future from the past, it would seem necessary for the success of these projects, to obtain the consent of those who are to be "decomposed," which has not yet been done. Fulton was, therefore, never able to demolish an English ship, although he watched long and anxiously such as approached the French coast, for that purpose. The rulers of France being at length discouraged, and Fulton thinking that the all-important object was to blow up ships, and so that was effected, it was no great matter to what power they might happen to belong, turned his eyes for patronage to the English government—or they turned their eyes to him. Mr. Colden seems very properly aware that this conduct of his friend might make an unpleasant impression on the minds of those who were not, like his biographer, acquainted with the elevation and philanthropy of his views, and seeks to justify him by the following defence. It must be recollected, that Fulton's enthusiastic notions of the advantages of a universal free trade and liberty of the seas, had led to the inventions which he was then endeavouring to employ, and which as he supposed, would annihilate naval armaments, the great support in his estimation of what he calls the war system of Europe. He was persuaded, that if this system could be broken up, all nations would direct their energies to education, the sciences, and a free exchange of their natural advantages. He was convinced that if, on the contrary, the Europeans continued to cherish this war system, and to support and augment their great naval armaments, his own country would be driven to the necessity of protecting herself by similar establishments, which, as he thought, would be inimical to her republican institutions, and destructive of her happiness. Without reference, therefore, to the merits of the then existing contest, the grounds of which were constantly changing, without feeling a partiality or enmity to either of the belligerents, he was desirous of engaging one of the nations at war to give him an opportunity of trying the efficacy of his inventions. If they were proved to answer his expectations, he was indifferent as to the temporary advantages it might give either over the other. He believed that the result would be the permanent happiness of all, and that in the general good his own country would largely participate. He considered himself as introducing a new military science, which he wished to prove, and which he had a desire to perfect himself, for the benefit of his country and of mankind. His sentiments on this subject were not novel, nor without the sanction of the nations which they most immediately concerned. Neither France nor England has hesitated to encourage their citizens, with a view to their improvement in military science, to serve in the armies and navies of foreign states at war, where they have been neutral. " Whatever," says Mr. C. " may be the just force of this reasoning, it swayed the mind of Mr. Fulton to honest conviction." It is doubtful whether it will produce a similar effect on any other mind. From the following passage we infer that the negotiations between Fulton and the English ministry were clandestine, and were carried on at a time when he resided in France, and was ostensibly attached to her interests :—" It has been mentioned, that the Earl of Stanhope had taken great pains to inform himself as to Fulton's proceedings in France. This nobleman's mathematical and mechanical mind perceived what consequences might result from the application of Fulton's inventions. The information he obtained was communicated by the British cabinet and excited attention. It was determined by the British ministry, if possible, to withdraw Fulton from France. Lord Sidmouth, who was then one of the ministers, contrived to have a communication with Fulton, while he was in Paris, and obtained his consent to meet an agent of the British government in Holland. In October, 1803, Fulton went from Paris to Amsterdam for this purpose, but the agent with whom he was to confer did not arrive ; and after being in Amsterdam three months he returned to Paris. We cannot resist the impression that some light is thrown upon Fulton's conduct by the evidence adduced for another purpose by Mr. Colden from Lord Stanhope, his early friend and correspondent. In a speech on American affairs, made by Lord Stanhope in the house of lords, soon after these experiments were made, he is reported in an English newspaper to have said, ' it was not perhaps sufficiently known, that at that very moment exertions were making in America to carry into effect a plan for the disclosure of which an individual had, a few years before, demanded of the British government fifteen thousand dollars, but had been refused. He alluded to a plan, he said, for the invisible destruction of shipping, and particularly men-of-war. That the inventor of this scheme was then in America, and it was ascertained that it would not, on an average, cost twenty pounds to destroy any ship whatever.' While he was labouring for his new employers, some of the torpedoes were thrown from British boats upon French vessels, but they exploded without effect—a circumstance which Fulton attributed to a slight, and easily rectified mistake. To evince the correctness of his opinion, in October, 1805, he did blow up with complete success a brig provided for the purpose. Still, however, the British ministry were incredulous, and Fulton, wearied with incessant applications, disappointments and neglect, at length embarked for this country." Mr. Colden here fairly states—it would be doing injustice to the memory of Fulton, as well as that of another ingenious native American, not to notice, before we leave this subject, that Fulton did not pretend to have been the first who discovered that gunpowder might be exploded with effect under water, nor did he pretend to have been the first who attempted to apply it as the means of hostility. He knew well what had been done by Bushnel in our revolutionary war. He frequently spoke of the genius of this American with great respect, and expressed a conviction that his attempts against the enemy would have been more successful, if he had had the advantages which he himself derived from the improvements of nearly forty years in mechanics and mechanical physiology. We cannot but think, that it is a very exaggerated estimate of the efficiency of Fulton's contrivances, which induces Mr. Colden to suppose, that the "British ministry never truly intended to give Fulton a fair opportunity of trying the effects of his engines." The object may have been to prevent their being placed in the hands of an enemy ; and if that was accomplished, it was the interest of England, as long as she was ambitious of maintaining the proud title of mistress of the seas, to make the world believe that Fulton's projects were chimerical. Nothing could be more likely to produce this effect, than abortive attempts to apply them. This would prevent other nations from making similar experiments and discourage the inventor. In June, the British ministry appointed a commission to examine Fulton's projects. The commissioners were Sir Jos. Banks, Mr. Cavendish, Sir Home Popham, Major Congreve and Mr. John Rennie. Many weeks passed before Fulton could prevail on them to do any thing, and finally, when they met, they reported against the sub-marine boat as being impracticable. In a letter to the ministry, Fulton complains that this report was made without his having been called for any explanations, and although the gentlemen who made it had before them no account of what had been done. Indeed, in the first interview which Fulton had with Mr. Pitt and Lord Melvile, the latter condemned the Nautilus without a moment's consideration. If these engines were, in truth, terrible as the biographer imagines, it would not be strange that the British ministry should choose to preserve the navy by almost any means from entire demolition; and they might oppose the introduction of a mode of warfare which though, in the first instance, it was exerted against their enemies, would infallibly re-act against themselves with greater effect in proportion to the superiority of their naval force. But no such motives can be ascribed to the French republican government, and they rejected it—no such suspicion can be against Bonaparte, and after a full trial he relinquished it ; or against the Dutch government, and they declined it ; no such policy is to be attributed to our administration, and still we are told by Mr. Colden, " Mr. Fulton's plan for sub-marine warfare met with no countenance from the government. He had not been able to inspire the executive officers with any confidence in them."

We presume also, that Commodore Rodgers is not to be accused of connivance in a similar design. Besides, Mr. Colden should have weighed the matter well before he made a charge which necessarily implies that all the experiments made by such men as Mr. Cavendish, Sir Home Popham, Major Congreve and Mr. Rennie, (the commissioners appointed by the British ministry) were intended to be deceptive, and that their report was meanly fraudulent and false. Mr. Colden has so far suffered his imagination to predominate over his better judgment upon this subject, that he seems really to have supposed, that during the late war it was the main object with the British navy to ascertain the part of the coast where Fulton might reside, and to avoid it as the particularly fulminating point of this terrific submerged thunder. Fulton arrived in New York, in December, 1806, and immediately renewed the pursuit of the objects upon which he had recently been engaged in Europe, that is, sub-marine war and steam navigation.

He was encouraged by the American government, and in the summer of 1807, made several experiments, and one of them upon a large bulk brig, (an unresisting subject,) was completely successful. The narrowness of our limits—the necessary length of this article—and the notoriety of these attempts, which were made in the vicinity of New York, render it unnecessary for us to detail them with minuteness. In March, 1810, congress passed an act making an appropriation for trying the use of torpedoes and submarine explosions. Commissioners were appointed to observe the success of the experiments, of which the sloop of war Argus, commanded by Captain Lawrence, was to be the subject. These commissioners differed considerably in their reports of the results to the government—Chancellor Livingston, with whom, as we before mentioned, Fulton had formed a very intimate acquaintance and connection in France, which subsisted during their joint lives, was rather favourably impressed. General Lewis ("whose long military services, and experience," Mr. Colden thinks, "renders his judgment on this subject deserving of the highest consideration") was very sanguine of their ultimate success; and such, also, was the opinion of the biographer, then one of the commissioners. Commodore Rodgers also made a report, which contained a journal of the daily proceedings of Fulton and the committee, and very minute descriptions of the machines and experiments. His opinion was entirely against Fulton's system, and he concludes that every part of it would be found totally impracticable. A great portion of the work is occupied by a statement of Fulton's merits and those of his chief friend and associate Chancellor Livingston, in relation to steam navigation. The information prevalent on the subject—the legal discussions which have already been had, and which may hereafter arise in relation to it—and, to speak honestly, a little distrust of our own judgment, induce us to refrain from a minute examination of the claims which are advanced in favour of those gentlemen. It is but fair, however, to remark, that even if it be admitted that Fulton has done no more than reduce to successful practice previously existing theories upon a subject of such paramount importance, he is entitled to praise enough to fully satisfy the ambition and affection of his friends. The increased facility of intercourse in many parts of the world, and especially on this continent, is such that twenty years ago it would have required a bold imagination to conceive. Can any man doubt that Fulton has been mainly instrumental in accelerating, if he did not exclusively produce, this state of things? The whole progress of the arts show that the first discovery of a principle is usually very remote from the perfection of the practice. This is strongly exemplified by some facts stated by Fulton himself. In 1320, gunpowder was discovered: one hundred and fifty years after that period, iron bullets were first used; muskets were unknown until two hundred years from the same time; and in these, the cumbrous match-lock did not give place to the fire-locks till the beginning of the seventeenth century, that is two hundred and eighty years after the first knowledge of gunpowder. In the year sixteen hundred and sixty-three, the Marquis of Worcester discovered the expansive power of steam. Thirty-three years afterwards, Savory took out a patent for a steam engine to pump the mines of Cornwall. In seventeen hundred and five, Mr. Newcomen thought of a piston to the cylinder; but he worked at it nine years before it was sufficiently improved to give it a fair prospect of utility. Fifty-two years after Newcomen's discovery, Mr. Watt thought of another improvement, which was the separate condenser. Thus it was an hundred years from the time of the Marquis of Worcester, till Mr. Watt's discovery gave the steam engine, in any degree, its present perfection; and rendered it so simple, familiar, and useful, as to be adapted to the many important purposes to which it is now applied. Another striking illustration to the same effect, and which may serve to exemplify the nature, as well as to manifest the degree of Fulton's benefactions to the public, is to be found in the gradual improvements effected in his steam boats since their establishment. We believe the average passage of the first boat between Albany and this city, fell little short of thirty-six hours, and in some of the present boats, it does not exceed twelve hours. Fulton's attention was strongly attracted, during several parts of his life, to the subject of improving internal navigation by means of canals; and in particular he entered, with his characteristic enthusiasm, into the magnificent project which our legislature is now attempting to realise. In 1811, he was appointed one of the commissioners upon the subject, but he did not sanction the report which in the subsequent year was returned to the legislature. It is not claimed by the biographer, that either this scheme in particular or generally this branch of improvement, has received any eminent benefit from the genius or industry of Fulton. In February, 1814, he addressed a letter to Governeur Morris, president of the board of commissioners, in which he shows what would be the advantages of the proposed canal, and exhibits very interesting and curious calculations of the comparative expense of transportation upon land, upon rivers, and upon canals. The same year, Fulton, with the other commissioners, made another report to the legislature; this is the last service he rendered this magnificent project. We presume that our readers will readily excuse our omission of any account of Fulton's well known and very extensive experiments in relation to the various modes which he devised for submarine attack, and for transferring a large portion of naval warfare beneath the surface of the ocean. We are told by Mr. Colden that the steam frigate, that imposing if not effective engine of war, owes its origin to these experiments, although it is not apparently connected with them. The untimely death of Fulton; the cessation of the war; and the imperfections inseparable from the infancy of all improvements, may have prevented the full development of the powers which, perhaps, this invention is hereafter destined to display. The occasion and manner of Fulton's death is thus related. In January, 1815, Mr. John Livingston, who owned the steamboat which plied between New York and New Jersey, but which was stopped by the operation of the New Jersey laws, petitioned the legislature of that state for their repeal. After hearing witnesses and counsel for several days, the laws were rescinded. It was upon this occasion Fulton was examined as a witness, as we have before stated. The weather, while he was at Trenton, where he was much exposed, in attending the hall of the legislature, was uncommonly cold. When he was crossing the Hudson to return to his house and family the river was very full of ice, which occasioned his being several hours on the water on a very severe day. Fulton had not a constitution to encounter such exposure, and upon his return found himself much indisposed from the effects of it.

He had at that time great anxiety about the steam frigate; and after confining himself for a few days, when he was convalescent he went to give his superintendence to the artificers employed about her: he forgot his debilitated state of health in the interest he took in what was doing on the frigate, and was a long time, on a bad day, exposed to the weather on her decks. He soon found the effects of this imprudence. His indisposition returned upon him with such violence as to confine him to his bed; his disorder increased, and on the 24th of February, 1815, terminated his valuable life. As soon as the legislature, which was then in session at Albany, heard of the death of Mr. Fulton, they expressed their participation in the general sentiment, by resolving that the members of both houses should wear mourning for some weeks. It will appear from the above slight sketch of the life of this valuable citizen, that the three great subjects of his attention and efforts were, the improvement in the art of making canals, submarine warfare and steam navigation. In relation to the first, we are not aware that he has effected much; in the second, he has displayed great talent and wonderful industry, the effects and utility of which time is hereafter to develope; and in the third he has done what should make his country proud, and the world grateful.

—

On the Origin of Steam Boats and Steam Wagons, by Oliver Evans.

About the year 1772, being then an apprentice to a wheel-wright, or wagon maker, I laboured to discover some means of propelling land carriages without animal power. All the modes that have since been tried (so far as I have heard of them), such as wind, treadles with ratchet wheels, crank tooth, &c., to be wrought by men, presented themselves to my mind, but were considered as too futile to deserve an experiment; and I concluded that such motion was impossible for want of a suitable original power. But one of my brothers, on a Christmas evening, informed me that he had that day been in company with a neighbouring blacksmith's boys, who, for amusement, had stopped up the touch hole of a gun barrel, then put in about a gill of water, and rammed down a tight wad; after which they put the breech in the smith's fire, when it discharged itself with as loud a crack as if it had been loaded with powder. It immediately occurred to me, that here was the power to propel any wagon, if I could only apply it, and I set myself to work to find out the means. I laboured for some time without success. At length a book fell into my hands describing the old atmospheric steam engine. I was astonished to observe that they had so far erred as to use the steam only to form a vacuum to apply the mere pressure of the atmosphere, instead of applying the elastic power of the steam for original motion ; the power of which I supposed irresistible. I renewed my studies with increased ardour, and soon declared that I could make steam wagons, and endeavoured to communicate my ideas to others ; but however practicable the thing appeared to me, my object only excited the ridicule of those to whom it was made known. But I persevered in my belief and confirmed it by experiments that satisfied me of its reality. In the year 1786 I petitioned the legislature of Pennsylvania for the exclusive right to use my improvements in flour mills, as also steam wagons in that state. The committee to whom the petition was referred heard me very patiently, while I described the mill improvements, but my representations concerning steam wagons made them think me insane. They however, reported favourably respecting my improvements in the manufacture of flour, and passed an act granting me the exclusive use of them, as prayed for. This act is dated March 1787. But no notice is taken of the steam wagons. A similar petition was also presented to the legislature of Maryland. Mr. Jesse Hollingsworth, from Baltimore, was one of the committee appointed to hear me and report on the case. I candidly informed this committee of the fate of my application to the legislature of Pennsylvania respecting the steam wagons ; declaring, at the same time, without the encouragement prayed for, I would never attempt to make them ; but that, if they would secure to me the right as requested, I would, as soon as I could, apply the principle to practice ; and I explained to them the great elastic power of steam, as well as my mode of applying it to propel wagons. Mr. Hollingsworth very prudently observed, that the grant could injure no one, for he did not think that any man in the world had thought of such a thing before ; he therefore wished the encouragement might be afforded, as there was a prospect that it would produce something useful. This kind of argument had the desired effect, and a favourable report was made May 21, 1787, granting to me, my heirs and assigns, for fourteen years, the exclusive right to make and use my improvements in flour mills and the steam wagons in that state. From that period I have felt myself bound in honour to the state of Maryland to produce a steam wagon as soon as I could conveniently do it. In the year 1789, I paid a visit to Benjamin Charles and sons, clock makers ; men celebrated for their ingenuity, with a view to induce them to join me in the expense and profits of the project. I showed to them my drafts, with the plan of the engine, and explained the expansive power of steam; all which they appeared to understand, but fearful of the expense and difficulties attending it, declined the concern. However, they certified that I had shown to them the drawings and explained the powers, &c. In the same year, I went to Ellicott's mills on the Patapsco, near Baltimore, for the purpose of persuading Messrs. Jonathan Ellicott and brothers, and connections, (who were equally famous for their ingenuity), to join me in the expense and profits of making and using steam wagons. I also showed to them my drawings, and minutely explained to them the powers of steam. They appeared fully to comprehend all I said, and in return informed me of some experiments they themselves had made, one of which they showed me. They placed a gun-barrel having a hollow arm, with a small hole on one side at the end of the arm, similar to Barker's rotary tube mill, as described in the books; a gill of water put into this barrel, with fire applied to the breech, caused the steam to issue from the end of the arm with such force, as by reaction, to cause the machine to revolve, as I judged, about one thousand times in a minute, for the space of about five minutes; and with considerable force for so small a machine. I tarried here two days, (May 10 and 11, 1789), using my best efforts to convince them of the possibility and practicability of propelling wagons on good turnpike roads, by the great elastic power of steam. But they also feared the expense and difficulty of the execution, and declined the proposition; yet they heartily esteemed my improvements in the manufacture of flour, and adopted them in their mills, as well as recommended them to others.

In the same year I communicated my project, and explained my principles, to Levi Hollingsworth, Esq., now a merchant in Baltimore. [I certify that Oliver Evans did about the year 1789, communicate a project to me, of propelling land carriages by power of steam, and did solicit me to join him in the costs and profits of the same. Levi Hollingsworth, Baltimore, Nov. 16th, 1812. I do certify, that some time about the year 1781, 31 years ago, Oliver Evans, in conversation with me, declared, that by the power of steam he could drive any thing; wagons, mills, or vessels, forward, by the same power, &c. Enoch Anderson, Nov. 15th, 1812.] He appeared to understand them; but also declined a partnership in the scheme for the same reasons as the former. From the time of my discovering the principles and the means of applying them, I often endeavoured to communicate them to those I believed might be interested in their application to wagons or boats. But very few could understand my explanations, and I could find no one willing to risk the expense of the experiment. In the year 1785 or 86, before I had petitioned the legislatures, I fell in company with Samuel Jackson, of Redstone; and learning of him that he resided on the western waters, I endeavoured to impress upon his mind the great utility and high importance of steam boats, to be propelled on them; telling him that I had discovered a steam engine so powerful according to its weight, that it would, by means of paddle-wheels (which I described to him) readily drive a vessel against the current of those waters with so great speed as to be highly beneficial. Mr. Jackson proves that he understood me well, for he has lately written letters declaring that about twenty-six years before their date, I did describe to him the principles of the steam engine that I have since put into operation to drive mills, which he has seen—and that I also explained to him my plan for propelling boats by my steam engine with *paddle wheels*; describing the very kind of wheels now used for this purpose; and that I then declared to him my intention to apply my engine to this particular object as soon as my pecuniary circumstances would permit. In the year 1800, or 1801, never having found a man willing to contribute to the expense, or even to encourage me to risk it myself, it occurred to me that though I was then in full health, I might be suddenly carried off by the yellow fever, that had so often visited Philadelphia; or by some other disease or casualty to which all are liable, and that I had not yet discharged my debt of honour to the state of Maryland by producing the steam wagon. I determined therefore to set to work the next day and construct one. I first waited upon Robert Patterson, Esq., professor of mathematics in the University of Pennsylvania, and explained to him my principles—as I also did to Charles Taylor, steam engineer from England. They both declared these principles to be new to them, and highly worthy of a fair experiment, advising me without delay to prove them; in hopes I might produce a more simple, cheap, and powerful steam engine, than any in use. These gentleman were the only persons who had such confidence, or afforded me such advice. I also communicated my plans to B. F. Latrobe, Esq., at the same time; who publicly pronounced them chi merical, and attempted to demonstrate the absurdity of my principles, in his report to the Philosophical Society of Pennsylvania, on steam engines; in which same report, he also attempts to show the impossibility of making steam boats useful, on account of the weight of the engine; and I was one of the persons alluded to, as being seized with the steam mania, conceiving that wagons and boats could be propelled by steam engines. The liberality of the members of the society caused them to reject that part of the report which he designed as demonstrative of the absurdity of my principles; saying they had no right to set up their opinions as a stumbling-block in the road of any exertions to make a discovery. They said I might produce something useful, and ordered it to be stricken out. What a pity they did not also reject his demonstrations respecting steam boats! for not-withstanding them, they have run, are now running, and will run: so has my engine, and all its principles, completely succeeded: and so will land carriages, as soon as these principles are applied to them, as explained to the legislature of Maryland in 1787, and to others long before. In consequence of the determination above alluded to, I hired hands, and went to work to make a steam wagon, and had made considerable progress in the undertaking, when the thought struck me, that as my steam engine was entirely different in form as well as in its principles from all others in use, that I could get a patent for it, and apply it to mills more profitably than to wagons; for until now I apprehended, that as steam mills had been used in England, I could only obtain a patent for wagons and boats. I stopped the work immediately, and discharged my hands, until I could arrange my engine for mills, laying aside the steam wagon for a time of more leisure. Two weeks afterwards, I commenced the construction of a small engine for a mill to grind plaster of Paris; the cylinder six inches in diameter, and stroke of the piston eighteen inches; believing that with $1000 I could fully try the experiment. But before I was done with experiments, I found that I had expended $3,700 —all that I could command. I had now to begin the world anew at the age of forty-eight, with a large family to support. I had calculated that if I failed in my experiment, the credit I had would be entirely lost; and without money or credit, at my advanced age, with many heavy encumbrances, my way through life appeared dark and gloomy indeed. But I succeeded perfectly with my little engine, and preserved my credit; I could break and grind 300 bushels of plaster of Paris, or 12 tons, in twenty-four hours; and to show its operations more fully to the public, I applied it to saw stone on the side of Market street, where the driving of twelve saws, in heavy frames, sawing at the rate of 100 feet of marble stone in twelve hours, made a great show, and excited much attention. I thought this was sufficient to convince the thousands of spectators of the utility of my discovery : but I frequently heard them enquire if the power could be applied to saw timber as well as stone, to grind grain, propel boats, &c.; and though I answered in the affirmative, I found they still doubted. I therefore determined to apply my engines to all new uses, to introduce it and them to the public. This experiment completely tested the correctness of my principles, according to my most sanguine hopes. The power of my engine rises in a geometrical proportion, while the consumption of fuel has only an arithmetical ratio; in such proportion that every time I added one fourth more to the consumption of fuel, the powers of the engine were doubled; and that twice the quantity of fuel required to drive one saw would drive sixteen saws at least; for when I drove two saws the consumption was eight bushels of coals in twelve hours, but when twelve saws were driven, the consumption was not more than ten bushels; so that the more we resist the steam the greater is the effect of the engine. On these principles, very light, but powerful engines, can be made, suitable for propelling boats and land-carriages, without the great incumbrance of their own weight, as mentioned in Latrobe's demonstrations.

In the year 1804, I constructed at my works, situate a mile and a half from the water, by order of the board of health of the city of Philadelphia, a machine for cleansing docks. It consisted of a large flat or scow, with a steam engine of the power of five horses on board, to work machinery to raise the mud into flats. This was a fine opportunity to show the public that my engine could propel both land and water carriages, and I resolved to do it. When the work was finished, I put wheels under it, and though it was equal in weight to two hundred barrels of flour, and the wheels fixed with wooden axle-trees, for this temporary purpose in a very rough manner, and with great friction of course, yet with this small engine I transported my great burthen to the Schuylkill with ease ; and when it was launched in the water, I fixed a paddle wheel at the stern, and drove it down the Schuylkill to the Delaware, and up the Delaware to the city, leaving all the vessels going up, behind me, at least half way, the wind being ahead.   Some wise men undertook to ridicule my experiment of propelling this great weight on land, because the motion was too slow to be useful. I silenced them by answering, that I would make a carriage, to be propelled by steam, for a bet of $3000, to run upon a level road against the swiftest horse they would produce. I was then as confident as I am now, that such velocity could be given to carriages. Having no doubt of the great utility of steam carriages on good turnpike roads, with proper arrangements for supplying them with water and fuel, and believing that all turnpike companies were deeply interested in putting them into operation, because they would smooth and mend the roads, instead of injuring them as the narrow wheels do. On the 25th September, 1804, I submitted to the consideration of the Lancaster turnpike company, a statement of the costs and profits of a steam carriage to carry one hundred barrels of flour, fifty miles in twenty-four hours—tending to show that one such steam carriage would make more net profits than ten wagons drawn by five horses each, on a good turnpike road, and offering to build such a carriage at a very low price. My address closed as follows:—
"It is too much for an individual to put in operation every improvement which he may invent. I have no doubt but that my engines will propel

boats against the current of the Mississippi, and wagons on turnpike roads, with great profit. I now call upon those whose interest it is to carry this invention into effect. All which is respectfully submitted for your consideration."

In the year 1805, I published a book describing the principles of my steam engine, with directions for working it, when applied to propel boats against the current of the Mississippi, and carriages on turnpike roads. And I am still willing to make a steam carriage that will run fifteen miles an hour, on level railways, on condition that I have double price if it shall run with that velocity ; and nothing for it if it shall not come up to that velocity. What can an inventor do more than to insure the performance of his inventions ? Or, I will make the engine and apparatus at a fair price, and warrant its utility for the purpose of conveying heavy burthens on good turnpike roads. I feel it just to declare that, with Mr. Latrobe, I myself did believe that the ponderous and feeble steam engine, now used in boats, could never be made useful in competition with sail boats, or to ascend the Mississippi, esteeming the current more powerful than it is. But I rejoice that, with him, I have been mistaken ; for I have lived to see boats succeed well with those engines, so as to induce the proprietors to exchange the old for the new, more cheap and more powerful, principles. I have been highly delighted in reading a correspondence between John Stephens, Esq. and the commissioners appointed by the legislature of New York, for fixing on the scite of the great canal proposed to be cut in that state. Mr. Stephens has taken a most comprehensive and very ingenious view of this important subject, and his plan of railways for the carriages to run upon removes all the difficulties that remained. I have had the pleasure, also, of hearing gentlemen of the keenest penetration, and of great mechanical and philosophical talents, freely give in to the belief that steam carriages will become very useful. John Ellicott proposed to make roads of substances such as the best turnpikes are made with, with a path for each wheel to run on, having a railway on posts in the middle, to guide the tongue of the wagon, and to prevent any other carriage from traveling on it. Then, if the wheels were made broad and the paths smooth, there would be very little wear. Such roads might be cheaply made; they would last a long time and require very little repair. Such roads, I am inclined to believe, ought to be preferred, in the first instance, to those proposed by Mr. Stephens, as two ways could be made in some parts of the country for the same expense as one would be with wood ; but either of the modes would answer the purpose, and the carriages might travel by night as well as in the day. When we reflect upon the obstinate opposition that has been made by a great majority to every step towards improvement: from bad roads to turnpikes, from turnpikes to canals, from canals to railways for horse carriages, it is too much to expect the monstrous leap from bad roads to railways for steam carriages. But why may not the present generation, who have already good turnpikes, make the experiment of using steam carriages upon them ? They will assuredly effect the movement of heavy burthens, with a slow motion of two and a half miles an hour, and as their progress need not be interrupted, they may travel fifty or sixty miles in the twenty-four hours. This is all that I hope to see in my time, and though I never expect to be concerned in any business requiring the regular transportation of heavy burthens on land, because if I am connected in the affairs of a mill it shall be driven by steam and placed on some navigable water, to save land carriage, yet I certainly intend, as soon as I can make it convenient, to build a steam carriage that will run on good turnpike roads, on my own account, if no other person will engage in it; and I do verily believe that the time will come when carriages propelled by steam will be in general use, as well for the transportation of passengers as goods, traveling at the rate of fifteen miles an hour, or three hundred miles per day. It appears necessary to give the reader some idea of the principles of the steam engine, which is to produce such novel and strange effects; and this I will endeavour to do in as few words as I can, by showing the extent to which the principles are applied already. To make steam as irresistible or powerful as gunpowder, we have only to confine and increase the heat by fuel to the boiler. A steam engine with a working cylinder only nine inches in diameter, and a stroke of the piston three feet, will exert a power sufficient to lift from 3,000 to 10,000 pounds perpendicularly, two and a half miles per hour. This power applied to propel a carriage on level roads or railways would drive a very great weight with much velocity, before the friction of the axle-tree or resistance of the atmosphere would balance it. This is not speculative theory, the principles are now in practice; driving a saw-mill at Manchacks on the Mississippi, two at Natchez, one of which is capable of sawing 5000 feet of boards in 12 hours; a mill at Pittsburgh able to grind twenty bushels of grain per hour; one at Marietta of equal powers; one at Lexington of the same powers; one, a paper mill, of the same; one of one fourth the power at Pittsburgh; one at the same place of three and a half times the power for the forge, and for rolling and splitting sheet iron; one of the power of twenty-four horses, at Middletown, Conn. driving the machinery of a cloth manufactory : two at Philadelphia of the power of five or six horses, and many making for different purposes; the principles applying to all purposes where power is wanted.

OLIVER EVANS.

Ellicott's Mills on the Patapsco, Nov. 12, 1812.

—

To the Honourable the Secretary of State, the Secretary of War, and the Attorney General; the petition of John Fitch, of the city of Philadelphia, humbly showeth :

That your petitioner, in the spring of the year 1785, conceived the idea of applying steam to the purpose of propelling vessels through the water: that, fully satisfied, in his own mind, of the practicability of such a scheme, of its great immediate utility, and the important advantages which would in future result therefrom, not only to America, but the world at large, if the scheme should be carried into effectual operation, he divested himself of every other occupation, and undertook the arduous task, not doubting, that when perfected he should be amply rewarded. In his first attempts to procure assistance from congress, and the legislatures of many of the states, from the peculiar situation of her finances, and the seeming impossibility of the success of his scheme, he met with no relief. Not entirely discouraged by these disappointments, he continued his application to his project, and prayed several of the states for an exclusive 'right to the use of fire and steam to navigation': that New Jersey, New York, Pennsylvania, Delaware, and Virginia granted him an exclusive right, agreeably to the prayer of his petition, for fourteen years. —That the impracticability of procuring experienced workmen in America, your petitioner's total ignorance of the construction of a steam engine, together with the necessary deviations from the form described in books, in order to accommodate its weight and bulk to the narrow limits of a vessel, have caused him not only to expend about eight thousand dollars in successive experiments, but nearly four years of some of his grants have expired, before he has been able to bring his engine to such a degree of perfection as to be carried into use.

That having, at length, fully succeeded in his scheme, proofs of which he is prepared to offer, he trusts he now comes forward, not as an imaginary projector, but as a man who, contrary to the popular expectation, has really accomplished a design which, on examination, will clearly evince the many and important advantages which must result therefrom to the United States, some of which your petitioner begs leave to enumerate.

The western waters of the United States, which have hitherto been navigated with difficulty and expense, may now be ascended with safety, conveniency and great velocity; consequently, by these means, an immediate increased value will be given to the western territory : all the internal waters of the United States will be rendered much more convenient and safe, and the carriage on them much more expeditious; that from these advantages will result a great saving in the labour of men and horses, as well as expense to the traveller.

Your petitioner also conceives, that the introduction of a complete steam engine, formed upon the newest and best principles, into such a country as America, where labour is high, would entitle him to a public countenance and encouragement, independent of its use in navigation; he begs leave to say that the great length of time, and vast sums of money, expended in bringing the scheme to perfection have been wholly occasioned by his total ignorance of the improved state of steam engines, a perfect knowledge of which has not been acquired, without an infinite number of fruitless experiments; for not a person could be found who was acquainted with the minutia of Bolton and Watt's new engine; and whether your petitioner's engine is similar or not to those in England, he is to this moment totally ignorant; but is happy to say, that he is now able to make a complete steam engine, which in its effects, he believes, is equal to the best in Europe; the construction of which he has never kept a secret.

That on his first undertaking the scheme, he knew there were a great number of ways of applying the power of steam to the propelling of vessels through the water, perhaps all equally effective; but this formed no part of his consideration, knowing, that if he could bring his steam engine to work in a boat, he would be under no difficulty in applying its force; therefore he trusts no interference with him in propelling boats by steam, under any pretence of a different mode of application, will be permitted; for should that be the case, the employment of his time, and the amazing expense attending the perfecting his scheme, would, whilst they gave the world a valuable discovery, and to America peculiar and important advantages, eventuate in the total ruin of your petitioner; for a thousand different modes may be applied by subsequent navigators, all of them benefiting by the expense and persevering labour of your petitioner, and thus sharing with him those profits, which they never earned; such a consequence he is confident will not be permitted by your honourable body.

Your petitioner therefore prays that your honours will take the subject of his petition into consideration, and by granting him an exclusive right to the use of steam navigation, for a limited time, do him that justice which he conceives he merits, and which he trusts will redound to the honour and add to the true interest of America: and your petitioner, as in duty bound, shall ever pray.   JOHN FITCH.

New York, 22d *June*, 1790.

CERTIFICATE.

District of Columbia, Washington county,

At the request of Dr. William Thornton, of this county, personally appeared before me, the subscriber, one of the justices of the peace for the said county, Oliver Evans of Philadelphia, who solemnly affirmed, that when John Fitch and his company were engaged in constructing their steamboat in Philadelphia, he, the said Oliver, suggested to the said John Fitch the plan of driving and propelling the said boat by paddle or flutter wheels at the sides of the boat; when the said Fitch or some other person, but he thinks it was Fitch, informed him that one of the company had already proposed and urged the use of wheels at the sides, but that he had objected to them. The said Oliver also states that he afterwards mentioned the same to Henry Voight, one of the members of that company, who said that Dr. William Thornton, also a member of the same, was the person who had proposed the said paddle or flutter wheels at the sides of the boat, but that both himself and John Fitch had objected to them.

The said Oliver further saith, that Robert Fulton, the patentee of steam boats in the state of New York, had observed to him, that he deemed it impossible to drive a boat or vessel, by steam, at a greater speed than five miles per hour: but the said Oliver says, he had understood Fitch's boat had far exceeded that speed, and that Fitch's experiment had completely succeeded to show that boats could be driven by steam to advantage; and also that when the said John Fitch was afterwards setting out for the western country, he called on the said Oliver at his house, and declared his intention to be to form a company, to establish steamboats on the western waters; of the advantages of which he appeared to have formed vast conceptions and great expectations. The said Oliver also saith, that some time about the years 1786, 1787, or 1788, the said Fitch informed him that he contemplated employing his steamboat on the lakes, and meant to construct them with two keels, to answer as runners, and when the lakes should freeze over he would raise his boat on the ice, and by a wheel on each side, with spikes in the rims, to take hold of the ice, he calculated it would be possible to run thirty miles an hour. And also that he meant to tow boats and other floats by steamboats.

(Signed)   OLIVER EVANS.

Affirmed to before the subscriber, one of the justices of the peace for Washington county, Columbia, this 16th day of December, 1814.

JOSEPH FORREST.

On the Origin of the Woollen Trade in England, &c.

Wool has been considered at all times as a valuable commodity; we find the use of wool in the earliest periods, and flocks of sheep are mentioned in the first ages of mankind; kings have not been ashamed to employ themselves in the care of them. The patriarch Abraham had flocks, and the Israelites of that early time employed themselves in the care of them; their neighbours, the Midianites, had such numbers, that the Israelites took among the spoil more than six hundred thousand; and two hundred and fifty thousand were taken from the Hagarites by the sons of Reuben. The Ethiopians had sheep; for when Asa conquered a part of their country, he carried them away in abundance. The Arabians at the same period had also sheep, for they brought more than seven thousand rams at one time to Jehoshaphat; and the Moabites must have bred them in great quantity, for Mesha, king of that country, rendered to the king of Israel a hundred thousand lambs, and a hundred thousand rams. These are passages of history delivered in the Old Testament; and by these we find that at this remote time the Israelites had sheep in great abundance, and that the Midianites and Hagarites, the Ethopians and the Arabians, and the Moabites, fed them also in vast numbers. There is an account of sheep bred, in a manner, all over the eastern quarter of the world; and we have occasional mention of the same creature making a chief object of the care, and a principal article in the rites, of the Amalekites, the Philistines, and the people of Damascus. We see a great part of the quarter of the world then most inhabited, devoted to the care of this useful animal. This creature was not bred only for its flesh; the mention of wool is made in some of these passages, and in others there are allusions to the implements of weaving, and of the method of preparing wool for the loom. That the Israelites fed sheep for the wool, may be seen by the tithe exacted on it. The first of the fleece is declared the due of the priest: and that other countries knew its value in the same manner is plain, from an instance in the present of the Moabitish king, before named, which is, that the rams were given with their wool. The staff of Goliah's spear is said to equal a weaver's beam. The fuller's field is mentioned in Isaiah, and by the prophet Malachi; and Ezekiel calls the people of Damascus, "merchants in white wool." These passages are the summary of what is said concerning flocks of sheep, their wool and its manufacture, in the scriptures; and they show that the shearing of sheep, the use of wool, the manufacturing into cloth, and the preparing that cloth by fulling, were articles known in the earliest time. It establishes the care of this animal, and the use of its fleece, upon a very great authority of ancient history; it produces examples that may animate all persons to interest themselves in the care and management of its fleece, and legislative powers to establish and encourage the manufacture of it. This attention of individuals and of public authority, is greatly wanting at present in America, for the advancement of our woollen manufactures; let those who sit in high places remember the " *wool-sack.*" All old historians mention the care of flocks, and value of their wool: the Greeks used it for the purposes of clothing, and they refer to times much earlier than their own, as familiar in the same use; the Tyrian purple was employed in dyeing woollen cloth, and the early expedition of the Argonauts to Colchis for what was called the golden fleece, was no more than a voyage in search of this commodity. Naturalists may suppose their voyage was in search of gold, and the adepts pretend the secret of the philosopher's stone was couched under this mystery; but plain reason and the most authentic accounts of this transaction say nothing more than this: that the people of Colchis understood the management of sheep, and the manufacturing of their wool, better than any other nation of that time, and that Jason and his partners in that expedition, after encountering many dangers at sea, brought back a quantity of the wool, and a number of the natives to manage the same article in their country. The city of Corinth became afterwards a general mart for wool; and after Pompey had dispersed the pirates, the same article was a very considerable branch of the commerce carried along the coasts of the Mediterranean. Spain is mentioned with great commendation for the wool it produced in those times, and the manufactures made from it; some attribute the invention of weaving woollen cloth to the people of that nation. Wool was received in early times from many parts of the Euxine; and the trade of the Baltic was, in a great measure, supported by it. The Armenians obtained wool and woollen cloths of the Turks, in exchange for horses; and Rome, in somewhat later times, received woollen manufactures from Alexandria. This all stands established on the best authorities, and is related by all the authors who have had occasion to mention the commerce of those ages. In the East they less regard the produce of wool now, because their principal manufactures are in silk and cottons, but there is a great deal of very fine wool in Asia, Syria, and Persia. They have a particular breed of sheep, whose wool is long and grayish, and they make certain peculiar manufactures of it, and those much esteemed. In China and the East Indies the produce of wool is so great, that they shear their sheep three times a year. One of the earliest notices we have of sheep in Britain, with respect to their value, is found in Stillingfleet, who tell us, that between 712 and 727, were made certain laws of King Ina, and in those a price was set upon sheep. The price of an ewe and her lamb together, till a fortnight after Easter, is set down at one shilling. The value of money was then very different from what it is now, but this, with all the allowance that can be made on that head, is but a very poor price. Alfred, famous for the care of arts and commerce, took no small pains to improve this manufacture, but it did not much succeed. In the year 885, he set about this great work, but wolves were too numerous in the island to let sheep be kept in safety. The consequence of the encouragement Alfred gave to the raising of sheep was seen in the succeeding years; for in 918, Edward, who had married the daughter of a country gentleman, distinguished by the regard he had shown to this great concern, and thence called by those who little understood what they read in earlier writers, a shepherd, had his own daughters instructed in the art of carding, spinning, and manufacturing wool. This double patronage bestowed by Edward, the countenance he gave to one who employed himself in breeding sheep, and to the example he set in making his daughters work the wool, was of so much assistance to the manufacture, that the pasturage of the southern countries became soon occupied in feeding sheep, and every one fond of recommending himself to the royal favour became a shepherd, or at least employed his attention greatly on that article. The value of the sheep rose in proportion to the number, for with the increase in quantity of wool the numbers of manufacturers increased, and the demand for it enlarged. Richard I. in the year 1173, returning from the holy war, was taken prisoner by the Duke of Austria. A vast ransom was required, and toward raising it one year's wool was demanded from two abbeys. This is a passage recorded by Rapin, and is supported on the best authorities; and this shows, though we have not had any regular account, that all the time the price of sheep was increasing, the value of wool was also rising, and that this was the principal cause of their increase of value. When quantities of wool began to be exported, the manufacturing of it at home increased; about thirty years after England found the way of serving her neighbours with wool, they improved in the art of dyeing. At first, wool was only wrought up in a coarse plain way, for the clothing of the farmer and his family; by degrees those who best understood the working it up, brought what they had to spare to market. But all this time the wool was only wrought up as it was furnished by the sheep, and all cloth was of the same colour; when the legislature encouraged its manufacture it continued to prosper.

We find by those accounts how little historians and others have considered this important work. Those who speak of the manufacture of broad cloths in England, follow one another in placing the time of their being first made at the year 1331. But we find they were made in 1220.

In 1284, foreign merchants were permitted to establish themselves in the kingdom, for the encouragement of the woollen manufactures. They had, till that time, only been allowed to board, and could not trade otherwise than by making their landlords their brokers; but now they were permitted to traffic in their own names; and the privilege granted to them was of the utmost benefit to the trade. So vastly did the trade increase and the manufacture flourish, that a few years after we find the traffic very flourishing in London, and several of the sea-port towns. From this period the woollen trade became an object, more than ever, of the public concern. Persons of all nations who could improve the manufacture of broad cloth, were encouraged to come over: and among numbers, brought under great encouragements from Flanders, Brabant, and Zealand, there were some so worthy of the advantages they received, that they soon set the trade upon a most respectable footing abroad, and upon the most profitable foundation at home. In consequence of the greater traffic in this article, the price rose; and more assistances were drawn from it for the state: in the reign of Edward III. we read of subsidy after subsidy, on wool: and in the reign of Richard II. more subsidies were demanded; the trades complained, and the matter being candidly examined, it appeared that though they were not without reason of complaint, the trade could bear more loads, and still make fortunes. In the reign of Richard III., though the traffic was encumbered with large subsidies, it increased continually. In the reign of Henry VII. the greatest regard was shown to trade in every article, and in none more than this: the exportation of wool was limited, and the manufacture of cloths increased accordingly. In the reign of Henry VIII. the produce of wool was greater than at any time before; and its price increased with the quantity; farmers were laid under limitations, as to the number of sheep they were to keep; but these were very extensive, and we may see by the account preserved of this transaction, and of the price of things at that time, to what an advance the care of that animal, and the price of its flesh and wool, had arisen.

Husbandry had been, in early times, little understood in England; but the regard to wool, the demand for which was so considerable, and the price so large, gave a spirit to the people, which has continued to the present time. The care of the pasturage grew with the number of enclosures, and the thriving of sheep and the price of wool rose with it. It sold, in this reign, dearer than in any of the preceding. Statutes were made, from time to time, to encourage the manufacture of cloths, and marts were established in different places. In the reign of Philip and Mary, the subsidies granted to Edward VI. were continued: many good statutes were enacted in favour of the woollen manufacture, in this reign; and it throve greatly under the prudent regulations which were established, and extended itself to many parts of the kingdom. In Queen Elizabeth's time a subsidy was granted for life, included in tonnage and poundage: many good statutes were made, and numbers of the French and Flemish, leaving their native country because of persecution, brought over their secrets, and increased our credit. In this reign, wool rose from its former price. We may establish the period from the end of the reign of Edward VI. to the end of Queen Elizabeth's, as the most flourishing of all times for the wool trade of England up to the last century.

The Worsted or Long Wool Manufacture.*

The reason why a long stapled, strong, and firm, though somewhat coarse wool, is best adapted for worsted stuffs, is because they require a fine smooth yarn, which shall have little or no tendency to shrink, curl, and felt, when made into cloth. Hence the fibres must not be entangled and crossed by carding, but on the contrary, be disposed as nearly as possible in parallel lines, by a peculiar combing operation. The yarn thereby producible will be comparatively level, slender, and hard, fit for warping and wefting into finer and more compact goods. The first process to which the long wool is subjected, in a worsted factory, is washing, which is performed exclusively by men, with soap and water. They are paid by quantity, each man being attended by a boy, who receives the wool as it issues from between the two rollers in front of the washer, which squeeze out the greatest part of the moisture. The wool is then carried by the boy, in large baskets, to the drying room, where it is spread upon the floor. The drying-room is generally placed over the boilers of the steam engine, and is thus kept at a high temperature. After drying, the wool is removed to a machine called the plucker, which is always attended by a boy. His business is to lay the tufts of wool even, in an endless web, on an apron, which, as it travels forward, delivers the wool to a pair of spiked rollers, by which it is carried to the interior apparatus, which is somewhat similar to the willow employed in the cotton factories, and thence it is blown out at the opposite side. The use of this mechanism is to clean and straighten the fibres of the wool, and to prepare it for the next machine, the comb-card. In the old routine of the trade, and

* Worsted is a thread spun of wool that has been combed, and which, in the spinning, is twisted harder than ordinarily. It was chiefly used formerly, either to be woven into stockings, caps, gloves, &c. Worsted has obtained its name from Worstead, a market town in the county of Norfolk, England; where the manufacture of the article was first introduced.

still for the finest description of work, the wool is not carded in the factory, but is given out to the wool combers, who comb it by hand.

Three implements are in common use for combing long wool :—1, a pair of combs for each workman : 2, a post to which either of the combs can be fixed : and 3. a comb-pot or small stove, for heating the teeth of the combs. Each comb is composed of two rows of tapering pointed steel teeth, disposed in two parallel planes ; of which one row is longer than the other. They are fixed into a wooden stock or head which is covered with horn, and has a handle fixed into it, perpendicular to the planes of the teeth-range. The space between these planes is only one-third of an inch at the bottom of the teeth. The combs used for the last combing have three rows of teeth, In the work shop a post is fixed, in order to support the combs occasionally during the process. An iron stem is fixed into it, which has an upturned point, for passing through a hole of the handle of the comb, while it has a staple pin at its inner end, for entering into the hollow extremity of the handle, and by the two fixtures holding it fast to the post. The stove consists of a flat iron plate, heated by a fire, or by steam, and surmounted by another plate for confining the heat. Into a small space left between the two plates, the teeth of the combs are introduced.

In combing the wool, 'the workman separates it into handfuls of about four ounces each, sprinkles it with oil, and rolls up in his hands, to smear it uniformly. The proportion of oil varies from a fortieth to a sixteenth of the weight in wool. Having fastened a heated comb to the post with its teeth upwards, the workman takes one half of that quantity of wool in his hand, and, throwing it over the points of the comb, draws it through them, and so repeatedly, a portion of wool remaining each time in the comb. When all the wool is gathered on the teeth, the comb is placed with its points in the stove, and the wool hanging on the outside receives a portion of the heat. The other comb, now hot, is fixed to the post, and filled in its turn, with the other half of the four ounces of wool, and is then removed to the stove, like the first. When both combs are properly warmed, the comber holds one of them, with his left hand over his knee, as he is seated on a low stool, and with the other comb, held in his right hand, he combs the wool upon the first, by introducing the points of the teeth of one comb into the wool contained in the other, and drawing them through it. This is repeated till the fibres are laid parallel. He always begins by introducing the points of the teeth of one comb first into the extremity of the fleece contained in the teeth of the other comb, and he then advances deeper at each succeeding stroke, till, eventually, he works the combs as closely together as possible without bringing their teeth into collision ; otherwise, he could not draw the comb through the wool without breaking its fibres, or tearing the wool out of the teeth of the comb. The short wool which remains on the teeth of the comb at last, because it does not reach the place where the comber grasps it, is called *noyl*, and is unfit for worsted spinning ; it amounts to about an eighth of the new wool by weight.

The wool which is drawn off from the comb forms a continuous sliver or band, with straight parallel fibres, but is still not ready for the spinning machine, till combed again at a somewhat lower temperature. When the process is complete, the wool is formed into parcels containing ten or eleven slivers each.

A great many self-acting machines have been contrived for performing the wool-combing operations. One was made the subject of a patent by John Platt, of Salford, 1827, being an invention communicated to him by a foreigner. This machine is intended to comb wool by means of two revolving combs or heckles. It consists of a square frame of iron mounted upon legs, and two axles, upon each of which one of the circular combs is mounted. These axles are not placed in horizontal positions, but are inclined at acute angles to the horizon, and in directions crossing each other. These combs are made in the form of ordinary wheels, with arms, of which the nave is attached to the axle by screws. The points or teeth are set in the edge of the rim, at right angles to the axis of the wheel, and are made to revolve in opposite directions by means of a crossed or twisted strap, running over a pulley on each axle; these being driven by a band and rigger, or power pulley, on the end of the axle. As the comb wheels go round they are made to approach each other slowly. This approach is caused by mounting the bearings of the axle in slots, which allow of their sliding, and enable that axle and its circular comb to be brought towards the circular comb on the axle. This traverse movement is effected by an endless screw and toothed wheel, or snail work, connected to the under part of the frame. This mechanism gradually moves the axle in a lateral direction, while the twisted strap which connects the two axles, and drives, by rotation, is kept at its proper tension, as the circular combs approach each other by means of a heavy roller, which hangs on a jointed lever. In putting this comb in operation, the proper quantity of wool, in its entangled state, is to be stuck between the teeth, and when the wheels are set in rapid rotary motion, the loose ends of the fleece will, by the centrifugal force, be thrown out in the direction of radii, and will catch against the points of the teeth of the other revolving comb, whereby the fibres will,be drawn out and straightened. The operation is to commence when the comb-wheels are at their greatest distance apart. As they slowly approach each other, the ends or fibres of the wool will be laid hold of by the teeth-points, at progressively increasing depths, until the wheels come near together; by which time the whole length of the staple will have been combed out smooth, and will be then drawn from the comb, by throwing the driving-belt, as usual, on a loose pulley. The *noyls*, or short refuse wool, which remains entangled among the teeth being removed, the machine is charged for another operation.

In one of these large machines, the comb-wheels are ten feet in diameter, and are furnished with hollow iron spokes filled with steam, which keep the whole apparatus at a proper combing heat. These wheels are made to revolve slowly, while a boy, seated on the ground, dresses one of them with wool; they are 'then made to revolve with great rapidity, by shifting the driving-belt on' the proper pulley, during which revolution they gradually approach each other. Such machines will supersede the hand comb.

The *breaking frame* is the next machine in the worsted manufacture, and is, in fact, a continuous form of comb or card, called by the French the *défeutreur*, from its opening out any felted fibres. It represents a vertical section of a breaking comb, for the purpose of explaining the principles of its action. A frame for carrying the machines, of which there are usually four alongside of one another, each from four to six inches broad. The front or feeding pair of rollers, three inches in diameter, the upper one bearing by a weight suspended to its axis on the under; the continuous lower comb, and the upper comb going with the same velocity as the lower. (See DR. URE on *Worsted*.) The rows of teeth slope gently forwards, and alternate with the teeth of the other comb; thus the row of the one corresponds to the middle of the two other rows. Fluted cylinders, which cause the rotation of the endless chain of combs. Counter cylinders, fluted in like manner. The forked bearings in which these turn are so mounted as to permit the comb-chain to be stretched. Small tension-cylinders, for giving a proper direction to each comb. The second pair of rollers, which takes the wool from the combs. These rollers are like the first, made of wood, and of the same diameter. The under one of this pair is kept clean by a brush. On its axis the fast and loose power pulleys are fixed, which give motion to the whole machine. The upper roller is furnished with wiper-wings; that is, its surface is covered with a series of small leaves of parchment, held by one of their edges with little clamps, or keys, in grooves cut lengthwise on their surface. The same cylinder is firmly pressed down on the lower one by a loaded steelyard.

The speed of the first pair of rollers is to that of the second as one to four, and the velocity of the comb-train is the geometrical mean between them, or two. Too great a velocity in these parts would be apt to knot and felt the wool; and it must not therefore exceed above five or six inches in a second. A copper funnel, or trumpet mouth, for conducting the sliver delivered by the second rollers. The third pair of rollers turning with a little more velocity than the second pair, only in consequence of having a diameter a little greater.

The comb of this continuous machine is formed of a series of small rectangular pieces of tin-plate, hinged together, the half of one overlapping that of the other, like slates on a roof. These pieces are struck out by a punch, which leaves at their four corners little discs which are afterwards bent back to a right angle by a pair of plyers, and which serve to make the hinge joints. (*Philosophy of Manufactures.*) While the chain is advancing in a straight line, the teeth soldered to the lower tin-plate present the whole of their projection, minus the thickness of the upper plate, which is here cleft; but in proportion as these plates come upon the fluted cylinders which drive them, the plates cease to lie flat on each other, and become inclined by the curvature of the cylinders. The part cut through for the passage of the teeth recedes, or turns out of the way, and thereby passes by the extremities of the teeth; thus getting disengaged from the fibres of the wool, and allowing them to be immediately seized by the second pair of rollers. In this way each piece of tin plate acts both as a tooth and a disengaging bar. It is obvious that the upper and the lower combs, during their parallel progress, by means of their alternate rows of teeth passing between each other, like the fingers of our two hands, perform a double combing at a single stroke upon the cardings introduced in pairs at the feeding rollers.

The sliver delivered by the roller, proceeds next to a large bobbin or cylinder, round which it is lapped, till the whole combing is entirely wound up. It is again passed through another chain-comb like the preceding, furnished with finer and closer-set teeth; and in this process the sliver, is doubled, to give greater uniformity to the fleece. The person who attends this machine, (invariably a young boy or girl,) is called the feeder. His business is to weigh the wool, and spread it in definite quantities on a traveling apron, which feeds the first pair of rollers. The attention of the feeder is necessarily invariable while the engine is at work, as the uniformity of the thread finally produced depends, in no small degree, on his accuracy. The film of wool at open drawing, on its delivery from its first pair of rollers is collected through a funnel mouth, and either lapped on a cylinder or received in a tin can, and broken off when the can is full. An empty can is then set in the place of the full one.

The machines for reducing, and at the same time equalising, by doubling the open drawings of long wool, are constructed on the same principle as the drawing frame of a cotton-mill, only the distance between the first and last pair of rollers is much greater, on account of the greater length of the wool-staple. The drawing operation is performed by the first pair of rollers moving more slowly than the last pair, whereby the soft woolly riband is extended in length proportionally to that difference of velocity.

Hitherto, no degree of torsion has been given to the slender fillet; but a little twist must now be introduced to preserve its cohesion, in its progression towards the state of a fine thread.

The following description of a roving apparatus for long wool will communicate a tolerably distinct idea of the process.

The sections of two pair of rollers, the lower ones being made of iron, and fluted; the upper being of wood, covered with leather. Pressure is exercised by the upper on the under ones by means of weights suspended by curved rods from the ends of the axes of the upper rollers. The first roller moves faster than the second, in the proportion of two and a half or three to one, according to the nature of the wool. The second roller rests on a moveable bearer, which permits it to be placed nearer to, or farther from, the first roller. A cylinder mounted with pins, which revolves very slowly on its axis, and delivers to the second roller, moving with a treble velocity, the open drawings of wool supplied by the feeding roller. A spindle, having one leg of its forked flyer tubular, through which the roving passes in its way to the bobbin. The spindle turns very slowly, so as to give no more twist to the filaments than may be necessary to secure the formation of an uniform soft cord during their extension. The up and down motion of the bobbin is given by an eccentric acting on the copping-rail.

The general manner of spinning long wool into a finer thread:—Here are three pairs of drawing rollers; the first two of which are supported on moveable bearings, or brass brushes, which allow of their being separated, more or less, from one another, and also from the other roller, to suit the staple of the wool. The ratio of the speed of the first and last pair of rollers is as one to four. The roller serves merely to bear up the fine roving; its velocity is therefore a mean between that of the other two. The bobbins filled with rovings made on the previously described machine, are arranged, behind the back drawing roller, in a creel-frame, so that three rovings together may pass through the funnel or eyelet, placed opposite the middle of this roller. The roving is never reduced to its ultimate fineness by passing through two or three such machines, but it passes successively through five or six of them, receiving not only extension, but an equalising combination every time. At last, the fine yarn is formed by a spinning frame, or throstle, which may contain two hundred and fifty-four spindles on each side, furnished with a four-fold set of drawing rollers. The back and the front pairs of rollers alone are loaded by a suspended weighted lever. The upper rollers of the two middle pairs are of lead, and press merely by their weight. The ratio of the velocities of the extreme pairs of rollers is here as one is to six, eight or ten, according to the fineness of the roving, and the number of yarn wanted. In this final spinning there is no doubling operation; but single bobbins are set on skewers in the reel in correspondence with the single spindles on the copping rail. The number of doublings in this process of drawing and roving long wool, may amount in certain cases to several thousand.

The spindles should revolve very quickly in the spinning frame, in order to give the requisite degree of twist to the worsted. The hardest twisted worsted is called *tammy* warp; and when its fineness is such as to contain twenty-four hanks to the pound weight, the twist is about ten or twelve turns in every inch length. The least twist is given to the hosiery worsted yarn, which runs from eighteen to twenty-four hanks to the pound weight. The twist is only from five to six turns per inch. The degree of twist is regulated by the size of the wharves or whorls upon the spindles, and the speed of the front rollers, in the spinning of which, on the fine mule, extraordinary nicety of adjustment is required.

A hank of worsted yarn contains five hundred and sixty yards; and it is divided into seven lays, of eighty yards each. Some count hanks of eight hundred and forty yards, like those of cotton yarn.

The roving frames have much fewer spindles than the fine spinning frame; some of them are two spindle, some of them four spindle, others six spindle-frames, &c., which all repeat, however, the similar process of doubling threads and passing under drawing rollers, so as to give successive draughts to the spongy cords, and to maintain their perfect equality of texture. Girls from sixteen to twenty and upwards, are generally employed at drawing, roving and spinning frames. At the former two they earn from 6s. to 7s. each, weekly; at the last, from 9s. to 10s.

—

Dates of Circumstances and Occurrences connected with Manufactures.

1756. Cotton velvets and quiltings first made in England.

1768. The stocking frame applied to make lace by Hammond.

1774. A bill passed to prevent the export of machinery used in cotton factories.

1779. Mule spinning, by Crompton.

1794. Sewing cotton made by S. Slater.

1803. First cotton factory in New Hampshire.

1810. Digest of cotton manufactures in the United States by Mr. Gallatin, and another by Tench Coxe, Esq; and public attention drawn to their growing importance.

1815. The power loom introduced into the United States, by Gilmore, (R. I.) afterwards more perfectly at Waltham, Massachusetts, where the latest improvements in machinery were obtained.

1822. First cotton factory erected at Lowell.

1825. Self-acting mule spinner patented in England, by Roberts. Same year the tube frame introduced there from America.

1826. First exports of American cotton manufactured to any considerable value.

1830. Mr. Dyer introduces a machine from the United States into England, to make cards.

1831. Calico Printing much improved in the United States.

1834. A patent for an improved spindle, by Charles Jackson, Esq. Providence R. I.

1835. April 20. " Died at Webster, Massachusetts, aged 67, Samuel Slater, long known as an enterprising and respected citizen of Rhode Island, and the father of the cotton manufacturing business in this country, in which he acquired a great estate. The first cotton manufactory in the United States, was built by Mr. Slater, at Pawtucket R. I., which was standing and in operation at the time of his death."—*American Almanac.*

1836. One hundred and twenty millions of yards of calico printed in the United States, during the year ending April 1, 1836.

———

INDIANS.

Their arts and manufactures were confined to the construction of wigwams, bows and arrows, wampum, ornaments, stone hatchets, mortars for pounding corn, to the dressing of skins, weaving of coarse mats from the bark of trees, or a coarse sort of hemp, &c. In summer, they wore little besides a covering about the waist; but in winter, they clothed themselves in the skins of wild beasts. For habitations, the Indians had wigwams. These consisted of a strong pole erected in the centre, around which, at the distance of ten or twelve feet, other poles were driven obliquely into the ground, and fastened to the centre pole at the top. Their coverings were of mats or bark of trees, so well adjusted as to render them dry and comfortable. Their domestic utensils extended not beyond a hatchet of stone, a few shells, and sharp stones which they used for knives, stone mortars for pounding corn, and some mats and skins upon which they slept. They sat, and ate, and lodged, on the ground.

1678. The colonists during this period, being chiefly occupied in gaining a subsistence, and in protecting themselves against their enemies, had occasion for few articles beyond the necessaries and comforts of life. Arts and manufactures could, therefore, receive but little encouragement, beyond the construction of such articles, and even those were principally imported.

In 1620, one hundred and fifty persons came out to Virginia to carry on the manufacture of silks, iron, potash, tar, pitch, glass, salt, &c. but they did not succeed. In 1673, Chalmer says of New England, " There be five iron works which cast no guns, no house in New England has above twenty rooms —not twenty in Boston have ten rooms each. All cordage, sailcloth, and mats, come from England—no cloth made there of any value—no alum, no copperas, no salt made by their sun. The first buildings of the settlers were made of logs and thatched, or were built of stone. Brick and framed houses were soon built in the larger towns; the frames and brick were, however, in some instances imported. The first mill in New England was a windmill, near Watertown, but it was taken down in 1632 and placed in the vicinity of Boston. Water mills began to be erected the next year. The first thing printed was the freeman's oath, the second an almanack, and the third an edition of the psalms. The bible was printed at Cambridge in 1664, translated into the Indian language. Notwithstanding the obstacles interposed by Great Britain to the progress of arts and manufactures, the coarser kinds of cutlery, some coarse cloths, both linen and woollen, hats, paper, shoes, household furniture, farming utensils, &c. were manufactured on a small scale, but not sufficient to supply the inhabitants; cloths were made in some families for their own consumption. In 1700, which was the time of the commencement of the first newspaper, there was but a moderate advance for some years. The trade with England during the revolutionary war being interrupted, the people were compelled to manufacture for themselves. Encouragement was given to all necessary manufactures, and the zeal, ingenuity, and industry of the people, furnished the country with articles of prime necessity, and in a measure, supplied the place of a foreign market. Such was the progress in arts and manufactures, that after the return of peace, when an uninterrupted intercourse with England was again opened, some articles, which before were imported altogether, were found so well and so abundantly manufactured at home, that their importation was stopped, and arts and manufactures attracted the attention of government. A. Hamilton, secretary of the treasury, made a report to congress on the subject, in which he set forth their importance to the country, and urged the policy of aiding them. Since that time the revenue laws have been framed with a view to the encouragement of manufactures, and their promotion has been considered as a part of the settled policy of the United States. Although the flourishing state of commerce attracted the attention, and absorbed the capital of the country in some degree to the exclusion of other subjects, still manufactures began to progress.

—

From Hallam's History of the Middle Ages.

The condition of internal trade was hardly preferable to that of agriculture, which was wretched. There is not a vestige perhaps to be discovered for several centuries of any considerable manufacture; I mean, of working up articles of common utility, to an extent beyond what the necessities of an adjacent neighbourhood required. Rich men kept *domestic* artisans among their servants; even kings, in the ninth century, had their clothes made by women upon their farms. The only mention of a manufacture, as early as the ninth or tenth centuries, is what Schmidt says, that cloths were then exported from Friseland to England and other parts. Venice took the lead in trading with Greece and more eastern countries. Amalfi had the second place in the commerce of those dark ages; the fine cloths of Constantinople were imported. It is an humiliating proof of the degradation of Christendom, that the Venetians were reduced to purchase the luxuries of Asia, by supplying the *slave-market* of the Saracens.

Netherlands, coasts of France, Germany, Scandinavia, and the maritime districts of England, were first animated by the woollen manufacture of Flanders. It is not easy either to discover the early beginnings of this or to account for its rapid advancement. Several testimonies to the flourishing condition of Flemish manufactures occur in the twelfth century, and even earlier. A writer of the thirteenth century asserts, that all the world was clothed from English wool wrought in Flanders; they were probably sold wherever navigation permitted them to be carried. Flanders was a market for the traders of all the world. England soon began to share in the trade.

The History of Norfolk speaks of a colony of Flemings settling as early as the reign of Henry II. at *Worsted*, and immortalised its name by their manufactures. There were several guilds of weavers during the reign of Henry II. Edward III. may almost be called the father of English commerce, a title more glorious than hero of Cressy. In 1331 he invited the manufacturers of Flanders into his dominions. They brought the finer manufacture of woollen cloths which had been unknown in England. Commerce became a leading object with parliament. There were inducements held out to the Flemings: " Here they should feed on fat beef and mutton, till nothing but their fulness should stint their stomachs; their bed should be good, and their bed-fellows better, seeing the richest yeomen in England would not disdain to marry their daughters unto them, and such the English beauties, that the most envious foreigners could not but commend them."

THE END.

PLATE X.

Silk Loom exhibiting Mr. Richards's improved Drawboy.

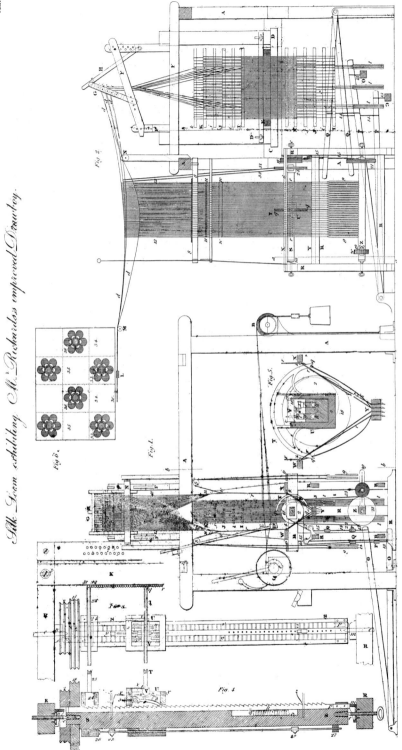

Fig. 2.

Fig. 1.

Fig. 6.

Fig. 5.

Fig. 3.

Fig. 4.

Heinz Mandl
Alan Lesgold

Editors

Learning Issues
for Intelligent
Tutoring Systems

Springer-Verlag

Cognitive Science

Series Editors:
Marc M. Sebrechts
Gerhard Fischer
Peter M. Fischer

Heinz Mandl   Alan Lesgold
Editors

Learning Issues for Intelligent Tutoring Systems

With 57 Figures

Springer-Verlag
New York Berlin Heidelberg
London Paris Tokyo

Dr. Heinz Mandl
Deutsches Institut für Fernstudien
  an der Universität Tübingen
7400 Tübingen
Federal Republic of Germany

Dr. Alan Lesgold
Learning Research and
  Development Center
University of Pittsburgh
Pittsburgh, PA 15260, USA

Library of Congress Cataloging-in-Publication Data
Learning issues for intelligent tutoring systems.
  (Cognitive science)
  Includes bibliographies and index.
  1. Intelligent tutoring systems.   I. Mandl, Heinz.
II. Lesgold, Alan M.   III. Series.
LB1028.5.L388   1988   371.3'9445   87-23449

Typeset by Best-set Typesetter Ltd., Hong Kong
Printed and bound by R.R. Donnelley & Sons, Harrisonburg, Virginia
Printed in the United States of America

9 8 7 6 5 4 3 2 1

ISBN 0-387-96616-1 Springer-Verlag New York Berlin Heidelberg
ISBN 3-540-96616-1 Springer-Verlag Berlin Heidelberg New York

Preface

Modern technological societies, with the demands they place upon people, make critical the improved teaching of higher-order skills such as reasoning, critical analysis, synthesis, problem solving, how to learn in various fields, and how to control and manage one's thinking (Lesgold, 1987). New technologies—particularly the computer—combined with better understanding of cognitive processes offer possibilities for the necessary improvements. This book focuses on these possibilities, attending especially to learning issues. The authors of the chapters were members of a group of cognitive scientists from various disciplines who gathered in Tübingen in 1985 to discuss the cognitive processes of learning and how those processes might be enhanced by intelligent instructional systems.

The promise of educational improvement through computers is not a new one. Computers have been used in education for almost 30 years. In the 1960s and 1970s, when computers began to appear in schools, a variety of computer-assisted instructional programs were developed. Generally, however, these did not meet the high expectations educators had for the new medium. Learning via computer was almost always based on inflexible presentations of didactic material. Moreover, these programs had only limited capabilities for adaptive diagnosis and feedback. Two things limited early teaching programs. First, the hardware then available had minimal memory capacity and computational speed. Second, the only theory available to guide instructional development was behavior theory, which poorly matched the cognitive goals of education.

Now both these limitations are being overcome. Recent prototype computer-based instructional systems are able to conduct an "intelligent" dialogue with the student and to provide screen-based learning environments that promote considerable self-initiated exploratory activity. These developments are possible partly because computer hardware is more powerful and there are better languages available for channeling that power. Further, the development of productivity-enhancing programming environments for object-oriented (e.g., Smalltalk and Loops) and rule-based (e.g., OPS5) program design has made it easier for psychologists

and educators to participate directly in software design. Further developments are likely in this growing area of the computer world (Bobrow & Stefik, 1986). The development of a technology for knowledge engineering and expert system design is also important. The early expert systems technology has played an important role in helping the world of education see what might be possible on a computer, although ultimately other contributions of artificial intelligence research will probably prove more relevant.

Finally, and most important, there have been great advances in the analysis of mental processes and in techniques for representing knowledge, including how it is acquired and how it changes over time. Work on machine learning of semantic networks, rule systems, and "mental" models (e.g., Michalski, Carbonell, & Mitchell, 1986) has provided useful insights, and work directly on human learning has flourished. Together, artificial intelligence and research on human cognition have provided a basis for a new generation of computer-based teaching programs. Like the human teacher, these programs attempt to model the knowledge of the student as learning takes place.

Now we have new expectations of computer-based instructional systems. They should be able to conduct a flexible and adaptive dialogue with the student through words or graphic interfaces. Students should be able to access information in varying forms and from varying viewpoints as they wish. This information should be presented according to the knowledge and skill level of the student, and should be grounded in the core mental models that are needed for the particular domain of instruction. Tasks for the student, and help in completing those tasks, should be selected based upon a continually updated model of the student's learning progress.

STRUCTURE OF INTELLIGENT TUTORING SYSTEMS

In this book, our colleagues join us in exploring the issues of learning that arise in building *intelligent tutoring systems*, systems that can make inferences about student knowledge and can interact intelligently with students based upon individual representations of what those students know. What do such systems look like? While they vary in architecture, intelligent tutoring systems tend to have four major components (cf. Lesgold, 1988, inter alia): the expert knowledge component, the learner modeling component, the tutorial planning component, and the communication component.

The *expert knowledge component* comprises the knowledge of experts: the facts and rules of a particular domain. Expert knowledge is represented in various ways, including semantic networks, frames, and production systems. It must include not only surface knowledge, but also the representational ability that is a critical part of expertise: the ability to

construct implicit representational understanding from explicit observations and other information. There are two different ways in which expert knowledge can be represented in a tutor. In earlier tutors, the knowledge was present only in "black box" form, which remained opaque to the learner. For example, the SOPHIE I tutor (Brown, Burton, & Bell, 1975; Burton & Brown, 1979) could answer any question a learner posed about electrical measurement values for any point in a complex circuit. However, because it used numerical simulation techniques to derive these test values, it could not explain to the learner why the values were as reported. Because such explanations seem very important to the acquisition of expertise, more recent work has focused on "glass box models" (Goldstein & Papert, 1977), whose knowledge is represented in a way that more directly matches human capability, affording richer possibilities for explanations to the learner.

The *learner modeling component* refers to the dynamic representation of the emerging knowledge and skill of the learner. This requires a diagnostic capability that can deduce the learner's knowledge from his interactions with the system as he tries to handle the educational tasks posed to him. Again, different approaches to this component can be observed in recent prototype systems and articles. One approach, the *overlay model*, represents the learner's knowledge as a subset of the expert's knowledge (Carr & Goldstein, 1977). An overlay model is useful only when the expert knowledge is represented in a form that reflects human learning and performance capabilities and limitations. For example, SOPHIE I could not have an overlay model of learner device knowledge because it used a complex mathematical simulation to generate device information; human knowledge of the device would not be organized as a system of mathematical equations.

An alternative approach is to include *deviations* from expertise in the model of the learner, since learners sometimes show incorrect inferences and systematic errors (Brown & Burton, 1978). Several approaches to deviation modeling have been taken. For example, following Anderson's (1983) theory of acquisition, one might represent deviations as incorrectly generalized or differentiated conditions in production rules. Or one might focus on the mental model as the unit of knowledge, with possible deviations from the expert view (e.g., White & Frederiksen, 1986).

The *tutorial planning component* is the part of an intelligent instructional system that designs and regulates instructional interactions with the learner. It is closely linked to the learner modeling component, using knowledge about the learner and its own tutorial goal structure to decide which instructional activities will be presented: hints to overcome performance impasses, advice and support, explanation, new material to be taught, different practice tasks, tests to confirm the learner model, etc. The tutorial component then is the source and orchestrator of pedagogical interventions.

One important distinction among tutorial strategies is that between didactic and discovery-oriented learning—between being told and learning from experience. The primary advantage of didactic approaches is that they are strongly goal-oriented. All activity focuses on the system's instructional goals, because the system initiates and controls activity. In discovery environments, some learners take a long time to make the discoveries that constitute the system's goals. Discovery environments are seen as having an advantage in that they allow new knowledge to be constructed in the learner's terms—in terms of the concepts and capabilities the learner already possesses—from direct concrete experience. Microworlds (see, for example, Lesgold, 1987, or Shute, Glaser, & Raghavan, in press) are one approach to discovery learning, and some recent microworlds tend to "guide" the discovery process in an effort to increase the efficiency of discovery learning. It is important to note that modeling the learner's knowledge becomes more difficult as his degrees of freedom are increased.

Finally, the fourth component of intelligent instructional systems is the *communication component*, which controls interactions between the system and the learner. For a variety of reasons, intelligent instructional systems have tended to use graphic interfaces heavily. Such interfaces provide greater concreteness in the information provided to the student, and they make the interaction with the student more "user-friendly" by substituting pictures and pointing for text and typing. We can expect to see intelligent instructional systems communicating with the learner primarily via graphics, since computer recognition and generation of written and spoken language, though becoming more feasible, are incomplete and computationally intensive. From a psychological viewpoint, this presents a quandary, since there is a much richer body of research on verbal processing than on the perception of and interaction with graphics. More work is needed on learning issues in the use of graphics, even though practical work using graphics flourishes. On the verbal side, Wahlster (1981) has pointed out relevant questions concerning the design of natural speech in dialogue systems.

RECENT EFFORTS

During the last few years, several intelligent instructional systems have been developed as research prototypes (e.g., GUIDON by Clancey, 1983; SOPHIE by Brown, Burton & de Kleer, 1982; WEST, by Burton & Brown, 1979; the BUGGY/DEBUGGY series by Burton, 1982; and Anderson's Lisp Tutor, Anderson, Boyle, & Reiser, 1985). Good overviews can be found in Wenger (1987), Barr & Feigenbaum (1982), and Sleeman & Brown (1982). Several of the most recent efforts, such as SMITHTOWN (Shute, Glaser, & Raghavan, in press) place special emphasis on discovery learning and on the coaching of metacognitive processes of learning.

Nonetheless, the development of intelligent instructional systems is still in its infancy, though like many infants it flourishes. What is needed are a stronger theoretical foundation based on deeper analysis of the acquisition of complex learning-to-learn, conceptual and performance knowledge, and a stable level of research funding that can attract more of the best cognitive science talent to this field. The same might be said for the entire field of intelligent systems science and technology (Hayes-Roth & Thorndyke, 1985). The infancy of this field has been very productive, however, and this book attempts to record what has been learned so far.

The first part of the book deals with fundamentals of learning and instruction that are especially relevant to the design of intelligent tutoring systems. It begins with a programmatic chapter by Allan Collins and John Seely Brown, on learning through reflection. Collins and Brown have called for a new wave of apprenticeship learning, in which the learner can reflectively compare his learning and problem-solving strategies and methods with those of an expert. They have used concrete screen displays that provide viewpoints on several different aspects of the learning or problem-solving process simultaneously, "reifying" the cognitive processing that has taken place. Having access to these concrete reifications of his own thinking, the learner is then more able to generalize metacognitive strategies from his, or the machine expert's, specific performances.

Kurt VanLehn (Chapter 2) proposes that impasses play a critical role in the learning of procedural skills. Building from his work on Repair Theory (Brown & VanLehn, 1980; VanLehn, 1981) VanLehn has developed a metalevel architecture for learning. When an impasse in performance occurs, the student either attempts to repair his performance using weaker methods or seeks help. When the chosen metaprocess succeeds in resolving the impasse, the student may then abstract the actions needed to deal with the kind of situation just encountered (see Rosenbloom & Newell, 1986, for another view of the abstraction process). To the extent that the student encounters impasses that he cannot resolve with his weak repair methods, repairs may tend to generate buggy subprocedures. To the extent that effective help is sought and received, impasses are the source of new learning in the VanLehn formulation.

Cognitive diagnosis is central to psychological research, to instruction, and to the construction of computer systems that adapt to their users' needs. Ohlsson and Langley, in Chapter 3, describe a diagnostic method for specifying the learner model for a procedural skill, given instances of the performance of that skill. The heart of the method is a set of psychologically motivated evaluation criteria for choosing between competing diagnoses. Ohlsson and Langley have implemented their method in a computer program that performs cognitive diagnosis for the domain of subtraction. They present selected computational results and discuss the power and limitations of their method.

Chapter 4, by Ipke Wachsmuth, stresses the problem of situation-specific knowledge that is straightforward in one domain but cannot be

applied in related situations. To use domain-specific knowledge in a broad range of situations, two things appear to be required: (1) a set of rules that support successful performance in a given subject domain, and (2) a set of situations of sufficient perceptual variation to span the range of circumstances in which the learner will be calling upon those rules. Wachsmuth proposes a computer-based learning model, LAKOS 1, which models different levels of student mathematical knowledge. Levels of specificity in the learner's knowledge are typified by certain language that influences the situations in which those rules will be effective. Wachsmuth also outlines how his approach can be adapted for use in intelligent tutoring systems.

The second part of the book deals with issues of learning systems design. William Clancey (Chapter 5) develops a basis for teaching students how to direct their own learning. He describes how a model of active learning is being developed and tested in a knowledge acquisition procedure for an expert system. The model is derived from modeling methods that knowledge engineers use to approach new domains and to acquire practical problem-solving knowledge. In particular, a knowledge engineer is good at detecting gaps in a knowledge base and asking focused questions that can lead to improved expert system performance. This ability stems from domain-general knowledge about problem-solving procedures and from knowledge of the categories of routine problem-solving and domain and task differences. Clancey examines different forms of metaknowledge and illustrates how it can be incorporated into an intelligent tutoring system. He presents a model of learning which describes how the knowledge engineer detects problem-solving failures and tracks them back to gaps in domain knowledge, which are then reformulated as questions to ask teachers.

Alan Lesgold (Chapter 6) presents an architecture for representing curriculum or goal knowledge in intelligent tutors. It is thus a first step toward a theory of curriculum to inform the design of intelligent tutoring and testing systems. He suggests that the knowledge in an intelligent tutor should be structured in three interconnected levels: (1) curriculum knowledge, a lattice of lessons or curricular subgoals connected by the prerequisite relation; (2) a network representation of the knowledge to be taught, from which explanations and student models can be generated; and (3) a representation of the enduring characteristics of the student (such as his metacognitive skills or aptitudes) to which instruction should be sensitive. To illustrate one way in which such a theory can sharpen ideas about intelligent tutoring, Lesgold focuses on the concept of *prerequisite*. He shows that both (1) the curricular level, and (2) the domain level of an intelligent system's knowledge base are needed to determine why a student had trouble with a lesson for which he knew all the prerequisites.

Gerhard Fischer (Chapter 7) considers the problem of users of powerful and complex computer systems when they lack the skills needed to use

such systems effectively and efficiently. From a general theory of incremental learning processes, he derives processes "which will be the dominant way to master systems of broad functionality." This approach is based on the paradigm of *increasingly complex microworlds* (Burton, Brown, & Fischer, 1983; Fischer, Burton, & Brown, 1978). The theory is complemented by several application systems that feature cooperative "critics" that follow a person's use of a system and intervene when they have advice or help that might be useful.

A further framework for learning systems design is provided by Norbert A. Streitz in Chapter 8. In describing human-computer interaction, he distinguishes a *content problem* of the learner who wants to acquire knowledge about a domain from the *interaction problem* that the learner has in interacting with a tutoring system. In his approach, Streitz builds upon Norman's "mental model zoo," distinguishing among a user's mental model, a system's realization, the psychologist's view, and the designer's view, and he introduces a formal notation that can help in distinguishing these viewpoints. He then goes on to discuss how to communicate conceptual models of a novel system to a new user, discussing metaphorical approaches that are as conflict-free as possible.

The third part of the book focuses on conditions that facilitate learning. Mark Lepper and Ruth Chabay (Chapter 10) argue that motivational components of tutoring strategies are as important as the cognitive components, and that truly personalized instruction must adapt to motivational as well as cognitive differences. They illustrate and compare interactions between computer tutors and learners on the one hand and between human tutors and learners on the other, discussing four aspects of tutorial intervention: control, timing, content, and style. The chapter continues with a discussion of whether *empathy* might be built into a computer tutor, whether part of an instructional system's intelligence might not relate to motivational aims. Some steps toward the development of empathetic computer tutors are outlined, emphasizing the variety of issues that arise in motivating children to engage in activities to foster learning.

A related issue is addressed in Chapter 9, by Peter Fischer and Heinz Mandl. They address the affective stresses that are placed on a learner by the feedback that an intelligent tutor might provide, discussing what is needed to model this aspect of the acquisition process adequately and reliably. They suggest that some of the stresses can be overcome by transforming any kind of covert feedback into deliberate, overt feedback. They then describe their KAVIS II interactive teaching-learning system, in which the learner is trained to make intelligent use of the feedback presented and to experience it positively. KAVIS II, like some of the other systems presented in the book, was created as both a learning and a research tool that might efficiently and sensitively detect ongoing cognitive processes.

The next two contributions have in common an experimental approach

and an emphasis on forms of representation for problem-solving techniques, the first in physics and the second in algebra. Both chapters discuss consequences of their findings for the design of intelligent instructional systems.

Eileen Scanlon and Tim O'Shea ask, in Chapter 11, whether multiple representations are really helpful, or whether they may sometimes hinder successful problem solving. They question the view of many artificial intelligence researchers that multiple representations of the same problem situation are helpful, showing evidence of cases where non-experts do less well in solving problems when multiple representations are presented. They suggest, based on their data, that *economical* use of alternative representations is important for effective problem solving, and go on to suggest that the relationship between different representations of the same problem situation ought to be taught explicitly.

Evelyne Cauzinille-Marmèche and Jacques Mathieu, in Chapter 12, proceed from the hypothesis that mapping between different representations from various microworlds is an important determinant of learning. They report results from three experiments on algebra learning, showing that (1) students approaching algebra for the first time spontaneously refer to different microworlds; (2) the different microworlds are not necessarily related to or coherent with each other; and (3) inducing students to change their representations and establishing links between representations can help the students make sense of newly introduced rules of algebra and master the domain of applicability for those rules. The conception of their system ALGIR is based on these ideas.

In Chapter 13 by Joachim Wedekind, a further important aspect of computers for learning is addressed, closing a circle back to the beginning of the volume. In addition to using the computer to record individual problem solving and learning paths, to model the learner, and to help him reflect on his cognitive activity, systems should help the student learn the process of modeling itself. Therefore, Wedekind argues that the structure and function of interactive simulation systems should match the ways in which people work in the domain being simulated, and presents an example of this approach, KOMPART.

Wedekind makes a statement that nicely reflects the overall theme of this book: "It is the computer that has to be changed, not the user." We thank our colleagues for providing such a useful range of examples of the work on issues of learning—issues that must be handled in order to have a new generation of instructional computer systems that are, not only intelligent, but also supportive and cooperative in facilitating learning.

Heinz Mandl
Alan Lesgold

REFERENCES

Anderson, J. R. (1983). *The architecture of cognition.* Cambridge, MA: Harvard University Press.

Anderson, J. R., Boyle, C. F., & Reiser, B. J. (1985). *Intelligent tutoring systems.* Pittsburgh, PA: Carnegie Mellon University, Advanced Computer Tutoring Project.

Barr, A., & Feigenbaum, E. A. (1982). *The handbook of artificial intelligence.* (Vol. II). Los Altos, CA: Morgan Kaufmann.

Bobrow, D. G., & Stefik, M. (1986). Perspectives on artificial intelligence programming, *Science, 231,* 951–957.

Brown, J. S., & Burton, R. R. (1978). Diagnostic models for procedural bugs in basic mathematical skills. *Cognitive Science, 2,* 155–192.

Brown, J. S., Burton, R. R., & Bell, A. G. (1975). SOPHIE: A step toward creating a reactive learning environment. *International Journal of Man-Machine Studies, 7,* 675–696.

Brown, J. S., Burton, R. R., & de Kleer, J. (1982). Pedagogical, natural language and knowledge engineering techniques in SOPHIE I, II and III. In D. Sleeman & J. S. Brown (Eds.), *Intelligent tutoring systems.* New York: Academic Press.

Brown, J. S., & VanLehn, K. (1980). Repair theory: A generative theory of bugs in procedural skills. *Cognitive Science, 4,* 379–426.

Burton, R. R. (1982). Diagnosing bugs in a simple procedural skill. In D. Sleeman & J. S. Brown (Eds.), *Intelligent tutoring systems.* New York: Academic Press.

Burton, R. R., & Brown, J. S. (1979). An investigation of computer coaching for informal learning activities. *International Journal of Man-Machine Studies, 11,* 5–24.

Burton, R. R., Brown, J. S., & Fischer, G. (1983, January). *Analysis of skiing as a success model of instruction: Manipulating the learning environment to enhance instructional acquisition.* Palo Alto, CA: Xerox Palo Alto Research Center.

Carr, B., & Goldstein, I. (1977). *Overlays: A theory of modeling for computer-aided instruction.* Cambridge, MA: Massachusetts Institute of Technology, Artificial Intelligence Laboratory.

Clancey, W. J. (1983). GUIDON. *Journal of Computer-based Instruction, 10,* 8–15.

Fischer, G., Burton, R. R., & Brown, J. S. (1978). Analysis of skiing as a success model of instruction: Manipulating the learning environment to enhance skill acquisition. In *Proceedings of the second national conference of the Canadian Society for Computational Studies of Intelligence.*

Goldstein, I. P., & Papert, S. (1977). Artificial intelligence, language, & the study of knowledge. *Cognitive Science, 1,* 1–21.

Hayes-Roth, B., & Thorndyke, P. W. (1985). Paradigms for intelligent systems. *Educational Psychologist, 20,* 4, 231–241.

Lesgold, A. (1987). Intelligent tutoring systems: Practice opportunities and explanatory models. In J. Barrett & J. Hedberg (Eds.), *Using computers intelligently in tertiary education.* Kensington, New South Wales: University of New South Wales, Continuing Education. (Proceedings of the 1987 meeting of the Australian Society for Computers in Learning, Sydney, December, 1987).

Lesgold, A. (1988). Intelligenter computerunterstützter Unterricht. In H. Mandl

& H. Spada (Eds.), *Wissenpsychologie: Ein Lehrbuch*. Müchen/Weinheim: Psychologie Verlags Union.

Michalski, R. S., Carbonell, J. G., & Mitchell, T. M. (Eds.). (1986). *Machine learning* (Vol. II). Los Altos, CA: Morgan Kaufmann.

Rosenbloom, P. S., & Newell, A. (1986). The chunking of goal hierarchies: A generalized model of practice. In R. S. Michalski, J. G. Carbonell, & T. M. Mitchell (Eds.), *Machine learning* (Vol. II). Los Altos, CA: Morgan Kaufmann.

Shute, V., Glaser, R., & Raghavan, K. (in press). Discovery and inference in an exploratory laboratory. In P. L. Ackerman, R. J. Sternberg, & R. Glaser (Eds.), *Learning and individual differences*. San Francisco: Freeman.

Sleeman, D., & Brown, J. S. (1982). *Intelligent tutoring systems*. New York: Academic Press.

VanLehn, K. (1981). *Bugs are not enough: Empirical studies of bugs, impasses and repairs in procedural skills*. Technical Report SSL-81-2. Palo Alto, CA: Xerox Palo Alto Research Center.

Wahlster, W. (1981). *Natürlichsprachliche Argumentation in Dialogsystemen. KI-Verfahren zur Rekonstruktion und Erklärung approximativer Inferenzprozesse*. Informatik-Fachberichte 48. Berlin: Springer-Verlag.

Wenger, E. (1987). *Artificial intelligence and tutoring systems*. Los Altos, CA: Morgan Kaufmann.

White, B. Y., & Frederiksen, J. R. (1986). Intelligent tutoring systems based upon qualitative model evolutions. *Proceedings of the Fifth National Conference on Artificial Intelligence*, 313–319.

Contents

Contributors

DR. JOHN SEELY BROWN
Xerox PARC, Palo Alto, California 94304, U.S.A.

DR. E. CAUZINILLE-MARMÈCHE
Laboratoire de Psychologie Génétique, Universite René Descartes 75005
Paris, France

DR. RUTH W. CHABAY
Department of Psychology, Stanford University, Stanford, California
94305, U.S.A.
Current address:
Center for the Design of Educational Computing, Carnegie-Mellon
University, Pittsburgh, PA 15213

DR. WILLIAM J. CLANCEY
Knowledge Systems Laboratory, Stanford University, Palo Alto, California 94304, U.S.A.
Current address:
Institute for Research on Learning, 3333 Coyote Hill Road, Palo Alto,
California 94304

DR. ALLAN COLLINS
Bolt, Beranek, and Newman, Inc., Cambridge, Massachusetts 02238,
U.S.A.

DR. GERHARD FISCHER
Department of Computer Science and Institute of Cognitive Science,
University of Colorado, Boulder, Colorado 80309-0430, U.S.A.

MR. PETER MICHAEL FISCHER
Deutsches Institut für Fernstudien an der Universität Tübingen, 7400
Tübingen, Federal Republic of Germany

DR. PAT LANGLEY
Department of Information and Computer Science, University of California, Irvine, Irvine, California 92717, U.S.A.

DR. MARK R. LEPPER
Department of Psychology, Stanford University, Stanford, California 94305-2130, U.S.A.

DR. ALAN LESGOLD
Learning Research and Development Center, University of Pittsburgh, Pittsburgh, Pennsylvania 15260, U.S.A.

DR. HEINZ MANDL
Deutsches Institut für Fernstudien an der Universität Tübingen, 7400 Tübingen, Federal Republic of Germany

DR. J. MATHIEU
Centre Mondial Informatique, 75008 Paris, France

DR. STELLAN OHLSSON
Learning Research and Development Center, University of Pittsburgh, Pittsburgh, Pennsylvania 15260, U.S.A.

DR. TIM O'SHEA
Institute of Educational Technology, Open University, Milton Keynes, England MK7 6AA

DR. EILEEN SCANLON
Institute of Educational Technology, Open University, Milton Keynes, England MK7 6AA

DR. NORBERT A. STREITZ
ACCEPT, Institute of Psychology, Aachen University of Technology, 5100 Aachen, Federal Republic of Germany
Current address:
Gesellschaft für Mathematik und Datenverarbeitung MBH, D-6100 Darmstadt, Federal Republic of Germany

DR. KURT VANLEHN
Department of Psychology, Carnegie-Mellon University, Pittsburgh, Pennsylvania 15213, U.S.A.

DR. IPKE WACHSMUTH
Fachbereich Mathematik/Informatik, Universität Osnabrück, 4500 Osnabrück, Federal Republic of Germany

DR. JOACHIM WEDEKIND
Deutsches Institut für Fernstudien an der Universität Tübingen, 7400 Tübingen, Federal Republic of Germany

1

The Computer as a Tool for Learning Through Reflection

ALLAN COLLINS
JOHN SEELY BROWN

Introduction

A unique aspect of computers is that they not only represent process but also naturally keep track of the actions used to carry out a given task, so that the process with its trace can become an object of study in its own right. One effect of this can be seen vividly in the sciences, where computers and computational languages have improved our ability to develop and test process theories of complex natural phenomena. Before powerful computers became readily available as scientific tools, process models were expressed in mathematical languages, such as differential equations—languages primarily effective in capturing a static "snapshot" of a process. Computation provided formal languages that are more flexible than mathematics but just as precise. In part because computation is itself dynamic, it provides an ideal medium for representing and testing richer, more varied, and more detailed theories of process. The use of this medium for process modeling has radically changed the nature of many current theories in both the physical and social sciences. Particularly in the arena of the cognitive sciences, computational techniques have proved to be powerful tools for both experimental and theoretical investigations of the mind.

The computational revolution in the sciences has a parallel in education. With a computational medium it becomes possible (and often easy) to capture directly the processes by which a novice or an expert carries out a complex task. Properly abstracted and structured, this process trace, or audit trail, can become a useful object of study for students who are trying to learn how to improve their performance on a task. By comparing the details and structure of their own performance with that of more expert performers, they can discover elements that need improving. In a sense the expert's audit trail provides an accessible example of the situated use of general reasoning strategies. Likewise, audit trails of students' own performances provide objects of study from which students can learn important self-monitoring and other metacognitive strategies.

It is because of its ability to record and represent process that we con-

jecture that the computer can become a powerful tool for learning through reflection, a new form of intellectual "bootstrapping." We suggest that the revolution in discovery learning heralded by Logo (Papert, 1980) will not fully materialize unless there is a way for students to study and explore their own problem-solving efforts. The students' problem-solving processes—their thrashings, false starts and restarts, and partial successes —should not be left implicit. A major value in solving problems occurs when students step back and reflect on how they actually solved the problem and how the particular set of strategies they used were suboptimal and might be improved. Of course, this ideal scenario seldom occurs, in part because students are not really motivated to perform the reflection and in part because the current problem-solving medium (i.e., paper and pencil) does not really lend itself to this activity. Our claim here is that the computational medium, properly structured, can provide a powerful, motivating, and as yet untapped tool for focusing the students' attention *directly* on their own thought processes.

This chapter reports on several steps in the direction of reflective learning. We begin by considering a familar skill, tennis, to illustrate the power and possibilities of reflective media for learning.

Types of Reflection

Let us consider the pedagogical strengths and weaknesses of different ways of representing a tennis swing and the different ways of reflecting on that representation.

IMITATION

The tennis coach can imitate a student's swing, highlighting those aspects of the swing that were correct or incorrect, while verbally describing the crucial properties of the swing as it progresses. He can slow the swing down and even stop at critical moments. However, imitations have their limitations as a pedagogical device. First, there are always distortions in any imitation, and the student may focus on them as the relevant features. Second, from a model of a swing, the student cannot be sure how much or exactly how to correct a particular movement. Nor can the student easily engage in a fine-grained analysis of his own swing. He may miss critical relationships that can only be seen in an abstracted replay or spatial reification.

REPLAY

Alternatively, the student's swing can be videotaped from different angles and replayed and discussed. The tape can be played as often as the student

wants, sped up or slowed down, or stopped in critical places for detailed discussion with the coach. The replay is accurate in its reproduction of the student's behavior. It has high physical fidelity and captures not only the swing itself but also the follow-through, the angling of the ball off the strings of the racquet, and so forth, so that the student sees the swing in context. Given split-screen technologies, students can even compare themselves to video recordings of experts and attempt to abstract how to alter their movements to approximate better the important aspects of the experts' swings.

The last notion highlights one of the fundamental limitations of exact replay for use in reflective learning. It is often difficult for students to know what to pay attention to unless a coach points out the important properties as they watch the replay. Indeed, without the student possessing a relevant set of distinctions about the process being observed, he is hard-pressed to remember or compare his performance with that of the expert, nor can he readily modify his performance to bring about the desired effects once he knows what they are. However, there are ways to focus the student's attention and to help set the stage for constructing a useful set of distinctions with which to observe and remember expert performance.

ABSTRACTED REPLAY

Suppose a reflective material is taped to critical points (e.g., the shoulder, elbow, wrist, handle, racquet head), and the motion of these different points recorded during the swing, perhaps from two angles (e.g., the side and the front). Such an abstracted replay attains both accuracy and the unambiguous highlighting of critical features, thus focusing the student's attention on the important parameters of the swing. Abstracted replay thus turns on the notion of "cognitive fidelity" rather than physical fidelity. This is especially crucial when there is too much data for the student to absorb in a full replay or imitation. The highlighting made possible through abstraction conveys information in a way that no verbal explanation can. Of course, if critical features (such as leg positions) are omitted, information is lost to the student that is available in the full replay condition.

As with the replay condition, comparison of the student's swing with that of the expert depends on the student's either remembering the expert's or using a side-by-side comparison with split screens. If a good abstraction can be constructed, it becomes possible to overlay the student's swing with a trajectory of an expert's swing.

SPATIAL REIFICATION

The trajectory of the critical points of a swing, say from the side angle or from other angles, can be plotted in a graph. This gives a static representa-

tion of the process unfolding in time that can be inspected and analyzed in detail. A spatial reification has many of the same properties as an abstracted replay; but because the dimension of time is now spatially represented, the student can analyze critical relationships over time more easily and can directly refer back to prior parts of the process. For example, the relative height of the racquet head at the beginning, middle, and end of the swing can be easily seen from the side plot. Students can directly compare their plot with a plot of expert performance without relying on memory. But again some critical features may be lost at the expense of others being reified. For example the timing of the swing is only implicit in the above representation scheme.

As a general principle, multiple representations are helpful. Students should be able to inspect their performance in different ways, so it makes sense to provide them capabilities for seeing full replays, abstracted replays, or spatial reifications. A critical ingredient of the Reciprocal Teaching Method (Palincsar & Brown, 1984) is that the students are able to compare their performance with expert performance in terms of the difficulties they are currently having and the distinctions they currently hold. This suggests showing simpler abstractions of their performance at earlier stages of learning.

Ideally, a coach could diagnose where the student is having difficulty and abstract those elements critical to overcoming the difficulty. For example, a student who is dropping his racquet head might see a replay where the relative position of the wrist and racquet head is highlighted, whereas a student who is bending his or her elbow too much might see a replay that highlights the positions of the shoulder, elbow, and wrist. This linking of correction to diagnosis is what gives coaching in general and the Reciprocal Teaching Method in particular much of their leverage.

Reflection on the Process of Problem Solving

Two recently developed tutoring systems use reifications of the student's problem-solving process as a major pedagogical device: Algebraland and Geometry Tutor.

ALGEBRALAND

Students are given algebraic expressions to solve for a particular variable (J. S. Brown, 1985). In Figure 1.1 students are to solve for N. They manipulate both sides of the equation by selecting an algebraic operator from the menu at the bottom right and a term in the equation in the record window on which the operator is to be applied. In Figure 1.1 the student first distributes 4 across $(2 + N)$ and then divides both sides by 4. In a special search space window, the program automatically forms a tree that represents the various problem-solving steps, halts, and continuations that

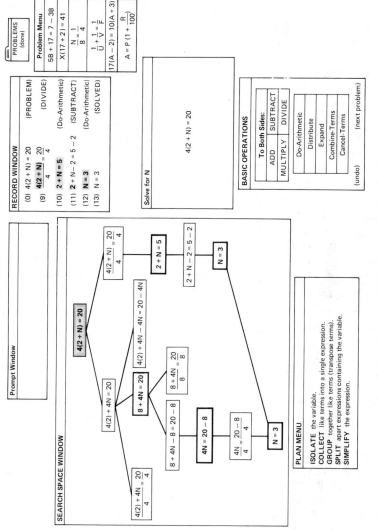

FIGURE 1.1. Layout of the screen for Algebraland.

the student has thus far taken in attempting to solve the problem. When students become stuck, they can return to an earlier node in the solution path by simply pointing at it and beginning a new path that they hope will lead to a solution. This branching process causes the resulting search space window to be a tree rather than just a single chain of nodes. The record window records each state (i.e., node) the student reached in the current solution path, and the algebraic operation that was used to move from one state to another in that chain.

The tree in the search space window is a reification of the student's problem-solving process. Students can see exactly where they backed up, where they reached the same state twice, where they were getting farther away from a solution, and so on. The structured representation of partial solution paths provides an opportunity to reflect on problem-solving and evaluation strategies in the context of their use, a context that reveals where they worked well and where they may have led the student astray. For example, reflecting on a choice point where the branch (i.e., operator) first chosen proved to be counterproductive, but where a different branch taken at that choice point (chosen at a later time) proved to be productive, provides grist for considering which features the decision process for that choice point should have focused on. That is, the student should ask himself what properties of the algebraic expression comprising the node could have alerted him to a better strategic choice.

Countless learning activities can be constructed around this reified problem space. For example, a student or team can be asked to study another student's (or team's) problem space with the aim of finding a shorter solution path to the problem. Among other things this kind of exercise helps to make explicit that there is no single "right" solution; there are many solutions, some of which are shorter and perhaps more elegant than others. Indeed, games can be constructed that turn on this simple idea. Alternatively, using a menu-based annotation editor, such as shown at the bottom left of Figure 1.1, a student might be asked to annotate the reasons why they made certain choices (see Bundy, 1983), a simple and rewarding exercise if the annotation menu has built into it strategic terms that can be readily selected and joined to the links in the reified problem space (Carolyn Foss, personal communication, March 1985—she is a Stanford graduate student who is writing a thesis on the role of reflection in the development of metacognitive skill and impasse-driven learning). Finally, students can examine their own floundering in order to formulate self-monitoring strategies that would help to detect and prune nonproductive approaches to similar problems.

GEOMETRY TUTOR

In another learning environment involving reflection (Anderson, Boyle, & Reiser, 1985), this one for learning the skill of doing proofs in geometry,

students are given a diagram of the problem at the top left of the screen and a set of "givens" at the bottom of the screen (Figure 1.2). In this example the goal is to prove the statement at the top of the screen. Students can work either forward from the givens (forward chaining) or backward from what is to be proved (backward chaining), as shown in the middle panel of the figure. The system alternates operators and states in the diagram it constructs. Again, as seen in the bottom panel, there is a trace of the problem-solving process. Although it is impossible to tell the order of the steps taken, the student can see dead ends and look for other possible proofs.

As Anderson, Boyle, Farrell, and Reiser (1984) point out, geometry proofs are usually presented in a fundamentally misleading way. Proofs on paper appear to be linear structures that start from a set of givens and proceed step by step (with a justification for each step) to the statement to be proved. But this is not at all how proofs are constructed by mathematicians or by anybody else. The process of constructing proofs involves an interplay between forward chaining from the givens and backward chaining from the goal statement. Yet, the use of paper and its properties encourage students to write proofs as if they were produced only by forward chaining—starting with the givens at the top of the page and working downward to the goal in a two column linear format (left column for the derived statements, right column for the logical justifications). If students infer that they should *construct* proofs this way, they will fail at any long proof. Properly designed computational learning environments can encourage students to proceed in both directions, moving forward, exploring the givens, and moving backward, finding bridges to the goals.

The representations in Algebraland and Geometry Tutor are abstractions of the problem-solving process in terms of "problem spaces." Both systems show the states in the problem space that the student reached and the operators used to reach each of those states. Simply seeing the steps toward a solution reified in this way helps to create a problem space as a mental entity in its own right. This, in turn, makes it possible, for both teachers and students, to characterize problem-solving strategies in terms of abstractions that *refer* to properties concretely manifested in the reified problem space. For example, in geometry it is a good strategy to forward chain at the beginning of a problem in order to understand the implications of the givens. Similarly, if you are stuck in backward chaining, and do not see a way to connect your backward chain to any of the givens, then either go back to forward chaining or go back to the goal state again and try backward chaining along a different path.

These problem-solving strategies are what are known as "metacognitive" strategies (A. L. Brown, 1978); students must learn these strategies to control problem-solving processes. Metacognitive strategies are what people use to detect and control "floundering," that is, moving through the problem space without getting closer to the goal. Figure 1.3 shows the

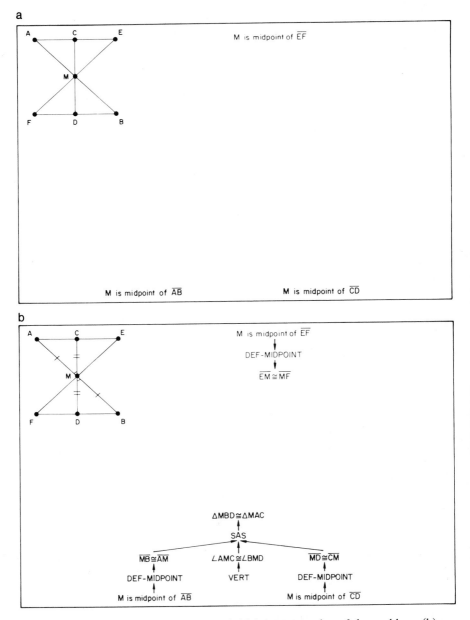

FIGURE 1.2. (a) The Geometry Tutor's initial representation of the problem; (b) a representation in the middle of the problem; and (c) a representation at the solution of the problem.

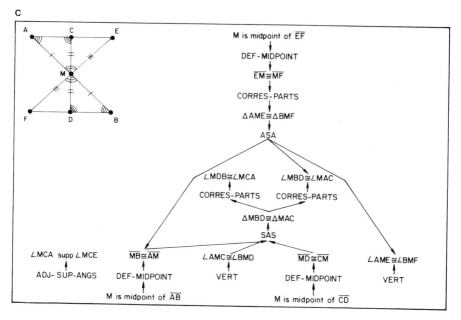

FIGURE 1.2. *Continued*

problem space of one of Foss's (personal communication, March 1985) subjects floundering while using Algebraland. The problem was to solve the equation for V. When the student first got to the state $\frac{1}{V} = \frac{1}{F} - \frac{1}{U}$, he tried a whole series of different operations (e.g., multiplying by 1, dividing by 1, subtracting 1, etc.). In that sequence he even tried the operation that eventually led to success (i.e., multiplying by V), but he failed to see that this step was a good one. The student was obviously floundering at the time. He was just trying operations without any clear plan and without considering where they might lead. As a result he was carrying out operations without apparently getting closer to the goal. Suddenly, however, he started over and solved the problem systematically as seen on the right-hand side of the figure.

Anderson et al. (1984) argue that the system should prevent students from going off the optimal solution path so that they never flounder. The authors argue that floundering leads to confusion, waste of valuable time, and loss of motivation. In contrast we argue that unless students flounder they will never have the opportunity to learn the kinds of metacognitive strategies suggested previously. We need to create environments where students can flounder and where the system helps students profit from this floundering by making it explicit and, if necessary, by having coaching systems highlight the floundering and help students discover or understand better metacognitive strategies grounded on their particular experience.

Perhaps a mixed pedagogical strategy would be ideal. When students

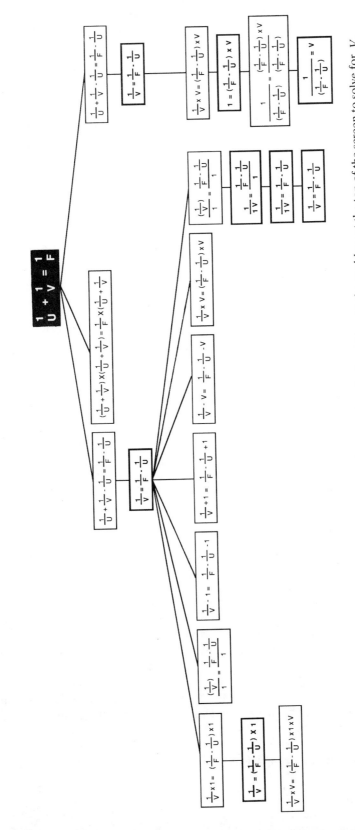

FIGURE 1.3. Algebraland reflection window showing the trace of an actual student working on the problem at the top of the screen to solve for V.

are learning the use and meaning of basic domain operators for moving through a problem space, the system should prevent students from floundering. In this way their time is being solely focused on mastering the basic tools of the trade. As students begin to tackle real problems, they need the elbow room to explore nooks and crannies of the problem space in order to gain insights into what makes a theorem true or a problem solvable. During this phase, however, the system should attempt to provide students guidance on how to examine their own floundering, helping them to detect inherently useless exploration. In this way learning moves naturally from domain skills to metacognitive strategies.

Reflection on the Process of Writing

We can illustrate the educational potential of reflection on the writing process in the context of the NoteCards system developed by Frank Halasz and Tom Moran (J. S. Brown, 1985). The NoteCards system is a multi-windowed authoring system based on the metaphor of the small note cards that writers sometimes use to capture, organize, and reorganize their thoughts. The NoteCards system allows writers to create notes including text and sketches on a topic they plan to write about. These notes can be indexed in any way desired by "filing" them in "fileboxes" by source, topic, and so on. The writer can also create labeled links between notes that characterize the relationships between the ideas such as comments, contradictions, elaborations, and so forth. The notes and their linkages to fileboxes or other note cards can be viewed in a link-icon browser, exemplified in Figure 1.4, using link-type selection as a mechanism for filtering the information in the note file. Thus, one might want to see only the cards that deal with the main thesis of the paper. Or one might want to view all the contradictions and support links for a given piece of text. The writer can also create an outline structure of the text and insert links to notes into it. Link icons that represent note cards can be moved freely around in the browser or in an outline, allowing either local or global restructuring of the ideas for the paper.

While the initial NoteCards system was under development, a history graduate student used the system to write a paper on the deployment of North Atlantic Treaty Organization (NATO) missiles in Western Europe. He read a number of documents and made notes on them in the system. After he had written about 30 notes and filed them in a topic hierarchy, he created a browser that reflected the structure of his initial thinking (see Figure 1.4). As he created more notes, he changed the structure of the browser several different times. When he had written about 500 notes, he decided he was ready to start writing. He created a text outline for the paper and inserted footnote links to particular notes. He then rewrote each note, inserting it as text into the outline, adding bridging sentences

Topics

- **TNF Doctrine**
  - **NATO TNF Modernization Plan**
    - Official NATO View of Deployments
    - Perception of Need for Modernization
    - HLG and TNF Modernization Plan
    - Decision to Adopt GLCM and Pershing II
  - **Arms Control: Proposals and Negotiations**
    - NATO Responses to Soviet Initiatives
    - Soviet Initiatives
    - Geneva INF Talks
  - **Proposals for TNF Change**
    - Critsisms of No First Use
    - No First Use Proposal
    - Nuclear Free Zone Proposal
  - **NATO TNF Doctrine**
    - Origins of NATO Doctrine
    - Criticisms of NATO Doctrine
    - ESECS Pln for Conventional Strengthening
    - NATO Conventional Forces
    - NATO Nuclear Structure
    - US Role in NATO

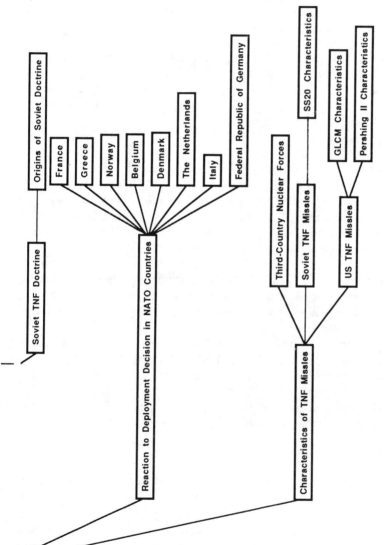

FIGURE 1.4. Screen from Notecards showing one of the browsers created by a graduate student working with the system.

and paragraphs as necessary. As he worked, he added new topics and subtopics to his outline. He proceeded in this way until he produced a complete draft.

It is now possible to look at the various structures he created while organizing and writing the paper (i.e., the notes, the various browsers, the outline). By adding a tracing program to the system, it would be possible to replay the actual process by which the paper was constructed, reflecting his strategies for producing a complex text based on many different sources.

People's strategies for writing vary widely. Some writers start with an outline and then produce notes or text to fill out the outline. Bereiter and Scardamalia (1985) argue that children tend to use a "knowledge telling" strategy, in which they write the first thing they think of as the first sentence of a text, then the second thing they think of, and so on. More experienced writers tend to separate idea generation (e.g., producing notes) from actually writing text (Flower & Hayes, 1980), as did the graduate student in the study. Although no one strategy is "correct," some are decidedly more effective than others.

The capability to record and replay the various notes, outlines, and pieces of text that students produce provides a new way for students to think about the process of writing. They might be able to look at the process by which different people produced articles in similar genres. Perhaps students might have access to models of how some classic texts of the future (i.e., by a future Shakespeare or Marx) were constructed using a system like NoteCards. Students could then systematically compare their writing process to a variety of different writers.

This possibility raises the issue of separating out for replay the critical aspects of the writing process. Students are not likely to spend the time to replay the entire process by which a text was produced, unless it is a short text. Instead they will want to see an abstracted replay or reification that highlights parts of the process.

The right set of abstractions (like the problem-space abstraction in mathematical problem solving) is needed to characterize the writing process.[1] Then students could observe and analyze abstracted replays of the writing process as practiced by themselves, other students, and more expert writers. An abstracted replay might use notes, outlines, browsers, and paragraph headings as elements in conjunction with operators such

---

[1] Actually, two kinds of abstractions need to be considered. The first concerns how to structure and present the problem-solving audit trail, the second concerns choosing the right "grain size" of events that are to be stored on the audit trail so that, metaphorically, the wheat can be easily separated from the chaff. In Algebraland this latter issue is solved by choosing a set of moderately high-level algebraic operators for the student to use in transforming mathematical expressions and to have all the arithmetic simplifications done by just one operator.

as rearrangement, deletion, and annotation as the level of process representation that students observe.

Reflection on the Process of Reading

Reading is a very difficult task in which to apply reflection, because the process goes by very quickly. In spite of this we would like to sketch the design of a system to tutor reading in which the kind of reflection we have described might be embedded, in order to show the range and power of this technique.

Researchers have proposed a number of methods for teaching reading that employ expert modeling as a component (Bereiter & Bird, 1985; Collins & Smith, 1982; Palincsar & Brown, 1984). Collins and Smith, for example, proposed that the teacher read aloud for the student in one voice while verbalizing her own thoughts about the passage in another voice. This technique results in something like a slow motion movie of the reading comprehension process. The teacher verbalizes many different kinds of thoughts: confusions over particular phrases, hypotheses about what a passage means, predictions about what will come later, summaries of what the text says, descriptions of ideas provoked by the text, guesses about the author's intentions, evaluations of the writing, and reevaluations of any of the preceding as they occur. In short, the goal of expert modeling in this proposal is to verbalize all the thoughts a skilled reader might have while reading.

There have also been several attempts in recent years to build computer-based systems that help people to learn to read (Collins, 1986). One class of systems provides interactive help to novice readers as they read texts: for example, systems that will pronounce any word or sentence that the reader indicates by pointing to it on the screen. We imagine extending systems like this so that the student tries to read the passage aloud. His reading is tape recorded and can be played back at any time. In addition the student would have access to tapes of well-known people with different accents and backgrounds (e.g., Vanessa Redgrave, Martin Luther King, and Ricardo Montalban). Thus students can compare how they read the passage to how more expert readers read the passage. Such a system might also ask questions at critical junctures in the student's reading to see what hypotheses, evaluations, and so on he had formed as an active problem solver trying to comprehend the passage.

In Aesop's "Stone Soup" fable shown in Figure 1.5, we have indicated questions that might be interjected while students read, as well as answers an expert might give to each question. In our proposed design the system would verbally ask readers each question when they had finished reading the prior sentence. The answer would be recorded. The student then could ask to hear answers to the same question by the same experts who were recorded reading the passage. At any time students could go back and

Stone Soup

A poor man came to a large house during a storm to beg for food. He was sent away with angry words. (Q. *Who do you think sent him away and why?* A. The owner because he didn't care about beggars.) But he went back and asked, "May I at least dry my clothes by the fire, because I am wet from the rain?" The maid thought this would not cost anything, so she let him come in. (Q. *Now who do you think sent him away at first and why?* A. The maid, because she didn't want to give away her master's property.) (Q. *What do you think will happen when he gets inside?* A. He will dry his clothes and maybe make friends with the maid.)

Inside he told the cook that if she would give him a pan, and let him fill it with water, he would make some stone soup. This was a new dish to the cook, so she agreed to let him make it. The man got a stone from the road and put it in the pan. (Q. *What good is a stone for making soup?* A. It is of no use.) The cook gave him some salt, peas, mint, and all the scraps of meat she could spare to throw in. (Q. *Why do you think he offered to make stone soup?* A. So he could get to eat all the scraps the cook threw in.) Thus, the poor man made a delicious stone soup, and the cook said, "Well done! You have made a wonderful soup out of practically nothing." (Q. *Why do you think that the man asked to dry himself inside?* A. So he could get inside in order to fool the cook into giving him food.)

FIGURE 1.5. Aesop's "Stone Soup" with inserted questions and expert answers.

replay either their own tapes or the expert tapes and even rerecord themselves for a second try.

One of the goals in this system design is to make direct comparison possible between what the student and the expert produce in the same situation. Thus, the student sees how an expert deals with the same problem he or she has just tried to solve. Palincsar and Brown (1984) argue that this is one of the critical reasons for the success of the Reciprocal Teaching Method. In Reciprocal Teaching the expert modeling is initiated when the student has difficulties producing a question or a summary for a text, and the teacher intervenes to help provide one. Initially, the teacher, as expert, provides a complete model of how to do the task and gradually turns over more and more of the task to the student, aiding him or her with leading questions, evaluation of the student's efforts, and encouragement. We do not have the technological capability to do the kind of individual shaping that teachers do in Reciprocal Teaching, but technology can provide expert models to students struggling with problems of pronunciation or interpretation of text.

Conclusion

The recording and replaying of the processes people use to perform tasks such as reading, writing, and problem solving has the capability to make

these processes objects of reflection, annotation, and communication. Using imitation, replay, abstracted replay, and reification, students can begin to think about, talk about, and experiment with their learning and problem-solving processes in a way not previously possible.

By way of summary, we can briefly reiterate some of the reasons why reflection is important to learning:

1. Students can compare their own process to the way more expert performers carry out the process.
2. With reification it is possible to reconfigure a process representation so that students can see separate aspects of the process together and can view the process itself from perspectives they have not seen before.
3. Students can derive abstractions about the process by comparing multiple performances simultaneously.
4. Abstractions can be constructed in a form that is critical to developing good metacognitive strategies.

When we design learning environments for any subject, be it history, language, or physics, we should consider how to record and abstract the problem-solving processes students use in these learning environments. We should then provide students with facilities for replaying and observing their own performance and the performance of other students. And finally we should provide process models of more advanced performance that students can compare to their own process.

Acknowledgements. This research was supported by the National Institute of Education under Contract No. US-NIE-C-400-81-0030 and by the Office of Naval Research under Contract No. N00014-C-85-0026.

REFERENCES

Anderson, J. R., Boyle, C. F., & Reiser, B. J. (1985). Intelligent tutoring systems. *Science, 228,* 456–468.

Anderson, J. R., Boyle, C. F., Farrell, R., & Reiser, B. J. (1984). Cognitive principles in the design of computer tutors. In *Proceedings of the sixth annual conference of the Cognitive Science Society* (pp. 2–19). Boulder: University of Colorado.

Bereiter, C., & Bird, M. (1985). Use of thinking aloud in identification and teaching of reading comprehension strategies. *Cognition & Instruction, 2,* 131–156.

Bereiter, C., & Scardamalia, M. (1985). Cognitive coping stategies and the problem of "inert knowledge". In S. F. Chipman, J. W. Segal, & R. Glaser (Eds.), *Thinking and learning skills* (Vol. 2). Hillsdale, NJ: Lawrence Erlbaum Assoc.

Brown, A. L. (1978). Knowing when, where, and how to remember: A problem of metacognition. In R. Glaser (Ed.), *Advances in instructional psychology* (Vol. 1, pp. 77–165). Hillsdale, NJ: Lawrence Erlbaum Assoc.

Brown, J. S. (1985). Process versus product: A perspective on tools for communal

and informal electronic learning. *Journal of Educational Computing Research, 1*, 179–201.

Bundy, A. (1983). *The computer modeling of mathematical reasoning*. Orlando, FL: Academic Press.

Collins, A. (1986). Teaching reading and writing with personal computers. In J. Orasanu (Ed.), *A decade of reading research: Implications for practice* (pp. 171–187). Hillsdale, NJ: Lawrence Erlbaum Assoc.

Collins, A., & Smith, E. E. (1982). Teaching the process of reading comprehension. In D. K. Detterman & R. J. Sternberg (Eds.), *How much and how can intelligence be increased?* (pp. 173–185). Norwood, NJ: Ablex.

Flower, L. S., & Hayes, J. R. (1980). The dynamics of composing: Making plans and juggling constraints. In L. W. Gregg & E. R. Steinberg (Eds.), *Cognitive processes in writing* (pp. 31–50). Hillsdale, NJ: Lawrence Erlbaum Assoc.

Palincsar, A. S., & Brown, A. L. (1984). Reciprocal teaching of comprehension-fostering and monitoring activites. *Cognition & Instruction, 1*, 117–175.

Papert, S. (1980). *Mindstorms: Children, computers, and powerful ideas*. New York: Basic Books.

2
Toward a Theory of Impasse-Driven Learning

KURT VANLEHN

Introduction

Learning is widely viewed as a knowledge communication process coupled with a knowledge compilation process (Anderson, 1985). The communication process interprets instruction, thereby incorporating new information from the environment into the mental structures of the student. Knowledge compilation occurs with practice. It transforms the initial mental structures into a form that makes performance faster and more accurate. Moreover, the transformed mental structures are less likely to be forgotten. At one time, psychology concerned itself exclusively with the compilation process by using such simple stimuli (e.g., nonsense syllables) that the effects of the communication process could be ignored. The work presented here uses more complicated stimuli, the calculational procedures of ordinary arithmetic. For such stimuli, the effects of the knowledge communication process cannot be ignored. Later in this chapter it is shown that certain types of miscommunication can cause students to have erroneous conceptions. The long-term objective of the research reported here is to develop a theory of the neglected half of learning, knowledge communication. The experimental methods employed are designed to show the effects of knowledge communication and hide the effects of knowledge compilation. Consequently, whenever the term *learning* appears, it is intended to mean knowledge communication.

Earlier work (Brown & VanLehn, 1980; VanLehn, 1982, 1983a, 1983b, in press) has shown that students often reach "impasses" while trying to use a procedural skill that they are acquiring. An impasse occurs when the step that they believe should be executed next cannot be performed. If they are in a test-taking situation, where they may not receive help, they perform a specific, simple kind of problem solving, called "repair." This chapter speculates about what happens when impasses occur during instructional situations, where help is available. The conjecture is that the help that the student receives—either from the teacher, from examining the textbook, or from other information sources—is reduced to the sequence

of actions that will get the student past the impasse. This action sequence is generalized to become a new subprocedure. The new subprocedure is inserted into the old procedure at the location where the impasse occurred. The proposed learning process is called impasse-driven learning.

The research presented here began with the "buggy" studies of Brown and Burton (1978). Those studies found that students of certain procedural skills, such as ordinary multicolumn subtraction, had a surprisingly large variety of bugs (i.e., small, local misconceptions that cause systematic errors). Early investigations into the origins of bugs yielded a theory of procedural problem solving, named Repair Theory (Brown & VanLehn, 1980). Among other accomplishments, Repair Theory predicted the occurrence of certain patterns of short-term instabilities in bugs. These instabilities were subsequently found (VanLehn, 1982). Recent research has investigated the relationship between the curriculum, the students' learning processes, and the acquisition of bugs. A learning theory has been added to Repair Theory, yielding an integrated explanation for the acquisition of correct and buggy procedures (VanLehn, 1983a; 1983b, in press). It describes learning at large "grain size." Given a lesson and a representation of what the student knows before the lesson, the theory predicts what the student's knowledge state will be after the lesson.

Recently, attention has turned toward describing learning at a finer grain size. The object of the current research is to describe the student's cognitive processing during a lesson. The research strategy is to augment Repair Theory, which already provides a fine-grained account of problem-solving processes during diagnostic testing sessions, so that it provides a fine-grained account of learning. If this strategy succeeds, the cognitive processes will account for both problem-solving behavior and lesson-learning behavior. In contrast to the old theory, the new theory will (1) provide a more integrated account of cognition and (2) describe learning behavior at a finer grain size. In order to make it easier to contrast old and new theories, the new theory is identified as RT2, and the old theory, which is a conglomerate of Repair Theory and the large-grained learning theory, is referred to as RT1.

This chapter introduces RT2. It is, for the most part, speculation. Unlike RT1, RT2 has not been implemented as computer simulation, nor has its internal coherence and empirical accuracy been scrutinized with competitive argumentation (VanLehn, Brown, & Greeno, 1984). Although the ideas behind RT2 are simple extensions of the principles of RT1, they seem capable of explaining much about human behavior. Moreover, they relate to current research in machine learning and language acquisition. A discussion of RT2, even in its current underdeveloped form, should be at least timely, and perhaps interesting as well.

The chapter begins with a discussion of the task domain and the kinds of behavior one finds students displaying. It then introduces the old theory, RT1. Readers who are familiar with RT1 from earlier publications may

safely skip the first two sections. The remainder of the chapter presents RT2 and discusses its relationship to other work in cognitive science.

Learning Elementary Mathematical Skills

The goal of this research is to develop a rigorously supported theory of learning by taking advantage of the new modeling power of artificial intelligence (AI). The long-term research strategy is to begin by studying a particular kind of cognition, then if all goes well, to test the theory's generality on other kinds of cognition. The initial studies focused on how elementary school students learn ordinary, written arithmetic calculations. The main advantage of arithmetic procedures, from a methodological point of view, is that they are virtually meaningless to most students (Resnick, 1982). Most students treat arithmetic procedures as arbitrary formal manipulations (i.e., "symbol pushing"). Although this may frustrate teachers, it allows psychologists to study a complex skill without having to model a whole world's worth of background knowledge.

This section introduces the domain. First, it describes the instruction that students receive, and then it describes the behavior they produce. The theory's main job is to explain what kinds of mental structures are engendered by that instruction and how those structures guide the production of the observed behavior.

Learning From Lesson Sequences of Examples and Exercises

In a typical American school, mathematical procedures are taught incrementally via a lesson sequence that extends over several years. In the case of subtraction, there are about 10 lessons in the sequence that introduce new material. The lesson sequence introduces the procedure incrementally, one step per lesson, so to speak. For instance, the first lesson might show how to do subtraction of two-column problems. The second lesson demonstrates three-column problem solving. The third introduces borrowing, and so on. The 10 lessons are spread over about 3 years, starting in the late second grade (i.e., at about age 7). These lessons are interleaved with lessons on other topics, as well as many lessons for reviewing and practicing the material introduced by the 10 lessons. In the classroom a typical lesson lasts an hour. Usually, the teacher solves some problems on the board with the class, then the students solve problems on their own. If they need help they ask the teacher, or they refer to worked examples in the textbook. A textbook example consists of a sequence of captioned "snapshots" of a problem being solved (Figure 2.1). Textbooks have very little text explaining the procedure, perhaps because young children do not read well. Textbooks contain mostly examples and exercises.

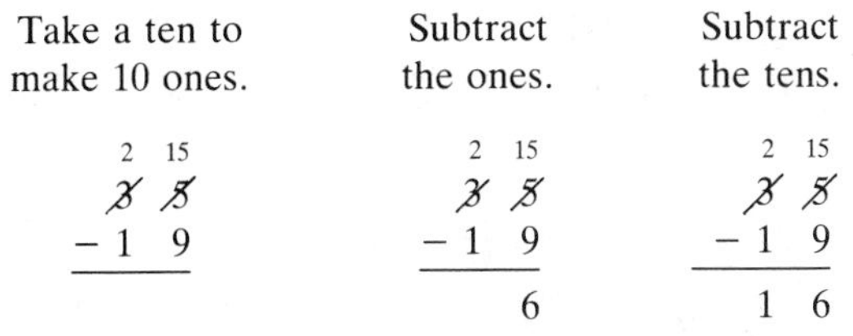

Take a ten to make 10 ones.	Subtract the ones.	Subtract the tens.
2 15	2 15	2 15
$\not{3}$ $\not{5}$	$\not{3}$ $\not{5}$	$\not{3}$ $\not{5}$
− 1 9	− 1 9	− 1 9
	6	1 6

FIGURE 2.1. A typical textbook example.

DESCRIBING SYSTEMATIC ERRORS WITH "BUGS"

The observable output of the students' learning process is their performance while solving exercise problems. Error data are a traditional measure of such performance. There have been many empirical studies of the errors that students make in arithmetic (Ashlock, 1976; Buswell, 1926; Brueckner, 1930; Brownell, 1935; Cox, 1975; Roberts, 1968; Lankford, 1972). A common analytic notion is to separate systematic errors from slips (Norman, 1981). Systematic errors appear to stem from consistent application of a faulty method, algorithm, or rule. Slips are unsystematic, "careless" errors (e.g., facts errors, such as $7 - 3 = 5$). Since slips occur in expert performance as well as student behavior, the common opinion is that they are due to inherent "noise" in the human information processor. Systematic errors, on the other hand, are taken as stemming from mistaken or missing knowledge, the product of incomplete or misguided learning. Only systematic errors are used in testing the present theory. See Siegler and Shrager (1984) for a developmental theory of addition slips.

Brown and Burton (1978) used the metaphor of bugs in computer programs in developing a precise, detailed formalism for describing systematic errors. A student's errors are accurately reproduced by taking a formal representation of a correct procedure and making one or more small perturbations to it, such as deleting a rule. The perturbations are called bugs. A systematic error is represented as a list of one or more bugs. Bugs describe systematic errors with unprecedented precision. If a student makes no slips, then his or her answers on a test exactly match the buggy algorithm's answers, digit for digit. Bug data are the main data for testing this theory.

Burton (1982) developed an automated data analysis program, called Debuggy. Using it, data from thousands of students learning subtraction were analyzed, and 76 different kinds of bugs were observed (VanLehn, 1982). Similar studies discovered 68 bugs in addition of fractions (Shaw, Standiford, Klein, Tatsuoka, 1982), several dozen bugs in simple linear equation solving (Sleeman, 1985), and 57 bugs in addition and subtraction of signed numbers (Tatsuoka & Baillie, 1982).

It is important to stress that bugs are only a notation for systematic errors and not an explanation. The connotations of "bugs" in the computer programming sense do not necessarily apply. In particular, bugs in human procedures are not always stable. They may appear and disappear over short periods of time, often with no intervening instruction, and sometimes even in the middle of a testing session (VanLehn, 1982). Often, one bug is replaced by another, a phenomenon called bug migration.

Mysteries abound in the bug data. Why are there so many different bugs? What causes them? What causes them to migrate or disappear? Why do certain bugs migrate only into certain other bugs? Often a student has more than one bug at a time—why do certain bugs almost always occur together? Do co-occurring bugs have the same cause? Most importantly, how is the educational process involved in the development of bugs? One objective of the theory is to explain some of these bug mysteries.

Another objective is to explain how procedural skills are acquired from multiyear curricula. This objective seems to require longitudinal data, where each student in the study is tested several times during the multiyear period. Such data are notoriously difficult to acquire. Bug data are readily available and nearly as good. The bug data discussed here were obtained by testing students at all stages in the curriculum. Thus, the bug data are like between-subjects longitudinal data. Instead of testing the same student at several times at different stages of his or her learning, different students at different stages are tested just once. As shown later, such data can perform nearly as well as longitudinal data in testing a learning theory, and yet they are much easier to collect.

An Introduction to the Model: Explaining Always-Borrow-Left

Most of the mental structures and processes proposed by the theory can be introduced and illustrated by going through an explanation for a certain subtraction bug, called Always-Borrow-Left. Students with this bug always borrow from the leftmost column in the problem no matter which column originates the borrowing. Problem A shows the correct placement of borrow's decrement. Problem B shows the bug's placement.

$$
\text{(A)} \quad \begin{array}{r} 5 \\ 3\ \cancel{6}\ {}^{1}5 \\ -\ 1\ 0\ 9 \\ \hline 2\ 5\ 6 \end{array}
\qquad
\text{(B)} \quad \begin{array}{r} 2 \\ \cancel{3}\ 6\ {}^{1}5 \\ -\ 1\ 0\ 9 \\ \hline 1\ 6\ 6 \end{array}
\qquad
\text{(C)} \quad \begin{array}{r} 5 \\ \cancel{6}\ {}^{1}5 \\ -\ 1\ 9 \\ \hline 4\ 6 \end{array}
$$

Always-Borrow-Left is moderately common. In a sample of 375 students with bugs, six students had this bug (VanLehn, 1982). It has been observed

for years (Buswell, 1926, p. 173, bad habit number s27). However, this theory is the first to offer an explanation for it.

The explanation begins with the hypothesis that students use induction (generalization of examples) in learning where to place the borrow's decrement. All the textbooks used by students in our sample introduce borrowing using only two-column problems, such as in preceding problem C. Multicolumn problems, such as A, are not used. Consequently, the student has insufficient information to induce an unambiguous description of where to place the borrow's decrement. The correct placement is in the left-adjacent column, as in A. However, two-column examples are also consistent with decrementing the leftmost column, as in B.

The next hypothesis of the theory is that when a student is faced with such an ambiguity in how to describe a place, the student takes a conservative strategy and saves all the relevant descriptions. When inducing from two-column problems (e.g., C), the student describes the borrow-from column as "a column that is both left-adjacent to the current column and the left-most column in the problem."

Suppose that our student is given a diagnostic test at this point in the lesson sequence and that the test contains borrowing problems of all kinds. Suppose the student is faced with solving problem D.

$$\text{(D)} \quad \begin{array}{r} 3\ 6\ 5 \\ -\ 1\ 0\ 9 \\ \hline \end{array} \qquad \text{(E)} \quad \begin{array}{r} 3\ 6\ {}^1 5 \\ -\ 1\ 0\ \ 9 \\ \hline \end{array}$$

The student starts to borrow, gets as far as E, and is suddenly stuck. The student's description of where to borrow from is ambiguous because there is no column that is *both* left-adjacent and the leftmost column. In the terminology of the theory, getting stuck while problem solving is called reaching an *impasse*.

It is hypothesized that whenever students reach an impasse on a test, they engage in *local problem solving*. Local problem solving is just like classical puzzle solving (Newell & Simon, 1972) in that there is an initial state, a desired final state, and state-change operators. Here, the initial state is being stuck, and the desired final state is being unstuck. Unlike traditional problem solving, in local problem solving the state-change operators do not change the state of the exercise problem. Instead, they change the *state of the interpreter* that is executing the procedure. The operators do things like pop the stack of goals or relax the criterion for matching a description to the exercise problem. They do not do things like writing digits on the test paper. Because the local problem solver modifies the state of the procedure's interpretation, it is a kind of *metalevel* problem solving. The sequences of metalevel operators that succeed in getting students unstuck are called *repairs*. Note that what is being repaired is, roughly speaking, the impasse. Repairs do not change the procedure. To

put it in terms of Newell's (1980) problem space hypothesis, the procedure works in one problem space, and local problem solving works in a second problem space that is "meta" to the base problem space. Returning to our stuck student, three common repairs to the impasse follow:

$$
(F) \quad \begin{array}{c} {\scriptstyle 2} \\ \not{3}\,6\ {}^{1}5 \\ \underline{-1\ 0\ 9} \end{array}
\qquad
(G) \quad \begin{array}{c} {\scriptstyle 5} \\ 3\ \not{6}\ {}^{1}5 \\ \underline{-1\ 0\ 9} \end{array}
\qquad
(H) \quad \begin{array}{c} 3\ 6\ {}^{1}5 \\ \underline{-1\ 0\ 9} \\ 6 \end{array}
$$

In F, the student has relaxed the description of which column to borrow from by ignoring the restriction that the column be left-adjacent to the current column. The remaining restriction, that the column be the leftmost column in the problem, has the student decrement the hundreds column, as shown in F. This is one repair. It generates the bug Always-Borrow-Left. Another repair is shown in G. Here, the student has relaxed the borrow-from description by ignoring the leftmost requirement. The decrement is placed in the left-adjacent column, yielding G. This repair generates a correct solution to the problem. In H, the student has chosen to skip the borrow-from entirely and go on to the next step in the procedure. This repair generates a bug that is named Borrow-No-Decrement-Except-Last, because it only executes a borrow-from when it is unambiguous about where to place the decrement; and that occurs only when the borrow originates in the last possible column for borrow. To sum up, three different repairs to the same impasse generate two different bugs and a correct version of subtraction.

As mentioned earlier, students' bugs are not like bugs in computer programs, because students' bugs are unstable. Students shift back and forth among bugs, a phenomenon called bug migration. The theory's explanation for bug migration is that the student has a stable underlying procedure but the procedure is incomplete in such a way that the student reaches impasses on some problems. The student can apply any repair she can think of. Sometimes she chooses one repair, and sometimes she chooses others. The different repairs manifest themselves as different bugs. So some bug migration is caused by varying the choice of repairs to a stable, underlying impasse. In particular, the theory predicts that the three repairs just discussed ought to show up as a bug migration. In fact they do. Figure 2.2 is a verbatim presentation of a diagnostic test showing the predicted bug migration.

This discussion of the bug Always-Borrow-Left illustrates many of the assumptions of the theory. First, procedures are the result of generalization of examples, rather than, say memorization of verbal or written recipes. The main evidence for this assumption is that there are accidental, visual characteristics of the examples, namely, the placement of the de-

A
```
   7 12
   9̷2̷
 - 4 3
 ─────
   3 9
```
B
```
   4 10
   8̷0̷
 - 2 3
 ─────
   2 7
```
C
```
 1 0 9
 -  7 0
 ─────
   3 9
```
D
```
 X̷5 6 4
 -  8 8 7
 ───────
   1 8 7
```
E
```
      12
 1 0̷2̷
 -  3 9
 ─────
   7 3
```
F
```
   1 17
   2̷7̷
 -   8
 ─────
   1 9
```
G
```
 9 0 0
 - 6 8 8
 ───────
   2 2 2
```

H
```
 7 1 6
 - 5 9 8
 ───────
   1 1 8
```
I
```
 3 1 1
 - 2 1 4
 ───────
     9 7
```
J
```
 8 8 5
 - 2 0 5
 ───────
   6 8 0
```
K
```
        4
      8̷ 15  11
   6̷8̷9̷X̷
 - 2 6 9 7
 ─────────
   2 9 0 4
```
L
```
 8 3 5 5
 -     3
 ─────────
   8 3 5 2
```
M
```
      6   10 11
   8̷0̷0̷X̷
 -       4 3
 ─────────
   6 0 6 8
```

N
```
     2
   X̷ 10  15
   X̷0̷X̷X̷
 -   6 0 7
 ─────────
   2 4 1 8
```
O
```
 6 3 7
 -  3 5
 ─────
   6 0 2
```
P
```
   4 10
   8̷0̷X̷
 -     4
 ─────
   4 0 6
```
Q
```
   6   12
   7̷0̷X̷
 - 1 0 3
 ─────
   6 0 9
```
R
```
            12
   X̷0 0 1 X̷
 -       2 1 4
 ─────────
     2 0 8
```
S
```
   6   12
   7̷4̷X̷
 - 1 3 6
 ─────
   6 1 6
```

FIGURE 2.2. Verbatim presentation of a test by subject 8 of class 17 showing three repairs to the same impasse. On problems D, E, and G, one repair generates the bug Borrow-No-Decrement-Except-Last. (N.B., The subject does not always use scratch marks to indicate borrowing.) On problems H and I, another repair generates the correct borrow-from placement. On problems K, M, N, P, Q, R, and S, a third repair generates the bug Always-Borrow-Left. There are slips on problems D, P, Q, and S. There is a second impasse in processing the hundreds column of problem R.

crement, that a nonexample source of instruction, such as a verbal recipe, would not mention. The appearance of these visual characteristics in the acquired procedure is evidence that they were learned by induction (see VanLehn, (1986) for a full defense of this idealization).

A second assumption is that learning occurs in the context of a lesson sequence and that many bugs are caused by testing students who are in the middle of the lesson sequence on exercise types that they have not yet been taught how to solve. Perhaps such bugs should be welcomed as signs of a healthy learning process that may eventuate in a correct understanding of the procedure. Such a view of bugs is radically different from the traditional view, which considers bugs to be "bad habits" that need to be remediated. On the other hand the bad-habit view may be appropriate for older students, some of whom have bugs long after the lesson sequence has been completed (VanLehn, 1982).

Another set of assumptions involves the notions of interpretation, impasses, and repairs. A particularly important hypothesis is that repairs occur at the metalevel and change only the state of the interpretation. This hypothesis predicts the existence of bug migration. In fact, this prediction was made before any evidence of bug migration had been found (Brown

& VanLehn, 1980). The surprising success of this forecast and the fact that it is an almost unavoidable consequence of the hypothesis provide strong support for the theory.

The Stable Bug Problem

Although some students' behaviors can be characterized as bug migrations, other students appear to have the same bug throughout a test. When such students are tested again 2 days later, they often have the same bug (VanLehn, 1982). Some students even show the same bug when tested twice 6 months apart (VanLehn, 1982). Such data encourage the interpretation that some students have learned their bugs. That is, their bugs have become a part of the knowledge structure they use to encode their procedure. Such relatively permanent bugs are called "stable" in order to differentiate them from bugs that may exist only for a short time, then migrate/change into other bugs[1].

Stable bugs present a problem for Repair Theory. Repairs do not modify the core procedure, but instead modify the state of the interpreter that is executing the core procedure. After a repair has been accomplished and the interpreter is running again, there is no trace of the effects of repair on the core procedure. Bug migrations are explained by assuming that the students apply different repairs at different occurrences of the impasse. In order to explain a stable bug, one must assume that the student chooses to apply the same repair every single time the impasse occurs. Intuitively, this seems quite unlikely.

One way to explain stable bugs within the RT1 framework is to assume that the set of possible repairs is different for different individuals. Some students may only know about one repair, so they always choose that repair at an impasse. They will appear to have a stable bug. However, this hypothesis has difficulties. There are stable bugs that can only be generated by assuming that the students have two different impasses and that the student repairs the first one with one repair and the second one with a different repair. Students with such bugs must know at least two repairs, yet they consistently choose the same one at each choice point. Assuming that different students have different repairs does not help explain such multi-impasse stable bugs.

---

[1] The proportion of students whose errors are due to stable bugs varies significantly with the grade level. In one study, 49% of the third graders had stable subtraction bugs versus 27% of the fourth graders and 13% of the fifth graders (VanLehn, 1982). The variation is due to the fact that more older children know the correct algorithm: 19% of the third graders were bug free versus 39% of the fourth graders and 60% of the fifth graders.

The Patch Hypothesis

As another potential explanation of stable bugs, one could augment RT1 by assuming that there is some memory of previous episodes of impasses and repairs. Stable bugs are generated by assuming that the student recognizes the impasse as one that has occurred before and recalls the repair that was selected before and employed successfully. To perform such recall, the student must have some memory of the impasse and the repair. That is, the student's knowledge of the skill must consist of a set of impasse-repair pairs in addition to the core procedure. Such pairs are called patches (Brown & VanLehn, 1980). Thus, if the students have a stable bug, then they have a patch for that impasse. If they do not have a patch, then the impasse will cause bug migrations.

There are problems with the hypothesis that the student's knowledge consists of patches as well as the core procedure. First, it seems inelegant and unparsimonious. Patches are essentially, condition–action rules. The condition is a description of particular interpreter states (i.e., a certain kind of impasse). A patch's action is some modification to be made to the interpreter's state. The core procedure is also made up of condition—action rules. The only differences between patches and the core procedure's rules are that the rules' conditions can test the external problem states (i.e., the state of a partially completed subtraction problem) and the rules' actions can modify the external problem state. That is, the patches operate exclusively on the interpreter's state, while core procedure's rules operate on the external problem state as well. Nonetheless, there are more similarities than differences between patches and rules. It would be parsimonious to combine them.

The second problem with patches is that they must be somewhat abstract in order to function properly. In order for the patch to apply to multiple occurrences of an impasse, it must be a *description* of the interpreter's state. Thus, if a patch is acquired from, say, the first occurrence of an impasse, then the condition half of the patch must be abstract. It must not mention details of the interpreter state that are idiosyncratic to this particular occurrence, such as the values of digits in the problem. Similarly, the repairs must also be abstract descriptions of the modifications that were performed to the interpreter's state. Consequently, acquiring a patch is not simply a matter of storing a state and a state change. Rather, patch acquisition requires nontrivial abstraction.

A third, more technical problem with patches is that they do not interface well with the pattern matching component of the interpreter. In order to represent descriptions of the external problem state, the procedure employs patterns. Such patterns are just like the usual ones found in, for instance the conditions of production rules. They consist of sets of relations whose arguments are variables or constants. To employ such patterns, the interpreter must have a pattern matcher. The matcher tries to fit the

pattern to the representation of the external problem state. If the pattern matches, then the objects matched by the variables are often "read" and become a part of the interpreter's state. We saw an instance of this earlier, in the discussion of the bug Always-Borrow-Left. A pattern is used to re-present the idea that the place to borrow from is (1) the leftmost column in the problem, (2) a column that is adjacent to the column that is the cur-rent focus of attention, and (3) a column that is left of the current focus of attention. Speaking very approximately, the pattern for this concept em-ploys three relations, one for each of the constraints listed previously. It has two variables; one for the current focus of attention and one for the column to be borrowed from. The following is an informal presentation of the pattern:

(Is-leftmost-column New-focus) and
(Is-adjacent-to New-focus Current-focus) and
(Is-left-of New-focus Current-focus)

If the pattern matches, the object that is matched to the New-focus vari-able, namely a particular column in the problem, becomes the focus of attention for the borrow-from subgoal. The bug Always-Borrow-Left is generated when this pattern fails to match. Such mismatching occurs when borrowing originates in the units column of problems with more than two columns. In such problems, there is no column that meets all three con-straints. The bug is generated when the second one is relaxed, allowing the pattern to match and picking out the leftmost column of the problem as the focus of attention for borrowing-from. This causes the student to borrow from the leftmost column, which is exactly what the bug Always-Borrow-Left does.

If the patch hypothesis is incorrect, then it should be possible to build a patch for Always-Borrow-Left. The impasse half of the patch can be quite simple. It can achieve the appropriate degree of abstraction by merely referring to the pattern. The description in the condition half of the patch would read, "The pattern that fetches the borrow-from column does not match." However, there are problems implementing the repair half of the patch. The following paragraphs present three possible implementations, all of which fail.

The repair could also be expressed in terms of the pattern. It needs to say something like "relax the second relation of the pattern." However, if this is taken literally, it means actually modifying the pattern by removing the second relation from it. Such modifications change the procedure itself. This makes it hard to explain bug migration—one would have to assume that the relaxation repair puts the deleted relations back, for instance.

A second possibility for the Always-Borrow-Left patch involves inter-rupting the pattern-matching process. In order to accomplish the requisite relaxation, the repair would have to interrupt the pattern matcher right when it was about to apply the second constraint of the pattern and some-

how cause the pattern matcher to skip over that relation. Expressing this repair as a patch is difficult. It would require a precise specification, at the theoretical level, of a pattern-matching algorithm, thus embroiling the theory in a layer of irrelevant detail.

A third option for the Always-Borrow-Left patch is to include a revised pattern that has all the relations except the second. The interpretation of this description is for the local problem solver to perform pattern matching using this pattern and substitute the results into the interpreter's state just as if the original pattern had been matched. This option works, usually. However, it has the flaw that on some occasions, the pattern stored in the patch does not match. This causes an impasse *inside* the local problem solver. That is, there can be an impasse while a person is trying to fix another impasse. The local problem solver is running "meta" to the interpreter, trying to repair the interpreter's impasse. We could assume that there is a meta-meta level, where another local problem solver runs, trying to repair the impasse that occurred inside the metalevel local problem solver. Such "towers" of metalevel interpreters have begun to appear in AI (Smith, 1982), but their properties are largely unexplored at this time. It is probably best to avoid postulating such multilevel architectures of students until they are better understood computationally.

In summary, there are three methods for representing the repair half of the patch: (1) modifying the core procedure by deleting a relation from the pattern, (2) having the repair cause the pattern matcher to ignore the relation, and (3) storing a substitute pattern in the patch and matching it from inside the local problem solver. Because all these methods have defects, it seems that patches cannot represent the stability of bugs that, like Always-Borrow-Left, depend on pattern relaxation in their repairs. This is just one problem with the patch hypothesis. The others, mentioned earlier, are its lack of parsimony, since patches are quite similar to rules, and the fact that nontrivial abstraction is required for patches to be acquired.

REPRESENTING STABLE BUGS WITH MALRULES

The new version of the theory, RT2, takes the position that there are no patches. The student's knowledge of the skill consists only of a procedure. In order to represent stable bugs, the core procedure has "malrules."[2] Malrules are identical in format and function to the core procedure's regular rules. The difference is only that they cause the student to answer incorrectly, rather than correctly. Furthermore, RT2 assumes that malrules

---

[2] Derek Sleeman coined the term "malrule" for his method of describing bugs in an objective, theoretically neutral fashion (Sleeman & Smith, 1981). Although the malrules of RT2 are interpreted as lying at a deeper, more psychologically plausible level, the use of the term seems just as descriptive of how the rules function.

are acquired by the same learning mechanism as regular rules. Regular rules are acquired by induction of the teacher's examples. Malrules are acquired by induction from the "malexamples" produced by local problem solving.

Malrules are a much more parsimonious solution to the stable bug problem than patches. They are identical to rules, and they are acquired by the same mechanism as rules. Thus, malrules escape the first objections raised against patches.

Another objection was that patches could not represent stable pattern-relaxation bugs. This objection is also resolved by the malrule hypothesis. To illustrate how, consider the bug Always-Borrow-Left again. In the normal course of events, students are first taught borrowing with two-column problems. Later they are taught how to solve three-column borrow problems. Recall that after the first lesson, the pattern is overconstrained:

(Is-leftmost-column New-focus) and
(Is-adjacent-to New-focus Current-focus) and
(Is-left-of New-focus Current-focus)

The second borrowing lesson shows that when borrowing originates in the units column of three-column problems, it is the tens column that one borrows from. The learning mechanism uses such examples to eliminate the first relation from the pattern. That is, the learning mechanism does pattern relaxation.

If, on the other hand, malexamples had been presented where the hundreds column was borrowed from, then pattern relaxation would delete the second relation. Such malexamples can be generated when the learner is tested between the first and second lessons on borrowing. The overconstrained pattern will cause impasses, and the repair of those impasses generates the malexamples. On this account, stable bugs like Always-Borrow-Left seem to be caused, ironically, by learning from one's mistakes.

Learning Occurs at Impasses

The introduction of this chapter promised a description of a fine-grained learning process. Although the responsibilities of the learning process have been increased, by including the generation of malrules as well as rules, the large-grained description of the learning process has not yet been refined. This section ventures a finer grained description.

If learning occurs as a result of local problem solving, then the learning process is likely to be interwoven with the local problem-solving process. The main hypothesis is that inductive learning occurs at impasses. The "at" is used here in two senses. Learning occurs when an impasse occurs.

If there is no impasse, there is no learning.[3] The second sense of learning "at" impasses is more subtle. When an impasse occurs, the student is "at" some place in the procedure. That is, the interpreter for the procedure is reading some part of the control structure of the procedure. The hypothesis is that the control location of the impasse is the place where the newly learned piece of procedure will be inserted. That is, if the control structure is visualized as laid out spatially, say as a tree, then the hypothesis that learning occurs "at" impasses takes on a spatial interpretation. The spatial location of the impasse is the place where the new subprocedure will be attached to the existing procedure. So, the hypothesis has two independent aspects: (1) learning occurs "at" impasses in the temporal sense and (2) learning occurs "at" impasses in the control structure sense.

First, let's examine the implications of the temporal aspect. According to the old theory, RT1, the only activity that occurs in response to impasses is repair. The goal of repair is merely to get the interpreter past the impasse in any way possible. In particular, repair is not concerned with answering the problem correctly. Consequently, repairs rarely modify the interpretation in such a way that the problems are solved correctly. However, the impasse-driven learning hypothesis is intended to explain the acquisition of regular rules as well as malrules. To do this, the theory must be amended to allow other activities in response to impasses. Once the history of this research is reviewed, it will be easy to see what those activities should be.

The bug data that initiated the theory were collected in testing situations. The students were asked to answer problems without help from their teacher, friends, or textbooks. If they got stuck, they would have to rely on their own knowledge to get unstuck. Thus, they repaired. However, students are not always in test-taking situations when they solve problems. Often, they solve practice exercises in class or at home. In such situations help is permitted. Indeed, students are encouraged to ask for help if they get stuck. So, the second kind of activity that may occur at impasses is receiving help.

Help seems to be the source of information that allows correct rules to be learned at impasses. For instance, suppose that a student gets stuck while doing seat work. He raises his hand. His teacher comes over. He asks, "I got to here and got stuck. What am I supposed to do next?" The teacher shows him what to do, saying, "You do this, and then this, then this." This short sequence of actions is just what the student needs. Not only does it get him around the impasse, but it is an example of a new subskill. The student may abstract the actions, leaving behind details that are specific to the particular problem that is being solved, such as the numerical values of the digits. The abstracted actions become a new subprocedure, which the student can attach to his existing procedure. Thus, correct

---

[3] Knowledge compilation may occur without impasses, but that is not the kind of learning that the theory describes.

rules can be acquired by the same mechanism that acquires malrules, provided that there is some way of obtaining help at impasses.

The actual method of delivering help is probably of secondary importance. The student can obtain help by comparing his solution to his friend's solution. The comparison isolates a subsequence of actions, illustrating the new subprocedure just as effectively as asking the teacher, but it may cost the student some effort to make the comparison. With slightly more effort, the student could generate a subsequence by drawing a "near" analogy to a worked problem in the textbook (Anderson, Farrell, & Saurers, 1984). The student may even be able to generate the subsequence from a "far" analogy, given a little coaching from the teacher (Resnick & Omanson, 1987). For instance, some teachers might have the student think of the problem's base-ten numerals as piles of pennies, dimes, and dollars. Under the teacher's prodding, the student maps the impasse over to the monetary representation, solves the impasse there without violating principles of fair exchange (i.e., always change a dime for 10 pennies), then maps those monetary manipulations back into paper-and-pencil actions in the written representation. Because the impasse was solved correctly in the monetary representation, the written analog of that solution should be a correct subsequence of actions. The point is that there are a variety of ways to obtain a written action subsequence. Demonstration, comparison, near analogy, and far analogy are only a few of the many possible ways, although they may be the most common.

As soon as one discovers that there are several kinds of inputs to a cognitive process, one wonders whether those differences make any difference. Does it matter whether the student receives help via individualized demonstrations, versus comparison, etc? The simplest hypothesis is that it is the subsequence of actions that determines the contents of the subprocedure and not the source for that subsequence of actions. If two methods of obtaining help yield the same subsequence of actions for the impasse, then the subprocedure that the student induces should be the same.

Like most simple hypotheses, this one is likely to be only half right, at best. The various methods of obtaining help may require different cognitive resources, and that may affect the inductive learning process. For instance, suppose far analogy takes longer and requires more problem solving of the student than attending to the teacher's demonstration. The heavier demands of far analogy could interfere with the retention of the interpreter's state at the time of the impasse. This may decrease or perturb inductive learning, because retaining (or reconstructing) the interpreter's state is necessary for determining where to attach the new subprocedure. This interference could be considered, however, a second-order or "performance" factor.

The second aspect of the hypothesis that learning occurs "at" impasses concerns the place where the new subprocedure will be attached to the existing procedure. The hypothesis is that the attachment point will be the

same as the location of the interpreter at the occurrence of the impasse. The notion of location is complicated by the fact that the student's procedures have a hierarchical control structure. That is, the procedure has goals, which call subgoals, which call sub-subgoals, and so on. There may even be recursion: a goal calling itself. Consequently, at the time of an impasse, there may be a whole stack of goals pending. However, it is the lowest goal, the one that is a subgoal of all the others, that is suffering from the impasse.[4] This has implications for where new subprocedures will be attached, given the hypothesis that subprocedures are attached at the place in the goal structure where the impasse occurred. Roughly speaking, new subprocedures will tend to be attached low in the goal tree. This prediction is a necessary implication of the hypothesis.

It is also a true prediction for the data available now. In order to predict the locations of subprocedure attachments, as inferred from the arithmetic bug data, RT1 had an ad hoc hypothesis, called the lowest parent hypothesis (VanLehn; 1983a). It simply stipulated that new subprocedures be attached as low as possible in the goal hierarchy. This hypothesis is no longer needed. The attachment points are predicted from an independently motivated hypothesis, namely, that learning occurs at impasses.

Implications for Remediation

One of the most obvious facts about arithmetic is that remediation of bugs tends to work. Many students have arithmetic bugs when tested in the early grades (e.g., 49% in the third grade). The proportion decreases with grade level. The proportion of adults with bugs is much smaller. Apparently, students' bugs are being remediated somewhere in the educational process. The question addressed in this section is how this remediation takes place. The section entitled Representing Stable Bugs With Malrules discussed how malrules are learned. The section entitled Learning Occurs at Impasses discussed how regular rules are learned. This section speculates about how regular, correct rules may be learned when they have to compete with malrules that were learned earlier.

Suppose a student enters a remedial session with a stable bug. The stability of the bug indicates that a malrule was learned during some prior

---

[4] Here is an informal proof that only the lowest goal can be stuck. Suppose that some goal other than the lowest goal is stuck. This means that there is some subgoal of it that is pending but not stuck. But if that lower goal is not stuck, then it can continue until it succeeds or fails. In either case it would be removed from the stack of pending goals. So the only goals left in the stack when interpretation is forced to stop are (1) the stuck goal and (2) all the goals that depend on its completion in order for them to complete, that is, the supergoals of the stuck goal. In short it is always the lowest goal on the stack that is the current locus of control when an impasse occurs.

episodes of local problem solving. Those impasses no longer occur because the malrule circumvents them. Consequently, the student can work all the relevant problems without reaching an impasse. As mentioned earlier, if there are no impasses, there is no learning. Yet, remediation works. How can the hypothesis be reconciled with the facts?

The simplest reconciliation is to assume that remediation occurs when the teacher stops the student just as the student makes a wrong move in the problem-solving process. For instance the teacher may be carefully watching the student do a borrow and may interrupt just as the student has placed a scratch mark where no scratch mark should occur. Suppose further that the student interprets the teacher's interruption in a similar fashion to an impasse. The student observes the subsequence of actions that the teacher suggests, abstracts them, and plugs them into the existing procedure as a new subprocedure. Treating interruptions in tutorial situations as impasses could extend the theory to cover remediation. Such interruptions are rare events, which explains why stable bugs are often found. However, if we postulate that such remediation is effective when it does occur, and that tutorial efforts persist for years, then the assumption also explains why stable bugs eventually disappear.

However, there is a small problem. Typically, the teacher's interruption occurs just after the first incorrect action instead of before it. Yet that action is the result of a malrule that is running in place of the impasse. We want the new subprocedure to be placed where the impasse used to occur, just as if the instruction had been delivered then instead of now. This would cause the new subprocedure to be attached correctly. However, the teacher's interruption is too late. The impasse place has been passed. In principle, the student could be asked to reason backward in order to locate the impasse place. However, a better remediation technique may be to have the student solve the same problem again (or a very similar one) and interrupt just before the incorrect action. This interruption would be at the impasse place, or at least much closer. This is, of course, a testable suggestion concerning the effectiveness of two remediation strategies.

There is a more significant problem with the kind of remediation proposed so far. Suppose the interruption is completed, and the student has installed the new subprocedure at the impasse place. There is already another subprocedure attached there, the malrule. It was generated in response to that impasse. So both the rule (subprocedure) and malrule are attached at the same impasse place. Subsequently, when the student comes to that place in solving a problem, how will the student know whether to execute the rule or the malrule? Since both were constructed in order to handle the same impasse, both will be applicable. All other things being equal, the student will pick the rule half the time and the malrule the rest of the time. This predicts a new kind of instability, where buggy problem solving alternates with correct problem solving.

There is anecdotal evidence that this prediction might be close to the

mark. The evidence concerns the spontaneous reappearance of bugs after their supposed remediation. Several teachers have told me that when students with bugs are shown the correct procedure in a remedial session, they pick it up easily. They can solve dozens of problems successfully in the session. Apparently, they have learned the correct procedure. However, when tested again several weeks later, these students are either back to using their old buggy procedure or alternating between their old buggy procedure and the correct procedure. Resnick and Omanson (1987) have carefully documented several cases of such bug regression in a study designed to investigate new remediation strategies. Bug regression occurred despite the fact that the remediation was particularly thorough. Nonetheless, Resnick and Omanson report that 60% of the students reverted to using their buggy procedures for answering written subtraction problems when tested about 4 weeks later.

Bug regression makes intuitive sense, given the cognitive process sketched earlier. Suppose the student has enough context during the remediation session to differentiate the newly learned rule from the malrule, which was learned some time previously. The similarity between the learning context and the application context allows the student to reliably differentiate the correct rule from the older rule and thereby apply the new rule throughout the remediation session. However, at a later testing session, the context during the session may not be similar enough to the remediation session that the student can recall which rule is the one to use. This would cause the student to be uncertain about which rule was correct. The student might alternate rules in order to maximize the test score. Another possibility is that the malrule was learned during a testing session. The present context, another testing session, may be more similar to the context in which the malrule was learned than the context in which the correct rule was learned. This may cause the student to use the malrule exclusively. Thus, depending on when the malrule was learned, the students may either apply the buggy procedure exclusively, or they may alternate between the correct procedure and their buggy one. The predictions of impasse-driven learning are in accord with the phenomenon of bug regression.

General Discussion

Many cognitive theories of learning have hypothesized that learning is some kind of automatic phenomenon. Mental activity leaves a trace that somehow makes it easier to perform that activity the next time. Automatic learning has been the dominant paradigm for the last few decades of psychology, if not longer. Particular examples of this kind of learning for skill acquisition are Anderson's (1983) ACT* theory, Laird, Rosenbloom and Newell's (1986–1987) SOAR theory, and Anzai and Simon's (1979) theory

of learning by doing. These theories feature automatic learning of new material (i.e., task-specific productions) by repeated usage of older material (i.e., weaker, more general productions).

Automatic learning theories have begun to draw fire from computer scientists who have noted that the lack of control over what is learned causes the system to acquire vast quantities of useless knowledge (Minton, 1985). For instance, Roger Schank (1982) has rejected automatic learning as a totally impossible way to acquire common sense knowledge about, for example, how to dine in a restaurant. He points out that most mundane thinking is so banal and disconnected that to remember it all would be pointless and a poor model of our introspective experience of learning. To put it in a phrase, automatic learning would generate mental clutter.

Impasse-directed learning does not generate mental clutter. Learning only occurs when the current knowledge base is insufficient. Moreover, it is not just any incompleteness that causes learning. The incompleteness must be relevant enough to the person's affairs that it actually generates an impasse. The person's problem solving must require a piece of knowledge that is not there. Consequently, one learns only when there is a need to learn. Mental clutter is avoided, and only pertinent knowledge is acquired.

RELATED MODELS OF SKILL ACQUISITION

Impasse-directed learning is a species of failure-driven learning. Failure-driven learning is a common theoretical idea in the learning literature. For instance, in Wexler and Culicover's (1980) theory of language acquisition, whenever the learning model cannot understand a sentence, it randomly deletes a rule from its grammar, or it makes a change in an existing rule by randomly choosing from a small class of legal perturbations. Their theory is typical of a class of learning theories where negative reinforcement of an internal kind causes a more-or-less random change in the learner's knowledge. Impasse-driven learning is more specific than these theories in that it postulates exactly what kinds of negative reinforcement cause learning (i.e., impasses) and exactly what kinds of changes the learner makes to its knowledge. The impasse-driven learning hypothesis is a new member of the class of failure-driven learning theories.

The idea of impasse-driven learning is central to the SOAR architecture (Laird, Rosenbloom, & Newell, 1986, 1987). SOAR is a production system. When SOAR reaches an impasse, it does some problem solving at the metalevel. As it returns from that problem solving, it automatically builds a new production rule, whose conditions are exactly the conditions pertaining at the impasse and whose actions are the results of the metalevel problem solving that was just completed. If ever those conditions occur again, the production will fire, thus saving SOAR the effort of reaching an impasse and resolving it at the metalevel. SOAR's authors call this kind of learning "chunking," and the productions built this way are called chunks.

SOAR's authors claim that chunking is the only kind of learning that people do. However, this claim is not very restrictive, because the SOAR architecture allows arbitrary metalevel problem solving at impasses. The chunking mechanism saves the results, but the programmer can generate those results any way she wants by writing the appropriate problem solving into SOAR's metalevel. RT2 will be more specific than that. The theory will describe in detail the metalevel problem solving qua learning that occurs at impasses.

The impasse-driven learning hypothesis has appeared in the literature on formal theories of natural language acquisition. Robert Berwick (1985) developed a theory of how English syntax is learned. His theory is strikingly similar to RT2, despite the fact that the two theories were developed independently. Berwick assumes that a person has a grammar and a parser. The grammar and parser are analogous, respectively, to the procedure and interpreter postulated by RT2. As internal state, Berwick's parser employs a stack and some other temporary structures. These have analogs in RT2 as well. In Berwick's theory the parser can get stuck because no grammar rules apply (the analog of reaching an impasse in RT2). One of four actions is taken. All four actions modify only the parser's internal state just as repairs would. Two of Berwick's four "repairs" have nearly exact analogs to the repairs found in RT2. So the architecture postulated by Berwick for understanding English is nearly isomorphic to the one described here for following procedures.

Berwick (1985) goes on to state his version of the impasse-driven learning hypothesis. Grammar rules are induced when the parser gets stuck. Which rules are induced depends on external information, namely, a perceptually given understanding of the sentence. To put it intuitively, if the child cannot understand a sentence, she figures out what it meant from context, then invents a rule that would both get her parser unstuck and be consistent with the sentence's meaning. This process is analogous to that postulated here, except that the typical learner may appeal to a blackboard, a Dienes Blocks algorithm (given an implementation of Resnick and Omanson's (1987) suggestion) or some other source of information about the skill, rather than inferring its meaning from context.

Summary

Impasse-driven learning has been put forward as a conjecture about how students learn procedural skills. It employs the metalevel architecture proposed by Repair Theory. It postulates additional processes that run at the metalevel. When an impasse occurs, the student can either repair or seek help; both processes run at the metalevel and fix the problem of being at the impasse. When the impasse is fixed, the student can choose either to abstract the actions taken to resolve it, or not. In general, inducing a new subprocedure from the actions taken at the impasse will result in either

a correct subprocedure, if help was sought, or a buggy subprocedure, if repair was used.

Impasse-driven learning seems to make the right sort of predictions about bugs and their stability. It predicts that bugs can migrate as well as be stable over long periods. It predicts that remediation of bugs will appear effective at the end of the remediation session, but that bugs will tend to reappear over time.

Impasse-driven learning also seems to correctly predict the shape of cognitive structures that are built by learning. It predicts that new subprocedures will be attached as deeply as possible in the goal-subgoal hierarchy of the student's procedures.

Impasse-driven learning is a form of failure-driven learning. Failure-driven learning has traditionally been advanced as more cognitively economical than automatic learning, its traditional opponent hypothesis, in that it predicts that new knowledge is acquired only when there is a need for that knowledge. Automatic learning tends to generate mental clutter—cognitive structures of little or no relevance to subsequent thinking.

Impasse-driven learning seems to have great potential generality. It has been investigated in a powerful general learning system, SOAR (Laird et al., 1986, 1987). It has been shown capable of learning English grammar (Berwick, 1985). The future of this hypothesis seems quite bright indeed.

Acknowledgement. This research was supported by the Personnel and Training Research Programs, Psychological Sciences Division. Office of Naval Research, under Contract No. N00014-86K-0349, Project Number 442a558. Reproduction in whole or in part is permitted for any purpose of the United States Government. Approved for public release; distribution unlimited.

REFERENCES

Anderson, J. R. (1983). *The architecture of cognition.* Cambridge, MA: Harvard.

Anderson, J. R. (1985). *Cognitive psychology and its implications.* New York: Freedman.

Anderson, J. R., Farrell, R., & Saurers, R. (1984). Learning to program in LISP. *Cognitive Science, 8,* 87–129.

Anzai, Y., & Simon, H. A. (1979). The theory of learning by doing. *Psychological Review, 86,* 124–140.

Ashlock, R. B. (1976). *Error patterns in computation.* Columbus, OH: Bell & Howell.

Berwick, R. (1985). *The acquisition of syntactic knowledge.* Cambridge, MA: MIT Press.

Brown, J. S., & Burton, R. B. (1978). Diagnostic models for procedural bugs in basic mathematical skills. *Cognitive Science, 2,* 155–192.

Brown, J. S., & VanLehn, K, (1980). Repair Theory: A generative theory of bugs

in procedural skills. *Cognitive Science, 4*, 379–426.

Brownell, W. A. (1935). Psychological considerations in the learning and teaching of arithmetic. In W. D. Reeve (Ed.), *The teaching of arithmetic*. New York: Teachers College, Bureau of Publications.

Brueckner, L. J. (1930). *Diagnostic and remedial teaching in arithmetic*. Philadelphia: Winston.

Burton, R. B. (1982). Diagnosing bugs in a simple procedural skill. In D. H. Sleeman, and J. S. Brown (Eds.) *Intelligent Tutoring Systems*. New York: Academic Press.

Buswell, G. T. (1926). *Diagnostic studies in arithmetic*. Chicago: University of Chicago Press.

Cox, L. S. (1975). Diagnosing and remediating systematic errors in addition and subtraction computation. *The Arithmetic Teacher, 22*, 151–157.

Laird, J. E., Rosenbloom, P. S., & Newell, A. (1986). Chunking in SOAR: The anatomy of a general learning mechanism. *Machine Learning, 1*, 11–46.

Laird, J. E., Rosenbloom, P. S., & Newell, A. (1987). SOAR: An architecture for general intelligence. *Artificial Intelligence, 33*, 1–64.

Lankford, F. G. (1972). *Some computational strategies of seventh grade pupils*. Charlottesville, VA: University of Virginia.

Minton, S. (1985). Selectively generalizing plans for problem-solving. In *Proceedings of IJCAI 85* (pp. 596–599). Los Altos, CA: Morgan-Kaufman.

Newell, A. (1980). Reasoning, problem solving and decision processes: The problem space as a fundamental category. In R. Nickerson (Ed.), *Attention and Performance VIII*. Hillsdale, NJ: Erlbaum.

Newell, A., & Simon, H. A. (1972). *Human problem-solving*. Englewood Cliffs, NJ: Prentice-Hall.

Norman, D. A. (1981). Categorization of action slips. *Psychological Review, 88*, 1–15.

Resnick, L. (1982). Syntax and semantics in learning to subtract. In T. Carpenter, J. Moser & T. Romberg (Ed.). *Addition and subtraction: A cognitive perspective*. Hillsdale, NJ: Lawrence Erlbaum Assoc.

Resnick, L. B., & Omanson, S. F. (1987). Learning to understand arithmetic. In R. Glaser (Ed.), *Advances in instructional psychology*. Hillsdale, NJ: Lawrence Erlbaum Assoc.

Roberts, G. H. (1968). The failure strategies of third grade arithmetic pupils. *The Arithmetic Teacher, 15*, 442–446.

Schank, R. (1982). *Dynamic memory: A theory of learning in computers and people*. Cambridge, England: Cambridge University Press.

Shaw, D. J., Standiford, S. N., Klein, M. F., & Tatsuoka, K. K. (1982). *Error analysis of fraction arithmetic-selected case studies* (Tech. Report 82-2-NIE). Urbana, IL: University of Illinois, Computer-based Education Research Laboratory.

Siegler, R. S., & Shrager, J. (1984). Strategy choices in addition: How do children know what to do? In C. Sophian (Ed.). *Origins of Cognitive Skill*. Hillsdale, NJ: Lawrence Erlbaum Assoc.

Sleeman, D. (1984). An attempt to understand students' understanding of basic algebra. *Cognitive Science, 8*, 387–412.

Sleeman, D. H. (1985). Basic algebra revisited: A study with 14-year olds. *International Journal of Man-Machine Studies, 22*, 127–149.

Sleeman, D. H., & Smith, M. J. (1981). Modeling student's problem solving. *Artificial Intelligence, 16,* 171–187.

Smith, B. C. (1982). *Reflection and semantics in a procedural language* (Technical Report MIT-TR-272). Cambridge, MA: M.I.T. Laboratory for Computer Science.

Tatsuoka, K. K., & Baillie, R. (1982). *Rule space, the product space of two score components in signed-number subtraction: An approach to dealing with inconsistent use of erroneous rules* (Tech. Report 82-3-ONR). Urbana, IL: University of Illinois, Computer-based Education Research Laboratory.

VanLehn, K. (1982). Bugs are not enough: Empirical studies of bugs, impasses and repairs in procedural skills. *The Journal of Mathematical Behavior, 3,* 3–71.

VanLehn, K. (1983a). *Felicity conditions for human skill acquisition: Validating an AI-based theory* (Tech. Report CIS-21). Palo Alto, CA: Xerox Palo Alto Research Center.

VanLehn, K. (1983b). Human skill acquisition: Theory, model and psychological validation. In *Proceedings of AAAI-83* (pp. 420–423). Los Altos, CA: Kaufman.

VanLehn, K. (1986). Arithmetic procedures are induced from examples. In J. Hiebert (Ed.), *Conceptual and procedural knowledge: The case of mathematics.* Hillsdale. NJ: Lawrence Erlbaum Assoc.

VanLehn, K. (in press). *Cognitive procedures: The acquisition and mental representation of basic mathematical skills.* Cambridge, MA: MIT Press.

VanLehn, K., Brown, J. S., & Greeno, J. G. (1984). Competitive argumentation in computational theories of cognition. In W. Kintsch, J. Miller, & P. Polson (Ed.), *Methods and tactics in cognitive science.* Hillsdale, NJ: Lawrence Erlbaum, Assoc.

Wexler, K., & Culicover, P. (1980). *Formal principles of language acquisition.* Cambridge, MA: MIT Press.

3
Psychological Evaluation of Path Hypotheses in Cognitive Diagnosis

STELLAN OHLSSON
PAT LANGLEY

Consider a human being at work locating a fault in a car, proving a mathematical theorem, playing chess—in short, carrying out a cognitive task of some kind. We can capture an individual's performance on the task by observing his or her actions and by listening to what he or she says. We wish to describe the mental processes that generated that performance. The problem of describing the mental processes of a particular person with respect to a particular task, given a performance record, is here called the problem of *cognitive diagnosis*. To the psychologist the problem of cognitive diagnosis is the problem of "research method"—how to process empirical observations of subjects. To the teacher it is the problem of "assessment" —how to evaluate the knowledge, or lack of knowledge, of students. To the computer scientist it is part of the problem of "user modeling"—how to construct interfaces that adapt to the individual user.[1]

It may seem as if the ability to infer a person's thoughts and intentions from what he does and says ought to be the basis of psychological expertise. In actual fact the problem of cognitive diagnosis has received scant attention from psychologists. The main research traditions, such as experimental psychology and test psychology, have not been interested in thought content, nor in the detailed description of single individuals. The main countertraditions, such as Gestalt psychology and the Piagetian tradition, produced *examples* of cognitive diagnoses but never proposed a *methodology* for how to perform such diagnoses.

A major step forward in cognitive diagnosis came when Newell and Simon (1972) proposed a method for the construction of information-processing models of problem solving on the basis of think-aloud proto-

---

[1] In the context of research on Intelligent Tutoring Systems, cognitive diagnosis is often called "student modeling." But inferring mental processes from performances is no different for students than for other human beings. Also, some types of cognitive diagnosis do not result in a model of the observed person, but in some other kind of description. Thus, this term obscures commonalities between research methodology, educational assessment, and interface design.

cols. Their method was carried out "by hand" and relied on the expert judgment of the diagnostician. A second breakthrough came when computer scientists in the field of artificial intelligence computerized the diagnosis of errors in arithmetic (Brown & Burton, 1978; Burton, 1982) and algebra (Sleeman, 1982). Currently, cognitive diagnosis is receiving attention from psychologists (e.g., Marshall, 1980, 1981; Siegler, 1981; VanLehn, 1983; Williams & Hollan, 1981), educators (e.g., Ginsburg, 1983; Hull, in press), and computer scientists (e.g., Bonar & Soloway, 1985; Attisha & Yazdani, 1984).

Our goal in this chapter is to present a diagnostic method that adapts the approach invented by Newell and Simon (1972) so that it can be applied to different kinds of empirical observations and to report on a computer implementation of that method. We develop our argument in four steps. First, we review the diagnostic method of Newell and Simon (1972) in order to separate their underlying approach from the particular method of analysis they proposed. Their method, we argue, is dependent on the peculiar properties of think-aloud data, while the underlying approach is not. Second, we propose an alternative method that allows the approach to be applied to answer data. Third, we focus on the central step in our method, namely the identification of solution paths. We propose a set of psychologically motivated criteria for how to perform this step and report on a computer program that uses these criteria. Fourth, we discuss which kinds of errors the method can handle, which task domains it can be applied to, which types of observations it can use, and how to extend and improve it.

The Problem-Space Approach to Cognitive Diagnosis

The diagnostic method of Newell and Simon (1972) was invented in the context of research on problem solving. Their main aim was to diagnose the problem-solving strategies of their subjects. Their method builds on their theory of problem solving, which says, in brief, that thinking occurs when a problem-solving strategy carries out a search through a problem space. The *problem space* for a particular problem is defined through three components: (1) a mental encoding of the problem situation, known as the *initial state*;[2] (2) a set of cognitive skills, called *operators*, which can be used to process the problem; and (3) a specification of what counts as an answer to the problem—we might call this a *termination criterion*. The termination criterion, most typically a goal, specifies the conditions under which

---

[2] The initial state presupposes a "vocabulary" of concepts in which the problem is described or encoded. When we describe a problem space without referring to a particular problem, as in Table 3.1, we list the conceptual "vocabulary" instead of describing the initial state.

the problem solver believes that he or she is finished with the problem. The problem space consists of all the situations, called *states*, that can be derived from the initial state by successive applications of operators until either no operator is applicable or the termination criterion applies. States in which the termination criterion applies are called *final states*. Problem spaces for challenging problems are very large, containing thousands, or even millions, of states. A problem space for multicolumn subtraction is shown in Table 3.1.

Searching a problem space is done by selecting one or more states (beginning with the initial state), applying one or more operators to each state, thus generating (or "visiting") several new states, selecting one or more other states, and so on, until a final state is reached. A sequence of state–operator pairs that leads from the initial state to a final state is called a *solution path*. The notion of a solution path is central to the work reported in this chapter.

The function of a problem-solving *strategy*, or search scheme, is to specify which of the alternative paths through the problem space are worth exploring. The search can be carried out so that all states in the space are visited, so-called *exhaustive search*. This is usually impractical for both man and machine because of the large sizes of problem spaces. The alternative

TABLE 3.1. A problem space for subtraction.

Representation
>The objects are digits, numbers, columns, and rows.
>The predicates are "left," "right," "above," "below," "being in (a row or column)," "current-column," etc.
>The rows are called "top-row," "middle-row," and "answer-row," respectively.

Operators
>Decrement (number, column). Takes the number in the top row of a column, and replaces it with the result of subtracting one from it.
>Add 10 (number, column). Takes a number in the top row of a column, and replaces it with the result of adding 10 to it.
>Find difference (number 1, number 2, column). Takes two numbers in a column, and writes the result of subtracting the second from the first in the answer row of that column.
>Find top (number, column). Takes a number in the top row of a column and writes that number in the answer row of that column.
>Skip zero (column). Takes a zero in the top row of a column and decides not to write anything in the answer row of that column.
>Shift left (column). Takes a column as input, and returns the column immediately to the left of it.
>Shift right (column). Takes a column as input, and returns the column immediately to the right of it.

Termination criterion
>The problem is finished when there is an answer in each column.

is *selective search*, in which only some paths are explored. A strategy may consist of rules that recommend some paths as more likely to lead to the problem solution than others, without offering any guarantee that their advice is correct every time it applies. Such heuristic strategies can be more or less selective. If the strategy is maximally selective, that is, if it specifies exactly one path through the problem space, then we usually talk about *algorithmic behavior*, rather than about search behavior. The original statement of the theory (Newell & Simon, 1972) should be consulted for a full discussion of these concepts.

The preceding conception of thinking implies that a description of the mental processes of a subject should consist of three components: (1) the problem space of the subject, (2) the subject's path through that space, and (3) the strategy that the subject used to generate that path. The diagnostic method proposed by Newell and Simon (1972) specifies how to derive these three parts of the description from the think-aloud protocol.

The problem space is identified by scanning the think-aloud protocol for evidence concerning the following:

The concepts that the subject used to encode the problem; knowledge of the conceptual "vocabulary" that the subject uses helps to determine the initial state.

The actions, or cognitive skills, that the problem solver applied to the problem; they become the operators.

The answer that the subject gave to the problem; this indicates the subject's termination criterion.

The solution path is identified by using the sequential information in the protocol to map the problem solver's stepwise progress onto a path through the problem space. The path can be represented in a so-called *Problem-Behavior Graph*, which shows each state, the operator applied to it, new conclusions and results, back-ups, goals, and so on. The Problem-Behavior Graph is a *path hypothesis*. In the section entitled Identifying Solution Paths in Diagnosis, we report on a computer program that generates Problem-Behavior Graphs.

The problem-solving strategy is identified by abstracting rules from the state–operator pairs in the solution path, such that the rules—taken together—will reproduce as many steps in the solution path as possible. The collection of rules is a *strategy hypothesis*.

We make the following observations. First, unlike most other data-processing methods in psychology, the method of Newell and Simon gets its rationale from their psychological theory (rather than from, say, statistics). If the theory turns out to be false, the method is inappropriate. Second, the method is a bottom-up, data-driven diagnostic technique. The problem space, the solution path, and the strategy represent successive levels of abstraction from the utterances in the think-aloud protocol,

each level building on the previous one. Third, the unit of analysis in this method is a single performance, rather than a set of performances. Fourth, the method is carried out "by hand"[3] and depends on the expertise of the analyst. A person who is unskilled in the formal analysis of human information processing is unlikely to discover anything interesting with this method. Fifth, the method is labor intensive. A single, relatively short think-aloud protocol may require weeks of analysis. Finally, in spite of the ubiquity of verbal protocols in current cognitive research, the Newell and Simon method of analysis is not widely used, most investigators preferring either informal treatment or categorization followed by statistical treatment.

The Newell and Simon method of analysis relies heavily on two features of think-aloud protocols, one of which they share with verbal protocols in general, and one of which they share with other kinds of trace data (e.g., video recordings of motor actions, eye-movement recordings, etc.). First, in talking about the problem in front of them, subjects reveal which aspects of the problem are salient to them. A paradigmatic case of this occurs in the task domain of cryptarithmetic, where some problem solvers realize that the concept of "parity" is important, while others do not (Newell & Simon, 1972). Thus, while thinking aloud, subjects give direct expression to some of the concepts they use to encode the problem. This information helps decide which problem space the subject is working in.

Second, trace data in general have the advantage of high temporal density. Each performance is represented by a long sequence of observations or data points, each of which provides some evidence as to what the subject was thinking at the corresponding point in time. If the temporal density of the trace is high enough, the information about the successive cognitive steps may be relatively complete. Thus, once the problem space is identified, a high-density trace may determine with a high degree of certainty which path through that space the subject took.

Newell and Simon (1972) accordingly did not propose any method for the evaluation of alternative path hypotheses for the same protocol. They proposed that a strategy hypothesis, that is, a set of rules, can be evaluated by the proportion of steps in the solution path it can account for. However, this is an evaluation of a strategy hypothesis *in relation to* a path hypothesis. In other words given the hypothesis that the subject took a particular path, this measure indicates how successful a particular rule set is in accounting for that path. This measure can be used to choose between alternative *rule sets*. However, Newell and Simon do not discuss any method for selecting between alternative *paths* to the same answer. In their method such conflicts are (implicitly) resolved in the bottom-up analysis that generated the path hypothesis in the first place. If the problem-space

---

[3] Or, rather, "by brain."

approach is to be applied to other kinds of data, alternative techniques must be found for resolving such conflicts. The main contribution of the present chapter is a list of principles for resolving conflicts between path hypotheses (see the section entitled Evaluation Criteria for Path Hypotheses).

In summary the theory of problem solving proposed by Newell and Simon (1972) implies that a cognitive diagnosis should consist of a problem space, a solution path, and a problem-solving strategy. We will call this basic idea the *problem-space approach* to cognitive diagnosis. The step-by-step, bottom-up analysis used by Newell and Simon to identify each of the three components relies on the peculiar properties of think-aloud data, or so we claim. If the problem-space approach is to be applied to other kinds of observations, we need to substitute other techniques for identifying the three components of a cognitive performance.

Extending the Problem-Space Approach

As discussed in detail in the previous section, the diagnostic method proposed by Newell and Simon (1972) was designed for the analysis of think-aloud protocols. However, in many situations in which it is desirable to be able to carry out cognitive diagnosis, most notably instructional contexts, think-aloud protocols are unlikely to be available. The diagnostic method to be defined here allows the problem-space approach to be applied to other kinds of data.

The Newell and Simon type of analysis is labor intensive and is carried out "by hand," relying extensively on expert judgment. Efforts to computerize the analysis of think-aloud protocols have not so far resulted in useful systems (Waterman & Newell, 1972). Large-scale use of cognitive diagnosis however, is impractical unless it can be computerized. The method to be defined here is implemented as a computer program.

The diagnostic method we propose resides within the problem-space approach. However, instead of identifying problem spaces, solution paths, and strategies through bottom-up analyses of think-aloud protocols, we propose to find them with the help of task analysis, search, and machine learning, respectively.

Looking first at the subproblem of identifying the problem space of the subject or student, answer data do not contain any direct evidence about problem spaces. However, for most tasks, there are only a few problem spaces that are psychologically plausible and also sufficient for solving the task. For instance, the problem space in Table 3.1 assumes that a subtraction problem is seen as a spatial grid of rows and columns, which is certainly plausible given the language that is used to teach subtraction. (It is certainly more plausible than the obvious alternatives: an unstructured set of digits, a set of columns but no rows, or two rows but no columns.) The

first three operators represent basic arithmetic skills that children certainly learn before they master multicolumn subtraction, and the last four operators represent even more basic sensorimotor skills.[4] The termination criterion refers to the structure of the problem display, in accordance with empirical evidence that children are concerned with the way answers "look" (e.g., Resnick, 1982). Finally, the space in Table 3.1 is demonstrably sufficient for doing multicolumn subtraction. If there exists an equally "natural" and nevertheless qualitatively different problem space for subtraction, we are unable to think of it. In short we suggest that for many task domains, we can find an adequate approximation to the subject's problem space through task analysis, informed by general psychological considerations.[5] The effect of this stance is to remove the problem space from the outputs of the diagnostic method and to allow it to be one of the inputs instead.

Looking next at the problem of finding the solution path, we propose to find it by *searching the problem space for the observed, possibly incorrect, answer*. This is the main topic of the present chapter and is discussed in the next section.

The third and final subproblem—given the solution path, find the rules that generated it—has received much attention from a field of research outside psychology since Newell and Simon (1972) originally proposed their diagnostic method. Artificial intelligence research into machine learning has lead to computational methods for the automatic construction of problem-solving rules. Such methods, usually called *learning mechanisms*, typically take one or more solution paths as inputs and generate rules that "cover" the steps in those paths. Examples of such learning mechanisms are "generalization," which finds the common elements of good problem-solving steps (Anderson, 1983), "discrimination," which finds the differences between good and bad problem-solving steps (Langley, 1983), and "chunking," which combines several problem-solving steps together into a single, higher order step (Rosenbloom & Newell, 1983). Machine learning is a rapidly growing field of research, and a variety of machine-learning methods are being investigated (Michalski, Carbonell, & Mitchell, 1983).

Machine-learning methods are designed to find rules that will generate *correct* answers to problems. Accordingly, they are given correct solution paths from which to construct the rules. In cognitive diagnosis, on the other hand, we are usually interested in finding out how an *incorrect*

---

[4] In principle one could imagine operators at either a finer grain of analysis, or a more aggregated level of analysis. See Ohlsson & Langley (1985) for a fuller discussion of how the level of analysis of the operators in Table 3.1 was chosen.

[5] In the long run we expect this makeshift procedure to be replaced by some technique based on a theory of the origin of problem spaces. As yet no theory for how to predict which space a particular problem solver will use for a certain task is available. The UNDERSTAND program of Hayes and Simon (1974) is a first approximation to such a theory, but it is not powerful enough for our purposes.

answer was produced. However, the machine learning methods that have been developed so far are "syntactical" in nature. They do not make use of the concepts of "correct" or "incorrect" in the construction of problem-solving rules. Therefore, the hypothesis arose[6] that if given an incorrect solution path, such learning mechanisms should be capable of finding rules that produce incorrect solution paths. This idea was tested by applying the SAGE learning system (Langley, 1983) to diagnostic problems (Langley & Ohlsson, 1984; Langley, Ohlsson, & Sage, 1984). We verified that the discrimination mechanism used by this system can indeed find incorrect problem-solving rules in order to account for specific erroneous solution paths. In short we claim that the diagnostic task of generating rule sets from one or more solution paths can be solved by the application of machine-learning methods.

In summary the problem-space approach reduces the problem of diagnosing the mental processes behind a performance to three subproblems: (1) find the problem space, (2) find the solution path, and (3) find the problem-solving strategy. We propose to deal with them in the following ways:

In principle the first problem remains unsolved. However, we suggest that useful approximations to subjects' problem spaces can be found through task analysis, informed and guided by general psychological considerations.

For the second problem we claim that solution paths to incorrect answers can be found through search. We support this claim with the analysis and computational results reported in the next section.

For the third problem we have demonstrated in previous research (Langley, Ohlsson, & Sage, 1984) that incorrect problem-solving rules can be generated from solution paths with the help of machine learning methods.

These applications of task analysis, search, and machine learning constitute a method for performing cognitive diagnosis within the problem space approach without dependence on think-aloud protocols. In the next section we focus on the second of the three subproblems.

Identifying Solution Paths in Diagnosis

The purpose of this section is to focus on the second of the three diagnostic problems within the problem-space approach, namely how to find the solution path of a subject. The first subsection introduces the basic idea of using search for this purpose, the second subsection outlines a computer program that performs the task of path finding, and the third lists

---

[6] In conversations with our colleague Derek Sleeman.

the evaluation criteria used by the program. The fourth and final subsection reports some selected computational results.

SEARCHING FOR INCORRECT ANSWERS

Suppose that we have identified the problem space used by a subject or student. We propose that one technique for finding the solution paths corresponding to an observed (typically incorrect) answer is to do a search through that problem space. Let us ask why search is an appropriate technique. Search is usually used to find the correct answer to some problem. How can we search for an *incorrect* answer?

Consider the problem space in Table 3.1, and any subtraction problem. If we search that space exhaustively, we are guaranteed to find the correct answer. Since every possible sequence of operators has been developed, by definition of "exhaustive search," the particular sequence of steps that leads to the correct answer must have been developed. However, by the same argument, the particular sequence of steps leading to many incorrect answers must have been developed as well. In fact every terminal state in the subtraction space, except those containing the correct answer, represents some incorrect solution to the problem.

The method of using exhaustive search for finding solution paths in diagnosis is attractive for several reasons. First, it is quite general. It can be applied to any performance that can be cast as a search through a problem space. Second, it is foolproof. If the problem space contains a particular wrong answer, the method is guaranteed to find a solution path to it. Third, it does not make any theoretical commitments other than the problem-space hypothesis. However, exhaustive search is an inefficient technique. We originally believed that problem spaces for simple task domains, such as multicolumn subtraction, were small enough so that exhaustive search could be practical to use. Experience has shown that this is not so. We therefore abandoned the idea of exhaustive search, in spite of its advantages.

The alternative to exhaustive search is, of course, selective search. To search the space selectively means that we do not develop all paths until they end in a final state. Some paths (the more the better) are rejected before they are fully developed. In order to do this, we must have some criteria by which we can recognize one path as a better hypothesis than another, before either path is fully developed.

A set of criteria by which we can evaluate the psychological plausibility of a solution path constitutes a definition of what is meant by a good psychological hypothesis. Clearly, such a definition must rest on psychological theory. In searching for such criteria, we should look to psychology for general principles that can be used to evaluate alternative hypotheses about a performance. (As we shall see later, there are disappointingly few psychological principles that can be used for this purpose.)

In summary we propose to find the solution path of a particular subject by performing a search through the subjects' problem space, guided by a collection of psychological principles. After describing the particular search scheme we have implemented, we put forward a list of such principles.

COMPUTER IMPLEMENTATION

We have implemented our method for problem-space analysis in a computer program called the Diagnostic Path Finder (DPF). A full report on this program is given elsewhere (Ohlsson & Langley, 1985). A brief description must suffice here. The program takes the following as its inputs:

1. A problem space (i.e., a conceptual "vocabulary" for describing a problem, a set of operators, and a termination criterion)
2. A particular problem (described in the notation mentioned previously)
3. A procedure for deriving the correct solution path for that problem in that particular space
4. An answer to the problem (correct or incorrect)

It delivers as its output a solution path in the given space that leads from the problem to the answer.

The main module of the DPF program carries out a best-first search through the subject's problem space. The standard format for a best-first search is as follows: A list of unexpanded states is retained. A selection procedure iterates through the unexpanded list, applies an *evaluation function* to each state, and selects those that have the highest value. The evaulation function measures the "worth" of a state; the higher the value, the more interesting it is to expand that state. The selected states are expanded and then removed from the unexpanded list. Their descendents are then added to the unexpanded list, and the process continues until a complete path hypothesis has been found (i.e., until some path ends with the observed answer).

In standard applications of best-first search, the alternative paths are evaluated with respect to the possibility that they lead to an answer to the problem. The evaluation function typically computes a distance between a state and the final state. But in our application, the selection procedure applies psychological principles. In other words the evaluation function measures the psychological plausibility of a state (or of the path that leads to a state). The criteria listed in the next subsection constitute the evaluation function of our program. This is appropriate, because we are not interested in finding the most efficient route to the answer but in finding the solution path that has the highest probability of being used by the subject or student being diagnosed.

EVALUATION CRITERIA FOR PATH HYPOTHESES

The search scheme described in the previous section tries to find the psychologically most plausible solution path. Its main tool for doing this is an evaluation function that consists of a collection of evaluation criteria. The purpose of this section is to describe these criteria. We begin with three principles of rationality that constitute a basic platform for cognitive diagnosis (and for computer simulation in general).

Assumption of Causal Closure

When DPF expands a state in the problem space, it considers only those operator applications that have all their arguments available in that state. These may be available either because they are part of the givens of the problem, or because they have been produced by some earlier operator. Expressed differently, we are considering only paths in which the arguments to the operators have some rational connection with the task. We do not consider paths in which arguments to operators are generated through imagination (or "divine intervention").

It is important to note that this assumption is sometimes false. For instance a child doing arithmetic may get a digit by peeking at his neighbor's work sheet. However, the ambition to account for inputs to operators gives discipline to the diagnostic process. If operators can take arbitrary arguments, then any solution path can produce any answer.

Assumption of Purposefulness

We are assuming that operators are executed because their outputs are needed for some purpose; in other words, they will be used as inputs to some other operator, or they occur in the final answer. DPF rejects paths in which several intermediate results have not been used by any subsequent operator, even if these paths arrive at the desired answer. We do not consider paths with superfluous steps.

Again, this assumption is sometimes false. It is possible, almost certain, that subjects or students are executing all kinds of unnecessary operators, the outputs of which are not used for anything. However, the very fact that the outputs are not used for anything makes it impossible for us to know anything about them. We cannot evaluate hypotheses about extra and unnecessary steps that have no effects on subsequent processing and, in particular, no effect on the answer. Also, the space of such paths is clearly infinite. Therefore, we choose to ignore such path hypotheses.

Assumption of No Duplication

We assume that subjects do not derive intermediate results that are already available. If an expression is available in a knowledge state, we do not consider operator applications that generate that expression as output.

Again, this assumption is certainly false in some cases. However, steps that produce already available knowledge items have no effect on the future processing, because they do not produce any new possibilities for action. Thus, their existence is also impossible to determine. Again, the set of possible paths becomes infinite if we allow repeated derivations of the same result within a path.

Note that the preceding three assumptions lead to *absolute* evaluation criteria rather than relative. They are not used to evaluate whether one path hypothesis is better than another. Paths that violate any of these criteria are simply rejected. However, the DPF also employs *relative* criteria that rank order the various hypotheses.

Criterion of Memory Load

One of the few general principles that has emerged from cognitive psychology relates to the limited capacity of human short-term memory. There is still considerable debate about the cause of this capacity limitation, but for our purposes, it is enough to know that such a limitation exists. Given this knowledge, a path hypothesis that requires a small short-term memory load is more plausible than a hypothesis that requires a larger memory load. Thus, given two hypotheses that are comparable on other criteria, DPF prefers the one with the smaller memory load.

We compute memory load as the number of unused intermediate results at each state along the path. An intermediate result that is not used immediately must be kept in memory. Thus, the number of operator outputs that have not yet been used as inputs to any operator at a particular time is a reasonable estimate of memory load at that time.

Criterion of Subgoaling

A second psychological principle of some generality is that human thinking is goal oriented. We assume that the different parts of the goal (in the case of subtraction, the different digits) are subgoals for the subject or student. In its evaluation DPF prefers paths that have more subgoals satisfied.

The user also has the option of specifying some preferred order in which the subgoals are most likely to be satisfied. For the subtraction domain we specified right-to-left as the most plausible ordering of the subgoals. During evaluation DPF prefers paths that have the subgoals in the specified order, rather than in some other order. (Notice, however, that this is a relative, not an absolute, criterion. Paths with the subgoals in some other order will be considered, if they have high scores on some other evaluation dimension.)

Criterion of Productivity

A third psychological principle of general importance is that skills of all kinds are continuously being made more efficient through a process called

automatization. Several different mechanisms have been proposed to explain how automatization occurs. For present purposes the exact mechanism behind automatization is not important. It is enough to know that there are processes in human cognition that continually look for short-cuts and weed out unnecessary steps. We take this to imply that in diagnosis we should prefer a path with a higher degree of productivity to one with a lower degree. We compute productivity as the number of satisfied subgoals divided by the number of operator applications in the path (i.e., as "results per effort").

The DPF also uses criteria related to the notions of simplicity and parsimony, to which we now turn.

Criterion of Minimal Error

We want to ascribe to the subject or student as few errors as possible, consistent with the subject's erroneous answers. This follows one of the oldest methodological canons of science: Do not complicate an explanation more than necessary. Furthermore, given two path hypotheses, DPF prefers the one that is more similar to the correct path.[7] We compute the similarity between a path hypothesis and the correct path as the average length of the maximal common subsequences of the two paths.

Criterion of Minimal Length

A second measure of simplicity involves the *length* of the path hypothesis. Given two path hypotheses, DPF prefers the shorter path, other things being equal. Length is defined as the number of operator applications.

These eight criteria constitute our definition of what we mean by a good path hypothesis. One way to text whether or not they constitute a useful definition is to run the program that uses them and observe whether it generates plausible diagnoses. We report selected computational results in the next subsection.

SELECTED COMPUTATIONAL RESULTS

We have applied the DPF program mainly to the domain of multicolumn subtraction with regrouping, using the problem space shown in Table 3.1. We used both ideal data, that is, data with certain bugs planted in them, and empirical data, that is, observations of children. Ohlsson and Langley (1985) discussed the runs made with the program. The results can be summarized as follows:

- When applied to ideal data—answers to a 17-item subtraction test with 10 different high-frequency subtraction bugs planted in them—the DPF

---

[7] This use of the correct path is one reason why the correct procedure is given as one of the inputs to the program.

program found plausible diagnoses on 64 out of 74 runs (86%), producing weird or implausible diagnosis in 10 cases.

- When applied to empirical data—answers to the same subtraction test produced by three different school-children—the DPF program showed a mixed picture of successes and failures. It discovered a new subtraction bug. The DPF program, however, does not generalize across solution paths in the derivation of its diagnoses and therefore overlooks some regularities in the data.
- Demonstration runs have been made with a problem space for addition and one for verbal reasoning, verifying that the task-specific parts of the program reside in the definition of the problem space and not in the search mechanism.

Let us next look at three examples of specific path hypotheses proposed by DPF to account for particular incorrect answers.

Example 1

Consider the following problem:

$$
\begin{array}{r}
513 \\
- 268 \\
\hline
\end{array}
$$

Correct answer: 245
Incorrect answer: 355

The incorrect answer, 355, is consistent with (at least) two different subtraction bugs. Referring to the bug library in VanLehn (1983), they are called Borrow-No-Decrement and Smaller-From-Larger. The Borrow-No-Decrement bug predicts that the answer 355 is produced in as follows:

1. Add 10 to 3 in the rightmost column (without decrementing the 1 in the adjacent column).
2. Subtract the 8 from the 13 in the rightmost column, giving 5 as the answer in that column.
3. Add 10 to the 1 in the second column from the right (again without decrementing the 5 in the adjacent column).
4. Subtract the 6 from the 11 in the middle column, giving 5 as the answer in that column.
5. Subtract the 2 from the 5 in the leftmost column, giving 3 as the answer in that column.

However, when run on this problem with 355 as the given answer, the DPF program preferred the Smaller-From-Larger bug, which corresponds to the following solution path:

1. Subtract the 3 from the 8 in the rightmost column, giving 5 as the answer in that column.

2. Subtract the 1 from the 6 in the middle column, giving 5 as the answer in that column.
3. Subtract the 2 from the 5 in the leftmost column, giving 3 as the answer in that column.

The solution path for the Small-From-Larger bug is indeed simpler.

Example 2

The following example is taken from empirical data:

$$3,005$$
$$-28$$

Correct answer:	2,977
Observed incorrect answer:	2,087

When this problem was given to the DPF program together with the observed incorrect answer, it produced the following solution path:

1. Add 10 to the 5 in the first column from the right.
2. Subtract the 8 from the 15, giving 7 as the answer in the first column from the right.
3. Add 10 to the 0 in the second column from the right.
4. Subtract the 2 from 10, giving 8 as the answer in the second column from the right.
5. Copy the 0 in the third column from the right as the answer for that column.
6. Decrement the 3 in the last column, and write the resulting 2 as the answer in that column.

This solution path can be interpreted as follows: The student added 10 to any column where it was needed, and then *"paid back" all their "borrows" at once with a single decrement in the last column*. It is of some interest to note that this bug—perhaps to be called "Add-Ten-Freely-Decrement-Last"—is not included in the bug library of VanLehn (1983).

Example 3

The previous two examples show two successful diagnoses produced by DPF. It is less clear how to evaluate the following diagnosis.

$$800$$
$$-168$$

Correct answer:	632
Incorrect answer:	542

When DPF is given this problem with the incorrect answer *542*, it suggests the following solution path:

1. Shift to the leftmost column, and decrement the 8 there, giving 7 as the new top number in that column.
2. Shift back to the second column from the right, and add 10 to the 0 there.
3. Shift back to the first column from the right, and add 10 to the 0 there.
4. Subtract the 8 from the 10 in the first column from the right, giving 2 as the answer in that column.
5. Subtract the 6 from the 10 in the second column from the right, giving 4 as the answer in that column.
6. Decrement the 7 in the leftmost column, giving 6 as the new top number in that column.
7. Subtract the 1 from the 6 in the leftmost column, giving 5 as the answer in that column.

In effect the DPF program explains the faulty answer in two steps. First, it suggests that the student forgot to decrement the 10 added to the second column, which seems plausible enough. However, to get the 5 in the leftmost column, the program postulates that the student decremented this column twice, once correctly when he or she did the borrow, and once again when he or she processed that column. This diagnosis is logically correct, in the sense that the path offered by the program explains the observed answer. However, how plausible is the "extra" decrement operation? This question cannot be settled within the context of a single solution path; only evidence from other problems solved by the same student could be used to decide whether or not this is a good hypothesis. Since the DPF program does not take interpath regularities into account, it cannot gather evidence for or against its rather creative, but somewhat implausible, explanation for the observed behavior.

Discussion

In summary, the problem-space approach to cognitive diagnosis claims that an intellectual performance should be described as a search through a problem space. We propose that such descriptions can be generated with a combination of task analysis, selective search, and those artificial intelligence techniques known as machine-learning mechanisms. In the present work we focussed on the problem of identifying solution paths. We proposed a set of psychologically motivated criteria that can be used to choose between alternative path hypotheses. These criteria have been embedded in a computer program, called DPF, which performs the path-finding task in the domain of multicolumn subtraction. The program generates plausible path hypotheses for a variety of incorrect answers to subtraction problems.

We will briefly discuss the kinds of *behavior* that can be handled in this

form of diagnosis, the kinds of *task domains* that it can be applied to, the kinds of *data* it can be applied to, and finally, how one would go about improving it.

A central issue is which kinds of behaviors our method can deal with. Of course, in cognitive diagnosis, we are usually interested in explaining why the subject or student we have observed made an error. The principle that underlies our method is that *errors arise from the incorrect or inappropriate application of correctly learned cognitive operations*. A person is equipped with a large number of cognitive skills and operations that he or she knows how to execute correctly. In solving problems a person makes use of those subskills. However, he or she may apply them to the wrong arguments, in the wrong contexts, or in the wrong order. The outcome is an incorrect answer. We might characterize such errors as *strategic errors*. The main remedy is to learn the correct rules for applying the operators.

There are three classes of errors that do not naturally fit into this framework. First, there are *memory failures*. This class includes failure to retrieve information from long-term memory, as well as failure to keep task-important information in short-term memory. Second, there are *misperceptions*. A subject or student does not perceive a task in the way it was intended. This type of error may not be common in arithmetic and other tasks with simple displays, but it can be expected to occur in tasks with more complex stimuli, such as algebra. Finally, there are *distractions*, external events that intrude on problem solving. A distraction might cause a break in the sequence of operators, or introduce task-irrelevant information that becomes confused with task information. None of these three error types can be characterized in terms of the incorrect application of operators. In summary, our method is oriented toward strategic errors rather than memory failures, misperceptions, and distractions.

It is worthwhile to ask *why* the method we are proposing is successful. Recall that Newell and Simon (1972) argued that diagnosis of cognitive strategies can be made only on the basis of temporally dense trace data. Their reason for turning to think-aloud protocols was that we need to monitor the successive steps of the problem solver closely in order to identify the strategy that is used. And yet the DPF program (as well as other diagnostic computer systems, e.g., Burton, 1982; Sleeman, 1982) performs cognitive diagnosis on the basis of answer data only. Why are these systems successful? Under what conditions can one infer a cognitive strategy from observed answers?

One way to approach this question is to look at subtraction, the task domain in which diagnosis based on answer data has been most successful. We suggest that the following three properties of the subtraction domain are necessary conditions for this success:

First, notice that in a subtraction problem, the answer is not given with the problem statement. This is in contrast to other types of tasks, such as move tasks and proof tasks, in which the goal object is given as part of the

problem statement. In such problems the "answer" to the problem, that is the goal object, does not in itself carry any information about the problem solver. Therefore, one could not do diagnosis on the basis of answers in those domains.

Second, the answer to a subtraction problem is chosen from a very large universe of possible answers (i.e., all numbers). This is in contrast to many other tasks used in cognitive research, such as verbal reasoning tasks, where the answers may be chosen from a small set of objects or names. (An example would be the famous selection task, in which the subject decides which of four cards to turn over in order to test a rule. See Wason & Johnson-Laird, 1972.)

Third, the answer to a subtraction problem consists of parts (the digits) with relations to each other (left-to-right ordering). The answer has *internal structure*. This is in contrast to many other task types, such as judgmental tasks in which the answers often are indivisible responses, such as "Yes" or "No."

In summary, we want to suggest that cognitive diagnosis on the basis of answer data will succeed only in task domains in which the answers are not given with the problem statement, in which the answer in chosen from a very large set of possible answers, and in which the answer has internal structure. In those cases the given answers might contain enough information about the problem solver to make the diagnostic inference possible.

It is useful to be able to diagnose on the basis of answer data, because in many situations they are the only data available. Answer data, however, contain less information than other types of psychological observations. It is therefore important that the method we have described does not *exclude* the use of other kinds of data. Recall that in our method the solution path of the subject or student is found through a selective search, guided by an evaluation function that applies psychological principles to estimate the plausibility of a path. Suppose that some trace of the performance to be diagnosed is available, such as a video recording of problem-solving actions, written scratch marks in the domain of arithmetic, or the like. The evaluation function of the search program can be extended so as to estimate how much of the trace is "covered" or accounted for by any particular path hypothesis. For instance, given a set of scratch marks for an arithmetic problem, the evaluation function may count the number of such marks that a path hypothesis accounts for. A path will then be judged according to two considerations: its ability to account for whatever trace data happen to be available and its psychological plausibility. Thus, although the method can be used even when only answer data are available, it nevertheless affords a mechanism through which trace data, if available, can be brought to bear.

One important methodological consequence of this is that *trace data do not have to be complete in order to support diagnosis.* Since the DPF program can find a path hypothesis without *any* help from a trace, the tem-

poral density and completeness of the trace are not as crucial as they are when the trace is the sole resource for finding the solution path. Even an incomplete trace might be helpful in focusing the search on the most plausible alternatives. In summary our version of the problem-space approach can be used in conjunction with many different kinds of data.

Finally, one might want to consider how the method could be extended and improved. Let us first consider applying the DPF program to another task domain. What must be changed? The DPF system separates cleanly into two components, the problem space and the search scheme that tries to find a psychologically plausible path through the problem space. The search scheme is content-independent, and the evaluation criteria it uses are general psychological considerations that ought to be valid across task domains. The problem space holds *all* the domain-specific information given to the program.

To support the preceding claim, we have run the DPF system on a problem space for addition, in which it diagnosed the error of forgetting to carry, and on a problem space for verbal reasoning. No task information other than the problem space was necessary to make the program run on these domains, nor any tuning of the search mechanism. Thus, these runs verified that the task-specific input to the program is limited to the problem space. Applying the DPF program to a new task domain is then a matter of supplying it with a new problem space, which is not an overwhelming task (see Table 3.1 for an example of a problem space).

A more fundamental extension of the program would be to add new evaluation criteria to make the search for the best path hypothesis more selective. Any psychological principle can be turned into an evaluation criterion. Thus the bottleneck here is not our ideas about diagnosis *per se* but the state of cognitive theory. Currently, disappointingly few generally accepted principles have emerged from research in cognitive psychology. Therefore, our list of evaluation criteria is short. However, as the theory of human cognition develops, we will be able to add further criteria to the diagnostic system. We find this coupling between progress in theory and progress in diagnosis appealing. It seems reasonable that as we gain in knowledge and understanding of mental processes, our capacity to diagnose such processes accurately should increase. If it increases enough, the vision of psychological competence as the ability to infer mental processes from observations of what a person does and says may eventually become a reality.

Acknowledgement. This research was supported by Contract N00014-83-K-0074, NR 154-508, from the Personnel and Training Research Program, Psychological Sciences Division, Office of Naval Research.

REFERENCES

Anderson, J. R. (1983). *The architecture of cognition*. Cambridge, MA: Harvard University Press.

Attisha, M., & Yazdani, M. (1984). An expert system for diagnosing children's multiplication errors. *Instructional Science, 13*, 79–92.

Bonar, J., & Soloway, E. (1985). Pre-programming knowledge: A major source of misconceptions in novice programmers. *Human–Computer Interaction, 1*, 133–161.

Brown, J. S., & Burton, R. R. (1978). Diagnostic models for procedural bugs in basic mathematical skills. *Cognitive Science, 2*, 155–192.

Burton, R. (1982). Diagnosing bugs in a simple procedural skill. In D. Sleeman & J. S. Brown (Eds.), *Intelligent tutoring systems* (pp. 157–183). London: Academic Press.

Ginsburg, H. P. (1983). Cognitive diagnosis of children's arithmetic. *Issues in Cognition: Proceedings of a Joint Conference in Psychology*. Washington, DC: National Academy of Sciences and American Psychological Association.

Hayes, J. R., & Simon, H. A. (1974). Understanding written problem instructions. In L. W. Gregg (Ed.), *Knowledge and cognition* (pp. 167–200). Hillsdale, NJ: Lawrence Erlbaum Assoc.

Hull, G. (in press). Research on error and correction. In B. W. McClelland & T. R. Donovan (Eds.), *Perspectives on research and scholarship in composition*. New York: Modern Language Association.

Langley, P. (1983). Learning search strategies through discrimination. *International Journal of Man-Machine Studies, 18*, 513–541.

Langley, P., & Ohlsson, S. (1984). Automated cognitive modeling. *Proceedings of the National Conference on Artificial Intelligence*.

Langley, P., Ohlsson, S., & Sage, S. (1984). *A machine learning approach to student modeling*. (Tech. Rep. CMU-RI-TR-84-7). Pittsburgh: Carnegie-Mellon University, The Robotics Institute.

Marshall, S. P. (1980). Procedural networks and production systems in adapative diagnosis. *Instructional Science, 9*, 129–143.

Marshall, S. P. (1981). Sequential item selection: Optimal and heuristic policies. *Journal of Mathematical Psychology, 23(2)*, 134–152.

Michalski, R. S., Carbonell, J. G., & Mitchell, T. M. (Eds.). (1983). *Machine learning: An artificial intelligence approach*. Palo Alto, CA: Tioga Press.

Newell, A., & Simon, H. A. (1972). *Human problem solving*. Englewood Cliffs, NJ: Prentice-Hall.

Ohlsson, S., & Langley, P. (1985). *Identifying solution paths in cognitive diagnosis* (Tech. Rep. CMU-RI-TR-85-2). Pittsburgh: Carnegie-Mellon University, The Robotics Institute.

Resnick, L. B. (1982). Syntax and semantics in learning to subtract. In T. P. Carpenter, J. M. Moser, & T. A. Romberg (Eds.), *Addition and subtraction: A cognitive perspective* (pp. 136–155). Hillsdale, NJ: Lawrence Erlbaum Assoc.

Rosenbloom, P. S., & Newell, A. (1983, June). The chunking of goal hierarchies: A generalized model of practice. *Proceedings of the International Machine Learning Workshop*, Monticello, IL.

Siegler, R. S. (1981). Developmental sequences within and between concepts.

Monographs of the Society for Research in Child Development, 46 (2, Serial No. 189).

Sleeman, D. (1982). Assessing aspects of competence in basic algebra. In D. Sleeman & J. S. Brown (Eds.), *Intelligent tutoring systems* (pp. 185–199). London: Academic Press.

VanLehn, K. (1983). *Felicity conditions for human skill acquisition: Validating an AI-based theory* (Tech. Rep. No. CIS-21). Palo Alto, CA: Xerox PARC.

Wason, P. C., & Johnson-Laird, P. N. (1972). *Psychology of reasoning: Structure and content.* Cambridge, MA: Harvard University Press.

Waterman, D. A., & Newell, A. (1972). *Preliminary results with a system for automatic protocol analysis* (CIP Rep. No. 211). Pittsburgh: Carnegie-Mellon University, Department of Psychology.

Williams, M. D., & Hollan, J. D. (1981). The process of retrieval from very-long term memory. *Cognitive Science, 5,* 87–119.

4

Modeling the Knowledge Base of Mathematics Learners: Situation-Specific and Situation-Nonspecific Knowledge

IPKE WACHSMUTH

Introduction

This chapter describes an approach to modeling the domain-specific knowledge of mathematics learners in a predicate-logic formalism suited for computer implementation. Two hypotheses are central to this approach. First, a person's cognitive behavior is a *knowledge-based process* that evolves from relatively simple component processes of an inferential nature. The complexity of a person's observed behavior in a domain depends on the knowledge base: how many facts and rules he or she has and how these facts and rules are organized. Second, a person's behavior in a task situation is generally not supported by the total body of his or her long-term knowledge. Rather, it is assumed that knowledge must be *activated* to be used in a given situation and that the accessibility of particular knowledge depends on contextual cues in the situation. The degree to which particular knowledge is contextually bound with respect to a set of specific situations is called *situation specificity.*

The activation of particular knowledge may depend on various kinds of contextual information. Significant context information is carried by the language involved in communicating a task situation. Language is a primary carrier of instructional transactions and is thus a dimension to be considered in modeling the knowledge of mathematics learners along with the dimension of operational knowledge as captured by the rule-based approach. This discussion focuses on the linguistic dimension.

The chapter begins with a brief discussion to motivate and exemplify the issue of situation specificity. A short introduction to computerized learner models follows. The major part of the chapter presents a logical programming approach to modeling student knowledge on the basis of a representation system implemented in the PROLOG (PROgramming in LOGic) language. Principles followed in modeling student knowledge are presented and discussed. Finally, an outline is given of how the approach

could lead to the development of a student modeling component in an intelligent tutoring system.

Situation Specificity and Inconsistent Student Behavior

It is a frequent observation in mathematics instruction that learners who master a task when it is posed in a standard setting may stumble when the "same" task is embedded in a new context; for example, an applied situation. A possible effect is that a learner gives different answers to a mathematical question posed in different contexts. In this sense the learner's behavior can be inconsistent across different situations involving the same sort of mathematics.

Empirical investigations have shown that learners' ability to apply knowledge of a subject domain cannot be considered independently of the context in which that knowledge was acquired (Seiler, 1973). When subjects have had to demonstrate their knowledge in settings that deviated from the situational context of instruction, they have not always been able to do so. While formal thinking structures arise from the individual's experience with specific problems in specific situations, they rarely reach an unrestricted, universal generality. Without further guidance an individual may not be able to apply a given rule in novel situations. Further, it is very probable that in one individual and with respect to one subject domain, different thinking structures can coexist that can become activated alternately, depending on the symbol system primarily triggered or cued by a situation (in particular *cf.* Seiler, 1973, p. 268).

From clinical research in the realm of rational number learning, Wachsmuth (1985a, 1985b) has presented examples that illustrate some of the points mentioned previously. One fifth-grade subject's behavior in comparing the size of several fractions gave evidence of having knowledge but being unable to use it optimally in an applied situation. The evidence indicated that the activation of knowledge was inhibited by the latency of, and a lack of mutual access to, relevant subdomains of fraction knowledge. It was hypothesized that the subject used one repertory of rules to make judgments about the equivalence or nonequivalence of fractions and another repertory of rules to determine the sequence (in magnitude) of nonequivalent fractions. When the second repertory was employed heavily in arranging a set of 12 fractions according to their order relationship as numbers (represented by different gray shadings), some fractions that had originally been recognized as being equivalent were treated as unequal. The activation versus nonactivation of the different sets of rules might explain why the subject exhibited inconsistent behavior with respect to stating the equivalence of certain fractions.

On the basis of another fifth grader's performance, two competitive

domains of fraction knowledge, specific to situations governed by certain language, were identified. Triggered by contextual cues, each domain could be activated independently of the other, but a connection across the different situations was lacking. When the interviewer contrasted contradictory answers given in the different contexts, the inconsistency in the subject's knowledge base caused a cognitive conflict to occur.

With respect to the psychology of learning, the issue of inconsistency is crucial. First, any serious attempt to improve instruction must recognize and deal with the fact that isolated, possibly incompatible, domains—"islands" of knowledge—can exist in the human mind and give rise to inconsistent behavior. Second, the discovery of inconsistencies can yield important hints about flaws in a learner's knowledge base and indicate where to invest remedial efforts. Identifying the conditions and laws of a student's inconsistent behavior prepares the grounds for remediation. Remediation so grounded will promote mature conceptions that are consistent and stable across a broad range of situations.

In summary it is the intent of any instruction to bring about knowledge that is widely applicable. That knowledge tends to remain situation specific seems to require particular instructional attention. Such restriction in a learner's developing cognitive structure might be overcome by intelligent guidance that diagnoses the learner's condition and evaluates appropriate tutorial strategies. A central requirement for such an effort is that the cognitive structures of a learner be understood in terms of a framework that allows precise description of deficits.

Learner Models

Good teaching requires an understanding of the learner's thinking. A good teacher's instructional efforts are not restricted to preplanned behavior but can respond to a diagnosis and remediation of the learner's misconceptions. To make decisions about pedagogical interventions successfully, teachers must be able to put themselves in the learner's place, that is, make a model of the student's current thinking.

The construction and use of formal learner models is expected to pay off in improved instruction through better understanding of the organization of the learner's subject knowledge. Computerized learner models have become very important in attempts to apply artificial intelligence techniques for educational purposes in intelligent tutoring systems. In such a system a computer tutor diagnoses the student's errors and leads the student to an understanding of them. To do this the system uses the collected knowledge base of experienced teachers of the subject domain.

Three components comprise the general framework of an intelligent tutoring system (cf. Barr & Feigenbaum, 1982, pp. 229–235):

1. An "expert" component, which is charged with the task of generating problems and evaluating the correctness of the student's solutions
2. A student-model component, which is to represent the student's current understanding of the material to be taught
3. A tutoring component, incorporating knowledge about natural-language dialogues, teaching methods, and the subject area

The core of this approach is to compare, in a given problem situation, the student's actual response with an ideal interaction generated by the expert component (Figure 4.1). The difference will then be evaluated in order to make a decision about appropriate tutorial strategies.

In most instances so far, work has concentrated on the construction of single components of an intelligent tutoring system. Learner models are regarded as one of the most important components in the construction of intelligent tutoring systems but also have been found to be among the most difficult. A number of approaches have attempted to model individual students' understanding of the material to be taught; for example, by keeping catalogs of the student's response history or by setting "learned/not learned" flags in the rule base or in a subject-matter semantic net. Other approaches have modeled student knowledge as a deviation from expert knowledge. (For a more extensive review of this field cf. Barr & Feigenbaum, 1982, pp. 231–232). The issue of situation specificity is scarcely captured by such approaches, because they focus mainly on facts and rules, while the context-bound quality of such "particles of knowledge" is of concern here.

The notion of a learner model is concretized for the present purpose as follows: *A learner model is a system that makes concrete assumptions about a student's way of acting in specific situations.* The generality versus

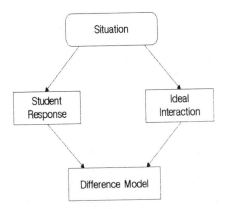

FIGURE 4.1. Difference model: Learner's suboptimal performance is explained as deviation from optimal performance.

specificity of a particular way of acting is then captured by the range (i.e., number and sort) of situations associated with it.

In order to design a computer-implementable representation for learner models, the first goal is to specify a *representation language* that can express pieces of student knowledge and model the use of such knowledge. A second goal of particular importance with respect to intelligent tutoring systems is the design of a component that generates and updates actualized hypotheses of individual learner knowledge.

As a means to describe and analyze the representation and use of domain-specific knowledge concisely, a formalized learner model, LAKOS, was developed at the University of Osnabrüeck. (LAKOS is an acronym standing for the German translation of logical analysis of cognitive organizational structures.) Its main intent is to derive hypotheses about the cognitive structures of individual learners. Such hypotheses, expressed in terms of the model, should provide "logical" explanations for learners' behavior even if the behavior appears irrational at first glance. A computerized version of the model, based on the technique of logical programming, has been developed. It models learner knowledge in terms of network structures as formulated by a human experimenter.

The LAKOS model emphasizes the following:

1. The linguistic competence of the learner, in the sense of what words are available to the learner, what meanings are associated with these, and in which contexts they are available and understood
2. The operational competence of the learner, in the sense of what abstract ways to act (rules) are available to the learner and in which situations they can be activated and used
3. The organization of the learner's knowledge as a basis for the flexibility of his or her performance
4. The disparity or connectedness of knowledge substructures
5. The generality or specificity with respect to the class of situations in which particular rules can be used

Although so far the construction of learners' knowledge structures must be accomplished by a human experimenter, these efforts can be an important precursor for conceptualizing intelligent tutoring systems. Whether our goal is to improve instructional strategies or to develop computerized teaching systems, the main objective of modeling a learner's knowledge structures remains the same: to obtain hypotheses about the learner's misconceptions and suboptimal behavior such that the teacher, or the system, can intervene in a corrective manner. In the same way that a good teacher should be able to understand the behavior of a learner, especially where it deviates from ideal behavior, intelligent tutoring systems should be able to diagnose origins of behaviors in terms of a learner model on which to base decisions about tutorial interventions.

Description of the LAKOS Model

The first implemented version of the model is the LAKOS1 system. It was conceptualized as a deductive question-answering system (Black, 1968) not restricted to a specific subject matter and was implemented in the PROLOG language (a Micro PROLOG version, MLOG, was used; Gust & Gust, 1984). The system can hold natural language dialogues of a restricted, standardized form with a user. The user proceeds by asking questions or probing behavior as if in a diagnostic interview. The computer takes the role of a person, some rudiments of whom are modeled in the machine, and answers questions or executes commands from the person's point of view. The system's responses are displayed on the terminal. They represent the actions or answer statements of the person as predicted by the model. If the user asks WHY the computer model gives a reason for its most recent answer.

The design of any such system requires both the specification of a representation scheme for bodies of facts and a method for deriving conclusions. In the LAKOS1 system, the representation scheme is a combination of formal logic and a network approach, and the reasoning method is deductive inference based on the resolution procedure (Robinson, 1965). As "world-dependent" components the knowledge base and the parser and generator need to be specified with respect to a specific application.

The reactions of the LAKOS1 system are generated as knowledge-based processes. The elements in the knowledge base are formulated as rules and facts. The rules are conditional statements, each consisting of one or more phrases, the antecedent(s), followed by an arrow, followed by another phrase, the consequent. Facts are included as rules without antecedents. In this approach there is no clear distinction between declarative and procedural knowledge. A rule has a declarative meaning as a descriptive statement about its constituents. In addition it has a procedural meaning by virtue of being executable by the interpreter. As is usual in the PROLOG language, rules are written in reverse, beginning with the consequent, interpreted as a goal that recurs on the antecedents as subgoals.

A prototypical instantiation of this model is the TERRI program, which was first presented in 1984 at the 5th International Congress on Mathematical Education in Adelaide (Carss, 1986; for more information cf. Wachsmuth, 1985a). Due to the economy of PROLOG, this program runs on an Apple II micro computer (with Z80 processor). It models responses from an uncertain pupil, not only to "straight" questions such as "Which is greater, $\frac{1}{4}$ or $\frac{1}{3}$?" but also to questions asking why the student gave a particular answer, for example, "$\frac{1}{4}$ is greater than $\frac{1}{3}$ [sic] because they have the same number on top and 4 is greater than 3." The student responses are not necessarily mathematically consistent but are modified in

the light of what wordings are used or what questions have already been asked by the user. Empirical clinical data from a long-term experimental teaching study carried out in the United States (the *Rational Number Project*[1]) served as a basis for the instantiation of the model.

As is seen in Figure 4.2, the LAKOS1 system consists of a dialogue interface, a knowledge base referred to as *long-term memory*, and three processes, PARSE, EVALUATE, and RESPONSE, which constitute components in the cognitive processing carried out by the system. Because of the limited subject matter for the TERRI program, it was possible to design a relatively simple natural language interface. (A parsing routine for arbitrary English sentences would be far more complex than the entire deductive system.) Further components of the system are a (semantic) *short-term memory* and a mechanism regulating the activation of knowledge coded in long-term memory, referred to as *focus*.

A working cycle of the system consists of three major steps:

1. PARSE transforms an input sentence into an expression in the representation language, activating a subset of the knowledge recorded in long-term memory.
2. EVALUATE searches the activated part of the knowledge base for relevant information and makes inferences to produce an answer internally.
3. RESPONSE generates a language answer and returns it to the terminal.

The results of the most recent inferences are kept in short-term memory for possible use in the evaluation of further queries. If the process fails at any step, an appropriate message is put out.

The knowledge in long-term memory is organized in the form of a *knowledge network*. The nodes in this network contain lexical language records and knowledge of a particular field of discourse in the form of rules that are interpreted as abstract ways to think and act. A single record in a node of the knowledge network is referred to by the term *knowledge element*. A knowledge element can be employed when it is marked active and when the data or part of the data of an input string match its structure.

The activation of knowledge is realized through the focus mechanism, which tags the network nodes that are currently accessible. The focus can shift along the links in the network during a dialogue in progress, causing a dynamic partitioning of the knowledge network into active and inactive knowledge. In this sense access structures are determined by the topology of the network. When a whole working cycle is completed, the focus re-

---

[1] Data and findings used stem from the Rational Number Project, which was in part supported by the National Science Foundation under Grants No. SED 79-20591 and No. SED 81-12643. Any opinions, findings, and conclusions expressed here are those of the author and do not necessarily reflect the views of the National Science Foundation.

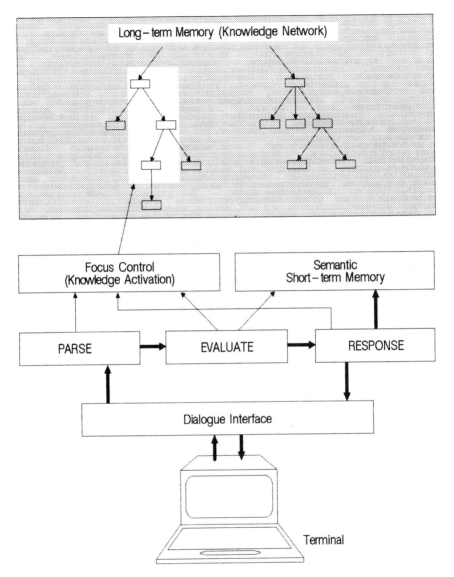

FIGURE 4.2. The LAKOS1 dialogue system. Light arrows denote access; heavy arrows denote information flow. Shaded region refers to inactive knowledge.

mains at the current node as starting focus for the next input which one could interpret as a "mind set".

The central idea of this modeling approach is that the potential actions an individual is able to perform are determined by his or her knowledge network. The explanatory power of the model thus lies in the fact that its

actions in the course of a simulated dialogue arise from the organizational structuring of its knowledge base.

Principles in the Modeling of Student Knowledge

As the basis for the model, it is assumed that individual structures of human memory—the "knowledge network"—are constituted by (1) sets of knowledge elements ("packets of knowledge") and (2) connections between these ("organizational network"). A knowledge packet is composed of a single node or a subnet consisting of several nodes (that is, a knowledge packet can be further structured). In the first instance only tree-structured networks were assumed; if there is a theoretical reason to do so, more general structures can also be represented.

The modeling of learner knowledge was exemplified in the realm of rational number learning with particular respect to size comparisons of fractions. Students' ability to make relative size judgments about fractions has been found to be an indicator for their development of a quantitative understanding of rational numbers (Behr, Wachsmuth, Post, & Lesh, 1984).

Based on the general model discussed previously, the hypothetical knowledge structures of individual learners concerning size comparisons of fractions were described in a tree-structured network. Modular pieces of learner knowledge were derived from subject answers given in clinical interviews and were captured in rules that were stored in indexed memory nodes. We present the general guidelines we followed to represent the operational competence of particular students:

1. Partition the subject domain into subclasses that require specific ways to act.
2. Select test items to assess the student's performance with respect to these subclasses.
3. Formulate rules based on the student's explanations.
4. Specify an appropriate node index to integrate a rule in the knowledge network.

For example, the following major subclasses of the particular subject domain, size comparisons of fractions, were distinguished (cf. Behr et al., 1984):

SN: Comparison of same-numerator fractions, for example, $\frac{3}{4}$ and $\frac{3}{5}$

SD: Comparison of same-denominator fractions, $\frac{6}{15}$ and $\frac{12}{15}$

GE: Comparison of general fractions, $\frac{5}{6}$ and $\frac{8}{9}$ or $\frac{4}{6}$ and $\frac{6}{9}$

Some words of explanation just for the first two subclasses: While children's early performance is frequently found to be dominated by whole-number schemas (e.g., "one third is less than one fourth because three is less than four"), they will eventually need to separate their thinking from the whole-number schemas and acquire a rule that puts fractions with the same numerators in the reversed order relation with respect to their denominators. In contrast the order relation of same-denominator fractions is consistent with the order relation of the whole numbers in the numerators. But here it is sometimes observed that at one stage the new rule that puts same-numerator fractions in correct order is overgeneralized and used to order same-denominator fractions in reversed fashion (e.g., "three fifths is less than two fifths"). At a later stage this kind of overgeneralization may be prevented by way of further discrimination of task characteristics (same numbers in the numerators vs. in the denominators).

TABLE 4.1. Formulation of rules based on subject responses to items in fraction subclasses early in teaching experiment.

Sample answers in subclass SN

$\frac{3}{6}$ and $\frac{3}{8}$

"Three eighths [is less]." *Explain.* "It takes more to cover."

$\frac{3}{6}$ and $\frac{3}{8}$

"One is less. Three eighths." *Explain.* "It would take more to cover the unit."

Source

Items B1-3.1 and B1-3.6, Bert (age 10;0)

Verbal description

"The second one of two fractions with equal numerator is less, if the first denominator is less than the second one."

Rule

$(> (*X*Y) (*X*V)) < = (\text{LESS}*Y*V)$

Sample answers in subclass SD[a]

$\frac{3}{5}$ and $\frac{5}{6}$

"One's less. Five sixths." *Explain.* "It would take more to cover."

$\frac{3}{6}$ and $\frac{5}{6}$

"Three sixths." *Explain.* "Oh, no, five sixths is less" (shakes his head in his hands). *Explain.* "It takes more to cover the unit."

Source

Items B1-4.1 and B1-4.6, Bert (age 10;0)

Verbal description

"The second one of two fractions with equal denominator is less, if the first numerator is less than the second one."

Rule

$(> (*X*Y) (*U*Y)) < = (\text{LESS}*X*U)$

SD, same denominators; SN, same numerators.
[a] Incorrect ordering of SD fractions due to overgeneralization of reversed order relation.

Such stages in the gradual development of a learner's ability to master tasks in the item classes mentioned can be captured in the model by different knowledge networks that model different levels of the learner's competence with respect to the taxonomy of the tasks. Tables 4.1 and 4.2 show basic examples of how student answers were used to obtain rules.[2]

Rules of thumb were derived from the experimental use of the model with the objective of reproducing protocols from interview sessions with subjects. Such "rules of thumb" were used to specify the node indexes. For example:

- Rules that are older with respect to the student's learning history are put in "higher" nodes, whereas rules acquired more recently are put in subordinate nodes.

TABLE 4.2. Formulation of rules based on subject responses to items in fraction subclasses later in teaching experiment.

Sample answer in subclass SN[a]

$\frac{5}{12}$ and $\frac{5}{9}$

"One's less. Five twelfths." *Explain.* "Well, the pieces, the twelfths are smaller, so ... but the ... that means they're smaller, the larger number on the bottom or top is smaller.... If the top number is the same, then the larger number on the bottom means that's smaller."
Source
    Items II-2.2, Bert (age 10;2)
Verbal description
    "The first one of two fractions is less if the numerators are equal and the second denominator is less than the first one."
Rule
    $(< (*X*Y) (*U*V)) < = (EQ*U*X) (LESS*V*Y)$

Sample answer in subclass SD[a]

$\frac{6}{7}$ and $\frac{9}{7}$

"One's less. Six sevenths." *Explain.* "There are not as many pieces covered or shaded."
Source
    Item II-3.1, Bert (age 10;2)
Verbal description
    "The first one of two fractions is less if the denominators are equal and the first numerator is less than the second one."
Rule
    $(< (*X*Y) (*U*V)) < = (EQ*Y*V) (LESS*X*U)$

SD, same denominators; SN, same numerators.
[a] Differentiation between size of pieces (reflected by denominator) and number of pieces (reflected by numerator) prevents overgeneralization.

---

[2] Terms like "cover", "pieces", etc. refer to imagined physical representations of fractions as were used in the instruction.

- Rules that are observed in a common context are given the same node index.
- Rule nodes that are observed to be accessible from one another are linked to lie on a path.
- Rule nodes that are observed to be disparate are given separate access paths from the superordinate node.

As explained in the introduction, the contextual dependency of a learner's operational competence is (partly) reflected in the way that the student understands certain words. The representation of learner knowledge uses the following guidelines to incorporate this linguistic aspect:

- Identify "significant" words with respect to the subject domain, that is, words that possess a specific meaning as distinguished from everyday language or words that are observed to trigger certain behavior. (Significant words serve to activate parts of the knowledge base.)
- "Rules of thumb":
  The more generally available a significant word, the "higher" is the node index for integrating the word in the knowledge network; in the extreme, a word that is observed to be available in all contexts with the same meaning is put in the highest node.

  The more specific a significant word, the "lower" is the node index for the word; in the extreme, a word available in only one context ("key word") is put in a leaf node (cf. Table 4.3).

  Two words, each of which is observed to be available in only one context at the same degree of generality/specificity, obtain the same node index.

Whereas words that are understood across different contexts give access to a larger part of the knowledge base, key words limit the rules available for inferences to the rules on the path to the leaf node that holds the key word. With respect to the network representation, there is no principal distinction between language knowledge and operational knowledge other than declaring particular entries to be of type TALK or type RULE. As "elements" of a learner's knowledge, both types of entries may be put in the same node. Thus, particular words may be associated with particular ways to act.

Toward a Learner Module in an Intelligent Tutoring System

The LAKOS model was developed primarily with a psychological intent, namely, to obtain a better notion of the way in which the organizational structuring of the "knowledge base" of a learner gives rise to particular kinds of behavior. So far, a human experimenter formulates the descrip-

TABLE 4.3. Identification of key words based on situational dependence of subject response to items within subclass SD.

Question was: (fraction1) and (fraction2), are they *equal* or is *one less*?

$\dfrac{9}{24}$ and $\dfrac{7}{24}$

"They're equal. Same size pieces and it takes the same amount to cover and the same size pieces. [gestures] "They're equal." *OK, what about the 9?* "That'd be nine pieces and seven pieces.... They're equal." *What exactly do you mean by "they are equal"?* "They have the same size pieces, so you know."

$\dfrac{6}{15}$ and $\dfrac{12}{15}$

"They're equal. Because they have the same denominator."

Source
  Items VII-2.4 and VII-3.2, Terri (age 11;6)
Key phrase
  EQUAL OR ONE LESS

Directions were to arrange fractions in *order*

$\dfrac{6}{15}$ and $\dfrac{12}{15}$

(Puts $\dfrac{6}{15}$ left of $\dfrac{12}{15}$) *Explain* "Because 6 comes before 12 so I thought that's the way you do it."

Source
  Item VII-3.1, Terri (age 11;6)
Key word
  ORDER

SD, same denominators.

tions that specify the knowledge base of an individual student on the basis of assessments of the student's performance and explanations. To do this the experimenter makes judgments about how to capture particles of the student's knowledge in rules and about how to integrate them in a knowledge network. In a sense the experimenter acts as an expert in the formalization of student knowledge, using heuristics, rules of thumb, and so on as previously described.

The following discussion explores how the approach presented could lead into the construction of a learner-model module to be incorporated in an intelligent tutoring system. Although these ideas are preliminary and none has yet been implemented in such a system, they may help to clarify possible directions for further work.

The question to be attacked in the context of intelligent tutoring systems is how to go about having an automated learner-modeling component generate hypotheses about a learner's domain-specific knowledge in the course of instructional sessions. Two things are necessary. First, the design of a representation system for learner knowledge and, second, the design of processes to generate and update assumptions about the user of the tutoring system during teaching dialogues and diagnostic assessments.

Although the modeling approach presented in the preceding sections seems to cover some of the requirements for a representation system, the second topic has yet to be dealt with. In principle it requires that the experimenter's expertise in representing learner knowledge be made explicit enough to be captured in rules that can be executed by a computer.

A hard approach, which certainly would involve a lot of effort, might be to let the system conduct diagnostic dialogues with the user on the basis of which the rules are inferred by the system. Technically, it does not seem totally absurd to parse students' explanations to obtain strings in the semantic representation language. These could then serve to be generalized into rules. But if this idea were technically realized, it would probably be at high cost, at least on the basis of the technology currently available for the processing of natural language. Furthermore, bounds would probably be reached when students could not sufficiently explain their actions.

A way that seems much more feasible at the present stage is the following. An empirical screening in the particular field of subject matter will make known many strategies that students use. Some strategies—both correct and incorrect—will be common to many learners. Such data are available from the Rational Number Project (e.g., Behr et al., 1984), and probably from work in a number of other areas. A catalog of possible rules formally describing such strategies can then be incorporated into the system, grouped by subclasses within which they are ordered by increasing sophistication (e.g., in terms of the number of subgoals in a rule). The following steps could yield a description of a learner's current knowledge in the domain:

- Match the student's performance on selected test items with rules in the relevant subclass.
- For each item choose the first (i.e., simplest) rule that produces the same response as the student.
- Choose an adequate node index (according to the subclass), and integrate the rule in the knowledge network.

Although a rule selected in this way may not completely mimic the student's actual thinking, it at least captures the student's behavior in the sense of an "axiomatic characterization."

A major problem to be dealt with in this approach occurs when a student uses idiosyncratic rules with outcomes that are not produced by any of the rules in the catalog. Another problem appears when a student exhibits inconsistent behavior even within a subclass of items without variation of contextual conditions. For example, a student may know that $\frac{1}{2}$ equals $\frac{2}{4}$ but will order less familiar equivalent fractions according to some whole number relationships of numerators and denominators, like $\frac{4}{6}$ less than $\frac{6}{9}$.

Although this case could be dealt with by creating subnodes that allow further discrimination of item characteristics, great problems would occur when a student responded inconsistently to different presentations of the same test item with no situational variations observable.

The next question would be how to change the rule base when changes are observed in consecutive diagnostic assessments carried out by the system. So far, in the psychological approach to the implementation of a reproductive simulation model, no rule previously employed is ever taken off the network. (This allows modeling processes of "backsliding" to seemingly eradicated behaviors.) Rather, if a "new" rule is diagnosed that produces different behavior in situations that were already included in the model, a constraint is imposed on the "old" rule, which intercepts its employment when inadequate by making finer discriminations of situational characteristics. Although the justification for this way of modeling is explicitly psychological, it would probably be sensible for an intelligent tutoring system to keep track of students' "old" rules in order to recognize fallbacks.

This article raised the issue of situation specificity to make an argument that tutoring must not be approached too naively. If the aim of a tutoring system is to bring about progress in a learner's ability to utilize knowledge in a broad range of situations, then the following two general objectives for such a system should be taken into account:

- To help the learner master a set of rules that can support successful performance in the subject matter in question
- To enable the learner to use these rules in a sufficiently varied set of situations to ensure that the learner's rules will be evoked in a variety of contexts

These objectives are derived from the following pragmatic assumption: *Only when learners exhibit consistent success with a variety of applied situations involving a subject matter can they be assumed to have developed a sufficiently general understanding of the subject matter to predict success in an even broader class of situations.*

Consequently, the question arises, how shall we represent situational characteristics of learner knowledge in the student module of an intelligent tutoring system? Earlier we suggested that situational competence is characterized by the learner's command of certain language. A possible way to model the situation specificity of a learner's rules, then, might be the following: We need to link a node holding rules of operations relevant to certain situations as a superordinate to nodes holding linguistic units that characterize those situations. Then the relevant rules would become active by activation of any subordinate node. In case only a single situation node can trigger activation of a rule node, that knowledge would have to be regarded as situation specific. The more specific situations are represented in nodes subordinate to a rule node, the broader the range of situations

in which that knowledge can be activated. If all in a predetermined set of situational descriptions selected for instructional tutoring are found to be linked to the corresponding rule node, then that knowledge would be termed situation nonspecific (with respect to the objectives of the tutoring system).

In the LAKOS model as prototypically specified, levels of different specificity of a student's rules can be distinguished with respect to situations typified by certain language. We have presented some ideas about how this approach could be developed into a student-model module of an intelligent tutoring system. These ideas are still far from full realization and exploitation. Probably the hardest problem to be dealt with is the diversity of reasons that cause learners to make errors (see the illuminating discussion of this issue by Davis, 1982). At the present stage one may be modestly optimistic that progress in the modeling of student knowledge will make some sort of "intelligent" tutoring possible upon further advancement of current developments.

Acknowledgement. The author is grateful to Helmar Gust, University of Osnabrüeck, for making available his PROLOG system MLOG and helping to implement the computerized version of the LAKOS model.

REFERENCES

Barr, A., & Feigenbaum, E. A. (Eds.). (1982). *The Handbook of Artificial Intelligence* (Vol. 2). Los Altos, CA: Kaufmann.

Behr, M. J., Wachsmuth, I., Post, T. R., & Lesh, R. (1984). Order and equivalence of rational numbers: A clinical teaching experiment. *Journal for Research in Mathematics Education, 15*, 323–341.

Black, F. (1968). A deductive question-answering system. In M. Minsky (Ed.), *Semantic Information Processing* (pp. 354–402). Cambridge, MA: MIT.

Carss, M. (Ed.). (1986). *Proceedings of the Fifth International Congress on Mathematical Education*. Boston: Birkhäuser.

Davis, R. B. (1982). The diversity of errors in mathematics. *Journal of Mathematical Behavior, 3*, 73–77.

Gust, B., & Gust, H. (1984). *Einführung in das PROLOG-System MLOG*. Osnabrück, West Germany: Authors.

Robinson, J. A. (1965). A machine-oriented logic based on the resolution principle. *Journal of the ACM, 12*, 23–41.

Seiler, T. B. (1973). Die Bereichsspezifität formaler Denkstrukturen—Konsequenzen für den pädagogischen Prozess. In K. Frey & M. Lang (Eds.), *Kognitionspsychologie und naturwissenschaftlicher Unterricht* (pp. 249–283). [Summary: The range-specificity of formal structures of thinking; The consequences for the construction of instruction processes] (pp. 284–285). Bern: Huber.

Wachsmuth, I. (1985a, April), *Logical analysis of cognitive organizational structures: The LAKOS Project (Part A). A computer model of student performance (Part B)*. Paper presented at the Annual Meeting of the American Educational

Research Association, March 31 to April 4, Chicago. (ERIC Document Reproduction Service No. Ed. 257 635)

Wachsmuth, I. (1985b). Inconsistent student behavior in applicational situations of mathematics. In L. Streefland (Ed.) *Proceedings of the Ninth International Conference for the Psychology of Mathematics Education* (Vol. 1, pp. 362–368). Utrecht, the Netherlands: State University of Utrecht.

5

The Knowledge Engineer as Student: Metacognitive Bases for Asking Good Questions

WILLIAM J. CLANCEY

A knowledge engineer can be viewed as a special kind of student. Her goal is to develop computational models of complex problem solving by watching and questioning an expert and incrementally testing her model on a set of selected problem cases.[1] Characteristically, the knowledge engineer (KE) is in complete control of this process. Her construction of a problem-solving model is almost completely self-directed; she is an active learner. The KE thus provides us with an excellent basis for studying methods that any student might use for approaching new problem domains and acquiring the knowledge to solve a set of practical problems.

Although there is some self-selection among KEs, so that people who are naturally quick learners are attracted to this profession (and there are some dilettantes), the knowledge engineering process is a skill that can be taught. In essence a KE learns how to ask good questions by learning useful representations of knowledge and by practicing the art of directing an expert to teach her what she needs to know. The activity of incrementally improving a computational problem-solving model (the expert system) on a well-defined sequence of cases focuses the learning activity. An intelligent tutoring system focuses learning in a similar way by engaging a student in case-method dialogues. Can we teach a student to play an active role in directing the tutoring program during these dialogues, in the same way a knowledge engineer directs her teacher?

This chapter studies the knowledge-acquisition process by reviewing a variety of KE interview and knowledge-base critiquing heuristics. Generalizing from these examples, we show how learning heuristics are intimately related to and derived from particular knowledge representation languages (presented as an introductory framework). Finally, we consider how the general model of learning that emerges can be formalized in a knowledge acquisition program and then used as a standard for inter-

---

[1] In this paper we use feminine pronouns to refer to KEs, though there are as many men in the profession; for symmetry we refer to students with masculine pronouns.

preting and guiding a student's behavior. Relation to current work in machine learning and philosophical problems are considered in the final sections of the paper.

BASING TEACHING ON A MODEL OF LEARNING

It is generally accepted that development of teaching programs should proceed from a model of the learning process. One approach is to design a teaching program so that it encourages the student to improve his understanding, such as by making predictions about some phenomenon and formulating experiments to test them (Crovello & McDaniel, unpublished). Although most computer-aided instruction programs of this type provide the student with a simulation of a physical process (e.g., an electronic circuit), artificial intelligence (AI) programming techniques enable us to provide a model of a problem-solving process as well. In particular an expert system can be presented as an object of study, as in GUIDON (Clancey, 1982, 1987).

In our previous research we have developed methods by which a model of the diagnostic process can be explored by a student (Richer & Clancey, 1985). This program, called GUIDON-WATCH, is designed to facilitate understanding the knowledge organization and diagnostic strategy of the underlying expert system, NEOMYCIN (Clancey & Letsinger, 1984), presented as a model for the student to study and emulate. A window-menu system for browsing a knowledge base overprints taxonomics and tables to show the flow and history of reasoning. Experience shows that GUIDON-WATCH is quite useful for a knowledge engineer debugging NEOMYCIN and for short lecture-style demonstrations to students and other researchers (e.g., using a blinking display to show the strategy of "looking up" and "looking down" through disease categories). However, we have not formalized or built into the program what a student using GUIDON-WATCH should be trying to do. While we have reified the process of diagnosis—making it concrete so it can be studied—we have not made explicit the *goal structure* of a student who is studying the program. Specifically, what is the learning process involved in studying and understanding a model of problem solving, in this case an expert system?

We are already familiar with the process of learning by studying an expert problem solver—this is what a KE does. The symmetry is shown in Figure 5.1. The KE actively probes the expert, listening to and organizing explanations in order to improve her model of problem solving, the expert system. By analogy, a student actively probes a computer tutor, listening to and organizing explanations in order to improve his own problem-solving performance. Our thesis is that by studying and modeling what a KE does, we will be able to formulate a model of learning that can be incorporated in the design of a computer tutor. In particular we are interested in modeling the learning process involved in interacting with an expert–teacher,

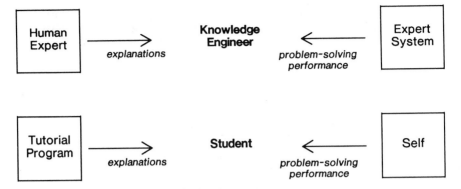

FIGURE 5.1. Analogy of learning by a knowledge engineer and by a student: Both attend to and solicit explanations in order to improve problem-solving performance.

in order to replicate his behavior in some well-defined problem domain.

This study is the precursor to developing a *learning apprentice* knowledge acquisition program (Mitchell, Mahadevan, & Steinberg, 1985) to assist in debugging NEOMYCIN. We then intend to develop a tutorial program that conveys this model of learning to a student while he is diagnosing medical problems. Thus, we follow the knowledge-based tutoring paradigm of first formalizing a program that can do what we will ask a student to do, specifically, to detect inadequacies in problem-solving performance and transform them into good questions for a teacher. The learning apprentice thus serves as a model for the student to study and emulate, as well as provides the tutorial program with a basis for assisting and evaluating his performance.

Origins in Previous Learning Research

This research is strongly influenced by other attempts to teach general problem-solving methods, such as Schoenfeld's work in mathematical problem solving (Schoenfeld, 1981) and Brown's work in algebra problem solving (Brown, 1983). However, we expect our model of learning to be better articulated and substantiated through the process of developing a simulation program. Furthermore, by working in a nonmathematical domain, we are dealing with complex knowledge structures, which we believe will better demonstrate what problem-solving knowledge transfers across domains. Current expert systems research suggests that abstract knowledge-base structures, such as relations used in the causal reasoning of diagnosis, recur in different domains (Bennett, 1983; Clancey, 1985; Chandrasekaran, 1984). These recurrent structures enable us to reuse knowledge representation languages and reasoning procedures in different

expert systems, forming the basis of expert system tools called "generic shells" (Chandrasekaran, 1986), of which HERACLES, a generalization of NEOMYCIN, is an example.

The particular model of learning developed here has its basis in our previous study of expert systems (Clancey, 1988b). We describe complex problem solving in terms of a *system* being reasoned about (such as an electronic circuit) and a *task* by which the system is to be manipulated (e.g., diagnosis, design, control). Unlike other current research in knowledge acquisition, which uses models of knowledge organization and inference processes to direct a learning process (e.g., Mitchell et al., 1985; Smith, Winston, Mitchell, & Buchanan, 1985), we need to make the learning process itself explicit so that it can be reasoned about by the tutorial program. A computational model alone is not sufficient; its representation must be well-structured. Specifically, according to the model of learning we are developing, we must make the *model-building process* in performing some task on a system explicit. For example, in diagnosis problems we must make explicit the constraints that a good diagnostic model must satisfy, so we can articulate problem-solving failures to a student and relate them to the subtasks of diagnostic reasoning. None of this would necessarily be explicit in a typical expert system or learning program.

A complex domain, such as medical diagnosis, requires a complicated reasoning procedure, which provides us with many examples of how knowledge about knowledge organization is used to focus reasoning and to formulate good questions when reasoning tasks fail. As our examples will make clear, problem domains like geometry theorem proving and algebraic equation simplification are comparatively impoverished. These domains provide little *content* that is general, and hence provide minimal leverage for learning about other problem domains. In comparison, experience with medical diagnosis provides a substantial basis for learning about diagnosis in other areas, such as electronic diagnosis. It is precisely this domain-general knowledge that makes a KE an efficient learner.

In particular we want to teach a student the organization of diagnostic knowledge and how it is used. In our research on NEOMYCIN, we have developed a model of diagnosis in which the procedure of how to do diagnosis is separated from the domain facts (Clancey & Letsinger, 1984; Clancey, 1986a, 1988a). Thus, at each point what the program is trying to do, called a *subtask*, is translated into a question about what the program needs to know. For example in refining a hypothesis H the program asks, "What are the subtypes of H? What could cause H?" The essential idea in the NEOMYCIN model of diagnosis is that a sequence of requests for problem data (e.g., "Does the patient have a fever?" "Has he travelled?") can be abstracted in terms of *operators* for manipulating a *situation-specific model* that describes the physical processes by which the patient's symptoms were produced (Clancey, 1986a, 1988a). This knowledge about what the problem solver is trying to do and the structure of his experiential

knowledge, as abstracted from diagnostic practice and formalized in NEOMYCIN, is the essential *metacognitive knowledge* we seek to exploit. The sequence of knowledge engineering examples in the section on learning heuristics builds up to this model of diagnosis, illustrating how knowledge about diagnostic knowledge and its use, a form of metacognition, provides a basis for active learning in the KE.

LIMITATIONS IN THE ANALOGY BETWEEN A KNOWLEDGE ENGINEER AND A STUDENT

It is important to realize that there are significant differences between a typical student's task and a KE's task. A KE is constructing a computer program, she is not learning how to solve a problem independently. Specifically, a KE does not have to remember everything she puts into a program. In working with an expert, she gains very little experience in proficiently integrating everything she has been told. Rather, she tends to view facts and problem-solving procedures in isolation, as they apply in specific cases. The implications of this difference are not immediately clear, but must be attended to later in evaluating the model of learning we develop. If we are lucky, the only difference will be the practice effect of solving problems from memory, and the program and student who follows the KE's model of directed learning will exhibit no difference in content of what is learned or in problem-solving ability.

We also know that students generally have a substantial background of factual knowledge about a domain. For example, medical students have 2 years of general learning about disease processes before they focus on practical, clinical problem solving. In contrast the KE has comparatively less specific knowledge about physiological processes, and the computer program has essentially none. Thus, another weakness in our analogy and potential barrier in our attempt to automate the KE's learning process is the absence of general knowledge about physical processes that a student, and to a lesser extent the KE, can draw on. If we are lucky here, this will impoverish the model of learning we develop, but not detract from the general form of the model (e.g., its basis in problem-solving failure) or the specific results concerning the learning of routine problem-solving knowledge (e.g., the emphasis on well-defined relations that carry across domains), which we focus on.

On the other hand, the essence of our approach is that a KE learns by filling in a schema, his knowledge representation, which is rarely known explicitly by a medical student. This is the KE's strong suit, which we seek to exploit and articulate in a simulation model of learning.

Another difference between the typical student and KE is that the theory of problem solving developed by the KE is the result of experience in different domains. It is not immediately clear whether we can make

the KE's problem-solving abstractions understandable within the context of a limited set of problems in just one domain. If we are lucky, the value of these abstractions will be apparent; and possibly the process of formalizing them from our experience in constructing the first expert systems was just a one-time difficulty that other people will not need to repeat.

We also start with the hypothesis that a student does not need to know a diagnostic strategy explicitly to become proficient. Indeed, medical expertise has certainly advanced and teachers have been effective without being able to articulate the diagnostic process to the extent that it is formalized in NEOMYCIN. We argue that knowledge of the diagnostic process is useful not for routine problem solving, but for recovering from failures, the essence of the model of learning we describe. A corollary is that we are teaching a method of learning that medical students typically do not use or at least do not use systematically.

One advantage of studying KEs, versus typical medical students, is that a KE is always working with a formal representation (the knowledge base). We can directly observe how she manipulates this representation and relate her behavior to the current state of her computer model. The formal representation provides a language for systematic description of what the KE is doing, which we view as a learning process. In developing a tutoring system, we will investigate the benefits of giving a student similar written notations to use in recording his understanding and solution to particular problems.

To recapitulate, we argue that the KE's interview ability and program-development process follows from her representation of how knowledge is organized and used in solving routine problems. This metaknowledge is coupled with a procedure for detecting knowledge gaps that critiques incomplete problem solutions. From this basis a problem solver can direct her own learning by formulating good questions—those that are directed at what she needs to know.

The Map Metaphor: Representations, Models, and Problem Solving

Before considering complex examples of metacognitive knowledge and how it is used in learning, it is useful to develop our intuitions by considering a familiar example. In particular a road map nicely illustrates the nature of representation and inference procedures. The familiar nature of a map is extremely useful for revealing the way in which an expert system's knowledge representation is a model of the world. This is especially important in our argument because the idea that an expert system knowledge base contains a model of the world is mostly ignored by AI researchers, to the extent that the term "model" is generally only used to

refer to simulations of processes. A few of these ideas are explored here; others are developed in (Clancey, 1988b).

Figure 5.2 is a portion of a road map. A map, like any *representation*, makes a commitment about the existence of particular classes of objects and relations in the world. That is, the map's notation—the particular symbols used in the map—allow certain statements to be made about the world and do not provide for others. For example, the map in the figure allows different kinds of buildings, roads, and facts about how they are related to be represented. We see that the faculty club is on Lagunita Drive and that Memorial Hall is adjacent to the Graduate School of Business. However, this particular notation does not provide a means of indicating the kinds of soils found on this land or possible ore-bearing deposits. This is a suitable representation for moving a car around campus, but not for drilling for oil. Thus, a map categorizes the world in a certain way; only certain distinctions can be expressed.

More formally, a map notation is defined by a set of terms (objects or spaces) and relations among them (notably connectivity, size, and distance). These terms and relations constitute a language for articulating propositions (believed statements) about the world, called the *representation language*. A specific map is a *model* of the world. Crucially, to this point, everything we have said about maps is true about expert system knowledge bases.

The *semantics* of a map concerns its meaning, that is, how it relates to the world. For example, the closed solid figures stand for or represent buildings in the world. Considerable philosophic debate concerns whether it is possible to represent the semantics of a map (e.g., what is a building?). While not irrelevant to this paper, the topic goes beyond the scope of what we can consider.

Maps, like knowledge representations, are not just artwork that we carry around in our pockets. Instead, there is always some accompanying procedure for using the map to solve practical problems. For example, a road map is associated with procedures for planning a trip from one location to another. We call such interpretation procedures *inference procedures*. This procedure (or program) makes extensive use of the language of the map. The inference procedure indicates how to use the map to solve a practical problem.

Sometimes we describe an inference procedure in terms of how it controls search (thus, the synonym, "control knowledge"). Of all the possible questions we might ask about the world (data we might find useful for solving a problem), and out of all the possible inferences we might draw from our map, which ones should we consider first? And which after that? An inference procedure *orders* data gathering and assertions about the world. (Note that searching the knowledge representation itself—e.g., determining whether there is a fire station on campus—is a different issue, pertaining to *encoding* of the knowledge, that is, how it is stored and retrieved.)

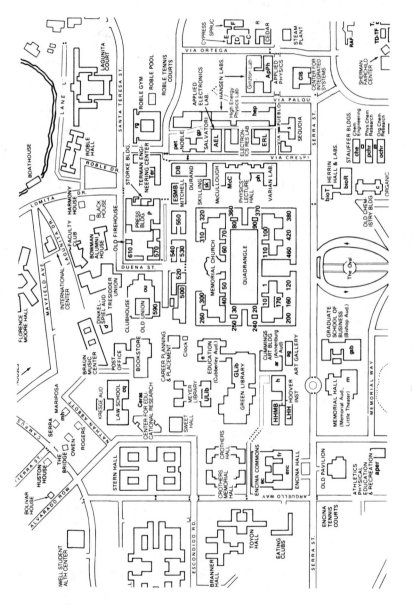

FIGURE 5.2. Portion of a map.

For example consider using the map in Figure 5.2 for moving your car from the Old Pavilion to the Faculty Club. Which parts of the map do you look at first? What controls those observations? What partial plan do you first construct? Why do you form those pieces first? This procedure, which tends to recur when we solve similar problems, is the inference procedure. In this example it is a planning procedure. Different kinds of problems have different characteristic inference procedures. Perhaps the most well-known is the procedure for diagnosis, also called a diagnostic strategy (Clancey, 1988a).

Inference procedures constitute a form of experiential knowledge. To develop this point, consider first that the representation language (to be contrasted with a particular map or knowledge base) is associated with operators for making inferences (often called *inference rules*). For example, if we need to determine the distance between two sites, we use the distance and adjacency information implicit in the map. Thus, we make a statement about the world by piecing together more primitive relations, as well as by extracting implicit facts. For any given map in a particular language, used for a particular kind of problem, a given set of operators will be useful. For example, in using roadway maps, we repetitively need to determine distances, the nearest object of type X to a given object, the shortest path between two objects, and a few others. The number of operators of this form is not necessarily large.

An often referred to distinction is that some inference operators are *heuristic*, as opposed to *definitional*. For example, "If classes are changing, do not attempt to cross Escondido Road by car" is a heuristic that could affect the solution of the parking problem. Characteristically, such a heuristic does not follow from the meaning of the map (the definitions of the symbols), but involves experiential information about cause–effect relationships, involving other objects in the world that are not represented in the map.

Crucially, the way in which inference operators are chained together in making inferences (to construct a plan) tends to recur. Thus, in moving from one place to another, we generally tend to consider the shortest path, depending on our mode of transportation, and will build a path from one end to the other, using methods like finding the largest artery between the two locations and anchoring the path by other places we wish to see along the way. These methods are to be contrasted with a comparatively unintelligent process of constructing multiple paths and making unuseful inferences, such as considering the distance between arbitrary points unrelated to the movement under consideration. Similarly, in planning a walk, different questions will be asked about the world. For example, we will be less concerned with unmarked roadblocks and traffic congestion, and perhaps more interested in where people tend to sit or congregate, so we can have a more pleasant *passeggiata*.

In summary the inference procedure indicates heuristically how to ex-

tract useful facts in order to solve the problem at hand. A domain-general inference process is focused on what we are trying to do and most specifically on the constraints we seek to satisfy. Other considerations that we cannot consider in detail here concern the nature of the situation-specific model (e.g., do we write down our problem solution in some notation?) and the nature of implicit facts in the notation. Finally, as a representation of the world constructed for a particular purpose, the map is a selective model of the world. It simplifies the world in a particular way so that problem solving can proceed efficiently. Representations are therefore biased by the degree to which they are specialized for particular tasks.

Briefly, to make the analogy with knowledge representations more explicit, NEOMYCIN's knowledge representation language consists of a set of terms (e.g., finding, hypothesis, test) and relations among them (subtype, cause, abnormal finding). The language is associated with an inference procedure that solves diagnostic problems by the general method we call *heuristic classification* (Clancey, 1985). The language is biased (specialized for diagnosis) and is more familiar to physicians than engineers. In a rough sense, knowledge-base networks of concepts and relations organized into hierarchies and transition graphs are analogous to the objects and lines of a road map. A knowledge-base representation language makes distinctions that are useful for solving particular classes of problems by particular inference procedures.

Here we are most concerned with the value of a representation language for learning practical problem-solving knowledge, not arbitrary facts about the world. Furthermore, we are concerned with how a *given* representation is useful, not with the process of modifying a representation. This is an *assimilative model of learning*, assuming no representation change.

The first key observation is that a given representation literally provides a language for asking questions about the world. Consider using the map language to learn about a new area. In learning that a building is in a certain location, you might ask what roads are closest to it, where is the nearest parking lot, and what buildings are adjacent to it. The language critically influences what we know about the world. (The much-debated philosophic point, generally associated with Whorf (1956), about how language shapes knowledge and experience shapes language, goes beyond the scope of this paper.)

The second observation is that construction of a specific model is intimately tied to the goal of solving a problem. That is, we realize gaps in our knowledge of the world when we are applying an inference procedure and find that the required facts are missing; there are gaps in our map of the world. For example, a medical student might conclude that a patient has a chronic-meningitis infection and know that this is not specific enough for prescribing therapy. His inference procedure indicates that he has not solved the problem, and he should now apply the operator for refining a disease hypothesis (to make it more specific). Yet, at this point he may

realize that he does not recall the subtypes or causes of chronic meningitis. He realizes that there is a critical gap in his knowledge, an *impasse* (following the terminology of Brown & VanLehn, 1980, an analogy with subtraction we develop later). This example illustrates that, by definition, useful distinctions—what you need to know about the world—are not based on gaining knowledge for its own sake, but arise in solving a particular problem and are directly related to the inference procedure being applied.

To recapitulate, the model of learning developed in this paper concerns how knowledge about a representation language and inference procedure enable the learner to articulate what knowledge he needs to know and hence to formulate a specific question for a teacher (e.g., "What are the subtypes of chronic meningitis?"). We will return to a more specific description of this process after considering how knowledge about representations and inference procedures is used by KEs.

Learning Heuristics Used by Knowledge Engineers

This section briefly surveys a variety of heuristics used by KEs for learning about a new domain and improving a knowledge base. This learning process is typically called *knowledge acquisition*. The sequence of examples presented here illustrates how the nature of active learning changes with the available representation. In particular we observe the progression from the terms of the rule-based representation language of MYCIN to the heuristic classification language of NEOMYCIN. The final example, in which diagnosis is described as a model-construction process, illustrates the advantages of abstracting the inference procedure so that the representation or map of the world is stated declaratively, as facts, that are separated from the procedure for using them. This separation makes explicit the representation language as an abstraction that is available for use in new problem domains.

GUIDON Orientation Tutoring

In approaching a new domain, a KE developing an EMYCIN system might ask the following sequence of questions over the course of several interviews with the expert and continue to pursue them while watching the expert solve particular cases:

What is the goal rule?
What is the main subgoal structure?
What do premises of the rules look like? Are there patterns?
What are the important input data? What kinds of judgments are required of the person supplying data to the expert system?
What are some typical outcomes for the major subgoals, and what are some typical rules to conclude about these outcomes?

When introducing a new problem to a student or discussing a subproblem, GUIDON (Clancey, 1987) provides orientation by effectively inverting the preceding questions, presenting the same material an experienced KE familiar with the EMYCIN rule language actively seeks from an expert (her teacher). In addition to showing the goal rule, the program indicates the general subgoal structure for the case at hand (indicating only subgoals used by or concluded by a large number of rules) (Figure 5.3). Each new major topic is introduced by a definition, outline of major subgoals (called a *rule model*), and typical values (Figure 5.4). This information helps a

Sketch of the tree of subgoals for determining the therapeutic regimen of J. Smith:

7a. The therapeutic regimen of J. Smith
    7b. The organisms (other than those seen on cultures or smears) which might be causing the infection
        7c. Whether J. Smith has a head injury defect
        .
        .
        .
        7d. The infection which requires therapy
        .
        .
        .
        7e. The type of the infection
            7f. The diagnoses of J. Smith
            .
            .
            .
        7g. Whether organisms were seen on the stain of the pending csf culture (CULTURE-1)
        .
        .

7h. Whether the organisms isolated from the pending csf culture (CULTURE-1) should be considered for therapy
.
.

7i. The organisms that will be considered to be causing the meningitis (INFECTION-1) for the purposes of therapy selection
.
.
.

You can produce a full tree of subgoals for any topic by the SUBGOALS option.

FIGURE 5.3. Guidon's presentation of subgoals for a given case

You should now proceed to ask questions that will enable you to make an hypothesis about the organisms that might be causing the infection.

A pathogenic organism which was not seen on a culture or smear but which might be causing an infection in the patient and therefore requires antimicrobial therapy is an organism to "cover for."

CULTURE-1 is a pending culture. In this context, when we are considering the organisms that might be causing the infection, we generally find it useful to consider:

8a. the infection which requires therapy
8b. the type of the infection
8c. whether organisms were seen on the stain of the culture
8d. whether a smear of the culture was examined

There are 93 rules used by MYCIN to conclude about this topic. Altogether there are 29 factors considered in these rules.

Some sample values for the organisms that might be causing the infection are: proteus-non-mirabilis, streptococcus-group-b, proteus-mirabilis and neisseria-meningitidis, etc.

FIGURE 5.4. Guidon's orientation for a new topic

student understand how the diagnostic problem has been formalized into objects and relations.

INTERVIEWING AN EXPERT: STRUCTURE, STRATEGY, AND SUPPORT

In the process of studying MYCIN's knowledge base to determine how it might be improved to be more effective as a basis for teaching, we developed a framework based on an expert's explanations of diagnostic reasoning. Explanations are analyzed according to *knowledge roles*—how knowledge is used in relation to other knowledge (Clancey, 1983b):

1. The *heuristic rule*, a relation between data and diagnoses or therapies
2. *Structure*, subsumption relations among data, diagnoses, and therapies
3. *Strategy*, the procedure for applying rules
4. *Support*, the justification for rules

These categories provide guidance for listening to and directing a teacher. They provide a means for understanding how a teacher's statements are related, so the student can organize what he is hearing and focus the teacher to fill in other connections he needs to know. In particular it is useful to cut short detailed support justifications and instead focus the teacher on structural overviews and their strategic motivations.

For example when the KE asks a physician who is solving a diagnostic problem, "Why did you request that information?" she classifies his answer into one of these categories. If he tells her, "Well I'm not going to

prescribe tetracycline because the patient's age is less than seven," she is being told what assertions were made from given information (i.e., a heuristic rule: If the age is less than seven, tetracycline is contraindicated). If she asks him why, and is given an explanation having to do with chelation, then she is being given the justification for the assertion (i.e., support, a chelation process causes teeth discoloration). If the expert says, "This is just one of the *contraindications* I'm going to consider," then he's telling the KE about the organization of his knowledge, the categories he uses for focusing (i.e., structure, undesirable physical changes are contraindications for drug therapy). Next, if he tells her *when* he considers contraindications and *how* he considers each type, then she is being told the inference procedure (i.e., strategy, after hypothesizing a drug therapy, attempt to rule it out by considering contraindications).

The strategy-structure-support categories can be restated as more active, specific heuristics for directing a teacher. We collected such heuristics by analyzing protocols of interactions between a KE and a physician-teacher. The KE's questions are classified to reveal her methods for actively critiquing, testing, and refining her understanding, while watching the teacher solve a problem.

Strategy
> Ask about ordering of data requests.
> Determine specificity of reason for data request (a general question or directed at a particular problem solution?)
> Track hypotheses and detect when focus changes.

Structure
> Ask for typical and atypical problem examples (cases).
> Listen for exceptions immediately after a general rule is stated.
> Detect synonyms.
> Summarize your understanding.
> Beware of implicit assumptions (what is the expert inferring from context?)

Support
> Ask for cases with inconsistent findings; listen for rationalizations of these in terms of possible misconceptions or misunderstanding (e.g., "I might be wrong about the prevalence of this symptom").

As always, the distinctions drawn here presuppose a model of useful knowledge relations (e.g., "inconsistent findings"). In particular many of the preceding heuristics might be justified by a model of knowledge organization, that is, a description and generative explanation for the recurrence that occurs in the expert's memory associations. (Another philosophic consideration beyond the scope of this paper argues that such associations are not *prestored* but rather *generated at the time of knowledge articulation*, as suggested by Winograd & Flores, 1985, and reflect general properties of narratives, as suggested by Bruner, 1986.) The knowledge

organization and inference procedure implicit in the preceding heuristics are partially formalized in the heuristic classification model of diagnosis.

KNOWLEDGE ACQUISITION FOR HEURISTIC CLASSIFICATION

The rule and goal language of EMYCIN has been specialized in the heuristic classification model of problem solving (Clancey, 1985). Distinctions are made between findings, hypotheses, and classifications of these (concerning type, causality, abnormality, location, etc.). Distinctions are made between definitional rules and causal rules. In addition goals and rules that represent the inference procedure are called tasks and metarules. This language structures the knowledge base, providing a more specific language for articulating the cause of problem-solving failures. In particular the following set of ordered heuristics was developed from the experience of constructing several knowledge bases in the HERACLES language (Clancey, 1984):

1. *Problem selection:* Selecting a domain, task, and scope for the expert system.
   - Look for problem types that can be solved by classification: Are the solutions enumerable and stereotypic (configurations, plans, diagnoses, etc.)?
   - Decompose problems into sequences of classification problems. Treat them separately, but work backward from the final problem. For example needs/requirements analysis may be solved by classification, with a solution heuristically related to ultimate solutions (products, services, etc.). Work backward from these solutions. Another common example: Consider what kinds of repair are possible before analyzing the associated diagnosis problem.
   - Early on, define the problem in terms of input and output and the kinds of relations. Try to distinguish between substances and processes. What is observable? Does causality play a role? For diagnosis, is there a disorder or abnormal state network? Is there a hierarchy of disorder processes (what can go wrong)?
2. *Knowledge-level analysis:* A structured way for identifying terms and relations.
   - List all possible solutions the program may output. Organize into classes and hierarchies if appropriate. Be clear about what the solutions are: plans, processes, configurations, and so on. A confusion at this point may mean that there are separable problems. Be clear about *types*, that is, do not mix different kinds of things (e.g., descriptions of diseases with descriptions of people). All solutions should at a high level belong to a single class.
   - List classes of data that will be input to the program (no need to be exhaustive at this point, unless the list is under a few dozen items);

will any data be numeric? Organize into classes and hierarchies to the extent possible.

- Identify relations among the data: generalizations, definitions, and qualitative abstraction. Exact attention to relations is difficult but essential to be sure the problem is adequately decomposed. For example, take care to distinguish *an abstraction of data* according to definition from *an abstraction of the solution* that is matched by direct identification of some features. (For example, "white blood count less than 2,500" is the *definition* of leukopenia [a data abstraction]; "gram-negative rod" *matches the features* of *Escherichia Coli* [a diagnostic solution].) A common problem is that the expert will leave out qualitative abstractions, stating associations in terms of numeric data, or vice versa, not indicating until later that data are actually numeric.

- Establish the heuristics that link data to solutions *after* establishing the network of solutions. To avoid identifying a solution as a datum, be aware that some rules may relate solutions to one another nonhierarchically (in diagnosis this is called a *complication*).

- Treat the inference process separately. It is essential to model the expert's inference structure (terms and relations) but not as important to model the inference process he uses. For example a program may use top-down refinement within a hierarchy of solutions, while the expert may use a more opportunistic, hypothesis-formation approach. Modeling inference ordering is much more difficult and is in general not necessary for efficiency in expert programs of the size constructed today.

3. *Implementation:* It is advantageous to use a programming language that allows relations to be made explicit, especially hierarchies. Top-down refinement can be easily encoded by ordering rule premise clauses, but this approach leads to redundant, more complex rules, with a loss of explanation capability. Better engineering suggests separating the inference and process structure (Clancey, 1983b).

4. *Knowledge-base refinement:* The classification model suggests selecting cases that will test the program's ability to discriminate among solutions, consistent with the usual approach of improving the knowledge structure by testing the program on a variety of problems. One might begin with classic cases corresponding to each solution, then systematically pick problems with similar input but different solutions.

Note that this is a framework for systematically describing knowledge, not for eliciting it. For example the order of knowledge-level analysis given here (basically, a bottom-up, output-to-input approach) may be a useful organization for the learner, but the expert may find it difficult to directly describe what he knows in this way. It may be preferable to present problems to the expert and quiz him about what he is doing.

The distinctions given here can be viewed as specializations of the pre-

viously discussed explanation categories, in which structure and strategy are the relations and tasks, respectively, of the heuristic classification inference procedure. This model of experiential knowledge is very general. It is a much more useful description of what we need to teach a student than is provided by EMYCIN's knowledge representation language, in which we can only say that knowledge consists of rules, goals, input data, values, and so on, and specific instances of these.

Constructing a Causal State Network

The heuristic classification model can be specialized for diagnostic tasks. For such problems the findings are symptoms, and the hypotheses are abnormal processes or states in a system being diagnosed. Further relations characterizing findings include "red-flag finding," "normal value," and "causal prerequisite finding." The inference process is specialized from the language of inference graphs to the language of diagnosis; rather than saying "backward chaining," we say "reasoning from symptoms to abnormal states to abnormal processes." Operators for traversing the network of hypotheses (a kind of map) include refine, test, rule-out, group, and discriminate.

Active-learning heuristics using this knowledge representation and inference procedure language include the following (using examples from CASTER, a sandcasting diagnosis program built in the HERACLES shell (Thompson & Clancey, 1986)):

- *Identify the fundamental terms and relations in the domain before writing rules.* For example, sandcasting involves substances like sand, water, gases, and metals; processes like melting metal, designing a pattern, building a mold, and pouring metal; forces like gravity and gas pressures. After these domain terms are introduced, the KE is ready to learn about causality between processes, and refine her knowledge of disorder types.
- *Ask about categories of substances and processes.* Often the heuristic (causal) relations between data and solutions are stated as generalizations relating these categories (e.g., different kinds of bubble defects are caused by gas, which has different sources).
- *Describe abnormal events in terms of temporal phases.* For example in manufacturing, abnormal events can be categorized according to the processes that cause them. For example the problem of inadequate feeding of iron in sandcasting occurs during the freezing process.
- *Identify abnormal properties of substances, then seek causes.* For example metal contamination is a serious problem in casting. After identifying a number of possible contaminants, such as aluminum, silicon, and phosphorus, it is appropriate to consider how each type of contamination might occur and evidence for specific types (their manifestations).

Patterns will enable learning specific relations more easily by analogy if the categories are established first.

- *Identify possible malfunctions, determine the corrections for those problems, and then causally reformulate the relationship.* For example for the problem of "feed shut off," we ask what possible changes could remedy the situation. These include making the gates bigger, the neck of the riser bigger, fillets larger, the metal hotter, and so on. These repairs are then reformulated in terms of how they will change the manufacturing process, and hence how the previous processes caused defects.
- *Establish causality between findings and malfunctions, then expand intermediate relations.* By making relations explicit (as measured by need in actual cases), it is possible to discover generalizations that collapse many specific heuristic associations into a common mechanism.

In summary the preceding heuristics can be viewed as things to do to improve a causal model—ways of usefully critiquing a partial model of disorders. Reflecting back on the examples given of GUIDON's orientation, it should be obvious that these heuristics can be turned around for presenting information to a student or probing his understanding. More in keeping with the active model of learning we are developing here, these heuristics could be applied by a student himself to articulate to a teacher what he needs to know, which is precisely what the KE does.

GRAPHIC REPRESENTATIONS

Although it is well-known that a good representation can greatly affect problem-solving efficiency and even the possibility of solving a problem, the most common examples involve puzzles such as the problem of tiling a checkerboard (Jackson, 1974), rather than the kinds of representations used in expert systems. Here we illustrate how graphics can be used to make salient the patterns (relations) among objects, prodding a student to formulate a *generative model*, which explains why objects fall together in the same group. These graphics are contrasted with the "modular," linear form of individual rules, which provide no basis for realizing the presence of patterns, let alone expressing them explicitly. This point is clearly illustrated by the shift from MYCIN's goal-rule language to classification relations in NEOMYCIN, which articulates and explains subgoal patterns in MYCIN's rules (Clancey, 1983a).

Viewing Process Similarities by Overlapping Line Graphs

A striking example of the inadequacy of a verbal representation for revealing knowledge relations is a typical tabular rule in MYCIN, "the cerebrospinal fluid (CSF) protein rule" (Figure 5.5). Faced with the difficulty of understanding this rule, we graph it, expressing the same knowledge by a pictorial representation (Figure 5.6). It is now apparent that some disease

RULE500
If: 1) The infection which requires therapy is meningitis,
2) A lumbar puncture has been performed on the patient, and
3) The CSF protein is known

Then: The type of the infection is as follows:
If the CSF protein is:
a) less than 41 then: not bacterial (.5), viral (.7), not fungal (.6), not tb (.5);
b) between 41 and 100 then: bacterial (.1), viral (.4), fungal (.1);
c) between 100 and 200 then: bacterial (.3), fungal (.3), tb (.3);
d) between 200 and 300 then: bacterial (.4), not viral (.5), fungal (.4), tb (.4);
e) greater or equal to 300 then: bacterial (.4), not viral (.6), fungal (.4), tb (.4);

FIGURE 5.5 The CSF Protein rule, illustrating EMYCIN tabular rule format

processes are similar. That is, the representation indicates no distinction between them over certain CSF protein ranges, within a certain tolerance of change. The physician-teacher stated the principles this way, "If the protein value is low, I think of an acute process; if it is high, I think of a severe or long term process." (Bacterial meningitis is a severe, acute [short-term] problem, while fungal and TB meningitis are problems of long

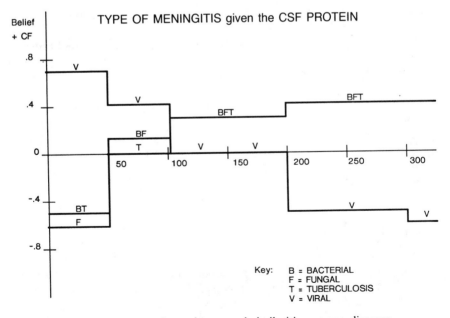

FIGURE 5.6. A graph used to reveal similarities among diseases

[chronic] duration.) Generalizing this further he describes the common mechanism, "An infection in the meninges stimulates protein production."

This example illustrates again how a given representation will naturally lead us to generate certain kinds of questions about the world. In a graph of this form, these questions include:

What accounts for maximums? (Is it unusual for the CSF protein to be greater than 300? Why is belief concerning bacterial meningitis never greater than 0.4?)

What accounts for zeroes? (Why do TB and fungal cross from negative to positive belief at 41 mg/ml?)

What accounts for patterns? (What do bacterial, fungal, and TB have in common that is not true about viral?)

The use of graphs for scientific theory formation is well-known. Such representations structure facts about the world, revealing patterns that we can then seek to understand. A representation provides a means for articulating our experience, structuring what we believe to be true about the world. By biasing the patterns that can be expressed, different representations reveal different similarities, leading us to ask different questions about the world (why certain patterns exist). In contrast with the well-known scientific techniques, the model of learning we are developing is couched in terms of a simulation model of problem solving. That is, our aim is not to merely seek and explain patterns, but to solve practical engineering problems.

One effect of detecting new patterns is that we add new relations to our language to express them, changing our representation. For example useful abstractions for understanding the CSF protein rule include "high protein" and "chronic process." The original patterns (the graph) can be generated from this more abstract representation, which is what happens when NEOMYCIN replicates patterns in MYCIN's rules when it refines hypotheses, generalizes data requests, checks to see if a test is done before requesting specific results, and so on. (The process of changing a representation by abstracting an inference procedure is described in Clancey, 1986a).

Viewing a Diagnosis as an Explanation Graph

The second striking example of the value of graphics over linear rules for expressing knowledge is the use of a graph to reveal the evidence relations between findings and hypotheses in NEOMYCIN (Figure 5.7). By this perspective, a diagnosis is not the name of a disease, but *an argument* that causally relates the manifestations that need to be explained (because they are abnormal) to the processes that brought them about. Our knowledge representation is thus further refined to classify diseases as kinds of *processes* and to view findings as *events* in the world. The inference procedure

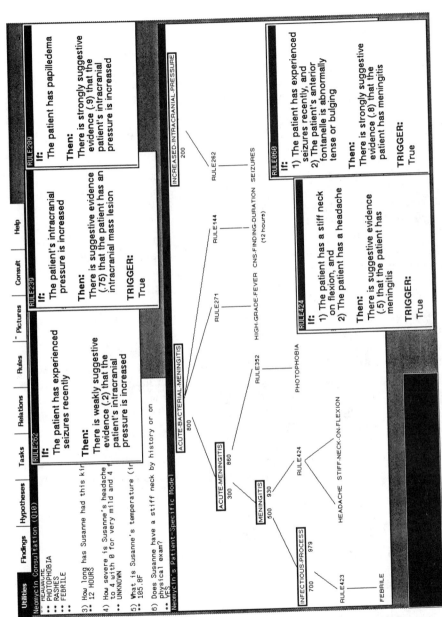

FIGURE 5.7. A diagnosis expressed as a patient-specific model in the form of a graph.

"copies over" these general concepts and relations of the domain knowledge base to construct a *case-specific model* (Patil, 1981). This network links manifestations and diseases, constituting a model of a particular sequence of events in the world (also called a situation-specific model).

Diagnostic operators (HERACLES subtasks) examine and modify the *differential* (the set of most specific diseases under consideration), linking and refining state and process descriptions to construct a situation-specific model. A causal explanation thus has the structure of a geometry proof. It must account for all of the findings and must be coherent and consistent. The situation-specific model must be a connected graph with one process at the root (assuming a single fault). These are the constraints the diagnosis must satisfy, the *form of a solution.*

For the purpose of teaching, this graph could be an effective way to reify the process of diagnosis. For several years, inspired by Brown's emphasis on "process versus product" (possibly derived from Dewey, 1964), we have been searching for some written notation that we could use, something analogous to algebra, to make visible what the operators of diagnosis (HERACLES subtasks) are doing. The analogy with geometry turns out to be stronger than the analogy with algebra because each inference itself relies on a proof, analogous to the causal arguments behind each link of the situation-specific model. In algebra the inference rules are axioms.

Giving this window to the expert-teacher, the KE directs him to explain his diagnosis by posting his hypotheses and linking them to the known findings. Each step along the way, there are visible problems to be solved that the KE and expert-teacher can use to focus their respective questions and explanations. The use of this perspective for constructing a computational model of active learning is developed next.

Model of the Active Learner

To this point the most specific representation we have presented is the substance/process language developed while improving the CASTER knowledge base. However, the inference procedure of HERACLES, the most developed available to us, does not use this language, but rather the more general language of heuristic classification. For example rather than referring to "substances" and "processes," it uses the terms "findings" and "hypotheses." The model of learning we develop from HERACLES therefore will be somewhat more general and less powerful (from the sense of focusing the learner's articulation of missing knowledge) than our more informal understanding of the knowledge and reasoning process of diagnosis.

Furthermore, even within the more general language of HERACLES, the view of inference operators as model-construction operators, as developed in the previous section, is not captured. Without this perspective

our model of learning is impoverished, since it does not make explicit the constraints that problem solving seeks to satisfy. This is reflected in the fact that NEOMYCIN does not detect that it has not explained findings or offer any evaluation about the adequacy of its solutions (beyond the strength of the "evidence" for hypotheses). Therefore, although we include in the model of learning developed here the view of problem solving as a model construction and application process, the reader should keep in mind that implementing this will require modifications to the HERACLES shell, as detailed following.

In the discussion that follows, notice that "the student" and "NEOMY-CIN" are interchangeable.

FORMALIZING THE LEARNING PROCESS AS A KNOWLEDGE-ACQUISITION PROGRAM

We want to teach the student domain knowledge that will enable him to solve problems by heuristic classification, a specific knowledge representation and inference procedure in terms of which all knowledge will be expressed. For example in the language of HERACLES, the student will learn classifications of findings and heuristics to relate them to classifications of solutions. He will learn to recognize and discriminate these prototypes. Using knowledge of the heuristic classification representation and inference procedure, the student will explain his failure to solve problems and direct a teacher to supply him with the facts about the world that he needs to know. A basic assumption is that learning will be more efficient by having the student determine what he needs to know than by having the teacher build a model of his knowledge, present factual lectures, and test him on cases. However, the student might *direct the teacher* to do any of these in the process of actively directing his learning.

In contrast with the model developed in GUIDON, we are not using the knowledge-acquistion heuristics to present information to the student, who must read facts and store them away. Instead, we focus on learning that occurs and is motivated by problem-solving failures. In contrast with GUIDON's original design, this is not a strategy for "filling in a knowledge based on knowledge of what he is trying to do (the form of an adequate request an *orientation* at particular times, just as the knowledge engineer applies these methods early in the knowledge acquisition process.

Just as for a knowledge engineer, the student's learning is failure driven, based on knowledge of what he is trying to do (the form of an adequate solution) and what failures occurred. Specifically the learning procedure is as follows:

Know what you are trying to do: constraints to satisfy (the form of a solution) and how to satisfy them (model-manipulation tasks).

Detect possible failures (unsatisfied constraints) in the inferred, situation-specific model:

Unable to test or refine a hypothesis.

Unable to explain finding.

Finding explained by two or more hypotheses.

Two or more hypotheses explain exactly the same findings and evidence does not discriminate between them, or they explain findings uniquely.

Situation-specific model hypotheses are not specific enough to select or construct action plans.

Reason backward to say what task, if it had succeeded, would have prevented this failure, and what facts (the hypothesized gaps in the domain knowledge), if true or proved false, would allow the metarule to succeed.

Prune alternative explanations using knowledge of what beliefs typically could be wrong or might be true, but which were not explicitly learned before.

Ask the teacher questions to gain missing knowledge or validate hypothesized facts.

For example, referring to Figure 5.7, we consider the diagnostic constraint that every abnormal finding must be explained by the most likely hypothesis. We observe that the seizure finding is not explained. Relating this constraint to subtasks, we see that the HERACLES subtasks Test Hypothesis (applied to acute bacterial meningitis) and Process Finding (applied to seizures) have associated inference rules (metarules) that would have satisfied this constraint if they had succeeded. Examining these metarules, we find that a domain rule linking seizures to acute bacterial meningitis (among others) would enable one or more of the metarules to succeed. Stating this hypothesized fact as a question, the student would ask, "Could acute bacterial meningitis cause seizures?"

To emphasize again the limitations and complications of this model of learning:

It is based on a fixed knowledge representation language and inference procedure.

It requires making explicit the constraints of a solution and how they relate to diagnostic tasks and metarules.

It requires a search procedure to work causally backward from failed constraints.

It might require domain knowledge or domain-general knowledge about disorder processes in order to focus the search for plausible facts, if many possibilities are generated.

It may be necessary to relax the constraints imposed on the situation-specific model, given the pragmatic requirements of how the model will

be used (e.g., the action plans it must discriminate between) and the inability to confirm hypothesized facts (e.g., lack of scientific understanding of causal mechanisms).

Resolving these uncertainties and filling in details are good reasons for implementing the model as a simulation program.

APPLYING THE MODEL TO TUTORING

To apply this model to tutoring, we should place the student in an environment that is amenable to detecting failures, realizing gaps in knowledge, and hypothesizing and testing new facts.

Giving the student a problem to solve forces him to construct a situation-specific model. By making the model an explicit object for the student, we make the task less threatening, moving the problem outside of the student onto the screen in the form of a graph. Thus, we exploit the advantage of the KE as student—she is not wrong, it is the evolving computer program that is wrong. Yet, the KE naturally translates the program's deficiencies to deficiencies in her own understanding.

In addition to forcing the student to articulate his knowledge, we must teach him about the knowledge representation and inference procedure we expect him to apply. Assuming for a moment that this is an adequate model of human problem solving for routine problems, it is evident that our model of learning must recur. We are arguing that a specific learning process will lead the student to learn medical problem-solving facts, but how will the student learn the learning process itself?

The student must realize when solving the problem that he needs to articulate the process of diagnosis itself, in order to apply the learning process of working backward from a failure. Presumably, at this level, the tutor could actively prompt the student to lead him to criticize the solution and relate it to failed tasks. In particular we must adjust our model of active learning to make clear the role of a teacher who prods the student, probes his understanding, and redirects his behavior.

What might go wrong with this instructional design? First, we face constant difficulties with level of detail. Explanations will have to carefully interweave specific and abstract descriptions so the diagnosis terminology is meaningful. Second, it is important to realize that NEOMYCIN has limited introspective ability to explain its design and reasoning. Human intervention may be necessary to explain the framework and its limitations. Other problems include the possible need to articulate the learning process itself (to explain the tutor's advice) and to allow the student to provide his own explanations of the diagnostic model for the tutor to respond to.

With this foundation we are now developing a tutorial program, named GUIDON2, to convey the NEOMYCIN model of problem solving and (yet to be implemented) active model of learning to a student. There

are three phases in the tutorial interaction: GUIDON-MANAGE, GUIDON-WATCH, and GUIDON-EXPLAIN.

GUIDON-MANAGE

The student solves a diagnostic problem by abstracting his requests for data in terms of HERACLES tasks (Rodolitz, 1987). For example, rather than asking if the patient has a fever, he might give the command to GUIDON-MANAGE, "Test the hypothesis of infectious process." In one sense the student directs the diagnosis by providing the strategies to follow, while NEOMYCIN provides the tactics, using its metarules to apply domain knowledge. The result is a form of cooperative problem solving in which the student can rely on the program's domain knowledge, but must interpret the implications of the evolving solution and direct the problem solving. By being forced to use the HERACLES task language, the student is led to observe that each request for data has a more abstract characterization in terms of model building, and he learns the specific meaning of the diagnostic tasks encoded in HERACLES by observing what they do. In the most general sense, he learns that the diagnostic process has a recurrent structure, and he can start to rely on this when he gets stuck and is not able to proceed automatically.

GUIDON-WATCH

The student then watches NEOMYCIN solve the same problem. Knowing that NEOMYCIN follows a certain procedure, the student is now in a position to interpret the program's actions. That is, his experience with GUIDON-MANAGE provides him with a vocabulary for explaining why NEOMYCIN requests patient data.

GUIDON-EXPLAIN

(Proposed)
The student and tutor then engage in a mutual explanation process in which they investigate significant differences in how the student solved the problem in the GUIDON-MANAGE phase and how NEOMYCIN solved the same problem in the GUIDON-WATCH phase. The tutor takes an active role of probing the student's understanding, while articulating its basis for criticizing a diagnostic solution so the student can realize his own failures and articulate his own missing knowledge.

By this instructional design we are teaching the process of knowledge engineering, not the product (the contents of a knowledge base). We are investigating how explaining, performing, and criticizing problem-solving behavior are interrelated and enhanced by the metacognitive ability to articulate the representation of diagnostic knowledge and how it is interpreted.

Related Learning Research

The model of learning described here relates educational research focusing on metacognition (e.g., Schoenfeld, 1981) to explanation-based learning within AI (DeJong & Mooney, 1986; Dietterich, Flann, & Wilkins, 1986, Mitchell et al., 1986). In this section we consider briefly how our study extends machine learning research and constitutes a model of failure-driven, explanation-based learning (EBL) for nonformal domains.

The basic idea of explanation-based learning is that a surprising or unusual fact about the world is explained by the learner in terms of his a priori knowledge, making the fact explicit or more efficiently accessible for future use (Dietterich et al., 1986). For example, the given information might be the features of an object, which could be used to infer that the object is a member of a certain class. This inference, which explains why the example satisfies the previously known definition of the class, takes the form of a proof, which is then generalized so that similar examples in the future can be more readily recognized.

Keller's explanation-based learning approach (Keller, 1986) resembles the model of active learning presented in this paper. His program uses contextual knowledge about how concepts are used, in order to formulate which concepts need to be learned. Keller's program incorporates knowledge about the "performance procedure and objective," which corresponds to the diagnostic procedure and constraints on the form of a diagnosis in HERACLES. The objective provides a criterion for determining the usefulness of a concept, called the *operationality criterion*. For most explanation-based learning, which focuses on deriving a relation that is already implicit in the knowledge base, the operationality criterion concerns efficiency of the inference procedure. That is, the goal of learning is to make the program able to solve a search problem that was previously too time-consuming.

The model of learning described here does not involve simply chaining together previously known facts and procedures, but conjecturing new facts or conjecturing the need for a certain type of knowledge. The operationality criterion is the description of a diagnostic solution, particularly its form as a causal model and how it will be used to select action plans (repairs). Learning is driven by failure to satisfy these constraints. It cannot automatically refine or generalize a previously known concept, as in previous explanation-based learning. Rather, the explanation of problem-solving failure is analyzed to determine the concepts or relations that could prevent the failure, which must then be confirmed or supplied in more detail by an expert-teacher. This analysis is a form of *goal regression*, a technique found in many EBL programs. We reason from the failed goal (unsatisfied diagnostic model constraint) to the task that could have satisfied the goal if it succeeded, back through failed metarules and failed metarule preconditions to other failed subtasks, eventually reaching ground

facts about the world that are not in the knowledge base (e.g., the subtypes of a disease or what might cause it).

This model of learning thus extends previous EBL in several ways. (1) Goal regression involves reasoning through the problem-solving procedure itself (tasks and metarules), rather than a separate description of the procedure (as in Keller's program). (2) The operationality criterion is described in terms of the form of a solution and how it will be used, rather than in terms of computational efficiency. (See Dietterich et al., 1986 for discussion of the distinction between learning new knowledge vs. chunking, compiling, or making computationally accessible what is already known.) (3) Learning is based in explaining problem-solving failures, as detected by the program itself, not in explaining why a supplied example is correct. That is, the model involves determining what must be learned in order to properly solve problems, not just to increase problem-solving speed. Thus, this model bridges a gap between EBL and failure-driven learning (Kolodner & Simpson, 1984; Schank, 1981). (4) The problem-solving procedure involves a schema-model of the world (the diagnostic relations of the knowledge base), which constitutes an incomplete theory, in contrast with the definitional model in domains like calculus (see Clancey, 1986b, for further discussion).

Generating plausible conjectures about missing knowledge is on the edge of learning research. Collins' early work in *plausible reasoning* suggests that metaknowledge about patterns in a knowledge base could be useful (Collins, 1978). Of special interest are the heuristics for conjecturing propositions that would lead to a consistent, parsimonious model of the world, if they were true. In this sense, a knowledge base is not just a set of isolated statements, but a model providing a coherent, functional map of some system in the world. Examples from CASTER suggest that a KE's metaknowledge includes such general facts about causal models, which are generalizations about different domains in the form of recurrent terms and relations. For example knowledge about manufacturing problems takes the form of a causal network relating abnormal structures (or substances) to abnormal functions (or processes), metaknowledge that goes well beyond a representational description that is merely in terms of goals and rules (as in TEIRESIAS; see Davis & Buchanan, 1977) or states and causal-associational links (as in CASNET; see Weiss, Kulikowski, Amarel, & Safir, 1978).

Related research in knowledge acquisition includes (1) MORE (Kahn, Nowlan, & McDermott, 1985) builds an initial knowledge base using a representation language and heuristics for improving a domain model that combine knowledge about the inference procedure and how to elicit knowledge from the expert. (2) MOLE (Eshelman, Ehret, McDermott, & Tan, 1986) goes further by debugging a situation-specific model by comparing it to an expert's diagnosis and makes clearer the nature of the inference procedure and knowledge elicitation strategies it relies on. (3) The

LEARNING APPRENTICE SYSTEM (LAS) (Smith, Winston, Mitchell, & Buchanan, 1985) explains failures (described by an expert) in terms of errors in its rules, reasoning about the justifications of rules and possible kinds of errors. Of programs in nonformal domains, LAS is distinguished by attributing errors to assumptions that justify its causal reasoning. By reasoning about which assumptions are substantiated and which are likely to be wrong in certain contexts, the program engages in a sophisticated form of plausible reasoning.

Again, the major difference between this work and the active model of learning described in this chapter is that we consider how a problem solver can *detect his own failure* to solve a problem and how he *reasons through his inference procedure* to explain how additional domain knowledge might have prevented the failure. The inference procedure is either implicit in learning heuristics used by the preceding programs or redundantly encoded in both the performance and learning programs. VanLehn's program, SIERRA (VanLehn, 1987) does reason through the inference procedure itself. However, its learning task is quite different. It is learning the inference procedure itself, not domain facts; its inference procedure is algorithmic, not heuristic; its domain is axiomatized; it learns by explaining how an expert solved the problem; and its learning is constrained by assuming that a sequence of examples is designed by the teacher to convey a single point.

The connection with Repair Theory (Brown & VanLehn, 1980) is particularly interesting. One wonders whether adults having trouble with subtraction would simply make up answers and continue by patching their incomplete knowledge in the manner described by Repair Theory, or would they attempt to articulate the nature of their knowledge deficiency as a question for the teacher if given a chance? Indeed, perhaps repairs might lead to conjectures about a correct procedure, which are tried and modified in solving later problems in an exam. An essential question is whether the subtraction inference procedure is articulated by the student in the course of recovering from failure or whether the procedure attributed by Repair Theory is just an abstraction that describes patterns in student behavior. The active model of learning has the advantage of describing problem solvers as active hypothesizers who use general knowledge about the form of a solution and constantly learn while solving problems, which is closer to the model of SIERRA.

Finally, we might relate the active model of learning to comments by Bruner about the nature of learning (Bruner, 1983). He emphasizes that learning is "going beyond the information given. . . . 'Learning' is figuring out how to use what you already know in order to go beyond what you currently think." (p. 183). We have elaborated on this to show the advantages of describing "what you currently think" in diagnosis as a model of processes in the world. "What you already know" corresponds to the representation language, inference procedure, and support for beliefs.

Viewing thinking as a form of perception, learning how to think means developing strategies for perceiving. "Selective perception" is another way of describing the process of asking good questions. Crucially, Bruner emphasizes the importance of learning knowledge relations, what we have called the map language or the knowledge representation language: "The structure of knowledge permits us to grasp and retain and transform the world in a generative way not tied to the learning of details." (1983, p. 279).

Conclusions

Generalizing a variety of learning heuristics used by KEs, we have described a model of learning, which provides a basis for designing a knowledge-acquisition program. We propose to incorporate this in an instructional program as a model of what we want to teach a student, a means of evaluating and responding to his performance, and a model of his learning.

In constructing expert systems and incrementally improving our language for describing knowledge bases, we have adopted a view of learning and problem solving that is based in critiquing, improving, and applying models of the world. Model improvement, equated with learning, occurs after failure to model the world, that is, when a specific problem cannot be solved. A KE is continuously involved in this task, and we conjecture that other students could be taught the metacognitive knowledge to direct their own learning in a smiliar way. This learner-centered orientation should be contrasted with the prevalent concern of most intelligent tutoring research of attempting to understand the student by watching him solve problems and with the equally strong concern in traditional educational research of question generation *by the teacher* (Bloom, 1956).

The analysis is complicated and violates many of our preconceptions about the design of teaching programs, because it is so different from what can occur in a typical crowded classroom. It focuses on the main strengths of knowledge-based tutoring: individualized instruction, driven by a single student's needs, and a simulation model of problem solving. The simulation model provides a basis for assisting and evaluating the student (in GUIDON-MANAGE) as well as providing a basis by which the student can learning by watching (in GUIDON-WATCH). Throughout, we maintain the paradigm that a knowledge-based tutor must be able to do what it asks the student to do. Thus, we must include a formal model of failure-driven learning (as described here), as well as a model of learning by watching concurrently developed in the ODYSSEUS program (Wilkins, Clancey, & Buchanan, 1986).

This chapter is not a traditional AI research article, because it surveys and studies AI practice and existing programs without describing a new

implemented program. In large part the novelty of the research direction requires this chapter as a statement of the model, so the difficulties and relation to other research can be explored first. Furthermore, theoretical connections tend to jump into place more quickly than we can complete implementations.

Consider for example the ramifications of applying the active model of learning to a model of explanation. In an important sense the explanation program is the teacher responding to the active learner's question. The teacher might apply the learning model in reverse: Given a question from the student, what inference failure is the student coping with? What is the question asker trying to do? What representation language is he using to accomplish what tasks? What is his problem-solving procedure? This is a very difficult problem for the teacher, particularly when the student is experiencing a breakdown in his representation. Some of the difficulties were mentioned parenthetically in this chapter as questions about the nature of knowledge and representation languages.

Consider further the justifications for the interview heuristics discussed in the section on interviewing an expert. What inherent problems in communication, deriving from the nature of knowledge and cognition, are these heuristics designed to cope with? Knowledge engineering methods go beyond designing notations for writing down what experts know; they touch on the very problem of the nature of knowledge itself.

For the moment it is sufficient to look back and observe that much progress has been made. We have come far from the simple capabilities of TEIRESIAS, which had no basis for detecting problem-solving failures on its own or relating them to MYCIN's model of the world, representation language, or inference procedure. TEIRESIAS could only say, "I couldn't conclude about the organisms that therapy should cover for," which is far from the well-focused question: "If I knew about the subtypes of chronic meningitis, I might be able to contrast it with brain abscess and perhaps produce a single diagnostic explanation for both the headache and the double vision." This active process of learning, rooted in metacognitive knowledge, might be summarized by the aphorism, "A good question is more than halfway to a new understanding."

REFERENCES

Bennett, J. (1983). *ROGET: A knowledge-based consultant for acquiring the conceptual structure of an expert system.* HPP Memo 83–24. Stanford, CA: Stanford University.

Bloom, B. S. (1956). *Taxonomy of educational objectives: The classification of educational goals.* New York: David McKay.

Brown, J. S. (1983). *Process versus product—A perspective on tools for communal and informal electronic learning.* In *Education in the Electronic Age, proceedings of a conference sponsored by the Educational Broadcasting Corporation, WNET.*

Brown, J. S., & VanLehn, K. (1980). Repair theory: A generative theory of bugs in procedural skills. *Cognitive Science, 4*, 379–415.

Bruner, J. S. (1983). *In search of mind: Essays in autobiography.* New York: Harper & Row.

Bruner, J. S. (1986). *Actual minds, possible worlds.* Cambridge, MA: Harvard University Press.

Chandrasekaran, B. (1984). Expert systems: Matching techniques to tasks. In W. Reitman (Ed.) *AI applications for business* (pp. 116–132). Norwood, NJ: Ablex.

Chandrasekaran, B. (1986). *Proceedings of the workshop on high level tools for knowledge-based systems.* Columbus, OH: Ohio State.

Clancey, W. J. (1982). GUIDON. Applications-oriented AI research: Education. In A. Barr & E.A. Feigenbaum (Eds.), *The handbook of artificial intelligence.* (pp. 267–278). Los Altos, CA: Kaufmann.

Clancey, W. J. (1983a). The advantages of abstract control knowledge in expert system design. In *Proceedings of the national conference on artificial intelligence.* (pp. 74–78). Washington, DC: Los Altos, CA: Morgan-Kaufmann.

Clancey, W. J. (1983b). The epistemology of a rule-based expert system: A framework for explanation. *Artificial Intelligence, 20*, 215–251.

Clancey, W. J. (1984). Knowledge acquisition for classification expert systems. In *Proceedings of ACM annual conference* (pp. 11–14).

Clancey, W. J. (1985). Heuristic classification. *Artificial Intelligence, 27*, 289–350.

Clancey, W. J. (1986a). From Guidon to Neomycin and Heracles in twenty short lessons (ONR Final Report 1979–1985). *AI Magazine, 7*, 40–60.

Clancey, W. J. (1986b). Qualitative student models. In *Annual Review of Computer Science*, (pp. 381–450). Palo Alto, CA: Annual Reviews, Inc.

Clancey, W. J. (1987). *Knowledge-based tutoring: The Guidon program.* Cambridge, MA: MIT Press.

Clancey, W. J. (1988a) *Acquiring, representing, and evaluating a competence model of diagnosis.* In M. Chi, R. Glaser, & M. Farr (Eds.), *The Nature of Expertise.* Hillsdale: Laurence Erlbaum.

Clancey, W. J. (1988b). Viewing knowledge bases as qualitative models. *IEEE Expert*, in press.

Clancey, W. J. (in press). Representing control knowledge as abstract tasks and metarules. In M. J. Coombs, & L. Bolc (Eds.), *Computer expert systems*, New York: Springer-Verlag.

Clancey, W. J., & Letsinger, R. (1984). NEOMYCIN: Reconfiguring a rule-based expert system for application to teaching. In W. J. Clancey, & E. H. Shortliffe (Eds.), *Readings in medical artificial intelligence: The first decade* (pp. 361–381). Reading, PA: Addison-Wesley.

Collins, A. (1978). Fragments of a theory of human plausible reasoning. In *Proceedings of the 2nd Conference on Theoretical Issues in Natural Language Processing.* D. L. Waltz (ed.) Urbana-Champaign University of Illinois. Theoretical Issues in Natural Language Processing (pp. 194–201).

Crovello, T., & McDaniel, M. *An artificial intelligence-based introduction to the scientific method.* Unpublished manuscript.

Davis, R., & Buchanan, B. G. (1977). Metal-level knowledge: Overview and applications. In *Proceedings of the Fifth International Joint Conference on Artifical Intelligence-77* (pp. 920–927).

DeJong, G., & Mooney, R. (1986). Explanation-based learning: An alternative view. *Machine Learning, 1*, 145–176.

Dewey, J. (1964). The process and product of reflective activity: Psychological process and logical form. In R. D. Archambault (Ed.), *John Dewey on education: Selected writings* (pp. 243–259). New York: Random House.

Dietterich, T. G., Flann, N. S., & Wilkins, D. C. (1986). *A summary of machine learning papers from IJCAI-85.* Technical Report 86-30-2, Oregon State University, Corvallis.

Eshelman, L., Ehret, D., McDermott, J., & Tan, M. (1986). MOLE: A tenacious knowledge acquisition tool. In *Proceedings of knowledge acquisition for knowledge-base systems workshop* (pp. 13-1–13-12).

Jackson, P. C. (1974). *Introduction to Artificial Intelligence.* New York: Petrocelli Books.

Kahn, G., Nowlan, S., & McDermott, J. (1985). MORE: An intelligent knowledge acquisition tool. In *Proceedings of the ninth international joint conference on artificial intelligence* (pp. 581–584).

Keller, R. M. (1986). *Deciding what to learn.* Technical Report ML-TR-6, Rutgers University, New Brunswick, NJ.

Kolodner, J. L., & Simpson, R. L. (1984). Experience and problem solving: A framework. In *Proceedings of the sixth annual conference of the Cognitive Science Society* (pp. 239–243). Boulder, CO.

Mitchell, T. M., Keller, R. M., & Kedar-Cabelli, S. T. (1986). Explanation-based generalization: A unifying view. *Machine Learning, 1*, 47–80.

Mitchell, T. M., Mahadevan, S., & Steinberg, L. I. (1985). LEAP: A learning apprentice for VLSI design. In *Proceedings of the ninth international joint conference on artificial intelligence* (pp. 573–580).

Patil, R. S., Szolovits, P., & Schwartz, W. B. (1981). Causal understanding of patient illness in medical diagnosis. In *Proceedings of the seventh international joint conference and artificial intelligence* (pp. 893–899).

Richer, M. H., & Clancey, W. J. (1985). GUIDON-WATCH: A graphic interface for viewing a knowledge-based system. *IEEE Computer Graphics and Applications, 5*, 51–64.

Rodolitz, N. (1987). *Tutoring for Strategic Knowledge.* KSL Report 87–38. Stanford University.

Schank, R. C. (1981). Failure-driven memory. *Cognition and Brain Theory, 4*, 41–60.

Schoenfeld, A. H. (1981, April). *Episodes and executive decisions in mathematical problem solving.* Technical Report, Hamilton College, Mathematics Department. Presented at the 1981 AERA Annual Meeting.

Smith, R. G., Winston, H. A., Mitchell, T. M., & Buchanan, B. G. (1985). Representation and use of explicit justifications for knowledge base refinement. In *Proceedings of the ninth international joint conference on artificial intelligence* (pp. 673–680).

Thompson, T., & Clancey, W. J. (1986). A qualitative modeling shell for process diagnosis. *IEEE Software, 3*, p. 6–15.

VanLehn, K. (1987). Learning one subprocedure per lesson. *Artificial Intelligence, 31*, 1–40.

Weiss, S. M., Kulikowski, C. A., Amarel, S., & Safir, A. (1978). A model-based method for computer-aided medical decision making. *Artificial Intelligence, 11*,

145–172.

Wilkins, D. C., Clancey, W. J., & Buchanan, B. G. (1986). An overview of the Odysseus learning apprentice. In T. M. Mitchell, J. G. Carbonell, & R. S. Michalski (Eds.), *Machine learning: A guide to current research*. Orlando, FL: Academic Press.

Winograd, T., & Flores, C. F. (1985). *Understanding computers and cognition: A new foundation for design*. Norwood, NJ: Ablex.

Whorf, B. L. (1956). *Language, thought, and reality*, J. B. Carroll (Ed.). New York.

6

Toward a Theory of Curriculum for Use in Designing Intelligent Instructional Systems

ALAN LESGOLD

Implicit in the approaches being taken by current efforts to create intelligent computer-based instruction is the notion that curriculum is almost an epiphenomenon of knowledge-driven instruction. Early computer-based instruction had little control structure other than an absolutely rigid curriculum and was insensitive to the subtleties of different students' partial knowledge. As a result there was a reaction in the direction of representing the students' knowledge as a subset of the target or goal knowledge to be taught and simply deciding de novo after each piece of instruction what piece of missing knowledge to teach the student. I am convinced that goal knowledge is as important to intelligent machine activity as it is to human activity and that it also must be well understood and explicitly represented in an instructional system if that system is to be successful in fostering learning.[1] This chapter presents an architecture for representing curriculum or goal knowledge in intelligent tutors and is thus a first step toward a theory of curriculum that can inform the design of such systems. To illustrate one way in which such a theory can sharpen our ideas about learning and instruction, the later part of the chapter focuses on the concept of *prerequisite* that is the basis for existing computer-assisted instruction and shows how that concept has been inadequate in the past. A new approach, in which the prerequisite relationship is always dependent on the instructional subgoal (curriculum) context, is introduced.

Current Practice

Programs that preceded the entrance of artificial intelligence into instruction prespecify the content of lessons. In some cases the order of the specific lessons to which a student is exposed is computed as instruction proceeds. However, the content of a lesson, in terms of knowledge it is

---

[1] I thank David Merrill for making this clear to me in his comments after a presentation I made at an American Educational Research Association meeting in 1983.

trying to teach, tends to be fixed. In currently used programs lesson assignment is viewed as a more-or-less knowledge-free subgoaling problem. We have a list of things to be taught, and we teach each in turn. If instruction is unsuccessful, we try again. The assignment of lessons can occur in several different ways. The *frame* approach organizes instruction into very microscopic units, characteristically one screen "frame" each in size. Each frame contains some instruction, some means for testing the student's performance, and decision rules for deciding, on the basis of that performance, which frame the student should see next. The *pretest–post-test* approach is organized at a higher level, the level of the *lesson*. Before each lesson, a pretest is given. If the pretest is passed, the lesson is skipped; otherwise it is presented. After each lesson a post-test is given. If the student passes the post-test, he goes on to take the pretest for the next lesson.

There is a certain amount of inefficiency in the pretest–post-test approach. In many cases the student spends most of his time taking tests, and many testing methods are not very effective instruction. More important, there usually is not much difference between the lesson taken initially by a student and the one he receives if he fails the post-test and is recycled. A number of efforts have been made in specific programs to ensure that novel material is presented or that the repeated lesson is taught more slowly, with more examples and more practice. In terms of content, however, it is the same old lesson being repeated again. As we shall see this may be a fundamentally incorrect approach to teaching.

There are many rationales for the pretest–post-test approach. Of these, perhaps the strongest is the learning hierarchy theory of Robert Gagné (1962). Gagné gave very clear directions for deciding on the content and sequencing of instruction, and these directions continue to have strong influence on the design of instruction and training today. The basic approach is to start with the capability that is the goal of the training being designed.[2] One is then to ask the question:

> *What kind of capability would an individual have to possess if he were able to perform this task successfully, were we to give him only instruction?* (Gagné, 1962, p. 356)

That is, what does the trainee have to know so that simple verbal advice is sufficient to get him to apply that prior knowledge to the task at hand? This methodology can, of course, be applied recursively to further decompose the target capability into smaller and smaller prerequisite capabilities. It is, after all, nothing but the generic problem-solving method of progressive refinement, splitting a complex goal into several pieces, splitting the pieces into still smaller pieces, and so on. This approach works as long

---

[2] I mean to address both school instruction and technical training needs with the ideas presented in this essay. For ease of exposition I shall use the term *training* to refer to both of these activities.

as we pick as units pieces that are small and coherent enough to cover in single lessons and as long as there are no dangerous interactions between achieving one lesson subgoal and achieving another.

These two criteria of subgoal internal coherence and linearity are extremely important to the success of the method of progressive refinement. By internal coherence we mean that the subgoal can be achieved sensibly by itself, without duplicating effort across subgoals unnecessarily. For example, if we decided to mow the lawn by dividing it into a checkerboard of square regions, first mowing every other region and then mowing the ones in between, our refinement of the lawn task into doing first the red squares of the board and then the black ones wastes effort. We must move over the entire lawn twice instead of once. Further, lifting the mower to avoid cutting certain sections that are being postponed for later is also unnecessary work.

Note that internal coherence is a function of the specifics of subgoal contents and not a general principle alone. For example, although the checkerboard approach to mowing the lawn is inefficient, making two passes over the lawn, one to mow and one to remove weeds, may be quite sensible. This is because the microacts of pulling one weed and mowing a small patch are incompatible, producing extra thinking and physical work if they must be continually alternated, while the microacts of mowing successive small regions are quite compatible, saving work over doing one patch, then mowing it, doing the next, and so on. It might be argued that the current approach of teaching subtraction of two-digit numbers and then waiting as long as a year before taking up subtraction of three-digit numbers also violates the internal coherence rule.

The linearity criterion is also important. For example, if we want to build a house, we can split the task into laying a foundation, putting up walls, and putting on a roof. Only one order of those three steps makes sense. The other orders fail. Some orderings are impossible: One cannot put on a roof if there are no walls to support it. Other orderings involve early steps that interfere with later ones, such as putting up the walls before the foundation. Linearity problems can also arise in learning. For example, if one requires students to type their essays beginning in fifth grade, and typing is not taught until seventh grade, then there will be some conflict. Students will acquire, on their own, patterns of typing that conflict with the behaviors used in efficient typing methods; there could be negative transfer.

Gagné (1971) undertook to prescribe some principles of learning that would help instructional designers achieve internal coherence and linearity in their development of hierarchical goal structures (which he called learning hierarchies) for training courses. He developed a variety of specific learning forms that could be used to constrain the parceling of pieces of instruction into separate lessons or curriculum subgoals. Implicit in his work is the principle that, in learning, the whole is more than the sum of its parts. That is, the lowest-level subgoals in a goal hierarchy do not, as a

group, contain all the knowledge implied by the highest level goal. The instructions that are given as subgoals are assembled into larger units of capability that result in new learning. This new learning is not part of any subgoal's knowledge. Rather, it is emergent when multiple subgoals are combined, just as a theorem in geometry is not present in the premises from which it is derived but is, rather, new knowledge.

Unfortunately, the belief that the whole is simply the sum of its parts has too often guided the task analyses that have generated training curricula. Rational task analysts have tended to look at an instructional subgoal, intuitively decide whether it can be taught in a single lesson, and if not, split it into a few sub-subgoals each to be treated by a separate lesson. Gagné's (1962) criteria, that we should be able to provide the "glue" needed to tie together the pieces of knowledge from prerequisite lessons using only simple instructions and that these instructions should be based on a theory of learning, are generally not given adequate consideration. For example, designers of training for technicians make intuitive decisions that a good technician must know some of the theory of operation for the devices he maintains and that he must know some specific rules for fixing those devices. A current technical curriculum therefore may cover primarily decontextualized theory and device-specific operating algorithms. No effort appears to have gone into determining the cognitive glue that allows concepts learned in one context to be applied in another, such as finding a fault in a nonworking device, which may require problem-solving heuristics rather than specific algorithms.

Intelligent computer-assisted instruction attempts to represent all the knowledge that constitutes the expertise that is to be taught. Interestingly, though, it generally does not possess an explicit curriculum based on a theory of learning and instruction. Where conventional instruction has an explicit curriculum but fails to have an explicit and complete representation of the knowledge that is to be taught, intelligent instructional systems have tended to represent the target knowledge explicitly but not to represent explicitly that body of knowledge that specifies the goal structure for instruction, the curriculum. For example, the WEST tutor (Burton & Brown, 1982) contains a method for determining how close to optimal a player's performance is and a set of issues to be considered. These issues constitute part of a curriculum knowledge structure but fail to have any relational structure tying them to each other or to a representation of target knowledge. In other cases, such as the geometry and lisp tutors being developed by John Anderson (Anderson, Boyle, Farrell, & Reiser, 1984), there are problem sequences that are preset, but again there is no explicit representation of curriculum knowledge.

To summarize, traditional computer-based instruction, whether organized into frames or into larger lesson units, tends to have an explicit representation of curricular structure, though often a shallow one, and at best, only an implicit representation of the kowledge being taught, while intel-

ligent instructional systems developed to date have explicit representation of the target knowledge but at best only implicit representations of the curriculum knowledge, the scope and sequencing of lessons.

Weaknesses in Current Approach

We can now restate and elaborate two problems inherent in current approaches to instructional design. First, there is no clear method for differentiating how to present material to remediate a problem discovered after a lesson has been taught from how it should be presented when taught initially. Second, the knowledge that represents the "glue" connecting the contents of related lessons is not clearly specified, nor is it assigned to be part of the content of any specific lesson. I consider each of these problems in turn.

"REDO" IS THE ONLY STRATEGY IT SUPPORTS

In current training systems the curriculum is at least implicitly a goal structure. One proceeds to teach the prerequisites (or subgoals) for a given lesson before teaching that lesson itself. The student should always be able to infer the missing knowledge that integrates those pieces of prerequisite knowledge into a broader skill. However, this does not always work. Lesgold's Two Fundamental Laws of Instruction (shown in Table 6.1) often apply, resulting in incorrect decisions about whether or not a trainee has mastered a given lesson. A lesson can appear to be mastered although the knowledge that has been acquired is too specific and cannot transfer from the context of the prerequisite training to the context in which it must be used (missing "glue"), resulting in the circumstance described by the First Law. On the other hand a lesson can appear to be unlearned because the context of testing does not match the context of instruction, even if the learned knowledge is adequate to the contexts for which the lesson is prerequisite. The result is the circumstance described by the Second Law. For example, there are mechanics whose formal knowledge of electrical principles is not sufficiently developed to pass tests but who understand more about a car's electrical system than many people who have studied physics.

Because we are never able to establish with certainty that a lesson has been learned and because excessively high criteria for post-testing can be

TABLE 6.1. Lesgold's two fundamental laws of instruction.

First Law: Not everyone who passes a test on a topic knows what appears to have been tested.

Second Law: Not everyone who fails a test on a topic lacks the knowledge that appears to have been tested.

very wasteful of instructional time (the student could fail despite having adequate knowledge), it is inevitable that occasions will arise in which it was assumed that a student has mastered a prerequisite when in fact he has not. It is important to note that this will occur whether the criteria for passing out of a lesson are prespecified or determined through some inferential process as the lesson is being taught, whether they are superficial (a cutoff score on a test) or deep (based on a detailed student model fitted to all of the student's performance in the relevant recent past).

When the student does need remediation because the assumptions of prerequisite knowledge have proven wrong, current systems generally replay the same instruction that did not work the first time. Sometimes different problems are assigned as examples or for practice, but they are generally of the same type as were used before. Sometimes the lesson proceeds more slowly, taking smaller steps and providing more practice at each step. In a few of the most recent intelligent computer-assisted instructional systems (e.g., Bonar, 1985; Burton & Brown, 1982), it is possible to estimate which specific pieces of knowledge targeted by the lesson are most likely not to have been learned and to concentrate on those. In every case, however, the goals of the lesson can and should be adapted to specific needs that arise only during remediation.

It should be noted that a number of theorists have proposed the view that learning in a domain is a process of successively replacing primitive conceptions, or personal theories, of the domain with more advanced constructions of it. This view subsumes the important insight that the knowledge structure of the student, rather than simply being incomplete, may actually be wrong, that he may hold a misconception, a different and conflicting theory of the task domain from the one the trainer would like him to have (for example, see Carey, 1985; Glaser, 1984; Shaughnessy, 1977; Young & O'Shea, 1981). The approach I am taking in this chapter is complementary to this view, concentrating on a somewhat more microscopic level of analysis.

No One Is Responsible for the Likeliest Failures of Instruction

A second problem with current approaches to remediation is that they fundamentally ignore the nonlinearities between lessons, the "glue" that holds lessons together. This is a problem particularly when responsibility for different parts of a training regimen is divided among multiple instructors. In such a regimen the content of a lesson always tends to be abstracted to its core, both in teaching it and in deciding how to test it. Consequently, the amount of between-lesson glue for which none of the course instructors takes responsibility can be substantial. Even worse, such division of responsibility is most common in technical training courses, where the trainees are often less likely to be facile at inferring the missing

content. However, it occurs between grades in school and between courses in college curricula as well.

The loss of the fringe content between lessons, the glue, produces a variety of pathologies that we see every day. The teacher in third grade feels that the only reason students do poorly in her class is that the second grade teacher failed to teach what was required. The second grade teacher points to high test scores and disclaims responsibility. The trainer providing on-the-job practice to technicians claims that they do poorly only because they were not taught fundamental principles of electricity, while the instructor for the course on fundamentals of electricity has abundant test data showing that they learned everything in the curriculum. Of course, what they were likely to forget after testing is exactly the fringes of the knowledge they were taught, the relations that glue it to the content of other lessons.

Overall, both of the previously cited problems seen to arise because there is a lack of distinction between the content of training and the curriculum or goal structure for training. Merely checking off subgoals as they are taught fails to account for the tendency of declarative knowledge to suffer high forgetting at its fringes, to shrink to a coherent, highly interconnected core. Simply reteaching prerequisite lessons when problems arise later fails to take account of what has already been learned and what has just been shown specifically to be weak.

In the next section I introduce a knowledge architecture for intelligent tutoring systems that has driven considerable current work on intelligent instructional systems that Jeffrey Bonar, Robert Glaser, and I (cf. Bonar, 1985; Glaser, Lesgold, & Lajoie, in press) have been conducting. The architecture's components are still being shaped by various projects each of us is conducting, but the basic ideas are well enough evolved to help supply what is missing from current instructional systems.

The Structure of Knowledge in an Intelligent Tutor

As previously discussed, a fundamental problem with existing architectures for instructional and training systems is that they fail to explicitly represent either the knowledge that they are designed to teach or the curriculum (goal structure) for teaching it. In setting out to develop an architecture that represents both content and curriculum, one quickly discovers that there are other issues that must be considered. First, there is other knowledge that a good teacher looks for in the student, knowledge we might call aptitude or metacognitive skill. That is, some students are more able to learn with facility from particular forms of instruction than others, and awareness of a student's learning capabilities can well shape the instructional approach a good teacher takes. Second, there are more domain-specific capabilities that represent both the broad outcomes desired from

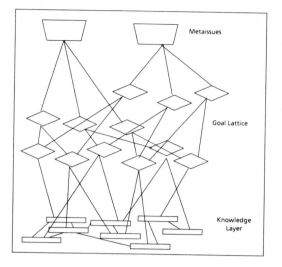

FIGURE 6.1. The three layers of an intelligent tutor.

the training and some specific capabilities for learning. For example, in a course on troubleshooting, general knowledge of electrical principles is both a useful prerequisite and something that should be enhanced by practice in finding faults in circuits.

These needs suggest that the knowledge in an intelligent tutor must be of three different types: (1) a representation of the knowledge to be taught (goal lattice), from which explanations and student models can be generated; (2) curriculum knowledge, a subgoal lattice of lessons connected by the prerequisite relation; and (3) a representation of the more enduring characteristics (metaissues) to which the instruction should be sensitive. Figure 6.1 shows the architecture symbolically.

THE KNOWLEDGE LAYER

The knowledge layer, highlighted in Figure 6.2, should contain a representation of the knowledge the system is trying to teach. One way to think about that knowledge is that it is a model of expert capability in the domain. Such knowledge includes both procedures and concepts (i.e., both procedural and declarative knowledge). Some constraints on its structure can be inferred from several things we know about human expertise. For example, we know that experts, in contrast to novices, tend to represent problems according to the underlying situations they involve, according to their deep structure, whereas novices tend to have more superficial representations (Chi, Feltovich, & Glaser, 1981; Larkin, McDermott, Simon, & Simon, 1980). We also know that, in contrast to intermediate-level per-

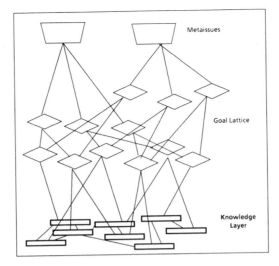

FIGURE 6.2. The knowledge layer.

formers, experts tend to know exactly what to do in a given situation rather than being dependent on inference from first principles (Chase & Simon, 1973; de Groot, 1965). That is, they are able to represent the situation more completely and richly and then to invoke the precisely appropriate method for dealing with it. In order to do this, experts' knowledge must be richly interconnected and, to some extent, redundant.

Before discussing how to deal with this problem, let me pause and give an example or two to illustrate the importance of the bridging connections between coherent bodies of knowledge. Consider the field of medicine. It is driven by several sciences: physiology, biochemistry, pharmacology, and even physics and chemistry. The relative roles of different portions of its scientific backing will differ for different disease problems. For this reason medicine is organized into specialties, each of which is internally very coherent. The ties between these specialties are much more complex and, relatively speaking, ad hoc.

A friend who is an attorney is handling a malpractice case involving a man who arrived at a hospital with severe back pain and several other symptoms. A very inexperienced intern was in the emergency room. He sent the patient to the orthopedics department. The specialists there found no skeletal problems and, after a lengthy examination, sent him back to the emergency room again. It then occurred to the intern that the man might have a tumor producing the pain. So, he was sent to oncology. While waiting for his turn there, he collapsed and died of a renal artery aneurysm. In essence the diagnosis process, decentralized according to the primary joints in the body of medical knowledge, failed to make adequate use of the linking knowledge that might have led from the symptoms, which

seemed to involve the back or the organs near the painful spot, to knowledge of various sorts of vascular problems. What was missing from the process was exactly the ad hoc interconnections between the conventional units of knowledge. Part of the specialty of emergency medicine is knowledge of the limits of the diagnostic processes that different specialties use, that is, knowledge of what happens at the "fringes" between specialized diagnostic approaches.

One can find other less dramatic examples throughout the curriculum. For example, in teaching elementary arithmetic, we teach children about place value, concentrating on the 1s, 10s, and 100s places in numbers. We also teach them algorithms for addition and subtraction of multicolumn numbers. Not all of the ties between these two related pieces of knowledge are explicitly taught, and not all seem to be universally learned (as demonstrated by the "Buggy" line of research; Brown & Burton, 1978; Brown & VanLehn, 1980; VanLehn, 1983). Some of what is not universally learned also has the character of being in the gap between the two pieces of instruction.

How do we deal with such gaps? One approach is a small extension of the original Gagné (1971) learning hierarchy ideas. The lowest levels of lessons in such a hierarchy correspond to the regions of the knowledge layer into which the total body of expert knowledge has been split. Higher levels of lessons are more than just the sum of what was taught in the lower level lessons. They have the specific task of ensuring that the conceptual glue between the lower level pieces is acquired. It is in this sense that teaching the whole of a body of material is more than just teaching its parts; the goal for the whole includes not only the parts but also a specific focus on the ties between those parts.

THE CURRICULUM GOAL LATTICE LAYER

The curriculum goal lattice layer is the central layer of the proposed architecture. As the goal structure for the instructional system, it is, more or less, in control of the system. Ordinarily, goal structures are trees, representing the progressive decomposition of each layer of subgoals into still smaller sub-subgoals. An example tree is shown in Figure 6.3. It shows the decomposition of a basic course in resistor network concepts into two main goals, knowledge of Ohm's law and knowledge of Kirchhoff's law. Those goals are then broken into subgoals, which are then decomposed further. The diagram becomes rather complex visually, but its underlying structure is still straightforward. Each subgoal is either a lesson that can be taught completely as a unit or it is further decomposable into sub-subgoals.

This kind of goal structure is exactly the sort of concept that Gagné (1971) was introducing in his discussions (see preceding section) of learning hierarchies. Further, he felt that psychological laws of learning would determine when subgoals had to be further subdivided and when they

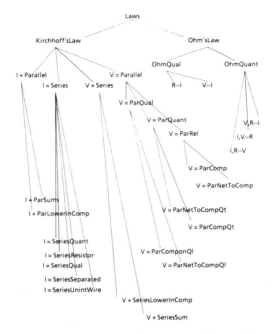

FIGURE 6.3. Goal hierarchy for basic resistor network laws. (Comp, Component; Compon, Component; I, Current; Net, Network; Par, Parallel; Ql, Qualitative; Qt, Quantitative; Qual, Qualitative; Quant, Quantitative; Rel, Relative; Sum, Sums; Unint, Uninterrupted; V, Voltage; R, Resistance.)

could be taught as single lessons. His analyses were in terms of the verbal association theory prominent at the time. More recently, VanLehn (1983) has advanced at least one different sort of criterion for deciding on such a subdivision, namely that a single lesson should not require the student to learn a rule with disjunctive conditions. Clearly, if the structure of curriculum is simply a subgoal tree, we are well on the way to understanding how to develop such a tree and how detailed its arborization must be.

However, in the first efforts by Jeffrey Bonar, his students Cynthia Cosic and Leslie Wheeler, and I to employ a curriculum goal hierarchy in an intelligent tutor, things were not as simple as we had hoped. For example, while one valid way to think of the resistor networks course is in terms of scientific laws presented, which leads to the decomposition shown in Figure 6.3, there are other equally valid ways. One might start with the basic measurable properties of such networks: current, electromotive force (voltage), and resistance. This leads to a goal lattice such as that shown in Figure 6.4. What is noteworthy is that the lowest level units in the tree, the simple lessons, are the same as in Figure 6.3, but the organization into higher order goals is entirely different, and the apparent purpose of the course may be different.

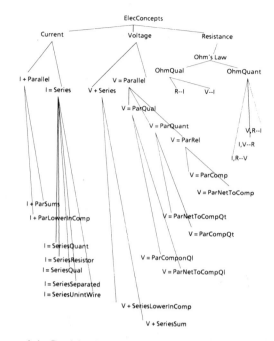

FIGURE 6.4. Goal lattice for basic resistor network measures.

So far in our own work, we have found four different viewpoints on the instruction that we want to present, each of which gives rise to a hierarchy that projects onto the same simple lessons. Figure 6.5 shows these viewpoints. We can partition our lessons into those that deal with series circuits and those that deal with parallel circuits, which is a quite reasonable organization, given that students often have different conceptual problems with parallel circuits. Or, we can partition our lessons according to the type of problem we present to the student: qualitative problems, quantitative problems, and problems that involve making a relative judgment about one part of a circuit relative to another. There are, of course, also the two viewpoints discussed previously, laws and measurable properties.

This leads us to a new view of the structure of curriculum knowledge in the knowledge base of an intelligent tutor. The curriculum knowledge has the structure of a *goal lattice*. There are a number of viewpoints on the goals of the instruction. With respect to each viewpoint, one can identify a subset of the curriculum lattice that is a true subgoal tree structure. So, from any specific point of view, there are clear pathways that determine the sequencing of instruction, though of course there are alternate approaches to such sequencing. For example, one can proceed depth first. In the case of Figure 6.4's viewpoint, this would mean perhaps doing all the lessons relating to current, then all those relating to voltage, and finally all those

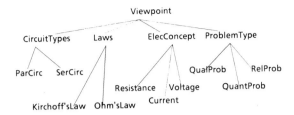

FIGURE 6.5. Viewpoints on resistor network instruction.

relating to resistance. Or, one might proceed breadth first, going through all the lowest level lessons, then the next level, and so on. There may be individual differences in aptitude or preference for these two approaches.

Of course, when all of the viewpoints are considered at once, there is much more complexity to the task of deciding what the appropriate sequencing for the lessons of the curriculum should be. To some extent the decision can be made on the basis of rational task analysis, but our experience has been that empirical work driven by cognitive theory is often necessary (Lesgold et al., 1986). Some of the lessons will tend to be difficult and others easy. By taking the various viewpoints, it should be possible to organize knowledge about lesson difficulty sufficiently to use it in deciding on appropriate orderings through the curriculum. Another approach may be to tell the student which lessons he is "eligible" to take next, based on prerequisites completed, and let him decide for himself. As discussed in this chapter in the section entitled "Context-Specific Prerequisite Content," there are even more sophisticated possibilities to consider in deciding how to handle sequencing.

To summarize, the goal lattice layer is a lattice structure in which are embedded a number of goal hierarchies, each corresponding to a fundamental viewpoint on the task of teaching the course content. Figure 6.6 shows the goal lattice for the resistor networks course we are implementing. This multiple viewpoints approach, incidentally, has implications for what constitutes an appropriate course, in terms of the *completeness, coherence,* and *consistency* of its curriculum lattice. Presumably, the resistor networks course as shown in Figure 6.6 is a reasonably sensible selection of content for a course. The course is *coherent,* in that each simple lesson is relevant to all of the viewpoints we have taken. It is *locally complete,* in that each viewpoint seems to be completely teachable with the set of simple lessons we currently have implemented. It is *globally complete* to the extent that the viewpoints represented include all of the viewpoints routinely held by experts and any others that are important to learning the domain content. Finally, it is relatively *consistent,* in that the prerequisite relationships all run in the same direction. There are no cases where lesson X is prerequisite to lesson Y from one point of view while lesson Y is prerequisite to lesson X from another.

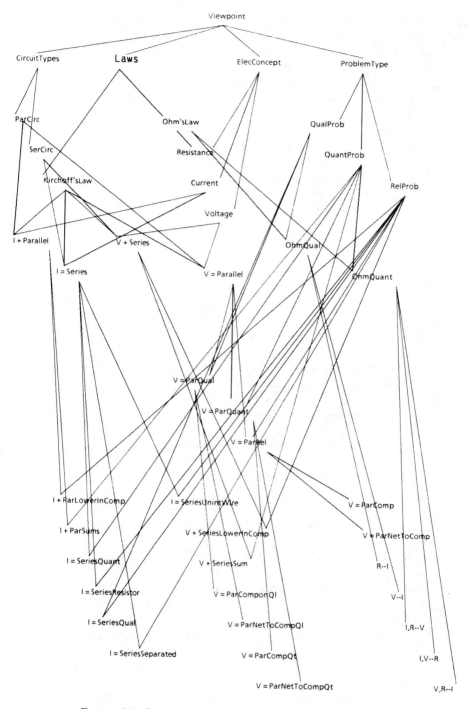

FIGURE 6.6. Goal lattice layer for resistor networks course.

It is not inevitable that courses will have these three properties. For example, consider the sort of introductory psychology course suggested by most current textbooks. There is little sense of completeness; lessons are included simply because of marketing needs and current fashion. There is no sense in which the simple lessons at the bottom of the hierarchy represent the simple foundations of concepts. Similarly, there is little coherence; the differing viewpoints, social, behavioral, cognitive, clinical, do not cover the same set of underlying basic concepts. Finally, there may not even be consistency. From one viewpoint, it may be best to teach sensory physiology before teaching about mental imagery; from another point of view a reverse ordering may seem obvious.

It seems appropriate to advance, as a hypothesis for future research, that knowledge-driven instructional systems will work best and be most implementable for those courses that have more or less coherent, consistent, and complete goal structures.

THE METAISSUE LAYER

The third layer of the proposed architecture for instructional knowledge is the metaissue layer. Once again, it is useful to recount some of our reasoning in deciding on the need for such a layer and on what should be in it. Initially, we were motivated by a single issue: the conflict between the sorts of data used by very good teachers to decide on how to proceed with a given student and the data and reasoning used by the few expert instructional systems that have been built. In giving students assignments teachers tend to rely on very broad representation of aptitude combined with a detailed knowledge of the curriculum. A child is "a good student," " a fast learner," "good in math," and/or "on page 93 in the book." In contrast, intelligent instructional systems, as envisioned by artificial intelligence researchers (e.g., Burton & Brown, 1982; Goldstein & Carr, 1977) construct a detailed student model that represents the best guess about exactly what a student does and does not know of the specific material targeted by the course, for example, "borrowing across zero," "adding single-digit integers," and so on.

There is at least modest evidence (Burton & Brown, 1982) that teachers cannot determine microscopic representations of student knowledge status nearly as well as intelligent computer systems can, so the first hope for an approach that would be sensitive to the detailed specifics of changing student knowledge is probably an intelligent instructional computer system. This prompted us to think about how to represent aptitude data. We were, in this thinking, heavily influenced by the object-oriented approach we were taking (we discuss this approach in the following section). Basically, we were led to the following point of view.

Attending to a specific aptitude or some other metaissue in shaping the activities presented for the trainee in any lesson is simply a special case of

shaping a lesson according to a specific viewpoint. That is, just as we might attend to differences between series and parallel circuits in our resistor network tutor and expect some students to have trouble with parallel circuits even after they have mastered series circuits, we could attend to differences among students in, say, reading ability or verbal facility and thus tailor our teaching to each student's capabilities seen from the verbal facility point of view. This has led us to the architecture shown in Figure 6.7, in which the metaissue layer is simply the collection of goal nodes that are the origins of various viewpoint hierarchies embedded within the curriculum lattice.

Lesson Objects

So far, we have rather mysteriously presented descriptions of various structures of knowledge, implying that these structures are organized into lessons that can be considered from a variety of different viewpoints. Also, we have suggested that, somehow, the lessons or subgoals of the curriculum are connected with a representation of the knowledge they are trying to teach. Nowhere have we said just what a lesson is, just what the structure within one of these graphs might be like. To this I now turn.

Our fundamental approach to designing architectures for intelligent instructional systems is object oriented. That is, we see the design task as one of specifying a set of intelligent fragments of computer program and then orchestrating the interactions among these fragments. This approach originated with Smalltalk (Goldberg & Robson, 1983), a language de-

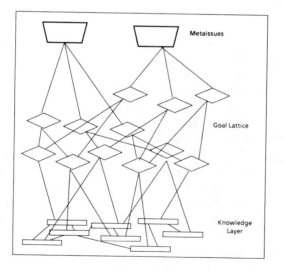

Figure 6.7. The metaissue layer.

veloped in the course of trying to determine ways in which powerful personal work stations could change education. In conventional computer programs the primary means of controlling the order in which computations take place, the task discipline, is by the sequencing of instructions. In object-oriented programming control is passed when objects, "entities that combine the properties of procedures and data since they perform computations and save local state" (Stefik & Bobrow, 1986, p. 41), send messages to other objects.

So, for example, the way in which our resistor network tutor might be started is for the student to point to a box on the screen that says "*Start.*" That box would actually be a menu operated by an object. The object would perhaps respond to the student's action by telling one of the meta-issue nodes in the tutor to teach the student. For example, if the approach favored by the designer were to teach primarily the relevant laws of electrical circuits, the "menu" object might send the "laws" object (see Figure 6.3) a message to teach everything for which it is responsible. The "laws" object would, in turn, ask its first prerequisite object, Kirchhoff's Law, to act, and that object might in turn tell the "I+parallel" object, which teaches that current sums across the branches of a parallel circuit, to act. The "I+parallel" object would then send messages in turn to its two prerequisites—dealing with current summing over branches and the notion that the current in a branch of a parallel network is always less than the current passing through the network as a whole—to teach their stuff. At each level, when one subgoal of a goal was satisfied, the next would be sent a message to act, and so on.

This requires that each object contain all the data and all of the methods needed to completely achieve the goal to which it corresponds. This is not as cumbersome as it may sound; it is not necessary for each object to be a complete instructional computer program. Rather, objects can "inherit" some of their methods from higher level objects. So, for example, if there are many objects that should teach their content via an exploratory electrical circuits simulation environment, they can all have a pointer to a single higher level object that includes the program for such a simulation. Each object using the simulation might specialize it either by setting the values of variables to which the simulation program refers or by including specializing information in a message it sends to the simulator when it invokes that approach. The object-oriented approach is valuable largely because it provides for a clear, understandable, and flexible means of ensuring that the goals an instructional program has to achieve are clearly delineated and clearly "tasked" by relevant pieces of program code, even if the content to be taught under various circumstances must be determined dynamically.

Table 6.2 lists the contents that each goal lattice object must have in the kinds of instructional systems we are currently building. The list is split into two parts. *Declarative knowledge* is the data that an object must have (or

TABLE 6.2. The contents of a lesson object.

Declarative knowledge

    Variables that identify how a given lessons' goals relate to the goals of other lessons (i.e., which lessons are prerequisite to the current one)

    Variables that identify how the knowledge a lesson is trying to teach relates to the knowledge other lessons are trying to teach (pointers to the knowledge layer)

    Variables that represent the student's mastery of the knowledge the lesson intends to teach (the student model)

Procedural knowledge

    Functions (methods) that generate instructional interventions based on the student model held by the given object, including both manipulations of the interactive learning environment (perhaps a simulated laboratory or a problem generator) and various forms of coaching or advising

    Functions that decide if the given object is to blame for problems that arise while other lesson objects for which it is prerequisite are in control

be prepared to accumulate during interactions with the student), what it is able to know. *Procedural knowledge* is the set of methods or programs that the object must have, what it is able to do. Each entry represents a specific kind of knowledge that must be present either explicitly, by being included in the object, or implicitly, via a pointer to the knowledge as part of a "parent" object.

The declarative knowledge must include knowledge that places the object in the curriculum lattice, showing what its prerequisites are and also which objects assume it as a prerequisite. It must also include a specification of the specific parts of the knowledge layer (the representation of the target knowledge to be taught by the course) it is responsible for teaching. From this representation it can provide explanations to the student. Finally, there must be a student model, that is, a representation of diagnostic information: which pieces of the target knowledge for the lesson does the student appear to know and how certain is that diagnostic information?

The procedural knowledge each object must have is of two primary types. First, an object must (again, either explicitly or implicitly) be able to teach its target knowledge. Second, it must be able to decide whether a student's failure to perform adequately in learning a lesson for which it is prerequisite might be due to inadequate learning of its target knowledge. We call this *blame-taking* capability. The idea is that if things are going poorly in a lesson, the object teaching that lesson might ask each of its prerequisite objects to find out whether what it was supposed to teach is what the student is missing. With the curriculum structures discussed so far, that would seem to imply something like readministering pieces of the lesson post-test. However, there are more interesting possibilities to consider.

The goal object lattice structure, as discussed so far, bears striking resemblance to current practice. If one looks at a current elementary or high school textbook, one finds that each topic, and the exercises associated

with it, is treated only once. One problem with curricula that actually follow such books (and most teachers do) is that the conditions of applicability for pieces of fact and process that students are taught are never reliably delineated. Students too often form rules for carrying out problem solving that are perfect for passing a unit test but maladaptive in the long run. For example, a student in elementary school given a set of arithmetic word problems might learn that it is not really necessary to read or understand the problem. If one finds words like *altogether*, one adds the numbers stated in the problem; if one finds words like *less*, one subtracts the smaller number from the larger; and so on. Scanlon and O'Shea (see Chapter 11) found similarly superficial strategies for use of specific equations that had recently been taught.

The way to avoid, or at least eventually remediate, such superficial learning is to combine different types of problems, to ensure that problems occur in a variety of superficial contexts, so that the successful cues for various actions are cues based on deep understanding of the problem. Jeffrey Bonar has been working on an extension of the architecture I describe here that tries to do this. In essence, higher level curriculum objects keep a list of lower level objects that have recently been taught. Occasionally, a few problems are created that require various unpredictable combinations of this knowledge for their solution. This forces the student to look more deeply at the problem situation and work, like an expert, from deep understanding rather than from surface appearances.

However, the blame-taking problem becomes somewhat different in such cases. Rather than giving individual lesson post-tests, testing for prerequisite knowledge in the original limited context used to present it, one wants to determine which pieces of knowledge that appear to have been mastered do not generalize to new situations. This appears to require a strategy of responding to a student's failure to handle a complex, multi-lesson problem either by giving hints or by giving a simpler problem, so that some of the candidate knowledge generalization failures can be ruled out. Work on how to do this is still proceeding; I mention it only because it may help give a sense of the character of blame-taking processes that we envision.

Context-Specific Prerequisite Content

I turn now to the final issue I wish to address, the complex nature of the prerequisite relationship. In particular I want to show that the domain knowledge for which a lesson object is responsible is specific to the curricular context in which the lesson is invoked. That is, the knowledge that should be presented by a lesson depends on the context in which that lesson is taught. To do this I must compare the core content of a lesson being taught for the first time with its remedial content.

The Core Content of a Lesson

The target knowledge of a lesson object can be thought of as a set of pointers from that object to nodes in the knowledge layer. The subset of the domain (or expert) knowledge layer defined by those nodes and their relations to other nodes will generally not have a sharp boundary, because expert knowledge is highly interconnected. As can be seen in Figure 6.8, some of the nodes in a lesson's target knowledge will be connected to each other, while others will be outlying orphans, whose operational meaning, that is, the set of connections from a concept to node to other concept nodes, is defined primarily outside the target subset. I use the term *core content* to refer to the subset of a lesson's target knowledge that is coherent, in the sense that its nodes are interconnected, with relatively few connections from a node to others outside that subset.

When a lesson is taught initially, its core content should be presented. That is, a coherent subset of the knowledge subsumed under the lesson should be taught. The density of detail in that coherent subset can vary with the aptitudes of the learner. Some learners should be taught all of the core content explicitly, while others can be expected to make at least the most direct and obvious inferences. In either case it is impossible to teach explicitly the fringes of the target knowledge without also introducing knowledge outside the target subset, so it can be assumed that these fringe pieces of knowledge have not been taught during the lesson's initial presentation. If a course, whether presented by human or by machine, is well taught, then the fringe knowledge for one lesson will be covered in another overlapping lesson or will be so immediately inferable from what is taught that it is optimal to assume that the student will learn it. Part of the artistry

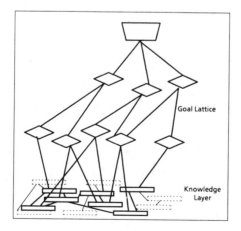

Figure 6.8. A curriculum goal object subsumes a region of the knowledge layer including more than core content.

of curriculum design is to split the knowledge to be taught into pieces that cover the total set of target knowledge with no more overlap than the usual student will require.

Further, there must be some mechanism for verifying how well the student is doing at learning what he is taught explicitly and completely and at inferring what it was hoped he would infer. In the design my colleagues and I have been evolving, *blame taking* provides this mechanism. When a lesson is proceeding poorly, an effort is made to determine which prerequisite material was not well presented, and that material is then retaught. Further, arbitrary objects can be created dynamically from time to time whose task it is to compose problems that require synthesis of several different pieces of already-taught knowledge and to test the student with them. When such problems fail one or more of the lessons they were based on should be reconsidered (i.e., the instructor or machine should consider reteaching them).

THE CONTENT OF A REMEDIAL LESSON

When a lesson is retaught remedially, generally there will be information to guide the selection of content that should be emphasized. In contrast to the emphasis placed on core content when a lesson is originally taught, it is crucial to teach the knowledge that links the core content of the to-be-remediated lesson with the core content of the lesson whose failure produced the need for remediation. We can make this point clearer by resorting to a graphical representation.

Figure 6.9 represents the interface between the goal lattice layer and the

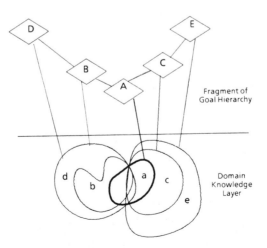

FIGURE 6.9. Higher level objects' projections do not necessarily cover the projections of their "children."

domain knowledge layer. Its point is that prerequisites are usually only partially overlapped by their superordinate lessons' domain knowledge. For example, the projection in the knowledge layer of lesson A (region a), is only partly contained in the projection of lesson C (region c), for which it is prerequisite. It has a different overlap with the projection of lesson B (region b), for which it is also prerequisite.

We can now proceed to define what content of a lesson should be taught when it is remediated. Basically, the emphasis should be on the nodes in the overlap between the projection of the superordinate lesson that failed and the projection of the prerequisite lesson that has taken blame. Figure 6.10 illustrates the area of goal A's content that should be taught when A has taken blame for the failure of superordinate goal B. Further, this overlap region should not be trimmed completely to produce a coherent core. Rather, its connections into the prerequisite lesson should also be pursued during remediation and perhaps also its connections into the superordinate lesson that failed. This gives us a clear distinction between the lesson as originally taught, which emphasized core content, and the lesson as remediated, which involves contextually relevant content.

I conclude by noting that this specification of what should be taught in remedial instruction is probably not foreign to the master teacher, who undoubtedly makes such determinations intuitively. However, instructional machines must have principles to guide their performance, and the principles just stated seem reasonable candidates for inclusion in the teaching knowledge of such machines. In implementing this approach I am sure that other candidates will also emerge. Finally, I suspect that the concerns we have had will be worth bringing to the attention of new teachers, who

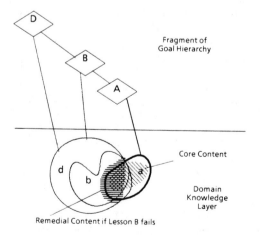

FIGURE 6.10. The appropriate content of a lesson when first taught is not the same as when it is remediated.

may not have a good idea of what the differences are between good remediation and simple repetition of instruction that failed the first time. I also note that I have not considered another principle that seems worthy, namely that instruction should build from strength. This is not because I disagree with that principle but rather because I have nothing new ready to say yet. A good instructional system, especially when remediating, will want to order the knowledge that is presented so that it builds from knowledge the student is known to have already. I hope that my colleagues and I will have something to say soon about how this should be done.

Acknowledgements. The work in this paper was collaborative research involving Jeffrey Bonar, Marilyn Bunzo, Cindy Cosic, Bob Cunningham, Marty Kent, Susanne Lajoie, Debra Logan, Mary Ann Quayle, Peter Reimann, Paul Resnick, Valerie Shute, William Weil, Leslie Wheeler, and others. It was supported by the Air Force Human Resources Laboratory, the Office of Naval Research, and the National Institute of Education. None of my collaborators nor the funding agencies cited necessarily endorse or agree with the views expressed.

REFERENCES

Anderson, J. R., Boyle, C. F., Farrell, R., & Reiser, B. J. (1984). *Cognitive principles in the design of computer tutors* (Report No. ONR-84-1). Pittsburgh, PA: Carnegie-Mellon University, Advanced Computer Tutoring Project.

Bonar, J. (1985). *Bite-sized intelligent tutoring.* Technical Report. Pittsburgh, PA: University of Pittsburgh, Learning Research and Development Center, University of Pittsburgh.

Brown, J. S., & Burton, R. R. (1978). Diagnostic models for procedural bugs in basic mathematical skills. *Cognitive Science, 2,* 155–192.

Brown, J. S., & VanLehn, K. (1980). Repair theory: A generative theory of bugs in procedural skills. *Cognitive Science, 4,* 379–426.

Burton, R. R., & Brown, J. S. (1982). An investigation of computer coaching for informal learning activities. In D. Sleeman & J. S. Brown (Eds.), *Intelligent tutoring systems* (pp. 79–98). Orlando, FL: Academic Press.

Carey, S. (1985). Are children fundamentally different kinds of thinkers and learners than adults? In S. F. Chipman, J. W. Segal, & R. Glaser (Eds.), *Thinking and learning skills: Vol. 2. Research and open questions.* Hillsdale, NJ: Lawrence Erlbaum Assoc.

Chase, W. G., & Simon, H. A. (1973). Perception in chess. *Cognitive Psychology, 4,* 55–81.

Chi, M. T. H., Feltovich, P., & Glaser, R. (1981). Categorization and representation of physics problems by experts and novices. *Cognitive Science, 5,* 121–152.

Gagné, R. M. (1962). The acquisition of knowledge. *Psychological Review, 69,* 355–365.

Gagné, R. M. (1971). *Conditions of learning*. New York: Holt Rinehart & Winston.

Glaser, R. (1984). Education and thinking: The role of knowledge. *American Psychologist, 39*, 93–104.

Glaser, R., Lesgold, A., & Lajoie, S. (in press). Toward a cognitive theory for the measurement of achievement. In R. R. Ronning, J. Glover, J. C. Conoley, & Witt, J. C. (Eds.), *The influence of cognitive psychology on testing*. Hillsdale, NJ: Lawrence Erlbaum Assoc.

Goldberg, A., & Robson, D. (1983). *Smalltalk-80: The language and its implementation*. Reading, MA: Addison-Wesley.

Goldstein, I., & Carr, B. (1977, October). The computer as coach: An athletic paradigm for intellectual education. *Proceedings of the 1977 Annual Conference* (pp. 227–233). Seattle, WA: Association for Computing Machinery.

de Groot, A. D. (1965). *Thought and choice in chess*. The Hague: Mouton.

Larkin, J. H., McDermott, J., Simon, D. P., & Simon, H. A. (1980). Expert and novice performance in solving physics problems. *Science, 208*, 1335–1342.

Lesgold, A. M., Lajoie, S., Eastman, R., Eggan, G., Gitomer, D., Glaser, R., Greenberg, L., Logan, D., Magone, M., Weiner, A., Wolf, R., & Yengo, L. (1986, April). *Cognitive task analysis to enhance technical skills training and assessment*. Technical Report. Pittsburgh, PA: University of Pittsburgh, Learning Research and Development Center.

Shaughnessy, M. (1977). *Errors and expectations*. New York: Oxford.

Stefik, M., & Bobrow, D. (1986). Object-oriented programming: Themes and variations. *AI Magazine, 6*, 40–62.

VanLehn, K. (1983). On the representation of procedures in repair theory. In H. P. Ginsburg (Ed.), *The development of mathematical thinking* (pp. 197–252). Orlando, FL: Academic Press.

Young, R. M. & O'Shea, T. (1981). Errors in children's subtraction. *Cognitive Science, 5* 152–177.

7

Enhancing Incremental Learning Processes With Knowledge-Based Systems

GERHARD FISCHER

In the past computer systems limited the user to modes of communication that made the machine's job easier. But now, as computer cycles become plentiful, our focus can shift to the users and how to make it easier, more productive, and less frustrating for them to cope with complex systems. Empirical investigations show that on the average only a small fraction of the functionality of complex systems is used. Figure 7.1 summarizes data based on careful observations of persons using systems like UNIX, EMACS, SCRIBE, LISP, and so on in our environment. It also describes different levels of system usage that typically can be found within many complex systems. The different domains correspond to the following:

D_1: the subset of concepts (and their associated commands) that the users know and use without any problems.

D_2: the subset of concepts that they use only occasionally. Users do not know details about them, and they are not too sure about their effects. Descriptions of commands (e.g., in the form of property sheets), explanations, illustrations (see the section on visualization techniques in prototypical system components) and safeguards (e.g., UNDOs) are important so that the user can gradually master this domain.

D_3: the mental model (Norman, 1982; Fischer, 1984) of the user, that is, the set of concepts that he or she thinks exist in the system. A *passive help system* (see the section on knowledge-based help systems in prototypical system components) is necessary for the user to communicate his or her plans and intentions to the system.

D_4: represents the actual system. Passive help systems are of little use for the subset of D_4, which is not contained in D_3, because the user does not know about the existence of these system features. *Active help systems* (see the section entitled Knowledge-Based Help Systems) and *critics* (see the section entitled The Code-Improver System), which advise and guide a user similar to a knowledgeable colleague or assistant are required so that the user can incrementally extend his or her knowledge to cover D_4.

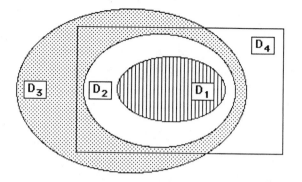

FIGURE 7.1. Levels of system usage.

As far as instructional strategies are concerned, it is important to note that only D_3 can be learned by using the methods of free exploration, whereas D_4 requires some guiding and coaching. The system's model of the user (see the section on using models to support incremental learning) will be used to determine the domains D_1 to D_4 for an individual user.

General Principles for Enhancing Incremental Learning Processes With Knowledge/Based Systems

THE PARADIGM OF "INCREASINGLY COMPLEX MICROWORLDS"

Over the last several years, we have developed a general paradigm for instruction that is best described as a sequence of increasingly complex microworlds (ICM) (Burton, Brown, & Fischer, 1983; Fischer, 1981; Fischer, Burton, & Brown, 1978).

The ICM paradigm was developed to capture instructional processes for complex skills that are difficult to learn because the starting state and goal state are too far apart. The student is exposed to a sequence of ICMs, which provide stepping stones and intermediate levels of expertise so that within each level the student can see a challenging but attainable goal. ICMs can also be used to provide protective shields for the novice that prevent him or her from being dumped into unfamiliar system areas (Figure 7.2). The paradigm requires a precise representation of the knowledge that is learned in a specific microworld and how to choose the next microworld. It serves well as a model to capture the essence of incremental learning processes.

In our application (the incremental learning of LISP skills; see the section on the application domain), the following microworlds can be defined:

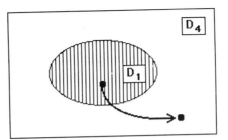

FIGURE 7.2. Protective shields.

- Use of an interactive environment with multiple windows, icons, pointing devices
- Dynamic and associative memory structures (e.g., lists and property lists)
- Applicative programming styles (e.g., little use of the assignment operators)
- Destructive versus nondestructive functions
- Macros (which can be used to create more problem specific representations; they reduce the cognitive complexity, because the goal structure of the problem domain can be more directly mapped onto the program)
- Use of existing tools (e.g., reader with real-time indenting, inspector, browser, trace and step package, *Kaestle, Code-Improver*, compiler, etc.)
- Use of existing building blocks in the construction of new programs (e.g., pattern matcher, window systems, packages to support an object-oriented style of programming, expert system shells)

In our future research we will extend the power of the *Code-Improver* (discussed later), so it can decide which microworlds are familiar to and have been mastered by individual learners. We will also develop a system component that will make suggestions to a student to move on to the next microworld.

The richness of powerful LISP systems (similar to the great variety of different slopes in skiing; Fischer et al., 1978) will allow people to learn first those parts of the system that are of immediate relevance to their tasks. Higher level programming formalisms and technological improvements (e.g., a pattern matcher, an expert system shell, a first-rate programming environment) have eliminated certain prerequisites to using computer systems successfully.

THE CRITICAL ISSUES

The three major goals of our research are (1) to enhance incremental learning processes with knowledge-based systems and to get a deeper

understanding of how people understand, learn, and operate complex systems; (2) to apply and test our general framework by implementing system components that will support the instructional process that the normal computer science student or software engineer has to go through when he or she learns to cope with complex LISP systems; (3) to evaluate empirically the effectiveness of the user support systems constructed, both to assess their effectiveness and to discover possibilities for improvement.

To achieve these goals we are investigating the following:

1. How can complex systems be constructed so that they have *no threshold and no ceiling*? It should be easy to get started (i.e., microworlds should provide *entry points*), but these systems should also offer a rich functionality for experienced users.
2. How can our theoretical paradigm of constructing *ICMs* be exploited to build complex systems that support incremental learning strategies?
3. What are the general principles that determine the right mixture of *free exploration* and *coaching*? How can we guarantee that systems take the initiative when necessary and at the same time are nonintrusive?
4. How can we turn "nonconstructive" bugs into "constructive" ones and develop a broad collection of *self-checking methods*?
5. How can we use *models of the user* to make systems more responsive to the needs of *different individual users*, and how does the system behavior reflect the *transition of a user from a novice to an expert*?
6. How can *explanations* be tailored to the user's conceptualization of the task?
7. What is the role and relative importance of *verbal* and *nonverbal* (e.g., graphic) explanatory material? When is the use of one preferred to the other?
8. How can we *evaluate* these systems?

We claim that knowledge-based systems with qualitatively new human–computer communication capabilities (see the section on system architecture) are one of the most promising ways to achieve our stated goal. We propose to extend the comprehensibility of systems by using a large fraction of the computational power of the machine to support sophisticated user-support systems (Figure 7.3).

In the past our efforts have concentrated on the incremental learning of *computer systems*, because they allow us to exploit the information structures already present in the machine and they do not require maintaining consistency between an outside world and a model of this world in the computer. In addition this problem domain is ideally suited for our purposes: it occurs in our daily work; a student pool for testing and evaluation is readily available; there is a growing interest in *LISP*-based systems and a serious shortage of appropriately trained persons.

However, we would like to emphasize that our concerns are of a more general nature. Computer systems are used as *vehicles* only to carry out

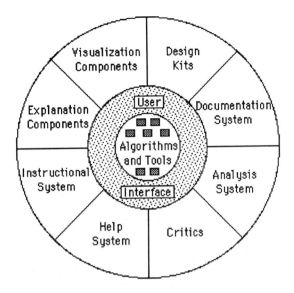

FIGURE 7.3. From tools to communication partners.

the work; the more general goals of our research are to develop theories and construct experimental systems that make a true contribution toward an improvement of instructional theories and processes in general.

Instructional Strategies

Our instructional strategies are oriented toward the *intermediate* user who has mastered a system to some extent (see Figure 7.1). This implies that reliance solely on tutorial strategies is not sufficient, but we must develop several ways to support a user:

1. A critic should "look" over a user's work and make suggestions for improvements.
2. A tutoring component (using some of our visualization techniques) can illustrate the advice given.
3. An explanation component can provide the rationale that leads to the improvement.

In our research we want to determine the balance between supporting an exploratory learning style of *learning by doing* (the basic philosophy behind the interest worlds in LOGO environments; (Papert, 1980) and a guided learning experience through *coaching assistance* (the primary instructional strategy supported by systems in intelligent computer-assisted instruction (Sleeman & Brown, 1982).

Learning by doing is tightly coupled with *learning on demand*. Users

are often unwilling to learn more about a system or a tool than is necessary for the immediate solution of their current problem. To be able to cope successfully with new problems as they arise requires a consultant who generates advice tailored to the user's specific need. This approach provides information only in relevant situations and eliminates the burden of learning a great deal in advance (i.e., at times when it is unknown if the information ever will be used or when it is difficult for the learner to imagine an application).

To get a deeper understanding of how to support *learning on demand*, our work on *knowledge-based help systems* (discussed later) serves as a starting point. We must be able not only to respond to errors but to notice—based on a model of the task and a model of the individual user—**suboptimal actions** of the user that serve as a basis for individual help. It is not always clear when a solution is suboptimal and hence should trigger an activity of the help system. A **metric** is necessary to judge how adequate a user's action is. Except for narrow problem domains (e.g., simple games; Burton & Brown, 1982), optimal behavior cannot be uniquely defined.

We will use the identification of a user with a specific microworld to prevent the system from using inadequate conceptualizations and knowledge structures that may lead to the following difficulties:

- The help offered may not be understood by the learner, because it refers to unknown concepts.
- The help offered may put too heavy a load on the learner's short-term memory.
- The help system may "force" the user to do something that he or she does not want to do. A possible solution to this problem might be to make the metric visible and to allow the user to change it; but we must be aware that this increases the control of the user as well as the complexity of the system. This increase in functionality will be of little use if we do not find adequate communication structures for it.

Our approach to the construction of instructional systems can be contrasted with some other approaches discussed following.

1. **The LISP Tutor.** Anderson and his research group (Anderson, Boyle, Farrell, & Reiser, 1984) address similar issues, but their work is oriented toward *tutoring*, which allows them to pursue a *predefined* course of action, whereas our actions are triggered by the behavior and the incremental learning process of individual users. Their system deals with the early phase of a skill-acquisition process in which it is important to provide guidance and correct the acquisition of "wrong" behavior as early as possible.

2. **The PROUST system.** Johnson and Soloway (Johnson & Soloway, 1984) provide systems with a *deep* understanding of programs and misconceptions of users about them. They look in great detail at very specific programs that they use as case studies in their work. Concentrating on a *very small* number of examples, they are able to create a very elaborate

("deep") representation of these objects. Their system is not able to take a basically arbitrary *LISP* program and criticize it as our *LISP-Critican*.

3. **The WEST system.** Brown's and Burton's work on the *WEST* system (Burton & Brown, 1982) as well as our joint work (Burton et al., 1983; Fischer, 1981; Fischer et al., 1978) have been very influential on the research described in this paper. Contrary to their approach in WEST, where one can rely on the evaluation of an arithmetic expression to determine a metric for "optimal" and "suboptimal" behavior, we have to model much more complex skills (e.g., how to write "good" *LISP* code), which require hundreds of rules (see the section entitled The Code-Improver System).

The following requirements can be derived from our desire to support the instructional strategies described:

The system must be able to support users on *all* levels of expertise (novices to experts);

It is *not restricted to a tutoring system* although tutoring aspects can be found;

It supports *learning on demand*; interesting new topics are introduced into the instructional process when there is a need for them; it should *take the initiative* when weaknesses of the user become obvious; not every recognized suboptimal action should lead to an intervention;

It ought to have *explanation capabilities*, because even the best advice is sometimes not understood; it should *give additional information*, which was not explicitly asked for but is likely to be needed in the near future;

It needs to have a model of its communication partner in order to be able to tailor its advice and explanations to the level of expertise of the user; *knowing what the user knows* the system may be able to predict the kind of problems the user is likely to encounter when tackling specific tasks;

It will be able to provide advice relating to the domains D_3 and D_4 in Figure 7.1; it will assist the user in the *stepwise extension* of his or her view of the system by making sure that basic concepts are well understood and by not introducing too many new features at once;

It should be *nonintrusive*; only frequent suboptimal behavior without the user being aware of it should trigger an action of the system.

The Application Domain: Enhancement of LISP Skills

Our system-building efforts have the goal of building a *LISP-Critic*. This system may be best thought of as a knowledgeable colleague, a consultant or an advisor of the programmer. It should be relevant in the standard situation that occurs among humans. Some person is working on a program, somebody else enters the room, and both persons start a dialogue on the program that is under development.

RATIONALE FOR THE SELECTION OF THE PROBLEM DOMAIN

The rationale for the selection of this problem domain is based on the following:

1. Relevance. There is a *great need* to train people to use complex *LISP* systems, which form the basis for the new tools of the fifth-generation computer systems; there are currently very few people around who can successfully exploit the computational power and broad functionality of high-performance personal work stations.
2. Complexity. The systems used are sufficiently *complex that nobody masters them completely*; incremental learning processes are a must.
3. Expertise. To train students and computer scientists has been our task for several years; we have a *good understanding of the problems* they encounter, and we have a large group of people around us to test our ideas and systems in a natural setting.
4. Appropriateness. We have enough *control* over these systems (because we built most of them ourselves) to augment them with knowledge structures (e.g., models of the task, models of the users, visualization techniques), which are required to enhance incremental learning.

A SCENARIO

The dialogue in Table 7.1 exemplifies some of the features that the system will have. It shows the functionality only, it does *not* show the user interface. We use a natural language dialogue to illustrate the main ideas;

TABLE 7.1. Computer and User Dialogue

Dialogue	Comments
	User types in some piece of new code.

```
(prog (line)
    (setq line (append
        (explode word) chars))
loop
    (cond ((null line)
        (return (terpri))))
    (princ (car line))
    (princ " ")
    (setq line (cdr line))
    (go loop))
```

Dialogue	Comments
I have some suggestions on how to improve your code, want to see them?	System steps in actively: Activist aspect.

TABLE 7.1. *Continued*

Dialogue	Comments

Yes
The code
    (prog (line)
      (setq line (append
        (explode word)
        chars))
    loop
      (cond ((null line) (return
        (terpri))))
      (princ (car line))
      (princ " ")
      (setq line (cdr line))
      (go loop))
could be rewritten by
  • *using the **msg**-macro and*
  • *replacing the **prog**-form by a*
    ***do**-form*
as:
    (do ((line (append (explode
      word) chars) (cdr line)))
      ((null line) (terpri))
      (msg (car line) B))
	System suggests using a macro and a higher level looping control structure than prog by using transformation rules contained in its domain knowledge base.

What does msg do? ***msg** is a* macro *that expands into more primitive* print *functions; "B" will print a blank; other arguments will be printed by 'princ'.*	User asks for explanation of a function. Passivist aspect. System generates explanation of "msg." The underlined words may be explained further. Note that the system does *not* print the whole manual entry for "msg" but instead gives the information on the "B" keyword only, which is relevant to the specific suggested improvement.
What is a macro? *A macro is . . .*	User asks for the explanation of a concept. System prints out explanation tailored to the knowledge state of the user.

Give me another example of a macro.
The Code
    (setq line (cdr line))
could be rewritten as:
    (unpush line)
 	
I have some suggestions on how to improve your code, want to see them?
	User asks for more examples of macros.
	
	System prints out another example generated from other portions of the user's code if possible.
	If the system's model of the user had been different, e.g., if the user were a more advanced person already knowing about macros and do-forms, the interaction might have been different.
	System steps in actively: Activist aspect.

Yes *The code* *(prog (line)*	Note that the system was able to generate a reasonable new name for the parameter of the

TABLE 7.1. *Continued*

Dialogue	Comments
(setq line (append	lambda-expression. This will be done through
(explode word) chars))	reference to other parts of the code or by having
loop	some knowledge about the user's naming style.
(cond ((null line) (return	
(terpri))))	
(princ (car line))	
(princ " ")	
(setq line (cdr line))	
(go loop))	
could be rewritten by	
• using the **msg**-macro,	
• replacing the **prog**-form by a	
mapc-form and	
• using a destructive function	
(nconc) instead of a copying	
one (append).	
as:	
(mapc ('lambda (char)	
(msg char B))	
(nconc (explode word)	
chars))	

Why replace append by nconc?

| *nconc is more efficient, because it* | System justifies its suggestion by referring to higher |
| *does not copy list structures.* | level concepts. |

Please explain!

You may start the Kaestle system	System suggests two approaches: the first involving
and execute	more activity on the side of the user, the second
(append (explode 'word)	being a prefabricated demonstration (that may use
'(c h a r s))	the current bindings of "chars" and "word"). The
and	system could have also chosen a textual
(nconc (explode 'word)	explanation by presenting the relevant manual
'(c h a r s))	information.
within the Kaestle-window or run	
the "nconc-append demo."	

Show the demo

The system runs the demo, which on the level of the internal representation of list structures shows how these are copied and modified by the two functions append and nconc, respectively (see Figure 7.4).

this form of interaction will be replaced or enhanced in the future by an interaction style that is more oriented toward direct manipulation (using windows, menus, icons, mouse, etc.). The system will not necessarily be used exclusively interactively; it may also be used in a batch mode, writing comments and suggestions for improvement into a separate file. One

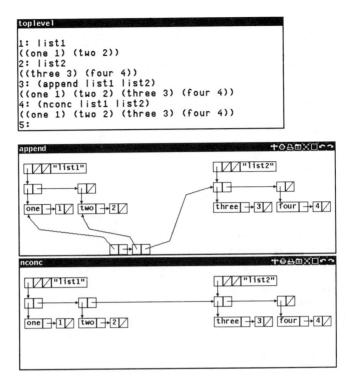

FIGURE 7.4. Illustration of append versus nconc.

alternative scenario is that before users log off the system in the evening, they ask the system to look over the work during the night.

The dialogue in Table 7.1 assumes that the user is not using the system the first time; from earlier sessions the system has incrementally built up a model of the user that reflects his or her knowledge state, preferred style of programming and so on. The table uses **bold type** for the user input and *italic type* for the computer output. Code is printed in a smaller **bold** or *italic* font.

A Conceptual Hierarchy of LISP Knowledge

The main question to be answered in order to provide intelligent help to a programmer is what does the system need to know to fulfill its job? What is the knowledge that the system can draw on, and how is it structured?

We are currently restricting ourselves to building a program that can assist the programmer up to the level of *application-independent knowledge* about programming; we do not try to model the knowledge that is specific to certain algorithms. The system also does not have an understanding of higher level programming constructs like loops, hashtables, and so on at

the level of Rich's and Shrobe's *Programmer's Apprentice* (Rich & Shrobe, 1978). Our approach can be compared with the *computer aids to writers* in the UNIX world (Cherry, 1981).

We formalize the programming knowledge using **Concepts, Goals,** and **Functions** as the basic representational entities. We are using *ObjTalk* (an object-oriented knowledge representation formalism; Lemke, 1985; Rathke, 1986; Rathke & Lemke, 1985) to represent this knowledge because it offers the right kind of descriptive power. Some basic knowledge types can be defined as the following classes: concepts, goals, and functions.

Concepts

A *concept* is an entity that is primitive in the sense that no action is associated with it; concepts are used to tie together the procedural knowledge that is embodied in the *goals*.

```
(ask class new: Concept
    (superc class)
    (descr (Superconcept (default 'LISP Knowledge))
        (Contrary Concept)
        (Related Concept)))
```

Goals

Goals specify normative categories for the LISP programmer. Goals embody procedural knowledge that can be applied to produce program code. *Goals* formulate the heuristics and higher order principles that may be followed to produce good software. There may be several layers of *goals*, that is, goals may have subgoals. *Goals* are used to represent individual *rules* that can be used to classify and transform program code.

```
(ask class new: Goal
    (superc class)
    (descr (Related Concept)
        (Supergoal)
        (Related Goal)
        (conflicting Goal)))
```

Functions

Functions capture the knowledge that is closely associated with the actual writing of LISP code.

```
(ask class new: Function
    (superc class)
    (descr (Superconcepts)
        (Pattern)
        (Subparts)
```

```
            (Related Functions)
            (Subconcepts)
            (Required Concepts)
            (Critics)
            (Specializers)
            (Generalizers)
            (Optimizers)))
```

The knowledge base will consist of a large number of instances of these primitive representational units. Some examples of instantiations of the classes follow:

Concepts
    (ask Concept new: LISP Knowledge (Superconcept Programming Knowledge))
    (ask Concept new: Control Structures (Superconcept Programming Knowledge))
    (ask Concept new: Data Structures (Superconcept Programming Knowledge))
    (ask Concept new: Readability)
    (ask Concept new: Macros (Superconcept Readability Speed Efficiency))

Goals
    (ask Goal new: Avoid Creating Garbage
        (Related Concept Garbage Collection))
    (ask Goal new: Avoid Multiple Evaluation of Identical Expression
        (Related Concept Speed Efficiency))
    (ask Goal new: Do not Copy Repeatedly
        (Related Goal Avoid Creating Intermediate ConsCells)
        (descr
            (Pattern) (Consequence) (Modifier) (Type)))

Figure 7.5 shows a typical *ObjTalk* representation of expert knowledge concerning the LISP function *do*.

The slots in this structure can be described as follows:

Superconcepts: a set of more general concepts that are instantiated through this function.

Pattern: the *LISP* syntax of the function. It can be used to recognize it from some piece of program code and conversely to generate code from an abstract description.

Subparts: lists of primitive blocks needed to build up a complete function.

Related Functions: functions that can be used to achieve similar functionality. They may be more special or more general.

Subconcepts: a list of more special uses of the function exploiting a certain part of the whole functionality. The example DoWithMultipleLoopVars addresses the issue that more than one loop variable can be used.

```
(ask Function renew: Do                          ;;; expert knowledge about the 'do' function
    (SuperConcepts                               ;;; links to higher level concepts
     Iteration ParallelEvaluation LambdaBinding SpecialForms
     SequentialProgramming)
    (Pattern                                     ;;; syntax of the function
     (do (?*DoDeclaration) ?DoExitClause ?*ProgBody))
    (SubParts
     DoDeclaration DoExitClause ProgBody)
    (RelatedFunctions                            ;;; 'do' can be transformed to these functions
     SimpleDo Prog MapFunctions)
    (SubConcepts
     DoWithMultipleLoopVars DoWithLocalVars DoWithUninitializedVars
     DoWithMoreThan1Var DoWithNoDoVar DoWithCondExitIdentical
     DoWithCondExit DoWithCondSomethingExit DoWithNilExitClause)
    (RequiredConcepts
     ProgBody UninitializedVarsAreNil ParallelAssignment
     LeftToRightEvaluationSequence)
    (Critics                                     ;;; recognize incorrect syntax
     MultipleDeclaredVariables IgnoredParallelAssignment MalformedExitClause
     MalformedDeclaration)
    (Specializers
     Do2Mapcar Do2Mapc DoWithTconc2Mapcar-1 DoWithTconc2Mapcar-2 Do2SimpleDo Do2Let)
    (Generalizers
     Prog2Do-1)
    (Simplifiers)
    (Optimizers))

;;; This special form of 'do' reflects the usage of more than one loop variable;
;;; It is used to recognize the use of this functionality.
(ask Function renew: DoWithMultipleLoopVars
    (SuperConcepts Do)
    (Pattern
     (do (?*vars1 (?v1 ?i1 ?r1) ?*vars2 (?v2 ?i2 ?r3) ?*vars3)
         ?test ?*body))
    (UsedIn
     Do2Mapcar DoWithTconc2Mapcar-1 DoWithTconc2Mapcar-2)
    (Examples ...)
    (Rating))

;;; Transformation rule from 'prog' to 'do' and vice versa.
(ask CriticRule renew: Prog2Do-1
    (FromFunction Prog)
    (ToFunction Do)
    (FromPattern (prog (?var) (setq ?var ?init) ?label:symbolp
                       (cond (?test (return ?result)))
                       ?*body (setq ?var ?rep) (go ?label)))
    (ToPattern (do ((?var ?init ?rep)) (?test ?result) ?*body)))

;;; Transformation rule: 'do' <--> 'mapc'
(ask CriticRule renew: Do2Mapc
    (FromFunction Do)
    (ToFunction Mapc)
    (FromPattern (do ((?var ?init (cdr ?var))) ((null ?var) ?*result) ?*body))
    (ToPattern (mapc '(lambda (?elem) ?*(replace: ?*body (car ?var) ?elem))
                     ?init) ?*result))
```

FIGURE 7.5. Representation of the *do* function.

Required Concepts: a link to concepts that are needed to understand how the function is working (i.e., links to previous microworlds).

Critics: patterns of program code that are clues to missing or incorrect concepts. Often these patterns are undetected by the *LISP* run-time system and the compiler because they are not explicitly erroneous. Examples are unreached pieces of code, code that computes a constant value, code that runs only interpretively, and so on.

Specializers, Generalizers, Simplifiers, and *Optimizers:* transformation rules that make the knowledge base operational. They allow the transition from a concept to a related concept and can also be used to generate explanations for this relation. The Prog2Do-1 generalizer connects this function to the related prog function and the Do2Mapc specializer provides the link to one of the higher level "map" functions.

The network of *concepts, goals,* and *functions* serves a variety of purposes. It may be used to make the relations between different parts of the programming knowledge explicit; to justify and thereby explain the improvements suggested by the rules (see the section entitled The Code-Improver System); to enable the student to actively browse through the conceptual space (e.g., to learn about similar concepts) of the application domain; to restrict the domain of tutoring to parts of the conceptual knowledge (i.e., criticize and advise relative to a subset of concepts and goals); to derive a model of the user (see the section entitled The Use of Models to Support Incremental Learning Processes).

Architecture of a System to Support Incremental Learning Processes

KNOWLEDGE-BASED HUMAN–COMPUTER COMMUNICATION

Knowledge-based systems are one promising approach to equipping machines with some human communication capabilities. Based on an analysis of human communication processes, we have developed the model shown in Figure 7.6.

The system architecture in Figure 7.6 contains two major improvements over traditional approaches. (1) The explicit communication channel is widened (e.g., we use windows, menus, pointing devices, etc.), and (2) information can be exchanged over the implicit communication channel.

The four domains of knowledge shown in Figure 7.6 have the following relevance:

1. **Knowledge of the problem domain** (see the preceding section entitled The Application Domain: Enhancement of LISP Skills): Intelligent behavior builds on large amounts of knowledge about specific domains. This knowledge imposes constraints on the number of possible actions and describes reasonable goals and operations. If, for example, in UNIX a user needs more disk space, it is in general not adequate help to advise him or her to use the command **rm**[1] (Wilensky, Arens, & Chin, 1984), although it would perfectly serve his or her explicitly stated goal. The user's goals and intentions can be inferred if we understand the correspondence between the system's primitive operations and the concepts of the task domain.

---

[1] The command deletes all files in the current directory.

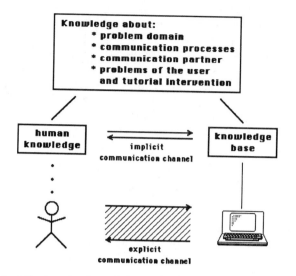

FIGURE 7.6. Architecture for knowledge-based human–computer communication.

2. **Knowledge about communication processes:** The information structures that control the communication should be made explicit, so the user can manipulate them.

3. **Knowledge about the communication partner** (see the next section): *The* user of a system does not exist; there are many different kinds of users, and the requirements of an individual user grow with experience.

4. **Knowledge about the most common problems that users have in using a system and about instructional strategies** (see preceding section entitled Instructional Strategies): This kind of knowledge is required if someone wants to be a good coach or teacher and not only an expert. A user support system should know when to interrupt a user. It must incorporate instructional strategies that are based on pedagogical theories, exploiting the knowledge contained in the system's model of the user.

THE USE OF MODELS TO SUPPORT INCREMENTAL LEARNING PROCESSES

To support incremental learning processes and learning on demand, the system must be able to represent for specific users information about the user's conceptual understanding of a system, the user's individual set of tasks for which he or she uses the system, the user's way of accomplishing domain-specific tasks, the pieces of advice given, whether the user remembered and accepted the advice, and the situations in which the user asked for help.

The domain chosen for this research is much more complex than the simple editing tasks considered in the *Activist* and *Passivist* systems (see section entitled Knowledge-Based Help Systems) or a simple game like

the WEST system (Burton & Brown, 1982). Although parametric models (i.e., ratings of the user in a small set of concepts) or overlay models, in the form of a one-to-one association of tasks and (expert) solutions, are sufficient for simple tasks, a network consisting of *programming concepts, LISP functions, data types*, and *transformation rules* must be developed to represent both the expert knowledge and the incomplete, suboptimal, and partly erroneous knowledge of the user.

The representation of the user's knowledge and skills is done as a modified subset of the system's expert knowledge. Compared to the system's expert knowledge, some of the concepts and transformation rules may be missing. Others may be present but incomplete or incorrect. In addition there may be erroneous subconcepts that were detected in code written by the user. An example of a user's representation of the *do* function (as hypothesized by the system) is given in Figure 7.7.

Given this detailed model of the user and the system's understanding of *LISP* knowledge, the following actions of the system become possible:

Select Appropriate Actions With Respect to the User

If the comparison of the user model and the system's expert knowledge reveals weaknesses in a specific area, the system should only become active if this area is adjacent (in terms of the ICM paradigm) to already known areas and does not require too many other areas unknown to the user.

Select Examples From the Domain the User is Familiar With

By using an executable form of representation, it is possible to generate illustrations out of areas that the user already understands and thus reduce the cognitive distance that has to be bridged.

```
(ask Function renew: Do
    (SuperConcepts                              ;;; fewer known superconcepts
     Iteration SequentialProgramming)
    (Pattern                                    ;;; less general form
     (do (?*DoDeclaration) (?test ?result) ?*LambdaBody))
    (SubParts                                   ;;; there is a lambda body instead of a prog body
     DoDeclaration DoExitClause LambdaBody)
    (RelatedFunctions                           ;;; many related functions are unknown or
     Prog)                                      ;;; not recognized as being related
    (SubConcepts
     DoWithMultipleLoopVars DoWithMoreThan1Var
     DoWithCondExit DoWithCondSomethingExit)
    (RequiredConcepts
     LeftToRightEvaluationSequence)
    (Critics
     MultipleDeclaredVariables IgnoredParallelAssignment MalformedExitClause
     MalformedDeclaration)
    (Specializers)                              ;;; no transformation rules available
    (Generalizers)
    (Simplifiers)
    (Optimizers))
```

FIGURE 7.7. A user's representation of the *do* function.

Present Only the Missing Pieces of Knowledge

In dialogues a large amount of time is spent to find out what each communication partner knows and does not know about the subject area. Provided a detailed user model, the system can concentrate on the very points where the user needs help.

Better Understanding of the User

Using knowledge about the user's understanding of a problem domain makes it much easier to find out about his or her real problem. We encountered many cases where a user had a problem that originated in a wrong decomposition of a higher level problem. Using knowledge about the user, it is possible to trace a problem back to its real roots.

The problem of knowledge acquisition for the user model is solved primarily using program code written by the user. Techniques, as described in the section entitled The Code-Improver System, will be extended from recognizing pieces of code that can be improved to recognizing both the goals of a piece of code and the existing and missing concepts that led to its generation. Because in only a very few cases a definitive assumption about the knowledge of the user can be made, it is important to have many clues that permit uncertain inferences when no specific evidence is available. Concepts grouped into a set of microworlds are such a clue. If, for example, the user has shown knowledge of a certain concept and there is no information about any of the prerequisite concepts, then it is very likely that the user also knows these concepts to some extent.

Prototypical System Components to Enhance Incremental Learning Processes

In this section visualization techniques, knowledge-based help systems, and the *Code-Improver* system are briefly described. These system components were developed over the last several years, have been in active use for some time, and will serve as important building blocks toward our goal to construct a *critic* for *LISP*.

VISUALIZATION TECHNIQUES

Our visualization tools were developed as extensions to the *FranzLISP* programming environment. All these tools display and visualize relationships among data and control structures that are otherwise invisible. Together they build a *software oscilloscope* that is used like the oscilloscope of the electrical engineer.

The most important data structure of *LISP* is the *list*. With *Kaestle* (Boecker, Fischer, & Nieper, 1986; Boecker & Nieper, 1985), the graphic

representation of a list structure is generated automatically and can be edited directly with a pointing device. By editing we do not mean changing the structure only but also changing the graphic representation, the layout, of the structure. *Kaestle* is integrated into a window system, and multiple *Kaestle*-windows may be used at the same time. The *user interface* is menu based (see Figure 7.8), and the *program interface* is realized through *ObjTalk* methods that can be triggered by sending messages to a *Kaestle*-window.

The user of *Kaestle* may take one of the following roles:

1. An *active* role: A graphic representation can be generated from whatever the user types in, and the user is encouraged in an exploratory style of learning.
2. A *passive* role: An inexperienced user does not know which structures and which operations on them lead to interesting effects. To display prestored examples (or even examples taken from the actual context),

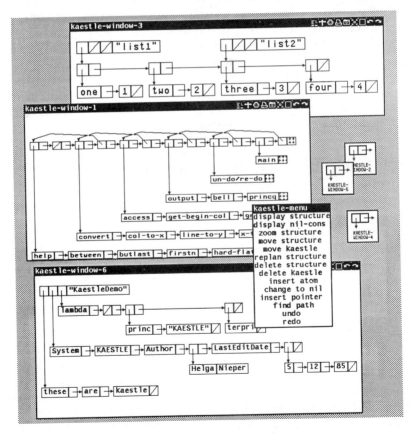

Figure 7.8. *Kaestle*: Visualization of data structures.

Kaestle can be used through a program interface, that is, programs can be written that generate graphic representations in a movielike manner.

Our visualization tools can be used to support different instructional strategies. *Kaestle* supports the graphic display of *data structures* to answer questions like: What are the (list) structures that the system is currently working on? How do they change through the execution of programs?

Kaestle is a tool that can be used by the *LISP-Critic* to illustrate explanations given by the system to answer questions such as the following:

What is the difference between several list creation functions (e.g., cons and list)?

What is the difference between equal and eq?

What is the difference between nondestructive and destructive functions (e.g., append and nconc[2])?

Why is it possible to transform (append (explode word) chars) to (nconc (explode word) chars)?

Why is it wrong to transform (append chars (explode word)) to (nconc chars (explode word))?

Why does nconc not work if the first argument is nil?

How is a stack implemented in *LISP*? What are push and pop doing?

We will adapt these and similar tools to help and explanation systems (see Figure 7.4), augmenting natural language by graphic and movie-like capabilities (Boecker et al., 1986).

KNOWLEDGE-BASED HELP SYSTEMS

Our knowledge-based help systems (for details see Fischer, Lemke, & Schwab, 1984, 1985) have created some of the basic ideas toward our goal to support learning by demand. Passivist, a passive, natural language-based help system, is implemented in OPS5 (Brownston, Farrell, Kant, & Martin, 1985). Flexible parsing using OPS5 is achieved by a rule-based bottom-up method. The consistent structure of the system as a set of productions and a common working memory allows the use of the same knowledge in several stages of the solution process. It uses a help strategy in which each step of the solution is presented and explained to the user, who then executes this step and immediately sees the resulting effects. Help is given as text generated from sentence patterns according to the goal structure of the problem-solving process, and key sequences and subgoals are displayed graphically.

Activist, an active help system for an EMACS-like editor, is implemented in *FranzLISP* and *ObjTalk*. Activist deals with two different kinds of suboptimal behavior. (1) The user does not know a complex command

---

[2] See Figure 7.4.

and uses suboptimal commands to reach a goal (e.g., deletes a string character by character instead of word by word). (2) The user knows the complex command but does not use the minimal key sequence to issue the command (e.g., types the command name instead of hitting the corresponding function key).

Like a human observer, *Activist* handles the following tasks:

Recognize what the user is doing or wants to do.
Evaluate how the user tries to achieve his or her goal.
Construct a model of the user based on the results of the evaluation task.
Decide (dependent on the information in the model) *when* and *how* to interrupt (tutorial intervention).

In *Activist* the recognition and evaluation task is delegated to 20 different *plan specialists* (Figure 7.9).

Each plan specialist recognizes and evaluates one possible plan of the problem domain. Such plans are for example *"deletion of the next word," "positioning to the end of line,"* and so on. A plan specialist consists of: (1) A transition network that matches all the different ways to achieve the plan using the functionality of the editor. Each transition network in the system is independent. The results of a match are the *used editor commands* and the *used keys* to trigger these commands. (2) An expert who knows the optimal plan including the *best editor commands* and the *minimal key sequence* for these commands.

Figure 7.10 displays the user model (consisting of all plan specialists) that *Activist* has built up. For each plan there is a pane that shows the performance of a specific user concerning this plan. Panes with black background indicate that the corresponding plan is currently not monitored by the active help system. A set of heuristics is used to focus the attention

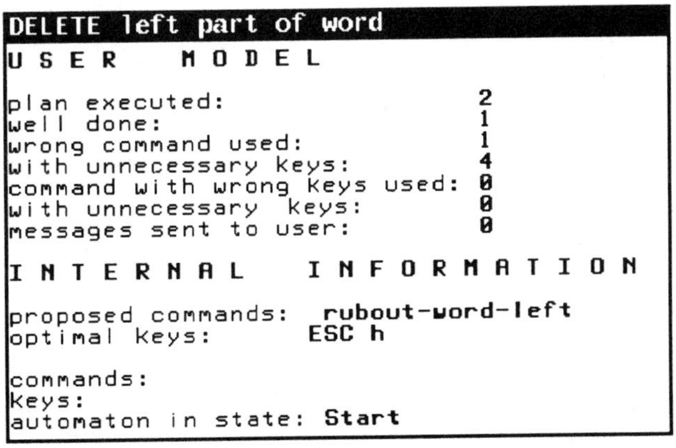

```
DELETE left part of word
U S E R      M O D E L

plan executed:                         2
well done:                             1
wrong command used:                    1
with unnecessary keys:                 4
command with wrong keys used:          0
with unnecessary  keys:                0
messages sent to user:                 0

I N T E R N A L    I N F O R M A T I O N

proposed commands:   rubout-word-left
optimal keys:        ESC h

commands:
keys:
automaton in state: Start
```

FIGURE 7.9. A detailed view of one plan specialist.

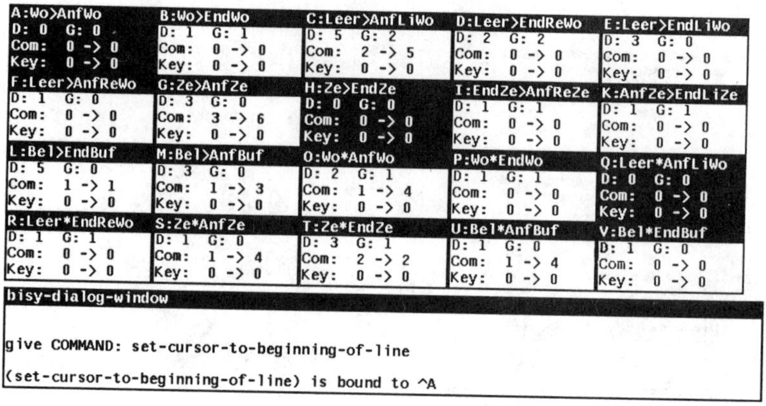

```
A:Wo>AnfWo         B:Wo>EndWo        C:Leer>AnfLiWo    D:Leer>EndReWo    E:Leer>EndLiWo
D: 0   G: 0        D: 1   G: 1       D: 5   G: 2       D: 2   G: 2       D: 3   G: 0
Com:  0 -> 0       Com:  0 -> 0      Com:  2 -> 5      Com:  0 -> 0      Com:  0 -> 0
Key:  0 -> 0       Key:  0 -> 0      Key:  0 -> 0      Key:  0 -> 0      Key:  0 -> 0
F:Leer>AnfReWo     G:Ze>AnfZe        H:Ze>EndZe        I:EndZe>AnfReZe   K:AnfZe>EndLiZe
D: 1   G: 0        D: 3   G: 0       D: 0   G: 0       D: 1   G: 1       D: 1   G: 1
Com:  0 -> 0       Com:  3 -> 6      Com:  0 -> 0      Com:  0 -> 0      Com:  0 -> 0
Key:  0 -> 0       Key:  0 -> 0      Key:  0 -> 0      Key:  0 -> 0      Key:  0 -> 0
L:Bel>EndBuf       M:Bel>AnfBuf      O:Wo*AnfWo        P:Wo*EndWo        Q:Leer*AnfLiWo
D: 5   G: 0        D: 3   G: 0       D: 2   G: 1       D: 1   G: 1       D: 0   G: 0
Com:  1 -> 1       Com:  1 -> 3      Com:  1 -> 4      Com:  0 -> 0      Com:  0 -> 0
Key:  0 -> 0       Key:  0 -> 0      Key:  0 -> 0      Key:  0 -> 0      Key:  0 -> 0
R:Leer*EndReWo     S:Ze*AnfZe        T:Ze*EndZe        U:Bel*AnfBuf      V:Bel*EndBuf
D: 1   G: 1        D: 1   G: 0       D: 3   G: 1       D: 1   G: 0       D: 1   G: 0
Com:  0 -> 0       Com:  1 -> 4      Com:  2 -> 2      Com:  1 -> 4      Com:  0 -> 0
Key:  0 -> 0       Key:  0 -> 0      Key:  0 -> 0      Key:  0 -> 0      Key:  0 -> 0

bisy-dialog-window

give COMMAND: set-cursor-to-beginning-of-line
(set-cursor-to-beginning-of-line) is bound to ^A
```

FIGURE 7.10. The user model of *Activist*.

of the system on the critical issues. The dialogue window at the bottom displays a help message given to the user. He or she has executed the command *set-cursor-to-beginning-of-line* by typing in the command name. *Activist* gives the hint, that this command is also bound to the key *CTRL-A*.

THE CODE-IMPROVER SYSTEM

The *Code-Improver* system (Boecker, 1984) can be used to get ideas on how to improve *LISP* code. The direction of improvements may be either of the following: (1) improvements that make the code more *cognitively* efficient (e.g., more readable or concise); or (2) improvements that make the code more *machine* efficient (e.g., smaller or faster); these improvements include those that can be found in optimizing compilers. The user must choose which kind of suggestions he or she is interested in.

The system is used by two different user groups for two slightly different reasons: (1) It is used by intermediates who want to *learn* how to produce better *LISP* code. We have tested the usefulness of the tool by gathering empirical, statistical data using the students of an introductory *LISP* course as subjects. (2) It is also used by experienced users who want their code to be "straightened out." Instead of doing that by hand (which these users in principle would be able to do), they use a system to carefully reconsider the code they have written. The system is used to detect optimizations and simplifications, and it has proven especially useful with code that is under development and is changed and modified continuously.

The system operates by using a large set of transformation rules (for examples see Figure 7.11) that describe how to improve code. The user's code is matched against these rules, and the transformations suggested by the rules are given to the user; the code is not modified automatically.

Saving Cons Cells

```
(rule append/.1-new.cons.cells-to-nconc/.1...        ;;; the name of the rule
  (?foo:{append appendl}                              ;;;
    (restrict ?expr                                   ;;; the condition
              (cons-cell-generating-expr expr))       ;;;
    ?b)                                               ;;;
  ==>
  ((compute-it:                                       ;;;
    (cdr (assq (get-binding foo)                      ;;;
            '((append . nconc)                        ;;; the action
              (appendl . nconcl)))))                  ;;;
  ?expr ?b)                                           ;;;
  safe (machine))                                     ;;; purpose and validity of the rule
```

Example:
```
(append (cdr (reverse a)) b) ---> (nconc (cdr (reverse a)) b)
```

Avoiding Unnecessary Comparisons

```
(rule eq/equal-predicate-t
  (?foo:{eq = equal}
    (restrict ?expr (predicate-expr expr))
    ?result:{nil t})
  ==>
  ?expr safe (people machine))
```

Example:
```
(eq (numberp a) t) ---> (numberp a)
```

An Unknown Function

```
(rule length.explode/n-to-flatsize
  (length (?foo:{explode exploden} ?a))
  ==>
  (flatsize ?a) safe (machine people))
```

Example:
```
(length (explode a)) ---> (flatsize a)
```

FIGURE 7.11. Some rules of the *Code-Improver* system.

It is important to note that the system is *not* restricted to a specific class of *LISP* functions or application domain. It accepts whatever *LISP* code is given to it. However, there is a trade-off. Because the system does not have any knowledge of specific application areas or algorithms, it is naturally limited in the kind of improvements that derive from its more general knowledge about programming. The improvements suggested by the system are of the following kind:

Suggesting the use of macros (e.g., (setq a (cons b a)) may be replaced by (push b a));

Replacing compound calls of *LISP* functions by simple calls to more powerful functions (e.g., (not (evenp a)) may be replaced by (oddp a));

Specializing functions (e.g., replacing equal by eq); using integer instead of floating point arithmetic wherever possible;

Finding alternative (simpler or faster) forms of conditional or arithmetic expressions;

Eliminating common subexpressions;

Replacing "garbage"-generating expressions by noncopying expressions (e.g., (append (explode word) chars) may be replaced by (nconc (explode word) chars));

Finding and eliminating "dead" code (as in (cond (...) (t...) (dead code)));

(Partial) evaluation of expressions (e.g., (sum a 3 b 4) may be simplified to (sum a b 7)).

The current version of the *Code-Improver* system runs in batch mode. Like the "writer's-workbench" UNIX tools, *diction* and *explain* (Cherry, 1981), it is given a file containing *LISP code and produces suggestions how to improve it.*

Conclusions

The scenario given previously characterizes our goals toward the construction of a *LISP-Critic*; the systems described in the preceding section (entitled Prototypical System Components to Enhance Incremental Learning Processes) serve as important stepping stones toward this goal.

Our approach toward the enhancement of incremental learning processes using knowledge-based systems does the following:

1. It applies the paradigm of ICMs to give people ideas and hints to improve their *LISP* skills.
2. It supports people in "real" working situations by using and *combining different system components for assistance.*
3. It is oriented toward the *intermediate user* who is already involved in his or her own doing and should not be restricted to a particular tutorial sequence or to a very small number of specific case studies.
4. It builds a bridge between *learning by doing* and *guided tutoring and coaching* by trying to combine the best of both worlds.
5. It supports a large variety of instructional strategies and represents a *substantial amount* of knowledge about *LISP* programming.
6. It uses our tools as object and medium (providing us with a large methodological advantage); *LISP* and *ObjTalk* provide a universal framework for representation and are the object of the incremental learning process.
7. It *exploits graphic, aesthetically pleasing interfaces* to illustrate structures and concepts and animate the dynamics of procedures.

Acknowledgements. This paper is based on a joint research effort with my colleagues Heinz-Dieter Boecker, Andreas Lemke, Helga Nieper, and Clayton Lewis, who have made major contributions to the ideas and system components described in this paper. This research was supported by grants from the Office of Naval Research (contract number: N00014-85-K-0842) and the University of Colorado, Boulder.

REFERENCES

Anderson, J. R., Boyle, C. F., Farrell, R., & Reiser, B. (1984). Cognitive principles in the design of computer tutors. In *Proceedings of the sixth annual conference of the Cognitive Science Society* (pp. 2–9). Hillsdale, NJ: Lawrence Erlbaum Assoc.

Boecker, H. D. (1984). *Softwareerstellung als wissensbasierter kommunikations- und designprozess.* Dissertation, Universitaet Stuttgart, Fakultaet für Mathematik und Informatik.

Boecker, H. D., Fischer, G., & Nieper, H. (1986). The enhancement of understanding through visual representations. In *Human factors in computing systems; Computer–human interface (CHI) conference proceedings* (pp. 44–50). New York: Association for Computing Machinery.

Boecker, H. D., & Nieper, H. (1985). Making the invisible visible: Tools for exploratory programming. In *Proceedings of the first pan Pacific computer conference* (pp. 583–579). Melbourne, Australia: The Australian Computer Society.

Brownston, L., Farrell, R., Kant, E., & Martin, N. (1985). *Programming expert systems in OPS5: An introduction to rule-based programming.* Reading, MA: Addison-Wesley.

Burton, R. R., & Brown, J. S. (1982). An investigation of computer coaching for informal learning activities. In D. Sleeman, & J. S. Brown (Eds.), *Intelligent tutoring systems* (pp. 79–98). Orlando, FL: Academic Press.

Burton, R. R., Brown, J. S., & Fischer, G. (1983). Analysis of skiing as a success model of instruction: Manipulating the learning environment to enhance skill acquisition). In B. Rogoff (Ed.), *Everyday cognition: Its development in social context.* Cambridge, MA: Harvard University Press.

Cherry, L. (1981). Computer aids for writers. *Proceedings of the ACM SIGPLAN SIGOA symposium on text manipulation (Portland, Oregon) SIGPLAN Notices, 16*(6), 61–67.

Fischer, G. (1981). Computational models of skill acquisition processes. In *Computers in education, 3rd world conference on computers and education* (pp. 477–481). Lausanne, Switzerland:

Fischer, G. (1984). Formen und funktionen von modellen in der mensch-computer kommunikation. In H. Schauer & M. J. Tauber (Eds.), *Psychologie der Computerbenutzung, Schriftenreihe der Oesterreichischen Computer Gesellschaft* (Vol. 22, pp. 328–343). Wien, Muenchen: Oldenbourg Verlag.

Fischer, G., Burton, R. R., & Brown, J. S. (1978). Analysis of skiing as a success model of instruction: Manipulating the learning environment to enhance skill acquisition. In *Proceedings of the second national conference of the Canadian Society for Computational Studies of Intelligence.*

Fischer, G., Lemke, A., & Schwab, T. (1984). Active help systems. In *Proceedings of the second European conference on cognitive ergonomics: Mind and computers.* New York: Springer-Verlag.

Fischer, G., Lemke, A., & Schwab, T. (1985). Knowledge-based help systems. In *Human factors in computing systems, Computer–human interface (CHI) conference proceedings* (pp. 161–167). New York: Association for Computing Machinery.

Johnson, W. L., & Soloway, E. (1984). PROUST: Knowledge-based program understanding. In *Proceedings of the seventh international conference on software engineering* (pp. 369–380).

Lemke, A. C. (1985). *ObjTalk84 reference manual* (Technical Report CU-CS-291-85). Boulder: University of Colorado.

Norman, D. (1982). Some observations on mental models. In D. Gentner, & A. Stevens (Eds.), *Mental models* (pp. 7–14). Hillsdale, NJ: Lawrence Erlbaum Assoc.

Papert, S. (1980). *Mindstorms: Children, computers and powerful ideas.* New York: Basic Books.

Rathke, C. (1986). *ObjTalk: Repraesentation von Wissen in einer objektorientierten Sprache.* Unpublished doctoral dissertation, Universitaet Stuttgart, Fakultaet für Mathematik und Informatik.

Rathke, C., & Lemke, A. C. (1985). *ObjTalk primer* (Technical Report CU-CS-290-85). Boulder: University of Colorado.

Rich, C., & Shrobe, H. E. (1978). Initial report on a Lisp programmer's apprentice, *IEEE Transactions on Software Engineering, SE-4*(6), 456–467.

Sleeman. D., & Brown, J. S. (Eds.), (1982). *Intelligent tutoring systems. Computer and people series.* Orlando, FL: Academic Press.

Wilensky, R., Arens, Y., & Chin, D. (1984). Talking to UNIX in English: An overview of UC. *Communications of the ACM, 27,* 574–593.

8

Mental Models and Metaphors: Implications for the Design of Adaptive User–System Interfaces

NORBERT A. STREITZ*

This chapter addresses two main issues. The first grew out of the observation that there is no agreed-on terminology for the different aspects and connotations of "model" in human–computer interaction research. Investigating the concept of "model" led to some new distinctions and to a classification schema that accounts for all possible concepts and combinations of different models. Moreover, this classification has a number of implications for how to go about systems design, for example, of adaptive user–system interfaces, and of tutoring systems.

The second issue concerns a problem-solving framework for representing human–computer interaction. We start out with this framework, and we use it all along in our discussion of the various models. It is relevant to our thesis on cognitive compatibility and in the sections on metaphors as communicators of conceptual models.

Different Purposes of Tutoring Systems

The term *intelligent tutoring systems* is applicable in at least three areas depending on the purpose they serve. Accordingly, three classes of intelligent tutoring systems should be distinguished.

The first-class, intelligent computer-assisted instruction (ICAI) is a kind of reborn old-fashioned computer-assisted instruction (CAI) that tries—it is hoped successfully—to avoid the mistakes that have been made in the past. (For a critical evaluation of CAI systems see, e.g., Nievergelt, 1975). Recently, the term "intelligent" has been used quite frequently, presumably to indicate that the new systems are comparable to a human tutor and

* Present address: Institute for Integrated Publication and Information Systems Gesellschaft für Mathematik und Datenverarbeitung (GMD) Postfach 104326 D-6100 Darmstadt, F.R. Germany.

to stimulate associations with artificial intelligence systems. The function of this kind of systems is to convey knowledge about a subject matter area to a learner. Their designers claim that such a system serves as a vehicle or tool for doing this in an "intelligent" way. This defines the most general class of tutoring systems.

Being hesitant to apply the term "intelligent" to a technical system, we prefer labels like knowledge-based tutoring system (KBTS) or adaptive tutoring system (ATS). In this context "knowledge" refers to the knowledge a system has about different domains and about the learner. The kind of knowledge concerns the following:

1. The domain of reality (e.g., physics, geography, programming)
2. The tutoring process (derived from a theory of teaching)
3. The learner (also with reference to his or her role as a user of a system)
4. The interaction process (modeling human–computer interaction).

About which of these aspects is a (tutoring) system supposed to be "intelligent," that is, "knowledgeable"? One hopes, of course, about all of them. But there is still a long way to go to achieve this goal. Our contribution is concerned with the third and fourth aspects, that is, the conditions of implementing knowledge in the user–system interface of tutoring systems.

The second class of systems is a subset of knowledge-based tutoring systems whose subject matter domain is any aspect of using an interactive computer system. Thus, the domain to be studied by the learner might be programming, text editing, graphics and spread sheet applications, or even a tutoring system. (Users must learn how to use tutoring systems, too.) The common elements of using interactive systems could be taught by a very "user-friendly" tutoring system. On the other hand the tutoring system might be a component of a larger computer system or application software package, thus dramatically extending elementary help functions available with present systems.

There is an important difference between learning about physics with a tutoring system and learning to use an application program running on a system. In the second case the vehicle of learning is identical with or contains the system to be tutored about. The consequence is that the learner —after successful learning—can apply the just-acquired knowledge on the same system that tutored him before. This will have a large impact on the motivational side of learning. In contrast learning physics with a tutoring system leads to leaving the tutoring system to apply the acquired knowledge in a new situation or context.

The third class of tutoring systems includes all kinds of help facilities, on-line manuals, and so on. This refers to a situation where the main goal is to use a computer system in some work activity. Being tutored or aided by the system is only an additional option. The latter aspect requires interaction with the tutorial component of the application program. Only in

those cases where the user is a new and/or casual user or is not able to continue his or her work (e.g., lacking knowledge about a certain command or procedure) will he or she draw on the tutoring system. There are again different ways how this help component might serve the user. Passive help systems can be called up by the user if he or she gets stuck, makes an error, or wants to find a better way to accomplish his or her work. Active help systems analyze and diagnose the interaction of the user and provide help—at appropriate points in time—in an adaptive way without being asked to do so (see G. Fischer, Chapter 7 in this volume).

All three categories of tutoring systems require a user–system interface that is specially oriented to the capabilities and needs of the users.

The users of the first category are not interested in or even concerned with learning how to use a tutoring system but with acquiring some knowledge about a content domain. They expect the tutoring system to take the initiative and are rather willing to follow through the various sections of the program. In addition they require that it be tailored to their specific needs. Thus, the interface must concentrate on content-related terminology and interaction modes.

For the second category learning how to use a particular application is of major concern. Again, the tutoring system for learning how to interact cannot expect any system-specific skills on the side of the user. Still, there is the advantage of having control over the sequence and units the learner will follow when starting with the tutoring system. For these cases one can assume that the learner is willing to follow, at least to a certain degree, a "guided tour" or other learning procedure proposed by the tutoring system.

In the third category one must take into account that turning to a tutorial or help component while using an application program is very different from the preceding two cases. There is no attempt by the user to learn systematically about the system but only to get (help) information on a very specific detail during the current interaction. When and where the user will call on the tutorial/help component is unpredictable. The user takes the initiative and is free to continue or to stop. Therefore, a very different strategy is necessary: having the user ask "correct questions" and then conveying the requested information as an "appropriate answer" to the user's question. Of course, this is different when dealing with active and adaptive help systems.

A Problem-Solving Framework for Human–Computer Interaction

In this section we outline a framework suited to describing human–computer interaction. Two major aspects are common to all three kinds of systems. (1) The learner's goal is to acquire knowledge about the domain

of study (e.g., physics), which we will call the *content domain*. Accordingly, the learner is confronted with what we shall call the *content problem*. (2) In order to acquire new knowledge, the learner must interact with an external source of information—in this case the tutoring system. This kind of interaction might be novel or at least different from the experience with a human tutor. In any case the user is confronted with an additional problem we shall call the *interaction problem*.

The distinction in describing user–system interfaces is part of a *problem-solving model of human–computer interaction* (proposed by Streitz, 1985a, 1985b; 1986a). Figure 8.1 shows a graphic representation of the relevant components of the model adapted to a learning or tutoring situation. Without going into much detail, we sketch only the underlying idea.

We start out with the assumption that the *learner* is set to acquire new knowledge about a given domain. Thus, he or she must build up a knowledge representation of the content domain by connecting new information to already existing pieces of information in his or her knowledge base. The new information is stored in the tutoring system as a representation of the domain in question (e.g., physics) and as certain procedures that control different ways of providing this information (content-specific tutoring strategies or didactic rules). The important thing to notice here is that the learner has no direct access to this knowledge base of the system. In order to obtain information from the system, the *learner* has to take the role of a *user* of an interactive system. Thus, he or she is confronted with the interaction problem, which requires that the learner—as a user—must build up a representation of the tutoring system, too. Reciprocally, the

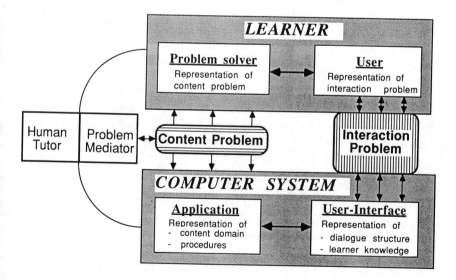

FIGURE 8.1. A problem-solving model of human–computer interaction.

computer system must have a component that represents the learner as a user or a member of a class of users. This representation (sometimes called *user model*, but see my comments on this terminology in the next section) should be related to the dialogue structure chosen for this type of interaction. Of course, there are many more details to this; we later return to the implications of the distinction between the *content problem* and the *interaction problem*.

As one can see from this description of the situation, the concept of representation is central. This is not new, but what has not been recognized is that different ways of designing systems have arisen from different views of the notion of representations or models. Therefore, this chapter addresses this question in more detail.

Another point must be mentioned. In addition to "learner" and "system," Figure 8.1 shows two more components, a *problem mediator* and a *human tutor*. The first reflects the fact that all too often the learner does not learn strictly on his or her own initiative but because some person (teacher, friend, employer) proposes a topic to be studied. This person functions as a problem mediator, that is, someone who conveys the content problem to the learner by suggesting an area or asking specific questions about a content domain. Especially in work situations where the superior gives an order or a task to be carried out by the employee, problem mediation plays an important role. The consequences are that the problem solver has to solve a problem that has been conveyed to him by somebody else. The conveyed formulation of the problem results in a new problem representation of the original problem. The encoding component of problem solving, however, which is based on text comprehension processes, depends on the specific conditions in which the problem is given. Thus, the learner might begin with a nonappropriate initial representation of the original problem, resulting in inadequate problem-solving strategies (Streitz, 1983, 1986b) and in some circumstances even in failure to find a solution.

The second additional component in Figure 8.1, the human tutor, also requires comment. It reflects the state of the art of existing systems. So far, most of them still need someone to introduce and to explain the system to the learner. In most cases this is because there still is a major "interaction problem" caused by an inappropriate learner–system interface (see also our previous comments on different categories of tutoring systems). With respect to the content problem, a human tutor seems to be desirable, too, providing guidance and additional information not available from the system. Sometimes we find the functions of a problem mediator and a human tutor combined in one person. For the future, of course, one should aim at a self-contained tutoring system that does not require a human tutor. Having mentioned different representations and models, one is ready to ask: Which models? Where do they come from? How do they relate to each other?

The Mental Model "Zoo"

In an often-quoted article, Norman (1983) makes "some observations on mental models." Starting out with a *target system*, *t*, he distinguishes between a *conceptual model, C(t)*, of that target, the user's *mental model, M(t)*, and a *scientist's conceptualization, C(M(t))*, of this mental model. Furthermore, he introduces the notion of a *system image*, that is, the image of the system seen by the user. The system image is a kind of surface representation presented to the user but based on C(t). The system image is the result of the design process, and it should be consistent with the instruction manuals and the teaching of the system. In this way Norman (1983) hopes, the mental model that the user builds up about the system will be consistent with C(t). One should add that in most cases of commercially available systems there is—for various reasons—no correspondence among the three models.

In a later discussion of these issues, Norman (1986) introduces a new terminology. He considers the following three concepts: (1) The conceptualization of the system held by the designer, called the *design model*; (2) the conceptual model constructed by the user, called the *user's model*; (3) the *system image* resulting from the *physical* structure that has been built (including documentation and instructions).

The first two are those that have been called *mental models*. In this context Norman (1986) remarks in a footnote that there is also another meaning of the term *user model*: a "typical user" model that the designer develops about the user to help in the formulation of the "design model." Norman admits to jumping between these meanings. Finally, he mentions the user model an "intelligent" program might construct of the person interacting with a system.

As one can see, the terminology used so far is ambiguous. Things become worse when we turn to other notions of "mental model" in the literature. Although we do not intend to provide a review of all, we mention some usages of the term "model" before proposing our own formal notation.

Young (1983) uses the term *user's conceptual model* (UCM) as "a more or less definite representation or metaphor that a user adopts to guide his actions and help him interpret the device's behavior." This corresponds to Norman's mental model M(t) in the 1983 version or his user's model in the 1986 version. Young (1983) remarks also that the designer and the psychologist may have different versions of the UCM—an aspect we elaborate in more detail in the section on higher order models. Furthermore, Young lists kinds of mental models, stressing differences in their nature or—as we view his list—in the theoretical framework used to describe them.

Carroll (1984) starts his overview of mental models with these statements: "Mental models are structures and processes imputed to a person's

mind in order to account for that person's behavior and experience. Ideally speaking, a mental model is a psychological theory that could give answers ..." (p. 1). In a further step he distinguishes between "the designer's model (that is, the understanding that the analyst develops of what it is that the user knows)" (p. 1) from the user's model. There is also a prescriptive sense of designer's model, namely, "the model that the user *should* acquire and refer to in using the designer's software" (p. 1).

At first glance Carroll's (1984) statements seem to mix the user's mental model and the psychological theory about this model. He tries to circumvent this problem by introducing the distinction between "model" as the object of a psychological investigation and "analysis" as the product of this investigation. (The same problem arises when Young, 1983, lists examples of both categories together in one list.) Later Carroll (1984) discusses the "user's conceptual model," thus being complete in using all available terms.

In the next section in order to resolve the confusion about what is what in this mental model "zoo," we introduce a formal notation derived from four basic categories. This framework provides a stringent classification of all possible "model" concepts appearing in this context.

In general we use the term *mental model* for an idiosyncratic, very personal model a user has about a given (technical) domain. You can think of it as a "subjective" knowledge representation about the domain. The term "subjective" is meant here to indicate that it does not have to be in agreement with an objective, scientific description of this domain. For the latter we reserve the term *conceptual model* developed by scientists and designers reflecting about the system and the user in a systematic way. Very often the conceptual model is expressed by means of a formal notation.

Of course, one must keep in mind that all models exist as mental models, that is, they are "in the head" of a person. Thus, a conceptual model also exists as a mental model. The difference is that conceptual models can be externalized and communicated in a standardized and systematic way. On the other hand "scientific" people also use personal mental models when actually working with an interactive system. Their mental models, one hopes, are then based on the correct conceptual model. Designers who are using a system not familiar to them, however, are in principle in the same position as everybody else. Their mental models may then show the characteristics of mental models listed by Norman (1983) for naive users: incompleteness, instability, unscientificness and overparsimoniousness. In the following section we systematize the different views of mental and conceptual models and introduce a new starting point for this discussion.

From Target System to Functionality

In his observations on mental models, Norman (1983) started out with a target system, **t**, leaving details of it more or less unspecified. Earlier we

observed that one must distinguish—at least—between the system's representation of the content domain and of the dialogue structure. Thus, one should start "earlier" or "at a lower level" than with the totality of an existing system.

A computer system is supposed to serve some purpose, that is, carry out actions by following given instructions. The user wants the system's actions to provide certain functions that aid him in achieving his primary goal within a given work or learning situation. This might be to write an article, to calculate his or her finances, to get information about the best ways to cross the Atlantic, to construct a piece of equipment, to paint a picture, to learn about the basic laws of physics, to learn how to use a new statistics package on the central computer system, and so on. Therefore, we propose to begin with the notion of an abstract *function*, *f*, as the *functionality* or the functional principle underlying an application program.[1] Examples of these basic functions can be derived from the preceding examples of goals people have: write, draw, correct (text, graphics), calculate, search, store, retrieve, compare (information), learn, and so on.

The next step is to consider a (computer) system that provides this functionality. Using a particular software running on a particular hardware configuration leads to what we will call S(f), the *system's realization* or implementation of the basic functionality. The user is thus confronted with a particular text-editing system, a spread-sheet program, an information retrieval system, a tutorial system on physics, and so on. (Within the context of this article, we refrain from discussing aspects of different hardware configurations and input–output devices, concentrating on the cognitive aspects of using an interactive computer system, i.e., software human factors or cognitive ergonomics.) To a certain degree S(f) might be identified with what Norman (1983, 1986) called the system image, although one probably has to differentiate here between the internal (hardware/software) implementation and the external surface presentation at the user–system interface.

The relevance of this distinction between f and S(f) will become more obvious as we go along. But dealing with tutoring systems in this volume, one can already see its relevance by observing that it has been shown that the acquisition of a particular skill or function is very much dependent on the given device, that is, a particular S(f). Learning addition with your 10 fingers is different from learning with paper and pencil, with a slide rule, or with a pocket calculator. By contrasting these different devices, I do not mean to refer to their "surface differences" in hardware but to the more fundamental differences in the conceptual model, leading to different im-

---

[1] In an earlier publication (Streitz, 1985a) on this topic, we used the letter *t* [from the original "target"] for the function as well. In order to avoid confusion, we prefer now *f* for the basic functionality.

plementations $S_i(f)$. This leads us naturally to the consideration of conceptual models and mental models.

But before introducing them, we still must mention two other aspects. First, one must think about the implications of introducing such a concept as an abstract function or functionality, f. Critics could argue that there "is" or "exists" no function f without a realization, $S(f)$. How then do we identify the purpose of a given device that we have not seen before but that performs a particular function familiar to us? One must assume that people are able to abstract the basic features of a function from their experience with a variety of system realizations, $S_i(f)$. In this way they arrive at a definition of the underlying abstract functional principle. (The admittedly simple position we take here does not concern itself with a discussion of the deeper philosophical issues involved.) At the same time a person's opinion of the defining features of a basic function may change with experience of a variety of very different system realizations. This leads to the user's mental model of f, $U(f)$.

Second, the transition $f \rightarrow S(f)$ implies that one again must consider the distinction between content problem and interaction problem. The content problem refers to the fact that a particular $S(f)$ provides a particular range of the functionality, f. It might be that not all possible aspects of f are implemented. On the other hand a particular system's realization, $S(f)$, also implies a particular interaction mode.

Take the example of "to calculate" and an artificial case of realizing this function—just to clarify the point. One realization might provide only addition and subtraction. If the user wants to do multiplication, he or she must transform the original task in terms of the provided possibilities, that is, repeated addition. Thus, the content problem results from different realizations of a given functionality and its domain in relation to doing the original task. This is different from the interaction problem resulting from the particular interaction mode and presentation of information chosen within one $S(f)$. Possible interaction modes might be typing a command line, thus specifying the operation (addition) and the objects (numbers) or clicking with a mouse device on the buttons of a calculator visually presented on the screen.

We consider now mental and conceptual models of the function, f. In order to indicate whose *mental model* we refer to, we use $U(f)$ for the *user's mental model* of f. By this model of the basic functionality, f, we mean the user's subjective representation of f as an abstraction that is based on his or her prior experience with a variety of realizations, $S_i(f)$. This is a different concept from the mental model mentioned by the other authors cited previously (Norman and Carroll). What they refer to is—in our terminology —$U(S(f))$, that is, the user's mental model of a particular system's realization. We discuss this model in the next section as an example of *second-order models*—as we call this type of model.

For *conceptual models* it seems important to us to distinguish between models by *designers*, D(f), and those by *psychologists*, P(f) (or ergonomists, human factors people). The differentiation is meant to account for the differences between conceptual models of a function to be implemented via S(f) and those models that appear in psychological theories and investigations of user's mental models. This distinction accounts also for differences in conceptualizations one can often observe in discussions between psychologists and system designers. The differences may not be prominent in discussions of the function f itself, but they become increasingly relevant at the level of second-order models (see the next section).

Thus, we must consider the four models U(f), S(f), D(f), and P(f). They represent four different perspectives of a given functionality, f, as illustrated in Figure 8.2.

It is important to realize that in principle the system's implementation, S(f), may not necessarily be in correspondence with D(f), although it is based on it. This will be the case because of additional boundary conditions for the whole system's design. Having this in mind, from now on we consider D(f) as the complete basis for S(f).

In addition one must note that the argument for S(f) with respect to the content and interaction problems is valid in the same way for the other three models. Let us look, for example, at the user's mental model U(f) of the function "to write." It has one part that represents the abstract concept of "writing," with features related to language, word meaning, correct syntax, orthography, and so on. It also has a representation of the

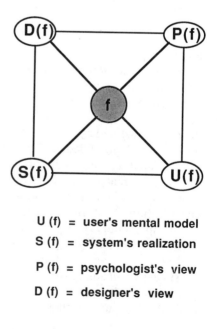

U (f) = user's mental model

S (f) = system's realization

P (f) = psychologist's view

D (f) = designer's view

FIGURE 8.2. Four perspectives of the functionality, f.

interaction aspect, consisting of features related to the situations of and tools for writing. For example, writing with a stick in the sand at the beach would be less prominently represented than writing with a pen on paper or using a typewriter. Similar statements can be made for the designer's and the psychologist's model.

Higher Order Models in Human–Computer Interaction

The situation illustrated in Figure 8.2 can also be described in terms of four operators, S, U, D, and P, and one operand, f, thus considering the different models (mental, conceptual, etc.) as the result of different mappings. From now on we will identify these by the term *first-order models*. Of course, one must observe that S, the system, is an operator that is somehow different from the three operators associated with people.

SECOND-ORDER MODELS

Extending the approach in a natural way, we arrive at *second-order models* by applying the operators S, U, D, and P on the operands S(f), U(f), D(f), and P(f).

Figure 8.3 shows all 16 combinations resulting from this operation as well as the 4 first-order models. Not all of them are equally relevant, but the classification matrix provides a complete picture of the situation. It is especially useful when we continue this approach by extending to models of the third and fourth order. We now discuss these models and their meaning in detail.

Let us first look at the elements in the diagonal of the 4 × 4 matrix of Figure 8.3. They are marked by an asterisk because this combination is of a very special nature. There are good reasons to label them "self-reflection" because an expression like U(U(f)) denotes the model a user has about his own mental model—a kind of metacognition. Of course, it is open for discussion whether S(S(f)) is—beyond formal arguments—a well-defined or justified expression. In any case it seems to make sense to introduce a slightly modified expression, S'(S(f)). This can be interpreted as a self-explanatory component of the system that provides information about the system's realization of the function, f, to the user. In other words this represents the help/tutorial component of a system. With reference to our classification of tutoring systems in the introduction, this is the third class of tutoring system.

Having clarified this special aspect, we now turn to the model that is central for our considerations, U(S(f)), that is, the *user's mental model of the system's realization of the function, f*. This is the model the user refers to when actually interacting with a system. The structure and quality of U(S(f)) is built up and then modified by interacting with the actual system,

Operator / Operand	S	U	P	D	Models of
f	++	++	++	++	1. order
S(f)	*	++	+	+	
U(f)	++	*	++	++	
P(f)	-	0	*	+	2. order
D(f)	-	+	+	*	

++ = very relevant, + = relevant, 0 = not relevant,
* = self reflection, - = does not exist (yet)

FIGURE 8.3. Classification of first- and second-order models in human–computer interaction.

reading manuals, and the like. During the acquisition phase, however, it is also determined by the mental model of his or her general idea about f, that is, U(f). The user compares his or her existing U(f) with the behavior of S(f), noticing similarities and contradictions. Thus, U(f) is especially important in the process of learning to use a new, unfamiliar system. In this phase U(S(f)) is very limited in range, unstable, and undergoes changes by incorporating new experiences with the system's behavior. The "poor" model is becoming enriched in a dynamic and interactive way. Later on, when the novice user is becoming more of an expert, the interaction will become controlled by a more complete, definite, and rather stable U(S(f)). Of course, this model is more elaborate and, hopefully, consistent with S(f) than that in the beginning. (We refrain at this point from indicating changes in time in our formal notation, but they definitely exist.)

On the other hand consider a user who became exposed to a variety of different $S_i(f)$ and consequently has acquired a number of $U(S_i(f))$. On the basis of them, the user constructs his or her U(f). In a next step the user will keep this U(f) as a common kernel of his or her knowledge representation and in addition a number of special rules accounting for the specific differences of the different systems, $S_i(f)$. Accordingly, in case of problems with the actual system, the user will "consult" his knowledge base derived from prior experience with different realizations, $S_i(f)$.

Also for the second-order models, we must consider the two aspects of content and interaction. By this time we are in a position to account for situations where somebody might be knowledgeable about the content domain and therefore has an appropriate mental model of it but is very deficient in his or her knowledge about using the interface of a particular system.

When interacting with S(f) and comparing it with his or her U(f), the user also makes inferences about the designer's conceptual model, D(f), as the basis of S(f). That is, the user develops a U(D(f)). Especially when encountering differences between S(f) and U(f), the user expresses this by asking him or herself such questions as "what might the designer have had in mind when designing the sequence of interaction this way?" U(D(f)) exists apart from U(S(f)) and stores the user's rationale of why the system might have been designed this way. It might help him to make inferences about the potential behavior of S(f) in situations where the system itself does not provide any clues.

The next two important second-order models are *conceptualization of the user's mental model:* D(U(f)) as the designer's and P(U(f)) as the psychologist's point of view about what users' mental models are like. Since at this level the operand is U(f) and not U(S(f))—this will be dealt with by third-order models—these are conceptualizations of users' general models about a certain function, f. They are aiming at the typical user and are meant to help in the formulation of the designer's model D(S(f)) of a new S(f) based on D(f) and thus, hopefully, on U(f). We will say more about the development process in the section on adaptive systems. The conceptual models are different from each other because of different techniques used to obtain them and their different purposes. We argue that P(U(f)) is based on psychological theories and empirical data about human cognition, whereas D(U(f)) results very often from designers' considering themselves and/or their colleagues as users and generalizing their introspections and impressions to novices and casual users. This kind of generalization is very often misleading for designing a system for nonexperts. On the other hand it should be noted that the format of the P(U(f)) models is not always suited to direct use for system design. Obviously, all this leads to very different ideas about the user and gives rise to controversies when discussing design issues between psychologists or human factors people and designers. Their controversies also result from differences in their opinions about each other, that is, D(P(f)) and P(D(f)). In any case one should aim at a cooperative approach because it is still the designer who does the implementation, although one observes fluid boundaries between the two.

Finally, the second-order model S(U(f))—that is, the model a system builds up about the user's mental model—is important for every adaptive system. The system, however, is not able to record and diagnose the user's general mental model, U(f), but only the specific mental model, U(S(f)), exhibited in the interaction with a particular system, S(f), resulting in

$S'(U(S(f)))$. This leads us to the terminology and classification of third-order models.

THIRD-ORDER MODELS

Now we consider the situation where a system, $S(f)$, has been built and a user develops a particular mental model, $U(S(f))$, by interacting with the system. This model is now the object of investigation, that is, it is considered as an operand for the operators introduced before. This procedure leads naturally to the next level of models, that is, *third-order models*. Considering all combinations of the second-order models as possible operands and the four operators, we get 64 models at this level. We discuss only a subset.

Psychologists and designers investigate the structure of $U(S(f))$, which results in $P(U(S(f)))$ and $D(U(S(f)))$. These models represent what psychologists and designers have in mind when they talk about how to consider mental models in evaluating existing user–system interfaces. Again, it is important to note that these models will be different from each other, depending on the kind of procedures and methods used for investigation and conceptualization. In addition they are not investigated in an isolated way but are judged on the basis of existing $P(S(f))$ and $P(f)$, $D(S(f))$ and $D(f)$, respectively. This aspect of design, that is, judging and evaluating mental models by comparing them with existing conceptual models (at different levels) and vice versa, has so far not been addressed in research on human–computer interaction. But it seems to be one of the important things to do if we take the objective of *user-oriented system design* seriously (see Streitz, 1987). This remark is especially true when one does not believe—and I do not—in the "pure goal" that only the mental model of the user will serve as the basis for the design of a system. As we will also see in our discussion of metaphors, there must always be a compromise between the various parties involved in the design process.

Another important third-order model is $S'(U(S(f)))$, which was already briefly mentioned. Of course, the system itself has no intention of analyzing the user's mental model. This terminology serves only to indicate that there is an automatic recording of the user's interaction with the system and that certain parameters are used for describing his or her behavior. There are different objectives for doing this.

One objective is to obtain data that are different from measures like "time on task" or thinking-aloud protocols and interviews. In this case the data are used for building (cognitive) models of the individual user in order to use this information for answering basic research questions or when designing a new version of the system or a completely new system.

Another objective goes beyond this and concerns the use of these data for providing adaptive help information to the user, for example, when the user is stuck or even for adapting the system to the current state of the

user (see the section entitled The Role of Models in Adaptive Systems). In real work or school situations this monitoring could also be used to control the user's or learner's performance at a very detailed level. Problems connected with this possibility—increasingly discussed by the unions in Europe—depend on the way this information is used by supervisors having access to these data. There are different proposals to keep the potential advantage of recording these data and at the same time circumvent the potential dangers of too much control. One example is for each user to have a personal disk where these data are stored. The disk would be carried around by the user, and no one else would have access to it.

Although it might be of less importance, one can continue to the next level, that is, to *fourth-order models*. For example, a user and a psychologist have a discussion about the user's mental model of a given system, that is, about their conceptualizations of this model. The objects of the conversation, then, are the user's self reflection, $U'(U(S(f)))$, and the psychologist's conceptualization, $P(U(S(f)))$. Since those are third-order models, communication about them results in fourth-order models. The same is true for a user who talks with a designer about a given system, his or her mental models, and ways to change the design in accordance with the user's mental model.

In summary of the last two sections, we can state that the notational framework derived from taking four different perspectives on the function, f, and extending them to multiple levels (higher order models) provides us with a clear-cut and complete classification schema of all combinations of models in this context. In the following sections, especially in that on adaptive systems, we see further applications of this framework.

Cognitive Compatibility and Adaptive User–System Interfaces

COMPATIBILITY AND USER ORIENTATION

The previous discussion of mental and conceptual models together with the fundamental role of knowledge representations in cognitive psychology suggests the importance of the relationship between the following models: $D(f)$, $S(f)$, $U(f)$, and $U(S(f))$.

Applying results from investigations in other areas of the relevance of initial knowledge representations for the processes and success of problem solving (Streitz, 1983, 1986b), we can formulate the following thesis regarding the extent of user orientation of systems as a demand for maximizing *cognitive compatibility* (Streitz, 1987).

An interactive computer system is more user-oriented when fewer discrepancies exist between the relevant knowledge representations (models) on either side of the interface. We consider discrepancies both before the

interaction (between S(f) and U(f)) and during the interaction (between S(f) and U(S(f))). This thesis requires some comment. In order to achieve compatibility, there must first be compatibility between D(f) and U(f). This means that the designer must take into account the user's general mental model about a function f before f is realized in the system. By our thesis, the precondition for compatibility between S(f) and U(f) is compatibility between D(f) and U(f). If this is achieved then the user will be able to develop an appropriate U(S(f)) that is compatible with the actual structure of S(f).

There are some problems with the application of this thesis to functions in a system where a user has no corresponding U(f). This will be the case with computer-specific functions that have no equivalent in the "outside" world. At this point the idea of providing metaphors for certain functions becomes relevant and critical at the same time. We discuss this in our section on metaphors.

THE ROLE OF MODELS IN ADAPTIVE SYSTEMS

If one intends to construct this kind of system, one should first specify whether one considers *adaptivity* or *adaptability*. The difference can easily be described within our framework. A system is *adaptable* when it allows the user ("the user as a designer") to transform an existing realization $S_i(f)$ into another realization $S_{i+1}(f)$. The index i points either to a sequence in time or to different versions of realization. This kind of *adaptable* system is easier to realize than *adaptive* systems because it does not require a component that models the user. It is very valuable to provide the possibility of configuring your system to your own preferences and progressing expertise. Adaptable systems, however, require the user to diagnose his or her own learning progress and to select an appropriate modification.

Adaptable systems differ from *adaptive systems*, which adapt themselves to characteristics of the user. In order to provide this function, they must be able to record and diagnose the behavior of users while interacting with the system. Based on an analysis of these data, the system represents the user in terms of a model, that is, $S'(U(S(f)))$. One must use this model and not $S(U(f))$, because the analysis is based on data from the interaction with a particular system's realization, S(f). It is not possible to diagnose the more general U(f) from the interaction with only one system, because this would require data on interactions with several different implementations, $S_i(f)$, of the function, f. (This subtle but important distinction is rarely made in the literature but arises naturally within our framework.)

In addition $S'(U(S(f)))$ must be conceptualized in a rather dynamic fashion because it must account also for the learning process of the user. This does not mean that it must be modified continuously but at a given rate of time or interaction units. The situation can be described as follows.

Adaptive systems react on the diagnosis of an identified $U_{i+1}(S_i(f))$,

which is evaluated as a change in relation to an earlier diagnosed $U_i(S_i(f))$ by offering a modified version $S_{i+1}(f)$ which, it is hoped, matches (corresponds) better with the just encountered $U_{i+1}(S_i(f))$. For implementation of such a system, one must specify the rate of diagnosis, measures of correspondence between $U(S(f))$ and $S(f)$ (cognitive compatibility), and rules of adaptation. There are still a number of problems on these aspects from the conceptual point of view as well as with the technical implementation. Other contributions in this volume address these questions in more detail.

Adaptive systems might—but do not need to—include a help or tutorial component offering additional information on the user's behavior and explanations of why a modification occurred. This is very close to the nature of the component we labeled earlier in the section entitled Second-Order Models as $S'(S(f))$.

With reference to another model entered in the diagonal of the classification matrix in Figure 8.3, we introduced earlier on a higher level $U'(U(S(f)))$ as the self-reflection of the user on his own mental model of $S(f)$. Feedback and tutorial information have to take this as a starting point, because by probing the self-reflection process of the user one can access and modify the mental model $U(S(f))$. This has a number of implications for all kinds of introductory and training courses.

Metaphors as Communicators of Conceptual Models

After our discussion of different types of models in human–computer interaction and our proposal of a classification schema, there seems to be no doubt about the relevance of mental and conceptual models for the design of user-oriented interactive systems. The general demand for cognitive compatibility and adaptive systems seems to show the direction. We are left with the following two questions, however: (1) What models should be used as conceptual models for systems design? (2) How do we communicate the conceptual model to the prospective user so that he or she can develop a compatible mental model of the system?

From the earlier discussion of cognitive compatibility, it seems to follow that the conceptual model, $D(f)$, leading to $D(S(f))$ should be *compatible* with the general mental model, $U(f)$, and with features of $U(S_i(f))$, the model the user has about the basic functions the system is supposed to realize. Of course, compatibility must be precisely defined in terms of the features of those objects and relations under consideration. We will return to this subject.

As for question 2, if the conceptual model, $D(f)$, is completely compatible with the prospective user's mental model, $U(f)$, there seems to be no need to communicate details of it to the user. One must only indicate which model was chosen as the basis for the system's design and no need exists to invent a new $D(S(f))$. Although this answer seems to be too

simple to be true, it has some heuristic value in terms of showing where to look.

The idea of using *metaphors* started from this idea, that is, trying to communicate a particular conceptual model by providing a description in terms of objects and operations familiar to the prospective user. This approach has been proposed and discussed within the last years in various ways. It is beyond the scope of this article to review the metaphor literature at this point (see e.g., Carroll & Mack, 1985; Carroll & Thomas, 1982). For a general discussion of the role of metaphors in thinking we refer to Ortony (1979), for related aspects of analogies to Douglas and Moran (1983), Gentner (1985), Gentner and Gentner (1983); and Halasz and Moran (1982). The implementation of this approach is best exemplified by the desk-top metaphor (e.g., Smith et al., 1982). We will use the desk-top example of the metaphor approach because it elucidates very clearly the general problems connected with the approach.

People working in offices are supposed to be familiar with using folders, filing documents or throwing them into wastebaskets, and so on. These users presumably have a mental model about how work is done in offices with appropriate office material and are able and motivated to apply this mental model to the desk-top world simulated on the computer screen.

This approach is accompanied by consequences for the realization of the functionality, because it requires that the functions be implemented in the way that is standard in a regular office. At first view this should not be a problem, because the starting point for designing such a system was to transfer work from the office to the computer. This way, things seem to be "compatible." But why does one want to transfer the functions used in a regular office to the computer? Probably because one wants to use the special properties of the computer to make things easier, faster, more efficient, and so on, than in a regular "paper" office. And this requires some new functionality not available with paper and pencil, folders, and typewriters. From these arguments it follows that there is a conflict between the extent of functionality we want to have on the computer system and the extent of compatibility between existing mental models and system realizations, if we want to keep the metaphor valid.

The idea of using metaphors to communicate underlying conceptual models about existing systems has the following psychological basis. It is assumed that the user has prior knowledge about a certain domain of reality related to the metaphor world on the new system. In order to learn about the new system, he or she must relate new (i.e., to-be-acquired) knowledge to old (i.e., already existing) knowledge. The choice of a particular metaphor is determined by the intention to provide a mapping from the old domain onto the new domain. Within the framework of problem solving, you can look at it as "providing the right cover story" for the new system and then trusting in the power of reasoning by analogy. Figure 8.4 shows the basic elements of the metaphor idea exemplified with the "desk-

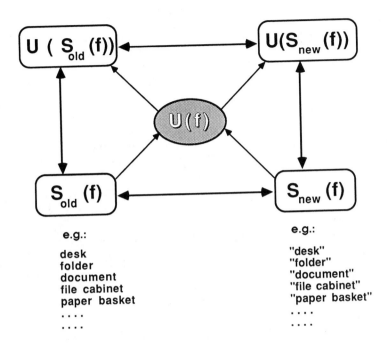

FIGURE 8.4. Basic mappings of structures when using metaphors.

top" metaphor world. (For reasons of simplicity, we have omitted the underlying conceptual models in this graphic representation.)

One begins with an "old" system's realization of the function, f. Prior knowledge through experience with $S_{old}(f)$ together with $U(f)$ has led to an existing mental model, $U(S_{old}(f))$. Confronting the user with a new system that realizes the functionality through $S_{new}(f)$ requires the user to build up a new mental model, $U(S_{new}(f))$. Basically, there are now two ways to build up this new model—the regular and the metaphor-aided way.

In the regular way the user tries to discover the properties and the structure of the new system by exploration. This exploration is guided by the user's general mental model, $U(f)$. The system's reaction on the user's manipulation provides feedback and information about correspondences and contradictions between $U(f)$ and $S_{new}(f)$. These interactions are always present when developing a new mental model. (For the moment the role of manuals and guided tours is neglected in our considerations).

The metaphor approach tries to shortcut this lengthy exploratory tour by presenting the system via a cover story in terms of the old system. This reference to a known system, that is, $S_{old}(f)$, is accomplished by using terms for objects and operations that are chosen from the metaphor world. Then the user is supposed to reason about the new system $S_{new}(f)$ by reason-

ing within his or her $U(S_{old}(f))$. In theory, and if the mapping is sufficient and complete, one could even say that $U(S_{new}(f))$ is identical in its structure to $U(S_{old}(f))$ except that it has a marker indicating "also applicable to new system." Of course, this will be never the case in reality. There are still a number of transformations necessary to provide the mapping of the objects of the domains onto each other. Both worlds still show differences on a number of dimensions. On the surface level we find very clear differences, as for example in the verbal and visual representation or even by having three-dimensional versus two-dimensional objects. More important, however, are differences that exist at the structural level.

At this point the question about the quality of the relationship between the two structures arises. Since we are, in principle, free to choose a metaphor world as a base domain for providing the description of a new system, we must identify criteria for choosing these worlds. The overall goal is to aim at rapid learning and transfer based on reasoning by analogy. Thus, an important criterion for the choice of a particular metaphor world should be that there is a minimum of conflicting features between the two structures, so that resulting mismatches are minimized. But as the reality of actual, commercially available metaphor world systems shows, this seems to be accomplished only partially and in rare cases or in restricted domains. What might be the reasons for this? Maybe it is in principle not possible. Our answer to this question is based on considerations about analogical problem solving. Due to the scope of this article and limitations of space it is not possible to present the formal treatment of it here (see Streitz, 1986c, for details).

CASE I AND CASE II ANALOGIES

We distinguish between case I and case II analogies. In the first the choice of the metaphor domain can be done in such a way that the mapping of the objects conserves the relational structure of the domain to be represented. This is the case if there is an isomorphic mapping of the complete domain.

In the more general case, II, the choice of the metaphor domain is accompanied by the effect that its objects "carry" features with them that would imply relations that are false in the domain to be represented.

Designers, of course, intend to provide case I analogies, but this very often fails and the metaphors turn out to be case II analogies. As a consequence structural properties (objects, relations) valid in the system are not correctly communicated by the chosen metaphor world. The user infers relations from his prior knowledge of this domain, that is, $S_{old}(f)$, and tries to apply them while using the new system. The inferred relations do not hold in the system, however. This results in a deficient understanding of the new system's structure and in high error rates. We say *the metaphor "collapses."* This is mainly caused by structural differences in the realization of functionality.

On the other hand as a designer one is trapped by the following problem. If the designer tries to make the new system completely compatible and consistent with the metaphor world, then one would deprive oneself of additional capabilities computer systems are able to offer. There are three possible answers to this dilemma, a radical one and two compromises. (1) Abandon the use of metaphors altogether. (2) Use metaphors, but accept the extra burden of having to teach modification rules for those aspects of the new system that are not in correspondence with the metaphor world but offer additional functionality. (3) Use different metaphors for different areas of functionality: multiple metaphor worlds.

Whether it is worthwhile to engage in the endeavor of using a metaphor and teaching its modification must be checked by a critical cost–benefit analysis. The analysis must show whether the advantages of metaphors for getting an early and rapid understanding of basic properties of a system are sufficient to justify the additional costs—including the mental costs—of modifying parts of the metaphor world at a later stage.

Arguing within a different framework, Halasz and Moran (1982) come to a related conclusion on the usefulness of analogies. They think that "analogy, used as a literary metaphor, is effective for communicating complex concepts to novices. But analogy is dangerous when used for detailed reasoning about computer systems—this is much better done with abstract conceptual models" (p. 36).

In any case one should aim for a high degree of consideration of the properties of user's mental models in the blueprint of the conceptual model for a new system.

Directions for Future Research and Concluding Remarks

Our treatment of the topic has a number of implications for research on the design of interactive systems as well as on tutoring and training of users (in this context, learners). First, one must diagnose the mental model of the user (or a class of users). This requires specific techniques to obtain valid data on knowledge representations of humans—a field of research still under heavy development and faced with a lot of problems. Second, one must have a (formal) method of description for representations that can be applied to $S(f)$ *and* $U(f)$, leading to $U(S(f))$. Otherwise, there is no way to derive a measure of discrepancy or degree of compatibility of representations. Third, one must have techniques available to transform data about users' mental models into design specifications leading to the desired structure of $S(f)$. This is the problem of presenting results of (cognitive) psychology research in a format that aids in designing systems. Fourth, one must take into consideration that $U(f)$ does not exist as one solid and consistent knowledge structure but that it is a combination of information based on an idea about the abstract functionality, f, and prior experience with other systems' realizations, $S_i(f)$, of this functionality.

Thus, in reality one is, of course, confronted with a variety of different mental models, $U(S_i(f))$.

Finally, we draw attention to a point beyond the topic of mental models. In a recent experimental study (Streitz, Lieser, & Wolters, 1986; Streitz, 1987), we investigated the effect of the two factors "metaphor world" and "dialogue mode" on the performance of users working with an interactive system. In a 2 × 2 design, we contrasted an office/desk-top metaphor with a computer metaphor and menu selection with control commands. The results showed an interesting interaction between the two factors. There was no advantage of the office/desk-top metaphor per se, but in combination with the dialogue mode menu selection, it was superior. The other three groups (desk-top metaphor/control commands; computer metaphor/menu selection; computer metaphor/control commands) showed significantly worse performance and did not differ from each other significantly.

We take this as a strong indication that one must be very careful when investigating the effects of metaphors in an isolated way and not in combination with other properties of the user–system interface. Generalizing this, we would like to argue for multi-factorial studies in this field that are more concerned with a broad perspective including all relevant facets of human–computer interaction.

Acknowledgements. This research was carried out in the ACCEPT-Group (Aachen Cognitive Ergonomics Project) at the Institute of Psychology of the Technical University Aachen and supported by the Bundesanstalt für Arbeits-schutz, Dortmund. I thank Uli Hoppe for his ideas in an early stage of developing the concept of different perspectives on basic functionality. Furthermore, thanks are due to Don Norman for providing valuable feedback—during his visit to Aachen—on the mental model sections. Finally, I must thank Edmund Eberleh, Tom Moran, and Yvonne Waern for useful comments on a draft version of this paper.

References

Carroll, J. M. (1984). *Mental models and software human factors* (IBM Research Report RC 10616). Yorktown Heights, NY: IBM.

Carroll, J., & Mack, R. L. (1985). Metaphor, computing systems, and active learning. *International Journal of Man-Machine Studies, 22*, 39–57.

Carroll, J., & Thomas, J. C. (1982). Metaphor and the cognitive representation of computing systems. *IEEE Transactions on Systems, Man and Cybernetics, 12*, 107–116.

Douglas, S., & Moran, T. (1983). Learning text editor semantics by analogy. In A. Janda (Ed.), *Proceedings of the CHI'83 Conference* (pp. 207–211). Boston: ACM.

Gentner, D. (1985). Structure mapping: A theoretical framework for analogy. *Cognitive Science, 7*, 155–170.

Gentner, D., & Gentner, D. R. (1983). Flowing waters or teeming crowds: Mental

models of electricity. In D. Gentner & A. L. Stevens (Eds.), *Mental models* (pp. 99–129). Hillsdale, NJ: Lawrence Erlbaum Assoc.

Halasz, F., & Moran, T. (1982). Analogy considered harmful. In T. Moran (Ed.), *Eight short papers on user psychology* (pp. 33–36). Palo Alto, CA: XEROX PARC.

Nievergelt, J. (1975). Interactive systems for education—The new look of CAI. In O. Lecarme & R. Lewis (Eds.), *Proceedings of the IFIP world conference "Computers in education"* (pp. 465–471). Amsterdam: North-Holland.

Norman, D. A. (1983). Some observations on mental models. In D. Gentner & A. L. Stevens (Eds.), *Mental models* (pp. 7–14). Hillsdale, NJ: Lawrence Erlbaum Assoc.

Norman, D. A. (1986). Cognitive engineering. In D. A. Norman & S. Draper (Eds.), *User centered system design: New perspectives on human–computer interaction* (pp. 31–61). Hillsdale, NJ: Lawrence Erlbaum Assoc.

Ortony, A. (Ed.), (1979). *Metaphor and thought.* Cambridge, England: Cambridge University Press.

Smith, C., Irby, C., Kimball, R., Verplank, B., and Harslem, E. (1982) Designing the Star user interface, BYTE; Vol. 7, No. 4, 242–282.

Streitz, N. A. (1983). The importance of knowledge representation in problem solving: An example from text comprehension and problem solving. In G. Lüer (Ed.), *Bericht über den 33. Kongress der Deutschen Gesellschaft für Psychologie* (S. 403–407). Göttingen, West Germany: Hogrefe.

Streitz, N. A. (1985a). Die Rolle von mentalen und konzeptuellen Modellen in der Mensch-Computer Interaktion: Konsequenzen fur die Software-Ergonomie? In H. J. Bullinger (Ed.), *Software-Ergonomie '85: Mensch-Computer Interaktion* (pp. 280–292). Stuttgart, West Germany: Teubner.

Streitz, N. A. (1985b). Kognitionspsychologische Aspekte der Gestaltung von Dialogstrukturen bei interaktiven Lehr-Lern-Systemen. In H. Mandl & P. Fischer (Eds.), *Lernen im Dialog mit dem Computer* (pp. 54–67). Munich: Urban & Schwarzenberg.

Streitz, N. A. (1986a). Cognitive Ergonomics: An approach for the design of user-oriented systems. In F. Klix & H. Wandke (Eds.), *Man–computer interaction research: MACINTER I* (pp. 21–33). Amsterdam: North-Holland.

Streitz, N. A. (1986b). *Subjektive Wissensrepräsentationen als Determinanten kognitiver Prozesse.* Institute of Psychology, Aachen, West Germany.

Streitz, N. A. (1986c). *Analogical problem solving: Case I and case II analogies.* Unpublished manuscript. Institute of Psychology, Aachen, West Germany.

Streitz, N. A. (1987) Cognitive compatibility as a central issue in human-computer interaction: Theoretical framework and empirical findings. In G. Salvendy (Ed.), *Cognitive engineering in the design of human-computer interaction and expert systems* (pp. 75–82). Amsterdam: Elsevier.

Streitz, N. A., Lieser, A., & Wolters, T. (1986, May). *User-initiated vs. computer-initiated dialogue modes: A comparative analysis of cognitive processes based on differences in user models.* Paper presented at the International Conference on Work With Display Units. Stockholm, Sweden.

Young, R. (1983). Surrogates and mappings: Two kinds of conceptual models for interactive devices. In D. Gentner & A. L. Stevens (Eds.), *Mental models* (pp. 35–52). Hillsdale, NJ: Lawrence Erlbaum Assoc.

9

Improvement of the Acquisition of Knowledge by Informing Feedback

PETER MICHAEL FISCHER
HEINZ MANDL

The Role of Feedback for Learning and the Acquisition of Knowledge

FEEDBACK AS A CENTRAL PRINCIPLE OF LEARNING

There is practically no recognized learning theory that neglects the role of feedback for acquisition of skill and knowledge. Any kind of human or animal learning depends on the shaping of behavior, especially the selection of appropriate behaviors necessary for any skilled, goal-directed behavior. The consequences and effects of an action determine whether a sequence of actions or operations becomes integrated into the evolving skill, the skill endowment or repertoire of the organism. Operations most likely to achieve this goal must be adopted and routinized by any organism in order to ensure survival. Feedback about the success (instrumentality) of a behavior or cognitive operation is information about the calibration and refinement necessary for the regulation of actions. "Learning by success" is synonymous for all learning that is regulated by its own outcome.

In the early behavioristic tradition, "learning via results" was a central issue in the regulation of behavior. Thorndike's "law of effect" (Thorndike, 1932) avoided the unfortunate separation of reinforcing qualities of feedback from informing qualities of feedback that were the result of a rigid Skinnerian conception of feedback. According to Thorndike an intrinsically motivated organism behaves and acts in response to the consequences of his action relative to goal attainment. Goal-achieving behaviors are selected on the basis of their efficiency. There is no need to distinguish, for example, between the reinforcing or informing aspects of behavioral outcomes. Only with the Skinnerian reduction of the (e.g., Holland & Skinner, 1961) status of behavioral consequences to solely reinforcing or nonreinforcing events (containing no information at all) does the full range of information inherent in the result of an action become reduced and dichotomized. Subsequently, the primary focus is not

now the achievement of the goal, instrumental for the organism, but the attainment of reward, regardless of preceding consequences. The organism controlled by reinforcement ceases to regulate its behaviors according to their inherent use or goal structure. Now it behaves and acts solely to attain reward. Reinforcement in Skinnerian terms conveys no information but loses itself in the external, metaoperational evaluation of action determined by some social reinforcing agency. Although the focus in Thorndike's theory concentrates on the cycle of behavior and behavioral effects, regardless of the informing or rewarding nature of its results, the focus in Skinner's theory shifts to the goal-extrinisic and separate events of reinforcement. Thus one could say that the behavioral results are externalized beyond their adaptive instrumentality for the organism. Figure 9.1 illustrates the two classic interpretations of behavioral effects.

Until the rise of the so-called "cognitive revolution" (or shall we say "cognitive renaissance"?), Skinnerism dominated psychological theorizing and consequently the impact of learning psychology on the design of learning devices or machines. After the publication of Miller, Galanter, and Pribram's *Plans and the Structure of Behavior* (1960) and Neisser's *Cognitive Psychology* (1967), the pendulum swung back. Feedback was now the central issue in action regulation. The two T(est)-components of the

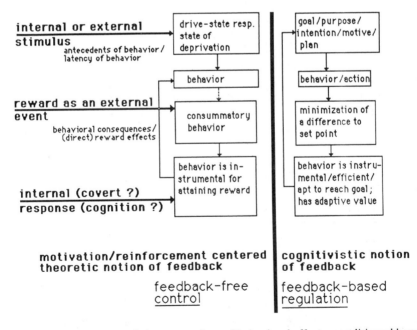

FIGURE 9.1. The two classic interpretations of behavioral effects: conditioned bond between a behavior and its instrumentality for attaining reward versus informational value of the effects of a behavior with respect to goal instrumentality.

T(est)-O(perate)-T(est)-E(xit) (TOTE) conception made feedback and the information it conveyed the center of attention. The first component in TOTE represents an entrance diagnosis that precedes any intended action. The second component in TOTE consists of an online diagnosis of current action until a match with the set point has been reached.

Further developments in action-regulation theories are almost exclusively based on the informational consequences of actions executed by the organism. This is especially true for those theories influenced by artificial intelligence using hierarchic and heterarchic models of thinking and action regulation. In essence Anderson's recent version of the ACT (adaptive control of thinking) model (1983) is an incarnation of cybernetic principles of action regulation. "Successful" productions are routinized and compiled, whereas failures or rarely used productions are abandoned. Learning according to Anderson is only possible when an internal and external agency exists that feeds information back to the user about the instrumentality of a given production and its subsequent increase in strength and maintenance.

Moreover, Flavell's (1970) and Brown's (1974) "metacognitive paradigm" was another reason that information concerned with the consequences of one's own action gained in importance. "Metacognition" or "thinking about one's own thinking" is a major source of information to be fed back into the course of regulated action. If metacognitions are a valid source of information for calibrating one's own actions, especially online monitoring, testing and checking of thinking and doing, and if they deserve psychological reality, then they must be turned into pillars capable of supporting heavy loads in instructions and self-instructions. Metacognition may be the central link to establish this, if one favors the shift from external control to internal regulation as a guiding principle of instruction.

The theoretical and methodological status of the term "metacognition" is ambiguous. Is metacognition the deliberate conscious tracking of one's own thinking and activity, or is it some extraordinary state of consciousness that happens when and only when thinking and/or acting encounter problems, that is, is it a kind of debugging state of consciousness?

There are some problems, however, with metacognitive self-regulation and monitoring. One problem is the duplication of mental burden and the widening of attentional focus. Even though metacognitions are thought of as a supplementary and assisting aid for thinking or thinking control, they may in fact interfere with the very act of thinking. The other problem is that metacognitions are not always integral, skilled elements of thinking or problem solving but—as is the case with young children and retardates— must be induced or evoked. There are even sufficient studies (e.g., Brown, 1975) done with "normal" adults showing that metacognitive regulation is not a widespread element of human mastery. Metacognitive activities therefore may draw off energy and strength from the real and primary cognitive task needed to solve the problem. Finally, when and how meta-

cognitions are used by the organism and how they are interpreted by the organism if they reach consciousness at all remains ambiguous. In the past metacognitive research reported astonishing results with young children or retardates heavily trained in actively monitoring their thinking and doing. They seemed to have been able to use metacognitions instrumentally as self-referent data (c.f., Brown, 1974; Cavanaugh & Borkowski, 1980; Schneider, 1982). Conversely, there are also studies showing the failures of induced metacognition, for example, with older adolescents (Buechel, 1980; Fischer & Mandl, 1981). Here metacognitive training resulted in a loss of learning efficiency and a distraction of self-attention away from the task toward the learner's state-oriented helplessness self-experience, causing failure rather than fostering learning, at least with learners possessing a poor performance record and especially with failure-oriented subjects.

INFORMING AND REINFORCING PROPERTIES INHERENT IN FEEDBACK

Skinnerism and the importation of reinforcing principles into programmed instruction resulted in the neglect of informative components of behavior as a data source for rational regulation; cognitivism led to a neglect of affective and motivational coprocesses in learning. Information about the results of one's actions was viewed almost exclusively as a continual matching between current state and set points. The rationally acting brute is no less fictitious than an animal staring fixedly at the expected reward.

Holding (1965) was one of the first who accounted for feedback effects by distinguishing between informative and incentive elements contained in feedback. According to Holding, based on R. B. Miller's (1953) distinction between action feedback and learning feedback, action feedback refers to immediate situation-specific knowledge concerned with success or failure, whereas learning feedback refers to intermediate situation-specific effects of prior learning, especially knowledge that deals with the individual's competence and capabilities (Figure 9.2).

Action feedback is a process and has a formative effect on learning; learning feedback is transsituational and has summative, evaluative effects. Another distinction made by Holding (1965) refers to "artificial" as opposed to "intrinsic" feedback. Artificial feedback refers to information about learning efficacy stemming from sources outside the acting person, that is, sources that are not proprioceptive. Conversely, intrinsic feedback refers to any self-experienced or self-generated data originating either directly from proprioceptive sensation or conscious self-monitoring. The more intrinsic, transsituational or temporally contingent such self-data are, the more efficient they are for action regulation. However, the more extrinsic, transsituational, or temporally remote feedback is, the more abstract and extraneous it becomes for the very learning process. Extrinsic feedback may be useful for post hoc, evaluative learning regulation, but

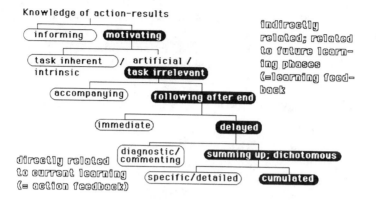

FIGURE 9.2. Holding's (1965) feedback differentiation.

in the course of adaptive learning regulation, it could interfere with intrinsic feedback, that is, shift the focus of attention away from action-relevant cues. Moreover, reward-centered feedback could possibly result in a fatal externalization if not seduction or corruption of both attention and motivation.

Condry and Chambers (1978), McCullers (1978), and McGraw (1978) deserve the credit for having accentuated the externalization of motivation by shifting the weight of situational saliences caused by material reward. A refined analysis of the effects of feedback on the learner was a result of the critique of Skinnerian reinforcement principles by Holding (1965), Lepper and Greene (1978) and colleagues, as well as by Stapf and collaborators (Stapf & Degner, 1981; Stapf & Mix, 1979). Meanwhile, feedback research is prepared to expect at least two possible effects of feedback and the probability that they may occur simultaneously: an instrumental informative effect that informs the individual about "hits" and "misses" of his action and a precise match between the current learning state and the set points of learning criteria, as well as an affective attributional effect. "Pride" could be the affective impact in mastery, and humiliation or "blame" could be the result of failure. The latter may occur especially when a learner is both success and failure oriented (success oriented on the one hand, that is, striving for good performance, and failure oriented on the other hand, that is, doubting that he might reach his goal) and interprets the feedback "misses" as punishment, an experience of decreasing self-worth, or even as a testimony of his own incompetence, after a series of failures. Punishing effects of performance feedback are also likely to occur for difficult tasks or in early learning phases with new, unfamiliar, or complex tasks or those tasks for which the learner tends to overestimate the difficulty subjectively. It is even plausible that the salience of feedback properties, that is, the interpretation and experience of feedback, are filtered by the learning history of a learner. Seligman's theory of "learned help-

lessness" (1975) and Kuhl's (1984) differentiation between "action" and "state" orientations account for the existence of such moderating or filter effects. Solely rationalistic concepts of action regulation by themselves are insufficient in explaining such negative side effects of feedback.

HIDDEN AND OVERT FEEDBACK IN DIAGNOSTIC SYSTEMS

Naturally, feedback principles are central components in current intelligent tutor systems (ITS) or intelligent computer-assisted instruction (ICAI). For an intelligent tutor system to be called intelligent depends mostly on the quality of its ability to perform online diagnosing and modeling for the learner. According to Wexler (1970) the former CAI systems were ad hoc frame-oriented (AFO) or "generative" because the responsiveness of the learning device was restricted to a fixed event space anticipated at the time of system construction. Recent ITSs, however, are flexible with respect to a wide range of unforeseen events. Their flexibility, which may be equated with the definition of their "intelligence," is based on their potency to diagnose. Koffman and Blunt (1975) define the intelligence of a system according to how well the system is able to reconstruct and hypothesize the sources of difficulty for a learner from the learner's recent learning history with the system. Correspondingly, the diagnostic component is one of the central elements of an ITS (see Figure 9.3).

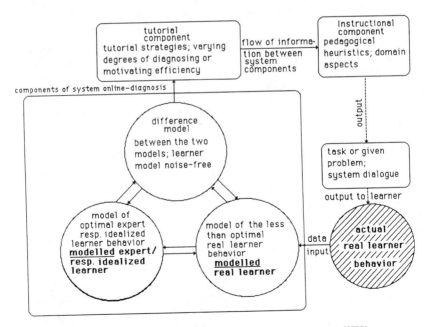

FIGURE 9.3. Prototype of an intelligent tutor system (ITS).

To make a tutorial intervention or instruction "intelligent," one must be able to precisely map and analyze the problem the learner is confronted with. This implies a normative model of idealized, bug-free understanding of the domain in question or a topic derived from that domain ("expert model"). This normative or expert model further implies a deeper insight into the concepts and relations within the domain (conceptual network) as well as an insight into the nature of the cognitive processes necessary to comprehend the domain. To estimate the distance between ultimate expert knowledge and the learner's current state of comprehension, a valid model of the learner's present state is required. Thus, content-valid diagnostic tasks and questions are needed. To be able to separate unsystematic "noise" from systematic learner data, some reliability is needed. Only by a series of diagnostic tasks with some retesting can a valid, noise-free learner model be obtained. Only then, by comparing learner and expert models, can a difference model evolve, which allows for a problem-sensitive tutorial intervention. A series of diagnostic questions should lead both to overt feedback (the tutorial intervention) and some portion of covert feedback from the learner ("I could [I failed to] answer the questions put to me"). In addition to the tutorial and pedagogic strategy as it is realized in the system design, the degree of reliability intended for the solution of the noise problem determines the system's obtrusiveness. According to Barr and Feigenbaum (1982, p. 233), the obtrusiveness in diagnosing the learner is a distinct feature of a system's architecture. Systems with aimed Socratic dialogue techniques, systems with bug-or-failure diagnosis overlays, coaching systems, and systems with "mixed initiative" differ and vary in their degree of obtrusiveness.

An ITS that places the stress on diagnostic effectiveness, as does Brown, Burton and Larkin's (1977) "BUGGY" (Figure 9.4), cannot avoid the burden of failure experience for the learner. To be able to exercise diagnostic acuity and to carefully depict the skill-or-bug lattice of the learner, the learner's cognitive limits must be tested repeatedly. Moreover, to escape the noise problem of unsystematic or unclear bug data, a more than thorough test–retest cycle must be installed in all BUGGY architecture. Although BUGGY contains no explicit feedback mechanism, in fact, a great amount of covert feedback for the learner may exist when he experiences failures with a series of difficult tasks that test his limits.

In a BUGGY-like ITS architecture, there is an interplay (and data exchange) between the expert model implemented, the set of domain-related issues derived from the expert model, the corresponding diagnostic tasks as presented to the learner by the problem generator, and the goodness of fit between systematic bugs and current learner data. If the issue recognizers yield an inconsistent or even contradictory, noisy picture of the learner's actual performance, which allows no clear-cut diagnosis of his competence, further tasks must be administered to settle the issue and to eliminate the noise that the mismatch yielded. The preliminary model

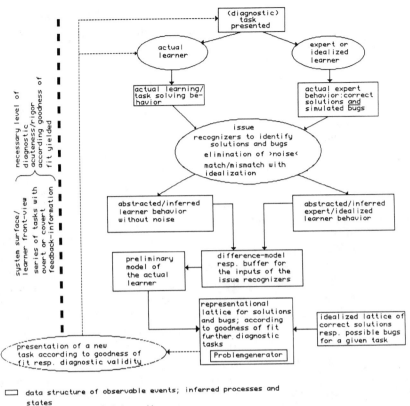

FIGURE 9.4. Flow of information in a BUGGY-like ITS (Brown et al., 1977).

of the learner's current competence, illustrating the degree of match–mismatch between a systematic bug and the idealized skill lattice, might decide whether further noise-eliminating questions or tasks are needed. Again, even the sheer fact of prolonged testing might "show" the learner that he lacks some knowledge or competence (covert self-feedback). If the ITS architecture lays heavy stress on a noise-free learner model, expanded testing and retesting and thus a certain degree of "obtrusiveness" is unavoidable.

Conversely Burton and Brown's (1978) WEST is an "enriched learning environment" which was constructed primarily with motivational considerations in mind. Feelings of punishment or boredom are avoided by implementing the principle that the learner's motivation should never suffer because of a series of failures. After a failure has occurred, the play strategy is changed and the winning criteria are lowered. However, the notion that it is better not to intervene than to intervene too much may at least partially lead to an extended or prolonged error on the side of the

learner. Stressing "hits" by simultaneously weakening or totally suppressing "misses" may result in an impoverished learning efficiency. Therefore, if a WEST architecture is restricted in diagnostic precision, it may sacrifice acuity in tradeoff between motivational impact and modeling or even tutorial ability.

Although BUGGY, as was shown in Figure 9.4, implies a test–retest loop until a precise, noise-free model of learner's current competence is reached, WEST is governed much more by the pedagogic heuristics and intervention strategies implemented. It is not the match–mismatch or goodness of fit dimension that determines further diagnostic tasks to be presented to the learner but rather the degree of diagnostic "stress" the implemented pedagogic heuristic is willing to impose on the learner (lower part of Figure 9.5). The nature of tasks and tutorial interventions to be presented to the learner is apart from any goodness-of-fit considerations. The problem generator is not governed by diagnostic validity and reliability principles but rather by motivational aspects. There is even a further complication. Because WEST aims both at a mastery of basic arithmetic skills and a satisfying course of the learner's interactions with the enriched learning environment, system interventions aim both at correct arithmetic solutions and "good moves." What is the informative and diagnostic value of a tutor feedback that tells the learner that he missed using shortcuts on his way to the WEST? To summarize: problem generator, dialogue generator, and instructions generator (lower part of Figure 9.5), which select the system's interventions, are not in the service of diagnostic power but rather in the service of other, relatively separate goals (learner motivation, winning strategies).

At present according to our knowledge, no empirical study has been done on the possible punishing or demotivating effects of a bug-diagnose series in a BUGGY system or has examined the possible lowered diagnostic power of a WEST architecture.

Consequences for the Design of Interactive Learning Systems

Thus far our review of BUGGY or WEST-like ITS has shown that there is a considerable amount of overt or covert feedback contained in such systems. Overt feedback, as is the case with WEST, may have been designed carefully to meet the learner's motivational and affective demands. (We might even suspect that too much is done with respect to motivation while diagnostic power suffers.) In a BUGGY-like architecture of an ITS, however, covert feedback may be of more harm than instrumental use to the learner. The very fact that diagnostic tasks of a given kind are repeated several times in the service of "noise elimination" may signal to him that he is "wrong." But being wrong without an apparent chance to advance may result in some inner state of "helplessness" (see Seligman,

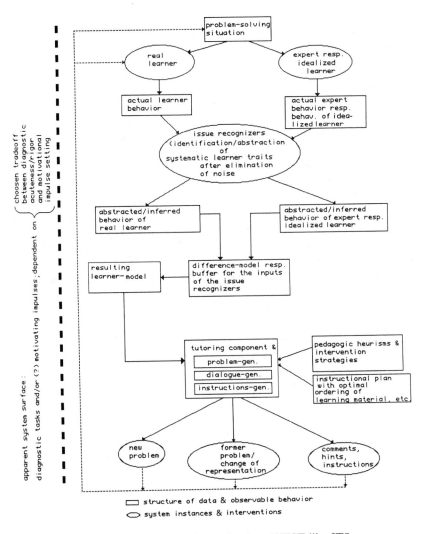

FIGURE 9.5. Flow of information in a WEST-like ITS.

1975; Kuhl, 1984). Covert feedback in an ITS then might impede and prevent learning rather than assist it.

In our view there is only one solution to overcome the dilemma of the diagnostic power needed to be able to model adequately and reliably without burdening affective stress on the learner. If we transform any kind of covert feedback in an ITS into deliberate overt feedback and train the learner to make intelligent use of it, we may be able to optimize both the diagnostic power of our systems and the learner's online monitoring without the former negative impact on his or her mood. The diagnostic component of an ITS then, necessary to depict the learner's current knowledge

state, can further serve as an essential component of the inner architecture of the ITS while it is seen and experienced from the perspective of the learner as an integral part of the instructional and tutorial component. To achieve this transformation of diagnosis into instructional and tutorial help, a thorough analysis of possible feedback effects and side effects is necessary.

Although ITS systems presently are in a prototypical state of development—to our knowledge at present there is no complete tutorial system with all components implemented—"more intelligent" AFO-type systems may bridge the gap. In addition to the major weakness of AFO systems—the need to have online analysis facilities prepared and predesigned outside the learning process—they are capable at least of sharing some portion of ITS's diagnostic power in online diagnosis and thus are able to collect large sets of user data in the service of forthcoming learner modeling.

The knowledge-acquisition video instruction system II (KAVIS II) interactive teaching–learning system described in the next section is essentially an AFO system. The following section outlines the hardware and software architecture of our KAVIS II interactive learning system, beginning with a systematic view of feedback. After a sketchy description of the domain in question, audiovisual (AV) material about plant cells, morphology and function of cells, and photosynthesis, the hardware and software architecture of the system is outlined.

The Architecture of KAVIS II

PRINCIPLES FOR THE DESIGN OF THE DIAGNOSTIC AND FEEDBACK COMPONENT WITH RESPECT TO LEARNING PHASES AND LEARNING CONTENT

When we consider acquisition of knowledge in terms of its temporal and process nature (cf., Figure 9.6) we can distinguish an early information processing or information intake phase, when isolated single facts are recorded and the learner attempts to associate the new pieces of information with those already stored in prior knowledge. Only later is the learner able to connect and tie this information together, that is, establish coherence, make sound inferences, discriminate, generalize, and transfer his knowledge gains. In addition to this dimension—comprising information ranging from intake of single, insular facts to the formation of an integrated whole—another dimension may exist with respect to affective experience in knowledge acquisition. In general new information, especially content material that is complex and unfamiliar, may be experienced as nonredundant, abstract, strange, and difficult to process. If a problem space is widely unstructured or not easily structurable for the learner, he may become confused and suffer feelings of a nonsovereign distance to the

Facts-factual knowledge ————→ comprehension/integration/cohesion

level of processes & results

cognitive resp. information-proc. level

- information intake & processing; integration with existing prior knowledge; abstraction of core content
- connecting & integrating of concepts and topic units; sophisticated integration into related concepts; inferences, discrimination, generalization, and transfer

affective & emotional-motivational level (self-evaluation & self-esteem)

- labilization by nonredundancy of topic material; high informational load and strangeness; experienced distance to content by the not-yet sovereign; unstructurability of problem-space; difficulty and/or helplessness phase; dependent on earlier failure/success & self-esteem, positive or negative affective mood
- increasing abstractness of content with concomitantly increasing mastery; paradoxical coexistence of nearness to content and sovereign distance. organization and structuredness of problem space; high objective difficulty accompanied by subjective feelings of easy understanding *dependent* on learner's failure/success on earlier learning phases; high or low self-esteem

moderation and filter-effect for the way corrective feedback is interpreted and processed

level of instructional intervention by feedback and/or guidance

- instrumental, solely informational factual AV feedback to convey missing or uncomplete facts; illustration and demonstration of elementary facts
- **regulative PROLOGue**
  (1) about (logical) nature of misconception or error;
  informative PROLOGue
  (2) with reference to concept in question
  AV information
  (3) detailed explanation and correction of misunderstanding

informing feedback

correcting and regulating differential feedback specific to bugs

time- & process-dependent ————→ intervention

FIGURE 9.6. Interdependence model. Interdependence between content level, process phase, and intervention.

subject matter he cannot master. Sometime later in the learning process when comprehension has increased and some mastery has occurred, when separate islands of facts grow together into aggregates of connected and cohesive, meaningful units (i.e., when the problem space becomes structured and integrated), then the learner should experience a feeling of familiarity and mastery. Thus, the more sovereign the learner becomes, the more abstract (and also the more mental) the distance to the content material will be.

Correspondingly, subjective estimates of content difficulty can be highest at the beginning of information intake, when the objective difficulty of factual information is paradoxically rather low, while a decrease in estimated task difficulty could occur when the objective complexity of the content material increases. According to Holding's (1965) opinion, state-oriented feedback, stemming from earlier learning and competence history, could interfere with the learning process as well as determine how feedback will be interpreted. Instead of viewing feedback as instructive information, it could be construed as reinforcement/reward/punishment, that is, praise/blame. When and how should we intervene with instructions and/or feedback? Stapf (1988) suggested stressing "hits" at the beginning of the learning process in order to avoid failure feedback and switching during the later stages of learning to an error- or bug-accentuated feedback style, when the learner has gained some mastery and self-confidence and may be able to stand criticism. A "double strategy" would be adequate then, when praise is stressed at the beginning by implementing a neutral feedback. With this kind of feedback, punishing consequences would be avoided or at least minimized. The switch to a bug-oriented, error-stressed feedback should be done at a later time in order to eliminate "mislearning," incorrect learning decisions, and the waste of learning time. As one can see in Figure 9.6, we distinguish between informing versus correcting feedback and regulating feedback. The former kind of feedback is constructed to be solely informative (and affectively neutral) and consists of illustrations and demonstrations of elementary facts missed or truncated by the learner in response to a given task. The latter kind of feedback contains a correcting and regulating component and performs instructive intervention. The instructive intervention not only clarifies and explains but also corrects explicitly an incorrect input that resulted from a misunderstanding or a defect in comprehension.

To foster the learner's constructive ability to learn from his failures, to avoid the learner's feeling as if he were treated as a child, and to aid metacognitive self-regulation, the first part of corrective feedback consists of a formative "PROLOGue" (our terminology). Based on a thorough and explicit analysis of the content material and comprehension testing questions, four main categories of errors and their combinations were covered: *omissions*, when important aspects of the subject matter are missing; *intrusions*, when irrelevant or minor aspects are taken as central points; *con-*

fusions, when disagreeing, conflicting, or even contradictory points are grouped together; and finally *combined omissions and intrusions*. These main error types, which primarily focus on the logical nature of the misconception in question, were further graded according to their severity with respect to their implication(s) for the topic in question and the number of buggy answer alternatives per item (which is different for 1 correct, 2 correct, and 3 correct multiple-choice items).

This categorization of errors was intended to allow for a later detailed mapping and modeling of students' bugs. It was also the main source of information to administer learning-concomitant, differential, online feedback. Finally, it was the guiding principle underlying the construction of differential feedback. As detailed later the PROLOGues were the only source of information available to the learner in one experimental condition, as opposed to a combined package of PROLOGue and subsequent related content information about the subject matter. Dependent on the experimental design, regarding its underlying feedback-intervention scheme, the PROLOGue should have differential effects (see following discussion). Although PROLOGue-only should stipulate the learner to correct his or her bug solely based on the regulatory information contained in the PROLOGue, PROLOGues as the yoked element of a PROLOGue and AV content feedback pair should have a different status. Serving as "advance organizers" for the subsequent AV feedback, the PROLOGues are intended to shape and direct attention to subsequent content aspects.

COURSE AND STUDY MATERIAL

Natural sciences information, in the good empirical tradition, consists largely of direct visual information stemming either from experimentation or laboratory preparation. Because of the expanding sophistication of the apparatus needed and its exploding costs, resulting in limitation of apparatus directly available to the student, only parts of the study material can be learned from immediate experience, whereas large amounts are conveyed by traditional print media. To expand the student's direct access, salient parts of visual materials could be transferred by AV material. To prevent the learner from passively consuming visualized content materials (as is the case when gazing at television) more "offensive," gripping forms of video learning can be administered by interactive video.

The Content Material: Audiovisual Learning Units About Plant Cells, Morphology and Function of Cells, and Photosynthesis

The curriculum, dealing with plant cells, morphology and function of cells, and photosynthesis, is thematically grouped into three LEARNing blocks: features of the plastids, morphology of the chloropolasts, and function of the chloroplasts and photosynthesis. Each of these topics was divided again

into subunits covering important details and principles. Each content block was highlighted by an instruction in order to focus the subject's attention on important relationships. After thorough multiple modification the script was audiovisualized with commentary by a professional radio announcer (the same procedure was applied to the two kinds of instructive DIALogue feedback material, which is discussed later). The central concepts contained in the LEARNing mode (menu-guided presentation of the AV material) and questions in the DIALogue mode exist on an elementary, factual level, two higher order comprehension levels, and on a transfer level. Individual video frames were available for any relevant aspects of a selected topic except for the DIAGnose mode, where no feedback was provided.

Kinds of Questions and the Derivation of Diagnostic Questions From the Content Material

As outlined later the diagnostic and feedback principles implemented in KAVIS II lead to a direct interfacing between teaching and LEARNing modes on the one side and DIAGnostic and DIALogue feedback modes on the other side. LEARNing—whether on the elementary, factual level in the beginning of information processing and material intake or in the advanced, inference-based integration and comprehension stages—always was accompanied by online diagnosis and feedback. To manage such an intimate connection between LEARNing and learning diagnosis by DIALogue and DIAGnosis, a thorough classification and typology of the questions and tasks used was needed. Fact-oriented and higher order comprehension test questions were used.

Fact-Oriented Questions

To test the knowledge of elementary facts and topic aspects, questions directly related to the AV content were derived from the definitory, terminological, or conceptual units of the curricular lesson. The online DIAL 1 test questions, the DIAG test questions, and the 15 fact-oriented questions pretest were constructed in different parallel versions. Fact-oriented questions were always directly and unambiguously related to one of the eight subunits, and their distractors directly or indirectly derived from the information contained in the unit. In LEARN it did not matter whether that statement was repeated, paraphrased, expressed as a synonym, negated, or mediated in the lesson in visual but not in verbal form.

Higher Order Comprehension Questions

Higher order comprehension questions were used in order to deepen the understanding of conceptual and semantic units of the lessons. The interrelationships and relations between them were constructed from an analysis of the lesson similar to that of Kintsch and Van Dijk (1978).

Comprehension questions required a connection between the information contained in at least two of the LEARN subunits. In contrast to the factual or knowledge items, they are not oriented to the text surface or textual content. Instead they aim at a particular scientific or conceptual mental model (cf., Norman, 1983), which is supposed to be conveyed by textual and/or visual information. One can answer a comprehension question only when one has constructed an adequate mental model on the basis of integrated text and picture information. One can distinguish three types of comprehension questions: rearrangement, generalization, and recognition of functional interrelations.

Rearrangement. Here, the information is scattered around, and the curriculum must be grouped and rearranged under a new common scope. For example the production of ATP (adenosine triphosphate) is described with the so-called Z-schema and as a structural model of thylacoides. The use of ATP, however, is described by the Calvin cycle. A rearrangement of the question would deal with the production and use of ATP.

Generalization. These questions require autonomous comparison, differentiation, abstraction, and generalization abilities. Statements referring to higher order relationships must be evaluated. For example the question "What is the difference between the two photoelectric systems?" (Calvin cycle and Z-schema) requires that the learner discover the difference(s) and allocate it (them) to one superordinate principle or concept. Moreover, he also must scan his knowledge acquired in the LEARN part, work out the differences, and delineate them.

Recognition of Functional Interrelations. Answering these types of questions requires knowledge and understanding of functional relationships (e.g., a functional mental model as suggested by Norman, 1983). For example on the Z-schema, whereas factual or knowledge questions ask for separate components or component processes, comprehension questions ask for the underlying rationale. For example those kind of questions would concern themselves with the function of absorption of light rays in the context of light-dependent processes. They would ask why two photosystems are necessary, or why these systems are arranged differently on the redox scale. Transfer-type questions, which are even more demanding, consist quite often of a combination of the three types of questions previously mentioned. For example a question dealing with the requisites and premises of electron transport requires the generalization of factual knowledge (e.g., transmitter molecules have different redox qualities) as well as the learner's ability to recognize that this information is relevant for electron transport.

The content of the video frames differed in detail and "spot characteristics," depending on whether they were used in the DIAL 1 mode (facts) or in the DIAL 2 mode (comprehension). To optimize the instrumental value

of the feedbacks given, especially in the more demanding comprehension and transfer parts, and to maximize their narrow tailoring to the special type of error done by the learner, an additional "feedback script" was written, detailing any important and bug-fallible aspects of the topics, both on the visual and auditory level.

KINDS OF FEEDBACK AND THE DERIVATION OF FEEDBACK COMMENTS FROM THE CONTENT MATERIAL AND THE EDUCATIONAL STRATEGY

As will be evident from the following overview of the system's architecture, the diagnostic and feedback principles implemented in KAVIS II are intended to result in a direct interfacing between teaching and learning. As outlined in the section on the design of the KAVIS II diagnostic and feedback component and in Figure 9.6, feedback is differentiated according to its possible effects in different learning phases and stages. On the elementary, factual level, in the beginning of information processing and material intake, feedback should not lay heavy stress on failures or errors but rather give help by informing the student in audiovisual form about the true matter in question. Only later, in the advanced, inference-based integration and comprehension stages when some mastery has occurred, failures and typical errors should be deliberately stressed to prevent erroneous learning. Feedback then should consist both in corrective "metacognitive" aids and in direct hints with respect to learning content to allow for an independent, autonomous self-correction. Only when the learner is unable to use this metacognitive PROLOGue information should more direct, material help in the form of AV informative feedback be given. To manage such an intimate connection between learning stages and differential feedback, a thorough classification and typology of the feedbacks to be administered was needed.

General/Global/Undifferentiated Feedback

The system was divided into both *process* organization, from the first information intake phase to the knowledge integration and comprehension and transfer stage, and a more local, curriculum- and/or system-based organization, that is, starting from a first knowledge-conveying part (presentation of content material in the AV LEARN mode (mode 1), knowledge-based learning DIALogue 1 (mode 2), free SELection of AV topics and/or DIAL 1 questions (mode 3), and the DIAGnosis followed by learning protocol (mode 4) and branching into a second comprehension part, comprehension-oriented learning DIALogue 2 in either linear, content-oriented sequence (mode 5), or randomized test sequence (mode 6). The overall organization of the learning system and its two main parts are shown in Figure 9.7. The left side or knowledge feedback was rather

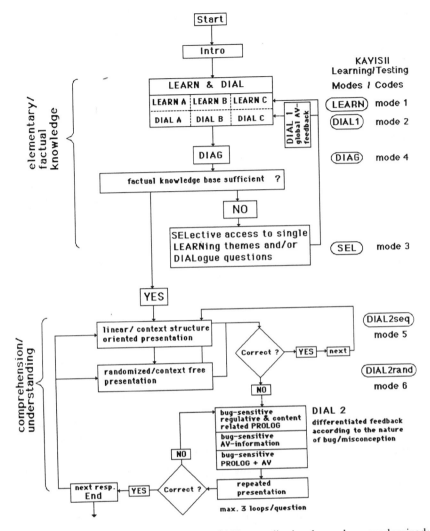

FIGURE 9.7. KAVIS learning structure. (AV = audiovisual; rand. = randomized; seq. = sequential)

general, global, or undifferentiated. It consisted of an excerpt or extract from the corresponding LEARN/AV subunit. The audio component of these feedbacks comprised a rough summary of the topic in question without highlighting or marking special aspects.

Differential/Bug-Sensitive or "PROLOGue" feedback

Comprehension-related, differential feedback aims to correct and clarify bugs or misconceptions. Corresponding to our bug taxonomy, the feedback applied here should cover precisely the narrow, circumscribed, rele-

vant point in question. Regardless of the experimental feedback condition a particular subject was exposed to (AV information only, PROLOGue only, or PROLOGue and AV information combined), any given feedback in the comprehension part of the system was detailed and distinguished according to the particular bug made by the subject. In the AV feedback or the AV component of the combined PROLOGue and AV information feedback, special aspects of the topic were highlighted by "zooms," flashing inserts, arrows at the level of the pictorial information, and by a special emphasis in the speaker's voice. Affirmation or negation/falsification was made especially salient, depending on the preceding bug.

As shown in Figure 9.6 PROLOGue feedback comprises two parts, regulative and informative PROLOGue feedback. Regulative feedback functions as an instructive intervention component by acting like an advance organizer and directing the attention of the learner to the detailed AV clarification and explanation. Furthermore, it can provide explicit correction of misunderstandings or defects in the learner's comprehension. The formative, corrective regulative PROLOGue was designed to foster metacognitive self-regulation, for example, facilitating learner activity in response diagnosis and training his constructive ability to learn from failure. The informative metacognitive PROLOGue component consists of a paraphrase of our error category. Its "linking" part previews special aspects of the topic to be channeled to the learner, directs and calibrates the learner's attention and focusing. Moreover, it informs the learner how to deal operationally with the relevant information. In a sense both formative and linking PROLOGue are directed at the cognitive operations required by the learner. The mastery of these cognitive operations is a prerequisite to comprehending the relevant aspects and integrating them into a consistent and coherent "cognitive map" or network of the topics.

Two Examples of Complete PROLOGues

To illustrate the essential nature of PROLOGue, two bug-dependent versions are presented:

1. *Intrusion bug. Formal/metacognitive PROLOGue*, "Your answer would be completely correct if it did not contain additional incorrect (superfluous/irrelevant information)." *Content-related PROLOGue*, "Would you try to differentiate between the production of ATP and the consumption of ATP."
2. *Combined omission and intrusion bug. Formal/metacognitive PROLOGue*, "Your answer is incomplete and in addition contains intrusions of incorrect (superfluous/irrelevant) information not pertinent for the topic." *Content-related PROLOGue*, "Try to consider all aspects contained in the structural model of thylacoides and specify the location of the two processes of photosynthesis!"

Any loop (repetition of the question) led to a new feedback and correspondingly to a new PROLOGue pair that was based on the preceding bug. As mentioned previously in the description of the learning course, questions could be repeated three times and were accompanied by feedback in DIAL 1 and DIAL 2 sequential and DIAL 2 random modes if the first or second answer was incorrect. After three incorrect answers there was a break off, and the next question was introduced. The last incorrect answer was commented with a neutral "O.K., let's go to the next question." To keep feedback as neutral as possible, bugs were only pointed out in the PROLOGue or for the AV-only condition by instructing the learner, "Get some additional AV information." Conversely "hits" were followed by the PROLOGue-like statement "Your answer is completely correct."

The Hardware and Software Architecture of KAVIS II

Preliminary Remark: Dissemination of Computers in West German Schools

There are several reasons why we tried so hard to implement such a demanding ITS-like structure on the smallest hardware conceivable (Apple II plus and *II*e) and in the seemingly simplest programming language (BASIC with assembly language parts) although there are much more powerful machines and much more potent higher level programming languages.

In West Germany mainframe, mini-, and personal computers have penetrated the business market considerably. Although small personal computers, capable of playing ATARI games, presently are expanding into households, educational use of small computers in the sense of "consumer electronics" is still in its infancy. With a coverage of three to five machines per class on the average, classrooms with more than 10 computers are a rare exception. Of the machines presently used, the Apple II plus and *II*e, Commodores, and IBMs are the most widely used. LOGO is the dominant programming language in primary and secondary education, while BASIC and PASCAL are less widely used. LOGO is the language for the teacher beginning programming without elaborated programming skills, and PASCAL is used especially by physics and information science teachers.

Presently, just a fraction of commercial "eduware" is available in Germany as compared with the United States. Public domain, or "shareware," is nearly unknown in Germany.

There is another very sensitive trend to be respected. German teachers are somewhat idiosyncratic in the way they use available learning and teaching material. Reluctant to use ready-made commercial material, they prefer their own product or at least to have material to which they can put the finishing touches.

Finally, we wanted to develop the interactive learning system on hardware that is widely available in schools and educational institutions and has a widely recognized reliability and capability.

Hardware Architecture

KAVIS II was developed on the basis of CAVIS I (Computer Assisted Video Instruction System), which we had developed at an earlier stage.

CAVIS I had been deliberately restricted to computer assemblies that were relatively inexpensive but nevertheless performed efficiently. Furthermore they were used extensively in our schools (cf., Fischer, Frey, & Jeuck, 1983; Fischer, Mandl, Frey, & Jeuck, 1984). Because the German Institute for Research and Development of Independent Education (DIFF) has at its disposal a rich selection of film and video material, especially in natural science, botany was selected as the subject matter. The content of the material presented to the subjects dealt with plant cells, morphology and cell functions, and photosynthesis. A VHS video recorder was used to allow for progressive modification and elaboration of the AV material presented. Figure 9.8 shows the hardware configuration of the KAVIS II learning system.

In essence there are three system components with which the learner is directly confronted: (1) A video monitor that displays the content material, the instructions, and the feedback; (2) a mouselike three-button control device that allows the learner system control; and (3) a printer for the output of diagnostic learning protocols. Since computer literacy is not as extensive in Germany as it is in the United States, direct computer control via keyboard was not made available to the learner. Another reason for excluding the keyboard was to ensure that maximum attention would be focused on the content material. Furthermore, it would minimize the effort necessary for system control. To provide optimal system–user interaction, the user interface was mostly isomorphic.

Commands for the mouse were shown in the left corner of the screen. The learner could control the system by feeding the correct sequence input into the computer. The instructions were faded in on the screen (Figure 9.9 illustrates the instructions, i.e., a part of the user interface). Instructions hanging on the wall informed the learner in outline form about the design of the system and the manner in which he could select the computerized curriculum.

TEACHWARE: THE LEARNING STRUCTURE IN THE KAVIS II ENVIRONMENT

As illustrated in Figure 9.6, the learner enters the system by a short AV introduction especially designed to promote motivation and mood to

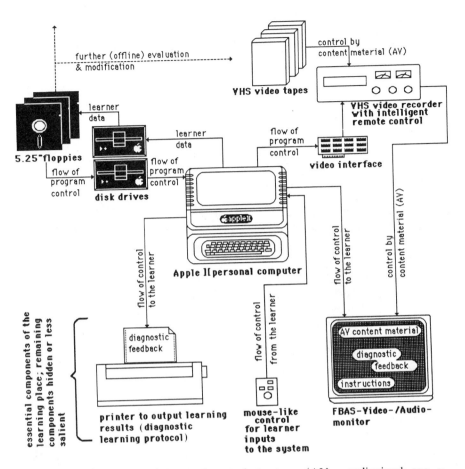

FIGURE 9.8. KAVIS hardware and control structure. (AV = audiovisual; seq. = sequential; rand. = randomized)

learn. Illustrated by a couple of photographs of outer space (the "desert" moon with astronant Neil Armstrong's dusty footprints and the "blue planet" with its invaluable atmosphere), the role of the plants and especially the plastids for respiration and life is sketched. The introduction ends with an overview of the learning unit and its significant sections.

The learner is then confronted with the system's first part, LEARN. He is shown a menu to take his choice from the content units with the "mouse" and is told that any move between the three main content parts is followed by a learning DIALogue (DIAL 1), which will present questions derived from the topics worked through thus far. Then he makes his first selection and works through some or all AV units of the respective thematic block, starting from any of the three blocks. After signaling to the system his willingness to move to another block, he is given the questions pertinent to the previous block units. He is informed that the questions

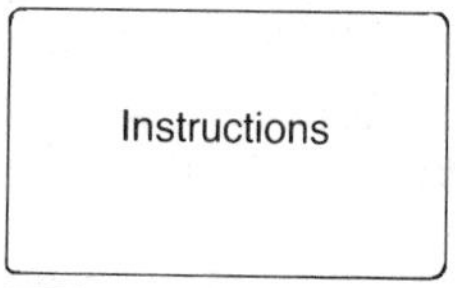

Instructions

The entire set of operations necessary at any time for you to input into the learning system with the control panel (left) are faded in the lower left corner of the screen in the correct sequence in abbreviated form.

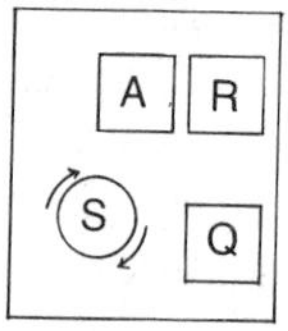

A

(*Advance*) = **A**dvance in the course of the program. **A** (stand alone) continues from any signboard on the screen giving instructions or hints.

S, A

(*Select, Assign*) = **S, A** means any selection or series of selections from a multiple set. **S**elect by turning the handle (cursor moves up or down) and **A**ssign your selection by pressing key **A**. E.g. by **S, A** you can choose topics from the topic menu.

S, A; R

(*Select, Assign, ...; Return*) **S, A; R** is the control sequence to choose from a set of items, e.g., multiple-choice alternatives. **S**elect (first) item you like to choose; **A**ssign it with key **A**; **S**elect next, **A**ssign it, etc. Complete series after your final choice/assignment by hitting **R**eturn.

Q

= **Q**uit/Correction: **Q** allows you to abandon chosen items after having assigned them. The last item in preparation when hitting the **Q**-key is repeated then.

Double Input

If you have selected and by chance chosen the same item twice, a dialogue box will prompt you. As is the case with hitting **Q**, double input results in a repetition of the item.

Less than **1** and more than **3** inputs and **A**ssign result in a prompt box, which informs you that less than 1 resp. more than 3 inputs aren't permitted.

FIGURE 9.9 KAVIS user interface.

used are of the multiple choice type (i.e., that one, two, or three answer alternatives can be correct), and he works through the questions. If he fails to give a correct or complete solution, informative AV feedback is given. To prevent the learner from "failure expectancies" or a punishing interpretation of the feedback event, the terms "error" or "bug" are never used. The learner instead is informed that his answer was incomplete or not fully complete. Immediate AV feedback, virtually without a delay, is then given from the AV player. After the third unsuccessful trial the next question is posed until the series is completed.

After the learner has dealt with at least one subtopic of the three thematic blocks, he is offered the choice of an interim DIAGnosis. If he passes the threshold, he is instructed to call the experimenter for further instructions. The instructions are in the form of a questionnaire. Should the learner fail to pass the threshold, he receives a printed diagnostic learning protocol, informing him where to look at AV units. Furthermore, depending on the severity and location of the bugs, questions dealing with the subject matter are presented to him. Following this phase of remedial learning, he can attempt to take the test again or to reengage once more with LEARNing topics or DIALogue questions.

After the learner passes the DIAGnostic examination and after filling out the feedback questionnaire, he is introduced to the consolidating comprehension part of the curriculum. Here he is confronted with two series of higher order questions. These questions are at a level of increased complexity and refer to different range inferences that are based on the "mental model" approach of Norman (1983). In case of a bug, the learner is given a differential DIALogue 2 feedback that relates exactly to the point where he committed the error. Depending on experimental conditions the learner is either presented with AV feedback, PROLOGue, or the combined package of PROLOGue followed by AV feedback. Any question can be repeated three times. The first two repetitions are followed by feedback, the last by a neutral statement announcing the next item. The first series of comprehension questions are presented in linear sequence or corresponding with the arrangements of content elements in the curriculum (DIAL 2 sequential). The second series of questions are presented in a randomized order scrambled between the thematic blocks (DIAL 2 randomized). This arrangement was made to facilitate information on bugs and to enable us to trace the learning progress in more detail. Moreover, such structuring was supposed to foster the broad, context-free retrievability of the relevant aspects and relationships. When the learner completed the randomized series of comprehension questions, he received a feedback questionnaire and an evaluation form. Here he had to rate the system's efficiency and possible weaknesses as he experienced them.

POSSIBLE RESEARCH DATA SOURCES MAPPED ONTO THE SYSTEM'S ARCHITECTURE

Figure 9.10 maps the system's main learning–testing parts against related research questions and data sources. Generally, any movement of the learner through the system, that is, his *learning path*, is of interest. Which topics will he choose from the LEARNing topics? In which order will he choose among them? Will his choice be influenced by success or failure on earlier, related topics in the DIALogue 1 mode? (As outlined previously any change from one learning unit to any other was accompanied by a set

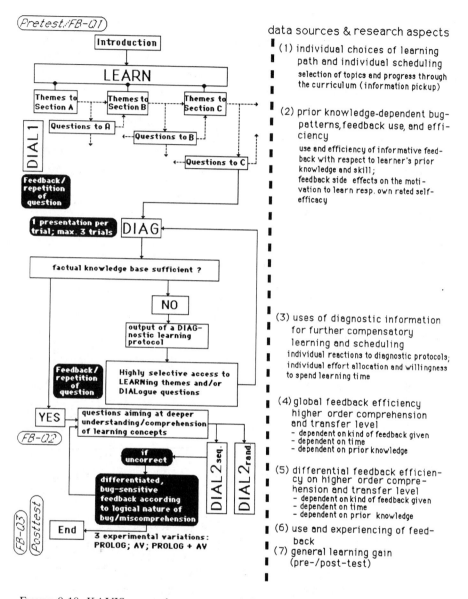

FIGURE 9.10. KAVIS research structure and data sources. (Rand. = randomized; seq. = sequential.)

of fact-oriented questions related to the last topic to secure a profound basis of *given* information before further *new* information could be acquired.) How will he use the diagnostic information contained in the printed output of the DIAGnostic test mode? Will he systematically compensate for his learning deficits with the help of the SELective topics/ques-

tions mode? How effective is AV feedback in general? Are the different feedback types in the comprehension–understanding part of the system of differential effectiveness both in terms of learning gains and economy? Are there any differences between learners of different prior knowledge in the ways they use the system and make use of its diagnostic/feedback information?

To make the system capable of being an efficient learning tool and to record online the learners' data as sketched, a double software design strategy was necessary: one to cover the teaching/learning and one to cover the online recording and analysis. The software developed to reach our goals correspondingly consists both of teachware and control of online data-recording. Additional auxiliary programs had to be written to transfer the recorded data to data-base and statistical analysis programs.

Hypotheses, Experimental Design, and Procedure

GENERAL RATIONALE

Any kind of ITS that deserves that name and that lays heavy stress on the online diagnosis and modeling of learner's current knowledge, comprehension, and skill regarding the bug lattice necessary to tailor the system's intervention and instruction must use a series of diagnostic tasks and questions to obtain a noise-free, valid learner diagnosis. A series of similar questions can be interpreted by the learner as indicating that he did not progress but rather stagnated. He then may attribute his or her actual performance and past competence as signs of personal failure or incompetence. Motivation lowering or even "helplessness feelings" may result. But if we must impose series of diagnostic questions to improve validity and reliability of our diagnosis, why not make a virtue of necessity and turn diagnosis into an explicit overt feedback tool for the learner to detect and correct his own bugs? An "offensive," explicit diagnostic feedback component then should result in considerable learning gains, especially for those learners who are unskilled and/or unused to online diagnosis of their learning. Inseparably yoked with the disclosure of diagnosis as overt feedback may be a second effect. If feedback diagnosing learning is deliberately designed so that its effects are controllable, unwanted diagnosis effects—emotional and affective, even motivational—should be eliminated or at least reduced, if not reversed, into a motivating, stabilizing stimulus.

RESEARCH OBJECTIVES

Interactive and/or tutorial learning systems rely heavily on diagnostic feedback, whether implicit in the covert system's diagnosis or explicit as

declared feedback. Although there is a commonsense attitude that feedback is efficient as a guiding principle in human learning, there are only scarce if any detailed studies of feedback efficiency in intelligent learning systems. We must take uncontrolled feedback effects into account as long as we have not investigated their possible effects both with regard to learning efficiency and emotional side effects. Clarification of feedback effects even could be a means to model cognitive processes. If we record and analyze how a given feedback and/or tutorial intervention influences further learning and knowledge formation, both cognitive processes can be modeled more precisely (in their interaction with implicit or explicit tutorial intervention), and feedback can be designed more narrowly tailored after the learner's needs. Our central focus of interest here thus is the efficiency of instrumental informative or corrective feedback on learning and knowledge acquisition.

The present study is concerned with the following two main goals. (1) How does feedback in general influence cognitive processes from the first information intake to deepened comprehension? How does it influence integration of new information into *knowledge* structures, and what effect has differential, bug-sensitive feedback on *comprehension*? (2) How does feedback in general influence affective and motivational coprocesses of learning, especially the learner's concomitant feelings of self-efficacy and success? With regard to the first question, the *impact of feedback on knowledge acquisition and comprehension*, two subclasses of questions can be derived: (1.1) What are the *general effects of global feedback on information intake and the growth of knowledge structures*? (1.2) What are the *differential effects of bug-sensitive feedback varying in intensity on comprehension for learners with different prior knowledge*?

With regard to the second main question, the *impact of feedback on affective and emotional coprocesses of learning*, a more global approach is undertaken here. Can learners of different abilities learn to profit from information about failures? Can we succeed in influencing the way feedback about success and failure is experienced, and can we turn feedback into a means to control and guide learning apart from the feedback's possibly punishing or aversive side effects? In the following two sections, hypotheses concerning the first and main goal of feedback effectiveness are elaborated. Hypotheses related to our second goal—the concomitant affective quality of learning feedback—are also outlined following.

Hypotheses Concerning the Differential Potency of Feedback Types Varying in Intensity and Content

To reiterate, we use the term *informing feedback* with the intention of providing the learner with information that is affectively neutral. The *informative* feedback is comprised of AV illustrations and demonstrations,

which present elementary facts of missed or truncated learner responses to a given task or question. Conversely *correcting and regulatory* feedback consist of a (self-) correcting and regulating component and an instructive intervention component, which in addition to AV clarification and explanations, also corrects misunderstandings and miscomprehensions (bugs). As outlined the first part of corrective feedback was delivered as a formative prologue to foster metacognitive self-regulation, that is, learner activity with regard to his response diagnosis in order to train his constructive ability to learn from failures.

With respect to the learner's prior knowledge, high-ability subjects should profit more from metaoperational control information, as is conveyed by the PROLOGue. This hypothesis holds for both kinds of feedback used: PROLOGue only and PROLOGue and AV. Differential efficiency of these two kinds of feedback should allow the teachware designer to decide which kind and intensity of feedback is better apt to control and guide comprehension. Because learning and the growth of knowledge is a cumulative process, one might even suppose that there may also be a phase-dependent differential feedback efficiency.

Poorer subjects should profit more from instructive, that is, supporting and aiding intervention. If one takes into account the temporal and process nature of knowledge acquisition as well as the increasing mastery of the content and its "sovereign distance," then less intriguing feedback intensities should become more efficient in later learning stages, while more intensive feedback should be more helpful at the beginning. If time-dependent shifts in feedback intensity are adequate, one could implement free choice among feedback kinds and intensities as an important feature in future ITS's. The learner himself—e.g., after an entrance diagnosis—may best decide whether a more or less intensive feedback level is suitable for him with respect to his current learning state.

Hypotheses Concerning the Differential Efficiency of Differential Feedback for Learners With Different Ability Level

The more intensive feedback is the more efficient it should be, provided it is bug sensitive and can be interpreted in a neutral, informative manner. The more able a learner is the more he should profit from feedback aimed at improving his self-regulating abilities.

Poorer subjects should profit more from aiding, assisting, and instructional-type feedback, that is, from our AV-only and/or PROLOGue *and* AV feedback and less from PROLOGue-only feedback, which may be too hard for them to process.

Better subjects should profit more from our self-regulatory *PROLOGue* type feedback. If there is an interaction between prior ability to learn from bugs, that is, ability to process the information contained in feedback, and its actual efficiency, learners with higher prior knowledge should profit

more from differential control feedback than poorer learners. If the training per se is efficient in shaping the learner's ability to process feedback, differences in the ability to process and use feedback should be reduced at later learning stages. Although it is possible that the cumulative effect of neutralizing the affective side effects of feedback by longer exposure to feedback reduces subjective stress, and although this neutralization could result in an increasingly better feedback use, the feedback's cognitive efficiency may be contaminated with general and unspecific decreasing stress effects, thereby interfering with learning.

The Emotional/Affective Qualities of Feedback for Different Learners

Affective side effects of feedback on learner motivation and self-esteem must be expected if one accepts the dual nature of feedback (informing/reinforcing). Similar to Kuhl's (1984) state versus action–orientation dichotomy, the filter of the learner's interpretation as installed via his or her learning history is a possible relevant moderator variable here. Feedback can be viewed as being instrumental for goal attainment or as an aversive confirmation of failure expectations. Holding (1965) would say "extrinsic vs. intrinsic dichotomy," and Condry and Chambers (1978) consider this state salience-shifting by external reward and/or punishment. The pattern of feedback interpretation for success-oriented learners (good learners) may be different from the pattern of failure-oriented learners (poor learners). The poor learner may interpret feedback as a source of aversive stimulation, preventing him from using the content properly; the successful learner, however, is skilled in using feedback information adequately. Differences between the two learner groups regarding the emotional or instrumental response to feedback should be eliminated during feedback-based practice if we would succeed in implementing an affectively neutral feedback. Correspondingly, one could expect that the more useful feedback becomes for adaptive learning regulation the more often it will be used as an instrumental tool by the learner. Additionally, the corrective type of feedback should then be regarded and experienced neutrally and contain no punishing qualities. With regard to the learner's prior ability, the following should be expected. If poorer subjects had "sad" experiences with self-efficacy, they should experience feedback much more emotionally than would higher ability subjects. Therefore, poorer subjects would rate feedback (tools) as less neutral and less instrumental, that is, view it as an external learning device. This emotionalized feedback could be eliminated if feedback could be experienced as something helpful. Less intensive types of feedback, at least for low-ability subjects, should be rated as less instrumental and more aversive than more intensive feedback. Less intensive feedback is defined as PROLOGue-only feedback, stating only that the learner's response was defective in a special sense.

GENERAL OUTLINE OF THE PROCEDURE

The study consisted of two parts, conducted in two sessions. The time elapsed between session 1 and session 2 was approximately 2 weeks. At the first experimental session, the pretest, a random sample of biology students was given booklets containing the pretest questions and the pretest feedback questionnaire. The students were informed that they would be given the opportunity to partake as paid testers and evaluators in a new AV biology curriculum. The booklets of those subjects willing to join were analyzed. The pretest questions were a set of 10 multiple-choice questions. The questions covered the factual knowledge supposedly gained from the previous term and used as prior knowledge for the experimental treatment. To test for existing prior knowledge with respect to the treatment content, three additional sets of multiple-choice questions were given. The first set consisted of 15 questions concerned with factual knowledge; the second of 10 questions covering target comprehension; and the third of 8 transfer questions on a high-comprehension level. Sets 2 (target comprehension) and 3 (complete comprehension) were parallel forms of corresponding items that appeared in DIAL 1, DIAG, or DIAL 2 sequential, DIAL 2 randomized, and the post-test. As in the pretest, the transfer set was also administered again in the post-test. The data of 96 subjects were analyzed and transformed into percentiles. The subjects were assigned to six experimental groups in such a way that the 2×3 prior knowledge/ability and treatment groups were completely homogeneous with respect to prior knowledge or ability. Table 9.1 shows the six experimental groups.

In the second experimental session, all subjects were treated individually. The subjects were given a small booklet, "Instructions on How to Use the System," through which they became acquainted with the hardware and study program. This was followed by a short explanation of the outline hanging on the wall as well as a demonstration of how to start up the screen and the first menu. The subject then proceeded to work on the LEARN, DIAL 1 and DIAG modes (cf., Figure 9.7). After having passed the threshold of DIAG, he was handed a feedback questionnaire. Once the questionnaire was filled out, he worked on the comprehension part (DIAL 2 sequential and DIAL 2 randomized, i.e., modes 5 and 6 of the system). Following completion of the comprehension section, the subject was given the second feedback questionnaire and a questionnaire in which he had to assess his learning and evaluate the features of the system. Because of a delay of about 30 to 45 minutes, which occurred between the last Learning mode (mode 6) and the completion of the feedback and evaluation questionnaire, the post-test was assigned delayed test status.

DATA SOURCES

The hardware and software architecture of a computerized instructional system like KAVIS II allows for a fine-grained learning-concomitant re-

TABLE 9.1. Feedback Assessment

Feedback content/event	Feedback interpretation	Statement to be rated as either "agree"/"disagree"
No feedback	Neutral-instrumental interpretation	If one monitors one's learning, one doesn't need other information.
	Affectively positive interpretation ("pride")	I feel relieved if I need not know how I do.
	Affectively negative interpretation ("shame")	If I have no opportunity to find out how I have done, I feel insecure.
Positive feedback "hit"/"correct"/"fine"	Neutral-instrumental interpretation	Feedback by another is a good means to control one's learning.
	Affectively positive interpretation ("pride")	If I get to know that I was right, I am proud.
	Affectively negative interpretation ("shame")	I feel ashamed when praised by another.
Negative feedback "missed"/"false"/"bad"	Neutral-instrumental interpretation	It is necessary to be informed about bugs to learn from them.
	Affectively positive interpretation ("pride")	Getting to know about my bugs just shows me how inefficient I am.
	Affectively negative interpretation ("shame")	If I hear that I was wrong I feel blamed.

cord of learner activities. As is shown in Figure 9.10, there are several sources of information with regard to learner's activities and several focuses possible when analyzing such data.

Except for the experimental control needed, the learner's approach to the content material is largely free and unrestricted. One source of information thus is his information intake from LEARN and his use of diagnostic information from DIAG, as evidenced by his further scheduling of learning.

With regard to feedback efficiency, there are several data sources. Overall feedback efficiency can be measured for the different feedback groups and the interaction between prior knowledge and treatment (see the outline of the experimental design following), and there is an overall comparison possible between pre- and post-test performance. In addition further comparisons are possible between unspecific factual feedback in DIAL 1 and the differential, error-sensitive feedback in the comprehension and transfer modes DIAL 2 sequential and DIAL 2 randomized as well as the corresponding interaction between prior knowledge and treatment. According to the typology that guided the system design, of possible feedback effects with respect to learning stages and the cognitive and affective processes involved, global, overall feedback efficiency on the one hand and differential stage-specific feedback effects on the other hand can be recorded. Finally, any individual bug can be recorded at any given point of time, and the effect of the correspondent feedback given on the next trial may be traced. Analyses of this latter kind allow for a detailed answer and bug modeling for the implementation of interactive computer tutors.

To obtain data from the different parts of KAVIS II, we recorded time and place of all learner–system interactions. Therefore, many movements of the learner within the system were traceable as was any learner input in response to a given question. Since we needed the "bug category" of any learner answer for immediate feedback, bug categories also were recorded. In order to supervise response latencies for the questions, tracing both learning gains and subjective certainty of the learner with respect to the answers but also to account for possible differences in answer styles (e.g. "impulsive" vs. "reflective"), both response latencies were recorded, starting with the first presentation of the question until the last answer alternative chosen. Moreover, "return-time," that is, the time spent between the last problem assignment and the return of the completed answer to the system, was recorded as well. Thus, our data allow for a precise, step-by-step monitoring of each individual learner.

As detailed in the dependent measures section concerning affective data, ratings on several seven-point scales of a feedback interpretation questionnaire were collected at three different points in the course of our treatment. Preceding any treatment (t_0) *global attitudes* about success or failure feedback in typical learning–studying tasks were probed. Further ratings of more narrowly *treatment-related* feedback statements were probed

at two significant points in our treatment. Directly after surpassing the knowledge threshold (in the mode 4 DIAGnosis) and before entering the comprehension part (modes 5 and 6) of the system, the subjects were asked to rate the feedback interpretation questionnaire (t_1). The same feedback questionnaire was again presented after quitting from the system after completion of mode 6, the randomized comprehension DIALogue 2, (t_2).

Variables

INDEPENDENT VARIABLES

As is evident from the experimental design (see Figure 9.11), there were two independent variables, ability and prior knowledge (A) and treatment/ type of feedback administered (B). Our differentiation between high prior knowledge and low prior knowledge subjects was based on a paper-and-pencil pretest that covered prerequisite elementary knowledge and related physics and chemistry concepts. This grouping measure, of course, is not further used in any of the following comparisons of learning gains. According to their percentile ranks, the 96 subjects were grouped in a high-ability group (A_1) and a low-ability group (A_2) and then were balanced across the three feedback groups (B_1 = PROLOGue only, B_2 = AV only, B_3 = PROLOGue and AV). Thus, six experimental groups were selected:

A_1B_1 = high ability/PROLOGue feedback only
A_1B_2 = high ability/AV feedback only
A_1B_3 = high ability/PROLOGue and AV feedback
A_2B_1 = low ability/PROLOGue feedback only
A_2B_1 = low ability/AV feedback only
A_2B_1 = low ability/PROLOGue and AV feedback

For any of the interesting dependent measures (Figure 9.11), a 2 × 3 analysis of variance (ANOVA) was done.

Dependent Variables and Measures Related to the Cognitive Feedback Effects

Our main rationale is that instrumental, bug-sensitive online feedback aids learning, that is, that feedback in general helps the student to master the psychologically difficult early steps in his or her first confrontation with still unfamiliar material in the phase of information intake and processing, whereas differential, bug-sensitive, online feedback guides and assists the later, more demanding stages of building integration and coherence. Accordingly, different classes of dependent measures can be derived.

Even knowing that one should not separate cognition from affect and

Experimental conditions and design.

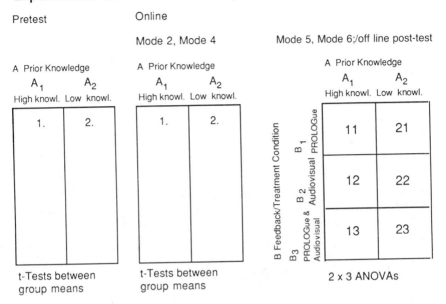

FIGURE 9.11. Experimental design and treatment; ANOVAs resp. *t* tests. Experimental conditions and design.

knowing that affective and cognitive coprocesses in learning are deeply intertwined, we can loosely group the dependent variables according to their dominant heritage either in *cognition* or in *affect* (see following discussion).

Feedback Efficiency as a Means to Foster Cognition and Comprehension

With regard to the instrumental role of feedback in general and the guiding and controlling effects of differential online feedback on comprehension and understanding, power and efficiency measures can be derived. Because our experimental design consisted of both online and offline diagnosis and because we have answer times, decision latencies, and total times for any online activities of the subjects, additional speed scores can be reported for any online tests, whereas power scores exclusively are restricted on the pre- and post-test. To reiterate: pretest does *not* refer to the prior-knowledge grouping measure used to separate the two knowledge groups. Because our treatment, at least as the PROLOGues involve metacognitive control, may have been influenced by both cognitive learning gains and metacognitive self-regulation in addition to power measures (score level), process measures were defined that may be indicative for process and control phenomena.

For any of the four main KAVIS II learning modes, the following dependent measures therefore were defined:

1. Sum of total score points. Power and level of learner performance.
2. Total learning time needed; total amount of learning time needed or spent (effort calculation).
3. Number of loops needed. The number of repetitions (loops) of a given question needed indicates the learner's needed effort as well as the efficiency of the feedback administered.
4. Learning time needed to get a score point. This effort measure is related to a standard score-point unit and indicates the learner's relative effort as well as relative feedback efficiency.
5. Score points per loop. This efficiency measure indicates the gain a learner can get from any presentation and/or repetition of a question.
6. Number of loops needed until a complete answer can be given. This again indicates the effort needed from the learner and the power of the feedback administered.

General feedback effects on knowledge acquisition and understanding–comprehension can be evaluated from a comparison between pre- and post-test. Differential effects of different kinds of feedback can be evaluated from a stage-related analysis. The following power and efficiency data correspond to our distinction between elementary knowledge (modes 2 and 4) and accumulated deeper understanding and comprehension (modes 5 and 6) and correspond to the kinds of feedback used—*uniform*, excerpt-like, short AV feedback in the knowledge-acquisition phase (modes 2 and 4) and *differential, bug-sensitive* feedback in varying intensities (PROLOGue-only, AV feedback-only, and combined PROLOGue and AV feedback).

Knowledge. General feedback effects on *knowledge acquisition* appear as results of absolute knowledge scores in the post-test (Table 9.2); relative differences in knowledge measured by learning gains in the pre- and post-test comparison (Table 9.3); differences in time- and treatment-dependent knowledge acquisition in power and efficiency scores from *mode 2/DIAL 1* (see following section entitled Online Measures From Mode 2 (DIAL 1) with respect to *mode 4/DIAG* (see following section entitled Online Measures From Mode 4 (DIAGnosis).

Understanding–Comprehension. General feedback effects on *understanding–comprehension* appear in the results of absolute comprehension scores in the post-test (Table 9.6); relative differences in comprehension concerning learning gains in the pre- and post-test comparison (Table 9.7); differences in time- and treatment-dependent and differential feedback effects in power and efficiency comprehension scores from *mode 5/DIAL 2 sequential* (Tables 9.11 to 9.13) regarding *mode 6/DIAL 2 random* (Tables 9.14 to 9.19).

As Figure 9.11 shows, dependent on the treatment conditions and independent variables design, either t tests for group differences or 2×3 ANOVAs were calculated.

Affectively Neutral Informative Feedback as a Means to Familiarize Learners With Basing Their Learning Control on Success/Failure Information

To measure feedback use and its effects on subjective feedback interpretation, a feedback questionnaire was constructed. Subjects had to rate their assertion or rejection of feedback-related statements on a seven-point scale. As is evident from Table 9.1, any theoretical, plausible conjunction of situation x feedback interpretation was rated in a carefully balanced order.

The rationale for the construction of the feedback questionnaire (as illustrated by Figure 9.11) is the following. Depending on the learner's learning history and his failure or success orientation, which may serve as a filter for the interpretation of feedback events, he may give feedback an affectively neutral, positive, or aversive interpretation. This holds for neutral, positive, or negative feedback. The resulting 3×3 grid covers any possible feedback–feedback-interpretation combination. A learner, for instance, might be given no feedback at all. He may then react either positively ("Fine: Don't think twice, it's alright"), negatively ("Without feedback I feel insecure whether I have hit the point"), or neutrally ("If I don't get feedback that doesn't matter"). Analogous feedback interpretations (feeling proud or ashamed when getting feedback that a performance was right or false) can be conceived the same way. With respect to instrumental, informative feedback, which by its very nature should be neutral in its affective quality, affectively neutral interpretations of feedback as useful information are apt to guide learning. Because it is plausible that a learner already has a learning history and thus has an interpretation filter "installed," one might look for an attitude change after exposure to instrumental feedback. To discriminate long-term attitude from situation-specific reactions, a feedback-interpretation questionnaire can be administered before, during, and after exposure to feedback.

In order to analyze preexisting feedback interpretations of subjects, a feedback questionnaire was also used in the pretest. It contained typical learning situations with which students are confronted when attending a university.

For each of the nine item types in Table 9.1, four learning situations were constructed. They were interspersed with "dummy" or "filler" items to avoid bias and to hide the intention of the questionnaire. The pretest feedback questionnaire was given to the subjects about 2 weeks before the experiment started. The two experimental questionnaires were presented after the subjects had been successful with the DIAGnosis and finished the last comprehension item (randomized order). Repeated measures from the

prior knowledge test phase *beyond treatment* (t_0) and from two significant learning stages (t_1 and t_2) *within treatment* should evidence any changes in feedback interpretation.

Results of *t* Tests and ANOVAs

In the following sections, results from all areas under investigation are reported: knowledge acquisition power and efficiency data, comprehension power and efficiency data, and subjective ratings of feedback interpretation and use. For an easier access to the results, only the ANOVA main effects and their interactions and the tables of cell means are reported. (More detailed results can be obtained from the authors).

KNOWLEDGE ACQUISITION DATA

Sum of Knowledge Score Points: Post-Test

There is a clear and highly significant superiority effect of higher prior knowledge against low ability. Because there is no significant treatment-feedback effect but a significant interaction between treatment and prior knowledge, we must assume that learner's prior knowledge governs the efficiency of using feedback for learning control. The AV feedback condition seemingly requires minimal skill; correspondingly, low-ability subjects here score like their high-ability counter-group. In the reverse case the most demanding treatment, PROLOGue only, and the next demanding, AV information organized in advance by PROLOGue, require some knowledge or skill to be used optimally. For both pairs of ability group means, there are significant differences. Whereas the high-ability subjects scored best in the AV and PROLOGue condition, low-ability subjects conversely scored best in the least demanding AV-only condition. Knowledge acquisition generally is aided by feedback, but some foregoing skill is required to be able to make full use of it.

TABLE 9.2. Sum of knowledge score-points; post-test (2 × 3 ANOVA)

Prior knowledge	Treatment			Σ	F ratios		P
	PROLOGue only	AV only	PROLOGue & AV				
High	39.9	39.7	41.9	40.5	F_A	$= 9.79$	$\leq .003$
Low	37.9	39.9	37.9	38.6	F_B	$= .98$	$\leq .38$
Σ	38.9	39.8	39.9	39.5	F_{AB}	$= 3.76$	$\leq .03$

Learning Difference in Knowledge Score Points: Pretest Versus Post-Test

There are clearly significant effects of both prior knowledge and feedback treatment (see Table 9.3). As is the case with the power score, knowledge

acquisition generally is aided by feedback but requires some foregoing skill to make full use of the information contained. With regard to learning gain, even high-ability subjects profited most from AV feedback only, followed by the combination of the two kinds of feedback. On the contrary the poorer ability group profited most from the less demanding simple AV feedback with substantial smaller gains both from PROLOGue-only and combined feedback. With regard to learning gain per se, the poorer subjects profited most from all kinds of treatments compared with the high-ability group. Even if this is due to a ceiling effect at the side of the high-ability subjects, the fact that the average post-test performance level of the high-ability group is below the maximal number of score points to be gained (45 points) indicates that this possible ceiling effect is restricted. Feedback thus is an effective means to foster poor subjects' acquisition of knowledge.

TABLE 9.3. Learning gains in knowledge score-points; pre-test–post-test (2 × 3 ANOVA)

| Prior knowledge | Treatment | | | Σ | F ratios | P |
	PROLOGue only	AV only	PROLOGue & AV			
High	12.8	16.1	17.1	15.4	F_A = 59.6	$\leq$ .001
Low	20.7	23.8	20.8	21.8	F_B = 5.3	$\leq$ .01
Σ	16.7	20.0	19.0	18.6	F_{AB} = 2.7	$\leq$ .07

Online Measures From Mode 2 (DIAL 1)

Due to the fact that feedback administered in mode 2 (DIAL 1) consisted in a uniform AV excerpt from the LEARNing topics, only prior knowledge differences can differentiate the groups here. Correspondingly, only t tests between the ability groups were calculated. Performance and efficiency differences here are due to both a general impact of prior knowledge and feedback efficiency in general (see Table 9.4).

TABLE 9.4. On-line measures from DIAL 1 (mode 2) (2 × 3 ANOVA)

| On-line measures | Prior knowledge | | | T | P |
	Total	High	Low		
Sum of score-points	55.2	54.9	55.4	−.50	$\leq$ .63
Learning time	967.1	918.8	1015.4	−1.45	$\leq$ .15
Loops needed	23.2	23.0	23.5	−.56	$\leq$ .59
Learning time per score-point	17.5	16.7	18.2	−1.40	$\leq$ .17
Score-points per loop	2.4	2.4	2.4	−.61	$\leq$ .55
Loops before 1st correct answer	1.9	1.8	1.9	−.71	$\leq$ .49

Sum of Score-Points/DIAL 1 (Mode 2)

Both ability groups performed equally well, indicating that the uniform AV instruction and DIALogue feedback treatment was apt to reduce existing knowledge differences. (see Table 9.4). To show what actually

happened in the first phase of information intake and integration, the following process data are revealing.

Learning Time/DIAL 1 (Mode 2)

Despite the nonsignificance of the difference between group means, there is at least some evidence that the low-ability group needed more total learning time to make up their original arrears in knowledge (see Table 9.4).

Loops Needed/DIAL 1 (Mode 2)

The low-ability subjects needed the same effort in number of repeated presentations and feedbacks (loops) as the high-ability group, indicating that they were indeed aided by the elementary AV feedback (see Table 9.4).

Learning Time Per Score Point/DIAL 1 (Mode 2)

Again—as was the case with total learning time—there was an insignificant trend indicating that the low-ability group invested or needed more time to exploit the feedbacks (see Table 9.4).

Score Points Per Loop/DIAL 1 (Mode 2)

The efficiency of exploitation of feedback information was not different in the two groups, indicating both that the feedback also was adequate for the low-ability group and that their arrears in knowledge could be made up (see Table 9.4).

Loops Before First Correct Answer/DIAL 1 (Mode 2)

Again, as was the case with the earlier process data, there is no significant difference between the two groups. There is no difference in the *level* of efficiency in using the learning and feedback information (see Table 9.4).

Summary of DIAL 1/Mode 2 Process Data

At an early stage of knowledge acquisition, the very first phase of information intake and integration, elementary AV feedback is efficient in reducing preexisting knowledge differences between ability groups. Low-ability subjects do not differ from high-ability subjects in terms of resulting performance, but they need more effort in terms of time needed to process the material or exploit a given feedback per given presentation.

Online Measures From DIAGnosis (Mode 4)

Mode 4, DIAGnosis, closes the stage of information intake and knowledge integration. After surpassing a predefined threshold of required knowledge score points, the subject is allowed to enter the comprehension and understanding part of the system. At the same time mode 4 is a more advanced

stage of information processing; data accessed here indicate a later, and, related to knowledge acquisition, final stage (see Table 9.5).

TABLE 9.5. On-line measures from DIAG (mode 4) (2 × 3 ANOVA)

On-line measures	Prior knowledge			T	P
	Total	High	Low		
Sum of score-points	39.9	40.7	39.1	2.24	≦ .03
Learning time	634.6	589.2	680.0	−1.74	≦ .08
Learning time per score-point	15.5	14.6	16.3	−1.51	≦ .13
Score-points per loop	2.7	2.7	2.6	2.25	≦ .03
Loops before 1st correct answer	1.8	1.7	1.9	−2.13	≦ .04

Sum of Score Points/DIAG (Mode 4)

Whereas the results from learning at an early stage (mode 2) indicated that the poor-ability group could draw level with the high-ability group, results here indicate that this was still unstable. High-ability subjects performed significantly better than the low-ability countergroup (see Table 9.5).

Learning Time/DIAG (Mode 4)

There is an insignificant trend that the poor-ability subjects needed more learning time to complete the knowledge diagnosis. This more global measure is highlighted by the following results of the loops analysis (see Table 9.5).

Learning Time Per Score Point/DIAG (Mode 4)

There is an insignificant trend that the high-ability group was better able to profit from LEARNing and feedback-based interactive DIALogue. They were better able to exploit feedback in the previous mode and now need less time to score (see Table 9.5).

Score Points Per Loop/DIAG (Mode 4)

Loop has a different and unparalleled meaning here. Although in any feedback-based interactive mode (modes 2, 3, 5, and 6) *loop* means that an item could be repeated maximally three times consecutively, a loop in the DIAGnostic mode means that the whole series of following questions could be run through maximally three times as a whole block of items presented. The low-ability group could gain less score points per loop than the high-ability group, indicating that the former were overall less efficient (see Table 9.5).

Loops Before First Correct Answer/DIAG (Mode 4)

Again in the unparalleled sense of *loop* used here, the loops-effort measure indicates the efficiency of what was gained from a series of questions. The

low-prior-knowledge subjects needed more loops to make an item correct. Because we scored answers that were deficient or incorrect at the end of the last series repetition with a count of 4, the number of loops required before an item could be fully completed indicates that a substantial number of poor-ability subjects could not complete some knowledge items (see Table 9.5).

Discussion of DIAGnosis/Model 4 and Previous DIALogue 1 Mode 2 With Uniform Feedback

In the early phase of learning, poor subjects are able to make comparable use from learning and interactive feedback even if they need more time per trial and on the whole. As the results from the later stage show, this catch-up in knowledge is not very stable. Short-period gains—if not even short-term memory effects—feign some temporary effect, which volatilizes soon. Longer lasting catch-up effects demand a more thorough, intensive training, as is the case in the following modes with bug-sensitive intensified feedbacks.

COMPREHENSION/UNDERSTANDING AND DIFFERENTIAL FEEDBACK DATA

Sum of Comprehension Score Points: Post-Test

Main effects, prior knowledge, and differential feedback are all significant without a significant interaction between them (Table 9.6). All three high-ability treatment groups scored equally well, with an insignificant tendency for the combined treatment to be the most powerful. The poor-ability subjects also scored best with the combined and the AV-only treatments with a minor insignificant advantage of the combined PROLOGue and AV treatment. Except in the AV-only treatment, where both groups performed equally well, the high-ability subjects scored better in the two other treatments. The equality of performance in the AV-only feedback indicates that this feedback requires less ability to be interpreted. Both treatments containing a PROLOGue indicate that some prerequisite skill is needed to make optimal use of feedback information.

TABLE 9.6. Sum of comprehension score-points; post-test (2 × 3 ANOVA)

Prior knowledge	Treatment			Σ	F ratios	P
	PROLOGue only	AV only	PROLOGue & AV			
High	23.6	23.7	24.6	24.0	$F_A = 7.67$	$\leq .01$
Low	20.9	22.9	23.4	22.4	$F_B = 3.20$	$\leq .04$
Σ	22.2	23.3	24.0	23.2	$F_{AB} = 1.08$	$\leq .35$

Learning Difference in Comprehension Score Points: Pretest and Post-Test

Again, both main effects are significant without a significant interaction (Table 9.7). Learning gains for the low-ability subjects are greater than those of all three high-ability groups. Even if there may have been a ceiling effect for the high-ability subjects, the fact that they did not succeed in achieving the maximal number of score points possible (30 score points; see Table 9.6) indicates that they were apart from top performance. High-ability subjects learned best with the combined feedback and equally well with the PROLOGue-only and AV-only feedback. Low-ability subjects, on the contrary, learned best and equally well with AV-only feedback and the combined PROLOGue and AV feedback.

TABLE 9.7. Learning gains in comprehension score-points; pre-test–post-test (2 × 3 ANOVA)

Prior knowledge	Treatment			Σ	F ratios			P
	PROLOGue only	AV only	PROLOGue & AV					
High	8.1	7.9	9.6	8.5	F_A	=	58.10	$\leq$ .001
Low	11.7	14.7	14.4	13.6	F_B	=	3.42	$\leq$ .04
Σ	9.9	11.3	12.0	11.0	F_{AB}	=	1.99	$\leq$ .14

Online Measures From DIAL 2 Sequential/Mode 5

Online measures from DIAL 2 sequential/mode 5 (and following mode 6/DIAL 2 random) are sensible for the effects of our differential feedbacks on comprehension and rate of progress in the different ability groups. By recording resulting bugs and series of bugs in the first, second, and possibly third repeated presentation of an item (loops), it is also possible to directly relate intervention by feedback to the growth of comprehension and understanding.

Sum of Score Points/DIAL 2 Sequence (Mode 5)

There is no significant effect of prior knowledge, indicating that the effects are due solely to treatment effects. Both ability groups performed better with AV only and PROLOGue and AV combined feedback, with slight but insignificant advantages of PROLOGue and AV feedback in the high-ability group and a significant advantage of the latter in the low-ability group. While PROLOGue *only* may be a too harsh, demanding treatment for the low-ability group, there may have been some kind of a "sleeper effect" for the combined treatment, which combined with AV factual information leads to better performance.

TABLE 9.8. Sum of score-points/DIAL 2 sequential (mode 5) (2 × 3 ANOVA)

Prior knowledge	Treatment			Σ	F ratios		P
	PROLOGue only	AV only	PROLOGue & AV				
High	36.4	38.9	39.0	38.1	F_A =	.43	≦.52
Low	38.1	38.9	39.8	38.6	F_B =	2.81	≦.06
Σ	37.3	38.4	39.4	38.3	F_{AB} =	1.26	≦.29

Sum of Learning Time/DIAL 2 Sequential (Mode 5)

The insignificance of prior knowledge again indicates the efficiency of feedback (Table 9.9). Subjects in both groups needed more time in the more demanding PROLOGue-only condition than in the remaining feedback groups with minor but insignificant advantages for the combined feedback. High-ability subjects in the AV-only condition needed the least learning time.

TABLE 9.9. Sum of learning time/DIAL 2 sequential (mode 5) (2 × 3 ANOVA)

Prior knowledge	Treatment			Σ	F ratios		P
	PROLOGue only	AV only	PROLOGue & AV				
High	956.6	726.8	787.9	823.8	F_A =	1.58	≦.21
Low	981.1	843.4	857.0	893.8	F_B =	4.04	≦.02
Σ	968.8	785.1	822.5	858.8	F_{AB} =	.23	≦.80

Sum of Loops Needed/DIAL 2 Sequential (Mode 5)

Both treatment and prior knowledge main effects were significant (Table 9.10). High-ability subjects needed fewer repeated presentations of items than the low-ability group. Again AV only and PROLOGue and AV feedback were less hard to process as compared with the demanding PROLOGue-only condition. Although there is a minor and insignificant advantage of PROLOGue and AV combined over AV only in the high-ability group, poor-ability subjects needed significantly fewer loops in the AV-only condition. This indicates again that processing of the PROLOGues is a task that may have been too demanding.

TABLE 9.10. Sum of loops needed/DIAL 2 sequential (mode 5) (2 × 3 ANOVA)

Prior knowledge	Treatment			Σ	F ratios		P
	PROLOGue only	AV only	PROLOGue & AV				
High	18.2	17.1	16.2	19.2	F_A =	8.60	≦.005
Low	21.1	17.3	18.9	19.1	F_B =	5.82	≦.005
Σ	19.7	17.2	17.5	18.1	F_{AB} =	1.76	≦.18

Learning Time Per Score Point/DIAL 2 Sequential (Mode 5)

The insignificance of the prior knowledge effect indicates that treatment is the crucial factor for what can be exploited from a given learning time

TABLE 9.11. Learning time per score-point/DIAL 2 sequential (mode 5) (2 × 3 ANOVA)

Prior knowledge	Treatment			Σ	F ratios		P
	PROLOGue only	AV only	PROLOGue & AV				
High	26.3	18.7	20.2	21.7	F_A	= 1.35	≦ .25
Low	26.4	22.4	21.6	23.5	F_B	= 6.27	≦ .003
Σ	26.3	20.6	20.9	22.6	F_{AB}	= .50	≦ .62

unit (Table 9.11). Score gains in the AV-only and PROLOGue and AV combined condition needed less learning time than the PROLOGue-only condition, i.e., they were more efficient. The fact that the low-ability subjects needed equal amounts of learning time in the AV-only and combined PROLOGue and AV conditions again may speak for some kind of sleeper effect in PROLOGue use.

Score Points Per Loop/DIAL 2 Sequential (Mode 5)

Both main effects reached (Table 9.12). significance. High-ability subjects in both the PROLOGue-only and PROLOGue and AV combined conditions could gain more score points per loop than their low-ability counterparts. Both ability groups could exploit more score points under the AV-only and PROLOGue and AV combined feedbacks than from PROLOGue only, which again was the most demanding feedback. The fact that there was no performance difference between the ability groups in the AV-only treatment, whereas the high-ability subjects performed significantly better with feedback containing a PROLOGue, indicates that some knowledge or skill is necessary to fully use this kind of feedback.

TABLE 9.12. Score points per loop/DIAL 2 sequential (mode 5) (2 × 3 ANOVA)

Prior knowledge (B)	Treatment			Σ	F ratios		P
	PROLOGue only	AV only	PROLOGue & AV				
High	2.1	2.3	2.4	2.3	F_A	= 9.41	≦ .003
Low	1.8	2.2	2.2	2.1	F_B	= 10.42	≦ .001
Σ	2.0	2.3	2.3	2.2	F_{AB}	= .08	≦ .48

Number of Loops Before First Correct Answer/DIAL 2 Sequential (Mode 5)

Both main effects were significant (Table 9.13). Both ability groups required fewer loops until they were able to fully complete an answer in treatment conditions AV only and combined PROLOGue and AV (with a small insignificant advantage of the latter). High-ability subjects again performed better in these two conditions than the low-ability groups; again the fact that this difference is not valid for AV-only treatment indicates that the PROLOGue component offers surplus information to those who are able to use it.

TABLE 9.13. Number of loops before 1st correct answer/DIAL 2 sequential (mode 5) (2 × 3 ANOVA)

Prior knowledge	Treatment			Σ	F ratios	P
	PROLOGue only	AV only	PROLOGue & AV			
High	2.0	1.8	1.7	1.8	F_A = 6.43	≤.01
Low	2.4	1.8	2.0	2.4	F_B = 8.62	≤.001
Σ	2.2	1.8	1.8	1.9	F_{AB} = 1.45	≤.24

Summary of DIAL 2 Sequential/Mode 5 Online Data

In those cases where the prior knowledge variable is significant, high-ability subjects in feedback types PROLOGue only and PROLOGue and AV combined consistently perform better or learn more economically than do the low-ability subjects. The combined PROLOGue and AV treatment then too has a small but insignificant advantage over AV-only feedback, indicating that the high-ability group at least to some degree could make use of the PROLOGue as an "advance organizer." In no measure is there a significant difference between high-ability and low-ability subjects with regard to AV-only feedback, indicating that AV-only feedback was adequate for the majority of the poor-ability subjects to reach some substantial learning and or economic gain. PROLOGue only consistently was too demanding for the low-ability group, indicating that their shortcomings in prior knowledge and/or metacognitive skill could not be overcome by the PROLOGue treatment at least in the form implemented here.

DIAL 2 Random/Mode 6 Online Data

Again, each presentation of an item was followed by one of the three feedback types if the answer was wrong or deficient. In a sense the *randomized* presentation of comprehension questions in mode 6 is a test of the stability of what was learned earlier. The linear ordering of questions correspondent with the sequential order of the learning themes may help recognition memory to reconstruct relations between correspondent units; since randomized order eliminates possible helpful sequential effects in reconstructive memory, it tests for true comprehension. At the same time mode 6 is the latest and final presentation of comprehension questions, so that here the deepest level of comprehension after maximally six presentations of each comprehension item is accessed.

Sum of Score Points/DIAL 2 Random (Mode 6)

Because of the insignificant two main effects, neither *t* tests for differences between cell means nor *t* tests for differences between correspondent ability/treatment means made sense (Table 9.14).

TABLE 9.14. Sum of score-points/DIAL 2 random (mode 6) (2 × 3 ANOVA)

Prior knowledge	Treatment			Σ	F ratios		P
	PROLOGue only	AV only	PROLOGue & AV				
High	34.1	33.4	33.0	33.5	F_A	= .54	≦ .47
Low	34.7	33.4	33.9	34.0	F_B	= 1.06	≦ .35
Σ	34.4	33.4	33.4	33.8	F_{AB}	= .16	≦ .85

Sum of Learning Time/DIAL 2 Random (Mode 6)

Only the treatment variable was significant (Table 9.15). Learners with AV-only and PROLOGue and AV combined feedback needed significantly less learning time than learners in the PROLOGue-only groups. This again indicates that the PROLOGue-only feedback was not easy to process for both ability groups. The fact that high-ability learners in the PROLOGue and AV combined treatment condition did not differ significantly from their AV-only counterparts indicates that the PROLOGue feedback component may be more helpful if it is accompanied by AV information. There is an interesting crossover effect for the high-ability group. Although high-ability learners consistently needed less learning time than low-ability learners in the previous measures/modes, high-ability learners now needed more learning time in the PROLOGue-only condition than the low-ability learners needed. This may indicate that the high-ability learners tried harder to process the most demanding feedback, whereas the poor learners may have allocated less effort here.

TABLE 9.15. Sum of learning time/DIAL 2 random (mode 6) (2 × 3 ANOVA)

Prior knowledge	Treatment			Σ	F ratios		P
	PROLOGue only	AV only	PROLOGue & AV				
High	559.3	337.4	390.4	442.3	F_A	= 1.75	≦ .19
Low	533.5	448.2	484.8	488.8	F_B	= 5.43	≦ .01
Σ	546.4	412.7	437.6	465.6	F_{AB}	= 1.09	≦ .34

Sum of Loops Needed/DIAL 2 Random (Mode 6)

Both prior knowledge and treatment reached significance (Table 9.16). The AV-only and PROLOGue and AV combined feedback resulted in less repetitions (loops) needed for both ability groups with a minor, insignificant advantage for the latter in the high-ability group. PROLOGue contained in a feedback and yoked with AV information may serve as an advance organizer for the processing of the AV component if the learner is able to make full use of it. High-ability subjects in treatment conditions PROLOGue only and PROLOGUE and AV combined also needed fewer loops than their low-ability counterparts.

TABLE 9.16. Sum of loops needed/DIAL 2 random (mode 6) (2 × 3 ANOVA)

Prior knowledge	Treatment			Σ	F ratios		P
	PROLOGue only	AV only	PROLOGue & AV				
High	14.9	12.4	11.8	13.0	F_A	= 7.58	≦.01
Low	17.4	13.5	13.9	14.9	F_B	= 9.79	≦.001
Σ	16.2	12.9	12.8	14.0	F_{AB} =	.33	≦.72

Learning Time Per Score Point/DIAL 2 Random (Mode 6)

Only the treatment/feedback variable was significant (Table 9.17). Both AV-only and the PROLOGue and AV combined feedback required less learning time to get a score point as compared with PROLOGue only. Consistent with the learning time data, high-ability learners needed more learning time in the PROLOGue-only condition than the poor learners. This may indicate that they tried harder to process the most demanding feedback than did the poor learners.

TABLE 9.17. Learning time per score-point/DIAL 2 random (mode 6) (2 × 3 ANOVA)

Prior knowledge	Treatment			Σ	F ratios		P
	PROLOGue only	AV only	PROLOGue & AV				
High	16.3	11.4	11.8	13.2	F_A	= 1.50	≦.22
Low	15.6	13.4	14.0	14.4	F_B	= 5.14	≦.01
Σ	16.0	12.4	12.9	13.8	F_{AB} =	.91	≦.41

Score Points Per Loop/DIAL 2 Random (Mode 6)

Treatment as well as prior knowledge were significant (Table 9.18). High-ability subjects could exploit more score points per loop than the low-ability groups. Again, there is an insignificant minor advantage for PROLOGue and AV combined feedback in the high-ability group, indicating that—provided some knowledge or skill—PROLOGue information can serve as an advance organizer.

TABLE 9.18. Score-points per loop/DIAL 2 random (mode 6) (2 × 3 ANOVA)

Prior knowledge	Treatment			Σ	F ratios		P
	PROLOGue only	AV only	PROLOGue & AV				
High	2.4	2.8	2.8	2.7	F_A	= 9.51	≦.003
Low	2.1	2.6	2.6	2.4	F_B	= 14.13	≦.001
Σ	2.2	2.7	2.7	2.5	F_{AB} =	.22	≦.81

Number of Loops Before First Correct Answer/DIAL 2 Random (Mode 6)

Again, both prior knowledge and feedback treatment were highly significant (Table 9.19). High-ability subjects needed fewer repeated presentations

of an item until they could complete it. For both ability groups AV only and PROLOGue and AV combined were more efficient than PROLOGue only. Again, there is a small insignificant advantage of the combined feedback for high-ability subjects.

TABLE 9.19. Number of loops before 1st correct answer/DIAL 2 random (mode 6) (2 × 3 ANOVA)

Prior knowledge	Treatment			Σ	F ratios			P
	PROLOGue only	AV only	PROLOGue & AV					
High	1.6	1.3	1.2	1.4	F_A	=	7.64	$\leqq .007$
Low	1.9	1.4	1.5	1.6	F_B	=	10.26	$\leqq .001$
Σ	1.8	1.3	1.3	1.5	F_{AB}	=	.43	$\leqq .66$

Summary of DIAL 2 Random/Mode 6 Online Data

With two interesting exceptions mode 6/DIAL 2 random replicates the findings from mode 5/DIAL 2 sequential. If the prior knowledge variable is significant, high-ability subjects consistently perform better or learn more efficiently than the low-ability subjects in feedback types PROLOGue only and PROLOGue and AV combined. Correspondingly, the combined PROLOGue and AV treatment then has a small but insignificant advantage over AV-only feedback. This indicates that the high-ability group at least to some degree could make use of the PROLOGue as an advance organizer. There was no significant difference between high-ability and low-ability subjects with regard to AV-only feedback. AV-only feedback was adequate for the majority of the poor-ability subjects to reach some substantial learning and/or economic gain. PROLOGue-only feedback consistently was too demanding for the low-ability group, indicating that their shortcomings in prior knowledge and/or metacognitive skill could not be overcome by the PROLOGue treatment, at least not in the form implemented here. The interesting exception is that the high-ability subjects, who needed consistently less learning time or fewer repeated presentations of an item for all three kinds of feedbacks in mode 5 now spend more learning time on the whole and need more learning time to get a score point in the PROLOGue-only feedback than the low-ability subjects need. This may indicate that the high-ability subjects made heavy use of the metaoperational PROLOGue information and tried harder to weed out their final shortcomings, whereas the low-ability group may have tried less or even may have given up.

DISCUSSION OF THE EFFICIENCY DATA

With regard to acquisition of knowledge, uniform informative AV feedback is apt to enhance learning gains and/or reduce learning effort for

both high- and low-ability subjects. The substantial learning gains of the low-ability group, especially at an early stage of learning, are promising. As the decrease in efficiency in mode 4 shows, the learning gains in fact were less stable than we had expected, indicating that feedback with only moderate not adaptive intensity may be insufficient to result in durable learning gains.

With regard to comprehension we succeeded in implementing an efficient learning aid by enhancing its usefulness/efficiency/availability for the learner. Thus he can use feedback as a means to identify bugs and to correct them. As predicted, feedback containing a regulatory component was useful for high-ability subjects but only when combined with content-related AV instructions. Whether this usefulness depends on underdeveloped metaoperational skills or a tendency to pretend to material aid cannot be settled. If regulative information as it is contained in the PRO-LOGues is combined, however, with AV information as a material aid, it can be used as advance organizer at least by subjects of higher ability and/or higher metaoperational skill. In any case there is a need to view feedback effects in a more differentiated manner, that is, according to the different cognitive levels of the target measure. It seems necessary to abandon expectations of an overall feedback efficiency regardless of learner ability and necessary cognitive operations involved. Whereas regulatory feedback may be too demanding for poorer learners (PROLOGue only), they can be helped efficiently with the remaining kinds of feedback. Low-ability subjects could achieve substantial learning gains with the instructional assistance of AV.

Our expectation with regard to a higher efficiency of regulatory feedback for *high-ability* learners was not substantiated. At present only regulatory feedback *combined* with aiding feedback seems to be efficient. We are also dissatisfied with the meager efficiency of the combined treatment as compared to AV only. Because the differential AV treatment was the same for the AV-only treatment and the combined PROLOGue and AV treatment, the special PROLOGue may have served as advance organizer and may have installed expectations not fulfilled by the accompanying AV information. This justifies giving still more weight to careful design of regulatory PROLOGues and material informative AV in order to tie AV feedback even more tightly to PROLOGue content (e.g. by blinking arrows highlighting aspects stressed in the PROLOGue).

At present, due to the tremendous amount of data, we were only able to analyze power, speed, and efficiency measures and unable to work on the processing of bug data. A further fine-grained analysis of the learners' bug patterns before and after feedback—that is of loop-related error detection, correction, and possibly new errors—will allow a more detailed modeling of the comprehension process of learners with different prior knowledge.

FEEDBACK EFFECTS ON AFFECT AND MOTIVATION: GENERAL EVALUATION OF THE SYSTEM

Feedback Interpretation

As described earlier there were two types of feedback-interpretation questionnaires: a more general one, covering more unspecific, "typical" study experiences with feedback (attitudinal level), and a situation-specific feedback-interpretation questionnaire dealing with spontaneous affects of the student when confronted with feedback (behavioral level). The former was administered at the time of the pretest, that is, about 2 weeks before the experimental sessions. The latter was presented both directly after the student had passed the "threshold test" (DIAGnosis; mode 4), switching from basic knowledge to the comprehension and coherence part, and after the last set of randomized comprehension questions (DIALogue 2 random, mode 6). Thus differences between attitude toward feedback and reactions on immediate, accumulated exposure to intensified feedback can be measured.

We distinguish between feedback as such (the feedback "event") and its subsequent interpretation by the learner, which we suppose to be moderated by current success; earlier learning history; and situational saliences, which again might be filtered by the learner's learning history. As outlined in Table 9.1, there are possibly nine types of feedback events, feedback interpretations, which should be open to impacts by the intensified feedback exposure. As detailed earlier there were three repeated measurements: one at the beginning of the pretest (t_0), one after finishing the first knowledge-threshold diagnosis in the knowledge and facts part (t_1), and one after leaving the comprehension–understanding part (DIAL 2 sequential resp. DIAL 2 random t_2). Since the first feedback-interpretation questionnaire focused on more broad, attitudinal feedback-interpretation habits, it should serve as a kind of baseline. The latter two questionnaires, with their more situational content, might serve as direct indicators of any shifts in feedback-interpretation after stepwise, accumulated exposure. Differences between t_0 and t_1 resp. t_2 as well as differences between t_0 and t_2 resp. t_1 and t_2 might reflect any change in the learner's feedback-interpretation style.

The following feedback event/feedback interpretation measures reached significance (probabilities for F ratios resp. t scores $\leq .05$).

0/0 (No Feedback/Miss of Important Correction/Bug Information)

From the six treatment/ability groups, PROLOG only (1) and PROLOG and AV combined feedback (3) consistently scored higher than the AV-only group with the less intensive feedback (2). Regardless of subject's ability, intensified exposure to feedback leads to assertions of missing information.

−/0 (Feedback Stating Error or Bug ("False")/Interpreted as Important Information About One's Learning Efficiency

PROLOG only (1) subjects and PROLOG and AV combined feedback (2) subjects agreed to a substantial degree. Again, there was no substantial difference between high- and low-ability subjects.

0/+ (No Feedback/Feelings of Relief)

This negative attitude toward feedback ("don't think twice, its alright") was reduced significantly more in the low-ability group which, as our efficiency data show, had most profit from the feedback. There is a clear gradient with respect to feedback intensity: The PROLOG and AV combined feedback group (3) scored lower than the AV-only feedback (2) and PROLOGue-only (1) groups, which earlier asserted that "no feedback spares you care." There is a remarkable trend in the data that accumulated treatment leads to an accumulating decrease of negative attitudes toward feedback.

−/− (Feedback Stating Error or Bug ("False")/Interpreted as Harm or Punishment)

No doubt, feedback harms. Low-ability subjects to a significant degree interpret negative feedback as punishing or blaming. The low-ability subjects, however, also recovered most from aversive feelings and experienced instrumental feedback as helpful and necessary the more they were exposed to it.

All in all we did not succeed fully in freeing feedback from its emotional burden, but we were able to increase its informative interpretation significantly. Perhaps some harm is necessary in order to foster success-related feelings of self-efficacy. We had intended to strengthen the informative aspects of feedback with no increase in the aversive negative feedback. In this respect our goal was reached. As proposed there is sound reason to neutralize system feedback in order to control for its effects when basing learning on online feedback or correspondent tutor components.

General Evaluation of the System

Generally, the system's transparency and clearness was rated very high and positive. The learning system was experienced as easy to handle and as transparent, regardless of groups or treatment. The learning modes, that is, the opportunity of switching, was experienced by the learner as very flexible and beneficial for learning. The opportunity to learn by DIALogue was evaluated very positively. Interestingly, the repetition of the comprehension questions in randomized order—though one could assume that randomization makes the task more difficult—was viewed by low-ability subjects in a very positive manner. Both high- and low-ability

subjects thought that DIAL and DIAG questions were necessary and efficient.

Ratings concerning treatment evaluations of feedback were most important for us. All learners and treatment groups rated the opportunity to attain information about the current learning state as very helpful because it gave them a feeling of security. DIALogue-based feedback was rated informative and helpful instead of harmful or ego deflating. It seemed as if the AV-only condition in mode 2 (DIAL 1) was interpreted and evaluated on the basis of experience made with PROLOGue only and combined PROLOGue and AV feedback in the comprehension part. Both were generally rated higher than the AV-only feedback (a depreciation which contrasts with the actual efficiency of AV feedback in the low-ability group). After experiencing detailed, bug-related prompts positively, "simple" feedback is now devalued. The feedback evaluations differed according to the treatment ability conditions, which is consistent with our hypotheses.

Generally, PROLOGue-only feedback was considered to be a marginal aid, experienced as frustrating because no actual help was provided. Thus, it was not surprising that low-ability subjects rated this dimension as aversive and experienced this feedback as punishing. Nevertheless, PROLOGue only still received a better rating than undifferentiated, global feedback, because PROLOGue only still provides hints about where the bugs are located and motivates the learner to rethink the task and use his own initiative.

Differential AV-only feedback (DIAL 2, modes 5 and 6) was rated much higher than undifferentiated feedback (DIAL 1, mode 2). Futhermore it was criticized by low-ability subjects who said that "highlighting" techniques like flashing arrows were not used often enough. On the contrary high-ability subjects rated feedback according to the details it furnished regardless of illustrative techniques implemented.

PROLOGue and AV combined feedback was rated very positively by all groups, regardless of prevailing treatment.

The preparation provided by the PROLOGue, that is, considering AV information in a different manner, was welcomed by all subjects, especially by low-ability subjects. Of course, high-ability subjects of the PROLOGue-only group gave higher ratings than their high-ability counterparts in the combined condition.

Altogether, differential feedback was generally rated as a very positive experience. Its evaluation is clearly influenced by the learner's prior knowledge. The less help a learner needs, the more willing he is to work with a demanding feedback and vice versa. Regulatory feedback seemed to have fostered and strengthened feelings of mastery and autonomy, especially for high achievers. We expect interesting shifts in feedback evaluation with a planned version of KAVIS where the choice of feedback intensity is left to the learner.

General Discussion

Our aim was to create both a learning and research tool able to investigate the course and processes of learning, starting with the intake of elementary facts and proceeding to more thorough understanding. This results in increasingly cohesive, integrated building blocks of knowledge with respect to a concrete domain.

There is good evidence that our main goals could be reached. KAVIS II is an efficient learning tool, especially able to facilitate impressive learning gains for both high- and low-ability subjects. It is equally apt in providing us with a deeper understanding of the cognitive processes involved in the acquisition of knowledge. Future studies and analyses may further investigate the use of the metaoperational PROLOGue component that was used in two of our feedbacks.

Processed fine-grain data which indicate how a learner proceeds after any given corrective feedback (i.e., sequences of bug-feedback intervention—connection or next bug in the three possible loops) may reveal deeper insights into the way different kinds and intensities of feedback can be used by learners with different prior ability. The presently still incomplete analysis of bug patterns and loop-related series of bugs can explain both feedback efficiency on a more detailed and qualitative level and open up more enlightenment on interdependencies between content material and comprehension. This analysis also will allow for a critical check of our AV feedback materials by revealing items that still could not be completed even by high-ability subjects after combined PROLOGue and AV feedback.

With regard to the way instrumental feedback is affectively experienced and interpreted, there is a need to develop more situation-specific online access methods. Accessing affective states by questionnaire may have elicited broader attitudes and settled longer lasting attitudes toward feedback instead of actual feelings.

By yoking basic research and educational application, differential feedback can become a very efficient tool and sensitive detector for ongoing cognitive processes. Moreover it could be demonstrated that intensified research feedback need not result in motivational losses but instead can stabilize and strengthen learners' motivation to study and learn in a self-controlled, mature manner.

Acknowledgement. The work reported in this paper was collaborative research involving Dr. H. D. Frey (Arbeitsbereich Naturwissenschafen), Ing.grad. Josef Jeuck (Arbeitsbereich Medienforschung), Dipl.Psych. Olaf Schröder (Arbeitsbereich Lernforschung), cand.Psych. Klaus Ackermann (Arbeitsbereich Lernforschung). It was supported by the Deutsche Forschungsgemeinschaft (Ma 978/1-1).

REFERENCES

Anderson, J. R. (1983). *The architecture of cognition.* Cambridge, MA: Harvard University Press.

Barr, A., & Feigenbaum, E. A. (1982). *The handbook of artificial intelligence* (Vol. 2). London: Pittman.

Brown, A. L. (1974). The role of strategic behavior in retardate memory. In N. R. Ellis (Ed.), *International review in mental retardation* (Vol. 7, pp. 55–110). New York: Academic Press.

Brown, A. L. (1975). The development of memory: Knowing, knowing about knowing, and knowing how to know. In H. W. Reese (Ed.), *Advances in child development and behavior* (Vol. 10, pp. 103–152). New York: Academic Press.

Brown, J. S., Burton, R. R., & Larkin, K. M. (1977). Representing and using procedural bugs for educational purposes. *Proceedings of the 1977 annual conference of the ACM, Seattle* (pp. 247–255).

Buechel, F. (1980). *Der Transfer von Lernstrategien.* Berichte und Arbeiten aus dem Institut fuer Psychologie der Universitaet Basel No. 3. Basel, Switzerland.

Burton, R. R., & Brown, J. S. (1978). An investigation of computer coaching for informal learning activities. In D. Sleeman & J. S. Brown (Eds.), *Intelligent tutoring systems* (pp. 79–98). Orlando, FL: Academic Press.

Cavanaugh, J. C., & Borkowski, J. G. (1980). Searching for metamemory-memory connections: A developmental study. *Developmental Psychology, 16,* 441–453.

Condry, J., & Chambers, J. (1978). Intrinsic motivation and the process of learning. In M. R. Lepper & D. Greene (Eds.), *The hidden costs of reward: New perspectives of the psychology of human motivation* (pp. 61–84). Hillsdale, NJ: Lawrence Erlbaum Assoc.

Fischer, P. M. (1985). Wissenserwerb mit interaktiven Feedbacksystemen. In H. Mandl & P. M. Fischer (Eds.), *Lernen im Dialog mit dem Computer* (pp. 68–82). Baltimore, MD: Urban & Schwarzenberg.

Fischer, P. M., Frey, H. D., & Jeuck, J. J. (1983). *Entwicklung und Erprobung eines computerunterstuetzten Video-Instruktionssystems fuer den naturwissenschaftlichen Unterricht* (Forschungsbericht No. 22). Tübingen, West Germany: DIFF.

Fischer, P. M., & Mandl, H. (1981). *Metakognitive Regulation von Textverarbeitungsprozessen. Aspekte und Probleme des Zusammenhangs von metakognitiven Selbstaussagen und konkretem Leistungsverhalten* (Forschungsbericht No. 15). Tübingen, West Germany: DIFF.

Fischer, P. M., Mandl, H., Frey, H. D., & Jeuck, J. J. (1984). *DFG-Projekt: Beeinflussung und Foerderung des Wissenserwerbs mitt naturwissenschaftlichen AV-Medien bei kontingenter Rueckmeldung. Darstellung des Forschungsvorhabens* (Forschungsbericht No. 26). Tübingen, West Germany: DIFF.

Flavell, J. H. (1970). Developmental studies of mediated memory. In H. W. Reese & L. P. Lipsitt (Eds.), *Advances in child development and behavior* (Vol. 5, pp. 181–211). Orlando, FL: Academic Press.

Holding, D. H. (1965). *Principles of training.* New York: Pergamon Press.

Holland, T. G., & Skinner, B. F. (1961). *The analysis of behavior: A program for self-instruction.* New York, Toronto, London: McGraw-Hill.

Kintsch, W., & Van Dijk, T. A. (1978). Toward a model of text comprehension and production. *Psychological Review, 85*, 363–394.

Koffman, E. B., & Blount, S. E. (1975). Artificial intelligence and automatic programming in CAI. *Artificial Intelligence, 6*, 215–234.

Kuhl, J. (1984). *Motivation, conflict, and the control of action.* New York: Springer-Verlag.

Lepper, M. R., & Greene, D. (Eds.). (1978). *The hidden costs of reward: New perspectives of the psychology of human motivation.* Hillsdale, NJ: Lawrence Erlbaum Assoc.

McCullers, J. C. (1978). Issues in learning and motivation. In M. R. Lepper & D. Greene (Eds.), *The hidden costs of reward: New perspectives of the psychology of human motivation* (pp. 5–17). Hillsdale, NJ: Lawrence Erlbaum Assoc.

McGraw, K. O. (1978). The detrimental effects of reward on performance: A literature review and a prediction model. In M. R. Lepper & D. Greene (Eds.), *The hidden costs of reward: New perspectives of the psychology of human motivation* (pp. 33–60). Hillsdale, NJ: Lawrence Erlbaum Assoc.

Miller, G. A., Galanter, E., & Pribram, K. H. (1960). *Plans and the structure of behavior.* London: Holt, Rinehart & Winston.

Miller, R. B. (1953). *Handbook of training and training equipment design* (U.S. Air Force W.A.D.C. Technical Report 53–136). Washington, DC: U.S. Air Force.

Neisser, U. (1967). *Cognitive psychology.* New York: Appleton-Century-Crofts.

Norman, D. A. (1983). Some observations on mental models. In D. Gentner & A. L. Stevens (Eds.), *Mental models* (pp. 7–14). Hillsdale, NJ: Lawrence Erlbaum Assoc.

Schneider, W. (1982). *Developmental trends in the metamemory-memory behavior relationship: An integrative review.* Unpublished manuscript. Max Planck Institut für Psychologische Forschung, Munich.

Seligman, M. E. P. (1975). *Helplessness: On depression, development and death.* San Francisco: Freeman.

Stapf, K. H. (1988). *Motivationale Faktoren der Lernsteuerung.* Stuttgart, West Germany: Kohlhammer.

Stapf, K. H., & Degner, U. (1981). *Experimentelle Untersuchungen verschiedener Rueckmeldungsmodalitaeten beim Lernen.* Berichte aus dem Psychologischen Institut der Universitaet Tübingen No. 5.

Stapf, K. H., & Mix, R. (1979). *Zur relativen Wirksamkeit positiver und negativer Rueckmeldung. Eine Latenzzeit-Analyse.* Berichte aus dem Fachbereich Psychologie der Philipps-Universitaet Marburg/Lahn.

Thorndike, E. L. (1932). *The foundations of learning.* New York: Teachers College.

Wexler, J. D. (1970). Information networks in generative computer-assisted instruction. *IEEE Transactions on Man–Machine Systems, 11*, 181–190.

10

Socializing the Intelligent Tutor: Bringing Empathy to Computer Tutors*

MARK R. LEPPER
RUTH W. CHABAY

"In all things we learn only from those we love." —Goethe

The computer, it has been said, is a once-in-several-centuries invention—a technology potentially capable of transforming the process of education (Brown, 1985; Kay, 1977; Papert, 1980; Simon, 1983; Suppes, 1966). Indeed, as the computer has begun to infiltrate primary as well as college classrooms, the array of educational uses to which it has been put is impressive (Kleiman, 1984; Lepper, 1985). It can serve, simultaneously, as a tool for facilitating the performance of a variety of mundane tasks (such as word processing, data analysis, or information retrieval), a device for creating and presenting complex simulations and rich exploratory-learning environments, and a means of providing practice of skills and testing of knowledge in many content areas.

Computers as Tutors

Perhaps the most prevalent and persistent metaphor concerning the use of computers in education, however, remains the idea of computers as tutors—devices for providing students with explicit instruction, presenting them with appropriate problems, and offering them informed guidance and feedback contingent on their performance on these problems. At first such

* Preparation of this paper was supported, in part, by research grant HD-MH-09814 from the National Institute of Child Health and Human Development and by the Sloan Foundation Grant to Stanford University's Cognitive Science Program. Ruth Chabay is now at Carnegie-Mellon University.

computer tutors were very simple, basing their responses to students on simple and straightforward algorithms, such as "If the student makes an error, then say 'no' and give the correct answer." Later, computer-assisted instruction (CAI) systems began to draw, in increasingly sophisticated ways, on psychological research concerning the processes of learning (e.g., Atkinson, 1972, 1974; Suppes & Morningstar, 1969). Indeed, one of the pioneers in this area (Suppes, 1966) captured clearly the goal of this enterprise with the following vision:

> One can predict that in a few more years millions of school children will have access to what Phillip of Macedon's son Alexander enjoyed as a royal prerogative: the personal services of a tutor as well-informed and responsive as Aristotle (p. 207).

More recently, the instructional possibilities offered by the computer have again expanded, as newer principles and techniques, drawn from research in cognitive science, have been incorporated into computer-based tutors (Sleeman & Brown, 1982). The Handbook of Artificial Intelligence (Barr & Feigenbaum, 1982) describes intelligent tutoring systems (ITS) or intelligent computer-assisted instruction (ICAI) systems as having three components: an expert, capable of solving the kind of problems presented to the student; a diagnostician or student model builder, capable of diagnosing a student's bugs and misconceptions and of mapping discrepancies between the student's knowledge and strategies and those of an expert; and a tutor, whose strategies determine what guidance or feedback to provide to the student. There are now a number of well-known examples of programs that are expert problem solvers and sophisticated diagnosticians. For example, there are programs that can identify multiple bugs, or erroneous rules, in students' procedures for subtraction with borrowing (Burton, 1982; Brown & Burton, 1978) and for solving algebraic equations (Sleeman, 1982). Other systems can solve complex diagnostic problems, in domains as diverse as medicine and electronics, and can evaluate students' diagnostic strategies in those areas (Brown, Burton, & de Kleer, 1982; Clancey, 1982).

Despite this dramatic increase in the sophistication of computer-based expertise and diagnostic capabilities, however, the tutor module in most computer-based tutors generally remains an ad hoc construction. Only very limited information is available to help one decide what principles ought to underlie the rules by which a tutor decides how to interact with a student. Almost all of this information, moreover, is focused on cognitive, rather than motivational or social, aspects of the tutoring process. By contrast it is on the tutor, and some of its more affective functions, that we focus in this paper.

We will argue that cognitive principles alone do not provide an adequate basis for determining what a tutor should do, or how, or when. We assert that *motivational* components of tutoring strategies are as important as

cognitive components, and more generally, that truly personalized instruction must be individualized along motivational as well as cognitive dimensions (Lepper & Malone, 1987). Hence, we suggest that important benefits may arise from a serious consideration of techniques for creating computer tutors that display "empathy," as well as intelligence, in their interactions with students.

The Tutoring Process

What does research tell us about the principles of tutoring? Turning to the literature on human tutoring, the first thing we note is that research concerning the *process* of tutoring is highly limited. Most research on teaching has concerned the traditional classroom, studying the ways that teachers cope with the pressures of dealing simultaneously with 30 children (e.g., Brophy & Good, 1986; Cazden, 1986; Clark & Peterson, 1986; Doyle, 1986; Wittrock, 1986). Moreover, even those formal studies explicitly concerned with tutoring strategies have typically focused on the cognitive goals and strategies of tutors, whether in inquiry-oriented activities (e.g., Collins & Stevens, 1982) or straightforward didactic sessions (e.g., Putnam, 1985a, 1987).

Studies of teachers' actual classroom plans and priorities, however, clearly indicate that student interest and affect rank high in importance to teachers (Clark & Peterson, 1986; Clark & Yinger, 1979). Similarly, "how-to" books on tutoring and reports on school-tutoring programs deal extensively with affective issues and place great emphasis on motivational goals and strategies in tutoring (e.g., Koskinen & Wilson, 1982; Moore & Poppino, 1983). Our own preliminary observations of tutors and analyses of tutoring-session transcripts also suggest that motivational components of tutoring strategies are indeed important and that many decisions made by human tutors appear to be based as much on the tutor's sense of the student's feelings as on the tutor's assessment of the student's knowledge and skills (Lepper & Chabay, 1985).

What implications does this have for the design of effective intelligent computer tutors? How might the increased intelligence of current tutoring systems be harnessed to interest and motivate students during the process of instruction? Does it make sense to ask a computer to "empathize" with a student? Our observations of students from preschool through college age working with educational software support Turkle's (1984) report that children using computers respond to them as in some sense alive or imbued with personalities. It therefore appears important to ask what motivational principles and strategies can and should be incorporated into computer tutors and how the "personality" of a computer tutor might affect students' learning and performance.

ILLUSTRATIVE TUTOR–STUDENT INTERACTIONS

To begin, let us consider three excerpts from dialogues between tutors and students. Attisha and Yazdani (1984) describe an ITS that is able to diagnose students' errors in multiplication. When the student works a two-digit multiplication problem incorrectly, the system responds as follows:

$$\begin{array}{r} 87 \\ \times\ 43 \\ \hline 32 \end{array}$$

Your answer is wrong.

Possible causes of error:
1. You multiplied the number in the multiplicand by the number directly beneath it in the multiplier, and you wrote down the carried number, ignoring the units number.

Here the system clearly displays its complex diagnostic capabilities. But on what basis did the computer tutor choose to give this particular type of feedback? How would the fourth graders trying to solve the problem react to this information? Would they be able to make use of it? How would the children feel—would they want to try again?

Putnam (1985b, 1987) collected protocols of experienced elementary school teachers tutoring children who had difficulty with carrying in addition. In contrast to the preceding computer tutor, the following excerpt illustrates one teacher's approach to dealing with a student's error:

$$\begin{array}{r} 1 \\ 68 \\ +\ \ 999 \\ \hline 1{,}057 \end{array}$$

T: Check it and see.
T: There's a mistake there. Can you find your mistake?
S: What?
T: Well, let's look and see. How much is nine and eight? [points to numbers]
S: Nine and eight is seventeen.
T: We put a seven [points] and carry the ten, right? Now add this column. [points]
S: [erases the 5 in the answer]
T: Good for you.

A different teacher in the same study proceeded this way:

$$537$$
$$+\ \ 23$$
$$\overline{5510}$$

T: Now, look at that again. Can you put two numbers down in one column here?
S: No.
T: All right, what do you think? What did you do that was not correct?
S: I think that this "one" [pointing] should be up here.
T: Can you correct that?
S: Yeah.

Certain differences in the approaches of these computer and human tutors are striking. Instead of presenting a complete error diagnosis, both human tutors helped students to find and correct their own errors. They prodded unresponsive students, helped focus their attention on relevant pieces of the problem, and praised their success. They were tactful, never saying "No, your answer is wrong," and seemed to attempt to provide support rather than to deliver criticism.

Again, we ask the same questions: How did these teachers decide what to say? How did the students react? Was the feedback useful to the students? How did the students feel?

To explore these questions further, we have been looking at tutoring sessions conducted by human tutors experienced at one-on-one interactions with students. Our sources for these tutoring sessions included detailed transcripts of elementary school teachers tutoring second graders in addition with carrying (Putnam, 1985b) and videotapes of teachers coaching fourth graders on computer games involving fractions or graphing (Stillinger & McIsaac, 1986).

Motivational Goals of Tutors

What is it that human tutors do, then, besides the obvious informational functions of providing new information and tuition, diagnosing and correcting student errors, and presenting appropriate problems for solution? Our preliminary analyses suggest a fairly high level of agreement, across tutors, in their motivational goals, but a fairly low level of agreement concerning the methods by which those goals might be accomplished.

A first important point about human tutors is that they virtually all share a concern with motivating, as well as instructing, children. Indeed, they frequently discuss the two processes as intimately related to one another. In addition to a straightforward belief that good performances and obvious improvements deserve to be rewarded and that poor per-

formances require correction,[1] human tutors seem to have three sorts of additional motivational goals in their interactions with students.

Perhaps the most widely shared social goal of tutors is to keep pupils from becoming so discouraged, frustrated, or alienated that they give up on the task at hand (Koskinen & Wilson, 1982; Moore & Poppino, 1983; Wood, Bruner, & Ross, 1976). Tutors who believe that their students are approaching such a state are quick to reassure, commiserate, exhort, and encourage their charges. Closely related is a second general goal. Tutors seek to encourage in their students high levels of attention and effort. When tutors believe that students are not investing great effort in their studies, they are likely to goad, provoke, or reprove their pupils.

Other motivational goals seem to involve a somewhat higher level of analysis concerning the conditions that promote intrinsic motivations for learning. Thus, one finds tutors, on occasion, seeking to enhance children's feelings of challenge, curiosity, or control (cf., Malone, 1981; Malone & Lepper, 1987). To promote a sense of continuing challenge, for example, tutors may try to help children set appropriate performance goals for themselves or may describe tasks in a manner that highlights their diagnosticity concerning the child's competence at the activity. To provoke curiosity, on the other hand, tutors will often provide children with hints or incomplete information or may point out inconsistencies in the children's own approaches to similar problems. To maintain their pupils' feelings of control, by contrast, they may make a deliberate choice to refrain from intervening at each and every point at which the students seem in danger of making an error.

Motivational Choice Points for Tutors

In contrast to the fairly high level of agreement concerning the goals that tutors share for motivating the students they teach, there is a fairly high level of diversity in the techniques that tutors use, and believe to be effective, in accomplishing these goals. From this perspective important decision points in the tutoring process seem to concern four aspects of tutorial interventions: *control, timing, content,* and *style.*

CONTROL

Who should initiate tutorial interventions: the tutor or the student? Should the student be allowed to make errors or follow an unproductive path?

---

[1] Even this obvious presumption by tutors reflects more than a simple belief in "reinforcement theory." Quite explicitly tutors appear to base their reactions to the child's success or failure on inferences concerning the difficulty of the task for the child and the level of effort that the child invested in it (Weiner, 1979).

Research on intrinsic motivation has consistently identified a sense of personal control and self-determination as an important motivational factor (Condry, 1977; deCharms, 1968; Deci, 1975, 1981; Nuttin, 1973). Other research on learner control of instructional sequence has indicated that students frequently make poor choices which may actually interfere with learning (Atkinson, 1974; Steinberg, 1977; Tennyson, Park, & Christensen, 1985). Furthermore, it is clear that there is a great deal of individual variation. Some students seek a great deal of control over their work, whereas others prefer to be directed constantly by the teacher.

The choices are therefore complex. Should the tutor intervene *only* when requested to do so by the student, or at any time when he or she perceives that the student is having a problem? Should the tutor *always* intervene when the student requests help, or should some evidence of effort and independent work be demanded first? The decision is complicated by the fact that some students are reluctant to ask explicitly for help; others, however, taking the path of least effort, will request help right away before attempting a problem on their own (Anderson, Kulhavy, & Andre, 1971). Even the mere availability of the problem solution may undermine a student's sense of challenge. Students in one college physics course who were required to do homework problems on a computer complained vehemently because answers were available at the touch of a key. They were mollified, however, simply by the addition of a display showing the number of requests for hints or answers in each problem, providing a salient measure of the level of challenge each student had chosen (B. Sherwood, personal communication, April 1986).

TIMING

If the tutor chooses to intervene, is the best time to do so before the student makes an error or after the first error, or the second, or the third? Or is it when the student's strategy, though adequate, is not optimal? Here the primary motivational factors to consider are curiosity and challenge. Berlyne (1960, 1966) and others (Hunt, 1961, 1965; Kagan, 1972; Piaget, 1952), for example, have discussed the inclination to explore, seek surprises, and resolve discrepancies and incongruities. White (1959) and others (Csikszentmihalyi, 1975; Harter, 1978), similarly, have taken perceived challenge and the establishment of competence or mastery as a prime determinant of intrinsic motivation.

In each case, two sorts of errors seem possible. One could easily imagine that unsolicited interventions from a tutor could frustrate a student seeking to master a problem independently, and undesired guidance or structure could undermine the satisfaction of exploring a new domain and constructing one's own hypotheses (Brown, 1985; Burton & Brown, 1979). Conversely, excessive complexity, too much novelty, or too great a level of

challenge can be detrimental. For example, Dweck (1975, 1986; Dweck & Elliott, 1983) and others have studied the phenomenon of learned helplessness (Seligman, 1975), in which certain students who fail repeatedly to solve difficult problems become unable to solve even simple problems that they had previously solved without difficulty. Other students, however, redouble their efforts, and in fact evolve more sophisticated problem-solving strategies in the face of repeated failure (Anderson & Jennings, 1980).

In the tutoring sessions that we have analyzed, tutors' approaches to the control and timing of interventions varied considerably. Table 10.1 illustrates patterns of intervention for three of Putnam's (1985b) addition tutors on problems in which the child made one or more errors. Tutor C almost always allowed the child to complete a problem before saying anything, but tutor B usually intervened at the first error. Since each tutor in this study worked with only one child, it is not clear how much of this variation can be attributed to tutors' assessments of individual children's needs, and how much to overall differences in teaching style. In Stillinger and McIsaac's (1986) videotapes of teachers coaching fourth graders on computer math games, one tutor initially began by announcing to the child that her "official teaching style" was "not to teach," and that he would have to ask for help if he needed it; a second tutor intervened four or five times before allowing her extremely capable student to press a single key. Both tutors modified their styles somewhat as the sessions progressed. The first began volunteering help when the student looked puzzled or confused, or when he appeared to be guessing randomly, and pushed him to choose problems at a lower level of difficulty. The second tutor, though still apparently concerned about engineering success at the game, eventually began to hold off on her comments for a little while and allow the student, who was quite competent, an opportunity to figure out moves for herself, and even to make a few mistakes.

CONTENT

What should a tutor say when a student makes an error? Many different kinds of feedback and information are possible, among them, providing correct answers, diagnosing errors, instructing the student what to do next, and giving hints. How can a tutor determine what feedback is most appropriate for a given student in a given situation? How much does it matter? To a student who is determined to figure out a problem independently, is it frustrating to be handed the answer after one or two errors? To a student who is discouraged, does an error diagnosis simply undermine confidence further? To a student who has given up in frustration, can a hint seem like a taunt or a refusal to help instead of an expression of the tutor's confidence in his or her ability to solve the problem? At times teachers in both studies (Putnam, 1985b; Stillinger & McIsaac, 1986) simply asked the students

TABLE 10.1. Intervention patterns for three tutors, from Putnam (1985b).

Tutor	No help	Prompt starting column	Intervene in middle	Step by step
A	3	4	3	2
B	1	1	5	5
C	6	0	1	0

Note. Intervention patterns for three different tutors in Putnam's study on problems in which students made errors. Columns indicate (1) problems in which student was allowed to complete the problem without intervention even though an error had been made, (2) problems in which the teacher reminded the student to start with the ones' column, but gave no other help, (3) problems in which the teacher intervened to correct an error in the middle of the problem, and (4) problems in which the teacher worked through the problem step by step with the student.

whether they would like a particular kind of help, while at other times the teachers chose a particular approach without consulting the student explicitly.

STYLE

In addition to comments conveying information about the task at hand, tutors made many comments to students that were purely sociable or affective, or that mixed cognitive and motivational content. Among human tutors with differing styles and personalities, certain common themes emerged from a collection of noninformational comments, gathered from all the tutoring sessions (Putnam, 1985b; Stillinger & McIsaac, 1986). It was clear that tutors responded to students' feelings as well as to their performance. To students who acted discouraged, tutors offered commiseration, reassurance, encouragement, and exhortation. If students appeared distracted or did not seem to be working hard, teachers responded by setting goals, marking progress, providing explicit challenges, and even by expressing impatience or deliberate provocation. Successes, or even just serious efforts, brought praise and acclaim from teachers, whereas low achievement due to low effort was especially likely to bring reproach (cf., Weiner, 1974, 1979). Such comments formed a significant part of tutors' discourse. On the average about 35% of tutors' comments had strong motivational or affective content as well as cognitive content.

The roles human teachers chose to play in tutoring sessions also varied widely, from drill sergeant, demanding responses to problem after problem, to cheerleader, urging increased effort and vigorously applauding progress. At times tutors were collaborators, working with the student toward shared goals; at others they acted as playful competitors, encouraging the student to try to beat or outwit them. In some situations teachers assumed the role of lecturer, explaining and amplifying facts and concepts; sometimes they were Socratic tutors, trying to induce students to work through a chain of reasoning on their own; and at other times they

acted as coaches, providing hints and strategies for improving performance.

It makes sense to ask, then, what cast we would like to give to the relationship between student and computer tutor. Should the computer's "personality" be warm or cold, directive or nondirective, demanding or permissive? For a given student and activity, how does one determine the most effective role for the computer to play?

The Empathetic Computer?

Human tutors are able to empathize with students' feelings—to pick up nonverbal cues from students and to imagine how they themselves would feel in the same situation. Their decisions about when, where, and how to intervene seem based, in part, on their empathetic responses. Computers, of course, lack these capabilities. It may still prove informative, however, to ask whether a certain degree of "empathy" might be built into a computer tutor—to see whether the increased intelligence of current tutors might be harnessed to promote motivational, as well as cognitive, aims. What additions might we be able to make to an intelligent tutoring system to provide it with an empathetic component as well?

GENERAL SOCIAL KNOWLEDGE

A first step might be to provide the tutor with some general rules concerning the appropriateness of different sorts of social and motivational remarks in various situations. One might like an intelligent tutor to understand, for example, that especially enthusiastic congratulations would be appropriate when a student has finally succeeded at a particularly difficult or complex problem or has just solved a problem that he or she had failed in the past. A socially intelligent tutor should recognize that commiseration and reassurance are most well suited to situations in which students have made substantial progress toward a goal but have fallen just short of complete success. It ought, similarly, to know when it might be appropriate to challenge the student with a difficult problem or when it might be useful to focus the child's attention on signs of the progress he or she has already made.

A sophisticated computer tutor should also know *how* to phrase comments and provide feedback so as to create and sustain student motivation (Malone, 1981; Malone & Lepper, 1987). It should provide "informational" specific feedback on performance rather than "controlling" feedback (Deci, Schwartz, Sheinman, & Ryan, 1981; Deci, Spiegel, Ryan, Koestner, & Kauffman, 1982), for instance, and it should know how to present feedback in a fashion that maintains the learner's sense of competence and control (Dweck, 1975, 1986; Harter, 1978; Weiner, 1979).

SPECIFIC BACKGROUND KNOWLEGE

A second step might be to arm the computer with some of the sorts of background information about individual students that a human teacher would be given or could pick up in talking and working with them. The results of various aptitude tests and motivational measurement scales, as well as human teachers' assessments of the students, could be supplied to the computer tutor before its first session with a student. Thus, the computer could begin a session able to take advantage of the knowledge that Jenny really likes to work out problems by herself, but Johnny needs constant help and encouragement to succeed. It could be aware that Jessica enjoys math, but not history, whereas Joan is interested in both. Or, it could draw on the knowledge that Josh loves competitive learning situations and Jerry cooperative ones. Such information should help the tutor to anticipate and take advantage of aptitude-treatment and attitude-treatment interactions in learning (e.g., Snow, 1986, 1987).

STUDENTS' CHOICES AND RESPONSES

Third, the computer could occasionally ask the student directly whether he or she would like help or not, would prefer harder or easier problems, would rather cooperate or compete, and so on—questions asked from time to time by human tutors. Because a student's preferences are not always the most effective pedagogical strategies (Atkinson, 1972; Steinberg, 1977; Tennyson & Buttrey, 1980; Tennyson, et al., 1985), and because students' feelings can change during the course of a session, the computer would need a set of tutoring rules to determine when in a session to try changing strategies and what modifications to try.

Indeed, given a sufficiently intelligent system, one might imagine the computer being given the task of creating a diagnostic model of the student, along motivational dimensions, to be used, like its cognitive counterpart, to identify the best tutoring techniques to use with an individual student.

The Research Agenda

In this chapter we have tried to accomplish two basic goals: to illustrate the variety and prevalence of motivational issues that arise when humans attempt to tutor children and to suggest the potential importance of these same issues for the design of computer-based tutors that attempt to accomplish these same aims. In the absence of a functioning tutorial system involving some concrete instantiation of such principles, of course, our account has been necessarily speculative. Thus, it may be important to consider some of the potential difficulties likely to arise in any serious attempt to implement an "empathetic" computer tutor.

Two major obstacles to the creation of motivationally sophisticated computer tutors seem paramount. First, there is extremely little relevant research concerning the affective aspects of the tutoring process, on which one might base decisions regarding optimal procedures for enhancing student motivation. Although one may sometimes draw on related literatures for guidance, the answers to the questions we posed earlier concerning the control, timing, content, and style of tutorial interventions are largely unknown. Even our own analyses to date speak only to the question of what tutors do, and not to the question of how effective their practices might be. Second, even if one knew precisely how an expert human tutor ought to behave, there would be questions concerning the extent to which this knowledge could be automatically translated into the design of computer-based tutors. If the most critical determinants of tutors' effective interventions were their observations of the facial expressions of the student, for example, it would not be possible to employ analogous techniques with the computer.

Viewed positively these potential limitations can be seen as defining an important agenda for further research into the process of tutoring. Moreover, the study of these issues in the computer domain may have interesting repercussions for the study of teaching more generally. Historically, it has proved quite difficult for researchers both to control and to vary teacher behavior along these sorts of dimensions (e.g., Shavelson, Webb, & Burstein, 1986). By taking advantage of the computer's capabilities, however, it may be possible to conduct more efficient and more effective research into these issues.

From a more negative perspective, of course, these potential limitations raise the question of whether *any* of the variations in motivational approach that computers might take would actually make a difference in terms of students' learning.[2] We believe that there is already presumptive evidence of the potential importance of the sorts of variables we have been discussing in the history of the design of a number of recent tutorial systems. Burton and Brown's (1979) computer-based "coach," designed to help children learn more effectively from the educational math game "How the West Was One + Three × Four" (Seiler, 1973), for example, comes perhaps the closest in aims to the hypothetical empathetic tutor we have been discussing. In their presentation Burton and Brown discuss at considerable length the motivational difficulties occasioned by their initial, highly knowledgeable yet highly intrusive, coach; and they present, in the end, an elaborate set of rules of thumb that they feel should be generally applied in the design of such systems to prevent negative affective results.

---

[2] In fact, immediate learning from the program is only one measure of interest here. Children's later retention of the material and ability to transfer that learning to other settings, along with their later intrinsic interest in the subject being taught, would also be of importance (Lepper & Chabay, 1985).

We believe, in short, that motivational factors may often prove as critical as cognitive factors in determining the results of a tutorial interaction. Attention to these affective factors, normally disregarded in the cognitive science community, may therefore pay important dividends for those interested in designing intelligent computer tutors for use with school children. Had Aristotle possessed the limited social skills of some of today's computer tutors, his pupil Alexander might not have had such success in conquering the Mediterranean world.

Acknowledgements. We wish to express our deep appreciation to Ralph Putnam (1985b) and to Constance Stillinger and Lynn McIsaac (1986) for making available to us their original transcripts and videotapes of tutoring sessions.

REFERENCES

Anderson, C. A., & Jennings, D. L. (1980). When experiences of failure promote expectations of success: The impact of attributing failures to ineffective strategies. *Journal of Personality, 48*, 393–407.

Anderson, R. C., Kulhavy, R. W., & Andre, T. (1971). Feedback procedures in programmed instruction. *Journal of Educational Psychology, 62*, 148–156.

Atkinson, R. C. (1972). Ingredients for a theory of instruction. *American Psychologist, 27*, 921–931.

Atkinson, R. C. (1974). Teaching children to read using a computer. *American Psychologist, 29*, 169–178.

Attisha, M., & Yazdani, M. (1984). An expert system for diagnosing children's multiplication errors. *Instructional Science, 13*, 79–92.

Barr, A., & Feigenbaum, E. A. (1982). Applications-oriented AI research: Education. In A. Barr & E. Feigenbaum (Eds.), *The handbook of artificial intelligence* (Vol. 2, pp. 229–235). Los Altos, CA: William Kaufmann.

Berlyne, D. E. (1960). *Conflict, arousal, and curiosity.* New York: McGraw-Hill.

Berlyne, D. E. (1966). Curiosity and exploration. *Science, 153*, 25–33.

Brophy, J. E., & Good, T. L. (1986). Teacher behavior and student achievement. In M. C. Wittrock (Ed.), *Handbook of research on teaching* (3rd ed., pp. 328–375). New York: Macmillan.

Brown, J. S. (1985). Process versus product—A perspective on tools for communal and informal electronic learning. *Journal of Educational Computing Research, 1*, 179–201.

Brown, J. S., & Burton, R. R. (1978). Diagnostic models for procedural bugs in basic mathematical skills. *Cognitive Science, 2*, 155–192.

Brown, J. S., Burton, R. R., & de Kleer, J. (1982). Pedagogical, natural language and knowledge engineering techniques in SOPHIE I, II, and III. In D. Sleeman & J. S. Brown (Eds.). *Intelligent tutoring systems* (pp. 227–282). Orlando, FL: Academic Press.

Burton, R. R. (1982). Diagnosing bugs in a simple procedural skill. In D. Sleeman & J. S. Brown (Eds.), *Intelligent tutoring systems* (pp. 157–184). Orlando, FL: Academic Press.

Burton, R. R., & Brown, J. S. (1979). An investigation of computer coaching for informal learning activities. *International Journal of Man–Machine Studies, 11*, 5–24.

Cazden, C. B. (1986). Classroom discourse. In M. C. Wittrock (Ed.), *Handbook of research on teaching* (3rd ed., pp. 432–463). New York: Macmillan.

Clancey, W. J. (1982). Tutoring rules for guiding a case method dialogue. In D. Sleeman & J. S. Brown (Eds.), *Intelligent tutoring systems* (pp. 201–226). Orlando, FL: Academic Press.

Clark, C. M., & Peterson, P. L. (1986). Teachers' thought processes. In M. C. Wittrock (Ed.), *Handbook of research on teaching* (3rd ed., pp. 255–296). New York: Macmillan.

Clark, C. M., & Yinger, R. J. (1979). Teachers' thinking. In P. L. Peterson & H. J. Walberg (Eds.), *Research on teaching: Concepts, findings, and implications* (pp. 231–263). Berkeley, CA: McCutcheon.

Collins, A., & Stevens, A. L. (1982). Goals and strategies of inquiry teachers. In R. Glaser (Ed.), *Advances in instructional psychology* (pp. 65–119). Hillsdale, NJ: Lawrence Erlbaum Associates.

Condry, J. C. (1977). Enemies of exploration: Self-initiated versus other-initiated learning, *Journal of Personality and Social Psychology, 35*, 459–477.

Csikszentmihalyi, M. (1975). *Beyond boredom and anxiety.* San Francisco: Jossey-Bass.

deCharms, R. (1968). *Personal causation.* Orlando, FL: Academic Press.

Deci, E. L. (1975). *Intrinsic motivation.* New York: Plenum Press.

Deci, E. L. (1981). *The psychology of self-determination.* Lexington, MA: Heath.

Deci, E. L., Schwartz, A. J., Sheinman, L., & Ryan, R. M. (1981). An instrument to assess adults' orientations toward control versus autonomy with children. *Journal of Educational Psychology, 73*, 642–650.

Deci, E. L., Spiegel, N. H., Ryan, R. M., Koestner, R., & Kauffman, M. (1982). Effects of performance standards on teaching styles: Behavior of controlling teachers. *Journal of Educational Psychology, 74*, 852–859.

Doyle, W. (1986). Classroom organization and management. In M. C. Wittrock (Ed.), *Handbook of research on teaching* (3rd ed., pp. 392–431). New York: Macmillan.

Dweck, C. S. (1975). The role of expectations and attributions in the alleviation of learned helplessness. *Journal of Personality and Social Psychology, 31*, 674–685.

Dweck, C. S. (1986). Motivational processes affecting learning. *American Psychologist, 41*, 1040–1048.

Dweck, C. S., & Elliott, E. S. (1983). Achievement motivation. In E. M. Hetherington (Ed.), *Handbook of child psychology* (Vol. 4, pp. 643–691). New York: Wiley.

Harter, S. (1978). Effectance motivation reconsidered: Toward a developmental model. *Human Development, 1*, 34–64.

Hunt, J. McV. (1961). *Intelligence and experience.* New York: Ronald Press.

Hunt, J. McV. (1965). Intrinsic motivation and its role in psychological development. In D. Levine (Ed.), *Nebraska symposium on motivation* (Vol. 13, pp. 189–282). Lincoln, NE: University of Nebraska Press.

Kagan, J. (1972). Motives and development. *Journal of Personality and Social Psychology, 22*, 51–66.

Kay, A. C. (1977). Microelectronics and the personal computer. *Scientific American, 237*, 230–244.

Kleiman, G. M. (1984). *Brave new schools: How computers can change education*. Reston, VA: Reston Publishing.

Koskinen, P. S., & Wilson, R. M. (1982). *Tutoring: A guide for success*. New York: Teachers College Press.

Lepper, M. R. (1985). Microcomputers in education: Motivational and social issues. *American Psychologist, 40*, 1–18.

Lepper, M. R., & Chabay, R. W. (1985). Intrinsic motivation and instruction: Conflicting views on the role of motivational processes in computer-based education. *Educational Psychologist, 20*, 217–230.

Lepper, M. R., & Malone, T. W. (1987). Intrinsic motivation and instructional effectiveness in computer-based education. In R. E. Snow & M. C. Farr (Eds.), *Aptitude, learning, and instruction: Vol. 3. Conative and affective process analysis* (pp. 255–286). Hillsdale, NJ: Erlbaum.

Malone, T. W. (1981). Toward a theory of intrinsically motivating instruction. *Cognitive Science, 4*, 333–369.

Malone, T. W., & Lepper, M. R. (1987). Making learning fun: A taxonomy of intrinsic motivations for learning. In R. E. Snow & M. C. Farr (Eds.), *Aptitude, learning, and instruction: Vol. 3. Conative and affective process analysis* (pp. 223–253). Hillsdale, NJ: Erlbaum.

Moore, D. P., & Poppino, M. A. (1983). *Successful tutoring: A practical guide to adult learning processes*. Springfield, IL: Charles C. Thomas.

Nuttin, J. R. (1973). Pleasure and reward in human motivation and learning. In D. E. Berlyne & K. B. Madsen (Eds.), *Pleasure, reward, preference*. New York: Academic Press.

Papert, S. (1980). *Mindstorms: Children, computers, and powerful ideas*. New York: Basic Books.

Piaget, J. (1951). *Play, dreams, and imitation in childhood*. New York: Norton.

Piaget, J. (1952). *The origins of intelligence in children*. New York: International University Press.

Putnam, R. T. (1985a). Teacher thoughts and actions in live and simulated tutoring of addition. Unpublished doctoral dissertation, Stanford University.

Putnam, R. T. (1985b). [Live tutoring of addition: protocols]. Unpublished data.

Putnam, R. T. (1987). Structuring and adjusting content for students: A study of live and simulated tutoring of addition. *American Educational Research Journal, 24*, 13–48.

Seiler, B. A. (1973). How the west was one + three × four. [PLATO computer-assisted instruction lesson]. Urbana, IL: University of Illinois.

Seligman, M. E. P. (1975). *Helplessness*. San Francisco: Freeman.

Shavelson, R. J., Webb, N. M., & Burstein, L. (1986). Measurement of teaching. In M. C. Wittrock (Ed.), *Handbook of research on teaching* (3rd ed., pp. 50–91). New York: Macmillan.

Simon, H. A. (1983). The computer age. In A. M. Lesgold & F. Reif (Eds.), *Computers in education: Realizing the potential* (Report of an OERI-sponsored research conference, Pittsburgh, PA, November 1982) (pp. 37–60). Washington, DC: U.S. Government Printing Office.

Sleeman, D. (1982). Assessing aspects of competence in basic algebra. In D. Sleeman & J. S. Brown (Eds.), *Intelligent tutoring systems* (pp. 185–200). Orlando, FL: Academic Press.

Sleeman, D., & Brown, J. S. (Eds.). (1982). *Intelligent tutoring systems*. Orlando,

FL: Academic Press.

Snow, R. E. (1986). Individual differences and the design of educational programs. *American Psychologist, 41*, 1029–1039.

Snow, R. E. (1987). Aptitude complexes in education. In R. E. Snow & M. C. Farr (Eds.), *Aptitude, learning, and instruction: Vol. 3. Conative and affective process analysis* (pp. 11–34). Hillsdale, NJ: Erlbaum.

Steinberg, E. R. (1977). Review of student control in computer-assisted instructions. *Journal of Computer-Based Instruction, 3*, 84–90.

Stillinger, C., & McIsaac, L. (1986). Teachers helping students playing educational games. Unpublished data.

Suppes, P. (1966). The uses of computers in education. *Scientific American, 215*, 206–221.

Suppes, P., & Morningstar, M. (1969). Computer-assisted instruction. *Science, 166*, 343–350.

Tennyson, R. D., & Buttrey, T. (1980). Advisement and management strategies as design variables in computer-assisted instruction. *Educational Communication and Technology Journal, 28*, 169–176.

Tennyson, R. D., Park, O. C., & Christensen, D. L. (1985). Adaptive control of learning time and content sequence in concept learning using computer-based instruction. *Journal of Educational Psychology, 77*, 481–491.

Turkle, S. (1984). *The second self: Computers and the human spirit.* New York: Simon & Schuster.

Weiner, B. (1974). *Achievement motivation and attribution theory.* Morristown, NJ: General Learning Press.

Weiner, B. (1979). A theory of motivation for some classroom experiences. *Journal of Educational Psychology, 71*, 3–25.

White, R. W. (1959). Motivation reconsidered: The concept of competence. *Psychological Review, 66*, 297–333.

Wittrock, M. C. (Ed.). (1986). *Handbook of research on teaching* (3rd ed.). New York: Macmillan.

Wood, D., Bruner, J. S., & Ross, G. (1976). The role of tutoring in problem solving. *Journal of Child Psychology and Psychiatry, 17*, 89–100.

11

Cognitive Economy in Physics Reasoning: Implications for Designing Instructional Materials

EILEEN SCANLON
TIM O'SHEA

In this chapter we discuss observations arising from our work with think-aloud protocols of novices' attempts at kinematics problems. We report on some general observations made on their problem-solving techniques and examine one key issue in detail, namely whether multiple representations are a help or hindrance to problem solving. Modeling the successful and unsuccessful problem-solving behavior of pairs of students has led us to formulate the hypothesis of cognitive economy. Novices solving a physics problem can more easily achieve success when they restrict themselves to using only one representation of the problem. The cognitive economy hypothesis has consequences for the design of intelligent tutoring systems (ITS). In particular it implies that imposing constraints on the learning environment, rather than being a wholesale limitation of conventional intelligent tutors, is a positively helpful act.

The chapter is divided into four main sections. The first section describes our motivation for studying the domain of physics and introduces a principle—cognitive economy—that we believe is essential in accounting for the various apparently strange behaviors students exhibit while solving problems. The first section also describes various approaches to teaching problem solving and gives a brief review of the cognitive science/artificial intelligence literature in this area. The second section deals with data collection. We are convinced that the accumulation of good-quality data on individuals' attempts to solve problems is a prerequisite for work in this area. We describe our data-collection methods, the type of problems we use, and two studies involving data from individuals and pairs. The third section of the chapter discusses a key experiment that we have recently conducted. Pairs of students were presented with a problem that forced them to shift from one representation to another. We analyze these data and discuss a production rule framework that we used to construct models to account for the observed behavior. The last section discusses the results,

the most surprising of which is that multiple representations of a problem can actually impede students who are not expert in the chosen domain. We also discuss our future work and list the consequences of our findings for ITSs. These consequences are stringent, requiring the designer of such systems to make subtle distinctions in the student model about how much facility a student may have with the different knowledge sources.

MOTIVATION AND BACKGROUND

Like many other researchers we have chosen to work in the area of physics problem solving. The attractions of physics are clear. Although it is not a "toy" subject area, students' procedures can easily be evaluated because physics is expressed using conventional mathematical notation and because the student has a relatively small number of high-level laws and principles to guide his or her work. The other obvious attraction of physics as a domain is that at high school level the main "model" that students use is the real world. What distinguishes our work from others' is that we deal with genuine novices who make mistakes at a variety of different levels and that our primary long-term concern relates to improving the design of instructional materials. In fact we believe that in order to account for much student behavior it is necessary to consider the exact nature of their physics instruction in addition to considering more conventional notions, such as mental models of physical processes and mathematical reasoning skills. However, our working methods are those of the contemporary cognitive scientist and involve the analysis of fine-grained protocols of problem-solving behavior and the construction of production rule models.

We studied the question of the utility of multiple representations by collecting think-aloud protocols from eight pairs of 17-year-old high school students solving a physics problem that requires both algebra manipulation knowledge and graph interpretation knowledge. In contrast to the beliefs of most artificial intelligence (AI) researchers and of educators, the main conclusion that we tentatively draw is that the use of multiple representations in problem solving can hinder the nonexpert student. We suggest, in fact, that one important aspect of effective problem solving is the *economical* use of alternative representation schemes. This is our cognitive economy hypothesis, which we adopt in our explanatory framework in addition to other elements, such as problem-solving skills and effects of the curriculum.

This study followed the analysis of protocols of 50 individual novices solving kinematics problems. Our overall motivation is to construct an explanatory framework that can be used to describe the behavior of students in detail. This detail must be sufficient to lead to substantial improvement in the quality of instructional materials for physics and mathematics. We have described elsewhere (Scanlon & O'Shea, 1982) how mastery of mathematical technique and assumptions about the curriculum affect

problem-solving behavior. Our current enterprise is to examine how limits on cognitive processes affect problem-solving behavior. Because we express our models using production rules, the obvious way of modeling resource limitation would be to decide that the working memory be limited in size in traditional Miller-ish (Miller, 1956) style. However, we have no evidence for such a fixed-size working memory in our data and, in fact, find that in order to model our data we have to employ more than one set of production rules, each with an associated working memory. Instead of limiting memory size, it makes more sense to model effective use of the knowledge expressed in production rules by principled invocations of one set of rules from another. Following this approach we argue that when the metarules expressing these invocations are inappropriate (e.g., by being overgeneral or overspecific), a particularly chaotic style of problem solving is exhibited. This leads us to our cognitive economy hypothesis.

Our cognitive economy hypothesis is that one important component of expertise in problem solving or learning is the ability to control and hence minimize shifts from one type of knowledge representation or problem-solving technique to another. As novices acquire this type of expertise, their efficiency as problem solvers or learners increases. According to this view, experts try to be as economical as possible in the number of transitions from rule set to rule set. On the other hand novices often behave in a spendthrift way and flip from one rule set to another. For example a novice may go from reading the problem to solving it, from problem solving to using expectations about school work, from using graphs to using equations, and so on. The uneconomical path of least resistance leads the novice to change representations rather than back-track when stuck. The instructional implication of the cognitive economy hypothesis is that some teaching should focus on precisely when it is appropriate for a learner to switch from one representation to another.

LITERATURE REVIEW

Several other workers have examined the characteristics of problem solving in physics. In an exhaustive review Chi, Glaser, and Rees (1982) summarized the conclusions of a number of studies to outline what is meant by expertise in problem solving. Their hypothesis as a result of this review follows:

> ... problem solving difficulties of novices can be attributed mainly to inadequacies of their knowledge base and not to limitations in either the architecture of their cognitive systems or processing capabilities (such as the inabilities to use powerful search heuristics or the inability to detect important clues in the problem statement). (p. 71)

They believe that the examination of issues concerning the novice's knowledge base and problem representations are the most potentially fruitful.

Among physics educators, research has been concentrated on establishing the alternative conceptions that students bring to the formal study of physics concepts (e.g., L. C. McDermott, 1984).

Numerous theoretical models have been constructed to simulate the processes of problem solving. J. H. Larkin has been involved in the construction of a variety of psychological models (J. H. Larkin, McDermott, Simon, & Simon, 1980). The particular feature of the models developed so far concentrates on the difference between the sequences of calculations generated by experts and by novices. Experts work forward, but novices work backward. In these models it is assumed that experts work forward because their backward-working solution procedure becomes automated with learning. The models usually avoid the question of initial problem representation. One model, PH632 (J. McDermott & Larkin, 1978), does aim to model the use of problem representations by an expert solver. In PH632 four representational stages of a problem are postulated: verbal, naive, scientific, and mathematical.

Whatever deficiencies Larkin's models may have (J. H. Larkin et al., 1980) they are models of the learner. Her former co-worker, Fred Reif, has continued his study of physics problem solving by presenting a model of good performance, a prescriptive model of human physics problem solving; the strength of such a model being that it contains a knowledge base structured to facilitate problem solution (Reif & Heller, 1981). No one has presented a detailed model of physics instruction. As Reif says, as well as a model of good performance, such an instruction model must also "incorporate a model of the student's initial functioning and a model specifying the instructional transformational process". We know of no physics equivalent of the felicity conditions for skill acquisition in arithmetic (Van Lehn, 1983).

The issue of representation occurs in the construction of AI models whose aim is simply to construct a program that will solve a physics problem. An example of such a program is MECHO (Bundy, Byrd, Luger, Mellish, Milne & Palmer, 1979). Psychological claims are also made for MECHO (Luger, 1980), and an attempt has been made to make it the basis of a student model for an intelligent teaching system (Priest, 1981). MECHO is particularly interesting because it works with two different types of representation. When given a problem expressed in English, it generates a mathematical representation of the problem statement that can be manipulated by a problem solver. This problem solver itself, however, consists of a general collection of metalevel inference rules, so in some sense MECHO models both the process of reading and understanding a problem and the process of solving it. However, as a cognitive model it suffers from the obvious deficiency that it encompasses neither the various misunderstandings a student might develop on reading a problem nor the various faulty (e.g., underspecialized and overgeneralized) strategies that students actually seem to possess. Priest has attempted to develop a ver-

sion of MECHO that can be more accurately used to mimic different types of human problem-solving behavior via the incorporation of "malrules." This approach is obviously viable for characterizing some faulty problem-solving strategies, but does not easily lend itself to the characterization of behavior that depends on the student's use of unlikely metaphors or analogies; nor does it capture the role of what Priest describes as the "hidden curriculum assumption." This assumption is the basis on which a student may, for example, reject a possible solution path as being too complex for a problem that should typically be solved in, say, 15 minutes.

TEACHING PROBLEM SOLVING AT A DISTANCE

The immediate educational context to which we wish to apply our research is the British Open University. This University currently has an enrollment of 120,000 adult students studying part-time. Correspondence texts are the main medium of instruction, supplemented by television programs, home experiment kits, audio material, and a limited number of face-to-face tutorials. There are no prerequisites for entry into the Open University system, and many students find the mathematics in general and physics problem solving in particular extremely hard. The two main groups of Open University academics responsible for instruction in physics and mathematics adopt quite different approaches.

The physicists rely on very large amounts of practice, with feedback on accuracy of solution provided via answers at the back of correspondence texts, computer-marked assignments, and marked work returned by human tutors. The mathematicians adopt a quite different approach, aiming to teach problem-solving explicitly. Beginning students are required to undertake exercises that help them reflect on their own ways of trying to solve problems. In the course of these activities, they acquire a vocabulary that distinguishes levels of confidence: enactive, iconic, and symbolic, and terms for problem-solving states and processes: mulling, insight, checking, and so on. They are also taught to distinguish generalizing from specializing and the difference between various proof methods, including elimination, induction, and proof by counterexample. Toward the end of their introductory course, they are taught a seven-stage model of the mathematical modeling process that is recursive and is based on the idea of progressively refining problem solutions. The subsequent applied mathematics course includes a 40-hour (Berry & O'Shea, 1984) modeling project, and the students are helped by examples of real student work and video material depicting groups of experts trying to solve surprise problems.

One of our motivations in this research is to examine in detail the way students actually solve problems so that we are better able to compare the value of the Open University physics "practice makes perfect" approach to

the mathematicians' approach to teaching mathematical problem-solving techniques and vocabulary directly.

Data Collection

Our view is that much of the previous work is flawed by lack of sufficient data to support the conclusions drawn. Often it depends on a single protocol from a collaborator. Our novices are real novices. We have devised methods for collecting high-quality protocols and devoted time to trying out a variety of different types of problem with students working singly or in pairs.

We collected think-aloud protocols on a physics problem that requires both algebra manipulation knowledge and graph interpretation knowledge. After a pilot study with adult students, we collected protocols from eight pairs of 17-year-old high school students as they worked on the problems. We then constructed eight distinct production rule models for student behavior on this problem.

METHODS

Two episodes of data collection are described in this paper, both involving the collection of think-aloud solution protocols from students. The first set of subjects were seven 1st year Open University students who had just completed 3 weeks of study on elementary mechanics. Their backgrounds varied from no previous experience of physics to freshman university-level physics. Open University students are adults returning to study after some work experience. Using adult students has advantages for the attempt to attain an understanding of problem-solving skills in physics. Skill at solving physics problems is not a natural competence but a learned skill, and one learned with considerable difficulty. Adults' language competence is fully developed, so the notorious difficulty of achieving adequate verbalization in protocols should be simplest with them. The second set of subjects were 16 *pairs* of high school students attempting to solve some standard textbook kinematics problems. The students were aged 16 and 17 years.

The equipment consisted of a "summagraphics" kit pad and microphone connected via an interface box to a stereo cassette recorder. This equipment, based on the Open University CYCLOPS technology, allows recordings of paper-and-pencil work to be made on one track of the cassette tape while any words spoken during the process are recorded on the other track. The system combines in a convenient form the student's voice with a synchronized dynamic record of what he or she writes. Adolescent students were less forthcoming when working alone, so matched pairs of students were used, and we found that this decreased the self-consciousness of ado-

lescent students made to perform in this way. The replay facility was used at the end of some experimental sessions to discuss with students some of their problem-solving decisions.

The replay of the tape, the replication of the handwritten steps, the sequence of operations, timing information on each individual step, and the verbal protocol give rich information about the problem-solving processes employed by the subjects.

THE PROBLEMS

The adults in the pilot study were presented with 10 problems in basic kinematics selected from *Physics and the Physical Universe* by Jerry B. Marion (1978). The main problem set of 16 problems was obtained after searching several standard physics texts. Two of the simpler problems follow. Problem 1: A resultant force of 10 newtons acts on a mass of 2 kg. Find the acceleration. Problem 2: An automobile moves uniformly a distance of 20 m in 2 s; during the next 3 s it moves only 10 m. What was the average speed a) during the first 2 s, b) during the next 3 s, c) during the 5 s intervals? d) Compute the average speed for the first 3 s.

Problem 1 is fairly trivial, but to solve it the student must recognize that $F = ma$ is the appropriate equation to use, substitute the values for F and m, and solve for a. It is typical of many problems where recognition of an equation is followed by simple manipulation. The second problem requires some of the same skills. It requires the subject to know that average speed is calculated by dividing distance traveled by time taken to cover that distance. Answers to parts *a* and *b* follow by substituting the appropriate distance and time values from the question. In part *c* the subject must recognize that average speed will be given by calculating the total distance traveled in the 5-s interval and that this will be obtained by adding to the distance traveled in the first 2 s the distance traveled in the next 3 s. To answer part *d* more interpretation of the situation described in the problem is required.

THE ADULT PILOT STUDY

The adult students experienced many difficulties with the problems. Trowbridge (1979) describes student problems with the concepts of velocity and acceleration. These adults also had a very hazy notion of acceleration and constantly confused it with velocity. Velocity was confused with speed and average speed. They also made many mistakes, because they did not read the problem statement carefully. They misread distances for speeds and final speeds for average speeds and, despite the fact that these mistakes led them into numerous problems, never looked back to check. Having struggled through to an answer to the problem, they failed to check whether the answer made sense in terms of the original problem statement.

They mostly started by writing down the equation they knew, in contrast to the finding by Simon and Simon (1978) that novices work backward by writing down equations, including the equation they want to find. Real world checking, for example, to see if the size of the answer made sense, did not occur. A certain collusion with the experimenter to promote the illusion that they were really trying to solve the problem was noticeable. The main conclusion of the pilot study arose from the surprising observation that these students seemed to exhibit some way of doing problems. The protocols are littered with statements like "This is how I always do problems," "I always draw diagrams," ". . . write down the equations I know," or ". . . write down everything as if it was in sentences." This coping strategy is reminiscent of K. H. Larkin's (1978) experience of adults doing arithmetic problems. They could remember how to do some things; her subjects had "islands of knowledge" (K. H. Larkin, 1978). Our adult subjects had "islands of tactics." They were not basing their behavior on any understanding of physics but on some sort of coping strategy.

The Student Pairs Data

We have categorized the problems arising in our student pairs study as follows:

- Problems in knowing *how to go about it*—behavior to do with reading the problem statement and the subject's general attitude to doing the problems.
- Problems in knowing *what to do once you have started*—these include problems in understanding the subject matter and the problems applying an appropriate strategy.
- Problems in *finishing* appropriately—when and how to check and how to select the appropriate units.

How To Go About It

A feature of the protocols that was immediately noticeable was the amount of reading and rereading of problems. The high school subjects reread the whole problem, sentences, and parts of sentences. We have not yet achieved a description of how and when people read, but a large part of the behavior seemed to occur when a student got stuck and was looking for new inspiration. Accompanying this "getting unstuck" behavior was the habit of writing down odd phrases from the problem statement. Some words used in the problems caused difficulty for our A-level students, *deploy* and *interval*, for example. Several students thought the phrase "time taken for the parachute to deploy" meant the time between the parachutist's jumping out of the airplane and pulling the ripcord rather than the time between the pulling of the cord and the parachute opening.

Another feature of behavior apparent at this beginning stage was the

whole class of expectations the students had about what physics problems were like. One surprising expectation expressed by the adolescent subjects was that the problems would be more difficult than they appear on the surface. Comments like "it must be harder than this" litter the protocols. It is interesting to speculate on what may be the source of this expectation. Because these students have successfully passed physics exams and have continued their study of physics, they must have had some experience of successfully completing problems. One interpretation of the comments is that they refer to the circuitous route you sometimes must follow to solve the problem, for example, "We might have to find the acceleration first or something like that."

Another piece of physics problem-solving folklore is that equations are not worth remembering. Many of the adolescents (and the adults as well) seemed appalled that they were being expected to remember any equations. Some of the adults coped by working out the problems from first principles, that is, definitions of velocity and acceleration, and some of the children coped by dredging their memories. Related to this expectation was the surprise generated by problems where the subjects had to combine equations about force with equations about velocity and acceleration. This was regarded as completely against the rules. Equations about force *and* acceleration should not arise. We also noticed some peculiarities in the protocols arising from perceptual interference effects of the problems preceding the ones we were looking at. For example a problem that used g as *grams* preceding a problem where g was used as the acceleration due to *gravity* caused occasional confusions. On one particular problem the repeated generation of $v^2 - u^2 = 2ax$, an inappropriate equation, seems to be due to the fact that it was the only constant acceleration equation that had not been used in the problem set at that point.

What You Do Once You Get Started

Once the student pairs had started the problems, two sorts of difficulties arose—one set arising from the physics content of the problems and the other from the strategies used in attempting them.

Problems with the content in physics problems have usually been discussed in terms of students' misconceptions (di Sessa, 1980; Trowbridge, 1979). So we were prepared to find some evidence for these. However, what we found more commonly was evidence of a sloppiness of expression. Subjects haphazardly interchanged descriptions of quantities such as meters, meters per second and meters per second squared—both novices and experts. This did not seem to be symptomatic of an underlying confusion between distance, velocity, and acceleration. However, there were some obvious confusions. There was little appreciation among the school children of the distinction between average velocity and instantaneous velocity, and there was no evidence that they understood what it actually

meant for an object to be accelerating, though they could handle equations with a in them competently. Some students think that uniform acceleration means the same as constant velocity. Describing a body as undergoing uniform acceleration seems unnecessary to them, because they never do calculations that would involve nonuniform acceleration. Apart from not remembering the equations of motion, they did not characterize them as equations of constant acceleration—probably because, as noted previously, the notion of nonuniform acceleration is completely unimaginable.

In contrast to the adults, who showed evidence of possessing strategies—often inappropriate ones—for solving physics problems, among the school children no strategies for dealing with the problems were apparent. Examples of writing down either the knowns or unknowns were uncommon, and no sign of advice as to how to proceed on these problems was apparent. One strategy that was in common use was that of drawing a graph. The school children drew graphs when they could not think of what else to do. Graphs would often have the meaning of their axes shifted in full flight. For example a subject would draw a distance–time graph and then treat it as a velocity–time graph and vice versa or would draw a distance–time set of axes but fill in details of velocity versus time. Having drawn the graph, the subject would often not know what to do with it. Some *very general* facts about graphs are known. For example, you can read something from a graph using lines drawn across it; gradient equals something; something is the area under a graph. These facts allowed subjects great opportunity for continuing work on a problem, doing things they knew would turn out to be useful.

There was no sign of the students' appreciating the connection between the graphs and the equations of motion they represent. Indeed, one more-experienced subject who worked out the relationship between $s = ut + 1/2at^2$ and his distance–time graph was very surprised and pleased with himself. Where the average velocity might be found on a velocity–time graph was not known.

Finishing

None of the subjects ever estimated what their result should be. Only once or twice was any checking done, but this was not any elaborate "double-check your answer by working it out another way." One answer turned out to be $7\frac{7}{9}$ and this was rejected by two subjects who decided to check their arithmetic because the non-neatness of the answer worried them. Only one student used units to check his answer. There was an overall impression that the students were writing down things that would gain marks rather than using the paper to reflect their thinking about the question. In some cases very little of what is thought or said on our voice track is reflected in what is written down on the page.

Graph/Algebra Experiment

One particular feature of the protocols that we selected for further study was the use of graphs. Students' attitudes to and use of graphs varied enormously. Educators and psychologists agree that students should and often do use more than one representation of a domain in which they may be solving problems. However, to date work on the cognitive modeling of problem-solving processes has focused on single representations. This criticism applies to our own past work on problem solving in physics (Scanlon, Hawkridge, Evertsz & O'Shea, 1984; Scanlon & O'Shea, 1982) and arithmetic (Young & O'Shea, 1981). Accordingly, we considered protocols of students solving a physics problem that had been designed to force the pupils to use two different representations of the problem and to express these two different representations with pencil and paper. The problem chosen requires the use of both graphs and algebraic equations.

METHODOLOGY AND DATA

The students were presented with the following problem, taken from a high school physics test book (Abbott, 1964):

> Explain the difference between speed and velocity. Draw a graph of velocity against time for a body which starts with an initial velocity of 4 meters second and continues to move with an acceleration of 1.5 meter/second² for 6 seconds. Show how you would find from the graph a) the average velocity, b) the distance moved in the 6 seconds.

We will concentrate on the answers to the third part of the problem. In solving the first part of the problem, the students wrote an answer like, "speed is a scalar and velocity is a vector." Then they drew a velocity–time graph. After discussion all the pairs of pupils wrote down a definition and drew a graph.

ANALYSIS

The graphs of velocity against time were constructed in two ways. (1) Starting with an initial velocity of 4 m/s, they plotted the velocity attained after each second by adding 1.5 m/s to get $5\frac{1}{2}$, 7, $8\frac{1}{2}$, 10, $11\frac{1}{2}$, and finally 13 m/s. (2) Starting with an initial velocity of 4 m/s, they used $v = u + at$, substituted values, and calculated the final velocity of 13, and used the point (13, 6) with (4, 0) to construct the straight line.

Six of the eight graphs were drawn correctly. (The correct graph is given in Figure 11.1.) For the two incorrect graphs, in one the students had calculated the correct final velocity using $v = u + at$, but the students had simply marked the point (13, 6) and constructed a rectangle. Each pair

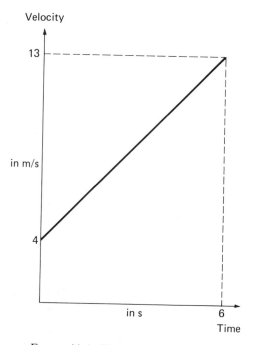

FIGURE 11.1. The velocity–time graph

of students produced a different way of finding average velocity. Four obtained the correct answer and four did not, but all eight pairs wrote down a final answer. Table 11.1 illustrates the eight methods for solving the problems. The protocols are given in full in Scanlon, Hawkridge, and O'Shea (1983). Some of the novice strategies are either overgeneralized or overspecialized. Some students who make errors or get into difficulty while reasoning using one representation tend not to recognize their situation but instead immediately switch to one of the other representations available.

This analysis focuses on student work on part 3 of the problem. The student has already attempted parts 1 and 2, so the velocity–time graph has already been constructed. A typical protocol has about 20 utterances with eight written steps in the problem solution. Subjects produce two types of utterance. The first type consists of generating a hypothesis or equation or suggesting an interpretation of the graph or suggesting a manipulation of an equation that has been written down. The second type of utterance consists of a challenge, confirmation, criticism, or check to some piece of reasoning or written statement that has previously been produced. These latter evaluative utterances are typically made about the previous generative utterance but occasionally involve challenges to the entire attempt to solve the problem. All eight protocols for part 3 can be broken down into four distinct phases: interpret, recall, manipulate, and check.

First, the students use their knowledge of school text books to interpret

TABLE 11.1. Eight methods used to solve a problem.

1. Use equation for av. vel. $= \dfrac{\text{total distance}}{\text{total time}}$

   Find total distance traveled from the area under the graph

   i.e., av. vel. $= \dfrac{51 \text{ m}}{6 \text{ s}} = 8.5$ m/s

2. As for 1, but find total distance using equation $s = ut + at^2$,
   i.e., not using graph skills.

3. Use definition of av. vel $= \dfrac{\text{initial vel.} + \text{final vel.}}{2}$

   $$= \dfrac{4 + 13}{2}$$

   i.e., concentrating on the notion of average rather than velocity.

4. Read answer from graph using fact that av. vel is given by midpoint.

The above methods give the correct answer. The following methods don't:

5. Use equation for av. vel. $= u + \dfrac{v - u}{2}$

   shortened to $\dfrac{v - u}{2}$

   (which is fine for a graph which goes through the origin, but not in this case—
   gives v = 4.5 m/s)

6. Use $v = u + at$ (inappropriate equation; solve for a to get $\dfrac{13 - 4}{6} = 1.5$)

7. Use fact that av. vel. is gradient of some graph (in fact, it's the distance time graph, not
   velocity, as is given here—

   gives $\dfrac{13 - 4}{6} = 1.5$)

8. Use equation av. vel. $= \dfrac{dv}{dt}$ (v similar to a)

---

part 3 of the problem. Then they recall an equation. The students generally draw on one of two sources of declarative knowledge, namely basic physical knowledge or school problem knowledge. In addition some students also use their graph interpretation skills in conjunction with one of the declarative sources of knowledge. Having recalled an equation, the students then use either their equation manipulation skills or their graph interpretation skills, but not both, to produce an answer. Then, according to the skill applied, they either roughly check their answer against the other variables in the equations or they check the answer approximately against the graph (see Table 11.2).

Using production rule models we developed a parsimonious account that generates the behavior of the eight pairs of students solving the problem. Each approach is distinct, and four yield correct solutions, and the other four incorrect solutions. In order to account for the observed behavior, we distinguished the five different types of knowledge used. The first three types of knowledge are essentially declarative, and the other two types are procedural. The student knows and can recall a variety of equations

TABLE 11.2. Four phases of work on the graph/algebra problem.

Interpret	Read problem	
	Use GIS to draw graph	
Recall	Use GIS, BPK, or SPK to recall equations from EK	
Manipulate	Use EMS to substitute values in equation	Use GIS to substitute values in equation
Check	Use size of answer to check	Use rough size checking against graph

BPK, basic physical knowledge; EK, equation knowledge; EMS, equation manipulation skills; GIS, graph interpretation skills; SPK, school problem knowledge.

(equation knowledge), the student has general commonsense knowledge (basic physical knowledge) about time, distance, velocity, and acceleration, and the student has knowledge about the type and difficulty of problems set in school textbooks (school problem knowledge). The student also has equation manipulation skills and graph interpretation skills. These different types of procedural and declarative knowledge are brought to bear by the students as they solve the problem.

It proved possible to break each of the eight protocols into the four phases described. Table 11.3 is an example of students using method 4 (see Table 11.1). By carefully looking at the utterances, it was possible to identify where the five different knowledge sources were brought to bear. We then tightened our analysis by devising a framework based on production rules to use in the construction of eight specific models to describe the various problem-solving behaviors.

THE PRODUCTION RULE FRAMEWORK

We are constructing these models in a packet-oriented production system (POPSI) (Evertsz, 1983), which we have used in the past (Scanlon et al.,

TABLE 11.3. A protocol.

S1: Velocity equals A over T.
   Yeah, that's right . . . that would come to 9.
S2: Up there . . . straight up.
S1: Show how you would find from the graph the average velocity.
S2: From the graph?
S1: Mm . . . isn't that 9–4 divided by 2?
S2: Yeah.
S1: Check that . . . $v = u + at$. Yeah, that's right. The average velocity equals 9–4 divided by 2 = 2.5. . . . No it doesn't! 9 + 4 over 2, 6.5.
S2: Would that be the same as taking it up from 3 seconds? It would, wouldn't it.
S1: No.
S2: How would you find it from the graph, then?
S1: I wouldn't.

1984) to construct parsimonious models of physics problem-solving behavior. POPSI was designed for use as a research tool in cognitive modeling and was implemented in MACLISP. We used the same type of reading rules and focus of attention rules based on selectors that we have used in our previous work. There are rules that relate the problem statement to the process of recalling equations, rules that map unbound variables onto the graph to yield bound variables, and rules for isolating the unknown, which are applied to solve equations when sufficient variable bindings are available. The working memory contains three types of elements. First, there are imperatives taken from the problem statements. Second, there are variables with bindings. Third, there are the labelings from the graph. We apply two conflict resolution principles: recency in working memory and refractoriness in rule memory. The production rule models are described further in Scanlon and O'Shea (1985) and summarized in Table 11.4.

THE MODELS

We have built eight distinct prototype models using the preceding framework. These models currently represent the behavior of the dominant student in the pair. The main difference between the models that arrive at correct solutions and those that arrive at incorrect solutions is that the processes that resulted in correct solutions used only one source of knowledge. In the models for behavior that achieved success, two out of four use basic physical knowledge for the recall of the equations, one uses school problem knowledge, and one uses graph interpretation skills. Two of the models depend entirely on equation manipulation skills and do not use the graph at all. One uses no equation manipulation, and the process is essentially one of graph interpretation; and one model incorporates both equation manipulation and graph interpretation. In summary three out of four of the models for correct solving behavior are very economical, using only one source of knowledge in the equation-recalling process and then employing either simple repeated equation manipulation or graph interpretation. The fourth model for correct behavior matches the approach taught in school and generates graph interpretation events and equation manipulations at the appropriate points.

The models for generating the four types of unsuccessful behavior are more complex. In each case the equation-recalling process depends on

TABLE 11.4. Production rule framework.

Reading rules
Focus of attention rules
Graph-drawing rules
Rules to relate problem statement to recalling equations
Rules mapping unbound variable to graph to yield bound variables
Equation-solving rules

the use of either basic physical knowledge or school problem knowledge in conjunction with graph interpretation skills. For example one model accounts for the way in which a student recalls equations with one unknown where all the other bindings are given by the graph. The other feature of these models is that they embody overspecialized or overgeneralized rules based on past experience and the use of either basic problem knowledge or school problem knowledge. These eight models are constructed using the same framework and differ from the model that embodies the standard approach taught in school by at most two rules. It is not necessary for us to appeal to the notion of malrules (Sleeman & Brown, 1982) to account for the variations in behavior. It is, however, necessary for us to distinguish very carefully among the five types of knowledge that can be brought into play.

After constructing the models we examined the extent to which our framework and the models can be used to account for a further set of eight protocols on the problem. Five of the eight pairs solved the problem correctly. Three of these can be accounted for by the model based on method 1, one by method 2, and one by the model based on method 3. Two of the unsuccessful-solver protocols were accounted for by method 6 and 7, while the eighth pair did not make a serious attempt at the problem. So the framework can be applied to the "other half" of our data. We are currently examining the extent to which our framework and the models we have described in this chapter can be used to account for a further set of eight protocols on the problem. We are attempting to adapt our models to describe the behavior of pairs rather than of the dominant individual. This involves using multiple working memories.

Results and Discussion

The results we are reporting are based on small numbers of subjects—albeit more subjects than most other workers in the field use. Therefore, it is sensible to treat the results that follow with caution. We believe, however, that the results have important implications for work on physics problem solving if they hold true with more subjects.

The initial intention of this research was to extend our work on the modeling of physics problem solving to cope with situations requiring more than one representation. We assumed that the subjects would find an extra representation helpful. To our surprise we find that to successfully describe the four different examples of correct behavior we must assume that the students do *not* use all the available sources of knowledge when they are recalling equations. Further we must assume that three out of four of our pairs in completing the problem deliberately *restrict* themselves to either equation manipulation skills or graph interpretation skills. The models for incorrect behavior are more complex, and in these cases we

must assume that the students are using more than one source of knowledge when they recall equations as well as being subject to the normal problems of overgeneralization and overspecialization seen in novices.

The surprising conclusion that we come to as a result of this study is that although two representations can help students with mastery of both to come quickly to a correct solution, two representations can be a hindrance for students with limited understanding because they are able to generate incorrect solutions more easily. This result challenges some conventional wisdom in AI and education (e.g., Sleeman & Brown, 1982). Implementors of large AI systems frequently argue for multiple representations. Many educators regard a student's ability to map between equivalent but superficially different problem representations as a key step in understanding. More than one representation, however, may make novice problem-solving processes too robust, and hence errors or sources of difficulty may be much harder to isolate and detect. Our initial results indicate that both educators and implementors of large AI systems should be very cautious about advocating the use of more than one representation in situations where less than perfect performance is likely. Given the complexity of shifting from one representation to another, it is not easy to account for the student behavior we have observed without evoking our cognitive economy hypothesis.

CONSEQUENCES FOR INTELLIGENT TUTORING SYSTEMS

Our observations show that novices have a tendency, when experiencing difficulties on a problem, to shift to another representation (e.g., from graphs to equations). Also, during problem solving novices make sudden leaps guided by expectations based on their school experience of what sort of behavior is required. This procedure is particularly noticeable in the rapid switching between reading the problem and apparently less than sensible problem-solving moves. Our conclusion from these observations is that instruction should be designed to provide constraints and to facilitate orderly moves from one inference process, representation, or knowledge source to another. None of our students seemed clear about the precise relationship between a velocity–time graph and an equation of motion. They came unglued when moving from one to another, so we believe the relationship between different representations like these ought to be explicitly taught.

A particular consequence from our research on the design of intelligent teaching systems is the nature of a student model that would reflect the behavior previously described. An adequate student model would need to have some way of characterizing the process by which students chose to work in a different representation and the ways in which work in one representation interacted with work in another.

Anderson (1983) has come to some similar conclusions in the course of

applying his ACT theory to the design of tutors for LISP and geometry. Our approach, which, like his, has involved production rule formalisms (O'Shea & Sleeman, 1973), stresses the importance of the problem-solving context and of minimizing student working memory load. However, in contrast to Anderson, the approach we advocate is not based on allowing the student to make only one deviation from the "correct" path; nor do we assume that the student possesses a single homogenous representation of the problem being tackled. Instead, like Kimball (1973), we regard the amount of "freedom" to be given students to be a function of their expertise, and we view changing the knowledge representation of a reasoning process as a cognitive act to be explicitly allowed for in the design of intelligent computer tutors.

Future Work

Our main objective is to relate the various findings in our studies of physics problem solving to the different approaches for constructing student models. To this end we are building a physics tutor that can operate with quite different styles of student models. We intend to make a careful comparison of the malrule approach as exemplified by Sleeman (1982), Brown and Burton (1978) and others with the "perturbation" approach as exemplified by Young and O'Shea (1981).

These comparative studies will be underpinned by longitudinal data on physics problem solving collected from pairs using our CYCLOPS apparatus. In this way we hope to produce a principled account of the role of multiple representation in physics problem solving.

Acknowledgements. We thank Caroline Hawkridge for assistance with data collection and Benedict du Boulay, Barbara Hodgson, and Richard Young for insightful comments.

References

Abbot, A. (1964). *Ordinary level physics.* Oxford: Oxford University Press.

Berry, J., & O'Shea, T. (1984). Mathematical modelling at a distance. *Distance Education, 5,*(2): 163–173.

Brown, J. S., & Burton, R. B. (1978). Diagnostic models for procedural bugs in basic mathematical skills. *Cognitive Science, 2,* 155–192.

Brown, J. S., & de Kleer, J. (1984). The origin, form and logic of qualitative physical laws. *Proceedings of the eighth international joint conference on artificial intelligence* (Vol. 2, 1158–69). Los Altos, CA: William Kaufmann.

Bundy, A., Byrd, L., Luger, G., Mellish, C., Milne, R., & Palmer, M. (1979). *Mecho: A program to solve mechanics problems* (Working Paper 50). Edinburgh: University of Edinburgh, Department of Artificial Intelligence.

Chi, M., Glaser, R., & Rees, E. (1982). Expertise in problem solving. In R. J.

Sternberg (Ed.), *Advances in the psychology of human intelligence* (Vol. 1, pp. 7–76). Hillsdale, NJ: Lawrence Erlbaum Assoc.

di Sessa, A. (1980). *Understanding Aristotelian physics: A study of knowledge-based learning* (D.R.S.E. Internal Report). Cambridge, MA: M.I.T.

Evertsz, R. (1983). *The POPSI manual* (Open University Internal Report). Milton Keynes, UK: The Open University.

Kimball, R. B. (1973). *Self optimizing computer-assisted tutoring theory and practice* (Technical report No. 206). Palo Alto, CA: Stanford University, Institute for Mathematical Studies in the Social Sciences.

Larkin, J. H., McDermott, J., Simon, D. P., & Simon, H. A. (1980a). Expert and novice performance in solving physics problems. *Science, 208*, 1335–1342.

Larkin, J. H., McDermott, J., Simon, D. P., & Simon, H. A. (1980b). Models of competence. *Cognitive Science, 4*, 317–345.

Larkin, K. H. (1978). *An analysis of adult procedure synthesis in fraction problems* (ICAI report No. 14). Cambridge, MA: Bolt, Beranek and Newman.

Luger, G. (1980). Human problem solving and the Mecho trace. *Proceedings of the Artificial Intelligence Society of Britain*. Amsterdam.

Marion, J. B. (1978). *Physics and the physical universe*. Orlando, FL: Academic Press.

McDermott, J., & Larkin, J. H. (1978). Representing textbook physics problems. *Proceedings of the 2nd national conference of the Canadian Society for Computational Studies of Intelligence* (pp. 156–164). Toronto: University of Toronto Press.

McDermott, L. C. (1984, July). Research on conceptual understanding in mechanics. *Physics Today*, 24–32.

Miller, G. A. (1956). The magical number seven plus or minus two: Some limits on our capacity for processing information. *Psychological Review, 63*, 81–97.

O'Shea, T., & Sleeman, D. H. (1973). A design for an adaptive self improving teaching system. In J. Rose (Ed.), *Advances in cybernetics*. New York: Gordon & Breach.

Priest, T. (1981). A design for an intelligent mechanics tutor. In *Proceedings of CAL 81*. Leeds, England:

Reif, F., & Heller, J. (1981). *Knowledge structure in physics*. Internal Report, Sesame project. Berkeley: University of California.

Scanlon, E., Hawkridge, C., Evertsz, R., & O'Shea, T. (1984). Novice physics problem solving behavior. In T. O'Shea (Ed.), *Advances in artificial intelligence* (pp. 245–256). North Holland: Elsevier.

Scanlon, E., Hawkridge, C., & O'Shea, T. (1983). *Modeling physics problem solving* (Open University C.A.L. technical report No. 36). Milton Keynes, UK: The Open University.

Scanlon, E., & O'Shea, T. (1982). How novices solve physics problems. In *Proceedings of the fourth cognitive science conference* (pp. 131–134). Ann Arbor, MI.

Scanlon, E., & O'Shea, T. (1985). *Eight production rule models for a graph interpretation and equation manipulation problem*. (Open University C.A.L. working paper No. 54). Milton Keynes, UK: The Open University.

Simon, D. P., & Simon, H. A. (1978). Individual differences in solving physics problems. In R. S. Siegler (Ed.), *Children's thinking: What develops?* Hillsdale, NJ: Lawrence Erlbaum Assoc.

Sleeman, D. H. (1982). Malrules in children's algebra. In *Proceedings of Artificial*

Intelligence Society of Britain. Orsay, Paris: Proc. Society for the Study of Artificial Intelligence and the Simulation of Behavior.

Sleeman, D. H., & Brown, J. S. (Eds.) (1982). *Intelligent tutoring systems*. Orlando, FL: Academic Press.

Trowbridge (1979). An investigation of student understanding of the concept of velocity in one dimension. *American Journal of Physics, 48,* 1000.

VanLehn, K. (1983). *Felicity conditions for human skill acquisition; Validating an AI based theory* (Xerox PARC technical report, CIS-21). Palo Alto, CA: Xerox.

Young, R. M., & O'Shea, T. (1981). Errors in children's subtraction. *Cognitive Science, 5,* 153–177.

Additional References

de Kleer, J., & Brown, J. S., (1985). A qualitative physics based on confluences. In D. G. Bobrow (Ed.), *Qualitative reasoning about physical systems* (pp. 7–85). Cambridge, MA: MIT Press.

di Sessa, A. A. (1982). Unlearning Aristotelian physics: A study of knowledge-based learning. *Cognitive Science, 6,* 37–75.

12

Experimental Data for the Design of a Microworld-Based System for Algebra

E. Cauzinille-Marmèche
J. Mathieu

An analysis of observed errors and the choice of a level of interpretation of these errors is a prerequisite to the design of a remedial teaching or of an intelligent tutoring system (ITS). Many experiments (e.g., Brown & Burton, 1978, in the subtraction field; Matz, 1982, in algebra) have underlined the systematic characteristics of observed errors. A student's incorrect solution can often be analyzed either as a deviation from the correct procedure, with steps omitted or modified, or as the inappropriate use of otherwise correct procedures.

Once the student's difficulty is identified, we can propose two different instructional responses. (1) At the procedural level, practice and feedback can be designed to focus children's attention on the procedural rules and on their domain of validity. (2) At the conceptual level, we hypothesize that a relatively small number of conceptual misunderstandings lie at the heart of many different erroneous procedures. Therefore, we would emphasize the student's representation of the problem to be solved.

From this second point of view, which is the one we examine here, two tutorial strategies can be considered: (1) a straightforward method that places the emphasis directly on the structure of the studied problem or (2) an analogical approach where the problems that are the target of the instruction are related to other domains previously mastered by the student. The usefulness of this last approach is attested by various teaching experiments in domains such as electricity and electronics (Gentner & Gentner, 1982; Riley, Bee & Mokwa, 1981) and elementary mathematics (Resnick, 1982). Such instructional strategies, sometimes called "mapping instruction" (Resnick, 1982), rest on the hypothesis that mapping between different representations from various microworlds is a determining process in the acquisition of knowledge (Lawler, 1985).

Let us now return to the algebraic domain, for which we are designing a microworld-based system. There is considerable evidence that difficulties in learning algebra derive in part from students' and teachers' tendency to

treat algebra as a purely formal system, without reference to the number relationship and situational constraints that give it referential meaning. A large number of algebra malrules have been documented in studies of algebra learning and performance. According to several theories (Matz, 1982; Sleeman, 1984) malrules arise as deformations of the symbol manipulation rules taught in school; no attention to the quantities and relationships represented by the symbols needs to be attributed to learners in order to account for the pattern of observed malrules. Other research (Hinsley, Hayes & Simon, 1976) has shown that students can have considerable difficulty in relating algebra equations to basic ideas such as equivalence and functional relationships.

Our theory is that if students encounter such difficulties in assimilating the rules for rewriting expressions that characterize algebra at this level of instruction, it is because these rules seem to them an arbitrary collection, independent from each other and disconnected from their previous knowledge.

Here we report experimental results which attest that:

1. When the students approach algebra for the first time they spontaneously refer to different microworlds;
2. The different microworlds employed by students are not necessarily related to each other and do not form a coherent structure;
3. Inducing students to change their representation and to establish links between different representations can help them understand and use the newly introduced algebraic rules.

Weidenfeld (1985) is developing an ITS that rests on these experimental data.

Younger Students Spontaneously Refer to Different Microworlds

In the first experiment (Resnick, Cauzinille-Marmèche, & Mathieu, 1987), we conducted structured interviews with 20 students, 11 to 14 years of age, in order to test their comprehension of literal or numerical expressions of the form $a + b + c$, with or without brackets around either the ab or the bc portion of the expression.

For example, the task was to compare $a - (b - c)$ with $(a - b) - c$ or $12 - (7 - 2)$ with $(12 - 7) - 2$. The expressions to be compared exhibited only the properties of associativity and commutativity. Each type of problem was first presented in a literal form and then in a numerical form with the letters replaced by whole numbers.

The interviews reveal three types of responses, each calling on a different microworld. The first is *an arithmetical microworld*, where the expressions to be examined were analyzed as a chain of transformations applied

to an initial quantity. For example here is the response of a sixth class student (11 years old), when comparing $(a - b) + c$ to $a - (b + c)$, "It's not the same, because you take a from b, and then add c. And if you add b and c and take off . . . oh yes, it comes to the same thing." Some students (especially the younger ones, 11 to 12 years old) had apparent difficulties in representing the problem this way. It can involve qualitative reasoning, where the units are evaluated in terms of "little," "big. . ." But most frequently, only the operators of the two expressions to be compared were finally taken into account. The second microworld is *algorithmic*. Here the evaluation of the expressions to be compared necessitated the calculation of each one. If they were literal expressions the letters were replaced by numbers. The third is *a formal syntactic microworld*, where the expressions were analyzed as chains of symbols. The responses were verified by the rules of symbol manipulation. For example here is the response of a student comparing the expressions $(a - b) + c$ and $a - (b + c)$, "It's the same, you just change the brackets."

The first result of this research is that students, especially young ones, spontaneously refer to distinct microworlds. The context of the problem, whether numerical or literal, favors the use of one of the three microworlds. The algorithmic microworld is usually used if the expressions to be examined are numerical. The arithmetical and the formal microworlds are mainly used with respect to literal expressions. The second result is that errors are observed in the three microworlds even among the older students. In agreement with the results of Matz (1982), the errors can be interpreted for the most part as incorrect generalizations of the correct rules. The third main result of this research, that the different microworlds are unconnected in students' minds, is considered in the next section.

The Different Microworlds Are Not Necessarily Connected

We have seen that for similar types of exercise, students often refer to different microworlds in order to verify their answer. Often they refer to the arithmetical or the formal microworlds for the literal form of the exercise and to the algorithmic one for the numerical form of the same exercise. The main point is that in algebraically identical exercises, students can often arrive at contradictory conclusions. For example from the formal microworld, $a - (b - c)$ and $(a - b) - c$ are judged equivalent, "because you only change the brackets." From the algorithmic microworld, however, the same expressions, in a numerical form, are then judged to be different, $12 - (7 - 2) \neq (12 - 7) - 2$, because "$(7 - 2) = 5$, which you take from 12, that makes 7; $(12 - 7) = 5, - 2$, that makes 3. It's not the same thing."

These types of responses are frequent in our data. What is typical is that students do not recognize any contradiction between their responses, as

if the different microworlds were really independent. This occurs even though the students actually have in front of them the two successive answers from the same exercise, first presented in the literal form and then in the numerical one.

What happens if the experimenter points to be contradiction? Students usually conclude that they are more confident with numerals (even if they use buggy algorithms) and that they were wrong with the letters. Rarely did they attempt to analyze the source of the contradiction. For example, a student answers that $a + (b - c)$ and $a + (c - b)$ are equivalent. "It comes out the same, all you do is swap round the letters." But afterward, with the letters replaced by numerical expressions, he concludes that the expressions are different, $12 + (7 - 3) \neq 12 + (3 - 7)$. "It comes out the same, you've just changed.... Oh no, it doesn't come out the same, because here you do $7 - 3$, and that makes 4, and here $3 - 7$, which you can't do. It would be the same if it was $+$." This student thus makes clear that only addition is commutative and not subtraction. This is an interesting case of self-learning, through the coordination of different microworlds. Nevertheless, this case remains an exception. For the majority of students, the three microworlds that we have shown function independently.

The second experiment (Cauzinille-Marmèche, Mathieu, & Monteils, 1985) examines another algebraic concept, that of equation, with the following question. What meaning do children attribute to equations when they are introduced in the arithmetic context of word problems?

We comment here only on the results obtained from students from the fourth class (50 students aged 13 to 14 years). The students had already met equations at the time of the experiment but had not yet received systematic instruction on the solving procedures.

The task proposed to the students was twofold: classic solving tasks with one unknown, such as $10 (x - 2) = 480$ or $6x + 12 = 42$, and solving of word problems. In such cases subjects were instructed to choose the one out of three proposed equations that best represented the problem posed. Out of the three proposed equations for each word problem, only one was isomorphic to one of the equations given in the solving task just described and also conveniently represented the problem posed. Following is an example:

Olivier has 4 times as many cigarettes as Jerome.
He is given 16 more.
He now has 36.
How many cigarettes does Jerome have?

Circle the equation which best represents the problem

$4 + x + 16 = 36$
or $4x + 16 = 36$
or $4(x + 16) = 36$

Solve the chosen equation.

The main results of this experiment are the following. In the first task, the students most frequently used the method of guessing the value of x, choosing a value such that equality was maintained. More rarely, students transformed the equation to solve it, and the classic errors related to re-writing (about distributivity, changing of members, etc.) were noted. In the second task, although the students were already familiar with equation (as the results of the first task show), the method adopted by the students was arithmetical. First they solved the problem in an arithmetical way, then they chose the equation that best fitted with the surface features of the problem, and finally they checked the result in an arithmetical way, maintaining the chosen balance. We observed various difficulties with this method. In certain cases the student could not, or did not, solve the problem arithmetically. So no equation was selected, as if the equation had meaning for the subject only if the problem could be solved arithmetically. In other cases no equation existed among those proposed that corresponded exactly to the surface features of the word problem. So we observed either a hesitation in choosing the equation or a transformation of the arithmetical problem so that one of the equations then represented the new problem. These results therefore show in a different way the existence, in the beginner, of separate microworlds: (1) the algebraic microworld in which the transformation rules can be used and (2) the arithmetical microworld where the equation makes sense only if it corresponds to the word problem, word for word, and in the order indicated by the text. In this final case the equation strictly speaking is not solved; the value of x is found arithmetically.

The results of the two experiments that we have presented confirm the hypothesis that an important part of the difficulty encountered by students when beginning algebra stems from the fact that a new formal domain of knowledge is disconnected from the various domains of experience that they have previously mastered.

In the final part of this chapter we show the results of an experiment in which we wished to test in what ways didactic intervention, by encouraging links between the algebraic microworld and other microworlds, particularly the arithmetical one, could help the student toward a better understanding of the algebraic rules (Cauzinille-Marmèche, et al., 1985).

The Effect of a Tutorial Strategy That Favors Links Between Different Representations

Our study was centered around two particular algebraic rules, in the use of which we observed systematic errors. First is distributivity, when it should be used in expressions of the type $5(x - 2) = 5x - 10$, with the main associated error $5(x - 2) = 5x - 2$. Second is a parenthesis rule. How to remove the parentheses, taking into account whether the operator before the brackets is $+$ or $-$. As, for example, in $14 - (2 + x) = 14 - 2 - x$, with the main associated error, $14 - (2 + x) = 14 - 2 + x$.

These are rules that have been poorly mastered by students (even those of the third class). They are also rules for which one may relatively easily refer to arithmetical situations, possibly by using graphic representations.

The experiment dealt with about 10 students from the fourth class (13 to 14 years), each individually monitored during two or three interview sessions. We used students who had participated in the previously described experiments and whose errors in the application of algebraic rules had already been detected. The aim of the interviews was, with respect to each type of error, to encourage the student to modify his representation of problems.

Following we give two short excerpts from interviews showing that the intervention of the experimenter caused, at least in the short term, a modification of the student's comprehension of the algebraic rules in use.

EXAMPLE I: GAR, A STUDENT IN THE FOURTH CLASS

Algebraic Microworld: GAR made the typical error:

$$5(x - 2) = 5x - 2$$

Arithmetical Microworld: The experimenter posed the following arithmetical problem to GAR.

"I buy 5 records. On each one there is a reduction of 2 francs. In all I pay 240 francs. How much did each record cost?"

GAR easily solved the problem:

Forty-eight francs is the price of a record with the reduction. Fifty francs is the price of a record before the reduction.

Algebraic Microworld: The experimenter then asked the student to choose, from the three equations following, the one that best represented the arithmetical problem:

$$5 + x - 2 = 240$$
$$5x - 2 = 240$$
$$5(x - 2) = 240$$

GAR selected the correct equation, $5(x - 2) = 240$ and then hesitated over his choice.

Arithmetical Microworld: "That's not right, $5(x - 2) = 240$, because you take away $2f$, and you have to take away $10f$ because there are 5 records, and you've only taken away the reduction on one record, and you should take it from 5 records."

Algebraic Microworld: The experimenter then asked the student to remove the brackets in the expression $5(x - 2)$.

$$\text{GAR: } 5(x - 2) = 5x - 2$$

GAR checked this by replacing *x* with the value that he had previously found arithmetically:

$$5x - 2$$
$$5 \times 50 - 2$$
$$250 - 2$$
$$248$$

Arithmetical Microworld: GAR stated that this was not the expected answer, 240, and concluded: "It's not right, 5 times 50 should be the whole price without a reduction, −2 is the reduction on only one record. It should be −10."

Algebraic Microworld: The experimenter asked where −10 can be found in the expression $5(50 - 2)$

Arithmetical: GAR, "Five times 2. Oh yes, you use distributivity, that makes $250 - 10$. If you don't use distributivity it's as though you only make a reduction on one record."

Algebraic: "Distributivity is for the two terms in the brackets."

EXAMPLE 2: KAC, STUDENT IN THE FOURTH CLASS

Algebraic Microworld: This student made the error $19 - (3 + x) = 19 - 3 + x$.

Arithmetical Microworld: The experimenter asked the student what he had to subtract from 19 in the expression $19 - (3 + x)$.

KAC: "You need to take away 3 and *x*."

The experimenter then presented to the student the graphic presentation shown in Figure 12.1. He then asked the student how it could be expressed that from 19 you subtract 3 and *x*.

KAC: $19 - (3 + x) = 19 - 3 - x$.

Algebraic Microworld: Finally, the experimenter pointed to the initial expression, $19 - (3 + x) = 19 - 3 - x$.

These two examples, among others, attest to the hypothesis that em-

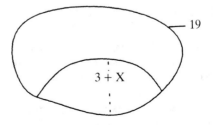

FIGURE 12.1. Graphic presentation for $19 - (3 + x)$.

phasizing the link between algebra and arithmetic can help the student to comprehend certain rules of algebraic rewriting.

The limitations of the completed study are, however, evident. Our interviews concerned only a few students. And the reference to the arithmetical microworld was proposed only for certain algebraic rules. Finally, and above all, the long-term effects of the strategy of intervention cannot be tested.

Conclusion

The data obtained in the three experiments briefly described here, even if they are very partial, suggest the usefulness of a didactic approach that enlightens subjects on the possible interaction between the different microworlds that cooperate to construct the new knowledge to be learned—algebra.

The system being developed by Weidenfeld (1985) rests on these ideas. This system will have a diagnostic module that will enable the automatic identification of the rules of rewriting, which have been so poorly mastered by the student in the domain of elementary algebra. It also will have a tutorial module for every type of badly learned rule, proposing to the student the rerepresentation of the problem in another microworld (such as word problems, or graphics).

REFERENCES

Brown, J. S., & Burton, R. R. (1978). Diagnostic models for procedural bugs in basic mathematical skills. *Cognitive Science, 2,* 155–192.

Cauzinille-Marmèche, E., Mathieu, J., & Monteils, N. (1985). *Le statut de l'équation dans deux micro-mondes: Le micro-monde arithmétique et le micro-monde algébrique* (technical report). Paris: Université Paris V, Laboratorie de psychologie génétique.

Gentner, D., & Gentner, D. R. (1982). Flowing waters or teeming crowds: Mental models of electricity. In D. Gentner & A. L. Stevens (Eds.), *Mental models* (pp. 99–129). Hillsdale, NJ: Lawrence Erlbaum Assoc.

Hinsley, D., Hayes, J. R., & Simon, H. A. (1976). From words to equations: Meaning and representation in algebra word problems. In M. Just and F. Carpenter (Eds.), Cognitive processes in comprehension. Hillsdale, NJ: Lawrence Erlbaum Assoc.

Lawler, R. W. (1985). *Computer experience and cognitive development.* New York: Wiley.

Matz, M. (1982). Toward a process model for high school algebra errors. In D. Sleeman & J. S. Brown (Eds.), *Intelligent tutoring systems* (pp. 25–50). New York: Academic Press.

Resnick, L. B. (1982). Syntax and semantics in learning to subtract. In P. P. Carpenter, J. M. Moser & T. A. Romberg (Eds.), *Addition and subtraction:*

A cognitive developmental perspective (pp. 136–155). Hillsdale, NJ: Lawrence Erlbaum Assoc.

Resnick, L. B., Cauzinille-Marmèche, E., & Mathieu, J. (1987). Understanding algebra. In J. Sloboda & D. Rogers (Eds.) *Cognitive processes in mathematics* (pp. 169–203). New York: Clarendon Press.

Riley, M. S., Bee, N. V., & Mokwa, J. J. (1981). *Representations in early learning: The acquisition of problem-solving strategies in basic electricity/electronics.* Unpublished manuscript. Pittsburgh: University of Pittsburgh, Learning Research & Development Center.

Sleeman, D. H. (1984). An attempt to understand students' understanding of basic algebra. *Cognitive Science, 8,* 387–412.

Weidenfeld, G. (1985, June). Paper presented at symposium on Learning Issues for Intelligent Tutoring Systems. Deutsches Institut für Fernstudien (German Institute for Distance Education) an der Universität Tübingen Hauptbereich Forschung. Tübingen, West Germany.

13

Computer-Aided Model Building

JOACHIM WEDEKIND

This chapter argues that learning the process of modeling should be an objective of science instruction. It outlines how the computer, by offering flexible simulation systems combined with a problem-oriented user interface, can be used to teach modeling.

The development and analysis of models or real systems is a basic scientific method, widely used in research development and planning. Many results of research on natural, social, or economic systems were worked out on models of these systems. It would be logical, then, to regard modeling as an integral part of science teaching. Students should be made aware of the role of models and should learn to use models in the process of scientific problem solving. They should have not only theoretical knowledge about modeling but also practical skills in the development, testing, validation, and analysis of models.

In research, modeling means the creation, modification, or choice of a model to correspond with a natural phenomenon or man-made system. Simulation is purpose-oriented work with a model of a system. In a computer simulation the model is formulated as an algorithm and programmed in a computer language to be run on a computer.

In an idealized case the scientist studies a natural phenomenon by observing it and by performing experiments in the field or laboratory (Figure 13.1A). For a better understanding and for communication with other scientists, he builds a model of the system. This is seldom done in one step but requires various cycles of revision (Figure 13.1B). This is the important phase of model validation. If the validated model can be put into an operational form (i.e., a computer program), simulation "experiments" can be performed (Figure 13.1C).

In most cases students learn science in a different way. In laboratory courses they learn how to set up experiments to cope with technical difficulties and how to evaluate the outcomes. However, they learn most areas of their discipline in a very abstract manner, by hearing lectures or reading books (Figure 13.1D). It is very rare that they learn how to relate experimental and theoretical work to each other.

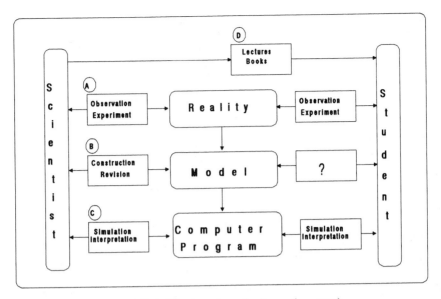

FIGURE 13.1. The learning of science (see text).

Computer Simulation

Computer simulation programs have proven to be valuable tools in teaching about theoretical models, especially when they use the possibility of visualization. Many models in the sciences are characterized by a high degree of complexity, abstraction, and mathematization. The graphic capabilities of computers, their computational speed, their interactive dialogue, and the variation of parameters possible for them can produce concrete material. Thus, they can enable the student to relate the theoretical model to the empirical background, which has often been obscured by theoretical formulas.

All computer simulation programs that are used in computer-assisted learning have a certain structure in common (Figure 13.2A). These programs have a large portion, the simulation environment, which is relatively invariant between different programs. It includes input–output routines, numerical routines to compute the mathematical equations, and routines for graphical or tabular output. Only a small portion of code is devoted to the specific model, including its equations and logical relationships (Figure 13.2B).

Such programs can be used to test models and to perform simulations, in that the students can vary parameters and investigate the results. But as in most cases of "canned software"—sometimes even with a list-protected program—the student cannot modify the model or simulate alternative

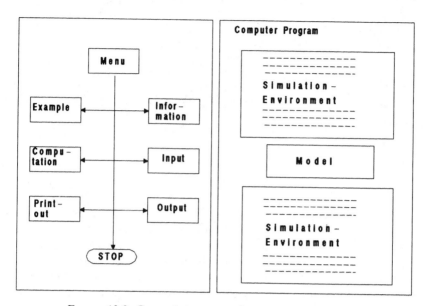

FIGURE 13.2. General structure of computer simulations.

models. To do this would require implementing a new program, knowledge of a high-level programming language, and knowledge of technical aspects of the computer (graphics, numerics). Such requirements are not related to the process of modeling itself. Computer-aided model building (CAMB) is a method whose aim is to overcome these limitations of simulation programs and to extend students' activities to more exploratory, activating, and motivating types of work. Its intention is to include model building in the curriculum and to bridge the gap between experimental and theoretical work.

Graphical Representations

One maxim of modern software development says that it is the computer that must be changed not the user. Using the computer should be as easy as working with other well-known tools. A computer's text editor should function like an ordinary typewriter; cut and paste functions should be similar to using scissors and tape. A data-base program should be organized like a filing cabinet, and a calculation program like a sheet of paper on the writing table.

There are a number of business software packages already on the market that are user friendly but are nevertheless flexible enough to cover a wide range of applications. The latest features are icon-driven menus, window-

ing, and so on, which allow the user to select a desired option simply by pointing at it and pressing a button, or even by pointing at it with a finger, if a touch-sensitive screen is available.

We have chosen this approach for our concept of CAMB. It is based on the fact that it is often possible to represent systems by drawing their structure. We can distinguish different levels of diagrams, including causal relationships (Figure 13.3), directions of operations, or exact metric relationships.

The Process of Modeling

Let us use the well-known biological predator–prey relationship as example for a description of the process of modeling. The learner has a naive mental model of the phenomenon, based on previous knowledge or on what has been taught so far (Figure 13.3A). This mental model can be verbalized. It is possible to give a description of the elements and their relationships (Figure 13.3B). To use the model for prediction, it will have to be formalized and quantifed. This is the important step of mathematization. In our example this is done by two linked differential (or difference) equations of first order (Figure 13.3C). This type of equation is typical for dynamic systems. Finally, to get the model into operation, it must be put onto the computer as a simulation program (Figure 13.3D). With the desired parameter values, the simulation program can be run, and the outcome must be interpreted (Figure 13.3E).

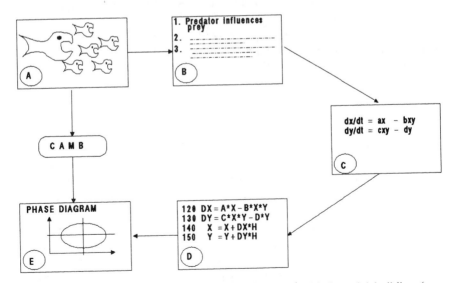

FIGURE 13.3. The process of modeling and computer-aided model building (see text).

This step of implementation requires tedious work and detailed knowledge that is not related to the real (biological) problem. For CAMB we have developed tools that require no such work and do not presuppose programming knowledge but allow the user to concentrate on the original task. We attempt to shorten the long way from the first model to the simulation program (A–B–C–D–E) to a direct path (A–E) by using a graphic representation of the system.

Diagrams may be used to implement such systems if they use precisely defined symbols and metric relationships. The diagrams may then be put together into block diagrams, from which the mathematical equations can be rederived by describing the system's behavior. Figure 13.4A is the causal loop diagram of our predator–prey example, showing the intrinsic growth of the prey population, the intrinsic decay of the predator population, and the mutual influence of both populations. With the symbolism used in a graphic interactive programming system (GRIPS), such a block diagram may be obtained from the causal loop diagram (Figure 13.4B), which looks similar.

Various symbolisms are used in different fields, and various interactive simulation systems use the construction of block diagrams on the screen as a step for implementing the model on a computer (i.e., CSMP III, DYNASIS, GRIPS). Interactive simulation systems should be as close as possible to the way people work within their field. This seems to be exactly the case for physicists with electronic circuits or with logic elements. But for biologists analog computing or DYNAMO are less natural. The ideal would be a simulation system that allows the user to think only in biological (or whatever) terms.

One severe difficulty in teaching about biological models is that we have to start with mathematical equations in order to get predictive results. With interactive simulation systems we can—in the first step—neglect the mathematization but try to transfer our concept directly into an operational form. Because of the isomorphism of the block diagram and the mathematical equations, it is even possible to deduce these equations from the diagram, thus making the students—in the second step—familar with the mathematization.

AN EXAMPLE: KOMPART

We illustrate this way of working with KOMPART, a simulation system for pharmacokinetic compartment models. Pharmacokinetics deals with the distribution of pharmaceuticals within the organism. Mathematical models have been developed to describe the kinetics of resorption, distribution, metabolism, and elimination of drugs. The organism is divided into different compartments, and the computational analysis deals with the change of the concentration of a drug within the compartments. Each compartment is characterized by an elimination constant (specific for every

a

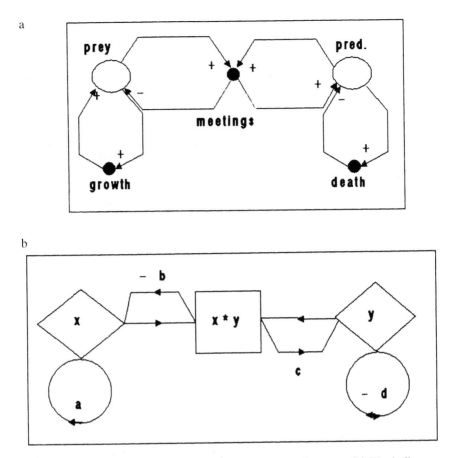

FIGURE 13.4. (a) Causal loop diagram of a predator–prey system. (b) Block diagram (GRIPS) of the predator–prey system.

drug), which determines the elimination of the drug. The velocity of elimination is proportional to the concentration, and the constant can be assumed to be a first-order velocity constant. The mean of medication (oral, subcutaneous, intravenous, etc.) can be incorporated into the model as external functions.

A basic pharmacokinetic model has stomach, blood, tissue, and urine compartments. A certain drug that the patient has swallowed is absorbed by the blood, transported to the tissue, resorbed again, and finally excreted via the urine. Figure 13.5A shows the paper-and-pencil version of this model, that is, the structure of the model, represented with symbols that are commonly used in pharmacology. Figure 13.5B shows the mathematical equations describing the time-dependent concentration within the different compartments. Figure 13.5C shows the model as it is implemented within KOMPART by simply putting together the symbols and defining

a

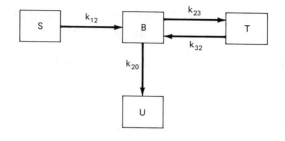

b

$$dS/dt = - k_{12}S$$
$$dB/dt = k_{12}S - k_{23}B + k_{32}T - k_{20}B$$
$$dT/dt = k_{23}B - k_{32}T$$
$$dU/dt = k_{20}B$$

c

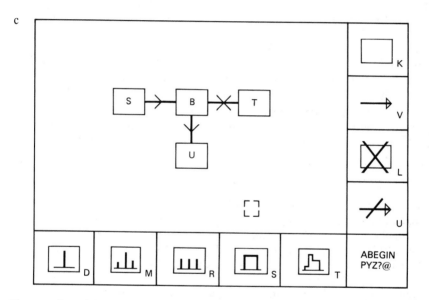

FIGURE 13.5. (a) Paper-and-pencil version of a basic pharmacokinetic model. (b) Differential equations describing the basic pharmacokinetic model. (c) Graphic representation of the basic pharmacokinetic model within KOMPART.

the numerical values (starting values for the variables, values for the velocity constants).

There is a limited syntax check within the program:

No input is accepted for external functions.

An arrow can be set only if there are two compartments that can be connected.

Only three inputs are allowed for each compartment.

Within the limitations of the screen (with a maximum of 20 compartments or functions), the user can define any model, even if it is nonsense from the pharmacological point of view. At present there are no tutorial components in KOMPART. Its use in the classroom depends mainly on the presence of a human tutor.

Learning by Doing in a Microworld

A microworld is a structure consisting of a set of states and transformations between states. It is important that transformations can be reversed in order to get the previous state, and the microworld includes homomorphisms to other structures that are representations of concrete actions (Groen, 1985). KOMPART and similar simulation systems can thus be classified as microworlds with one severe limitation. It is not possible to define new procedures.

The educational objectives of the use of KOMPART are twofold. First it is intended that the student learn about pharmacokinetics, second that he learn about the process of modeling itself. Both are supported by the active manner in which the student can modify a preset model or build new models (Brown, 1983). Empirical investigations, however, are needed to find out whether it is possible to transfer the writing table metaphor of modern computer–user interfaces to the learning of a scientific method.

REFERENCES

Brown, J. S. (1983). Learning by doing revisited for electronic learning environments. In M. A. White (Ed.), *The future of electronic learning*, (pp. 13–32). Hillsdale, NJ: Lawrence Erlbaum Assoc.

Englert, R., Goehring, R., & Wedekind, J. (1984). KOMPART—Ein interaktives Simulationssystem fur pharmakokinetische Kompartimentsysteme. *EDV in Medizin und Biologie, 15*, 1–4.

Groen, G. (1985). The epistemic of computer based microworlds. In *Program of 2nd international conference on artificial intelligence and education* (pp. 49–50). Exeter, England: The Society for the Study of Artificial Intelligence and Simulation of Behavior (AISB).

Wedekind, J. (1982). Computer aided model building and CAL. *Computer & Education, 6*, 145–151.

Wedekind, J. (1985). Einsatz von Mikrocomputern fur Simulationszwecke im Unterricht. In P. M. Fischer & H. Mandl (Eds.), *Lernen im Dialog mit dem Computer* (pp. 210–217). Munich: Urban & Schwarzenberg.

Author Index

Subject Index

Learning Issues for Intelligent Tutoring Systems arrays the most current and exciting research in this dynamic and growing area of cognitive science. A group of leading international scientists addresses important theoretical and practical questions that arise in the design and use of instructional systems. The chapters focus on uses of artificial intelligence approaches and offer complete and up-to-date reviews of the major research programs in computer-aided instruction and intelligent learning environments. *Learning Issues for Intelligent Tutoring Systems* is an important and useful introduction to this rapidly changing field.

ISBN 0-387-**96616**-1
ISBN 3-540-**96616**-1